Exam 70-642: Windows Server 2008 Network Infrastructure, Configuring

OBJECTIVE	CHAPTER	LESSON
1. CONFIGURING ADDRESSING AND SERVICES		
1.1 Configure IPv4 and IPv6 addressing.	Chapter 1	Lessons 2 and 3
1.2 Configure Dynamic Host Configuration Protocol (DHCP).	Chapter 4	Lessons 1 and 2
1.3 Configure routing.	Chapter 5	Lesson 1
1.4 Configure Windows Firewall with Advanced Security.	Chapter 6 Chapter 8	Lesson 1 Lesson 1
2. CONFIGURING NAMES RESOLUTION		
2.1 Configure a Domain Name System (DNS) server.	Chapter 2	Lesson 2
2.2 Configure DNS zones.	Chapter 3	Lessons 1 and 3
2.3 Configure DNS records.	Chapter 3	Lesson 1
2.4 Configure DNS replication.	Chapter 3	Lesson 2
2.5 Configure name resolution for client computers.	Chapter 2	Lesson 3
3. CONFIGURING NETWORK ACCESS		
3.1 Configure remote access.	Chapter 7	Lessons 2 and 3
3.2 Configure Network Access Protection (NAP).	Chapter 8	Lesson 2
3.3 Configure DirectAccess.	Chapter 7	Lesson 4
3.4 Configure Network Policy Server (NPS).	Chapter 7	Lesson 1
4. CONFIGURING FILE AND PRINT SERVICES		
4.1 Configure a file server	Chapter 11	Lessons 1 and 2
4.2 Configure Distributed File System (DFS).	Chapter 11	Lesson 2
4.3 Configure backup and restore.	Chapter 11	Lesson 3
4.4 Manage file server resources.	Chapter 11	Lesson 2
4.5 Configure and monitor print services.	Chapter 12	Lesson 1
5. MONITORING AND MANAGING A NETWORK INFRASTRUCTURE		
5.1 Configure Windows Server Update Services (WSUS) server settings.	Chapter 9	Lessons 1 and 2
5.2 Configure performance monitoring.	Chapter 10	Lessons 1 and 2
5.3 Configure event logs.	Chapter 10	Lesson 1
5.4 Gather network data.	Chapter 10 Chapter 6	Lessons 1, 2, and 3 Lesson 1

Exam Objectives The exam objectives listed here are current as of this book's publication date. Exam objectives are subject to change at any time without prior notice and at Microsoft's sole discretion. Please visit the Microsoft Learning website for the most current listing of exam objectives: *http://www.microsoft.com/learning/en/us /exam.aspx?ID=70-642&locale=en-us*.

Self-Paced Training Kit (Exam 70-642): Configuring Windows Server® 2008 Network Infrastructure (2nd Edition)

Tony Northrup
J.C. Mackin

PUBLISHED BY
Microsoft Press
A Division of Microsoft Corporation
One Microsoft Way
Redmond, Washington 98052-6399

Library of Congress Control Number: 2011924391

ISBN: 978-0-7356-5160-9

6 7 8 9 10 11 12 13 14   QGT 7 6 5 4 3 2

Printed and bound in the United States of America.

Microsoft Press books are available through booksellers and distributors worldwide. If you need support related to this book, email Microsoft Press Book Support at *mspinput@microsoft.com*. Please tell us what you think of this book at *http://www.microsoft.com/learning/booksurvey*.

Acquisitions Editor: Jeff Koch
Developmental Editor: Karen Szall
Project Editor: Carol Dillingham
Editorial Production: Online Training Solutions, Inc.
Technical Reviewer: Bob Dean; Technical Review services provided by Content Master, a member of CM Group, Ltd.
Copy Editor: Victoria Thulman; Online Training Solutions, Inc.
Indexer: Jan Bednarczuk; Online Training Solutions, Inc.
Cover: Twist Creative • Seattle

[2012-09-07]

Contents

Introduction   **xvii**

System Requirements. xvii

Using the CD xix

Acknowledgments xxii

Support & Feedback xxii

Preparing for the Exam   **xxiv**

Chapter 1   Understanding and Configuring TCP/IP   **1**

Before You Begin. 1

Lesson 1: Introducing Windows Networking. 2

    What Are Network Layers?   2

    Exploring the Layers of the TCP/IP Networking Model   5

    Configuring Networking Properties in Windows Server 2008 R2   14

    Lesson Summary   39

    Lesson Review   39

Lesson 2: Understanding IPv4 Addressing. 40

    The Structure of IPv4 Addresses   40

    Understanding Routing and Default Gateways   50

    Understanding IPv4 Address Ranges   51

    What Is Subnetting?   61

    Advantages of Subnetting   63

    The Subnet ID   65

    Creating Equally Sized Subnets   66

    Using Variable-Length Subnet Masks   67

What do you think of this book? We want to hear from you!

Microsoft is interested in hearing your feedback so we can continually improve our
books and learning resources for you. To participate in a brief online survey, please visit:

www.microsoft.com/learning/booksurvey/

Enumerating Subnets in an Address Space 68

Verifying Subnet Ownership and Configuration 76

Lesson Summary 84

Lesson Review 84

Lesson 3: Understanding IPv6 Addressing 86

Introducing IPv6 Addresses 86

Understanding IPv6 Address Types 87

IPv6 Transition Technologies 92

Working with IPv6 Subnets 96

Lesson Summary 103

Lesson Review 104

Chapter Review 105

Chapter Summary 105

Key Terms 106

Case Scenarios 106

Suggested Practices 107

Take a Practice Test 107

Chapter 2   Configuring Name Resolution   109

Before You Begin. 109

Lesson 1: Understanding Name Resolution
in Windows Server 2008 Networks 111

Name Resolution Methods in Windows 111

What Is Link Local Multicast Name Resolution? 112

What Is NetBIOS Name Resolution? 116

What Is DNS Name Resolution? 120

DNS Components 122

Understanding How a DNS Query Works 124

Understanding How Caching Works 131

Lesson Summary 134

Lesson Review 135

Lesson 2: Deploying a DNS Server. 136

Deploying a DNS Server on a Domain Controller 137

Deploying a DNS Server on a Stand-Alone or Member Server 139

Deploying a DNS Server on a Server Core Installation
of Windows Server 2008 R2   140

Configuring a Caching-Only DNS Server   142

Configuring Server Properties   143

Configuring DNS Socket Pooling   151

Configuring DNS Cache Locking   151

Lesson Summary   156

Lesson Review   156

Lesson 3: Configuring DNS Client Settings. 158

Specifying DNS Servers   158

Specifying a Computer Name and DNS Suffixes   160

Configuring a Suffix Search List   162

Configuring Dynamic Update Settings   165

Viewing and Clearing the DNS Client Cache   168

Lesson Summary   169

Lesson Review   170

Chapter Review 171

Chapter Summary   171

Key Terms   172

Case Scenarios   173

Suggested Practices   174

Take a Practice Test   174

Chapter 3   Configuring a DNS Zone Infrastructure   175

Before You Begin. 175

Lesson 1: Creating and Configuring Zones. 176

Creating Zones   177

Examining Built-in Resource Records   185

Creating Resource Records   189

Enabling DNS to Use WINS Resolution   195

Aging and Scavenging   196

Using a GlobalNames Zone   199

Lesson Summary   202

Lesson Review   203

Lesson 2: Configuring Zone Replication, Transfers, and Delegations 204

    Configuring Zone Replication for Active Directory–
    Integrated Zones   205

    Using Zone Transfers   210

    Understanding Zone Delegations   213

    Implementing Stub Zones   215

    Lesson Summary   221

    Lesson Review   222

Lesson 3: Implementing DNSSEC 223

    Understanding Public Key Cryptography in DNSSEC   224

    Understanding DNSSEC Name Resolution   227

    Configuring DNSSEC   234

    Lesson Summary   246

    Lesson Review   247

Chapter Review 248

    Chapter Summary   248

    Key Terms   249

    Case Scenarios   250

    Suggested Practices   251

    Take a Practice Test   251

Chapter 4 Creating a DHCP Infrastructure   253

Before You Begin 253

Lesson 1: Installing a DHCP Server 254

    Understanding DHCP Address Assignment   254

    Adding the DHCP Server Role   258

    Lesson Summary   268

    Lesson Review   269

Lesson 2: Configuring a DHCP Server 270

    Performing Post-Installation Tasks   270

    Understanding DHCP Options Classes   276

    Controlling DHCP Access Through MAC Filtering   279

    DHCP Delay Configuration   280

Using the DHCP Split-Scope Configuration Wizard 281
Configuring DHCP to Perform Dynamic DNS Updates for Clients 282
Installing and Configuring DHCP on a Server Core Installation 285
Lesson Summary 286
Lesson Review 287

Chapter Review 288
Chapter Summary 288
Key Terms 289
Case Scenarios 289
Suggested Practice 290
Take a Practice Test 290

Chapter 5 Configuring IP Routing   291

Before You Begin. 291

Lesson 1: Routing 292
Routing Overview 292
Examining Network Routes 294
Routing Protocols 295
Demand-Dial Routing 299
Static Routing 300
Lesson Summary 310
Lesson Review 310

Chapter Review 311
Chapter Summary 311
Key Terms 311
Case Scenarios 312
Suggested Practices 313
Take a Practice Test 313

Chapter 6 Protecting Network Traffic with IPsec   315

Before You Begin. 315

Lesson 1: Configuring IPsec. 316
What Is IPsec? 317
Using IPsec in Tunnel Mode 322

Authentication Methods for IPsec   323

Assigning a Predefined IPsec Policy   324

Creating a New IPsec Policy   325

Creating and Configuring a Connection Security Rule   330

Lesson Summary   342

Lesson Review   343

Chapter Review 344

Chapter Summary   344

Key Terms   344

Case Scenario   345

Suggested Practices   345

Take a Practice Test   346

Chapter 7   Connecting to Networks   347

Before You Begin. 348

Lesson 1: Configuring Network Policy Server 349

Wireless Security Standards   350

Infrastructure and Ad Hoc Wireless Networks   352

Configuring the Public Key Infrastructure   352

Authenticating Wireless Networks by Using
Windows Server 2008 R2   353

Connecting to Wireless Networks   361

Deploying Wireless Networks with WPA-EAP   362

Wired Network Security   363

Using NPS Templates   365

Lesson Summary   370

Lesson Review   371

Lesson 2: Configuring Network Address Translation 372

Network Address Translation Concepts   372

Configuring Internet Connection Sharing   374

Configuring Network Address Translation by Using Routing
And Remote Access   376

Troubleshooting Network Address Translation   378

Lesson Summary   380

Lesson Review   381

Lesson 3: Connecting to Remote Networks. 382
    Remote Access Overview   382
    Configuring Dial-Up Connections   385
    Configuring VPN Connections   391
    Troubleshooting VPN Connection Problems   395
    Configuring Connection Restrictions   395
    Testing Connectivity   397
    Lesson Summary   404
    Lesson Review   404

Lesson 4: Configuring DirectAccess. 405
    DirectAccess Connection Types   407
    Using DirectAccess on IPv4 Networks   408
    DirectAccess and Name Resolution   409
    The Network Location Server   410
    DirectAccess Requirements   410
    DirectAccess Limitations   412
    Firewall Configuration   412
    Running the DirectAccess Setup Wizard   413
    Lesson Summary   422
    Lesson Review   422

Chapter Review 423
    Chapter Summary   423
    Key Terms   424
    Case Scenarios   424
    Suggested Practices   426
    Take a Practice Test   427

Chapter 8   **Configuring Windows Firewall and Network Access Protection**   **429**

Before You Begin. 429

Lesson 1: Configuring Windows Firewall 430
    Why Firewalls Are Important   431
    Firewall Profiles   431
    Filtering Inbound Traffic   432

Filtering Outbound Traffic   434

Configuring Scope   435

Authorizing Connections   436

Configuring Firewall Settings with Group Policy   438

Enabling Logging for Windows Firewall   439

Identifying Network Communications   439

Lesson Summary   442

Lesson Review   443

Lesson 2: Configuring Network Access Protection 444

Network Access Protection Concepts   445

Planning a NAP Deployment   450

Installing and Configuring the Network Policy Server   450

Configuring NAP Enforcement   453

Configuring NAP Components   463

NAP Logging   474

Lesson Summary   480

Lesson Review   481

Chapter Review 482

Chapter Summary   482

Key Terms   482

Case Scenarios   483

Suggested Practices   484

Take a Practice Test   485

Chapter 9   Managing Software Updates   487

Before You Begin. 488

Lesson 1: Understanding Windows Server Update Services 489

WSUS Overview   489

Windows Update Client   490

WSUS Architecture   492

WSUS Requirements   494

Planning the WSUS Installation   495

Auditing Updates   496

Lesson Summary   497

Lesson Review   498

Lesson 2: Using Windows Server Update Services 499

    Installing Windows Server Update Services   499

    Configuring Windows Server Update Services   500

    Troubleshooting Problems Installing Updates   510

    Removing Updates   513

    Lesson Summary   516

    Lesson Review   516

Chapter Review 517

    Chapter Summary   518

    Key Terms   518

    Case Scenarios   518

    Suggested Practice   520

    Take a Practice Test   520

Chapter 10 Monitoring Computers   **521**

Before You Begin 521

Lesson 1: Monitoring Events 523

    Using Event Viewer   523

    Automatically Responding to Events   525

    Configuring Event Forwarding   526

    Lesson Summary   537

    Lesson Review   538

Lesson 2: Monitoring Performance and Reliability 539

    Using Performance Monitor   539

    Using Reliability Monitor   542

    Using Data Collector Sets   543

    Configuring Virtual Memory   549

    Lesson Summary   552

    Lesson Review   553

Lesson 3: Using Network Monitor and Simple Network
Management Protocol 554

    Installing Network Monitor   554

    Capturing and Analyzing Network Communications   555

Configuring SNMP	561
Lesson Summary	564
Lesson Review	564
Chapter Review	565
Chapter Summary	566
Key Terms	566
Case Scenarios	566
Suggested Practices	567
Take a Practice Test	568

Chapter 11 Managing Files   569

Before You Begin.	569
Lesson 1: Managing File Security	570
NTFS File Permissions	571
Encrypting File System	573
BitLocker	578
Lesson Summary	584
Lesson Review	584
Lesson 2: Sharing Folders	585
Installing the File Services Server Role	586
Quotas	587
Folder Sharing	592
Classification Management	596
Distributed File System	599
Offline Files	604
BranchCache	606
Lesson Summary	613
Lesson Review	614
Lesson 3: Backing Up and Restoring Files.	615
Shadow Copies	616
Windows Server Backup	617
Lesson Summary	626
Lesson Review	627

Chapter Review 627

    Chapter Summary   628

    Key Terms   628

    Case Scenarios   628

    Suggested Practices   629

    Take a Practice Test   630

Chapter 12 Managing Printers   631

Before You Begin. 631

Lesson 1: Managing Printers 632

    Installing the Print And Document Services Server Role   633

    Installing Printers   634

    Sharing Printers   638

    Configuring Print Server and Printer Permissions   640

    Adding Printer Drivers   640

    Configuring Printer Pooling   642

    Configuring Printer Priorities   643

    Managing Internet Printing   643

    Generating Notifications   644

    Deploying Printers with Group Policy   646

    Migrating Printers   647

    Managing Printers from a Command Prompt or Script   648

    Monitoring Printers   650

    Lesson Summary   653

    Lesson Review   654

Chapter Review 655

    Chapter Summary   655

    Key Terms   655

    Case Scenario   655

    Suggested Practices   656

    Take a Practice Test   656

Answers   657

Glossary   693

Index   697

About the Authors   725

What do you think of this book? We want to hear from you!

Microsoft is interested in hearing your feedback so we can continually improve our
books and learning resources for you. To participate in a brief online survey, please visit:

www.microsoft.com/learning/booksurvey/

Introduction

This training kit is designed for information technology (IT) professionals who work in the complex computing environment of medium-sized to large companies and who also plan to take Exam 70-642. We assume that before you begin using this training kit, you have a basic understanding of Windows server operating systems and common Internet technologies.

> **NOTE** **WINDOWS SERVER 2008 CERTIFICATION**
>
> Exam 70-642 is one of three required exams for MCSA: Windows Server 2008 certification. For a limited time, it is also valid for the MCTS certification, which will be retired. Please visit the Microsoft Learning website for the most current information about Microsoft certifications: *http://www.microsoft.com/learning/*

The material covered in this training kit and on the 70-642 exam relates to fundamental networking features such as addressing, name resolution, remote access, and printing. The topics in this training kit cover what you need to know for the exam as described in the Preparation Guide for the 70-642 exam, which is available at *http://www.microsoft.com/learning/en/us /exam.aspx?ID=70-642*.

By using this training kit, you will learn how to do the following:

- Configure IP addressing, routing, and IPsec.
- Configure name resolution by using Domain Name System (DNS).
- Configure remote and wireless network access.
- Configure Network Access Protection (NAP).
- Configure file and print services.
- Monitor and manage a network infrastructure.

Refer to the objective mapping page in the front of this book to see where in the book each exam objective is covered.

System Requirements

The following are the minimum system requirements your computer needs to meet to complete the practice exercises in this book and to run the companion CD.

Hardware Requirements

We recommend that you use a single physical computer and virtualization software to perform the exercises in this training kit. The physical computer should meet the following requirements:

- x64 processor.

- If you are using Hyper-V for virtualization software, the processor must support hardware-assisted virtualization, No eXecute (NX) bit technology, and data execution prevention (DEP).

- 2 GB RAM (8 GB is recommended).

- 100 GB of hard disk space (25 GB for each of three virtual machines plus 25 GB for the base system).

Software Requirements

The following software is required to complete the practice exercises:

- Windows Server 2008 R2. You can download an evaluation edition of Windows Server 2008 R2 at the Microsoft Download Center at *http://www.microsoft.com/downloads*.

- A web browser such as Windows Internet Explorer 7, Internet Explorer 8, or Internet Explorer 9.

- An application that can display PDF files, such as Adobe Acrobat Reader, which can be downloaded from *http://www.adobe.com/reader*.

Lab Setup Instructions

Most of the exercises in this training kit require two computers or virtual machines running Windows Server 2008 R2. (The exercises in Chapter 6, "Protecting Network Traffic with IPsec," several Lesson 4 exercises in Chapter 7, "Connecting to Networks," and Lesson 2 of Chapter 8, "Configuring Windows Firewall and Network Access Protection," require a third such computer or virtual machine.) All lab computers must be physically connected to the same network for most lessons. However, some lessons will describe different network configurations. We recommend that you use an isolated network that is not part of your production network to perform the practice exercises in this book.

To minimize the time and expense of configuring physical computers and networks, we recommend that you use virtual machines for the lab computers. To run computers as virtual machines within Windows, you can use Hyper-V or third-party virtual machine software such as the free VirtualBox. Both of these options allow you to run 64-bit guest operating systems in a virtual environment, and this feature is required to support Windows Server 2008 R2, which is 64-bit only. (Note that neither Virtual PC nor Virtual Server support 64-bit guests.) For more information about Hyper-V, visit *http://www.microsoft.com/hyperv*. To download VirtualBox, visit *http://www.virtualbox.org*.

Using a virtual environment is the simplest way to prepare the computers for this training kit. To isolate the lab computers within a single network, configure the settings in each virtual machine so that the network adapter is assigned to a private or an internal network. (Note that virtual network adapters are not assigned to such private or internal networks by default in either Hyper-V or VirtualBox.) In addition, some exercises need Internet access, which will require you to connect the network adapter to an external network. You can perform these exercises by temporarily connecting the network adapter to an external network, or you can perform them on another computer with Internet access.

Preparing the Windows Server 2008 R2 Computers

Perform the following steps to prepare the first Windows Server 2008 computer for the exercises in this training kit.

On the three lab computers, perform a default installation of Windows Server 2008 R2. Do not add any roles or adjust the networking settings. In Control Panel, use System to specify the computer name of the first computer as **Dcsrv1**, the second computer as **Boston**, and the third computer as **Binghamton**.

If you are using virtual machines, you should save a snapshot of the virtual machine after setup is complete so that you can quickly return the computer to that state.

> **NOTE** **TAKE SNAPSHOTS AFTER EACH EXERCISE**
>
> Virtual machine software allows you to take a *snapshot* of a virtual machine, which is the complete state of a virtual machine at any point in time. After each exercise, you should take a snapshot of any computers on which changes have been made. After Dcsrv1 is promoted to a domain controller, be sure to always take a snapshot of this virtual machine even when exercises are performed on another computer. (Changes made to member servers often modify settings on the domain controller.)

Using the CD

The companion CD included with this training kit contains the following:

- **Practice tests**   You can reinforce your understanding of how to configure Windows Server 2008 R2 network infrastructure by using electronic practice tests you customize to meet your needs from the pool of Lesson Review questions in this book. Or you can practice for the 70-642 certification exam by using tests created from a pool of about 200 realistic exam questions, which give you many practice exams to ensure that you are prepared.

- **Webcast**   To supplement your learning, the CD includes a webcast about IPsec.

- **eBook**   An electronic version (eBook) of this book is included for when you do not want to carry the printed book with you. The eBook is in Portable Document Format (PDF), and you can view it by using Adobe Acrobat or Adobe Reader.

> **Companion Content for Digital Book Readers:** If you bought a digital edition of this book, you can enjoy select content from the print edition's companion CD.
> Visit *http://go.microsoft.com/FWLink/?Linkid=215050* to get your downloadable content. This content is always up-to-date and available to all readers.

How to Install the Practice Tests

To install the practice test software from the companion CD to your hard disk, do the following:

1. Insert the companion CD into your CD drive, and accept the license agreement. A CD menu appears.

   NOTE IF THE CD MENU DOES NOT APPEAR

   If the CD menu or the license agreement does not appear, AutoRun might be disabled on your computer. Refer to the Readme.txt file on the CD-ROM for alternate installation instructions.

2. Click Practice Tests, and follow the instructions on the screen.

How to Use the Practice Tests

To start the practice test software, follow these steps:

1. Click Start\All Programs\Microsoft Press Training Kit Exam Prep. A window appears that shows all the Microsoft Press training kit exam prep suites installed on your computer.

2. Double-click the lesson review or practice test you want to use.

   NOTE LESSON REVIEWS VS. PRACTICE TESTS

   Select the (70-642) Configuring Windows Server 2008 Network Infrastructure (2nd Edition) lesson review to use the questions from the "Lesson Review" sections of this book. Select the (70-642) Configuring Windows Server 2008 Network Infrastructure (2nd Edition) practice test to use a pool of about 200 questions similar to those that appear on the 70-642 certification exam.

Lesson Review Options

When you start a lesson review, the Custom Mode dialog box appears so that you can configure your test. You can click OK to accept the defaults, or you can customize the number of questions you want, how the practice test software works, which exam objectives you want the questions to relate to, and whether you want your lesson review to be timed. If you are retaking a test, you can select whether you want to see all the questions again or only the questions you missed or did not answer.

After you click OK, your lesson review starts. The following list explains the main options you have for taking the test:

- To take the test, answer the questions and use the Next, Previous, and Go To buttons to move from question to question.

- After you answer an individual question, if you want to see which answers are correct— along with an explanation of each correct answer—click Explanation.

- If you prefer to wait until the end of the test to see how you did, answer all the questions and then click Score Test. You will see a summary of the exam objectives you chose and the percentage of questions you got right overall and per objective. You can print a copy of your test, review your answers, or retake the test.

Practice Test Options

When you start a practice test, you choose whether to take the test in Certification Mode, Study Mode, or Custom Mode:

- **Certification Mode**   Closely resembles the experience of taking a certification exam. The test has a set number of questions. It is timed, and you cannot pause and restart the timer.

- **Study Mode**   Creates an untimed test in which you can review the correct answers and the explanations after you answer each question.

- **Custom Mode**   Gives you full control over the test options so that you can customize them as you like.

In all modes, the user interface you see when you are taking the test is basically the same but with different options enabled or disabled depending on the mode. The main options are discussed in the previous section, "Lesson Review Options."

When you review your answer to an individual practice test question, a "References" section is provided that lists where in the training kit you can find the information that relates to that question and provides links to other sources of information. After you click Test Results to score your entire practice test, you can click the Learning Plan tab to see a list of references for every objective.

How to Uninstall the Practice Tests

To uninstall the practice test software for a training kit, use Add Or Remove Programs option (Windows XP) or the Program And Features option (Windows 7 and Windows Server 2008 R2) in Windows Control Panel.

Acknowledgments

This book was put together by a team of respected professionals, and we, the authors, would like to thank them each for the great job they did.

At Microsoft, Jeff Koch worked out our contracts as the acquisitions editor, Karen Szall was our developmental editor, and Carol Dillingham was our project editor.

Kathy Krause of Online Training Solutions, Inc., managed the editorial and production teams. Victoria Thulman, our copy editor, was responsible for making sure the book was readable and consistent, and Jaime Odell provided additional proofreading.

Bob Dean provided a technical review to help make the book as accurate as possible. Jan Bednarczuk created the index that you'll find at the back of the book.

Many people helped with this book, even though they weren't formally part of the team.

Tony Northrup would like to thank his friends, especially Brian and Melissa Rheaume, Jose and Kristin Gonzales, Chelsea and Madelyn Knowles, Eddie and Christine Mercado, Papa Jose, and Nana Lucy.

J.C. Mackin would like to thank his friends and family for always being so supportive.

It makes a huge difference when you consider the people you work with to be friends. Having a great team not only improves the quality of the book, it makes it a more pleasant experience. Writing this book was most enjoyable, and we hope we get the chance to work with everyone in the future.

Support & Feedback

The following sections provide information on errata, book support, feedback, and contact information.

Errata

We have made every effort to ensure the accuracy of this book and its companion content. If you do find an error, please report it on our Microsoft Press site at oreilly.com:

1. Go to *http://microsoftpress.oreilly.com*.
2. In the Search box, enter the book's ISBN or title.
3. Select your book from the search results.
4. On your book's catalog page, under the cover image, you will see a list of links.
5. Click View/Submit Errata.

You will find additional information and services for your book on its catalog page. If you need additional support, please email Microsoft Press Book Support at *mspinput@microsoft.com*.

Please note that product support for Microsoft software is not offered through the preceding addresses.

We Want to Hear from You

At Microsoft Press, your satisfaction is our top priority, and your feedback our most valuable asset. Please tell us what you think of this book at *http://www.microsoft.com/learning/booksurvey*.

The survey is short, and we read *every one* of your comments and ideas. Thanks in advance for your input!

Stay in Touch

Let's keep the conversation going! We're on Twitter: *http://twitter.com/MicrosoftPress*.

Preparing for the Exam

Microsoft certification exams are a great way to build your resume and let the world know about your level of expertise. Certification exams validate your on-the-job experience and product knowledge. Although there is no substitute for on-the-job experience, preparation through study and hands-on practice can help you prepare for the exam. We recommend that you augment your exam preparation plan by using a combination of available study materials and courses. For example, you might use the Training Kit and another study guide for your "at home" preparation, and take a Microsoft Official Curriculum course for the classroom experience. Choose the combination that you think works best for you.

CHAPTER 1

Understanding and Configuring TCP/IP

Like any communication system, computer networks rely on a set of standards that allow communicators to send, receive, and interpret messages. For the Internet, Windows networks, and virtually all other computer networks, that underlying set of standards is the suite of protocols known collectively as *Transmission Control Protocol/Internet Protocol* (TCP/IP), the core of which is IP.

In this chapter, you learn the fundamentals of TCP/IP and how to configure Windows Server 2008 and Windows Server 2008 R2 to connect to TCP/IP networks.

> IMPORTANT
> ### Have you read page xxiv?
> It contains valuable information regarding the skills you need to pass the exam.

Exam objectives in this chapter:
- Configure IPv4 and IPv6 addressing

Lessons in this chapter:

- Lesson 1: Introducing Windows Networking   **2**
- Lesson 2: Understanding IPv4 Addressing   **40**
- Lesson 3: Understanding IPv6 Addressing   **86**

Before You Begin

To complete the lessons in this chapter, you must have the following:

- Two virtual machines or physical computers, named Dcsrv1 and Boston, that are joined to the same isolated network and on which Windows Server 2008 R2 is installed. Neither computer should have any server roles added.

- A basic understanding of Windows administration.

Lesson 1: Introducing Windows Networking

This lesson introduces the basic concepts behind Windows networking. The lesson begins by introducing the concept of layered networking and then goes on to describe TCP/IP, the multi-layer suite of protocols upon which Windows networks are based. Next, the lesson describes how to configure basic networking properties in Windows Server 2008 and Windows Server 2008 R2. Finally, the lesson concludes by explaining how to perform basic network trouble-shooting with TCP/IP utilities.

After this lesson, you will be able to:

- Understand the four layers in the TCP/IP protocol suite.
- View and configure the IP configuration of a local area connection.
- Understand the concept of a network broadcast.
- Troubleshoot network connectivity with TCP/IP utilities.

Estimated lesson time: 100 minutes

What Are Network Layers?

Network layers are functional steps in communication that are performed by programs called *protocols*. As an analogy, consider an assembly line. If a factory uses an assembly line to create a product that is assembled, coated, packaged, boxed, and labeled, you could view these five sequential functions as vertically stacked layers in the production process, as shown in Figure 1-1. Following this analogy, the protocols in the assembly line are the specific machines (particular assemblers, coaters, packagers, and so on) used to carry out the function of each layer. Although each protocol is designed to accept a specific input and generate a specific output, you could replace any machine in the system as long as it remained compatible with the neighboring machines on the assembly line.

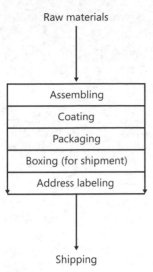

Raw materials

| Assembling |
| Coating |
| Packaging |
| Boxing (for shipment) |
| Address labeling |

Shipping

FIGURE 1-1 A layered view of assembly-line production

In a way, network communications really do resemble the creation of packaged products on an assembly line, because computers communicate with one another by creating and sending encapsulated (wrapped) packages called *packets*. Unlike assembly-line production, however, communication between computers is bidirectional. This means that the networking layers taken together describe a way both to construct *and deconstruct* packets. Each layer, and each specific protocol, must be able to perform its function in both directions. In the assembly line example, such a bidirectional model could be illustrated as shown in Figure 1-2.

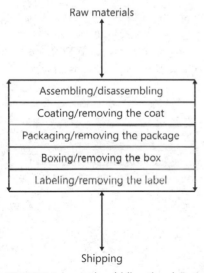

Raw materials

| Assembling/disassembling |
| Coating/removing the coat |
| Packaging/removing the package |
| Boxing/removing the box |
| Labeling/removing the label |

Shipping

FIGURE 1-2 Layers in a bidirectional, "assembly-disassembly" line

In computer networking, the layered model traditionally used to describe communications is the seven-layer Open Systems Interconnect (OSI) model, shown in Figure 1-3. You can see by their names that each of these seven layers was originally designed to perform a step in communication, such as presenting or transporting information.

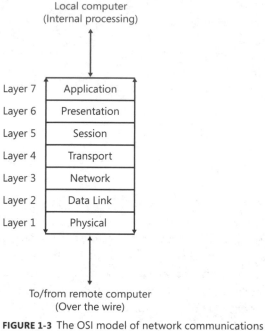

FIGURE 1-3 The OSI model of network communications

Although the particular protocols that originally instantiated the OSI model were never adopted in practice, the names, and especially the numbers, of the layers of the model survive to this day. As a result, even though TCP/IP is based on its own model, the four TCP/IP networking layers are often defined in terms of their relationship to the OSI model, as shown in Figure 1-4.

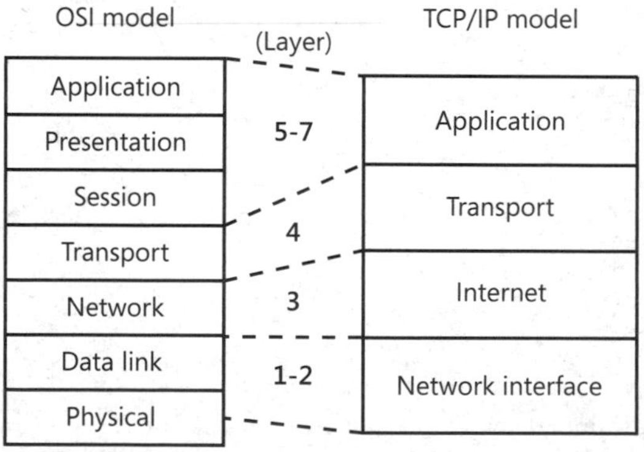

OSI model	(Layer)	TCP/IP model
Application		Application
Presentation	5-7	
Session		Transport
Transport	4	
Network	3	Internet
Data link	1-2	Network interface
Physical		

FIGURE 1-4 The TCP/IP networking layers are mapped to the OSI model.

Exploring the Layers of the TCP/IP Networking Model

The idea of a layered networking model allows individual protocols to be modified as long as they still work seamlessly with neighboring protocols. Such a protocol change has in fact recently happened with TCP/IP in Windows networks. Beginning with Windows Server 2008 and Windows Vista, and continuing with Windows Server 2008 R2 and Windows 7, Microsoft has introduced a new implementation of the TCP/IP protocol stack known as the *Next Generation TCP/IP stack*. This version of the TCP/IP stack features a new design at the Internet layer, but the protocols at the neighboring layers remain essentially unchanged.

The Next Generation TCP/IP stack is shown in Figure 1-5.

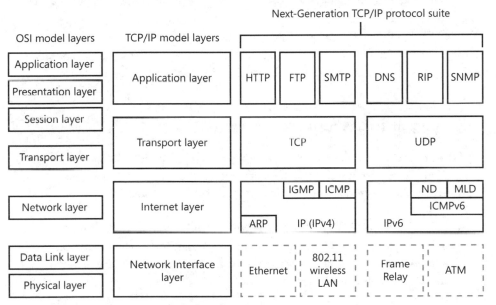

FIGURE 1-5 The Next Generation TCP/IP stack

NOTE TCP/IP LAYER NUMBERS

Although you will sometimes see the layers of the TCP/IP model assigned their own numbers independent of the OSI model, this book's terminology reflects the layer number usage that is far more current.

The following section describes in more detail the four layers of TCP/IP shown in Figure 1-5.

Network Interface Layer

The *network interface layer,* often also called *layer 2* or the *data link layer,* describes a standard method for communication among devices located on a single network segment. (A *network segment* consists of network interfaces separated only by cables, switches, hubs, or wireless access points.) Network interfaces use protocols at this layer to communicate with other nearby interfaces identified by a fixed hardware address (such as MAC address). The network interface layer also specifies physical requirements for signaling, interfaces, cables, hubs, switches, and access points; this subset of purely physical specifications can sometimes be referred to as the *physical* layer or *layer 1.* Examples of standards defined at the network interface layer include Ethernet, Token Ring, Point-to-Point Protocol (PPP), and Fiber Distributed Data Interface (FDDI).

> **NOTE A SWITCH OPERATES AT LAYER 2**
>
> Because a switch reads hardware addresses on the local network and restricts the propagation of network traffic to only those addresses needed, a switch is said to be a layer 2 device.

Looking at the Ethernet Protocol

Ethernet packets are known more specifically as frames. The following section includes an Ethernet frame that has been captured by Network Monitor, a protocol analyzer available for download from the Microsoft website.

> **NOTE PROTOCOL DETAILS ARE NOT COVERED ON MICROSOFT EXAMS**
>
> You don't need to understand the frame contents of any protocol type to pass the 70-642 exam. However, this type of in-depth knowledge can help you better understand and visualize protocols.

The first line, beginning with the word "Frame," precedes the captured frame and is added by Network Monitor to provide general information about the frame that follows. The Ethernet-only data (called a *header*) then follows; it has been expanded and highlighted.

Beneath the Ethernet header, if you scan the left side of the frame contents, you can see that the frame also includes headers for IPv4, TCP, and HTTP.

The last section of the packet is the HTTP header, which indicates an "HTTP GET Request" destined for a remote web server. The *ultimate* purpose of the entire Ethernet frame is therefore to request the contents of a remote webpage.

```
Frame: Number = 16, Captured Frame Length = 664, MediaType = ETHERNET

- Ethernet: Etype = Internet IP (IPv4),DestinationAddress:[00-1E-2A-47-
C2-78],SourceAddress:[00-15-5D-02-03-00]
  + DestinationAddress: 001E2A 47C278 [00-1E-2A-47-C2-78]
  + SourceAddress: Microsoft Corporation 020300 [00-15-5D-02-03-00]
    EthernetType: Internet IP (IPv4), 2048(0x800)
```

```
+ Ipv4: Src = 192.168.2.201, Dest = 216.156.213.67, Next Protocol = TCP,
Packet ID = 1134, Total IP Length = 650

+ Tcp: Flags=...AP..., SrcPort=49197, DstPort=HTTP(80), PayloadLen=610,
Seq=776410322 - 776410932, Ack=829641496, Win=32850 (scale factor 0x2) =
131400

+ Http: Request, GET /
```

Within the expanded Ethernet header, you can see a *DestinationAddress* and a *SourceAddress* value. These values represent MAC addresses, or fixed hardware addresses, assigned to network interfaces. The *SourceAddress* value is labeled "Microsoft Corporation" by Network Monitor because the first half of this MAC address (00-15-5D) designates Microsoft as the manufacturer of the network interface. (The local computer is in fact a virtual machine running inside the Microsoft Hyper-V virtualization platform, so the network interface in this case is actually a piece of software.) The second half of the MAC address is unique to this particular interface.

The "*DestinationAddress*" in this case refers to the default gateway on the local LAN, not the remote web server to which the packet contents are ultimately destined. Protocols such as Ethernet that operate at layer 2 do not see beyond the local network.

The *EthernetType* field designates the next upper-layer protocol contained within the frame. When a host operating system receives the frame, the value in this field determines which protocol will receive the data after the Ethernet header. In this case, the payload of data within the Ethernet frame will be passed to the IPv4 protocol for further processing.

As the packet moves from the local LAN and through the Internet toward its final destination at the remote web server, this layer 2 header will be rewritten many times to account for the new source and destination addresses within each network link. It can also be repeatedly revised to account for other network interface–layer technologies besides Ethernet, such as FDDI or Token Ring, that the packet might traverse.

Internet Layer

The Internet layer, also often called *layer 3* or the *network* layer, describes a global and configurable software addressing scheme that allows devices to communicate when they reside on remote network segments. The main protocol that operates at layer 3 is IP, and the network device that reads data at this layer is a router. *Routers* read the destination address written in a packet and then forward that packet toward its destination along an appropriate network pathway. If at this layer the destination address in a packet specifies a local network address or a local broadcast, the router simply drops the packet by default. For this reason, it is said that routers block broadcasts.

As previously mentioned, layer 3 is where the main changes have appeared in Microsoft's latest implementation of TCP/IP. Traditionally, IPv4 is the only protocol to appear at this layer. In the Next Generation TCP/IP stack, however, the IPv4 and IPv6 protocols now co-occupy layer 3. Just one set of protocols at the neighboring layers communicate with both IPv4 and IPv6.

- **IPv4** IPv4, or simply IP, is responsible for addressing and routing packets between hosts that might be dozens of network segments away. IPv4 relies on 32-bit addresses, and because of this relatively small address space, addresses are rapidly becoming depleted in IPv4 networks.

- **IPv6** IPv6 uses 128-bit addresses instead of the 32-bit addresses used with IPv4, and, as a result, it can define many more addresses. Because few Internet routers are IPv6-compatible, IPv6 today is used over the Internet with the help of tunneling protocols. However, IPv6 is supported natively in Windows Vista, Windows 7, Windows Server 2008, and Windows Server 2008 R2.

Both IPv4 and IPv6 are enabled by default. As a result of this dual-IP layer architecture, computers can use IPv6 to communicate if the client, server, and network infrastructure support it. Computers can also communicate over IPv4 with other computers or network services if IPv6 is not supported.

Looking at the IP Protocol

The following Ethernet frame is the same that was shown in the "Looking at the Ethernet Protocol" sidebar earlier in this chapter. However, the following output expands and highlights the IPv4 header in this frame:

```
Frame: Number = 16, Captured Frame Length = 664, MediaType = ETHERNET

+ Ethernet: Etype = Internet IP (IPv4),DestinationAddress:[00-1E-2A-47-
C2-78],SourceAddress:[00-15-5D-02-03-00]

- Ipv4: Src = 192.168.2.201, Dest = 216.156.213.67, Next Protocol = TCP,
Packet ID = 1134, Total IP Length = 650
    + Versions: IPv4, Internet Protocol; Header Length = 20
    + DifferentiatedServicesField: DSCP: 0, ECN: 0
      TotalLength: 650 (0x28A)
      Identification: 1134 (0x46E)
    + FragmentFlags: 16384 (0x4000)
      TimeToLive: 128 (0x80)
      NextProtocol: TCP, 6(0x6)
      Checksum: 0 (0x0)
      SourceAddress: 192.168.2.201
      DestinationAddress: 216.156.213.67

+ Tcp: Flags=...AP..., SrcPort=49197, DstPort=HTTP(80), PayloadLen=610,
Seq=776410322 - 776410932, Ack=829641496, Win=32850 (scale factor 0x2) =
131400

+ Http: Request, GET /
```

As with the Ethernet header, the most important data in the IPv4 header is the *SourceAddress* and *DestinationAddress*, both of which appear at the end of the highlighted section. Note, however, that in this case the addresses specified are IP addresses, and that the destination address specified is the ultimate destination (the remote web server).

Beyond the source and destination addresses, the IP header also contains information used for various other features of the protocol. The *DifferentiatedServicesField* section is broken into two fields, DSCP and ECN. The DSCP field, which is read only by some special routers, allows particular IP traffic to be designated as requiring priority handling. The ECN field signals congestion on a router to other downstream routers. *TotalLength* is the length in bytes of the IP packet (also called a "datagram"). This length includes all data from layer 3, 4, and up, including any data payload beyond the headers. In this case, the IP datagram is 650 bytes long. The *Identification* field is a number given to a packet so that if it is fragmented, it can be reassembled. (Packets are fragmented when their length exceeds a value called the Maximum Transmission Unit [MTU] size specified by computers, routers, and other devices.) The *FragmentFlags* section provides information that helps designate and reassemble fragmented IP datagrams. The *TimeToLive* value is set to 128 by default in Windows and is then decremented by 1 by each router that handles the IP datagram. If the value ever reaches 0, the datagram is discarded. The purpose of this feature is to prevent infinite looping of data on a network. *NextProtocol* specifies the upper-layer (layer 4) protocol that should handle the contents of the IP datagram. In this case, TCP is specified. The *Checksum* field contains the result of a mathematical function whose purpose is to check the integrity of the IP header. The checksum value of 0 here indicates that that the checksum value is being set and checked outside the TCP/IP stack.

IP datagrams can occur in one of two varieties: IPv4 and IPv6. IPv6 is a newer, alternative version of IP that is used in some network transmissions. The following Ethernet frame contains an IPv6 header that has been expanded and highlighted:

```
Frame: Number - 43, Captured Frame Length = 86, MediaType = ETHERNET

+ Ethernet: Etype = IPv6,DestinationAddress:[33-33-00-01-00-
03],SourceAddress:[00-15-5D-02-03-05]

- Ipv6: Next Protocol = UDP, Payload Length = 32
  + Versions: IPv6, Internet Protocol, DSCP 0
    PayloadLength: 32 (0x20)
    NextProtocol: UDP, 17(0x11)
    HopLimit: 1 (0x1)
    SourceAddress: FE80:0:0:0:D9C6:6B0E:BA3F:1FC9
    DestinationAddress: FF02:0:0:0:0:0:1:3

+ Udp: SrcPort = 53047, DstPort = Linklocal Multicast Name
Resolution(5355), Length = 32

+ Llmnr: QueryId = 0x862D, Standard, Query  for boston of type Host Addr
on class Internet
```

In the IPv6 header, *PayloadLength* indicates the length in bytes of the data carried within the IPv6 datagram. *NextProtocol* indicates the layer 4 protocol to which the IPv6 payload should be passed. The *HopLimit* value is the same as the TimeToLive value in IPv4. The value of 1 here indicates that the packet is destined only for the local LAN. The SourceAddress and DestinationAddress values specified here are 16-byte IPv6 addresses. The destination address in this particular case happens to be a multicast address that can be owned by more than one computer on the local LAN.

Transport Layer

The *transport layer* of the TCP/IP model, also called layer 4, defines a method to send and receive shipments of data among devices. Layer 4 also serves to tag data as being destined for a particular application, such as email or the web.

TCP and UDP are the two transport layer protocols within the TCP/IP suite.

- **TCP**   TCP receives data from an application and processes the data as a stream of bytes. These bytes are grouped into segments that TCP then numbers and sequences for delivery to a network host. TCP communication is two-way and reliable. The receiver acknowledges when each segment of a data shipment is received, and if the sender misses an acknowledgment, the sender resends that segment.

    When TCP receives a stream of data from a network host, it sends the data to the application designated by the TCP port number. TCP ports enable different applications and programs to use TCP services on a single host, as shown in Figure 1-6. Each program that uses TCP ports listens for messages arriving on its associated port number. Data sent to a specific TCP port is thus received by the application listening at that port.

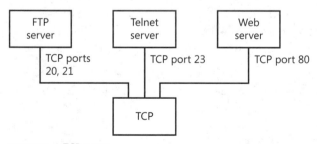

FIGURE 1-6 TCP ports

- **UDP**   Many network services (such as DNS) rely on UDP instead of TCP as a transport protocol. UDP enables fast transport of datagrams by eliminating the reliability features of TCP, such as acknowledgments, delivery guarantees, and sequence verification. Unlike TCP, UDP is a *connectionless* service that provides only best-effort delivery to network hosts. A source host that needs reliable communication must use either TCP or a program that provides its own sequencing and acknowledgment services.

Looking at the TCP and UDP Protocols

TCP and UDP are both transport-layer protocols, but only TCP is a connection-oriented protocol. *Connection-oriented* communication occurs within a two-way session; whenever one computer sends data to another through TCP, the receiver sends acknowledgments of the data received back to the sender.

A TCP session between two computers is first established by means of a three-step handshake. In the first step, the first computer sends a "synchronize," or SYN, message. The second computer then responds with a TCP packet (called a *segment*) that includes both an ACK (acknowledgment) and a SYN. Finally, the first computer responds to the second computer by sending an ACK segment.

This three-step handshake is shown in the Network Monitor capture in Figure 1-7. In the figure, notice the three TCP segments in a row. The three segments are exchanged between a first computer at address 192.168.2.201 and a second computer at the address 192.168.2.103.

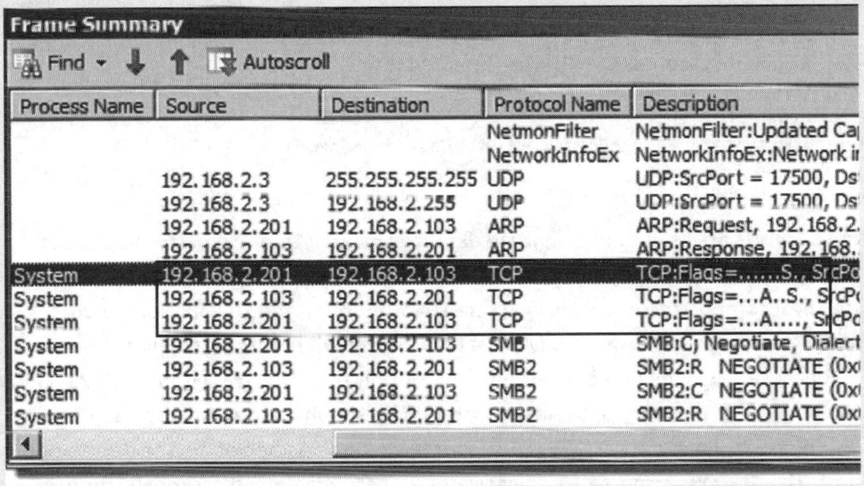

FIGURE 1-7 A TCP handshake

In the first TCP segment of the handshake, which is initiated by the first computer, a SYN is seen in Network Monitor by the description "TCP:Flags=......S.". The second computer then responds with a SYN-ACK segment, represented by the description "TCP:Flags=...A..S.". Finally, the first computer responds to the second with an ACK segment, shown by the description "TCP: Flags=...A....".

After the session is established, TCP can be used to transport data from one computer to another. The header of a TCP segment used within such a session can be seen in the section that follows. The following Ethernet frame is the same that was shown in the "Looking at the Ethernet Protocol" sidebar earlier in this chapter. However, the following output expands and highlights the TCP header within this frame:

```
Frame: Number = 16, Captured Frame Length = 664, MediaType = ETHERNET

+ Ethernet: Etype = Internet IP (IPv4),DestinationAddress:[00-1E-2A-47-
C2-78],SourceAddress:[00-15-5D-02-03-00]

+ Ipv4: Src = 192.168.2.201, Dest = 216.156.213.67, Next Protocol = TCP,
Packet ID = 1134, Total IP Length = 650

- Tcp: Flags=...AP..., SrcPort=49197, DstPort=HTTP(80), PayloadLen=610,
Seq=776410322 - 776410932, Ack=829641496, Win=32850 (scale factor 0x2) =
131400
    SrcPort: 49197
    DstPort: HTTP(80)
    SequenceNumber: 776410322 (0x2E4714D2)
    AcknowledgementNumber: 829641496 (0x31735318)
  + DataOffset: 80 (0x50)
  + Flags: ...AP...
    Window: 32850 (scale factor 0x2) = 131400
    Checksum: 0x73CE, Disregarded
    UrgentPointer: 0 (0x0)
    TCPPayload: SourcePort = 49197, DestinationPort = 80

+ Http: Request, GET /
```

In TCP, ports are used to differentiate data streams sent to or from various applications. The data carried by this particular TCP segment is an HTTP GET Request from the local computer to a remote web server. So, although the *SrcPort* (source port) 49197 of this request is randomly chosen, the destination port, or *DstPort*, must be 80 because this is the number reserved for HTTP traffic. The *SequenceNumber* relates to the order of *outgoing* data within a larger data stream carried by many segments. This number allows data received out of order to be reassembled by the destination host. The *AcknowledgementNumber* relates to *incoming* data: It essentially informs the sender of a TCP data stream which bytes of data have already been received. The *DataOffset* value indicates where the TCP header ends and the data payload begins.

The *Flags* are a series of eight bits. Each particular bit carries a special meaning when it is set (to 1 and not to 0). For example, an ACK is indicated by setting the fourth bit, and a SYN is indicated by setting the seventh bit. In this segment, the flags that are set indicate an ACK and a PSH (push). A push essentially sends data immediately to the upper-level protocol (here, HTTP) before the entire TCP buffer is full. Other important flag messages include RST (abort the TCP session), FIN (end the TCP session), and URG (urgent data included).

The *Window* value relates to data flow control. This value is sent by the receiver of a byte stream to notify the sender how many bytes of data the receiver can currently receive. Because this window varies from segment to segment, TCP is said to have *sliding windows*. The *Checksum* value is an integrity check of the data and operates the same way as the IP header checksum. The *UrgentPointer* value indicates where the urgent data is located when the URG flag is set.

Now, compare the feature-rich, connection-oriented TCP with its *connectionless* equivalent, UDP. The following Ethernet frame expands and highlights the UDP header:

```
 Frame: Number = 11, Captured Frame Length = 72, MediaType = ETHERNET

+ Ethernet: Etype = Internet IP (IPv4),DestinationAddress:[00-1F-C6-72-
80-C2],SourceAddress:[00-15-5D-02-03-00]

+ Ipv4: Src = 192.168.2.201, Dest = 192.168.2.2, Next Protocol = UDP,
Packet ID = 1131, Total IP Length = 58

- Udp: SrcPort = 65265, DstPort = DNS(53), Length = 38
    SrcPort: 65265
    DstPort: DNS(53)
    TotalLength: 38 (0x26)
    Checksum: 31269 (0x7A25)
    UDPPayload: SourcePort = 65265, DestinationPort = 53

+ Dns: QueryId = 0xDF04, QUERY (Standard query), Query  for www.bing.com
of type Host Addr on class Internet
```

What is most striking about the UDP header is how simple it is compared to TCP. The reason it is so simple is that UDP provides so few features. There is no sequence information, no acknowledgments, no flow control, and no message flags. UDP also includes no handshake process and no two-way session that starts and ends. The data transported by UDP is simply sent to a destination address and port, and if the receiver doesn't receive the byte stream, the data is lost.

Application Layer

The *application layer*, sometimes called layer 7, is the step at which network services are standardized. Application layer protocols are programs such as email that provide some service to a user or application. Besides email-related protocols such as POP3, SMTP, and IMAP4, some examples of application layer protocols native to the TCP/IP suite include HTTP, Telnet, FTP, Trivial File Transfer Protocol (TFTP), Simple Network Management Protocol (SNMP), DNS, and Network News Transfer Protocol (NNTP).

TCP/IP Encapsulation

By encapsulating data with each of the four layers described earlier in this chapter, TCP/IP creates a packet, as shown in the simplified example in Figure 1-8. In the figure, an email message of "Hello" is encapsulated with POP3 email (layer 7), TCP (layer 4), IP (layer 3), and Ethernet (layer 2) headers.

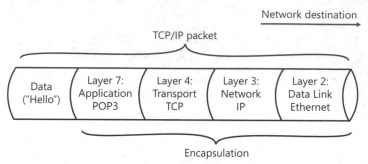

FIGURE 1-8 An example of a TCP/IP packet

NOTE   THE NUMBER OF PROTOCOLS IN EACH PACKET VARIES

The packet shown in Figure 1-8 is simplified because not every packet really includes data encapsulated by exactly four protocols. Many packets, for example, are designed to provide end-to-end communication only for lower layers such as TCP and therefore include fewer protocols. Other packets can have more than four protocols if they include more than one protocol at a given layer. For example, many higher-level application protocols and services can be used together at layer 4 within a single packet.

 Quick Check

1. At which networking layer is Ethernet found?
2. What do routers do to network broadcasts by default?

Quick Check Answers

1. Layer 2.
2. Routers block broadcasts by default.

Configuring Networking Properties in Windows Server 2008 R2

The Windows Server 2008 R2 interface includes two main areas in which to configure networking properties: Network and Sharing Center, and Network Connections. The following section describes these areas within the Windows Server 2008 R2 interface and the settings that you can configure in them.

Network and Sharing Center

Network and Sharing Center is the central dashboard for network settings in Windows Server 2008 R2. To open Network and Sharing Center, from the Start menu, right-click Network, and then select Properties. Alternatively, in the Notification area, right-click the network icon, and then choose Open Network And Sharing Center from the shortcut menu. As a third option, you can find Network and Sharing Center by browsing to Control Panel\Network and Internet\Network and Sharing Center.

Network and Sharing Center is shown in Figure 1-9.

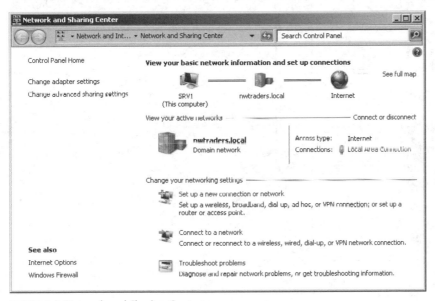

FIGURE 1-9 Network and Sharing Center

You can use Network and Sharing Center to review the basic network configuration and verify Internet access. You can also follow links to run a network troubleshooting wizard, open the status page of the Local Area Connection (or other active connection), create a new connection, and perform many other tasks.

Most of these options visible in Network and Sharing Center are self-explanatory. However, two options might require clarification: Change Advanced Sharing Settings and See Full Map.

Change Advanced Sharing Settings in Network and Sharing Center relates to the default settings on the local computer for network profiles, such as Home or Work, or Public. For each of these network profiles, you can configure the local computer to enable or disable Network Discovery (a protocol that enables browsing), File And Printer Sharing, Public Folder Sharing, and Media Streaming. However, these settings are mostly relevant for a workgroup environment and are not tested on the 70-642 exam. In a Domain environment, servers will automatically be set to the Domain network profile, and the default features enabled in the Domain network profile should be set for the entire domain by Group Policy.

The See Full Map option in Network and Sharing Center allows you to see the devices on your local LAN and how these devices are connected to each other and to the Internet. This feature is disabled by default in the Domain network profile, but it can be enabled in Group Policy. An example Network Map output is shown in Figure 1-10.

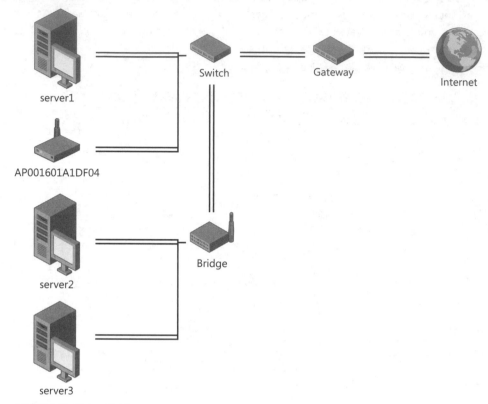

FIGURE 1-10 Network Map

Network Map relies on two components:

- The Link Layer Topology Discovery (LLTD) Mapper component queries the network for devices to include in the map.

- The LLTD Responder component responds to the queries from the Mapper I/O.

Although these two components are included only in Windows Vista, Windows 7, Windows Server 2008, and Windows Server 2008 R2, you can install an LLTD Responder component on computers running Windows XP so that they will appear on a Network Map on other computers.

EXAM TIP

Remember that to make a computer running Windows XP appear on the Network Map, you have to install the LLTD Responder on that computer.

Viewing Network Connections

Windows Server 2008 R2 automatically detects and configures connections associated with network adapters installed on the local computer. These connections are then displayed in Network Connections, along with any additional connections, such as dial-up connections, that you have added manually by clicking the Set Up A New Connection Or Network option in Network and Sharing Center.

You can open Network Connections in a number of ways. First, you can select the Server Manager node in Server Manager and then click View Network Connections. Also, in the Initial Configuration Tasks window, you can click Configure Networking. Next, in Network and Sharing Center, you can click Change Adapter Settings. Finally, from the command line, Start Search text box, or Run text box, you can type the command **ncpa.cpl.**

VIEWING DEFAULT COMPONENTS OF NETWORK CONNECTIONS

Connections by themselves do not allow network hosts to communicate. Instead, the network clients, services, and protocols *bound to* a connection are what provide connectivity through that connection. If you open the properties of a particular connection in Network Connections, the Networking tab of the Properties dialog box reveals the clients, services, and protocols bound to that connection.

Figure 1-11 shows the default components installed on a Windows Server 2008 local area connection. The check box next to each component indicates that the component is bound to the connection.

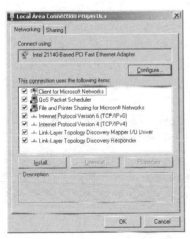

FIGURE 1-11 Default components for a connection

The following list describes the three types of network components that can be bound to a connection:

- **Network Clients** In Windows, *network clients* are software components, such as Client For Microsoft Networks, that allow the local computer to connect with a particular network operating system. By default, Client For Microsoft Networks is the only network client bound to all local area connections. Client For Microsoft Networks allows Windows client computers to connect to shared resources on other Windows computers.

- **Network Services** *Network services* are software components that provide additional features for network connections. File And Printer Sharing For Microsoft Networks and QoS Packet Scheduler are the two network services bound to all local area connections by default. File And Printer Sharing For Microsoft Networks allows the local computer to share folders for network access. QoS Packet Scheduler provides network traffic control, including rate-of-flow and prioritization services.

- **Network Protocols** Computers can communicate through a connection only by using *network protocols* bound to that connection. By default, four network protocols are installed and bound to every network connection: IPv4, IPv6, the Link-Layer Topology Discovery (LLTD) Mapper, and the LLTD Responder.

Bridging Network Connections

In some cases, you might want to combine multiple network connections on a given computer so that Windows will treat these connections as if they were on the same network (in one broadcast domain). For example, you might want to share a single wireless access point (WAP) with multiple and varying connection topologies, as shown in Figure 1-12.

In this example, an Internet connection is joined to a single WAP. The WAP then communicates with the wireless network interface card (NIC) in the server. Additionally, the server has an Ethernet connection and a Token Ring connection attached to other networks.

When you enable *network bridging* on this connection, all points entering the server (wireless, Token Ring, and Ethernet) appear on the same network. Hence, they can all share the wireless connection and get out to the Internet.

To bridge the networks, press Ctrl as you select multiple network connections on the server. Then, right-click and select Bridge Networks, as shown in Figure 1-13.

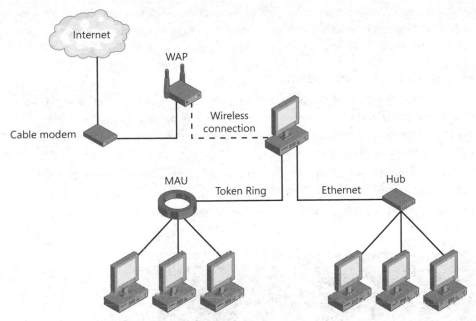

FIGURE 1-12 Example of network bridging

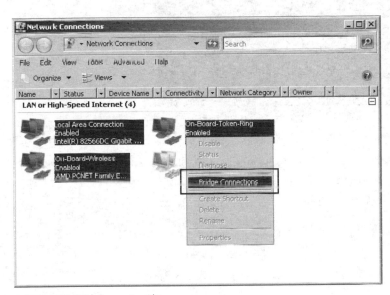

FIGURE 1-13 Bridging networks

When you configure network bridging, you allow traffic from the wireless, Ethernet, and Token Ring NIC to share the same network space. Hence, a single wireless NIC can be the outbound gateway to disparate networks.

Viewing an Address Configuration

The IP configuration of a connection consists, at a minimum, of an IPv4 address and subnet mask or an IPv6 address and subnet prefix. Beyond these minimal settings, an IP configuration can also include information such as a default gateway, DNS server addresses, a DNS name suffix, and WINS server addresses.

To view the IP address configuration for a given connection, you can use either the Ipconfig command or the Network Connection Details dialog box.

To use Ipconfig, type **ipconfig** at a command prompt. You will see an output similar to that shown in Figure 1-14.

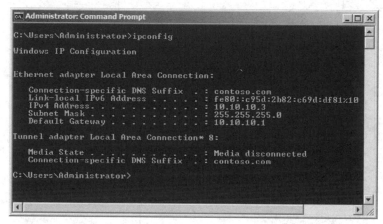

FIGURE 1-14 Viewing an IP address

To open the Network Connection Details dialog box, first click the connection in Network and Sharing Center to open the Status dialog box.

Then, in the Status dialog box, click the Details button, as shown in Figure 1-15.

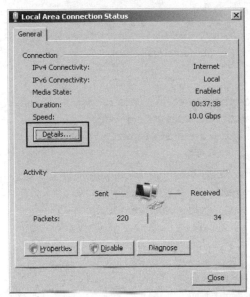

FIGURE 1-15 Local Area Connection Status dialog box

This last step opens the Network Connection Details dialog box, shown in Figure 1-16.

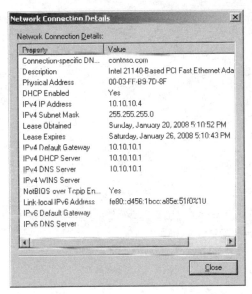

FIGURE 1-16 Network Connection Details dialog box

Assigning an IP Configuration Manually

A network connection can be assigned an IP configuration manually or automatically. This next section explains how to assign an IPv4 and IPv6 configuration manually.

ASSIGNING AN IPV4 CONFIGURATION MANUALLY

A manually configured address is known as a *static address* because such an address remains constant even after the computer reboots. Such static addresses are appropriate for critical infrastructure servers such as domain controllers, DNS servers, DHCP servers, WINS servers, and routers.

You can manually assign a static address and other IPv4 configuration parameters to a network connection by using the Internet Protocol Version 4 (TCP/IP) Properties dialog box. To access this dialog box, open the properties of the network connection for which you want to assign an IPv4 configuration. (To do this, you can right-click a particular network connection in Network Connections and then click Properties. Alternatively, you can click the connection in Network and Sharing Center, and then click Properties in the Status window.) In the connection's properties dialog box, double-click the Internet Protocol Version 4 (TCP/IPv4) from the list of components.

The Internet Protocol Version 4 (TCP/IPv4) Properties dialog box is shown in Figure 1-17.

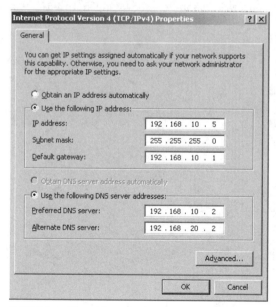

FIGURE 1-17 Manually assigning an IPv4 configuration

By default, network connections are configured to obtain an IP address and DNS server address automatically. To change this default and configure a static IP address, you need to select the Use The Following IP Address option and then specify an IP address, a subnet mask, and (optionally) a default gateway. To assign a static DNS server assignment to the connection, select the Use The Following DNS Server Addresses option, and then specify a preferred and (optionally) alternate DNS server address.

ASSIGNING AN IPV6 CONFIGURATION MANUALLY

In most cases, you do not need to configure an IPv6 address manually because static IPv6 addresses are normally assigned only to routers and not to hosts. Typically, an IPv6 configuration is assigned to a host through autoconfiguration.

However, you can set an IPv6 address manually by using the Internet Protocol Version 6 (TCP/IPv6) Properties dialog box. To open this dialog box, in the properties of the network connection, double-click Internet Protocol Version 6 (TCP/IPv6). The Internet Protocol Version 6 (TCP/IPv6) Properties dialog box is shown in Figure 1-18.

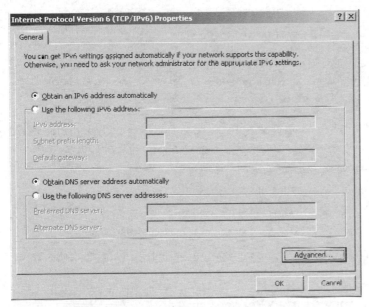

FIGURE 1-18 Configuring IPv6 settings

As with IPv4, network connections are configured to obtain an IPv6 address automatically and to obtain a DNS server address automatically. To configure a static IPv6 address, select the Use The Following IPv6 Address option and specify an IPv6 address, subnet prefix length (typically 64), and (optionally) a default gateway. Note that if you configure a static IPv6 address, you must also specify a static IPv6 DNS server address.

CONFIGURING IPV4 AND IPV6 SETTINGS MANUALLY FROM THE COMMAND PROMPT

You can use the Netsh utility to assign an IP configuration to a connection from the command prompt. To assign a static IPv4 address and subnet mask to a connection from the command prompt, type the following, where *Connection_Name* is the name of the connection (such as Local Area Connection), *Address* is the IPv4 address, and *Subnet_Mask* is the subnet mask:

```
netsh interface ipv4 set address "Connection_Name" static Address Subnet_Mask
```

For example, to set the IPv4 address of the Local Area Connection to 192.168.33.5 with a subnet mask of 255.255.255.0, you would type the following:

```
netsh interface ipv4 set address "local area connection" static 192.168.33.5
255.255.255.0
```

If you also want to define a default gateway along with the IPv4 configuration, you can add that information to the end of the command. For example, to configure the same IPv4 address for the local area connection with a default gateway of 192.168.33.1, type the following:

```
netsh interface ipv4 set address "local area connection" static 192.168.33.5
255.255.255.0 192.168.33.1
```

> **NOTE ALTERNATE NETSH SYNTAX**
>
> There are many acceptable variations in Netsh syntax. For example, you can type *netsh interface ip* instead of *netsh interface ipv4*. For more information, use Netsh Help.

To assign a static IPv6 address to a connection from the command prompt, type the following, where *Connection_Name* is the name of the connection and *Address* is the IPv6 address:

```
netsh interface ipv6 set address "Connection_Name" Address
```

For example, to assign an address of 2001:db8:290c:1291::1 to the Local Area Connection (leaving the default subnet prefix of 64), type the following:

```
netsh interface ipv6 set address "Local Area Connection" 2001:db8:290c:1291::1
```

The Netsh utility includes many other options for configuring both IPv4 and IPv6. Use Netsh Help for more information on the options and syntax.

Configuring an IPv4 Connection to Receive an Address Automatically

By default, all connections are configured to receive an IPv4 address automatically. When configured in this way, a computer owning this type of a connection is known as a *DHCP client*.

As a result of this setting, all network connections will obtain an IPv4 address from a DHCP server if one is available. If no DHCP server is available, a connection will automatically assign itself any alternate configuration that you have defined for it. If you have defined no alternate configuration, the connection will automatically assign itself an Automatic Private IP Addressing (APIPA) address for IPv4.

To configure a connection to obtain an IPv4 address automatically, select the appropriate option in the Internet Protocol Version 4 (TCP/IPv4) Properties dialog box, as shown in Figure 1-19.

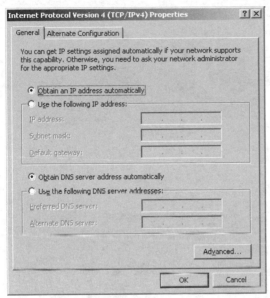

FIGURE 1-19 A connection configured to obtain an IPv4 address automatically (the default setting)

You can also use the Netsh utility to configure a client to obtain an IPv4 address automatically. To do so, at the command prompt, type the following, where *Connection_Name* is the name of the network connection:

```
netsh interface ipv4 set address "Connection_Name" dhcp
```

For example, to configure the Local Area Connection to obtain an address automatically, type the following:

```
netsh interface ipv4 set address "Local Area Connection" dhcp
```

UNDERSTANDING DHCP-ASSIGNED ADDRESSES

DHCP-assigned addresses always take priority over other automatic IPv4 configuration methods. A host on an IP network can receive an IP address from a DHCP server when a DHCP server (or DHCP Relay Agent) is located within broadcast range.

A network broadcast is a transmission that is directed to all local addresses. Such a broadcast propagates through all layer 1 and layer 2 devices (such as cables, repeaters, hubs, bridges, and switches) but is blocked by layer 3 devices (routers). Computers that can communicate with one another through broadcasts are said to be located in the same broadcast domain.

A network broadcast is illustrated in Figure 1-20.

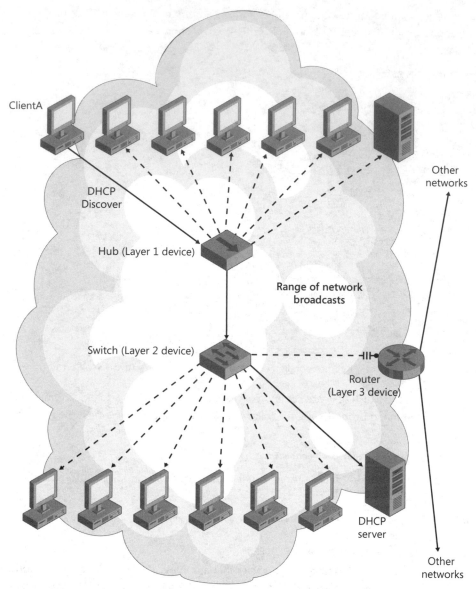

FIGURE 1-20 ClientA can obtain an IP address from the DHCP server because the two computers lie within the same broadcast domain. Note that the broadcast range extends only as far as the router.

DEFINING AN ALTERNATE CONFIGURATION

If no DHCP server is available within a client's broadcast range, a client that has been configured to obtain an address automatically will default to an alternate configuration if you have defined one.

You can assign an alternate configuration to a connection by selecting the Alternate Configuration tab in the Internet Protocol Version 4 (TCP/IPv4) Properties dialog box. This tab is shown in Figure 1-21. Note that the alternate configuration allows you to specify an IP address, subnet mask, default gateway, DNS server, and WINS server.

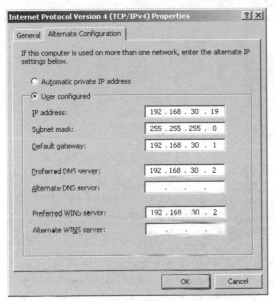

FIGURE 1-21 Specifying an alternate IPv4 configuration

Because an alternate configuration allows a computer to be assigned a specific and detailed IP configuration when no DHCP server can be found, defining an alternate configuration is useful for portable computers that move between networks with and without DHCP servers.

EXAM TIP
You need to understand the benefit of alternate configurations for the 70-642 exam.

UNDERSTANDING AUTOMATIC PRIVATE IP ADDRESSING
Automatic Private IP Addressing (APIPA) is an automatic addressing feature useful for some ad hoc or temporary networks. Whenever a Windows computer has been configured to obtain an IP address automatically, and when no DHCP server or alternate configuration is available, the computer uses APIPA to assign itself a private IP address in the range of 169.254.0.1 through 169.254.255.254 and a subnet mask of 255.255.0.0.

By default, all network connections are set to default to APIPA when no DHCP server can be reached. This setting is shown in Figure 1-22.

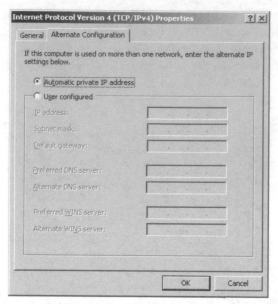

FIGURE 1-22 By default, network connections adopt an APIPA address in the absence of a DHCP server.

The APIPA feature is useful because it enables two or more Windows computers located in the same broadcast domain to communicate with one another without requiring a DHCP server or any user configuration. It also allows DHCP clients to communicate in the event of a DHCP failure. If the DHCP server later becomes available, the APIPA address is replaced by one obtained from the DHCP server.

EXAM TIP

When two client computers can see each other but cannot connect to anything else on the network (or the Internet), suspect APIPA. Either there is a problem with your network's DHCP server or there is a faulty connection to the DHCP server.

Although an APIPA address enables some local network communication, the limitations of being assigned such an address are significant. Connections assigned APIPA addresses can communicate only with other computers using APIPA addresses within broadcast range on the network; such computers cannot access the Internet. Note also that through APIPA, you cannot configure a computer with a DNS server address, a default gateway address, or a WINS server address.

An APIPA address configuration is shown in Figure 1-23.

FIGURE 1-23 An APIPA address is a sign of a network problem.

REPAIRING A NETWORK CONNECTION WITH IPCONFIG /RENEW AND THE DIAGNOSE FEATURE

If a connection has been assigned an APIPA address, it is typically a sign that the connection has not properly obtained an IP address from a DHCP server. Because connections assigned with APIPA addresses can communicate only with nearby computers that have also been assigned APIPA addresses, such addresses are usually undesirable. You should expect limited or no connectivity for a connection that has been assigned such an APIPA address.

If a connection has been assigned an APIPA address and no DHCP server is available on the network, you can either install a DHCP server or assign the connection a static IP configuration or alternate configuration.

If a connection has been assigned an APIPA address on a network on which a DHCP server is already operative, you should first try either to renew the IP configuration or to use the Diagnose feature with the connection. To renew the IP configuration, type **ipconfig /renew** at a command prompt. To use the Diagnose feature, in Network Connections, right-click the connection to which an APIPA address has been assigned, and then choose Diagnose from the shortcut menu. (Alternatively, you can click Troubleshoot Problems in Network and Sharing Center.) You will then be given a chance to repair the connection.

Should this strategy fail to provide the host with a new IP address, you should then verify that the DHCP server is functioning properly. If the DHCP server is functioning, proceed to investigate hardware problems, such as faulty or disconnected cables and switches, that might be occurring between the DHCP server and client.

> *NOTE* **RENEWING AN IPV6 CONFIGURATION**
>
> To renew an IPv6 configuration, type `ipconfig /renew6`.

TROUBLESHOOTING NETWORK CONNECTIVITY WITH PING, TRACERT, PATHPING, AND ARP

If neither the Diagnose feature nor the **Ipconfig /renew** command solves a network problem, you should use utilities such as Ping, Tracert, PathPing, and Arp to troubleshoot the connection. A description of these four utilities is described throughout the rest of this section.

- **Ping** Ping is the key tool used to test network connectivity. To use the Ping utility, at a command prompt, type **ping *remote_host,*** where *remote_host* is the name or IP address of a remote computer, server, or router to which you want to verify connectivity. If the remote computer replies to the ping, you know that connectivity to the remote host has been verified.

  Figure 1-24 shows a successful attempt to ping a computer at the address 192.168.2.2.

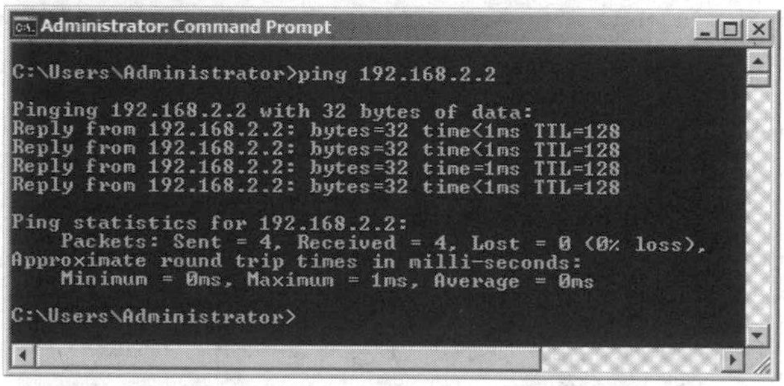

FIGURE 1-24 A successful ping demonstrating that the local computer can communicate with a computer at 192.168.2.2

In Figure 1-24, an IPv4 address was pinged, and the replies were received from the same IPv4 address. In certain cases, however, a ping attempt takes place over IPv6, such as when you ping a computer by name in a workgroup environment. This output is shown in Figure 1-25.

FIGURE 1-25 Ping sometimes uses IPv6 to communicate with a remote computer.

Looking at Ping Traffic

The Ping, Tracert, and Pathping utilities all rely on a layer 3 messaging protocol named Internet Control Message Protocol (ICMP). You can see ICMP in Figure 1-26, which shows a network capture of the same ping event shown in Figure 1-24.

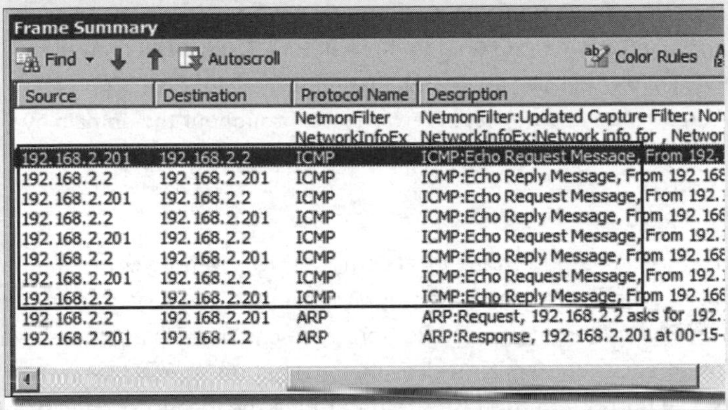

FIGURE 1-26 A network capture of a successful ping attempt

The network capture reveals eight ICMP messages. These eight messages amount to four simple ICMP exchanges in succession. In the first message of this exchange, an Echo Request Message is sent from the local computer (192.168.2.201) to a remote computer at 192.168.2.2. Then, in the second message of the exchange, the remote computer at 192.168.2.2 sends an Echo Reply Message back to the local computer. It is these four echo replies you see in this capture that correspond to the four "Reply from..." messages that appear in the command prompt output after you ping a remote computer. (Ping doesn't display each separate echo request.)

ICMP has a special version called ICMPv6 that is used over IPv6. The network capture of a ping event over IPv6 looks very similar to a ping event over IPv4, as shown in Figure 1-27. This figure reveals a network capture of the same ping event shown in Figure 1-25.

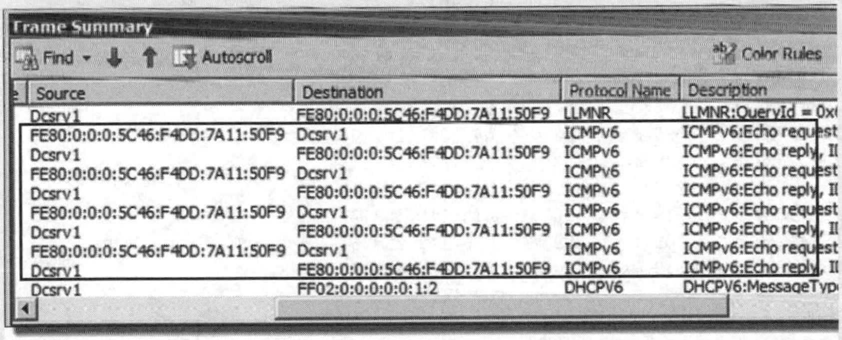

FIGURE 1-27 A network capture of a successful ping attempt over IPv6

- **Tracert** Tracert traces a path from the local computer to a remote computer and checks the status of each router along the way. For example, if the path from ServerA to ServerE crosses RouterB, RouterC, and RouterD, you can use Tracert to test whether each of those intermediate routers (as well as the destination ServerE) can respond to ICMP messages. The purpose of this test is to determine the location of any break in connectivity that might lie between the local computer and a remote destination.

  To use the Tracert utility, at a command prompt, type **tracert *remote_host,*** where *remote_host* is the name or address of a destination computer, server, or router to which you want to trace a path.

  An output of Tracert is as follows. Notice that the -d switch is used to speed up the test by preventing each IP address from being resolved to a name.

```
C:\Users\jcmackin>tracert -d 69.147.114.210

Tracing route to 69.147.114.210 over a maximum of 30 hops

  1     1 ms    <1 ms    <1 ms   192.168.2.1
  2   822 ms   708 ms   659 ms   67.142.148.2
  3   708 ms   649 ms   658 ms   67.142.131.209
  4   632 ms   619 ms   629 ms   67.142.131.254
  5   726 ms   698 ms   619 ms   67.142.128.246
  6   732 ms   679 ms   709 ms   65.46.24.177
  7   713 ms   650 ms   679 ms   207.88.81.245
  8   732 ms   719 ms   719 ms   71.5.170.41
  9   957 ms   739 ms   719 ms   71.5.170.34
 10   734 ms   736 ms   677 ms   64.212.107.85
 11   723 ms   690 ms   862 ms   64.208.110.166
 12   824 ms   849 ms   739 ms   216.115.101.137
 13   781 ms   799 ms   869 ms   216.115.101.152
 14   822 ms   719 ms   678 ms   216.115.108.72
 15   759 ms   709 ms   799 ms   216.115.108.61
 16   724 ms   819 ms  1479 ms   68.142.238.65
 17   775 ms   859 ms   739 ms   69.147.114.210

Trace complete.
```

- **PathPing** PathPing is similar to Tracert except that PathPing is intended to find links that are causing *intermittent* data loss. PathPing sends packets to each router on the way to a final destination over a period of time and then computes the percentage of packets returned from each hop. Because PathPing shows the degree of packet loss at any given router or link, you can use PathPing to pinpoint which routers or links might be causing network problems.

  To use the PathPing utility, at a command prompt, type **PathPing *remote_host,*** where *remote_host* is the name or address of a destination computer, server, or router on whose path to which you want to test intermittent data loss.

  The following shows a sample PathPing output:

```
D:\>pathping -n testpc1
Tracing route to testpc1 [7.54.1.196]
over a maximum of 30 hops:
0 172.16.87.35
1 172.16.87.218
2 192.168.52.1
3 192.168.80.1
4 7.54.247.14
5 7.54.1.196
Computing statistics for 25 seconds...
Source to Here This Node/Link
Hop RTT Lost/Sent = Pct Lost/Sent = Pct Address
0 172.16.87.35
0/ 100 = 0% |
1 41ms 0/ 100 = 0% 0/ 100 = 0% 172.16.87.218
13/ 100 = 13% |
2 22ms 16/ 100 = 16% 3/ 100 = 3% 192.168.52.1
0/ 100 = 0% |
3 24ms 13/ 100 = 13% 0/ 100 = 0% 192.168.80.1
0/ 100 = 0% |
4 21ms 14/ 100 = 14% 1/ 100 = 1% 7.54.247.14
0/ 100 = 0% |
5 24ms 13/ 100 = 13% 0/ 100 = 0% 7.54.1.196
Trace complete.
```

  Notice how the preceding output first lists the five hops on the path to the specified destination and then computes the percentage of data lost over each of these hops. In this case, PathPing shows that data loss at a rate of 13 percent is occurring between the local computer (172.16.87.35) and the first hop (172.16.87.218).

- **Arp** Arp is the name of both a utility and a protocol. The Address Resolution Protocol (ARP) is used to translate the IPv4 (software) address of a computer or router in broadcast range to the MAC (hardware) address of an actual interface across the network. In other words, the ARP protocol enables a computer to communicate physically with a neighboring computer or router represented by an IPv4 address. The Arp utility performs a related function. You can use it to display and manage a computer's ARP cache, which stores the IPv4-address-to-MAC-address mappings of other computers on the local network.

Because the connection to a computer within broadcast range depends on an accurate IPv4-address-to-MAC-address mapping of that computer in the local ARP cache, the Arp utility can help you fix network problems when an inaccurate mapping is the cause. For example, by displaying the cache with the **arp -a** command, you could reveal a problem—for example, with two neighboring virtual machines that have assigned themselves the same virtual MAC address. (This is fairly common.) You could also use the **arp -d** command to delete an entry in the ARP cache of a computer or virtual machine whose MAC address has just changed and that you know to be invalid.

In rare cases, you can also use the Arp utility to reveal a local hacker's attempt to poison your ARP cache by associating some or all local IPv4 addresses, most notably the local router's IPv4 address, with the hacker's own MAC address. This is a well-known technique that allows the hacker to secretly route your network connections through the hacker's computer.

An example of a poisoned ARP cache is shown in Figure 1-28. Notice how the IPv4 addresses 192.168.2.1, 192.168.2.52, and 192.168.2.53 are all associated with the same MAC address. If the hacker's own computer was represented as 192.168.2.52, this ARP cache would enable all connections to 192.168.2.1 and 192.168.2.53 to be intercepted. If 192.168.2.1 represented the IPv4 address of the local router, all Internet communications could be intercepted.

FIGURE 1-28 A poisoned ARP cache

NOTE **IS A DUPLICATE MAC ADDRESS LISTING IN THE ARP CACHE ALWAYS A SIGN OF A PROBLEM?**

Unless you have assigned two or more IPv4 addresses to a single network adapter somewhere on your local network (which is rarely done but is possible), each IPv4 address in the ARP cache should be associated with a unique physical address.

Looking at the ARP Traffic

Communication between two computers on the same network takes place over a layer 2 protocol such as Ethernet. If a first computer knows only the IP (layer 3) address of a second local computer, the first computer first needs to translate that IP address into a layer 2 (hardware) address before communicating with that second computer. The ARP protocol is what performs this translation.

Figure 1-29 shows a network capture of an ARP exchange used to determine the hardware address of a computer at 192.168.2.2.

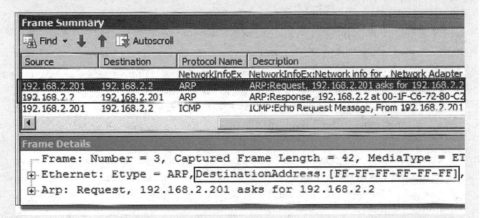

FIGURE 1-29 An ARP exchange consists of a broadcast request followed by a unicast response.

The ARP exchange consists of two packets. The first packet is an ARP Request from 192.168.2.201. Although the destination of the ARP Request is shown as 192.168.2.2 in the Frame Summary pane, the Frame details pane reveals that the destination address of the ARP Request is FF-FF-FF-FF-FF-FF. This Ethernet address is a broadcast address, which ensures that every network adapter on the LAN will hear the request. In the second packet of the ARP exchange, the network adapter owning the IP address 192.168.2.2 sends an ARP Response back to 192.168.2.201. This ARP Response includes the information requested: 00-1F-C6-72-80-C2, or the hardware address corresponding to 192.168.2.2. Once received, the hardware address is stored in the local ARP cache by the computer that performed the ARP Request.

In this practice, you configure a static IPv4 address for the local area connections on Dcsrv1, an alternate address for the local area connection on Boston, and finally a static address on Boston by using the command line. Until now, these connections have been assigned APIPA addresses. After configuring these addresses, you enable file sharing on both computers and test connectivity with Ping.

This practice assumes that you have performed the computer lab setup as described in the Introduction to this book, with the virtual network adapters in your virtual machines assigned to the same private or internal network (not a NAT network). On Dscrv1, Local Area Connection must be connected to the private lab network. On Boston, the Local Area Connection must be connected to the same private lab network. No other computers or servers should be on this private network. No server roles should be installed on either computer.

EXERCISE 1   Verifying Your Current IP Address

In this exercise, you review the current IP configuration on Dcsrv1.

1. Log on to Dcsrv1 as an administrator.

2. Open a command prompt by clicking Start and then choosing Command Prompt.

3. At the command prompt, type **ipconfig**, and then press Enter. This command is used to show your IP address configuration.

   The output shows your network connections. Below "Ethernet adapter Local Area Connection" and next to Autoconfiguration IPv4 Address, you will see the address of 169.254.y.z, where y and z refer to the host ID currently assigned to that connection. The subnet mask is the default of 255.255.0.0. Because a default Windows Server 2008 R2 installation specifies that the IP address of the host is assigned automatically, in the absence of a DHCP server, the host uses an APIPA address (assuming no alternate configuration has been defined). Note also that the same connection has been assigned a link-local IPv6 address beginning with fe80::. This address is the IPv6 equivalent of an APIPA address. Finally, you will also see tunnel adapter local area connections. These are associated with IPv6 and will be described in more detail in Lesson 3, "Understanding IPv6 Addressing."

EXERCISE 2   Configuring a Manual Address

In this exercise, you assign a static IP address to the Local Area Connection on Dcsrv1. A static IP address is needed for computers that will later host network infrastructure services such as DNS or DHCP.

1. While you are still logged on to Dcsrv1 as an administrator, at the command prompt, type **ncpa.cpl.**

2. In the Network Connections window, right-click Local Area Connection, and then choose Properties. This connection faces the private lab network.

3. In the Local Area Connections Properties dialog box, in the This Connection Uses The Following Items area, double-click Internet Protocol Version 4 (TCP/IPv4).

4. On the General tab of the Internet Protocol Version 4 (TCP/IPv4) Properties dialog box, select Use The Following IP Address.

5. In the IP Address text box, type **192.168.0.1**.

6. Select the Subnet Mask text box to place your cursor inside it. The subnet mask 255.255.255.0 appears in the Subnet Mask text box. Click OK.

7. In the Local Area Connection Properties dialog box, click OK.

8. At the command prompt, type **ipconfig**. You will see the new static IPv4 address associated with the Local Area Connection.

EXERCISE 3 Defining an Alternate Configuration

In this exercise, you alter the IP configuration on Boston so that in the absence of a DHCP server on the private lab network, Boston assigns the address 192.168.0.200 to the Local Area Connection.

1. Log on to Boston as an administrator.

2. In Server Manager, click View Network Connections.

3. In Network Connections, open the properties of the Local Area Connection.

4. In the Local Area Connection Properties dialog box, open the properties of Internet Protocol Version 4 (TCP/IPv4). On the General tab of the Internet Protocol (TCP/IP) Properties dialog box, notice that Obtain An IP Address Automatically and Obtain DNS Server Address Automatically are selected.

5. Click the Alternate Configuration tab. Automatic Private IP Address is selected. Because no DHCP server is available and this setting is enabled by default, Boston has automatically assigned the Local Area Connection an APIPA address.

6. Select User Configured.

7. In the IP Address text box, type **192.168.0.200**.

8. Click the Subnet Mask text box to place the cursor inside it. The default subnet mask of 255.255.255.0 appears in the Subnet Mask text box. Leave this entry as the default subnet mask.

9. Clear the Validate Settings, If Changed, Upon Exit check box. You have just defined an alternate IP address configuration of 192.168.0.200/24 for Boston. You can use this configuration until you configure a DHCP server for your network.

10. Click OK.

11. In the Local Area Connection Properties dialog box, click OK.

12. Open a command prompt and type **ipconfig /all**. Look for the IPv4 Address value in the Ipconfig output. Here, you will see the new alternate address you have just assigned. Next, look for the Autoconfiguration Enabled value. Note that it is set to Yes.

EXERCISE 4   Configuring a Static IPv4 Address from a Command Prompt

In the following exercise, you use the command prompt to configure for Boston a static IPv4 address of 192.168.0.2 and a subnet mask of 255.255.255.0.

1. While you are logged on to Boston as an administrator, open an elevated command prompt. (This step is not necessary if you are logged on with the account named Administrator. You can open an elevated command prompt by clicking Start, right-clicking Command Prompt, and then choosing Run As Administrator.)

2. At the command prompt, type the following:

   ```
   netsh interface ip set address "local area connection" static 192.168.0.2
   255.255.255.0
   ```

3. At the command prompt, type **ipconfig**. The Ipconfig output reveals the new IPv4 address.

EXERCISE 5   Enabling File Sharing

In Windows Server 2008 R2, enabling file sharing creates a firewall exception for ICMP that allows a computer to respond to pings. For this reason, you now perform this step in Network and Sharing Center on both Dcsrv1 and Boston.

1. While you are logged on to Dcsrv1 as an administrator, open Network and Sharing Center by right-clicking the network icon in the Notification Area and then choosing Network And Sharing Center. (The Notification Area is the area on the right side of the taskbar.)

2. In Network and Sharing Center, click Change Advanced Sharing Settings.

3. In the Advanced Sharing Settings window, in the area labeled the current profile, click Turn On File And Printer Sharing.

4. Click Save Changes.

   Note that this method of enabling a firewall exception for ICMP is only recommended for test networks. In a production network, it is preferable to enable firewall rules through the Windows Firewall With Advanced Security console or through Group Policy.

5. Repeat steps 1 through 4 on Boston.

EXERCISE 6   Verifying the Connection

In this exercise, you verify that the two computers can now communicate over the private lab network.

1. While you are logged on to Boston as Administrator, open a command prompt.

2. At the command prompt, type **ping 192.168.0.1**. The output confirms that Dcsrv1 and Boston are communicating over IP.

3. Log off both computers.

Lesson Summary

- Transmission Control Protocol/Internet Protocol (TCP/IP) defines a four-layered architecture, including the Network Interface or Data Link layer, the Internet or Network layer, the Transport layer, and the Application layer. Because of their position within the OSI networking model, these layers are also known as layer 2, layer 3, layer 4, and layer 7, respectively.

- Network and Sharing Center is the main network configuration tool in Windows Server 2008 and Windows Server 2008 R2. You can use Network and Sharing Center to perform functions such as setting the network location, viewing the network map, configuring Network Discovery, configuring file and printer sharing, and viewing the status of network connections.

- By using the properties of a network connection, you can configure a computer with a static address or with an automatically configured address. Automatically configured addresses are obtained from a DHCP server if one is available.

- When a connection is configured to obtain an address automatically and no DHCP server is available, that connection by default will assign itself an address in the form 169.254.x.y. You can also define an alternate configuration that the connection will assign itself in the absence of a DHCP server.

- Certain basic TCP/IP utilities are used to test and troubleshoot network connectivity. These utilities include Ipconfig, Ping, Tracert, PathPing, and Arp.

Lesson Review

You can use the following questions to test your knowledge of the information in Lesson 1, "Introducing Windows Networking." The questions are also available on the companion CD if you prefer to review them in electronic form.

> **NOTE ANSWERS**
>
> Answers to these questions and explanations of why each answer choice is correct or incorrect are located in the "Answers" section at the end of the book.

1. A user in your organization complains that she cannot connect to any network resources. You run the **Ipconfig** command on her computer and find that the address assigned to the Local Area Connection is 169.254.232.21. Which of the following commands should you type first?

   A. Ipconfig /renew

   B. ping 169.254.232.21

   C. tracert 169.254.232.21

   D. Arp –a

2. Which of the following address types is best suited for a DNS server?

    A. DHCP-assigned address

    B. APIPA address

    C. Alternate configuration address

    D. Manual address

Lesson 2: Understanding IPv4 Addressing

IPv4 is by far the most popular networking protocol in use. Although connecting computers to an established IPv4 network is straightforward (and often entirely automatic), to implement, configure, and troubleshoot IPv4, you need to understand basic concepts about IPv4 addressing.

After this lesson, you will be able to:

- Understand the structure of an IPv4 address, including the network ID and host ID.
- Understand the function of a subnet mask.
- Understand the function of a default gateway in IP routing.
- Understand and recognize the private IPv4 address ranges.
- Understand the concept of an address block.
- Determine the number of addresses in a given address block.
- Determine the address block size needed for a given number of addresses.
- Understand the benefits of subnetting.
- Enumerate subnets based on network needs and a given address space.
- Determine whether two addresses are configured in the same subnet.

Estimated lesson time: 180 minutes

The Structure of IPv4 Addresses

IPv4 addresses are 32 bits in length and are composed of 4 *octets* of 8 bits apiece. The usual representation of an IPv4 address is in *dotted-decimal* notation, with each of the four numbers— for example, 192.168.23.245—representing an octet separated from another by a period (dot). This common dotted-decimal notation, however, is only ever displayed for human benefit. Computers actually read IPv4 addresses in their native 32-bit binary notation such as the following:

    11000000 10101000 00010111 11110101

This point becomes important if you want to understand how IPv4 works. IPv4 is an addressing system—a system to help *find* devices—and not merely an identification system. Every IPv4 address on a network must be unique, but an address cannot be assigned randomly to a networked device because that would provide no way of finding the device. The way that IPv4 achieves both uniqueness and "findability" is by dividing addresses into two parts: the network ID and the host ID.

Network ID and Host ID

The first part of an IPv4 address is the *network ID*. The job of the network ID is to identify a particular network within a larger IPv4 internetwork (such as the Internet). The last part of an IPv4 address is the host ID. The *host ID* identifies an IPv4 host (a computer, router, or other IPv4 device) within the network defined by the network ID.

> **NOTE NETWORK ID + HOST ID = 32 BITS**
>
> If n = the number of bits in the network ID and h = the number of bits in the host ID, n + h is equal to 32.

Figure 1-30 shows a sample view of an IPv4 address (131.107.16.200) as it is divided into network ID and host ID sections. The letters w, x, y, and z are often used to designate the four octets within an IPv4 address. In this example, the network ID portion (131.107) is indicated by octets w and x. The host ID portion (16.200) is indicated by octets y and z.

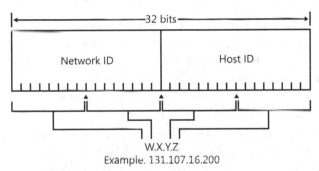

FIGURE 1-30 Network and host IDs

IPV4 ADDRESSES AND ZIP+4 COMPARED

This system of dividing the IPv4 address into a network ID and a host ID is reminiscent of the "ZIP+4" system used by most post offices in the United States Postal System. This system is used to route and deliver mail to individual post office boxes across the country.

Taken together, the 5-digit ZIP code (also known as a postal code) and the 4-digit box number represent a unique 9-digit ZIP+4 address similar in structure and function to the 32-bit IPv4 address. The first part of the ZIP+4 address—the 5-digit zip code—represents a findable area, not a unique address. The second part represents a specific 4-digit mailbox within the 5-digit ZIP code area, a mailbox to which the post office represented by the ZIP code has the responsibility to deliver mail.

However, ZIP+4 addresses are much simpler than IPv4 addresses in one respect. When you look at a ZIP+4 address, you know for certain which part of the address represents the post office (the ZIP code) and which part represents the individual mailbox (the +4). The dividing line between them never changes. The first five digits and the last four digits always have the same function.

The tricky thing about IPv4 addresses is that the size of the network ID and the size of the host ID vary. Just by looking at an IPv4 address such as 192.168.23.245, you cannot determine which of the 32 bits are used for the network ID and which are used for the host ID. To do this, you need an additional piece of information. That piece of information is the subnet mask.

Subnet Masks

The subnet mask is used to determine which part of a 32-bit IPv4 address should be considered its network ID. For example, when you write 192.168.23.245/24, the /24 represents the subnet mask and indicates that the first 24 of the 32 bits in that IPv4 address should be considered its network ID. For the IPv4 address 131.107.16.200 shown in Figure 1-30 earlier, the first 16 bits according to the picture are used for the network ID. Therefore, the appropriate subnet mask to be used by a host assigned that address is /16.

The two subnet masks just mentioned—/16 and /24—are relatively easy to interpret. Because their values are divisible by 8, these subnet masks indicate that the network ID is composed of, respectively, the first two complete octets and the first three complete octets of an IPv4 address. In other words, the network ID of a host assigned the address 131.107.16.200 /16 is 131.107, and the host's network address is therefore 131.107.0.0. The network ID of a host assigned the address 192.168.23.245/24 is 192.168.23, and host's network address is therefore 192.168.23.0. However, subnet masks are not always divisible by 8 and are not always so easy to interpret, as we shall see.

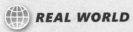
SUBNET MASK NOTATIONS

So far, the discussion has focused on subnet masks in slash notation—also known as Classless Inter Domain Routing (CIDR) notation or network prefix notation. Slash notation is a common way of referring to subnet masks both on the 70-642 exam and in the real world. However, subnet masks are represented just as commonly in 32-bit dotted-decimal notation.

In dotted-decimal notation, the subnet mask takes the form of a 32-bit IPv4 address. For example, the subnet mask /16 is represented in dotted-decimal notation as 255.255.0.0, and the subnet mask /24 is represented in dotted-decimal notation as 255.255.255.0.

To understand the connection between a subnet mask expressed by its slash notation and its dotted-decimal equivalent, you first have to translate the slash notation to binary notation. To begin, take the value after the slash in slash notation—for example, the 16 in /16—and represent it as an equivalent number of ones in binary notation, with a space after each 8 bits, or octet.

11111111 11111111

Then, to complete the 32-bit subnet mask in binary notation, add a string of 0s until the values of all 32 bits are represented (again with a space after each 8 bits):

11111111 11111111 00000000 00000000

Finally, convert this binary notation into dotted-decimal notation. Because 11111111 is the binary equivalent of the decimal 255, and 00000000 is the binary equivalent of the decimal 0, you can represent each octet as either 255 or 0. For this reason, /16 is equivalent to 255.255.0.0.

> **IMPORTANT WHAT HAPPENED TO ADDRESS CLASSES?**
>
> You might occasionally hear that a /8 address is called *Class A*, a /16 address is called *Class B*, and a /24 address is called *Class C*. These terms refer to an older system of IPv4 routing that is no longer used, even though its vocabulary is sometimes used informally. The 70-642 exam does not use these terms because they are technically defunct.

Converting Between Binary and Decimal Notations

t's not often that you need to convert between base-two and base-ten notations, and if you do, you could use a scientific calculator. However, when you don't have access to a calculator, it's good to know how to perform these conversions manually. It will certainly also help you understand the logic of IP addressing.

The key to understanding binary notation is to understand the value of each bit place. As with the base ten system, in which each place holds different values such as ones, tens, hundreds, and so on, a base two system holds potential values in each bit place, increasing from right to left.

Table 1-1 shows the scientific and decimal notation associated with each bit place within a binary octet. Notice that, as you move from right to left and begin with the eighth bit's potential value of 1, each successive bit represents double the potential value of the previous bit, with a maximum value of 128 for the leftmost bit. Knowing this pattern allows you to recall easily the potential value of each bit place.

TABLE 1-1 Potential Values in a Binary Octet

BIT PLACE	1ST BIT	2ND BIT	3RD BIT	4TH BIT	5TH BIT	6TH BIT	7TH BIT	8TH BIT
SCIENTIFIC NOTATION	2^7	2^6	2^5	2^4	2^3	2^2	2^1	2^0
DECIMAL NOTATION	128	64	32	16	8	4	2	1

Note that these numbers represent only the values that are held when the bit places contain a 1. When an octet contains a 0 in any bit place, the value of the bit is null. For example, if the first (leftmost) bit place is filled with a bit value of 1, the equivalent decimal value is 128. Where the bit value is 0, the equivalent decimal value is 0 as well. If all the bit places in an octet are filled with ones (1), the equivalent decimal value is 255. If all the bit places are filled with zeroes (0), the equivalent decimal value is 0.

Binary-to-Decimal Conversion Example

The following binary string represents an octet that could be used in an IPv4 address:

10000011

To understand the decimal equivalent of this binary octet, draw a simple conversion table, such as the one that follows, in which to enter the bit values of the octet.

128	64	32	16	8	4	2	1
1	0	0	0	0	0	1	1

By using this table as a reference, you can perform simple addition of each bit place's decimal equivalent value to find the decimal sum for this octet string, as follows:

128 + 2 + 1 = 131

Because the sum is 131, the octet with the binary value 10000011 is expressed as 131 in decimal form.

Decimal-to-Binary Conversion Example

You convert an octet from decimal to binary form by drawing the conversion chart and then adding a 1 in the octet's bit places from left to right until the desired target decimal value is achieved. If, by adding a 1, your total would exceed the target decimal value, simply note a 0 in that bit place instead and move to the next bit place. There is always exactly one combination of 1s and 0s that will yield the target value.

For example, suppose you want to convert the octet value 209 into binary form. First, draw the conversion table on scratch paper, as shown here:

128	64	32	16	8	4	2	1

Next, consider the potential value of the first (leftmost) bit place. Is 128 less than 209? Because it is, you should write a 1 beneath the 128 on your scratch paper and then write a 128 off to the side to keep tally of the running subtotal.

128	64	32	16	8	4	2	1	SUBTOTAL
1								128

Move to the next potential value. Is 128 + 64 less than 209? The sum of these values is only 192, so again, you should write a 1 beneath the 64 and then a 64 to your running subtotal.

128	64	32	16	8	4	2	1	SUBTOTAL
1	1							128 +64 =192

The next potential value is 32, but if you were to add a 1 here, you would achieve a subtotal of 224. This exceeds the target total of 209, so you must place a zero in the third bit place of the octet and not add anything to your running subtotal.

128	64	32	16	8	4	2	1	SUBTOTAL
1	1	0						128 +64 =192

Next, the fourth bit potential value is 16; adding this value to 192 results in a subtotal of 208. Is 208 less than 209? Because it is, you should add a 1 beneath the 16 and a 16 to your running subtotal.

128	64	32	16	8	4	2	1	SUBTOTAL
1	1	0	1					128 64 +16 =208

Because you need to add a value of only 1 to achieve the target value of 209, placing a 1 in the eighth bit place will complete the translation of the octet.

128	64	32	16	8	4	2	1	SUBTOTAL
1	1	0	1	0	0	0	1	128 64 16 +1 =209

The octet with the decimal value 209 is therefore written in binary notation as 11010001.

SUBNET MASK MIDRANGE VALUES

The subnet masks we have been looking at in dotted-decimal notation have octets whose values are represented as either 255 or 0. This limits our discussion to only three possible subnet masks: /8 (255.0.0.0), /16 (255.255.0.0), and /24 (255.255.255.0). In fact, these are the most common subnet masks used for addresses on the Internet (especially /24 or 255.255.255.0).

However, both on the 70-642 exam and in the real world, you will also encounter subnet masks such as /25 or /22 which, when expressed in dotted-decimal notation, include a mid-range value octet such as 128 or 252. This situation arises whenever the length of a network ID (expressed in bits) is not divisible by 8.

Figure 1-31 shows the binary representation of the IPv4 address 192.168.14.222 with a typical subnet mask of /24 or 255.255.255.0. For this address, the network ID is represented by the first 24 bits (first three octets), and the host ID is represented by the last 8 bits (the last octet).

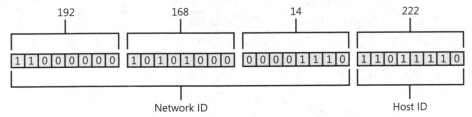

FIGURE 1-31 An IPv4 address with a /24 subnet mask

Now, consider the same IPv4 address with a 26-bit subnet mask, as shown in Figure 1-32. In this example, the network ID uses the first two bits from the last octet. The last octet is therefore dedicated partially to the network ID and dedicated partially to the host ID. In binary, the network ID is simply a 26-bit number, whereas the host ID is a 6-bit number.

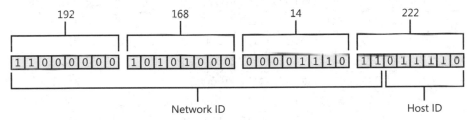

FIGURE 1-32 The same IPv4 address with a /26 subnet mask

Table 1-2 compares the slash, binary, and dotted-decimal notations for all subnet masks from /8 to /30. These are the only subnet masks you are ever likely to see. However, the subnet masks you will encounter most frequently (both on the 70-642 exam and in the real world) are in the /20 to /30 range.

IMPORTANT   STUDY THIS TABLE

This table presents information that most network administrators are expected to understand. Be sure to spend as much time as necessary browsing this table until you are comfortable with subnet mask values and how the three notations relate to one another.

TABLE 1-2 Subnet Mask Notations Compared

SLASH NOTATION	BINARY NOTATION	DOTTED DECIMAL NOTATION
/8	11111111 00000000 00000000 00000000	255.0.0.0
/9	11111111 10000000 00000000 00000000	255.128.0.0
/10	11111111 11000000 00000000 00000000	255.192.0.0
/11	11111111 11100000 00000000 00000000	255.224.0.0
/12	11111111 11110000 00000000 00000000	255.240.0.0
/13	11111111 11111000 00000000 00000000	255.248.0.0
/14	11111111 11111100 00000000 00000000	255.252.0.0
/15	11111111 11111110 00000000 00000000	255.254.0.0
/16	11111111 11111111 00000000 00000000	255.255.0.0
/17	11111111 11111111 10000000 00000000	255.255.128.0
/18	11111111 11111111 11000000 00000000	255.255.192.0
/19	11111111 11111111 11100000 00000000	255.255.224.0
/20	11111111 11111111 11110000 00000000	255.255.240.0
/21	11111111 11111111 11111000 00000000	255.255.248.0
/22	11111111 11111111 11111100 00000000	255.255.252.0
/23	11111111 11111111 11111110 00000000	255.255.254.0
/24	11111111 11111111 11111111 00000000	255.255.255.0
/25	11111111 11111111 11111111 10000000	255.255.255.128
/26	11111111 11111111 11111111 11000000	255.255.255.192
/27	11111111 11111111 11111111 11100000	255.255.255.224
/28	11111111 11111111 11111111 11110000	255.255.255.240
/29	11111111 11111111 11111111 11111000	255.255.255.248
/30	11111111 11111111 11111111 11111100	255.255.255.252

SUBNET MASK OCTET VALUES

Learning the sequence of nine possible octet values for a subnet mask will help you when you need to determine the size of an existing or planned network. To a large degree, in fact, the ability to perform such calculations in one's head is expected of a good network administrator.

Use Table 1-3 to help you memorize the values. Begin by covering the top row of the table. After you can recite without hesitation the decimal value associated with any number of 1-bits or binary values chosen at random from the bottom two rows, proceed to cover up the bottom two rows. When you can recite without hesitation the number of 1-bits associated with any decimal value chosen at random from the top row, proceed to memorize the sequence of decimal values from left to right and right to left.

TABLE 1-3 Subnet Mask Octet Values

DECIMAL VALUE	0	128	192	224	240	248	252	254	255
# OF 1-BITS	0	1	2	3	4	5	6	7	8
BINARY VALUE	00000000	10000000	11000000	11100000	11110000	11111000	11111100	1111110	11111111

Converting Subnet Masks Between Slash Notation and Dotted-Decimal Notation

You should normally use either memorization or a reference chart to convert between subnet mask notations when no software tools are available. However, you might be interested to know how to perform the conversion without relying on memorized values, a reference chart, or binary math. This method requires some practice and should not be your first choice for converting subnet mask notations on the 70-642 exam.

To convert a subnet mask expressed as /n to a subnet mask in dotted decimal notation, do the following:

1. Write out an octet of 255 for each time that 8 goes into n.

   For example, for a /19 network, 8 goes into 19 twice. You should therefore write out "255.255.".

2. Subtract the remainder of the previous operation from 8, raise two to the power of this difference, and then subtract this new value from 256. This calculation can be expressed mathematically as $256 - 2^{[8 - (n \bmod 8)]}$, where n is your /n value and *mod* is the operation that yields a remainder after dividing the preceding value by the following value. Place the result of this operation into the next octet. If any other octets remain, set them to 0.

   Following with the last example, $256 - 2^{[8 - (19 \bmod 8)]} = 256 - 2^{[8 - 3]} = 256 - 2^5 = 256 - 32 = 224$. You should therefore write out "224" for the third octet and "0" as the fourth octet. A /19 network therefore has a subnet mask of 255.255.224.0.

If you need to convert a dotted-decimal subnet mask to a subnet mask expressed as /n, do the following:

1. Multiply 8 times the number of octets in the subnet mask that are set to 255. If the other octets are all set to 0, put a slash in front of this value, and you are finished. Otherwise, keep this value as a subtotal, and proceed to the next step.

   For example, the octet 255.255.255.192 has three subnets of 255. 8 * 3 = 24. Because the fourth subnet has a midrange value, you will keep 24 as a subtotal.

2. For an octet with a value between 0 and 255, subtract the value of the octet from 256, convert the resulting value to an expression of 2 to an exponent, and finally subtract this exponent from 8. This calculation can be expressed mathematically as $8 - \log_2 (256-y)$, where y is the value of the octet and $\log_2$ is the binary logarithm, or the exponent required for 2 that would yield a value equal to the number that follows. Add the result of this operation to the subtotal from step 1, and put a slash in front of this value to obtain final the /n notation.

   Following with the previous example, 192 is the value of the midrange octet. $8 - \log_2 (256 - 192) = 8 - \log_2 (64) = 8 - 6 = 2$. Add 24 from the previous step to 2, and you have a final result of /26. Therefore, a subnet mask of 255.255.255.192 is equivalent to /26.

Understanding Routing and Default Gateways

The determination of the network ID by using the subnet mask is a vital step in IPv4 communication. This network ID essentially tells a computer how to handle an IPv4 packet. When a computer on a network needs to send an IPv4 packet to a remote address, the computer first compares its own network ID to that of the destination network ID specified in the IPv4 packet. (To determine these network IDs, the computer always uses its locally configured subnet mask.) If the two network IDs match, the message is determined to be local and is broadcast to the local subnet. If the two network IDs do not match, the computer sends the packet to a local router at the address known as the *default gateway*. The router at this default gateway address then forwards the IPv4 datagram in a manner determined by its routing tables.

Figure 1-33 illustrates this process of IP routing. In the figure, a computer whose address is 192.168.100.5/24 needs to send an IP packet destined for the address 192.168.1.10. Because the network IDs of the two addresses do not match, the computer sends the packet to the router specified by the default gateway address. This router consults its routing tables and sends the packet to the router connected to the 192.168.1.0 network. When the router connected to this network receives the packet, the router broadcasts the packet over the local subnet. The destination computer at the address 192.168.1.10 responds to the broadcast and receives the packet for internal processing.

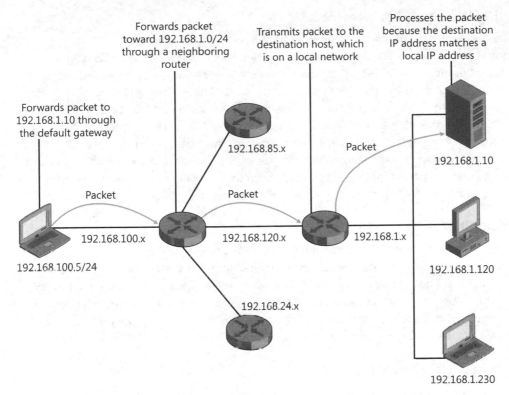

Forwards packet to
192.168.1.10 through
the default gateway

Forwards packet
toward 192.168.1.0/24
through a neighboring
router

Transmits packet to the
destination host, which
is on a local network

Processes the packet
because the destination
IP address matches a
local IP address

192.168.85.x

Packet

192.168.1.10

Packet

Packet

192.168.100.x   192.168.120.x   192.168.1.x

192.168.100.5/24

192.168.1.120

192.168.24.x

192.168.1.230

FIGURE 1-33 Routing an IP packet over an internetwork

Remember also these essential points about routing and default gateways:

- A default gateway must share the same network ID and be located within the same broadcast domain as the hosts it is serving.

- If a host has no default gateway setting configured, that host will be unable to connect to the Internet or to any computers beyond broadcast range. For example, a private internal server that occasionally needs to download content from the Internet needs to have a default gateway configured.

- Leaving the default gateway setting unconfigured on a host prevents access to that host from all points beyond the local subnet. In certain situations, therefore, you might in fact want to leave the default gateway setting unconfigured for security reasons

Understanding IPv4 Address Ranges

The vast majority of IPv4 addresses are *unicast*, which means they are assigned only to one host at a time. These IPv4 unicast addresses can be divided into three categories: APIPA (introduced in Lesson 1, "Introducing Windows Networking"), Public, and Private ranges. Whereas APIPA addresses are used only for temporary addresses or isolated computers, public and private ranges are divided into blocks that can be assigned to entire networks. These public and private ranges, along with the concept of address blocks in general, are described in the following sections.

Using Public IPv4 Addresses

Every IPv4 address on the public Internet is unique. To allow networks to obtain unique addresses for the Internet, the Internet Assigned Numbers Authority (IANA) divides up the non-reserved portion of the IPv4 address space and delegates responsibility for address allocation to a number of regional registries throughout the world. These registries include Asia-Pacific Network Information Center (APNIC), American Registry for Internet Numbers (ARIN), and Réseaux IP Européens Network Coordination Centre (RIPE NCC). The regional registries then allocate *blocks* of addresses to a small number of large Internet service providers (ISPs) that then assign smaller blocks to customers and smaller ISPs, who then provide public addresses to organizations paying for Internet service. Within these organizations, public addresses are typically reserved for Internet-facing routers and servers.

Using Private IPv4 Addresses

The IANA has also reserved a certain number of IPv4 addresses that are never used on the global Internet. These private IPv4 addresses are used for hosts that require IPv4 connectivity but that do not need to be seen on the public network. For example, you should not obtain public IPv4 addresses for use inside a private network, such as a home network or an internal business network. Private networks should use the address ranges shown in Table 1-4 to provide addresses for hosts on the network.

TABLE 1-4 Private Address Ranges

STARTING ADDRESS	ENDING ADDRESS
10.0.0.0	10.255.255.255
172.16.0.0	172.31.255.255
192.168.0.0	192.168.255.255

Hosts addressed with a private IPv4 address connect to the Internet through a server or router performing Network Address Translation (NAT). The router performing NAT can be a computer running Windows Server 2008 R2 or a dedicated routing device.

Understanding Address Blocks and Subnets

Most organizations use a combination of public and private addresses. Public addresses are usually reserved for Internet-facing routers and servers such as mail and web servers that require external access. The internal network composed of internal routers, servers, and clients should use private address ranges. What is most certain is that every organization that wants to communicate on the Internet must have at least one public address. This one public address can then be leveraged by many clients through NAT.

You obtain public IPv4 addresses from your ISP for all routers and servers that are directly facing the Internet. Although small organizations might be able to get by with only a single public IPv4 address, many organizations need far more than that. Organizations needing more than one public address usually purchase those addresses from their ISP as a block.

An *address block* is the complete group of contiguous IP addresses that shares any single network ID. For example, an organization may purchase from an ISP a /24 address block with network ID 206.73.118. The range of addresses associated with this address block is 206.73.118.0–206.73.118.255.

It is essential to understand that the addresses within an address block constitute a single network, and unless the network is subnetted—a possibility we will consider later in this lesson—that address block will serve a *single broadcast domain* with a single router, or way out of the network. The *default gateway* is the address assigned to that router within the same broadcast domain.

Stated another way, an address block by default is designed to serve a single subnet. A *subnet* is a group of hosts within a single broadcast domain that share the same network ID and the same default gateway address

Figure 1-34 displays a network served by the address block 206.73.118.0/24.

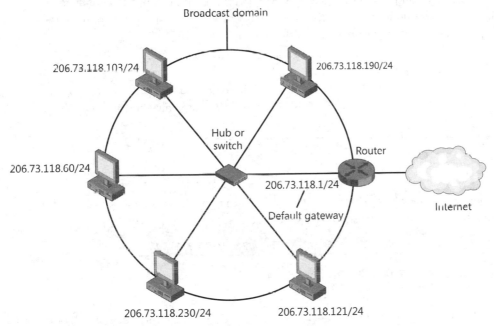

FIGURE 1-34 A single-subnet network

Creating an IPv4 Address Block Reference Chart

You should create a reference chart whenever you have to perform calculations related to IPv4 address blocks without the help of software tools. The chart will enable you to quickly solve problems related to addressing and is especially useful—even essential—in exam situations.

EXAM TIP

For the Microsoft exam, it's a good idea to draw this reference chart on the scratch pad provided by the testing site even before you click Start to begin the test. Doing so will give you the time you need to fill in the correct values without having to worry about the exam clock.

Rotate your scratch pad so that the longest side is horizontal, and then begin your reference chart by writing a 1 on the right side. Working from right to left, keep doubling and writing the values until you reach 256. Leave plenty of room on the left side of the scratch pad because you will be filling in more values later.

256	128	64	32	16	8	4	2	1

Next, draw a horizontal line above the row of numbers you have written and a vertical line to the left of 256. Label the row "Block size" to the far left, as shown here:

Block Size	256	128	64	32	16	8	4	2	1

Then, write the values /24 through /32 from left to right above the block size numbers you have just written. Your chart should now look like this:

	/24	/25	/26	/27	/28	/29	/30	/31	/32
Block Size	256	128	64	32	16	8	4	2	1

Each column in the chart represents a network of a distinct size. The block size value informs you of the number of addresses available within a given size network. For example, according to the chart, a /28 network provides 16 addresses.

Now, draw a horizontal line beneath the block size numbers. Subtract these same values from 256 and write the result in a row below the new horizontal line. (The results of this operation are the same subnet mask octet values shown in Table 1-3. If you have memorized these values, this step will be much faster.) Label the new row "Mask."

	/24	/25	/26	/27	/28	/29	/30	/31	/32
Block Size	256 -256	256 -128	256 -64	256 -32	256 -16	256 -8	256 -4	256 -2	256 -1
Mask	0	128	192	224	240	248	252	254	255

The Mask row value informs you of the last octet in the subnet mask for each network. The first three octets are 255.255.255 for all networks to the right of the vertical line. To determine the subnet mask of a /29 network, for example, begin with 255.255.255 and then add the Mask value for /29 shown on the chart (248) for the last octet. Therefore, the full subnet mask for a /29 network is 255.255.255.248.

At this point, you should fill in three or four more columns to the left of the vertical line, as desired. The networks to the left of this line are distinct because they have a value less than 255 in the third octet of the subnet mask.

In this example, you can fill in values for four more networks. To begin, write /20 through /23 to the left of /24 on the top row.

	/20	/21	/22	/23	/24	/25	/26	/27	/28	/29	/30	/31	/32
Block Size					256	128	64	32	16	8	4	2	1
Mask					0	128	192	224	240	248	252	254	255

In the Block Size row, continue to fill in each space by doubling the values from right to left. However, you should also now include a second expression of each block size value as a multiple of 256, as shown. You will use the factors paired with 256 for calculations related to the third octet of addresses. For example, you will use these factors to calculate address ranges on large block sizes and to fill in the Mask values in the next step.

	/20	/21	/22	/23	/24	/25	/26	/27	/28	/29	/30	/31	/32
Block Size	4096 256 x 16	2048 256 x 8	1024 256 x 4	512 256 x 2	256	128	64	32	16	8	4	2	1
Mask					0	128	192	224	240	248	252	254	255

For each factor you just paired with 256 in the Block Size row, subtract that factor from 256. (You can imagine replacing the multiplication sign with a subtraction sign in the multiple-of-256 expressions you have just written.) In other words, perform 256 – 16, 256 – 8, 256 – 4, and 256 – 2, and put the results of these four operations in the remaining spaces in the Mask row.

The completed reference chart will look as it does in Figure 1-35.

	/20	/21	/22	/23	/24	/25	/26	/27	/28	/29	/30	/31	/32
Block Size	4096 256 x 16	2048 256 x 8	1024 256 x 4	512 256 x 2	256	128	64	32	16	8	4	2	1
Mask	240	248	252	254	0	128	192	224	240	248	252	254	255

FIGURE 1-35 The IPv4 address block reference chart

To determine the dotted-decimal subnet mask for a network to the left of the vertical line, note that the Mask value in the chart for these networks refers to the value of the third octet in the subnet mask. The first two octets in these networks is always 255.255, and the last octet is always 0. For example, a /22 network has a Mask value of 252 in the chart. Therefore, the subnet mask for a /22 network in dotted-decimal notation is 255.255.252.0.

After you have completed the chart, be sure to refer to it for all questions related to IP addressing.

EXAM TIP

For manual calculations related to IP addressing, it's very useful to memorize the powers of 2 up to 2^{12}. If you have not memorized these values, you should create a power of 2 chart during the exam on the scratch pad provided by the testing site. These values are shown in the following list. The chart is easy and quick to create because each value is double the previous value. Note also that these values are the same as the block sizes, so if you prefer, you can add these 2^x expressions above the block size values in your reference chart.

$2^1 = 2$

$2^2 = 4$

$2^3 = 8$

$2^4 = 16$

$2^5 = 32$

$2^6 = 64$

$2^7 = 128$

$2^8 = 256$

$2^9 = 512$

$2^{10} = 1024$

$2^{11} = 2048$

$2^{12} = 4096$

Determining the Block Size for a /n Network

If your company purchases a block of addresses from an ISP, the size of that address block is often expressed by its subnet mask in slash notation. If you have not memorized these sizes, the easiest way to determine the number of addresses in a network expressed as /n is to use a reference chart such as the one shown in Figure 1-35. However, if you are in a location where you cannot create a chart, you can use the following formula:

$2^{(32-n)}$ = *number of addresses*

For example, a /27 network includes $2^{(32-27)} = 2^5 = 32$ addresses.

Figure 1-36 illustrates this mathematical relationship between the /n value and the number of addresses. Remember that every IPv4 address is a 32-bit address. If the first 24 bits are fixed as the network ID, 8 bits remain to be used as addresses in that network. You determine how many possible values exist within these 8 bits by calculating 2^8. Therefore 2^8, or 256, is the number of unique addresses for a /24 network.

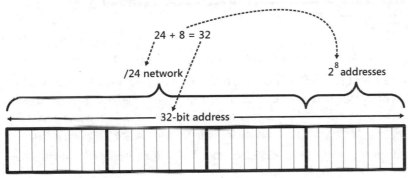

FIGURE 1-36 A /24 network leaves 8 bits for addresses.

Figures 1-37 and 1-38 illustrate the same concept for a /23 and /25 network, respectively.

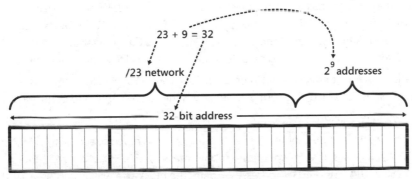

FIGURE 1-37 A /23 network allows for 2^9 or 512 addresses.

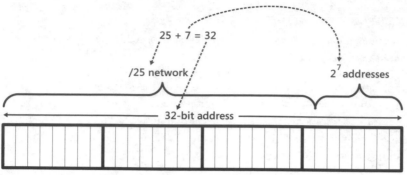

FIGURE 1-38 A /25 network allows for 2^7 or 128 addresses.

Determining the Block Size for a Dotted-Decimal Subnet Mask

Often you need to determine the size of an address block when the subnet mask for that network is given in a dotted-decimal format. Using memorized knowledge or a reference chart is the easiest way to solve this type of problem without software tools, but if you have not memorized the values and are in a location where you cannot create a chart, you can use the following method.

If the subnet mask value provided is 255.255.255.0 or greater, the calculation is fortunately very easy. Just use the following formula, where z is the value of the last octet:

$256 - z = number of addresses$

For example, if a network has a subnet mask of 255.255.255.240, the block size is 256 − 240 = 16 addresses. If a network has a subnet mask of 255.255.255.192, the block size is 256 − 192 = 64 addresses. If a network has a subnet mask of 255.255.255.0, the block size is 256 − 0 = 256 addresses. Remember that the block size will always be a power of 2, so if you have the powers of 2 memorized, you should be able to perform the calculation in your head.

If the subnet mask value for a network is between 255.255.0.0 and 255.255.255.0, the calculation is still fairly easy. Just use the following formula, where y is the value of the third octet:

$(256 - y) * 256 = number of addresses$

For example, if a network has a subnet mask of 255.255.252.0, the block size is (256 − 252) * 256 = 4 * 256 = 1024 addresses. If a network has a subnet mask of 255.255.240.0, the block size is (256 − 240) * 256 = 16 * 256 = 4096 addresses. Again, the block size will always be a power of 2, so if you have the powers of 2 memorized, you might still be able to perform the calculation in your head.

Network administrators rarely need to determine the address block size for a network with a subnet mask between 255.0.0.0 and 255.255.0.0, and you will not need to perform such a calculation on the 70-642 exam. However, for completeness, the formula is presented here (where x is the value of the second octet):

$(256 - x) * 256 * 256 = number of addresses$

Quick Check

- Does an address block get bigger or smaller when its subnet mask is lengthened? By how much?

Quick Check Answer

- An address block gets smaller by half for each 1-bit increment in the subnet mask.

DETERMINING HOST CAPACITY PER BLOCK

The host capacity of an address block is the number of addresses within that block that can be assigned to computers, routers, and other devices. In every address block assigned to a single broadcast domain and subnet, exactly two addresses are reserved for special use: the first, or all-(binary)-zeroes address, in the block, which is reserved as the address of the entire subnet; and the last, or all-(binary)-ones address in the block, which is reserved for the broadcast address. This means that the maximum host capacity of an address block is always two fewer than the number of addresses in that network.

For example, the network 192.168.10.0/24 has 256 addresses. The specific address 192.168.10.0 is reserved for the network address, and 192.168.10.255 is reserved for the network broadcast address. This leaves 254 addresses that can be assigned to network hosts.

Determining Block Size Requirements

If you are designing a network for a given number of computers, you often have to determine an appropriate subnet mask for that network. For example, if you are creating a new LAN that will be connected to a larger corporate network, you could request a block size expressed as /n from the central IT department of the company.

To determine block size requirements expressed in slash notation, first add 2 to the number of computers on the network you are planning for. This resulting value can be called a, or the number of addresses you need in the block. Then use either memorized knowledge of address block sizes or a reference chart such as the one in Figure 1-35 to determine the smallest network, expressed as /n, that has a block size of a or greater.

If you have not memorized the address block sizes and are in a location where it is impractical to create a reference chart, perform the following steps:

1. Determine the smallest value of x such that $2^x \geq a$. To express this step another way, ask yourself the following question: What is the smallest exponent for 2 that would yield a value equal to or greater than the number of addresses you need?

2. Subtract the x (exponent) value from 32 to get the n value of the subnet mask expressed as /n.

This procedure is illustrated on the following page.

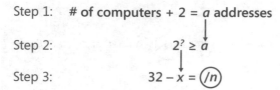

Step 1:   # of computers + 2 = a addresses

Step 2: $2^? \geq a$

Step 3: $32 - x = $ (/n)

For example, if you are designing a new network with 48 computers, you will need 48 + 2, or 50, addresses for the subnet. Because $2^5 = 32$ and $2^6 = 64$, the value 6 is the smallest exponent for 2 that would yield a value equal to or greater than 50. Finally, because $32 - 6 = 26$, you can determine that you need a /26 block to accommodate your new network.

To determine block size requirements expressed in terms of a dotted-decimal subnet mask, begin as always by adding 2 to the number of computers on the network you are planning for. We can call this result a. Then use memorized values of subnet masks or a reference chart such as the one in Figure 1-35 to determine the smallest network, expressed as a dotted-decimal subnet mask, that has a block size of a or greater.

If you have not memorized the address block sizes and are in a location where it is impractical to create a reference chart, perform the following steps:

1. Determine the smallest value that is a power of two (such as 128, 256, 512, and so on) and that is also greater than or equal to a. You can refer to this value as p.

2. If $p \leq 256$, set the first three octets to 255. Subtract p from 256, and then place this new value in the fourth octet.

This procedure when $p \leq 256$ is summarized here:

Step 1:   # of computers + 2 = a addresses

Step 2: $2^? \geq a$

Step 3:   256)
                                                    $-p$

255.255.255.

For example, if you are designing a new network with 30 computers, you need 30 + 2, or 32, addresses for the subnet. Because $2^5 = 32$, the value 32 is the smallest power of 2 that is big enough to accommodate your needs. 256 − 32 = 224, so you need a subnet mask of 255.255.255.224 to accommodate your new network.

If $p \geq 256$, set the first two octets to 255 and the fourth octet to 0. Then determine the following value and place it in the third octet: 256 − (p / 256).

This procedure when $p \geq 256$ is summarized as follows:

Step 1:   **# of computers + 2 = *a* addresses**

Step 2: $2^? \geq a$

Step 3:   256
                      − (*p*/256)
             255.255.___.0

For example, suppose you are designing a network for 2000 computers. In this case, you need 2002 addresses for the subnet. The smallest power of 2 that is equal to or greater than 2002 is 2048. 2048 / 256 = 8, and 256 − 8 = 248. Therefore, you need a network with a subnet mask of 255.255.248.0 to accommodate your needs.

EXAM TIP

Expect to see at least one question on the 70-642 exam in which you are given a specific number of computers and need to determine a subnet mask that will accommodate those computers. The answer choices might present subnet masks in either dotted-decimal or slash notation.

What Is Subnetting?

Subnetting refers to the practice of logically subdividing a network address space by extending the string of 1-bits used in the subnet mask of a network. This extension enables you to create multiple logical subnets or broadcast domains within the original network address space.

Assume that you have purchased from your ISP the address block 131.107.0.0 /16 for use within your organization. Externally, the ISP then uses the /16 (255.255.0.0) subnet mask on its routers to forward to your organization IPv4 packets that have been addressed to 131.107.*y.z.*

In a first scenario, suppose that you configure the subnet mask at its original 255.255.0.0 value on all internal hosts. In this case, all IPv4 addresses within the address space, such as 131.107.1.11 and 131.107.2.11, are logically seen by hosts to share the same network ID (131.107) and to belong to the same subnet. All hosts within this address space therefore attempt to communicate with one another by means of a broadcast. The configuration in this first scenario requires that internal to the network, only layer 1 and layer 2 devices such as hubs, switches, and wireless bridges that do not block broadcasts can be used.

In a second scenario, you decide to alter the subnet mask used within your organization to /24 or 255.255.255.0. In this case, internal hosts will read the addresses 131.107.1.11 and 131.107.2.11 as having different network IDs (131.107.1 vs. 131.107.2) and consider these addresses as belonging to different subnets.

To communicate with each other, the hosts assigned the addresses 131.107.1.11/24 and 131.107.2.11/24 send IPv4 packets to their respective default gateways, an address that must lie within the same broadcast domain. The router owning the default gateway address is then responsible for routing the IP packet toward the destination subnet. Hosts external to the organization continue to use the /16 subnet mask to communicate with hosts within the network.

Figure 1-39 and Figure 1-40 illustrate these two possible versions of the network.

Whereas the original /16 network address space in Figure 1-39 consisted of a single subnet including up to 65,534 ($2^{16} - 2$) hosts, using a /24 subnet mask everywhere internally, as shown in Figure 1-40, allows you to subdivide this original space into 256 (2^8) subnets with as many as 254 ($2^8 - 2$) hosts each.

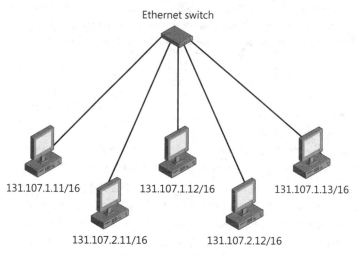

FIGURE 1-39 A /16 address space, not subnetted

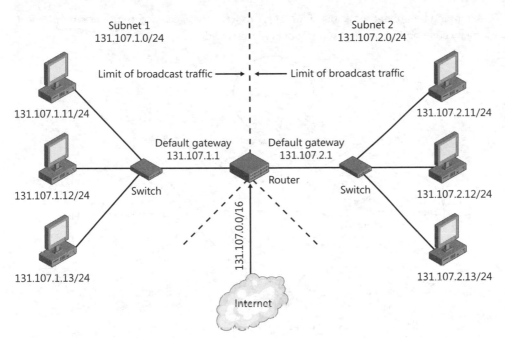

Subnet 1
131.107.1.0/24

Subnet 2
131.107.2.0/24

Limit of broadcast traffic ⟶   ⟵ Limit of broadcast traffic

131.107.1.11/24

131.107.2.11/24

Default gateway
131.107.1.1

Default gateway
131.107.2.1

131.107.1.12/24   Switch

Router

Switch   131.107.2.12/24

131.107.0.0/16

131.107.1.13/24

131.107.2.13/24

Internet

FIGURE 1-40 Subnetted /16 address space

Advantages of Subnetting

Subnetting is often used to accommodate a divided physical topology or to restrict broadcast traffic on a network.

Accommodating Physical Topology

Suppose you are designing or redesigning the address space for a campus network that has four public servers housed in each of four buildings. Each of the four buildings includes a router that connects to the rest of the campus network. If your ISP has allocated to you the /26 network 208.147.66.0, your address space includes 64 public addresses in the range from 208.147.66.0 through 208.147.66.63. Because of the physical topology, however, you cannot put all of these addresses in a single subnet. As illustrated in Figure 1-41, the routers in each building create eight separate physical segments that you have to accommodate with your IP address space design.

By extending the subnet mask in all four locations to /29, you can accommodate this physical topology by creating eight logical subnets of 8 addresses apiece.

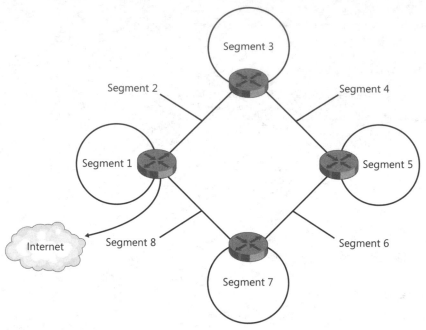

FIGURE 1-41 Each physical network segment requires its own logical subnet.

Restricting Broadcast Traffic

A broadcast is a network message sent from a single computer and propagated to all other devices on the same physical network segment. Broadcasts are resource-intensive because they use up network bandwidth and request the attention of every network adapter and processor on the LAN.

Routers block broadcasts and protect networks from becoming overburdened with unnecessary traffic. Because routers also define the logical limits of subnets, subnetting a network allows you to limit the propagation of broadcast traffic within that network.

> **NOTE** **VLANS ARE AN ALTERNATIVE TO SUBNETTING**
>
> As a means to restrict broadcast traffic in large networks, virtual LAN (VLAN) switches are becoming an increasingly popular alternative to subnetting. Through VLAN software that integrates all the VLAN switches on the network, you can design broadcast domains in any manner, independent of the network's physical topology.

The Subnet ID

Every 32-bit IPv4 address consists of a host ID and a network ID. When you obtain an address block from your ISP (or from your central network administrator in a large network), that address block contains a single network ID that cannot be changed. If you are given a /16 network, for example, the values of the first 16 bits of your address block are not configurable. It is only the remaining portion—the portion reserved for the host ID—that represents your configurable address space.

When you decide to subnet your network, you are essentially taking some of your configurable address space from the host ID and moving it to the network ID, as shown in Figure 1-42. This string of bits you use to extend your network ID internally within your organization (relative to the original address block) is known as the subnet ID.

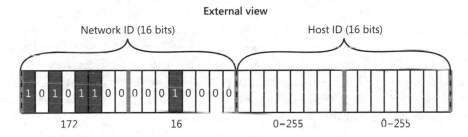

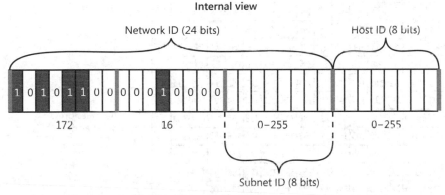

FIGURE 1-42 The Subnet ID is taken from the Host ID

Creating Equally Sized Subnets

The easiest way to subnet a network is to use one new and extended subnet mask on all computers within your internal address space. Doing so generates a number of subnets of equal size. When you subnet your network in this way, you can determine how many logical subnets have been created by using the formula

$$2^{(n2 - n1)} = number\ of\ subnets$$

where $n2$ is the length (in bits) of the new network ID used internally within the organization, and $n1$ is the length of the original network ID assigned externally to refer to the entire address block. For example, if you subnet a 10.0.100.0 /24 address space by using a /27 subnet mask on all hosts in your internal network, you generate $2^{(27-24)} = 2^3 = 8$ subnets. Each of these 8 subnets includes $2^{(32-27)} = 2^5 = 32$ addresses.

Figure 1-43 and Figure 1-44 provide a visualization of this address space and how it is affected by the subnetting. The address block shown includes 256 addresses, with each number in the large square representing one of the possible values of the last octet in the 10.0.100.0/24 address space. Figure 1-43 shows the address space before subnetting. The undivided address block represents a single broadcast domain. The 0 address (10.0.100.0) is reserved for the network address, and the 255 address (10.0.100.255) is reserved for the broadcast address. The network will use a single default gateway, typically at the 1 address.

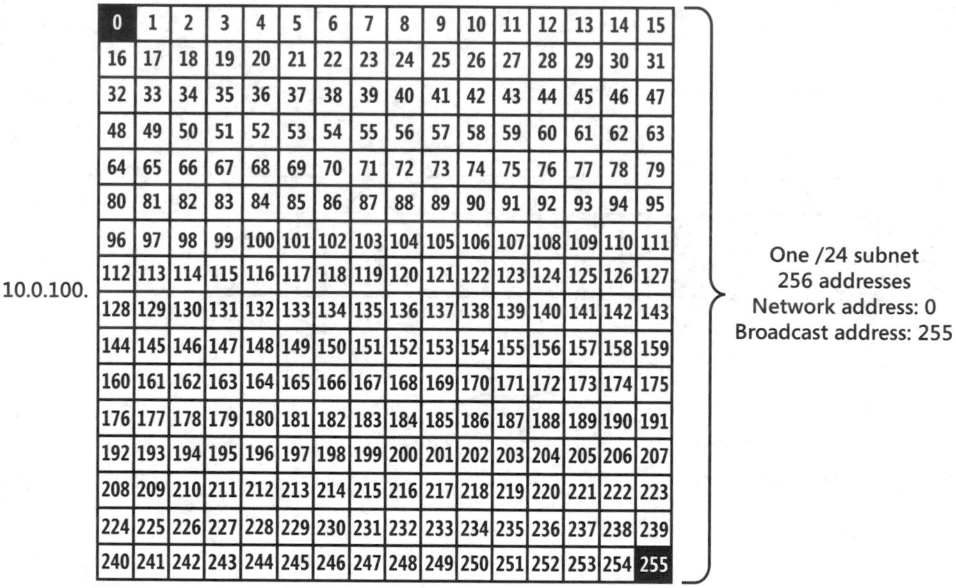

10.0.100.

One /24 subnet
256 addresses
Network address: 0
Broadcast address: 255

FIGURE 1-43 A /24 address space before subnetting

If all the computers within the address space change their subnet mask to /27, however, the eight subnets shown in Figure 1-44 are generated.

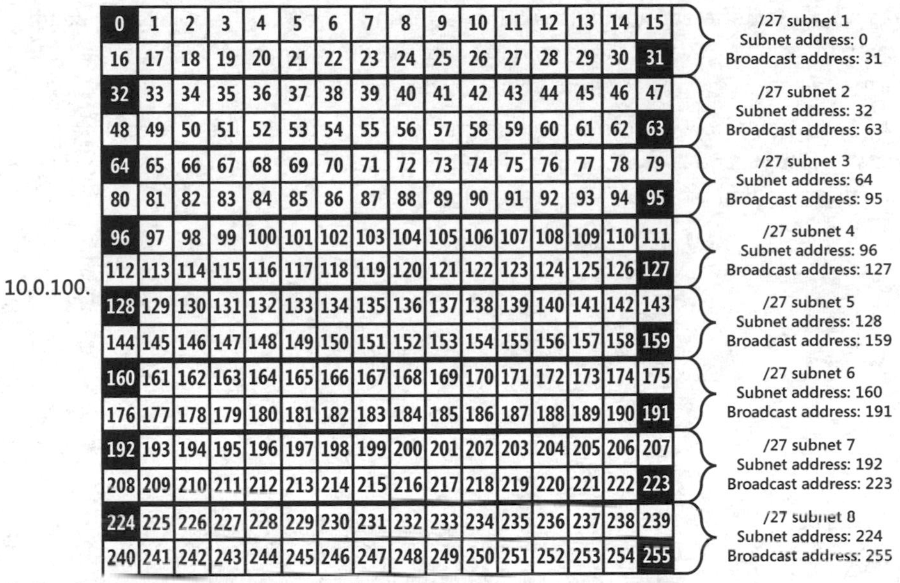

FIGURE 1-44 A /24 address space subnetted globally with a /27 subnet mask

A /27 network can accommodate only 32 distinct addresses, so as a result of subnetting, addresses such as 10.0.100.30 and 10.0.100.33 now belong to different networks. In addition, as shown in Figure 1-44, the first address in each subnet range acts as the network address, and the last address in each range acts as the broadcast address. Each range also requires one address to act as a default gateway.

Using Variable-Length Subnet Masks

It is common to configure an address space so that multiple subnet masks are used internally. Doing so enables you to use your network address space most efficiently.

For example, if you need one subnet to accommodate 100 computers, a second subnet to accommodate 50 computers, and a third subnet to accommodate 20 computers, this arrangement cannot be accommodated by any single internal subnet mask for a /24 address space. As Table 1-5 shows, any single default mask fails to accommodate either enough subnets or enough hosts per subnet to meet all your network needs.

TABLE 1-5 Subnetting a /24 Address Block with a Single Internal Subnet Mask

NETWORK ADDRESS	SUBNETS	HOSTS PER SUBNET
Internal subnet mask: 255.255.255.0	1	254
Internal subnet mask: 255.255.255.128	2	126
Internal subnet mask: 255.255.255.192	4	62
Internal subnet mask: 255.255.255.224	8	30

However, if you use different subnet masks for each subnet, you will be able to divide up the /24 address space in a way that accommodates your needs. This option prevents you from having to acquire new address space from your provider.

Figure 1-45 illustrates how you can use subnet masks of various lengths to accommodate three subnets of 100, 50, and 20 hosts, respectively. This particular network configuration leaves some space unused so that more subnets can be added later.

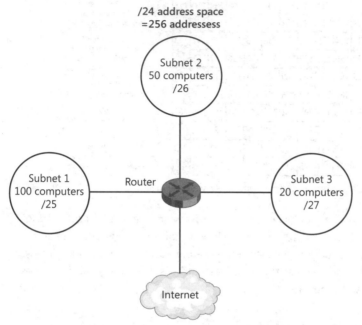

FIGURE 1-45 Using variable-length subnet masks (VLSMs) for flexible subnetting

Enumerating Subnets in an Address Space

When you subnet an address space, you need to know the address ranges of the subnets that are created by this subnetting process. For example, you might have a 192.168.10.0/24 address space and requirements for separate subnets of 20, 50, and 100 hosts. When you divide up your address space to accommodate your needs, you naturally need to determine the specific addresses and subnet masks that will be assigned to each of the three subnets.

To divide an address space and enumerate the address ranges of your subnets, first make sure you have written out an IP address block reference chart such as the one in Figure 1-35.

Then, create a subnet table that gives row headings on the left labeled from top to bottom as Entire Space, Subnet 1, Subnet 2, Subnet 3, and so on, respectively, for every network segment in the network, from largest to smallest. On the top of the table, create column headings from left to right for Addresses Needed, Block Size, First Address, Last Address, and Subnet Mask. The table should look like the one in Figure 1-46.

	Addresses needed	Block size	First address	Last address	Subnet mask
Entire space					
Subnet 1					
Subnet 2					
Subnet 3 ...					

FIGURE 1-46 Create a table to divide your address space into subnets.

After you create the table, simply proceed to fill in the data beginning with the "Entire Space" row. Remember that when filling in block size values > 256, fill in the value expressed as 256 multiplied by some factor, such as "512 = 256 x 2" or "2048 = 256 x 8." The factors will be used for calculations on the third octet.

As an example, we can use the requirements for the 192.168.10.0/24 address space mentioned earlier. The host requirements for its subnets are 100, 50, and 20 computers, or 102, 52, and 22 addresses. We can transfer this information to the table as shown.

	Addresses needed	Block size	First address	Last address	Subnet mask
Entire space	n/a		192.168.10.0		/24 255.255.255.0
Subnet 1	102		192.168.10.0		
Subnet 2	52				
Subnet 3	22				

In the first row, the block size of the entire space is 256 addresses for a /24 network. The last address of the entire space is therefore 192.168.10.255. This last address of the entire space is important. Use this value as a limit to let you know when your subnet requirements go beyond the address space you have available.

	Addresses needed	Block size	First address	Last address	Subnet mask
Entire space	n/a	256	192.168.10.0	192.168.10.255	/24 255.255.255.0
Subnet 1	102		192.168.10.0		
Subnet 2	52				
Subnet 3	22				

After the Entire Space row, you can fill in the remaining data in whichever order is easiest for you. You might find it easiest to fill in all the block sizes first and then continue to fill in the columns from left to right. In this example, we continue to fill the rows in from top to bottom. The method used to fill in any cell in the table is the same in either case.

This brings us to the second row, for Subnet 1. If 102 addresses are needed, you need a block size of 128. The associated subnet mask is /25 or 255.255.255.128, as shown in this table.

	Addresses needed	Block size	First address	Last address	Subnet mask
Entire space	n/a	256	192.168.10.0	192.168.10.255	/24 255.255.255.0
Subnet 1	102	128	192.168.10.0		/25 255.255.255.128
Subnet 2	52				
Subnet 3	22				

Now, add 128 to the last octet of the first address in Subnet 1. This will give you the first address of Subnet 2. To then get the last address of Subnet 1, subtract 1 from this last value, as shown here.

	Addresses needed	Block size	First address	Last address	Subnet mask
Entire space	n/a	256	192.168.10.0	192.168.10.255	/24 255.255.255.0
Subnet 1	102	(128)	192.168.10.0 → +128	192.168.10.127	/25 255.255.255.128
Subnet 2	52		192.168.10.128	-1	
Subnet 3	22				

Next, you can fill in Subnet 2. For 52 addresses, a block size of 64 is needed. The associated subnet mask is /26 or 255.255.255.192. If you add the block size to the first address of Subnet 2, you get the first address of Subnet 3. Subtracting 1 from this last address gives you the last address of Subnet 2, as you can see in the following table. (Note that you can also add the block size to the last address in the previous subnet to give you the last address in the current subnet, but the values are usually not as easy to work with.)

	Addresses needed	Block size	First address	Last address	Subnet mask
Entire space	n/a	256	192.168.10.0	192.168.10.255	/24 255.255.255.0
Subnet 1	102	128	192.168.10.0	192.168.10.127	/25 255.255.255.128
Subnet 2	52	(64)	192.168.10.128	192.168.10.191	/26 255.255.255.192
Subnet 3	22		192.168.10.192		

Next, you can fill in the data for Subnet 3. For 22 addresses, a block size of 32 is needed. The associated subnet mask is /27 or 255.255.255.224. When you add the block size to the first address in Subnet 3, you get 192.168.10.224. Because you have no more subnets, this address is the first in the range of unused addresses that lies at the end of the entire /24 address space. You can add a row named "Unused" to account for this space, and subtract 1 from the first unused address to determine the last address of Subnet 3.

The finished version of the subnet table is shown here.

	Addresses needed	Block size	First address	Last address	Subnet mask
Entire space	n/a	256	192.168.10.0	192.168.10.255	/24 255.255.255.0
Subnet 1	102	128	192.168.10.0	192.168.10.127	/25 255.255.255.128
Subnet 2	52	64	192.168.10.128	192.168.10.191	/26 255.255.255.192
Subnet 3	22	(32)	192.168.10.192	192.168.10.223	/27 255.255.255.224
Unused			192.168.10.224	192.168.10.255	

The division of this address space is illustrated in Figure 1-47. The black boxes represent the network addresses and broadcast addresses that cannot be assigned to individual hosts.

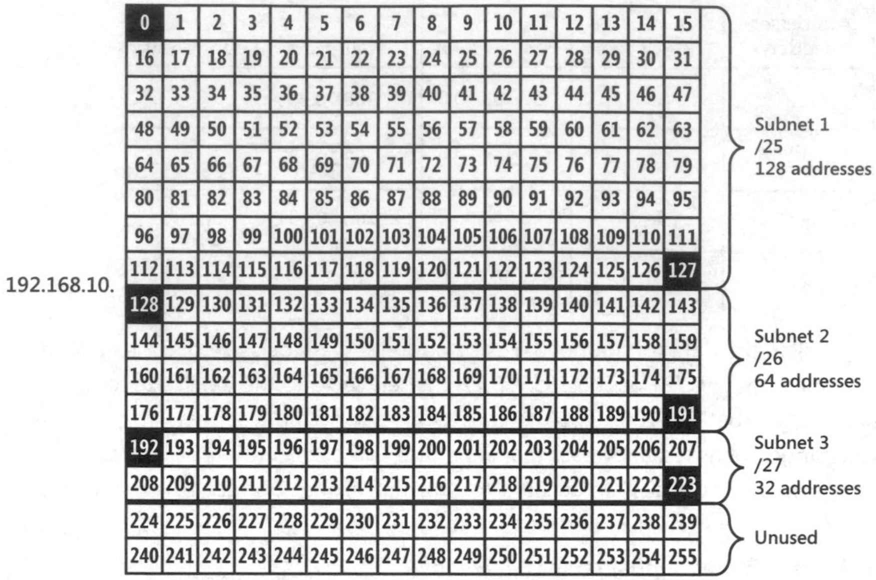

0	1	2	3	4	5	6	7	8	9	10	11	12	13	14	15	
16	17	18	19	20	21	22	23	24	25	26	27	28	29	30	31	
32	33	34	35	36	37	38	39	40	41	42	43	44	45	46	47	Subnet 1
48	49	50	51	52	53	54	55	56	57	58	59	60	61	62	63	/25
64	65	66	67	68	69	70	71	72	73	74	75	76	77	78	79	128 addresses
80	81	82	83	84	85	86	87	88	89	90	91	92	93	94	95	
96	97	98	99	100	101	102	103	104	105	106	107	108	109	110	111	
112	113	114	115	116	117	118	119	120	121	122	123	124	125	126	127	
128	129	130	131	132	133	134	135	136	137	138	139	140	141	142	143	
144	145	146	147	148	149	150	151	152	153	154	155	156	157	158	159	Subnet 2
160	161	162	163	164	165	166	167	168	169	170	171	172	173	174	175	/26
176	177	178	179	180	181	182	183	184	185	186	187	188	189	190	191	64 addresses
192	193	194	195	196	197	198	199	200	201	202	203	204	205	206	207	Subnet 3
208	209	210	211	212	213	214	215	216	217	218	219	220	221	222	223	/27 32 addresses
224	225	226	227	228	229	230	231	232	233	234	235	236	237	238	239	Unused
240	241	242	243	244	245	246	247	248	249	250	251	252	253	254	255	

192.168.10.

FIGURE 1-47 A /24 network subdivided into subnets of varying sizes

Next, we'll try a second, more complicated example. In this second example, assume that you have been allocated the 10.20.40.0 /22 address space and that you have to accommodate network segments of 300 nodes, 150 nodes, 75 nodes, and 22 nodes.

After you create a subnet table and fill in the information already given, the table should look like the following.

	Addresses needed	Block size	First address	Last address	Subnet mask
Entire space	n/a		10.20.40.0		/22 (255.255.252.0)
Subnet 1	302				
Subnet 2	152				
Subnet 3	77				
Subnet 4	24				

Now you can fill out the first row. A /22 network has a block size of 1024 addresses. Whenever the block size is greater than 256, you should also express the size as 256 times some factor and then use that factor to perform your calculations. In this case, you should write the block size as "256 x 4." Use the factor 4 in the 256 x 4 block size to assist you in determining the upper value of this address range. The factor 4 tells you that the very first address after the entire range must be 10.20.40 + 4.0, or 10.20.44.0. Consequently, the last address of the entire space must be the one before it, or 10.20.43.255. These values are entered into the following table.

	Addresses needed	Block size	First address	Last address	Subnet mask
Entire space	n/a	1024 256x④	10.20.40.0 → +4.0 ‾44.0	10.20.43.255 ‾-0.1	/22 (255.255.252.0)
Subnet 1	302				
Subnet 2	152				
Subnet 3	77				
Subnet 4	24				

For Subnet 1, the block size required is 512, or 256 x 2. The associated subnet mask is /23, or 255.255.254.0. To calculate the address range, use the block size factor of 2. The first address of Subnet 1 must be the same as the first address of the entire range, or 10.20.40.0. The factor 2 tells you that the first address of Subnet 2 is 10.20.40 + 2.0, or 10.20.42.0. Consequently, the last address of Subnet 1 is 10.20.41.255, as shown in this table.

	Addresses needed	Block size	First address	Last address	Subnet mask
Entire space	n/a	1024 256x 4	10.20.40.0	10.20.43.255	/22 (255.255.252.0)
Subnet 1	302	512 256x②	10.20.40.0 → +2.0	10.20.41.255	/23 255.255.254.0
Subnet 2	152		10.20.42.0 → -0.1		
Subnet 3	77				
Subnet 4	24				

For Subnet 2, the block size required is 256. The subnet mask is /24, or 255.255.255.0. This block size is easy to work with: You know that the last address must be 10.20.42.255, and the first address of Subnet 3 must increment the third octet by 1.0 to 10.20.43.0, like the following.

	Addresses needed	Block size	First address	Last address	Subnet mask
Entire space	n/a	1024 256x 4	10.20.40.0	10.20.43.255	/22 (255.255.252.0)
Subnet 1	302	512 256x 2	10.20.40.0	10.20.41.255	/23 255.255.254.0
Subnet 2	152	256x①	10.20.42.0 → +1.0	10.20.42.255	/24 255.255.255.0
Subnet 3	77		10.20.43.0 ── -0.1		
Subnet 4	24				

For Subnet 3, 77 addresses are needed, so the block size required is 128. This block size is associated with a /25 or 255.255.255.128 subnet mask. By adding the block size of 128 to the first address in Subnet 3 of 10.20.42.0, you learn the first address in Subnet 4 is 10.20.43.128 and that the last address in Subnet 3 is 10.20.43.127, as shown in this table.

	Addresses needed	Block size	First address	Last address	Subnet mask
Entire space	n/a	1024 256x 4	10.20.40.0	10.20.43.255	/22 (255.255.252.0)
Subnet 1	302	512 256x 2	10.20.40.0	10.20.41.255	/23 255.255.254.0
Subnet 2	152	256	10.20.42.0	10.20.42.255	/24 255.255.255.0
Subnet 3	77	128	10.20.43.0 → +128	10.20.43.127	/25 255.255.255.128
Subnet 4	24		10.20.43.128 ── -1		

For Subnet 4, 24 addresses are needed, so the block size required is 32. This block size is associated with a /27, or 255.255.255.224 subnet mask. Adding the block size to 10.20.43.128 reveals that there is unused space in the subnet; the resulting value of 10.20.43.160 is still lower than the last address in the entire space of 10.20.43.255. You can add a row named Unused to account for this first unused address, and you can then subtract 1 to arrive at the last address in Subnet 4 of 10.20.43.159.

The final version of the subnet table is shown here.

	Addresses needed	Block size	First address	Last address	Subnet mask
Entire space	n/a	1024 256x 4	10.20.40.0	10.20.43.255	/22 (255.255.252.0)
Subnet 1	302	512 256x 2	10.20.40.0	10.20.41.255	/23 255.255.254.0
Subnet 2	152	256	10.20.42.0	10.20.42.255	/24 255.255.255.0
Subnet 3	77	128	10.20.43.0	10.20.43.127	/25 255.255.255.128
Subnet 4	24	32	10.20.43.128 +32	10.20.43.159	/27 255.255.255.224
Unused			10.20.43.160	-1 10.20.43.255	

The division of this address space is illustrated in Figure 1-48.

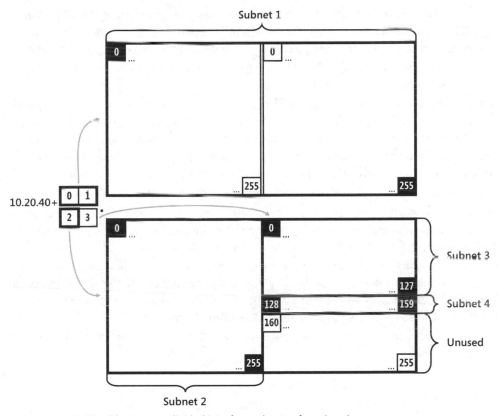

FIGURE 1-48 A /22 address space divided into four subnets of varying sizes

Verifying Subnet Ownership and Configuration

As an administrator of a multisubnet network, you need to ensure that individual computers are assigned an IP configuration that places them in the correct subnet with the correct default gateway. To verify the proper IP configuration for hosts, you need to be able to compare different addresses—such as a server address and its default gateway address—and determine whether they are on the same subnet.

To determine whether IP addresses are on the same subnet, first ensure that the hosts you are comparing have the same subnet mask configured. Then, compare the network IDs of the addresses.

For /8, /16, and /24 subnet masks, this comparison is easy: simply compare the IP address values of the first, the first two, or the first three octets, respectively. If and only if the values are identical, the computers are configured on the same subnet. For example, the addresses 192.168.5.1 /24, 192.168.5.32 /24, and 192.168.5.64 /24 are all on the same subnet because they all share the network ID 192.168.5.

For subnet masks of /25 and higher, divide the value of the last octet in each address by the address block size, and drop any remainder so that you are left with a whole number such as 0, 1, or 2. If and only if the resulting whole numbers are the same, the addresses are on the same subnet. For example, 192.168.5.1 /26 and 192.168.5.32 /26 are on the same subnet because the block size of a /26 network is 64, and if you discount the remainder, both $1 \div 64$ and $32 \div 64$ equal zero. However, 192.168.5.64 is on a different subnet because $64 \div 64 = 1$.

For subnet masks between /16 and /24, first convert the subnet mask to dotted-decimal notation by using a reference chart or by memorization. Subtract the value of the third octet in the subnet mask from 256, and then divide the value of the third octet in the IP addresses you want to compare by this resulting difference, dropping any remainders. If and only if the resulting values are the same, the addresses are on the same subnet. For example, if you want to compare 10.0.40.100 /21 and 10.0.41.1 /21, first determine that the dotted-decimal equivalent of /21 is 255.255.248.0, and then subtract 248 from 256 to obtain a value of 8. Finally, because $40 \div 8 = 5$ and $41 \div 8 = 5$ with some remainder, the two addresses are located on the same subnet.

Learning to Work with Address Blocks

In this practice, you perform exercises that help solidify your understanding of address blocks, subnet masks, and host capacity.

EXERCISE 1   Choosing an Appropriate Subnet Mask

You are adding a new server to each of the following subnets. Given the addresses of the existing computers on that subnet, determine which subnet mask you should assign the new server.

Question: Which subnet mask would you assign to the new server

SUBNET 1: EXISTING COMPUTERS
10.2.12.1
10.2.41.23
10.2.41.100
10.2.41.101

Answer Choices:

A. 255.0.0.0 (/8)

B. 255.255.0.0 (/16)

C. 255.255.255.0 (/24)

Answer: B

Question: Which subnet mask would you assign to the new server?

SUBNET 2: EXISTING COMPUTERS
192.168.34.1
192.168.34.55
192.168.34.223
192.168.34.5

Answer Choices:

A. 255.0.0.0 (/8)

B. 255.255.0.0 (/16)

C. 255.255.255.0 (/24)

Answer: C

EXERCISE 2   Converting Subnet Masks to Dotted-Decimal Notation

Convert the following subnet masks in slash notation to dotted-decimal by using your familiarity with the /16 subnet mask, the /24 subnet mask, and the nine possible subnet mask octet values. Write the final answer in each space provided.

SLASH NOTATION	DOTTED-DECIMAL
/18	
/28	
/21	
/30	
/19	
/26	
/22	
/27	
/17	
/20	
/29	
/23	
/25	

Answer:

SLASH NOTATION	DOTTED-DECIMAL
/18	255.255.192.0
/28	255.255.255.240
/21	255.255.248.0
/30	255.255.255.252
/19	255.255.224.0
/26	255.255.255.192
/22	255.255.252.0
/27	255.255.255.224
/17	255.255.128.0
/20	255.255.240.0
/29	255.255.255.248
/23	255.255.254.0
/25	255.255.255.128

EXERCISE 3 Converting Subnet Masks to Slash Notation

Using your familiarity with 255.255.0.0, 255.255.255.0, and with the nine possible values in a subnet mask octet, convert the following subnet masks in dotted-decimal notation to slash notation. Write the final answer in each space provided.

DOTTED-DECIMAL	SLASH NOTATION
255.255.240.0	
255.255.255.248	
255.255.192.0	
255.255.255.128	
255.255.248.0	
255.255.255.224	
255.255.252.0	
255.255.128.0	
255.255.255.252	
255.255.224.0	
255.255.254.0	
255.255.255.192	
255.255.255.240	

Answer:

DOTTED-DECIMAL	SLASH NOTATION
255.255.240.0	/20
255.255.255.248	/29
255.255.192.0	/18
255.255.255.128	/25
255.255.248.0	/21
255.255.255.224	/27
255.255.252.0	/22
255.255.128.0	/17
255.255.255.252	/30
255.255.224.0	/19
255.255.254.0	/23
255.255.255.192	/26
255.255.255.240	/28

EXERCISE 4 Determining the Host Capacity of Networks

For each of the given address blocks, determine the number of hosts that can be supported. Write down the answer in the space provided in the right column. (Hint: Remember to subtract 2 from the total number of addresses to determine the number of supported hosts.)

ADDRESS BLOCK	NUMBER OF SUPPORTED HOSTS
131.107.16.0/20	
10.10.128.0 Subnet mask: 255.255.254.0	
206.73.118.0/26	
192.168.23.64 Subnet mask: 255.255.255.224	
131.107.0.0 Subnet mask: 255.255.255.0	
206.73.118.24/29	
10.4.32.0/21	
172.16.12.0/22	
192.168.1.32 Subnet mask: 255.255.255.128	
131.107.100.48/28	
206.73.118.12 Subnet mask: 255.255.255.252	
10.12.200.128/25	
192.168.0.0 Subnet mask: 255.255.248.0	
172.20.43.0/24	
131.107.32.0 Subnet mask 255.255.255.240	
10.200.48.0 Subnet mask: 255.255.240.0	
192.168.244.0/23	
10.0.0.0 /30	
172.31.3.24 Subnet mask: 255.255.255.248	
206.73.118.32/27	
131.107.8.0 Subnet mask: 255.255.252.0	
192.168.0.64 Subnet mask: 255.255.255.192	

Answer:

ADDRESS BLOCK	NUMBER OF SUPPORTED HOSTS
131.107.16.0/20	4,094
10.10.128.0	510
Subnet mask: 255.255.254.0	
206.73.118.0/26	62
192.168.23.64	30
Subnet mask: 255.255.255.224	
131.107.0.0	254
Subnet mask: 255.255.255.0	
206.73.118.24/29	6
10.4.32.0/21	2046
172.16.12.0/22	1022
192.168.1.32	126
Subnet mask: 255.255.255.128	
131.107.100.48/28	14
206.73.118.12	2
Subnet mask: 255.255.255.252	
10.12.200.128/25	126
192.168.0.0	2046
Subnet mask: 255.255.248.0	
172.20.43.0/24	254
131.107.32.0	14
Subnet mask 255.255.255.240	
10.200.48.0	4094
Subnet mask: 255.255.240.0	
192.168.244.0/23	510
10.0.0.0 /30	2
172.31.3.24	6
Subnet mask: 255.255.255.248	
206.73.118.32/27	30
131.107.8.0	1022
Subnet mask: 255.255.252.0	
192.168.0.64	62
Subnet mask: 255.255.255.192	

EXERCISE 5 Determining Network Size Requirements in Slash Notation Terms

Each of the values in the left column of the following table refers to a number of computers that a given network must support. In the corresponding space in the right column, specify with a subnet mask in slash notation the smallest network address size that will accommodate those computers. The first row is provided as an example. (Hint: Remember to add 2 to the number of hosts to determine the number of addresses needed.)

NUMBER OF NETWORK HOSTS	SUBNET MASK (/N)
18	/27
125	
400	
127	
650	
7	
2000	
4	
3500	
20	
32	

Answer:

NUMBER OF NETWORK HOSTS	SUBNET MASK (/N)
125	/25
400	/23
127	/24
650	/22
7	/28
2000	/21
4	/29
3500	/20
20	/27
32	/26

EXERCISE 6 Determining Network Size Requirements in Terms of a Dotted-Decimal Subnet Mask

Each of the values in the left column of the following table refers to a number of computers that a given network must support. In the corresponding space in the right column, specify with a subnet mask in dotted-decimal notation the smallest network size that will accommodate those computers.

The first row is provided as an example. (Hint: Remember to add two to the number of hosts in order to determine the number of addresses needed. Then, use the halving-and-doubling or subtract-from-256 technique.)

NUMBER OF NETWORK HOSTS	SUBNET MASK (W.X.Y.Z)
100	255.255.255.128
63	
1022	
6	
1100	
12	
150	
2500	
20	
300	
35	

Answer:

NUMBER OF NETWORK HOSTS	SUBNET MASK (W.X.Y.Z)
63	255.255.255.128
1022	255.255.252.0
6	255.255.255.248
1100	255.255.248.0
12	255.255.255.240
150	255.255.255.0
2500	255.255.240.0
20	255.255.255.224
300	255.255.254.0
35	255.255.255.192

Lesson Summary

- An IPv4 address is a 32-bit number divided into four octets. One part of the IPv4 address represents a network ID, and the other part represents the host ID.

- The subnet mask is used by an IP host to separate the network ID from the host ID in every IP address. The subnet mask can appear in slash notation, such as /24, or in dotted-decimal notation, such as 255.255.255.0. As a network administrator, you need to be able to translate between these two forms of the IPv4 subnet mask.

- The calculation of the network ID by using the subnet mask tells a computer what to do with an IP packet. If the destination network ID of an IP packet is local, the computer broadcasts the packet on the local network. If the destination network ID is remote, the computer sends the packet to the default gateway.

- The IANA has reserved certain ranges of IP addresses to be used only within private networks. These ranges include 10.0.0.0 through 10.255.255.255, 17.16.0.0 through 17.31.255.255, and 192.168.0.0 through 192.168.255.255.

- You can obtain blocks of IP addresses from your provider. The block will be defined as a single address with a subnet mask, such as 131.107.1.0/24. As a network administrator, you need to be able to determine how many addresses are contained in address blocks defined in this manner. To meet your own needs for addresses, you also need to specify an appropriately sized address block in these terms.

- An address block can be subdivided into multiple subnets, each with its own router. To achieve this, you need to lengthen the subnet mask within your subnets so that computers see their subnet IDs as distinct.

Lesson Review

You can use the following questions to test your knowledge of the information in Lesson 2, "Understanding IPv4 Addressing." The questions are also available on the companion CD if you prefer to review them in electronic form.

> **NOTE ANSWERS**
>
> Answers to these questions and explanations of why each answer choice is correct or incorrect are located in the "Answers" section at the end of the book.

1. How many computers can you host in an IPv4 network whose address is 172.16.0.0/22?

    A. 512

    B. 1024

    C. 510

    D. 1022

2. You work as a network administrator for a research lab in a large company. The research lab includes six computers, for which central computing services has allocated the address space 172.16.1.0/29. You now plan to add 10 new computers to the research network. Company policy states that each network is granted address space only according to its needs. What should you do?

   A. Ask to expand the network to a /28 address block.

   B. Ask to expand the network to a /27 address block.

   C. Ask to expand the network to a /26 address block.

   D. You do not need to expand the network because a /29 network is large enough to support your needs.

3. You are a network administrator for your company. You have recently deployed a server that runs Windows Server 2008 R2. The server is provided with the following IP configuration:

   Address: 192.168.1.66

   Subnet Mask: 255.255.255.224

   Default Gateway: 192.168.1.1

   Users on remote subnets complain that they are not able to access the new server. Which of the following actions is most likely to resolve the problem?

   A. Change the server address to 192.168.1.62.

   B. Change the server address to 192.168.1.34.

   C. Switch to a 26-bit subnet mask.

   D. Switch to a 25-bit subnet mask.

4. Your company has obtained the 131.107.168.0 /21 address space from an ISP. You now need to design this address space to accommodate the following network segments.

   Segment A: 600 hosts

   Segment B: 300 hosts

   Segment C: 150 hosts

   Segment D: 75 hosts

   Which of the following addresses should you assign the networks?

   A. Segment A: 131.107.168.0/22, Segment B: 131.107.172.0/23, Segment C: 131.107.174.0/24, Segment D: 131.107.175.0/25

   B. Segment A: 131.107.168.0/22, Segment B: 131.107.174.0/23, Segment C: 131.107.175.0/24, Segment D: 131.107.176.0/25.

   C. Segment A: 131.107.168.0/23, Segment B: 131.107.172.0/24, Segment C: 131.107.174.0/25, Segment D: 131.107.175.0/26

   D. Segment A: 131.107.168.0/22, Segment B: 131.107.172.0/23, Segment C: 131.107.174.0/24, Segment D: 131.107.175.128/25

Lesson 3: Understanding IPv6 Addressing

IPv4 provides 4.3 billion unique possible addresses. This might sound like a large number, but because of the exponential growth of the Internet, the public IPv4 address space is starting to become exhausted. As of this writing, the IANA has already allocated the last available /8 IPv4 address blocks to regional Internet registries, and the first regional registries are expected to run out of IPv4 addresses in mid-2011.

IPv6 was designed primarily to resolve this problem of IPv4 address exhaustion. In place of the 32-bit addresses used by IPv4, IPv6 uses 128-bit addresses. This larger IPv6 address space provides 2^{128}, or 3.4 undecillion (3.4 x 10^{38}) unique addresses. Compared to the number of IPv4 addresses, this number is staggeringly large. If each address were a grain of sand, you could comfortably fit all IPv4 addresses into a small moving truck, but to fit all IPv6 addresses, you would need a container the size of 1.3 million Earths—or the entire Sun.

IPv6 is enabled by default in all versions of Windows since Windows Vista, and it often requires no configuration. However, you still need to become familiar with the various types and formats of IPv6 addresses.

This lesson introduces you to IPv6 by describing its addresses and the transition technologies used in mixed IPv4/IPv6 networks.

> **After this lesson, you will be able to:**
> - Recognize various types of IPv6 addresses, such as global, link-local, and unique local addresses.
> - Understand IPv6 transition technologies such as Intra-Site Automatic Tunnel Addressing Protocol (ISATAP), 6to4, and Teredo.
> - Enumerate IPv6 subnets according to a given network address space and prefix.
>
> **Estimated lesson time: 75 minutes**

Introducing IPv6 Addresses

Although there are other improvements in IPv6 compared to IPv4, such as built-in Quality of Service (QoS), more efficient routing, simpler configuration, and improved security, the increased address space of IPv6 is by far its most important feature. This large address space can be seen in its long addresses.

IPv6 addresses are written by using eight blocks of four hexadecimal digits. Each block, separated by colons, represents a 16-bit number. The following shows the full notation of an IPv6 address:

2001:0DB8:3FA9:0000:0000:0000:00D3:9C5A

You can shorten an IPv6 address by eliminating any leading zeroes in blocks. By using this technique, you can shorten the representation of the preceding address to the following:

2001:DB8:3FA9:0:0:0:D3:9C5A

You can then shorten the address even further by replacing all adjacent zero blocks as a single set of double colons ("::"). You can do this only once in a single IPv6 address.

2001:DB8:3FA9::D3:9C5A

Because IPv6 addresses consist of eight blocks, you can always determine how many blocks of zeroes are represented by the double colons. For example, in the previous IPv6 address, you know that three zero blocks have been replaced by the double colons because five blocks still appear.

> **NOTE   WHAT IS HEXADECIMAL?**
> Hexadecimal is a base 16 numbering system, with 16 possible digit values equivalent to 0 through 15 in decimal. The values 0–9 are represented the same as in normal decimal notation. The decimal values 10, 11, 12, 13, 14, and 15, however, are represented in hexadecimal by the letters A, B, C, D, E, and F, respectively. Note also that in hexadecimal, F + 1 = 10. The value 10 in hexadecimal is therefore equivalent to 16 in decimal notation.

The Structure of IPv6 Addresses

Unicast IPv6 addresses are divided into two parts: a 64-bit network component and a 64-bit host component. The network component identifies a unique subnet. The host component is typically either based on the network adapter's unique 48-bit Media Access Control (MAC) address or is randomly generated.

How Do IPv6 Computers Receive an IPv6 Address?

IPv6 was designed from the beginning to be easier to configure than IPv4. Although manual configuration is still an option (and is required for routers), computers will almost always have their IPv6 configurations automatically assigned. Computers can receive IPv6 addresses either from neighboring routers or from DHCPv6 servers. Computers also always assign themselves an address for use on the local subnet only.

Understanding IPv6 Address Types

IPv6 currently defines three types of addresses: global addresses, link-local addresses, and unique local addresses. The following sections explain these three address types.

Global Addresses

IPv6 global addresses are the equivalent of public addresses in IPv4 and are globally reachable on the IPv6 portion of the Internet. The address prefix currently used for global addresses is 2000::/3, which translates to a first block value between 2000–3FFF in the usual hexadecimal notation. An example of a global address is 2001:db8:21da:7:713e:a426:d167:37ab.

The structure of a global address, shown in Figure 1-49, can be summarized in the following manner:

- The first 48 bits of the address are the global routing prefix that specifies your organization's site. This portion of the address is assigned to you by your ISP and ultimately, by the IANA. (The first three bits of this prefix must be 001 in binary notation.)
- The next 16 bits are the subnet ID. Your organization can use this portion in whatever way it desires to specify unique subnets inside your organization.
- The final 64 bits are the interface ID and specify a unique interface within each subnet. This interface ID is equivalent to a host ID in IPv4.

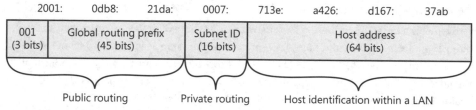

FIGURE 1-49 A global IPv6 address

Link-Local Addresses

Link-local addresses are similar to APIPA addresses (169.254.0.0/16) in IPv4 in that they are self-configured, nonroutable addresses used only for communication on the local subnet. However, unlike an APIPA address, a link-local address remains assigned to an interface as a secondary address even after a routable address is obtained for that interface.

Link-local addresses always begin with "fe80". An example link-local address is fe80::154d:3cd7:b33b:1bc1%13, as shown in the following Ipconfig output:

```
Windows IP Configuration

    Host Name . . . . . . . . . . . . : server1
    Primary Dns Suffix  . . . . . . . :
    Node Type . . . . . . . . . . . . : Hybrid
    IP Routing Enabled. . . . . . . . : No
    WINS Proxy Enabled. . . . . . . . : No
    DNS Suffix Search List. . . . . . : contoso.com
```

```
Ethernet adapter Local Area Connection :

    Connection-specific DNS Suffix  . : contoso.com
    Description . . . . . . . . . . . : Intel(R) 82566DC Gigabit Network Connection -
Virtual Network
    Physical Address. . . . . . . . . : 00-1D-60-9C-B5-35
    DHCP Enabled. . . . . . . . . . . : Yes
    Autoconfiguration Enabled . . . . : Yes
    Link-local IPv6 Address . . . . . : fe80::154d:3cd7:b33b:1bc1%13(Preferred)
    IPv4 Address. . . . . . . . . . . : 192.168.2.99(Preferred)
    Subnet Mask . . . . . . . . . . . : 255.255.255.0
    Lease Obtained. . . . . . . . . . : Wednesday, February 06, 2008 9:32:16 PM
    Lease Expires . . . . . . . . . . : Wednesday, February 13, 2008 3:42:03 AM
    Default Gateway . . . . . . . . . : 192.168.2.1
    DHCP Server . . . . . . . . . . . : 192.168.2.10
    DNS Servers . . . . . . . . . . . : 192.168.2.10
                                        192.168.2.201
    NetBIOS over Tcpip. . . . . . . . : Enabled
```

The structure of such a link-local address, illustrated in Figure 1-50, can be summarized as follows:

- The first half of the address is written as "fe80::" but can be understood as fe80:0000:0000:0000.

- The second half of the address represents the interface ID.

- Each computer tags a link-local address with a zone ID in the form "%ID". This zone ID is *not part of the address* but changes for each computer that refers to the address. This zone ID marks which local adapter faces the address in question if the address is located across the network. If the address is a local address, the zone ID refers to the adapter owning the address.

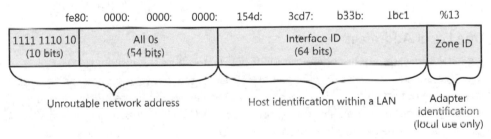

FIGURE 1-50 A link-local IPv6 address

What Are the Zone IDs After Link-Local Addresses?

Because all link-local addresses (LLAs) share the same network identifier (fe80::), you cannot determine which interface a link-local address is bound to merely by looking at the address. Therefore, if a computer running Windows has multiple network adapters connected to different network segments, the computer distinguishes the networks by using a numeric zone ID following a percent sign after the IP address, as the following examples illustrate:

- fe80::d84b:8939:7684:a5a4%7
- fe80::462:7ed4:795b:1c9f%8
- fe80::2882:29d5:e7a4:b481%9

The two characters after each address indicate that the preceding networks are connected to the zone IDs 7, 8, and 9, respectively. Although zone IDs can occasionally be used with other types of addresses, you should always specify the zone ID when connecting to link-local addresses.

Remember also that zone IDs are relative to the sending host. If you want to ping a neighboring computer's LLA, you have to specify the neighbor's address along with the Zone ID of *your* computer's network adapter that faces the neighbor's computer. For example, in the command `ping fe80::2b0:d0ff:fee9:4143%3`, the address is of the neighboring computer's interface, but the "%3" corresponds to the zone ID of an interface on the local computer.

The zone ID for a link-local address is assigned on the basis of a parameter called the *interface index* for that network interface. You can view a list of interface indexes on a computer by typing `netsh interface ipv6 show interface` at a command prompt.

Unique Local Addresses

Unique local addresses are the IPv6 equivalent of private addresses in IPv4 (10.0.0.0/8, 172.16.0.0/12, and 192.168.0.0/16). These addresses are routable between subnets on a private network but are not routable on the public Internet. They allow you to create complex internal networks without having public address space assigned. Such addresses begin with "fd". An example of a unique local address used in a large organization is fd00:9abf:efb0:1::2. An example of a unique local address used in a small organization is fd00::2.

The structure of a unique local address can be summarized in the following way:

- The first seven bits of the address are always 1111 110 (binary) and the eighth bit is set to 1, indicating a local address. This means that the address prefix is fd00::/8 for this type of address. (Note that in the future, the prefix fc00::/8 might also be used for unique local addresses.)

- The next 40 bits represent the global ID, which is a randomly generated value that identifies a specific site within your organization.
- The next 16 bits represent the subnet ID and can be used for further subdividing the internal network of your site for routing purposes.
- The last 64 bits are the interface ID and specify a unique interface within each subnet.

A unique local address is illustrated in Figure 1-51.

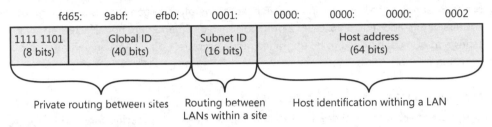

fd65:9abf:efb0:1::2

FIGURE 1-51 A unique local IPv6 address

EXAM TIP

Expect to see more than one question on the 70-642 exam about IPv6 address types. You need to be able to look at an IPv6 address and determine which type it is by name. You also need to understand the function of all three types and when they are used.

NOTE   WHAT ARE SITE-LOCAL ADDRESSES?

Site-local addresses in the fec0::/10 address prefix also provide private routing on IPv6 networks, but they have recently been deprecated (officially set on a path toward obsolescence) by RFC 3879.

States of an IPv6 Address

IPv6 hosts typically configure IPv6 addresses by interacting with an IPv6-enabled router and performing IPv6 address autoconfiguration. Addresses are in a *tentative* state for the brief period of time between first assigning the address and verifying that the address is unique. Computers use duplicate address detection to identify other computers that have the same IPv6 address by sending out a Neighbor Solicitation message with the tentative address. If a computer responds, the address is considered invalid. If no other computer responds, the address is considered unique and valid. A valid address is called *preferred* within its valid lifetime assigned by the router or autoconfiguration. A valid address is called *deprecated* when it exceeds its lifetime. Existing communication sessions can still use a deprecated address.

IPv6 Transition Technologies

IPv6 has a header format that is distinct from IPv4, and routers that have not been designed to support IPv6 cannot parse the fields in the IPv6 header. Therefore, organizations must upgrade their routers before adopting IPv6. Layer 2 protocols such as Ethernet are not affected, so layer 2 switches and hubs don't need to be upgraded, and computers on a LAN can communicate using existing network hardware.

Transition technologies, including the Next Generation TCP/IP stack in Windows, ISATAP, 6to4, and Teredo allow IPv6 to be used across a routing infrastructure that supports only IPv4. These technologies are described in the following sections.

Next Generation TCP/IP

The most fundamental transition technology is the architecture of the Next Generation TCP/IP stack, which is native to all versions of Windows since Windows Vista. With this technology, computers can use IPv6 to communicate if the client, server, and network infrastructure support it. However, they can also communicate with computers or network services that support only IPv4.

Intra-Site Automatic Tunnel Addressing Protocol

Intra-Site Automatic Tunnel Addressing Protocol (ISATAP) is a tunneling protocol that allows an IPv6 network to communicate with an IPv4 network through an ISATAP router, as shown in Figure 1-52.

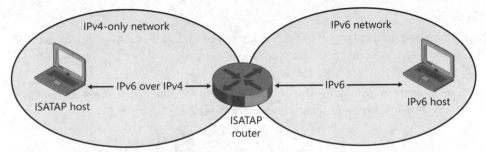

FIGURE 1-52 ISATAP routers help tunnel IPv6 traffic across an IPv4 intranet.

ISATAP allows IPv4 and IPv6 hosts to communicate by performing a type of address translation between IPv4 and IPv6. In this process, all ISATAP clients receive an address for an ISATAP interface. This address is composed of an IPv4 address encapsulated inside an IPv6 address.

ISATAP is intended for use within a private network.

6to4

6to4 is a protocol that tunnels IPv6 traffic over IPv4 traffic through 6to4 routers. 6to4 clients have their router's IPv4 address embedded in their IPv6 address and do not require an IPv4 address. Whereas ISATAP is intended primarily for intranets, 6to4 is intended to be used on the Internet. You can use 6to4 to connect to IPv6 portions of the Internet through a 6to4 relay even if your intranet or your ISP supports only IPv4.

A sample 6to4 network is shown in Figure 1-53.

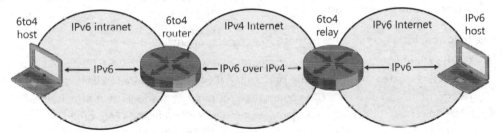

FIGURE 1-53 6to4 allows IPv6-only hosts to communicate over the Internet.

Teredo

Teredo is a tunneling protocol that allows clients located behind an IPv4 NAT device to use IPv6 over the Internet. Teredo is used only when no other IPv6 transition technology (such as 6to4) is available.

Teredo relies on an infrastructure, illustrated in Figure 1-54, that includes Teredo clients, Teredo servers, Teredo relays, and Teredo host-specific relays.

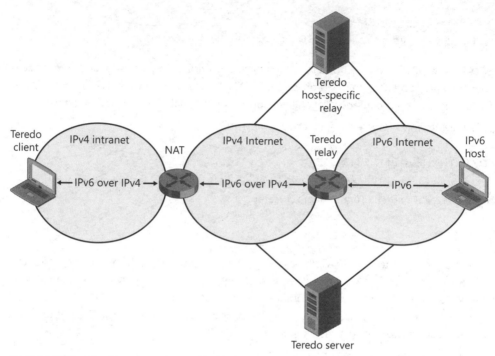

FIGURE 1-54 Teredo allows hosts located behind IPv4 NAT to use IPv6 over the Internet to communicate with each other or with IPv6-only hosts.

The following list describes each of these Teredo components:

- **Teredo client** A Teredo client is a computer that is enabled with both IPv6 and IPv4 and that is located behind a router performing IPv4 NAT. The Teredo client creates a Teredo tunneling interface and configures a routable IPv6 address with the help of a Teredo server. Through this interface, Teredo clients communicate with other Teredo clients or with hosts on the IPv6 Internet (through a Teredo relay).

- **Teredo server** A Teredo server is a public server connected both to the IPv4 Internet and to the IPv6 Internet. The Teredo server helps perform the address configuration of the Teredo client and facilitates initial communication either between two Teredo clients or between a Teredo client and an IPv6 host.

To facilitate communication among Windows-based Teredo client computers, Microsoft has deployed Teredo servers on the IPv4 Internet.

- **Teredo relay** A Teredo relay is a Teredo tunnel endpoint. It is an IPv6/IPv4 router that can forward packets between Teredo clients on the IPv4 Internet and IPv6-only hosts.

- **Teredo host-specific relay** A Teredo host-specific relay is a host that is enabled with both IPv4 and IPv6 and that acts as its own Teredo relay. A Teredo host-specific relay essentially enables a Teredo client that has a global IPv6 address to tunnel through the IPv4 Internet and communicate directly with hosts connected to the IPv6 Internet.

  Windows computers include Teredo host-specific relay functionality, which is automatically enabled if the computer has a global address assigned. If the computer does not have a global address, Teredo client functionality is enabled.

> **NOTE** **TUNNEL ADAPTER TEREDO TUNNELING PSEUDO-INTERFACE**
>
> Installations of Windows Server 2008 R2 include a Teredo tunnel interface by default. This interface is named "Tunnel Adapter Teredo Tunneling Pseudo-Interface."

IP-HTTPS

IP-HTTPS is a new protocol developed by Microsoft for Windows 7 and Windows Server 2008 R2. It enables hosts located behind a web proxy server or firewall to establish connectivity by tunneling IPv6 packets inside an IPv4-based Hypertext Transfer Protocol Secure (HTTPS) session. HTTPS is used instead of HTTP so that web proxy servers do not attempt to examine the data stream and terminate the connection. IP-HTTPS can be used as the fallback technology for clients when other IPv6 transition technologies are unavailable.

 Quick Check

1. Which technology is designed to allow an IPv4-only LAN to communicate with an IPv6-only LAN?

2. Which technology allows an a host on an IPv4-only network to communicate with the IPv6 Internet?

Quick Check Answers

1. ISATAP

2. 6to4

 EXAM TIP

IPv6 is compatible with all Windows clients since Windows XP. On Windows Vista and Windows 7, IPv6 is installed and enabled by default. In Windows XP, you need to install it manually.

Working with IPv6 Subnets

The first 64 bits of an IPv6 address represent the network ID. Organizations that have obtained global IPv6 address space from their ISP have only the first 48 bits (the first three blocks) of that 64-bit address space fixed by the ISP. As shown in Figure 1-49, the final 16 bits of the network ID portion of a global address (the fourth numeric block) represent the Subnet ID. These 16 bits can be used for subnetting in any way an organization chooses. For example, designers of a large network might use a hierarchical subnetting scheme. In this case, they can reserve the first three bits of the 16-bit subnet ID to designate 2^3, or 8, regional branches of the organization. Each branch is then left with 13 bits for local subnetting. Some of these regional branches might choose to use the next four bits to designate each of the 2^4 or 16 departments within the branch and then leave the remaining 9 bits for subnetting within those departments. As an alternative to this type of hierarchical design, smaller organizations can simply use a flat scheme that uses all 16 bits to designate up to 2^{16}, or 65,536, subnets starting from zero (0000000000000000).

If you work for a large organization that has implemented a hierarchical subnetting scheme within its IPv6 space, you need to know how to create and enumerate subnets within your portion of the address space. To perform this task, complete the following steps:

1. Determine the number of bits left to you in the 16-bit subnet ID.

2. Determine how many bits you need for subnetting.

3. Determine the new network prefix to be used within your subnetted portion of the network.

4. Use the number of bits remaining after subnetting to determine the hexadecimal increment between subnet addresses.

5. Use the hexadecimal increment to determine the network address of each subnet.

Each of these five steps is described in more detail in the next section.

Determining the Number of Bits Left in the Subnet ID

The network ID portion of an IPv6 address is 64 bits. Therefore, if a network engineer from a higher level of your organization assigns you an address space with a network prefix such as /51 or /53, you can simply subtract the value after the slash from 64 to determine how many bits are remaining in the subnet ID. Here is the formula:

64 – bits in the network prefix of your address space = bits available in the subnet ID

For example, if the network address assigned to you is 2001:CC1D:5A:C000::/51, you know that you have 13 bits remaining in the subnet ID, because 64–51 = 13. These 13 bits can theoretically be used for up to 2^{13}, or 8192, subnets, but you should only use the bits you need for your own subnetting. The remaining portion of the 13 bits should be left for future use.

Determining How Many Bits You Need for Subnetting

With this step, IPv6 subnetting is exactly like IPv4 subnetting. To determine how many of the available bits in the subnet ID you need to reserve for subnetting, ask yourself the following question: what is the lowest exponent for 2 that would yield a value equal to or greater than the number of subnets I need?

For example, if you need 5 subnets, you need 3 bits because $2^3 = 8$, and 3 is the lowest exponential value of 2 that yields a value equal to or greater than 5. If you need 4 subnets, you need 2 bits for subnetting, because $2^2 = 4$.

Naturally, the number of bits you can claim for subnetting can't be higher than the number of bits left available to you in the subnet ID. If your organization has designed its network space appropriately, it is unlikely that you will need more subnetting bits than are available.

Determining the New Network Prefix to Be Used Within Your Subnetted Portion of the Network

To determine the network prefix that will be used within your portion of the network after subnetting, add the number of bits you need for subnetting to the original network prefix assigned to you. For example, if you have been assigned the network address 2001:CC1D:5A:C000::/51 and you determine that you need 2 bits for subnetting, the new network prefix used internally will be /53. The network address of the first subnet will be 2001:CC1D:5A:C000::/53.

Determining the Hexadecimal Increment Between Subnet Addresses

To determine the hexadecimal increment between subnet addresses, subtract your new network prefix from 64, and raise 2 to the power of that difference. Finally, translate that value to hexadecimal. For example, if the new network prefix you have determined in the last step is 53, you need to translate 2^{64-53} or 2^{11} to hexadecimal.

To translate powers of 2 to hexadecimal, write out a conversion table. This table is easy to create if you draw it the right way.

Start at the top of a blank space by writing 1. Then keep doubling and writing the new values as you go down. However, every time you need to double a value with an 8, replace the 8 with a 10 and add any remaining zeroes. The sequence of numbers should look like this:

1

2

4

8

10

20

40

80

100

200

400

800

1000

2000

4000

8000

Then, add a column that labels these values as powers of 2, starting from 2^0. The final table should look like the one in Table 1-6.

TABLE 1-6 Powers of 2 Expressed in Hexadecimal

HEXADECIMAL VALUE	POWER OF TWO (2^x)
1	2^0
2	2^1
4	2^2
8	2^3
10	2^4
20	2^5
40	2^6
80	2^7
100	2^8
200	2^9
400	2^{10}
800	2^{11}

HEXADECIMAL VALUE	POWER OF TWO (2^x)
1000	2^{12}
2000	2^{13}
4000	2^{14}
8000	2^{15}

Use this table to determine the hexadecimal increment between subnets. If you have a /53 network prefix after subnetting, 11 bits are now remaining in the subnet ID, and your hexadecimal increment is 800. If you have a /55 network prefix after subnetting, then your increment is $2^{64-55} = 2^9$ or 200 in hexadecimal.

Using the Hexadecimal Increment to Determine the Network Address of Each Subnet

To enumerate the addresses of each new subnet you have created, first write down the name of each subnet in a column starting with Subnet 1, Subnet 2, and so on.

Then, write down the network address of each subnet next to each subnet name, starting with subnet 1. To determine the network address of subnet 1, write down the original address of your network space, but replace the original network prefix with the new network prefix you have determined in step 3. For example, if the original network address assigned to you is 2001:CC1D:5A:C000::/51 and you have used 2 bits for subnetting, the address of subnet 1 is 2001:CC1D:5A:C000::/53.

To determine the network address of subnet 2, start with the subnet 1 address and add the hexadecimal increment to the subnet ID portion of that address (the fourth numeric block). To determine the network address of subnet 3, start with the network address of subnet 2 and add the hexadecimal increment to the subnet ID of that address. To determine the network address of subnet 4, start with the network address of subnet 3 and add the hexadecimal increment to the subnet ID of that address. Continue adding the hexadecimal increment as necessary until you have written down the address for each subnet.

Adding the hexadecimal increment is easier than it might sound because you will be handling only a small number of possible values. To perform the addition, first write out the decimal values of A through F (10 through 15). Second, perform the addition as you would perform normal decimal addition, with the following exceptions:

- If a digit in any column is a value between A and F, replace it with the decimal equivalent.
- If the addition of digits within any column results in a sum between decimal 10 through 15, write a sum with the equivalent hex character A-F.
- If the addition of digits within any column results in the decimal value 16, write a sum of 0 and carry a 1 in the column to the left.

Note that adding the hexadecimal increment will never generate a sum greater than 16.

Working through an example can help you understand this hexadecimal addition procedure. Suppose your subnet 1 address is 2001:CC1D:5A:C000::/54 and the hexadecimal increment is 400. How would you find out what the addresses are for subnets 2 through 8?

First write out the decimal values of A through F:

A = 10

B = 11

C = 12

D = 13

E = 14

F = 15

Then, repeatedly add the increment to the fourth block of numbers in the address of subnet 1:

Subnet 2: C000 + 400 = C400 → Subnet 2 address = 2001:CC1D:5A:C400::/54

Subnet 3: C400 + 400 = C800 → Subnet 3 address = 2001:CC1D:5A:C800::/54

Subnet 4: C800 + 400 = C(12)00 → CC00 → Subnet 4 address = 2001:CC1D:5A:CC00::/54

Subnet 5: CC00 + 400 = C(12)00 + 400 = C(16)00 = (C+1)000 = D000 → Subnet 5 address = 2001:CC1D:5A:D000::/54

Subnet 6: D000 + 400 = D400 → Subnet 6 address = 2001:CC1D:5A:D400::/54

Subnet 7: D400 + 400 = D800 → Subnet 7 address = 2001:CC1D:5A:D800::/54

Subnet 8: D800 + 400 = D(12)00 = DC00 → Subnet 8 address = 2001:CC1D:5A:DC00::/54

Here is an example that illustrates the entire procedure. Suppose you have been allocated the network address 2001:3ADB:434F:E000::/51. You need to create four subnets in this space. Which addresses should you assign each subnet? Here is your solution:

1. Determine the number of bits left to you in the 16-bit subnet ID.

   64 − 51 = 13 bits

2. Determine how many bits you need for subnetting.

   4 subnets = 2^2 = 2 bits

3. Determine the new network prefix to be used within your subnetted portion of the network.

   /51 + 2 = /53

4. Use the number of bits remaining after subnetting to determine the hexadecimal increment between subnet addresses.

   Eleven bits remain after subnetting because 64 − 53 = 11. After creating a table like the one in Table 1-6, we can see that 2^{11} = 800 (hexadecimal). The hexadecimal increment is therefore 800.

5. Use the hexadecimal increment to determine the network address of each subnet.

   Subnet 1: 2001:3ADB:434F:E000::/53 (original network address + new network prefix)

   Subnet 2: E000 + 800 = E800 → Subnet 2 address = 2001:3ADB:434F:E800::/53

   Subnet 3: E800 + 800 = E(16)00= (E+1)000 = F000 → Subnet 3 address = 2001:3ADB:434F:F000::/53

   Subnet 4: F000 + 800 = F800 → Subnet 4 address = 2001:3ADB:434F:F800::/53

PRACTICE   Testing IPv6 Connectivity

In this practice, you will review IPv6 information in the Ipconfig output, ping a computer's IPv6 link-local address, and then specify a unique local address for both Dcsrv1 and Boston.

EXERCISE 1   Reading Ipconfig Output

In this exercise, you will use the Ipconfig /all command on the Boston computer to review IPv6 settings.

1. Log on to Boston. At a command prompt, type **ipconfig /all**.
2. Review the output, and then answer the following questions:

   Question: How many local area connections are assigned to your computer?

   Answer: If only one network adapter is connected to Boston, there should be three local area connections (software interfaces) at this time: one for the Local Area Connection corresponding to the physical network adapter, one for an ISATAP tunnel interface, and one for a Teredo tunnel interface.

   Question: Which local area connection corresponds to a physical adapter on the network?

   Answer: The first local area connection.

   Question: Which local area connection corresponds to a software interface for ISATAP?

   Answer: The second connection on a one-adapter computer will normally be assigned to ISATAP, but your particular configuration may vary.

   Note that because Boston is not communicating with an ISATAP router, the media state for this interface is shown to be disconnected.

   Question: Which local area connection corresponds to a software interface for Teredo?

   Answer: The third connection on a one-adapter computer will normally be assigned to Teredo, but your particular configuration may vary.

   Note that because Boston is not communicating on the Internet, it cannot obtain a Teredo address. The media state is therefore described as disconnected.

   Question: How many IPv6 addresses have been assigned to the computer?

   Answer: One. (It starts with fe80:: ...)

Question: What do the following addresses represent?

```
fec0:0:0:ffff::1%1
fec0:0:0:ffff::2%1
fec0:0:0:ffff::3%1
```

Answer: These site-local addresses are used for the autodiscovery of DNS servers when no specific DNS server address has been assigned to the local computer. To facilitate DNS autodiscovery, you can assign these addresses to the DNS servers in your organization.

EXERCISE 2   Pinging a Link-Local IPv6 Address

In this exercise, you will test IPv6 connectivity from Boston to Dcsrv1 by pinging Dcsrv1's IPv6 address. To do so, you will also specify the Boston adapter's zone ID.

1. Log on to Dcsrv1. At a command prompt, type **ipconfig**. Note the link-local IPv6 address assigned to Dcsrv1.

2. If you are not able to view the monitors of Dcsrv1 and Boston side by side, write down the link-local address of Dcsrv1's local area connection on a piece of scratch paper. Do not copy the zone ID (the "%" sign with a number following it).

3. Log on to Boston and open a command prompt.

4. At the command prompt, type **ipconfig**. Note the link-local Ipv6 address assigned to Boston and note the zone ID appended to it. You will use this zone ID in the next step.

5. At the command prompt, type **ping *IPv6addressZoneID***, where *IPv6address* = Dcsrv1's IPv6 address and *ZoneID* = the zone ID assigned to the local area connection on Boston. For example, if the link-local address on Dcsrv1 is fe80::1d63:a395:1442:30f0, and the zone ID assigned to the link-local address in Boston's local area connection is %10, type the following:

   ping fe80::1d63:a395:1442:30f0%10

   You will see four replies from Dcsrv1's IPv6 address.

EXERCISE 3   Assigning a Unique Local Address

In this exercise, you assign a unique local address to the local area connection on both Dcsrv1 and Boston.

1. While you are logged on to Dcsrv1 as an administrator, in the Search Programs And Files box, type **ncpa.cpl**, and then press Enter.

2. Open the properties of the local area connection, and then double-click Internet Protocol Version 6 (TCP/IPv6).

3. In the Internet Protocol Version 6 (TCP/IPv6) Properties dialog box, select Use The Following IPv6 Address, and then specify the following settings:

   IPv6 address: fd00::1

   Subnet prefix length: 64

Default gateway: (leave empty)

Preferred DNS server: (leave empty)

Alternate DNS server: (leave empty)

4. Click OK.

5. In the Local Area Connection Properties dialog box, click OK. (If necessary, also click Close in the Local Area Connection Status dialog box.)

6. Perform steps 1–5 on Boston, specifying an IPv6 address of fd00::2.

7. On Boston, open a command prompt, and type **ping fd00::1**. You will see four replies from the address fd00::1.

8. At the command prompt, type **ipconfig**, and then answer the following questions:

   Question: What is the name assigned to the address fd00::2?

   Answer: IPv6 Address.

   Question: Is a link-local address still specified?

   Answer: Yes. Unlike APIPA addresses in IPv4, link-local addresses in IPv6 are not replaced by other addresses.

9. Log off both computers.

Lesson Summary

- IPv6 is a technology designed to resolve the problem of IPv4 address exhaustion, although it also provides other advantages, such as improved security and simpler configuration.

- IPv6 addresses are 128-bit numbers written as 8 four-digit hexadecimal blocks, but the notation can be shortened. Leading zeroes within any block can be omitted, and once per address, any adjacent all-zero blocks can be replaced by a double colon "::".

- IPv6 hosts can obtain their address from a neighboring IPv6 router, from a DHCPv6 server, or from autoconfiguration.

- For unicast traffic, the first half of an IPv6 address is the network identifier, and the second half of the address is the interface (host) identifier.

- Three types of addresses are used for unicast traffic. Global addresses, which begin with a 2 or 3, are routable on the IPv6 Internet. Link-local addresses, which begin with fe80::, are not routable and are randomly assigned to each interface. Unique local addresses, which begin with "fd", are routable within a private network but not on the IPv6 Internet.

- Transition technologies have been defined to allow IPv4 and IPv6 to interoperate. With ISATAP, a special router negotiates directly between an IPv4-only and an IPv6-only LAN. 6to4 enables IPv6 hosts to tunnel over an IPv4 network such as the Internet. Teredo is a host-based technology that is used when no other option is available. It uses Internet servers to help create IPv6 tunnels over the Internet.

Lesson Review

You can use the following questions to test your knowledge of the information in Lesson 3, "Understanding IPv6 Addressing." The questions are also available on the companion CD if you prefer to review them in electronic form.

> **NOTE ANSWERS**
>
> Answers to these questions and explanations of why each answer choice is correct or incorrect are located in the "Answers" section at the end of the book.

1. You want an IPv6 address for a server that you want to connect to the IPv6 Internet. What type of IPv6 address do you need?

   A. A global address

   B. A link-local address

   C. A unique local address

   D. A site-local address

2. You want to create a test IPv6 network in your organization. You want the test network to include three subnets. What type of IPv6 addresses do you need?

   A. Global addresses

   B. Link-local addresses

   C. Unique local addresses

   D. Site-local addresses

3. You are an administrator for your company, which includes a headquarters and two branch offices. The corporate network uses both IPv4 and IPv6, and each office network is protected by a firewall that performs NAT. Currently, client computers in the separate locations cannot communicate with each other directly. What can you do to enable direct, peer-to-peer communication among client computers in the separate offices?

   A. Configure the firewalls with a global IPv6 address.

   B. Configure the firewalls to use Teredo.

   C. Configure all computers to use unique local addresses.

   D. Configure the firewalls to use ISATAP.

4. Your company has a private IPv6 network with 5 segments. You deploy a new server on one of these segments. Which of the following addresses could enable the server to communicate with clients on all 5 segments over IPv6?

   A. fa00::713e:a426:d167:37ab

   B. fb80::154d:3cd7:b33b:1bc1

   C. fd00::713e:a426:d167:37ab

   D. fe80::154d:3cd7:b33b:1bc1

5. You work as a branch network administrator of a large company with offices in many cities around the world. The corporate network is currently in the process of implementing global addresses for all hosts. The central IT department provides you with the global address space 3f04:4d12:95a5:a000::/52. Your network includes four subnets. Which address and network prefix should you assign the third subnet?

   A. 3f04:4d12:95a5:a800::/54

   B. 3f04:4d12:95a5:a800::/55

   C. 3f04:4d12:95a5:ac00::/54

   D. 3f04:4d12:95a5:ac00::/55

Chapter Review

To further practice and reinforce the skills you learned in this chapter, you can perform the following tasks:

- Review the chapter summary.
- Review the list of key terms introduced in this chapter.
- Complete the case scenario. This scenario sets up a real-world situation involving the topics of this chapter and asks you to create a solution.
- Complete the suggested practices.
- Take a practice test.

Chapter Summary

- IP provides routing and addressing for virtually all computer networks in the world. Windows clients by default are configured to obtain an IP address automatically. In this default configuration, the clients obtain an IPv4 address from a DHCP server if one is available. If one is not available, they assign themselves an address that offers only limited connectivity. Critical infrastructure servers, however, should be assigned addresses manually.
- To troubleshoot connectivity problems on IP networks, you should use tools such as Ipconfig, Ping, Tracert, PathPing, and Arp.
- If you need to implement IPv4 on a network or troubleshoot connectivity in a large network, you need to understand how IPv4 addressing works. An IPv4 address is a 32-bit number that can be broken down into a network ID and host ID, and the subnet mask is used to determine which is which.
- Some IP address ranges are reserved for use in private networks: 10.0.0.0–10.255.255.255, 172.16.0.0–172.31.255.255, and 192.168.0.0–192.168.255.255.

- Groups of addresses are known as address blocks, which you can obtain from your provider. To understand address blocks, you need to understand how many addresses are associated with each subnet mask. Two addresses in every subnet are reserved for special uses, so you always need at least two more addresses than computers for each subnet.

- Public IPv4 addresses are becoming exhausted, and the only long-term solution is a replacement protocol called IPv6, which is just beginning to be implemented. IPv6 addresses are 128-bit addresses. Global IPv6 addresses are usable on public networks. Unique local addresses are routable but are usable only on private networks, and link-local addresses are autoconfigured addresses that provide only limited connectivity.

Key Terms

Do you know what these key terms mean? You can check your answers by looking up the terms in the glossary at the end of the book.

- address block
- Automatic Private IP Addressing (APIPA)
- broadcast
- IPv4
- IPv6
- Network Address Translation (NAT)
- private address ranges
- subnet mask

Case Scenarios

In the following case scenario, you will apply what you've learned about IP addressing in this chapter. You can find answers to these questions in the "Answers" section at the end of this book.

Case Scenario: Working with IPv4 Address Blocks

You work as a network administrator for a company with 100 employees. Your company currently uses a total of six public IP addresses for its public servers and routers, all of which are hosted in a perimeter network on the company premises.

1. What is the smallest size address block that can support the servers and routers in your perimeter network? (Express the network size in slash notation and dotted-decimal notation.)

2. You have decided to deploy three new servers in the perimeter network and assign them each a public IP address. If your provider sells addresses in blocks only, what size block should you request to enable you to host all of your public servers on a single subnet? Express the size of the network with a subnet mask in both slash notation and dotted-decimal notation.

3. What is the maximum number of servers or routers you could deploy in this new address block?

Suggested Practices

To help you successfully master the exam objectives presented in this chapter, complete the following tasks.

Configure IP Addressing

Learning about IP addressing can give the impression that subnetting rules are abstract and not very useful to know in practice. For this reason, it's important to experiment with various combinations of subnet masks and addresses to see the very real effects they have on connectivity.

■ **Practice** In a physical or virtual environment, assign two neighboring computers a subnet mask of 255.255.255.252. Assign one computer an address of 192.168.0.1. Assign the second computer an address of 192.168.0.2 and ensure that the two computers can ping each other. Then, increment the address of the second computer and attempt to ping again. At what point does the connection break between the two? Use this method to determine the complete address range of the 192.168.0.0/30 block.

On two neighboring computers, disable IPv4, and then manually assign them unique local IPv6 addresses. Verify connectivity by using Ping.

Take a Practice Test

The practice tests on this book's companion CD offer many options. For example, you can test yourself on just one exam objective, or you can test yourself on all the 70-642 certification exam content. You can set up the test so that it closely simulates the experience of taking a certification exam, or you can set it up in study mode so that you can look at the correct answers and explanations after you answer each question.

> **MORE INFO** **PRACTICE TESTS**
>
> For details about all the practice test options available, see the "How to Use the Practice Tests" section in this book's Introduction.

CHAPTER 2

Configuring Name Resolution

Name resolution is the essential, endlessly repeated process of converting computer names to addresses on a network. In Windows networks, the primary name resolution system is Domain Name System (DNS), which is also the name resolution system of the Internet. DNS has a hierarchical structure that allows it to support networks of any size, and because DNS relies on point-to-point communication, it is blind to physical topology. DNS does not help clients resolve the names merely of computers that happen to be nearby; it helps clients resolve the names of all computers registered in the DNS server, regardless of location.

The DNS infrastructure is one of the most important areas of concern for Windows administration, but DNS is not the only name resolution system used in Windows. For reasons of history as well as user convenience, Windows relies on other name resolution systems in specific circumstances.

As a network administrator, you need to understand all name resolution systems. This chapter introduces them to you and gives the proper emphasis to DNS.

Exam objectives in this chapter:
- Configure a Domain Name System (DNS) server.
- Configure name resolution for client computers.

Lessons in this chapter:

- Lesson 1: Understanding Name Resolution in Windows Server 2008 Networks **111**
- Lesson 2: Deploying a DNS Server **136**
- Lesson 3: Configuring DNS Client Settings **158**

Before You Begin

To complete the lessons in this chapter, you must have:

- Two networked computers running Windows Server 2008 R2 and named Dcsrv1 and Boston, respectively.
- Assigned the IPv4 addresses 192.168.0.1/24 to Dcsrv1 and 192.168.0.2/24 to Boston.
- Assigned the IPv6 addresses fd00::1 to Dcsrv1 and fd00::2 to Boston.
- Enabled file sharing on both computers.

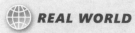

REAL WORLD

J.C. Mackin

DNS has served as the principal naming and name resolution provider in Windows networks since Windows 2000, but the older set of services that used to be responsible for names—NetBIOS—has been slow to disappear.

DNS upstaged NetBIOS for a good reason. NetBIOS networks resemble a world in which no family names exist and in which, to avoid ambiguity, everyone's first name has to be completely different from everyone else's. Because every computer in a NetBIOS network has only a single name tag, Windows networks before Windows 2000 were difficult to manage on a large scale. Aside from its lack of large-scale manageability, NetBIOS also has the limitation of providing too much transparency into corporate networks. If you watch the traffic on a NetBIOS network, you can see that it is noisy and, because of the information it broadcasts, not particularly secure. Finally, NetBIOS is incompatible with IPv6, a characteristic that will eventually restrict its deployment.

Despite these limitations, NetBIOS is enabled on network connections by default to this day, mostly for compatibility with older Windows clients. Unlike DNS, NetBIOS requires no configuration, so it has traditionally provided a backup name resolution method for Windows XP and earlier clients when DNS is unavailable. Also, for Windows XP and earlier clients, NetBIOS provides the only means to browse the local network (through My Network Places).

However, beginning with Windows Vista, a new replacement for NetBIOS appeared in Windows networks: Link Local Multicast Name Resolution, or LLMNR. Like NetBIOS, LLMNR doesn't require any configuration, and it allows you to browse the local network through the Network option in the Start menu. LLMNR doesn't carry any of the security risks or broadcasts of NetBIOS, and it's compatible with IPv6.

Is it time for you to start disabling NetBIOS on network connections? If your network includes computers running only Windows Vista, Windows 7, Windows Server 2008, or Windows Server 2008 R2, then yes, you should start testing network functionality with NetBIOS disabled. Disabling NetBIOS will reduce the attack surface of your network, and your users will probably not notice any change in network behavior. If by some chance users complain about an application not functioning correctly, however, you know it's still too early for you to leave NetBIOS behind.

Lesson 1: Understanding Name Resolution in Windows Server 2008 Networks

When you connect to a computer, you normally specify it by a name such as "www.microsoft.com" or "FileSrvB." However, computer names such as these are used only for human benefit. For a connection to be established to a remote computer, the name you specify must be translated into an IP address to which packets can be routed. In computer terminology, to *resolve* a computer name means to translate the name into an address, and the process in general is called *name resolution*.

Name resolution is one of the most important components in a network infrastructure. To be a Windows network administrator, you need to understand how names are resolved so that you can configure and troubleshoot this essential feature. In addition, it is a topic that is heavily tested on the 70-642 exam.

This lesson introduces the various name resolution methods used in Windows Server 2008 R2 networks.

After this lesson, you will be able to:

- Understand the function of Link Local Multicast Name Resolution (LLMNR).
- Understand NetBIOS name resolution methods.
- Understand the components in a DNS infrastructure.
- Understand the steps in a DNS query.

Estimated lesson time: 120 minutes

Name Resolution Methods in Windows

Windows Server 2008 R2 networks include no fewer than three name resolution systems: DNS, Link Local Multicast Name Resolution (LLMNR), and NetBIOS. Of these three, DNS is by far the most important because it is the name resolution method used to support Active Directory Domain Services, as well as the method used to resolve all Internet names. DNS is in fact the preferred name resolution method in Windows networks and is used whenever it is available.

However, because of the way that DNS works, it is not by itself sufficient to provide name resolution services for all Windows networks. A DNS infrastructure requires network-wide configuration for both servers and clients. Most small and informal networks lack such a DNS infrastructure. As a result, DNS cannot be used to resolve, for example, the names of computers in a workgroup with only default installations of Windows 7 and Windows Server 2008 R2. The other two name resolution services—LLMNR and NetBIOS—are the ones used in workgroups such as these.

The next sections describe these two fallback name resolution mechanisms.

What Is Link Local Multicast Name Resolution?

LLMNR is enabled by default on Windows Server 2008 R2 and Windows 7 clients. When enabled, LLMNR is always used to resolve computer names on the local subnet for the Network Map feature and for network browsing through Network on the Start menu. (These two features also require Network Discovery to be enabled in Advanced Sharing Settings, which you can access through Network and Sharing Center.)

In addition, LLMNR attempts to resolve computer names more generally in place of DNS when DNS is not configured. For example, suppose that you are working on a computer named Win7-01 that is running Windows 7 and that does not have a DNS server specified in its IP configuration. If you want to ping a computer running Windows Server 2008 R2 named WS08r2-01, your computer will first use LLMNR to attempt to resolve the name WS08r2-01. To do this, Win7-01 first checks the LLMNR cache of previously resolved names on the local computer. If no matching entry is found, Win7-01 immediately sends out two LLMNR query packets to the local network: first, to the IPv6 multicast address of FF02:0:0:0:0:0:1:3, as shown in Figure 2-1, and second, to the IPv4 multicast address of 224.0.0.252, as shown in Figure 2-2. All computers running versions of Windows since Windows Vista listen to traffic sent to these multicast addresses when LLMNR is enabled.

> **NOTE** **WHEN IS LLMNR ENABLED?**
>
> In Windows Vista and Windows Server 2008, LLMNR is enabled only when Network Discovery is enabled. However, in Windows 7 and Windows Server 2008 R2, LLMNR is enabled by default without Network Discovery. Unless it is specifically disabled in Group Policy, LLMNR is used as an active name resolution mechanism as long as IPv6 remains enabled. Finally, even when IPv6 is disabled, both Windows 7 and Windows Server 2008 R2 respond to LLMNR queries over IPv4.

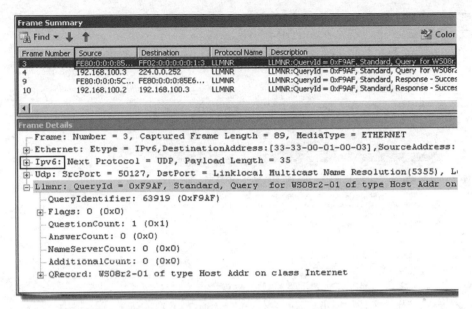

FIGURE 2-1 An LLMNR query to resolve the computer name "WS08r2-01" over IPv6

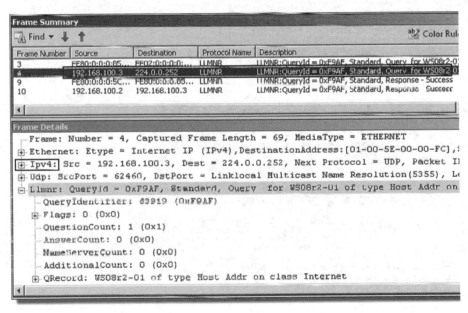

FIGURE 2-2 An LLMNR query to resolve the computer name WS08r2-01 over IPv4

If WS08r2-01 is located on the same subnet, the computer hears the query and responds to Win7-01 over IPv6 or IPv4, or over both, depending on which protocols are enabled on its network connection. By default, both are enabled, so the computer will respond over both protocols. These LLMNR responses providing the IPv6 and IPv4 addresses for the name WS08r2-01 are shown in Figure 2-3 and Figure 2-4.

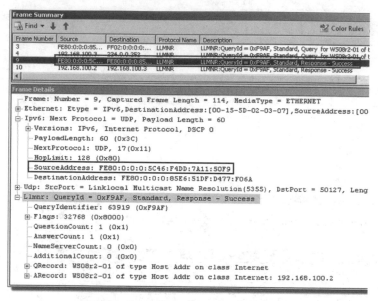

FIGURE 2-3 An LLMNR response over IPv6

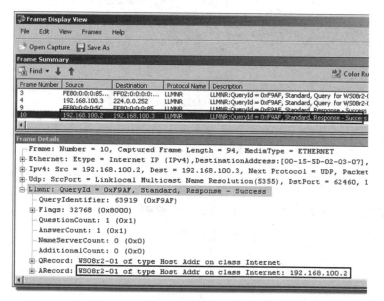

FIGURE 2-4 An LLMNR response over IPv4

The same two-part exchange is illustrated in Figure 2-5.

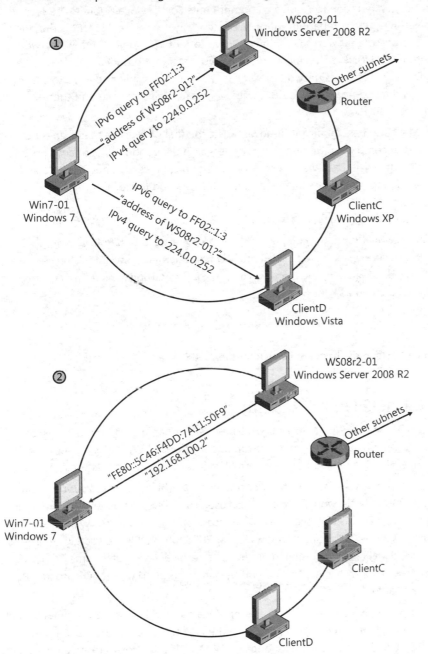

FIGURE 2-5 An illustration of the LLMNR name resolution shown in Figures 2-1 through 2-4

As a name resolution mechanism, LLMNR offers a few important advantages. The first is that it requires no configuration to resolve computer names on the local subnet. The second is that, unlike NetBIOS, it is compatible with IPv6. Essentially, therefore, LLMNR is the only name resolution protocol that works without configuration for IPv6-only Windows networks. Another advantage of LLMNR is that it uses multicasting instead of broadcasting to resolve computer names. This decreases network traffic and prevents possible network storms. A final advantage is that, compared to NetBIOS, it is a much smaller service and therefore has a reduced attack surface.

However, LLMNR also has significant disadvantages, the first of which is that it does not resolve the names of computers running Windows Server 2003, Windows XP, or any version of Windows earlier than Windows Vista. A second and significant disadvantage of LLMNR is that it cannot be used to resolve the names of computers beyond the local subnet.

> *NOTE* **DISABLING LLMNR ON A NETWORK**
>
> **You can disable LLMNR for many computers at a time by using Group Policy. In a Group Policy object (GPO), navigate to Computer Configuration\Policies\Administrative Templates\Network\DNS Client, and then search for the policy setting named Turn Off Multicast Name Resolution.**

EXAM TIP

You need to understand the basics of LLMNR for the 70-642 exam.

What Is NetBIOS Name Resolution?

NetBIOS, or NetBIOS-over-TCP/IP (NetBT or NBT), is an earlier naming and name resolution system used for compatibility with computers running versions of Windows earlier than Windows Vista. NetBIOS is enabled by default on all Windows operating systems.

On Windows operating systems prior to Windows Vista, NetBIOS is used to support computer browsing through My Network Places. It is also used to resolve computer names on these operating systems when DNS is unavailable. In more recent operating systems (Windows Vista, Windows 7, Windows Server 2008, and Windows Server 2008 R2), NetBIOS is used when DNS is not configured and LLMNR is either disabled or unable to resolve a computer name. In addition, computers running all Windows operating systems by default respond to NetBIOS broadcasts that query for their name.

Figure 2-6 shows a network capture of an attempt by a computer running Windows Server 2008 R2 to resolve the computer name Xpclient. In the first two packets, the server (at the IPv6 address "FE80:0:0:0:85..." and the IPv4 address 192.168.100.3) tries to resolve the name "Xpclient" by sending out LLMNR queries over IPv6 and IPv4. Xpclient is running Windows XP Professional, however, and doesn't respond to the LLMNR queries. Because the original computer doesn't receive a response, it then sends a third packet, a NetBIOS query broadcast over the local network. (The protocol name *NbtNs* refers to "NetBIOS-over-TCP/IP Name Service," and the local broadcast address used in this instance is 192.168.100.255.) In the fourth packet, the local computer receives a response from the computer that owns the name Xpclient, found at 192.168.100.4.

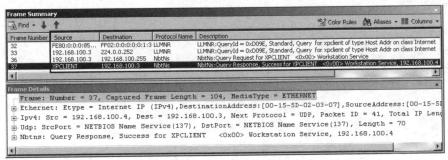

FIGURE 2-6 NetBIOS is used to resolve the name of a computer running Windows XP.

NetBIOS Name Resolution Methods

NetBIOS includes three name resolution methods: broadcasts, WINS, and the Lmhosts file.

NETBIOS BROADCASTS

The first name resolution mechanism enabled by NetBIOS is the use of NetBIOS broadcasts over IPv4. Computers using NetBIOS to resolve a name will send out broadcasts to the local network requesting the owner of that name to respond with its IPv4 address.

WINS

A WINS server is essentially a directory of computer names, such as Client2 and ServerB, and their associated IP addresses. When you configure a network connection with the address of a WINS server, you perform two steps in one. First, you enable the computer to use a WINS server to resolve computer names that cannot be resolved by DNS or LLMNR; and, second, you register the local computer's name in the directory of the WINS server. An important advantage of WINS over network broadcasts is that it enables NetBIOS name resolution beyond the local subnet.

LMHOSTS FILE

The Lmhosts file is a static, local database file that is stored in the directory *%SystemRoot%*\System32\Drivers\Etc and that maps specific NetBIOS names to IP addresses. Recording a NetBIOS name and its IP address in the Lmhosts file enables a computer to resolve an IP address for the given NetBIOS name when every other name resolution method has failed.

You must manually create the Lmhosts file. For this reason, it is normally used only to resolve the names of remote clients for which no other method of name resolution is available—for example, when no WINS server exists on the network, when the remote client is not registered with a DNS server, and when the client computer is out of broadcast range.

Enabling and Disabling NetBIOS

NetBIOS is enabled by default for IPv4 on every local area connection. To change NetBIOS settings, first open the properties of a local area connection. Then open the properties of Internet Protocol Version 4 (TCP/IPv4) and click the Advanced button to open the Advanced TCP/IP Settings dialog box. In this dialog box, click the WINS tab, shown in Figure 2-7.

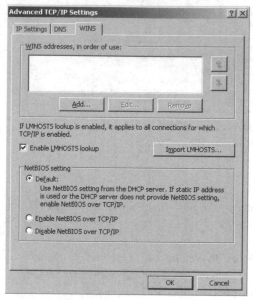

FIGURE 2-7 Adjusting NetBIOS settings

As shown in Figure 2-7, a local area connection will by default allow a DHCP server to assign its NetBIOS setting. A NetBIOS setting from DHCP does not merely enable or disable NetBIOS. The DHCP server can also configure a client as a specific NetBIOS node type.

NetBIOS Node Types

The mechanism or mechanisms that NetBIOS uses to resolve computer names depends on the NetBIOS node type that is configured for the computer. Four node types exist:

- **Broadcast (b-node)**   This node type uses only broadcast NetBIOS name queries for name registration and resolution. B-node has two drawbacks: first, broadcasts disturb every node on the network. Second, routers typically do not forward broadcasts, so only NetBIOS names on the local network can be resolved. This node type is most similar to LLMNR in its functionality.

- **Point-to-point (p-node)**   This node type uses point-to-point communications with a WINS server to resolve names. P-node does not use broadcasts; instead, it queries only the name server directly.

- **Mixed (m-node)** This node type uses broadcasts first (b-node) and then uses WINS queries (p-node) if broadcasts are not successful.

- **Hybrid (h-node)** This node type uses WINS queries first (p-node) and then uses broadcasts (b-node) as a fallback mechanism if no WINS server is configured, if a configured WINS server is unavailable, or if the queried-for name is not found in the WINS database. To reduce IP broadcasts, these computers also use an Lmhosts file to search for name-to-IP address mappings before using b-node IP broadcasts.

By default, Windows clients since Windows Vista are configured as hybrid nodes. You can determine the current node status assigned to a Windows computer by viewing the output of Ipconfig /all, as shown here. Note that the Node Type setting on this computer is set to Hybrid.

```
C:\Users\Administrator>ipconfig /all

Windows IP Configuration

    Host Name . . . . . . . . . . . . : WS08r2-01
    Primary Dns Suffix . . . . . . . :
    Node Type . . . . . . . . . . . . : Hybrid
    IP Routing Enabled. . . . . . . . : No
    WINS Proxy Enabled. . . . . . . . : No
    DNS Suffix Search List. . . . . . : nwtraders.local

Ethernet adapter Local Area Connection:

    Connection-specific DNS Suffix  . : nwtraders.local
    Description . . . . . . . . . . . : Microsoft Virtual Machine Bus Network Adapter
    Physical Address. . . . . . . . . : 00-15-5D-02-03-00
    DHCP Enabled. . . . . . . . . . . : Yes
    Autoconfiguration Enabled . . . . : Yes
    Link-local IPv6 Address . . . . . : fe80::5c46:f4dd:7a11:50f9%11(Preferred)
    IPv4 Address. . . . . . . . . . . : 192.168.20.103(Preferred)
    Subnet Mask . . . . . . . . . . . : 255.255.255.0
    Lease Obtained. . . . . . . . . . : Monday, November 06, 2010 7:38:53 AM
    Lease Expires . . . . . . . . . . : Tuesday, November 14, 2010 7:38:53 AM
    Default Gateway . . . . . . . . . : 192.168.20.1
    DHCP Server . . . . . . . . . . . : 192.168.20.2
    DHCPv6 IAID . . . . . . . . . . . : 234886493
    DHCPv6 Client DUID. . . . . . . . : 00-01-00-01-14-35-90-F9-00-15-5D-02-03-00

    DNS Servers . . . . . . . . . . . : 192.168.40.2
                                        192.168.20.2
    NetBIOS over Tcpip. . . . . . . . : Enabled

Tunnel adapter isatap.nwtraders.local:

    Media State . . . . . . . . . . . : Media disconnected
    Connection-specific DNS Suffix  . : nwtraders.local
    Description . . . . . . . . . . . : Microsoft ISATAP Adapter
    Physical Address. . . . . . . . . : 00-00-00-00-00-00-00-E0
    DHCP Enabled. . . . . . . . . . . : No
    Autoconfiguration Enabled . . . . : Yes
```

```
Tunnel adapter Teredo Tunneling Pseudo-Interface:

   Media State . . . . . . . . . . : Media disconnected
   Connection-specific DNS Suffix  . :
   Description . . . . . . . . . . : Teredo Tunneling Pseudo-Interface
   Physical Address. . . . . . . . : 00-00-00-00-00-00-00-E0
   DHCP Enabled. . . . . . . . . . : No
   Autoconfiguration Enabled . . . . : Yes
```

EXAM TIP

Expect to see a question about node types on the 70-642 exam.

Advantages and Disadvantages of NetBIOS

As a name resolution mechanism, the biggest advantage of NetBIOS is that by default it can resolve the names of computers running all Windows operating systems, including those prior to Windows Vista, without requiring any user configuration. In addition, when you add a WINS server to your name resolution infrastructure, NetBIOS can be used (like DNS and unlike LLMNR) to resolve the names of computers in neighboring subnets. (This is a particularly important option when those remote computers are not registered in a DNS zone.)

The biggest limitation of NetBIOS is that, although it provides a useful backup method for resolving computers within broadcast range and in small networks, it is impractical for very large networks. In NetBIOS, each computer is assigned only a single name or tag, and even if you use WINS to enable NetBIOS name resolution across subnets, each computer name on the entire network has to be unique. Another disadvantage of NetBIOS is that it is not recommended for high-security areas. NetBIOS advertises information about network services, and this information can theoretically be used to exploit the network. Finally, NetBIOS is not compatible with IPv6 networks.

EXAM TIP

When you have multiple WINS servers in a large organization, you must configure replication among them so that each WINS database remains up to date. In most cases, you want to configure push-pull replication among all WINS servers (often in a star configuration) so that they can efficiently and effectively update one another.

What Is DNS Name Resolution?

DNS enables you to locate computers and other resources by name on an IP internetwork. By providing a hierarchical structure and an automated method of caching and resolving host names, DNS removes many of the administrative and structural difficulties associated with naming hosts on the Internet and in large private networks.

DNS Namespace

The naming system on which DNS is based is a hierarchical and logical tree structure called the *DNS namespace*. The DNS namespace has a unique root that can have any number of sub-domains. In turn, each subdomain can have more subdomains. For example, the root "" (empty string) in the Internet namespace has many top-level domain names, one of which is com. The domain com can, for example, have a subdomain for the Lucerne Publishing company, lucernepublishing.com, which in turn can have a further subdomain for manufacturing called mfg.lucernepublishing.com. Organizations can also create private networks and use their own private DNS namespaces that are not visible on the Internet.

Domain Names

You can identify every node in the DNS domain tree by a *fully qualified domain name*, or FQDN. The FQDN is a DNS domain name that has been stated unambiguously to indicate its location relative to the root of the DNS domain tree. For example, the FQDN for the finance1 server in the lucernepublishing.com domain is constructed as finance1.lucernepublishing.com., which is the concatenation of the host name (finance1) with the primary DNS suffix (lucernepublishing.com) and the trailing dot (.). The trailing dot is a standard separator between the top-level domain label and the empty string label corresponding to the root. (In everyday usage and applications such as web browsers, the trailing dot is usually dropped, but the DNS Client service adds it during actual queries.)

The DNS root (the topmost level) of the Internet domain namespace is managed by Internet Assigned Numbers Authority (IANA), which itself is managed by the Internet Corporation for Assigned Names and Numbers (ICANN). These organizations coordinate the assignment of identifiers that must be globally unique for the Internet to function, including Internet domain names, IP address numbers, and protocol parameter and port numbers.

Beneath the root DNS domain lie the top-level domains, managed by ICANN, IANA, and country-specific registries such as Nominet in the United Kingdom and DENIC in Germany. Three types of top-level domains exist:

- **Organizational domains**   These domains are named using a code that indicates the primary function or activity of the organizations contained within the DNS domain. Some organizational domains can be used globally, although others are used only for organizations in the United States. Most organizations located in the United States are contained within one of these organizational domains. The best known organizational domains are .com, .net, .edu, and .org. Other top-level organizational domains include .aero, .biz, .info, .name, and .pro.

- **Geographical domains**   These domains are named using the two-character country and region codes established by the International Organization for Standardization (ISO) 3166, such as .uk (United Kingdom) or .it (Italy). These domains are generally used by organizations outside the United States, but this is not a requirement.

- **Reverse domains**   These are special domains, named in-addr.arpa, that are used for IP-address-to-name resolution (referred to as *reverse lookups*).

Beneath the top-level domains are the second-level domains that individuals, private organizations, or public entities can reserve through ICANN-accredited domain-name registrars such as GoDaddy, Enom, Tucows, and Network Solutions. Organizations such as Microsoft that have obtained a second-level domain can then assign names to hosts within their domains and use DNS servers to manage the name-to-IP-address mappings within their portion of the namespace. These organizations can also delegate subdomains to other users or customers.

Private Domain Namespace

In addition to the top-level domains on the Internet, organizations can also have a *private namespace*: a DNS namespace based on a private set of root servers independent of the Internet's DNS namespace. Within a private namespace, you can name and create your own root server or servers and any subdomains as needed. Private names cannot be seen or resolved on the Internet. An example of a private domain name is mycompany.local.

DNS Components

DNS relies on the proper configuration of DNS servers, zones, resolvers, and resource records.

DNS Servers

A *DNS server* is a computer that runs a DNS server program, such as the DNS Server service in Windows Server or Berkeley Internet Name Domain (BIND) in UNIX. DNS servers contain DNS database information about some portion of the DNS domain tree structure and resolve name resolution queries issued by DNS clients. When queried, DNS servers can provide the requested information, provide a pointer to another server that can help resolve the query, or respond that the information is unavailable or does not exist.

A server is authoritative for a domain when that server relies on locally hosted database data (as opposed to merely cached information from other servers) to answer queries about hosts within a given domain. Such servers define their portion of the DNS namespace.

Servers can be authoritative for one or more levels of the domain hierarchy. For example, the root DNS servers on the Internet are authoritative only for the top-level domain names, such as .com. As a result, servers authoritative for .com are authoritative only for names within the .com domain, such as lucernepublishing.com. However, within the Lucerne Publishing namespace, the server or servers authoritative for lucernepublishing.com can also be authoritative for both example.lucernepublishing.com and widgets.example.lucernepublishing.com.

DNS Zones

A *DNS zone* is a contiguous portion of a namespace for which a server is authoritative. A server can be authoritative for one or more zones, and a zone can contain one or more contiguous domains. For example, one server can be authoritative for both microsoft.com and lucernepublishing.com zones, and each of these zones can include one or more subdomains.

Contiguous domains, such as .com, lucernepublishing.com, and example.lucernepublishing.com, can become separate zones through the process of *delegation*, in which the responsibility for a subdomain within the DNS namespace is assigned to a separate entity.

Zone files contain the data for the zones for which a server is authoritative. In many DNS server implementations, zone data is stored in text files; however, DNS servers running on Active Directory domain controllers can also store zone information in Active Directory.

> *NOTE* **WHAT ARE FORWARD AND REVERSE LOOKUP ZONES?**
>
> Zones can occur in one of two varieties: forward lookup zones and reverse lookup zones. A *forward lookup zone* is the main type of zone, in which names are resolved to IP addresses. In a *reverse lookup zone*, an IP address is resolved to a name. Zone types are discussed in more detail in Chapter 3, "Configuring a DNS Zone Infrastructure."

DNS Resolvers

A *DNS resolver* is a service that uses the DNS protocol to query for information from DNS servers. DNS resolvers communicate with either remote DNS servers or the DNS server program running on the local computer. In Windows Server 2008 R2 and Windows 7, the function of the DNS resolver is performed by the DNS Client service. Besides acting as a DNS resolver, the DNS Client service provides the added function of caching DNS mappings.

Resource Records

Resource records are DNS database entries that are used to answer DNS client queries. Each DNS server contains the resource records it needs to answer queries for its portion of the DNS namespace. Resource records are each described as a specific record type, such as IPv4 host address (A), IPv6 host address (AAAA, pronounced "quad-A"), alias (CNAME), pointer (PTR), and mail exchanger (MX). These records are covered in more detail in Lesson 1 of Chapter 3.

Understanding How a DNS Query Works

When a DNS client needs to look up a name used by an application, it queries DNS servers to resolve the name. Each query message the client sends contains the following three pieces of information:

- A DNS domain name, stated as an FQDN. (The DNS Client service adds the suffixes necessary to generate an FQDN if the original client program does not provide them.)
- A specified query type, which can specify either a resource record by type or a specialized type of query operation.
- A specified class for the DNS domain name. (For the DNS Client service, this class is always specified as the Internet [IN] class.)

For example, the name could be specified as the FQDN for a particular host computer, such as host-a.example.microsoft.com., and the query type could be specified as a search for an A resource record by that name. You can think of a DNS query as a client asking a server a two-part question, such as, "Do you have any A resource records for a computer named host-a.example.microsoft.com?" When the client receives an answer from the server, the client reads the received A resource record and learns the IP address of the computer name originally queried for.

DNS Resolution Methods

DNS queries can be resolved in a number of ways. In the classic scenario, the DNS client contacts a DNS server, which then uses its own database of resource records to answer a query. However, a client can also answer queries by finding the needed information in its local cache first, before contacting a server at all. A third way that DNS queries can be resolved is through a DNS server cache. Like DNS clients, DNS servers store cached data from remote zones and use this cached information to attempt to answer queries before contacting other servers. A fourth way that DNS queries are often resolved is through recursion. Using this process, a DNS server can query other DNS servers on behalf of the requesting client in order to resolve an FQDN. DNS servers configured to perform recursion can resolve a name by making iterative queries to other DNS servers or by forwarding the query to a particular DNS server specified by an administrator.

DNS Query Steps

In general, the DNS query process occurs in two stages:

- A name query begins at a client computer and is passed to the DNS Client service for resolution.
- When the query cannot be resolved locally, the DNS Client service passes the query to a DNS server.

Both of these processes are explained in more detail in the following sections.

STEP 1: THE LOCAL RESOLVER

Figure 2-8 presents an overview of the default DNS query process, in which a client is configured to make recursive queries to a server. In this scenario, if the DNS Client service cannot resolve the query from locally cached information (which itself is preloaded with name-to-address mappings from the Hosts file), the client makes only a single query to a DNS server, which is then responsible for answering the query on behalf of the client.

In the figure, queries and answers are represented by Qs and As. The higher-numbered queries are made only when the previous query is unsuccessful. For example, Q2 is performed only when Q1 is unsuccessful.

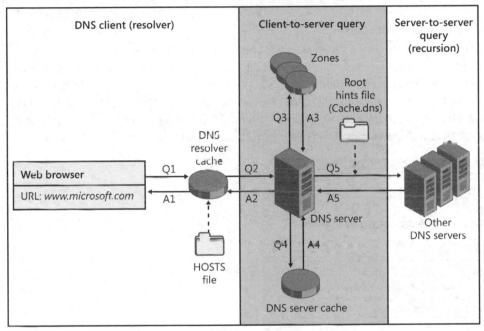

FIGURE 2-8 This overview of the default DNS query process shows a possible chain of events triggered by a DNS name query.

The query process begins when a DNS domain name is used in a program on the local computer. In the example shown in Figure 2-8, a web browser calls the FQDN *www.microsoft.com*. The request is then passed to the DNS Client service (the DNS resolver cache) to resolve this name by using locally cached information. If the queried name can be resolved, the query is answered and the process is completed.

The local resolver cache can include name information obtained from two possible sources:

- If a Hosts file is configured locally, any host-name-to-address mappings from that file are loaded into the cache when the DNS Client service is started and whenever the Hosts file is updated. In Windows Server 2008, the Hosts file is essentially provided as a means to add entries to the resolver cache dynamically.

- Resource records obtained in answered responses from previous DNS queries are added to the cache and kept for a period of time.

If the query does not match an entry in the cache, the resolution process continues with the client querying a DNS server to resolve the name.

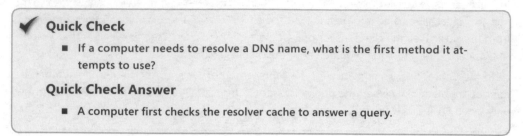

✔ **Quick Check**
- If a computer needs to resolve a DNS name, what is the first method it attempts to use?

Quick Check Answer
- A computer first checks the resolver cache to answer a query.

STEP 2: QUERYING A DNS SERVER

The DNS Client service uses a server search list ordered by preference. This list includes all preferred and alternate DNS servers configured for each of the active network connections on the system. The client first queries the DNS server specified as the preferred DNS server in the connection's Internet Protocol (TCP/IP) Properties dialog box. If no preferred DNS servers are available, alternate DNS servers are used. Figure 2-9 shows a sample list of preferred and alternate DNS servers, as configured in Windows Server 2008 R2.

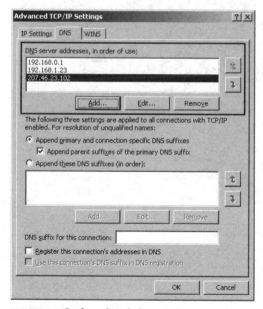

FIGURE 2-9 Preferred and alternate servers

When a DNS server receives a query, it first checks to see whether it can answer the query authoritatively—that is, on the basis of information contained in a locally configured zone on the server. If the queried name matches a corresponding resource record in local zone information, the server answers authoritatively, using this information to resolve the queried name.

If no zone information exists for the queried name, the server then checks to see whether it can resolve the name by using locally cached information from previous queries. If a match is found here, the server answers with this information. Again, if the preferred server can answer with a positive matched response from its cache to the requesting client, the query is completed.

 Quick Check

1. When a DNS server receives a query, how does it first attempt to resolve the name?
2. If a DNS server cannot resolve a query by using the first method, which method will it use next?

Quick Check Answers

1. A DNS server first attempts to resolve a query by using resource records stored in a locally configured zone.
2. If a DNS server cannot resolve a query by using zone data, it attempts to answer the query by using cached information.

Understanding Recursion

If the queried-for name does not find a matched answer at its preferred server—either from its cache or its zone information—the query process continues in a manner dependent on the DNS client and server configuration. In the default configuration for DNS clients in Windows, DNS queries are recursive, which means that the client requests the DNS server to perform recursion if necessary. *Recursion* in DNS refers to the process of a DNS server querying other DNS servers on behalf of an original querying client. This process of extending the query turns the original DNS server into a DNS client. By default, Windows-based DNS servers are configured to accept these recursive queries and perform recursion to resolve names on behalf of clients. When querying other servers, a DNS server then, by default, uses iteration. *Iteration* refers to the process of making repeated queries to different DNS servers to resolve a name.

If recursion is disabled on the DNS server, some DNS clients are able to continue the query. These clients perform iterative queries by using root hint referrals provided by the DNS server. However, Windows DNS clients are not configured to perform iteration by default. A DNS query initiated by the DNS Client service in Windows will therefore fail at this point if recursion is disabled on the DNS server.

Root Hints

To perform iteration properly, a DNS server first needs to know where to begin searching for names in the DNS domain namespace. This information is provided in the form of *root hints*, a list of preliminary resource records used by the DNS service to locate servers authoritative for the root of the DNS domain namespace tree.

By default, DNS servers running Windows Server 2008 R2 use a preconfigured root hints file, Cache.dns, that is stored in the WINDOWS\System32\Dns folder on the server computer. The contents of this file are preloaded into server memory when the service is started and contain pointer information to root servers for the DNS namespace. Figure 2-10 shows the default root hints file.

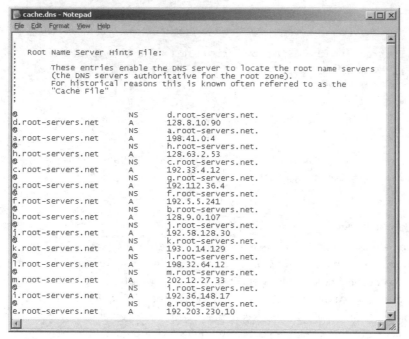

FIGURE 2-10 Root hints file

In Windows DNS servers, the root hints file already contains addresses of root servers in the Internet DNS namespace. Therefore, if you are using the DNS server to resolve Internet-based DNS names, the root hints file needs no manual configuration. If, however, you are using DNS on a private network, you can edit or replace this file with similar records that point to your own internal root DNS servers. Furthermore, for a computer that is hosting a root DNS server, you should not use root hints at all. In this scenario, Windows Server 2008 R2 automatically deletes the Cache.dns file used for root hints.

Query Example

The following example illustrates default DNS query behavior. In the example, the client queries its preferred DNS server, which then performs recursion by querying hierarchically superior DNS servers. The DNS client and the preferred DNS server are assumed to have empty caches.

In the example, a user working on a computer at the address 192.168.2.3 enters the address *http://bing.com* into a web browser. As a result of this action, the DNS client on the local computer attempts to resolve the name bing.com to an IP address. The process is illustrated in Figure 2-11.

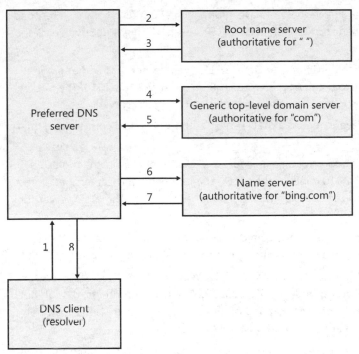

FIGURE 2-11 A DNS server performs iterative queries in the DNS namespace to resolve the name "bing.com" on behalf of a client.

When the DNS Client service on the client computer begins the query process, the following events take place:

1. The client contacts the preferred DNS server with a query for bing.com.

    This step is shown in the first frame in the Network Monitor capture in Figure 2-12. The client is found at 192.168.2.3, and the preferred DNS server is found at 192.168.2.110. You can see in the Description field that the client has queried for the name "bing.com".

2. The preferred DNS server checks its zones and chache for the answer but does not find it, so it contacts a server authoritative for the root of the Internet namespace with a query for "bing.com".

    This step is shown in the second frame in Figure 2-12. The preferred DNS server at 192.168.2.110 contacts an Internet root name server at 193.0.14.129, also known as k.root-servers.net. This root server address is obtained from the C:\Windows\System32\dns\cache.dns file on the preferred DNS server.

    You can see in the Description field for the frame that the local preferred DNS server has queried this root server for the name "bing.com".

3. The Internet root name server does not have information about bing.com, so it responds with a referral to a generic top-level domain (gTLD) server, which is authoritative for the "com" domain.

   This step is shown in the third frame in Figure 2-12. The Internet root name server at 193.0.14.129 responds to the local preferred DNS server at 192.168.2.110. The packet contents, though not shown, carry a referral to one of the gTLD servers.

4. The preferred DNS server contacts a gTLD server (authoritative for "com") with a query for "bing.com".

   This step is shown in the fourth frame in Figure 2-12. With this frame, the preferred DNS server at 192.168.2.110 contacts the gTLD server named l.gtld-servers.net. In the frame description, you can see that the local server has queried the gTLD server for the name "bing.com".

5. The gTLD server authoritative for the com domain does not know the answer, so it responds with a referral to a server authoritative for the bing.com domain.

   This step is shown in the fifth frame in Figure 2-12. With this frame, the gTLD server named l.gtld-servers.net responds to 192.168.2.110. The packet contents, though not shown, carry a referral to ns1.msft.net and other name servers such as ns2.msft.net and ns3.msft.net, which are all authoritative for bing.com.

6. The preferred DNS server contacts a server authoritative for the bing.com domain with a query for bing.com. In this case, the name bing.com is both the name of the domain and the name of a web server with at least one corresponding Host record in the DNS database.

   This step is shown in the sixth frame in Figure 2-12. With this frame, the preferred DNS server at 192.168.2.110 contacts ns1.msft.net, which is a name server authoritative for the bing.com domain. You can see in the Description field that the frame includes a query for the name "bing.com".

7. A server authoritative for the bing.com domain responds to the query with the requested IP address.

   This step is shown in the seventh frame in Figure 2-12. With this frame, the server ns1.msft.net responds to the preferred DNS server at 192.168.2.110. You can see in the Description field that the frame carries the address 65.55.175.254, which is the IP address associated with the name "bing.com".

8. The preferred DNS server responds to original querying client with the IP address for bing.com.

   This step is shown in the eighth and final frame in Figure 2-12. With this frame, the preferred DNS server at 192.168.2.110 responds to the original querying client at 192.168.2.3. You can see in the Description field that the frame carries the information that the client has requested: The name "bing.com" resolves to 65.55.175.254.

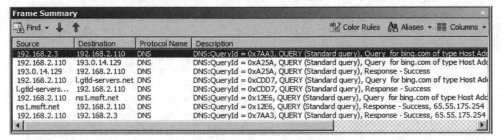

FIGURE 2-12 A DNS Server resolving the name bing.com on behalf of a client

 Quick Check

1. When would a DNS server contact a root server?

2. If a DNS server contacts a root server to resolve the name www.contoso.com and the root server cannot answer the query, how does the original server know which server to query next?

Quick Check Answers

1. A DNS server contacts a root server when it cannot answer a query with its own cached or authoritative data.

2. The root server responds to the DNS server with a referral for the address of the DNS server authoritative for the .com domain. The DNS server then contacts this server for which it has received a referral.

Understanding How Caching Works

Both the DNS Client service and the DNS Server service maintain caches. Caching provides a way to improve DNS performance and to substantially reduce DNS-related query traffic on the network.

DNS Client Cache

The DNS client cache is also called the DNS resolver cache. Whenever the DNS Client service starts, all host-name-to-IP-address mappings contained in a static file named Hosts are preloaded into the DNS resolver cache. The Hosts file can be found in WINDOWS\System32\Drivers\Etc.

> **NOTE** **HOW IS THE HOSTS FILE USED?**
>
> Whenever you add an entry to the Hosts file, that entry is immediately loaded into the DNS resolver cache.

In addition to the entries in the Hosts file, the DNS resolver cache also includes entries the client has received in response to a query from DNS servers. The DNS resolver cache is emptied whenever the DNS Client service is stopped.

EXAM TIP

For the 70-642 exam, you need to know the difference between the Hosts file and the Lmhosts file. The Hosts file helps resolve host names (essentially DNS names) to IP addresses, and the Lmhosts file helps resolve NetBIOS names to IP addresses.

DNS Server Cache

As DNS servers make recursive queries on behalf of clients, they temporarily cache resource records. These cached records contain information acquired in the process of answering queries on behalf of a client. Later, when other clients place new queries that request information matching cached resource records, the DNS server can use the cached information to answer these queries.

The DNS server cache is cleared whenever the DNS Server service is stopped. In addition, you can clear the DNS server cache manually in the DNS console—the administrative tool used for DNS administration—by right-clicking the server icon in the console tree and then choosing Clear Cache. Finally, you can clear the server cache at the command line by typing the command **Dnscmd /clearcache** at a command prompt.

TIME TO LIVE VALUES

A Time to Live (TTL) value applies to all cached resource records, whether in the DNS resolver cache or the DNS server cache. As long as the TTL for a cached resource record does not expire, a DNS resolver or server can continue to use that record to answer queries. By default, the TTL is 3600 seconds (1 hour), but you can adjust this parameter at both the zone and record levels.

PRACTICE **Exploring Automatic Name Resolution in Local Networks**

In this practice, you explore the name resolution mechanisms that are available in Windows networks before a DNS server is installed and configured. By turning on and off various features and then attempting to communicate with a computer by name, you will learn which features enable which functionality.

To begin this practice, on Dcsrv1 and Boston, File Sharing must be turned on so that an exception for ICMPv4 and ICMPv6 is created for both computers. Only a single local area connection should be enabled on both computers. Dcsrv1 should be assigned the IPv4 address 192.168.0.1/24 and the IPv6 address fd00::1. Boston should be assigned the IPv4 address 192.168.0.2/24 and the IPv6 address fd00::2.

EXERCISE Exploring LLMNR and NetBIOS Name Resolution

In this practice, you ping Boston from Dcsrv1, and then compare the effects by pinging again after disabling IPv6 and NetBIOS.

1. From a command prompt on Dcsrv1, type **ping boston**.

   You receive four replies from Boston's link-local IPv6 address. Only LLMNR can resolve single-tag names to IPv6 addresses, so you know that LLMNR has resolved the name "boston".

2. Switch to the Boston computer. In Network and Sharing Center on Boston, click Local Area Connection, and then click Properties to open the properties of the Local Area Connection.

3. In the Local Area Connection Properties dialog box on Boston, clear the Internet Protocol Version 6 (TCP/IPv6) check box, and click OK.

4. Switch back to the Dcsrv1 computer. From a command prompt on Dcsrv1, type **ping boston**.

   You again receive four replies from Boston, but this time from its IPv4 address. At this point, it is uncertain whether LLMNR or NetBIOS has been used to resolve the name "boston" to an IPv4 address.

5. On Dcsrv1, open Network and Sharing Center, click Local Area Connection, and then click Properties to open the properties of the Local Area Connection.

6. In the Local Area Connection Properties dialog box on Dcsrv1, double-click Internet Protocol Version 4 (TCP/IPv4).

7. Click Advanced to open the Advanced TCP/IP Settings dialog box, and then click the WINS tab.

8. On the WINS tab, select Disable NetBIOS Over TCP/IP, click OK three times, and then click Close to close all open dialog boxes.

9. From a command prompt on Dcsrv1, type **ping boston**.

   You again receive four replies from Boston's IPv4 address. This is a confirmation that LLMNR and not NetBIOS is still being used to resolve the name "boston" to an IPv4 address.

10. On Dcsrv1, open Network and Sharing Center and access the Local Area Connection Properties dialog box once again. Clear the Internet Protocol Version 6 (TCP/IPv6) check box, click OK, and then click Close.

11. From a command prompt on Dcsrv1, type **ping boston**.

    The ping attempt fails. LLMNR is turned off as a local name resolution mechanism whenever IPv6 is disabled.

12. On Dcsrv1, re-enable the default NetBIOS settings by opening the properties of the Local Area Connection, double-clicking Internet Protocol Version 4 (TCP/IPv4), clicking Advanced, clicking the WINS tab, and finally clicking Default. Click OK three times and then click Close to close all open dialog boxes.

13. From a command prompt on Dcsrv1, type *ping boston*.

    You again receive four replies from Boston's IPv4 address even though LLMNR is still disabled. In this case, NetBIOS is responsible for resolving the name "boston".

14. Re-enable IPv6 in the Local Area Connection on both Dcsrv1 and Boston, and log off both computers.

Lesson Summary

- To resolve a name means to translate the name of a computer to an IP address.

- Windows networks can perform name resolution by using any of three separate name resolution systems. DNS is the preferred name resolution service and is by far the most common, especially in large networks. However, because of the way DNS is designed, it requires configuration.

- In Windows Vista, Windows 7, Windows Server 2008, and Windows Server 2008 R2, LLMNR is the name resolution method used to enable the Network Map feature and network browsing through Network on the Start menu. (These features also require Network Discovery to be enabled in Advanced Sharing Settings.) In addition, LLMNR is used to attempt to resolve computer names when DNS is not configured on the local computer.

- NetBIOS is a protocol and naming system used to resolve the names of computers running versions of Windows earlier than Windows Vista. NetBIOS is also used as a backup name resolution mechanism in Windows Vista, Windows 7, Windows Server 2008, and Windows Server 2008 R2 when DNS is not configured and LLMNR is either disabled or unable to resolve a computer name. NetBIOS can resolve names by using network broadcasts, a WINS server, or a local Lmhosts file. NetBIOS is compatible only with IPv4 and not with IPv6.

- DNS provides a hierarchical name structure. In DNS, an FQDN is a domain name that has been stated unambiguously to indicate its location relative to the root of the DNS domain tree. An example of an FQDN is Client1.east.fabrikam.com.

- A *DNS zone* is a portion of a namespace for which a server is authoritative. When a server hosts a zone such as fabrikam.com, the zone contains resource records that map names to IP addresses within that namespace. For example, the DNS server hosting the fabrikam.com zone can authoritatively resolve names like client1.fabrikam.com and server2.fabrikam.com.

- In general, a DNS client that needs to resolve a DNS name first checks its local cache for the answer. If it doesn't find the answer, the DNS client queries its preferred DNS server. If the DNS server cannot resolve the query through authoritative or cached data, the DNS server will attempt to resolve the query by performing iterative queries against the DNS namespace, beginning with the root server.

Lesson Review

You can use the following questions to test your knowledge of the information in Lesson 1, "Understanding Name Resolution in Windows Server 2008 Networks." The questions are also available on the companion CD if you prefer to review them in electronic form.

> **NOTE ANSWERS**
>
> Answers to these questions and explanations of why each answer choice is correct or incorrect are located in the "Answers" section at the end of the book.

1. After the address of a remote computer is updated, you notice that a local DNS server is resolving the name of the computer incorrectly from cached information. How can you best solve this problem?

   A. At the DNS server, type the command **dnscmd /clearcache**.

   B. Restart the DNS Client service on the client computer.

   C. At the client computer, type **ipconfig /flushdns**.

   D. Restart all DNS client computers.

2. You are working on a Windows Server 2008 R2 computer named WS08A. You cannot connect to computers running Windows XP on the local network by specifying them by name in a UNC path such as \\computer1.

   What can you do to enable your computer to connect to these computers by specifying them in a UNC?

   A. Enable IPv6 on WS08A.

   B. Disable IPv6 on WS08A.

   C. Enable Local Link Multicast Name Resolution (LLMNR) on WS08A.

   D. Enable NetBIOS on WS08A.

3. Your company network includes a server named Research01 that contains confidential information. Research01 is assigned a static IP address in an isolated subnet and has NetBIOS disabled. Among other security measures you have taken to protect the server, you want to allow only five authorized computers to have network access to Research01 and to resolve the name Research01 to its IP address. The five authorized computers and Research01 are all located in different buildings on a large campus.

How can you prevent all but the five authorized computers from resolving the name Research01 to its IP address?

A. Do not specify a DNS server for Research01, and configure the HOSTS file on all five authorized computers with the name and address of the Research01 computer.

B. Specify a DNS server for Research01. At the DNS server, configure the properties of the A record for Research01 so that only the five authorized computers have read access to the record.

C. Configure Windows Firewall on Research01 to block DNS requests from all computers except the five authorized computers.

D. Configure IPsec on Research01 to block all connections except those originating from the five authorized computers.

Lesson 2: Deploying a DNS Server

Active Directory domains require DNS servers to enable domain members to resolve the names of computers and services. In most Windows networks, in fact, DNS servers are hosted on the Active Directory domain controllers themselves. Deploying a new DNS server on a domain controller requires very little administrative expertise, but you still need to know how to customize a DNS deployment to meet the particular needs of your organization.

This lesson introduces you to DNS server deployment and configuration. Whereas the topic of creating and configuring zones is covered in Chapter 3, this lesson focuses on configuring server-wide properties and features.

> **After this lesson, you will be able to:**
> - Deploy a DNS server on a new Active Directory domain controller.
> - Deploy a DNS server on a computer that is not a domain controller.
> - Deploy a DNS server on a Server Core installation of Windows Server 2008.
> - Configure DNS server properties.
> - Understand when to configure DNS forwarding.
>
> **Estimated lesson time: 60 minutes**

Deploying a DNS Server on a Domain Controller

Active Directory Domain Services (AD DS), which provides the unified management structure for all accounts and resources in a Windows network, is tightly integrated with DNS. In Active Directory, DNS is required for locating resources like domain controllers, and DNS zone data can optionally be stored within the Active Directory database.

When you deploy a DNS server within an Active Directory domain, you typically do so on a domain controller. Deploying DNS servers on domain controllers enables the zone to benefit from additional features, such as secure dynamic updates and Active Directory replication among multiple DNS servers. The best way to deploy a DNS server on a domain controller is to install it at the same time as you install the domain controller.

To promote a server to a domain controller for a new or existing domain, run Dcpromo.exe. This program first installs the AD DS binaries (the data elements common to all Active Directory domains) and then launches the AD DS Installation Wizard. The wizard prompts you for the name of the Active Directory domain, such as Fabrikam.com, for which you are installing the domain controller. The name you give to the Active Directory domain then becomes the name of the associated DNS zone. This page in the AD DS Installation Wizard is shown in Figure 2-13.

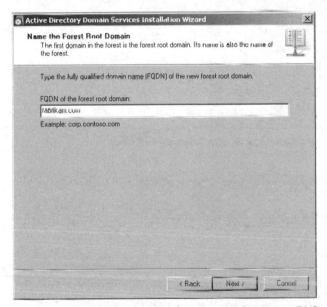

FIGURE 2-13 The Active Directory domain name becomes a DNS zone name.

> **NOTE** **WHAT IS THE ACTIVE DIRECTORY DOMAIN SERVICES SERVER ROLE?**
>
> Installing the AD DS binaries can require up to 5 minutes, and because of this time requirement, you might prefer to install the AD DS binaries as a separate step before running Dcpromo. To do so, use the Add Roles Wizard to add the Active Directory Domain Services server role. Note that this server role does not provide any functionality until you run Dcpromo.

Later in the wizard, you are given an opportunity to install a DNS server on the same domain controller. This option is selected by default, as shown in Figure 2-14.

If you do choose to install a DNS Server along with the new domain controller, the DNS server and the hosted forward lookup zone will automatically be configured for you. You can later review or manage these settings in DNS Manager, as shown in Figure 2-15, after the AD DS Installation Wizard completes. To open DNS Manager, click Start, point to Administrative Tools, and then choose DNS.

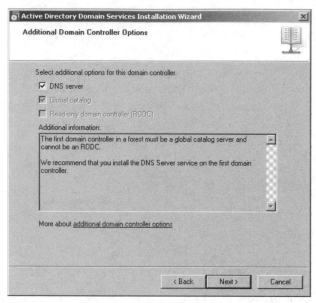

FIGURE 2-14 Installing a DNS server along with an Active Directory domain controller

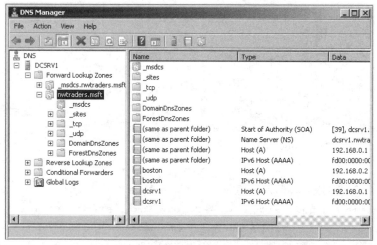

FIGURE 2-15 Dcpromo can automatically configure a locally hosted DNS server with a forward lookup zone for the domain.

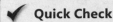
Deploying a DNS Server on a Stand-Alone or Member Server

Your name resolution infrastructure might require you to install a DNS server on a stand-alone server or on a member server in an Active Directory domain. In this case, you will need to install a DNS server without using Dcpromo.

To install a DNS server, use the Add Roles Wizard available in Server Manager or the Initial Configuration Tasks window. Then, in the wizard, select the DNS Server role (as shown in Figure 2-16) and follow the prompts.

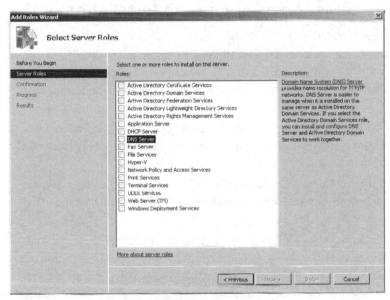

FIGURE 2-16 Installing a DNS server without AD DS

Installing the DNS server separately from AD DS requires you to configure the DNS server manually afterward. The main task in configuring a DNS server manually is to add and configure one or more forward lookup zones. To add a forward lookup zone, right-click the Forward Lookup Zones folder in the DNS Manager console tree, and then choose New Zone, as shown in Figure 2-17.

For more information about creating, configuring, and managing DNS zones, see Chapter 3.

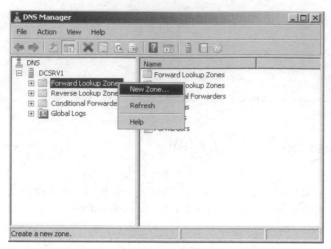

FIGURE 2-17 Adding a new zone

Deploying a DNS Server on a Server Core Installation of Windows Server 2008 R2

You can install a DNS server on a Server Core installation of Windows Server 2008 R2 along with AD DS by using Dcpromo, in which case the DNS server can be installed and configured automatically. You also have the option of installing the DNS server as a stand-alone or member server.

To install a DNS server along with a domain controller on a Server Core installation, use Dcpromo. However, no wizard is available to facilitate the process. You must specify an answer file with the Dcpromo command.

To install the Active Directory Domain Services role on a Server Core installation, at the command prompt, type **dcpromo /unattend:<unattendfile>**, where *unattendfile* is the name of a Dcpromo.exe unattend or answer file.

You can create the Dcpromo answer file by running Dcpromo on another computer that is running a full installation of Windows Server 2008 or Windows Server 2008 R2. On the last (Summary) page of the wizard, before the installation is actually performed, you are given an opportunity to export settings to an answer file, as shown in Figure 2-18. You can then cancel out of the wizard and use the answer file with Dcpromo on the Server Core installation.

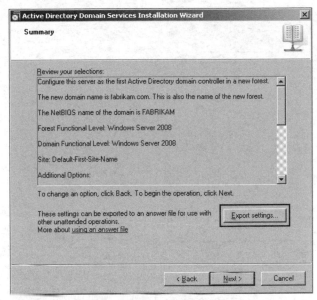

FIGURE 2-18 Creating an answer file for Dcpromo

If you want to install a DNS server on a stand-alone or member server running a Server Core installation of Windows Server 2008 or Windows Server 2008 R2, type the following command:

```
start /w ocsetup DNS-Server-Core-Role
```

To remove the role, type the following:

```
start /w ocsetup DNS-Server-Core-Role /uninstall
```

After you have installed the DNS server on a Server Core installation, whether by using Dcpromo or the Start /w ocsetup command, you can configure and manage the server by connecting to it through DNS Manager on another computer.

To connect to another server from DNS Manager, right-click the root (server name) icon in the DNS Manager console tree, and then choose Connect To DNS Server, as shown in Figure 2-19.

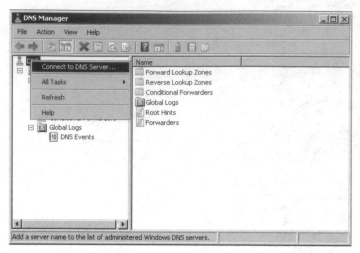

FIGURE 2-19 Using DNS Manager on a full installation to manage a DNS server installed on a Server Core installation

Configuring a Caching-Only DNS Server

All DNS servers include a cache of query responses. Although a DNS server initially contains no cached information, cached information is obtained over time as client requests are serviced. When a client queries a DNS server with a name resolution request, the DNS server checks to see if it can answer the query with local zone data and then checks its cache to see whether it has the answer stored. If the server can respond with information from resource records found in the local cache, the server response to the client is much faster.

Cached records stay alive in the server cache until they exceed their TTL value, until the DNS Server service is restarted, or until the cache is cleared manually.

Caching-only servers do not host any zones and are not authoritative for any particular domain. However, the mere availability of a DNS server cache that is shared by clients can be useful in certain network scenarios.

For example, if your network includes a branch office with a slow wide area network (WAN) link between sites, a caching-only server can improve name resolution response times because after the cache is built, traffic across the WAN link decreases. DNS queries are resolved faster, which can improve the performance of network applications and other features. In addition, the caching-only server does not perform zone transfers, which can also be network-intensive in WAN environments. In general, a caching-only DNS server can be valuable at a site where DNS functionality is needed locally but where administering domains or zones is not desirable.

By default, the DNS Server service acts as a caching-only server. Caching-only servers thus require little or no configuration.

To install a caching-only DNS server, complete the following steps:

1. Install the DNS server role on the server computer.

2. Do not create any zones.

3. Verify that server root hints are configured or updated correctly.

Configuring Server Properties

The DNS server properties dialog box allows you to configure settings that apply to the DNS server and all its hosted zones. You can access this dialog box in DNS Manager by right-clicking the icon of the DNS server you want to configure and then choosing Properties.

Interfaces Tab

The Interfaces tab allows you to specify which of the local computer's IP addresses the DNS server should listen to for DNS requests. For example, if your server is *multihomed* (has more than one network adapter) and uses specific addresses for the local network and others for the Internet connection, you can prevent the DNS server from servicing DNS queries from the public interface. To perform this task, specify that the DNS server listens only on the computer's internal IP addresses, as shown in Figure 2-20.

By default, the setting on this tab specifies that the DNS server listens on all IP addresses associated with the local computer.

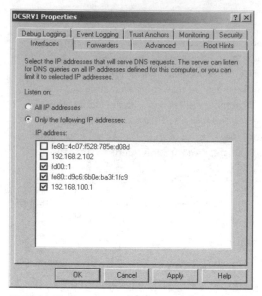

FIGURE 2-20 You can configure a multihomed DNS server to provide service to one network only. In this figure, the selected addresses are all associated with the same network adapter.

Root Hints Tab

The Root Hints tab contains a copy of the information found in the WINDOWS\System32\Dns \Cache.dns file. For DNS servers answering queries for Internet names, this information does not need to be modified. However, when you are configuring a root DNS server (named ".") for a private network, you should delete the entire Cache.dns file. (When your DNS server is hosting a root server, the Root Hints tab is unavailable.)

In addition, if you are configuring a DNS server within a large private namespace, you can use this tab to delete the Internet root servers and specify the root servers in your network instead. Figure 2-21 shows the Root Hints tab.

> **NOTE** **UPDATING THE ROOT SERVERS LIST**
>
> Every few years, the list of root servers on the Internet is slightly modified. Because the Cache.dns file already contains so many possible root servers to contact, it is not necessary to modify the root hints file as soon as these changes occur. However, if you do learn of the availability of new root servers, you can choose to update your root hints accordingly. As of this writing, the last update to the root servers list was made on June 17, 2010. You can download the latest version of the named cache file from InterNIC at *ftp://rs.internic.net /domain/named.cache*.

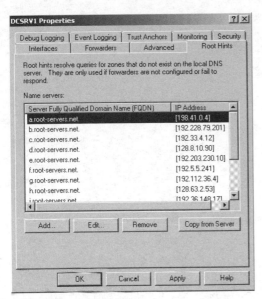

FIGURE 2-21 Root Hints tab

Forwarders Tab

The Forwarders tab allows you to configure the local DNS server to forward DNS queries it receives to upstream DNS servers, called *forwarders*. Using this tab, you can specify the IP addresses of upstream DNS servers to which queries should be directed if the local DNS server cannot provide a response through its cache or zone data. For example, in Figure 2-22, all queries that cannot be resolved by the local server will be forwarded to the DNS server 192.168.2.200. When, after receiving and forwarding a query from an internal client, the local forwarding server receives a query response from 192.168.2.200, the local forwarding server passes this query response back to the original querying client.

In all cases, a DNS server that is configured for forwarding uses forwards only after it has determined that it cannot resolve a query using its authoritative data (primary or secondary zone data) or cached data.

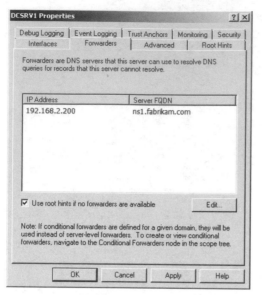

FIGURE 2-22 Forwarders tab

WHEN TO USE FORWARDERS

In some cases, network administrators might not want DNS servers to communicate directly with external servers. For example, if your organization is connected to the Internet through a slow link, you can optimize name resolution performance by channeling all DNS queries through one forwarder, as shown in Figure 2-23. Through this method, the server cache of the DNS forwarder has the maximum potential to grow and reduce the need for external queries.

Another common use of forwarding is to allow DNS clients and servers inside a firewall to resolve external names securely. When an internal DNS server or client communicates with external DNS servers by making iterative queries, the ports used for DNS communication with all external servers must normally be left open to the outside world through the firewall. However, by configuring a DNS server inside a firewall to forward external queries to a single DNS forwarder outside your firewall, and by opening ports only for this one forwarder, you can resolve names without exposing your network to outside servers. Figure 2-24 illustrates this arrangement.

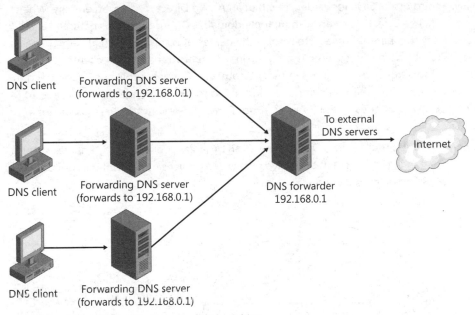

FIGURE 2-23 Using forwarding to consolidate caching

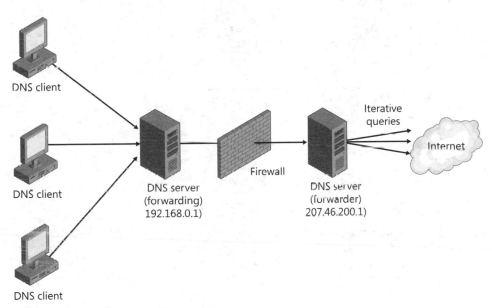

FIGURE 2-24 Secure iteration with forwarders

Finally, a third use of DNS forwarders is within an Active Directory forest hierarchy. When you have an Active Directory forest with multiple domains, DNS delegations naturally enable client queries within parent domains to resolve the names of resources in child (sub) domains. However, without forwarding, there is no built-in mechanism that allows clients in child domains to resolve queries for names in parent domains. To enable this necessary functionality, DNS servers in the child domains of multidomain forests are typically configured to forward unresolved queries to the forest root domain DNS server or servers, as shown in Figure 2-25.

Forwarding to the root domain DNS servers in an organization in this way enables client queries originating in child domains to resolve names of resources not only in the root domain, but also in all the domains in the forest.

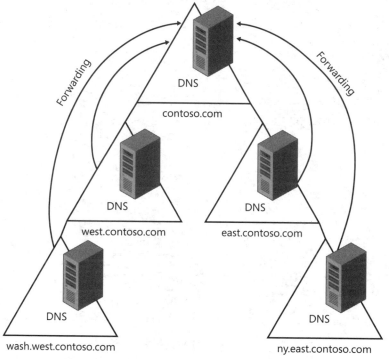

FIGURE 2-25 Forwarding queries within an Active Directory forest

WHEN TO USE CONDITIONAL FORWARDING

The term *conditional forwarding* describes a DNS server configuration in which queries for specific domains are forwarded to specific DNS servers.

One of the many scenarios in which conditional forwarding is useful is when two separate networks merge. For example, suppose the Contoso and Fabrikam companies have separate networks with Active Directory domains. After the two companies merge, a VPN is used to connect the private networks. For clients in each company to resolve queries for names in the opposite network, conditional forwarding is configured on the DNS servers in both domains. Queries to resolve names in the opposite domain will be forwarded to the DNS server in that domain. All Internet queries are forwarded to the next DNS server upstream beyond the firewall. This scenario is depicted in Figure 2-26.

Note that conditional forwarding is not the only way to provide name resolution in this type of merger scenario. You can also configure secondary zones and stub zones, which are described in Chapter 3. These zone types provide basically the same name resolution service that conditional forwarding does. However, conditional forwarding minimizes zone transfer traffic, provides zone data that is always up to date, and allows for simple configuration and maintenance.

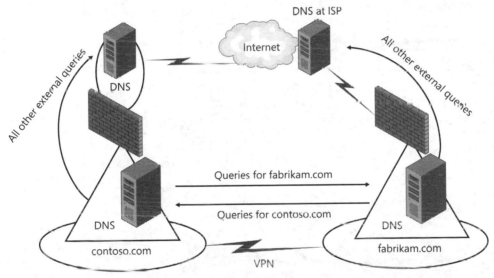

FIGURE 2-26 A conditional forwarding scenario

To configure conditional forwarding for a domain, you do not use the DNS server properties dialog box. You use the Conditional Forwarders container in the DNS Manager console tree. To add a new conditional forwarder, right-click the Conditional Forwarder container, and then choose New Conditional Forwarder, as shown in Figure 2-27.

Then, in the New Conditional Forwarder dialog box that opens, specify the domain name for which DNS queries should be forwarded along with the address of the associated DNS server. The New Conditional Forwarder dialog box is shown in Figure 2-28.

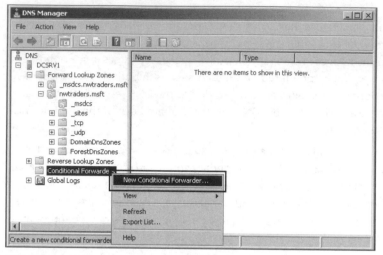

FIGURE 2-27 Adding a conditional forwarder

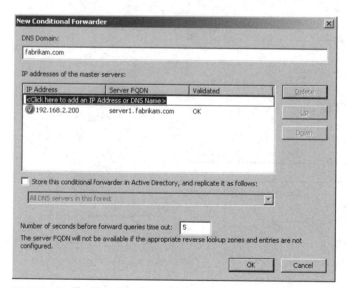

FIGURE 2-28 The New Conditional Forwarder dialog box

EXAM TIP

You will likely see a question about conditional forwarding on the 70-642 exam. Understand its purpose and the scenarios in which it might be useful.

Configuring DNS Socket Pooling

DNS socket pooling is a new feature in Windows Server 2008 R2 that randomizes the source port from which DNS servers perform queries. This randomization improves security because it helps prevent DNS spoofing and cache poisoning. By default in Windows Server 2008 R2, DNS socket pooling is enabled with the DNS source port chosen randomly from a pool of 2500 ports or sockets. (A *socket* is a combination of an address and port number.)

You can adjust the size of the pool of ports from which a random source port is chosen. To do so, type **dnscmd /Config /SocketPoolSize <*value*>** at an elevated command prompt, where <*value*> is a number up to 10000 indicating the pool size. Choosing a number higher than the default of 2500 improves security at the expense of increased memory usage.

If you need to exclude certain source ports from being used for DNS queries, you can type **dnscmd /Config /SocketPoolExcludedPortRanges <*excluded port ranges*>** at an elevated command prompt, where <*excluded port ranges*> is the series of port numbers or ranges of port numbers that you want to exclude as a possible source port for DNS server queries.

Although socket pooling is new to Windows Server 2008 R2, you can install this feature on servers running Windows Server 2000, Windows Server 2003, and Windows Server 2008 by applying a security update. This update is available at *http://www.microsoft.com/technet /security/Bulletin/ms08-037.mspx*. Note, however, that you can exclude DNS source port ranges only on Windows Server 2008 R2.

Configuring DNS Cache Locking

DNS cache locking is another new feature in Windows Server 2008 R2 that helps prevent DNS server spoofing and cache poisoning. By configuring cache locking, you can set a percentage of the TTL value for cached records during which time a record stored in the DNS server cache cannot be overwritten. This feature reduces the threat of DNS cache poisoning because it makes existing cached records less susceptible to being modified by an attacker.

To configure DNS cache locking, type the following command at an elevated command prompt on a DNS server running Windows Server 2008 R2:

  dnscmd /Config /CacheLockingPercent <*percent*>

where <*percent*> is a desired percentage of the cached records' TTL value. A value of 90 percent or greater is recommended.

PRACTICE **Exploring DNS in an Active Directory Environment**

In this practice, you create an Active Directory domain named Nwtraders.msft. During the process of creating this Active Directory domain, a DNS server is created for hosting the zone lookup information for Nwtraders.msft. You then explore this zone information along with the DNS server settings, create a domain administrator account for personal use, add the Boston computer to the domain, and observe the new DNS records created for Boston.

EXERCISE 1 Creating a Domain Controller

In this exercise, you use the Dcpromo program to create a domain controller for a new Active Directory domain named Nwtraders.msft.

1. Log on to Dcsrv1 with the account named Administrator.

2. In the Search Programs and Files box of the Start menu, type **dcpromo**, and then press Enter. A message appears indicating the Active Directory Domain Services binaries are being installed. After the binaries have been installed, the Active Directory Domain Services Installation Wizard appears.

3. On the Welcome page of the Active Directory Domain Services Installation Wizard, read all the text on the page, and then click Next.

4. On the Operating System Compatibility page, click Next.

5. On the Choose A Deployment Configuration page, select Create A New Domain In A New Forest, and then click Next.

6. On the Name The Forest Root Domain page, type **nwtraders.msft**, and then click Next. The forest name is verified to ensure that it is unique on the network, and then the NetBIOS name is verified.

7. On the Set Forest Functional Level page, select the Windows Server 2008 R2 forest functional level, read the text in the Details section, and click Next.

8. On the Additional Domain Controller Options page, verify that DNS Server is selected, read the text in the Additional Information section, and click Next. A dialog box appears and informs you that a delegation for this server cannot be created. You receive this message because you are creating a new DNS root domain and not a subdomain (for example, in the Internet namespace).

9. Click Yes to continue.

10. On the Location For Database, Log Files, And SYSVOL page, review the default settings, and then click Next.

11. On the Directory Services Restore Mode Administrator Password page, read all the text on the page, and then type a password of your choice in the Password and Confirm Password text boxes.

12. Click Next.

13. On the Summary page, review the summary information (especially the DNS server information), and then click Export Settings. You should always choose this option because it generates an answer file that you can later modify to use with Dcpromo on a Server Core installation. If you want to promote a Server Core installation to a domain controller, you must specify such an answer file.

14. In the Save Unattend File dialog box, specify a name, such as DCunattend, and then save the text file in the default location (the Documents folder). A message box appears, informing you that the settings were successfully exported.

15. Click OK.

16. On the Summary page of the Active Directory Domain Services Installation Wizard, click Next. The Active Directory Domain Services Installation Wizard dialog box appears while the DNS Server and Active Directory Domain Services are installed and configured. When the installation completes, the Completing page of the Active Directory Domain Services Installation Wizard appears.

17. Click Finish. A dialog box appears informing you that you need to restart your computer for the changes to take effect.

18. Click Restart Now.

EXERCISE 2 Reviewing DNS Server Information

In this exercise, you review the DNS server configuration on Dcsrv1.

1. After Dcsrv1 finishes restarting, log on to Nwtraders from Dcsrv1 as Administrator. After a few moments the Initial Configuration Tasks window appears.

2. If the Select Features page of the Add Features Wizard appears, click Cancel and then Yes to confirm the cancel.

3. In the Initial Configuration Tasks window, verify that the computer name is now dcsrv1.nwtraders.msft and that the domain is nwtraders.msft.

4. Open the DNS Manager console by clicking Start, pointing to Administrative Tools, and then choosing DNS.

5. In the DNS Manager console tree, navigate to DCSRV1\Forward Lookup Zones \nwtraders.msft. In the details pane, two records have been created for dcsrv1—a Host (A) record and an IPv6 Host (AAAA) record. These records point to the IPv4 and IPv6 addresses, respectively, of Dcsrv1.

6. Spend a few minutes browsing the contents of the other folders in the nwtraders.msft zone. Notice that many of the records in the zone are SRV records. These records point clients to the domain controller (Dcsrv1) when they query DNS for the location of a specific service such as Kerberos (which provides network authentication) or Lightweight Directory Access Protocol (LDAP). LDAP finds objects in Active Directory.

7. In the DNS Manager console tree, right-click the DCSRV1 node, and then choose Properties.

8. In the DCSRV1 Properties dialog box, review the information in the Interfaces tab. If your DNS server has multiple network interfaces or multiple addresses, you can use this tab to limit the sources of requests to which the server will respond.

9. Click the Forwarders tab.

10. Read the text in the tab, and then click the Edit button.

11. In the Edit Forwarders dialog box, read the text on the page. You would use this tab to specify a DNS server (a forwarder) to which unanswered queries should be forwarded. In a large organization, for example, the DNS servers for subdomains like east.contoso.local could forward queries to DNS server authoritative for the root zone (contoso.local) in the private DNS namespace.

12. Click Cancel to close the Edit Forwarders dialog box.

13. In the DCSRV1 Properties dialog box, click the Root Hints tab.

14. Read the text on the tab. Note that these name servers are the root DNS servers for the Internet. In a large organization, you might choose to replace this list with the root servers in your private namespace. (In such a case, the DNS servers in the corporate network could no longer resolve Internet names, but users could still connect to the Internet through the use of proxy servers.)

15. Click the Monitoring tab.

16. On the Monitoring tab, select the check box to test a simple query, and then click Test Now. In the Test Results area, an entry appears indicating that the simple query has passed. Do not perform the recursive test now. The recursive test would fail because this server is not yet configured with Internet access and cannot connect to the Internet root servers.

17. In the DCSRV1 Properties dialog box, click Cancel.

18. In the DNS Manager console tree, select and then right-click the Conditional Forwarders container, and then choose New Conditional Forwarder. (If the option appears dimmed, select the Conditional Forwarders container, and then right-click it again.)

19. In the New Conditional Forwarder dialog box, read all the text. Note that you use this dialog box to specify the addresses of remote DNS servers to which queries for specific domain names should be forwarded.

20. In the New Conditional Forwarder dialog box, click Cancel.

21. Minimize all open windows.

EXERCISE 3 Creating a Personal Administrator Account

In this exercise, you create a domain administrator account to use in future exercises.

1. Open Active Directory Users And Computers by clicking Start, pointing to Administrative Tools, and then choosing Active Directory Users And Computers.

2. In the Active Directory Users And Computers console tree, navigate to nwtraders.msft\Users.

3. Right-click the Users container, point to New, and then choose User.

4. In the New Object - User wizard, complete the fields by selecting a user name of your choosing for a personal administrator account.

5. Click Next.

6. On the second page of the New Object - User wizard, type a password of your choosing in the Password and Confirm Password text boxes, select or clear any options, and then click Next.

7. On the third page of the New Object - User wizard, click Finish.

8. In the Active Directory Users And Computers console, locate the user account you have just created in the details pane. (It should be visible when you select the Users container in the left pane console tree.)

9. Right-click your new user account, and then choose Add To A Group.

10. In the Select Groups dialog box, type **domain admins**, and then press Enter. A message box appears indicating that the operation was successfully completed.

11. Click OK.

12. Close Active Directory Users And Computers.

EXERCISE 4 Adding Boston to the Nwtraders Domain

In this exercise, you join Boston to the Nwtraders domain.

1. Log on to Boston as an administrator, and then open an elevated command prompt. (To open an elevated command prompt, right-click Command Prompt in the Start Menu (or the PowerShell icon in the Quick Launch menu), and then choose Run As Administrator. If you are logged on with the account named Administrator, you can merely open a Command Prompt or Windows PowerShell prompt because the prompt will already be elevated by default.)

2. At the command prompt, type **netsh interface ipv4 set dnsserver "local area connection" static 192.168.0.1**.

3. When the prompt reappears, type **netsh interface ipv6 set dnsserver "local area connection" static fd00::1**. These two commands configure Boston to look for the Nwtraders.msft domain by querying Dcsrv1.

> **NOTE** "LOCAL AREA CONNECTION"
> In the preceding Netsh commands, you should type "local area connection" only if that is the complete name of the local area connection on Boston. If the connection has been assigned another name such as "Local Area Connection 2", you should specify that name instead.

4. When the prompt reappears, minimize or close the command prompt.

5. In the Initial Configuration Tasks window, click Provide Computer Name And Domain. If the Initial Configuration Tasks is not open, you can open it by typing **oobe** in the Search Programs And Files box in the Start menu.

6. In the System Properties dialog box, click Change.

7. In the Member Of area of the Computer Name/Domain Changes dialog box, select Domain, and then type **nwtraders.msft** in the associated text box.

8. Click OK. A Windows Security prompt opens.

9. In the Windows Security prompt, specify the user name and password of your domain administrator account, and then click OK. After several moments (up to a minute), a message box appears welcoming you to the nwtraders.msft domain.

10. Click OK. A message appears indicating that you must restart your computer to apply these changes.

11. Click OK.

12. In the System Properties dialog box, click Close. A message appears again indicating that you must restart your computer.

13. Click Restart Now.

EXERCISE 5 Verifying New Zone Data

In this exercise, you verify that new resource records have been created in the Nwtraders.msft zone.

1. After Boston has finished restarting, switch to Dcsrv1.

2. While you are logged on to Dcsrv1 as a domain administrator, open DNS Manager.

3. In the console tree, navigate to the nwtraders.msft forward lookup zone.

4. Right-click the nwtraders.msft container, and then choose Refresh. Two records have been created for Boston—a Host (A) record mapped to 192.168.0.2 and an IPv6 Host (AAAA) record mapped to fd00::2.

5. Log off Dcsrv1.

Lesson Summary

- In most Windows networks, DNS servers are hosted on Active Directory domain controllers. You can install a DNS server together with a domain controller by running Dcpromo.exe. To install a DNS server without a domain controller, use the Add Roles Wizard to add the DNS Server role.

- You can install a DNS server on a Server Core installation of Windows Server 2008 or Windows Server 2008 R2. To do so on a domain controller, use Dcpromo and specify an answer file by using the command **dcpromo /unattend:<*unattendfile*>**. To install a stand-alone DNS server on a Server Core installation, type **start /w ocsetup DNS-Server-Core-Role**.

- The DNS server properties dialog box allows you to configure settings that apply to the DNS server and all its hosted zones.

- The Interfaces tab allows you to specify which of the local computer's IP addresses the DNS server should listen to for DNS requests. The Root Hints tab allows you to modify default root servers for the DNS namespace. The Forwarders tab allows you to specify the IP addresses of upstream DNS servers to which queries should be directed if the local DNS server cannot provide a response through its cache or zone data.

- You can use the DNS Manager console to configure conditional forwarding. In conditional forwarding, queries for specific domains are forwarded to specific DNS servers.

Lesson Review

You can use the following questions to test your knowledge of the information in Lesson 2, "Deploying a DNS Server." The questions are also available on the companion CD if you prefer to review them in electronic form.

1. You are configuring a new DNS server in your organization. You want to configure the new DNS server to specify the root servers in your organization as its root servers. What should you do?

   A. Replace the Cache.dns file with a new version specifying the company root servers.

   B. Configure a HOSTS file with the names and addresses of the root servers in your organization.

   C. Configure an Lmhosts file with the names and addresses of the root servers in your organization.

   D. Configure the new DNS server to forward queries to the root servers in your organization.

2. Your company includes a headquarters office in New York and a branch office in Sacramento. These offices host the Active Directory domains ny.lucernepublishing.com and sac.lucernepublishing.com, respectively. You want users in each office to be able to resolve names and browse the internal network of the other office. You also want users in each network to resolve Internet names. How should you configure the DNS servers in each office?

   A. Configure root servers in the New York office, and then configure the Sacramento servers to forward queries to the root servers in New York

   B. Configure the DNS server in each office to forward queries to an external forwarder.

   C. Use conditional forwarding to configure the parent DNS servers in the New York office to forward queries destined for the sac.lucernepublishing.com to the Sacramento DNS servers. Configure the parent DNS servers in the Sacramento office to forward queries destined for the ny.lucernepublishing.com to the New York DNS servers.

   D. Configure the parent DNS servers in the New York office to forward queries to the parent DNS server in the Sacramento office. Configure the parent DNS servers in the Sacramento office to forward queries to the parent DNS server in the New York office.

3. You want to improve security of your DNS server and reduce the threat of an attacker changing data that is stored on it. Which of the following commands will achieve this goal?

   A. dnscmd /Config /SocketPoolSize 2500

   B. dnscmd /Config /SocketPoolExcludedPortRanges 0-2000

   C. dnscmd /Config /CacheLockingPercent 90

   D. dnscmd /Config /LocalNetPriority 1

Lesson 3: Configuring DNS Client Settings

A DNS infrastructure requires configuration for clients as well as for servers. In a typical business network, DNS clients are configured through settings inherited through DHCP or from Active Directory domain membership. However, for computers with static IP configurations, as well as for some outside of an Active Directory environment, you need to define DNS client settings manually. This lesson describes the DNS settings that affect a computer's ability to resolve DNS names successfully and to have its own name resolved by other querying computers.

After this lesson, you will be able to:

- Configure a DNS client with a DNS server list.
- Configure a suffix search list.
- Configure a DNS client with a primary DNS suffix.
- Configure a DNS client with a connection-specific DNS suffix.
- Configure a DNS client to register its name and address with a DNS server.

Estimated lesson time: 45 minutes

Specifying DNS Servers

The most important configuration parameter for a DNS client is the DNS server address. When a client performs a DNS query, the client first directs that query toward the address specified as the client's preferred DNS server. If the preferred DNS server is unavailable, a DNS client then contacts an alternate DNS server, if one is specified. Note that the client does not contact an alternate DNS server when the preferred server is available yet merely unable to resolve a query.

You can configure a DNS client with a prioritized list of as many DNS server addresses you choose, either by using DHCP to assign the list or by manually specifying the addresses. With DHCP, you can configure clients with a DNS server list by using the 006 DNS Server option and then configuring the clients to obtain a DNS server address automatically in the TCP/IPv4 Properties dialog box, as shown in Figure 2-29. (This is the default setting.)

MORE INFO **DHCP OPTIONS**

DHCP options are discussed in Chapter 4, "Creating a DHCP Infrastructure."

To configure a DNS server list manually, you can use the Internet Protocol Version 4 (TCP/IPv4) Properties dialog box if you want to configure the local client with one or two DNS servers (a preferred and an alternate). However, if you want to configure a longer list, click the Advanced button, and then select the DNS tab. Use the Add button to add servers to the prioritized list of DNS servers, as shown in Figure 2-30.

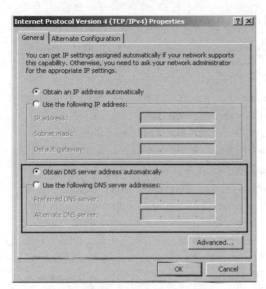

FIGURE 2-29 By default, IPv4 hosts are configured to obtain a DNS server address through DHCP.

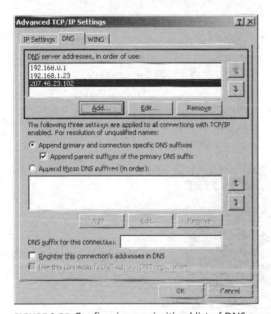

FIGURE 2-30 Configuring a prioritized list of DNS servers for a client to contact

Specifying a Computer Name and DNS Suffixes

When you install Windows Server 2008 R2, a computer name is generated automatically if you do not specify one in an answer file. You can later change this computer name after installation by using the System Properties dialog box (which you can open through the System control panel or by typing the **sysdm.cpl** command). In DNS, this same computer name is called a host name and is analogous to a person's first name or given name. An example of such a computer name or host name is ClientA. You can determine the computer's host name by typing the command **hostname** at a command prompt.

However, a client can take the fullest advantage of DNS name resolution services when it is configured with not just a host name, but also with a primary DNS suffix, which is analogous to a person's last name or surname (family name). The host name together with the primary DNS suffix creates the full computer name. For example, a computer named ClientA with a primary DNS suffix of contoso.com is configured with a full computer name of ClientA.contoso.com. Normally, the primary DNS suffix corresponds to the name of a primary (read-write) zone hosted on the locally specified preferred DNS server. For example, the client named ClientA.contoso.com would normally be configured with the address of a DNS server hosting the contoso.com zone.

The primary DNS suffix serves two specific functions. First, it enables a client to automatically register its own host record in the DNS zone whose name corresponds to the primary DNS suffix name. This host record enables other computers to resolve the name of the local DNS client. Second, the DNS client automatically adds the primary DNS suffix to DNS queries that do not already include a suffix. For example, on a computer configured with the DNS suffix fabrikam.com, the command **ping dcsrv1** would effectively be translated to **ping dcsrv1.fabrikam.com**. This appended query, demonstrated in Figure 2-31, would then be sent to the DNS server.

FIGURE 2-31 A computer configured with a DNS suffix appends that suffix to host names in its DNS queries.

Joining a computer to an Active Directory domain automatically configures the domain name as the computer's primary DNS suffix. To configure a primary DNS suffix outside of an

Active Directory domain, click Change on the Computer Name tab in the System Properties dialog box, and then click More in the Computer Name / Domain Changes dialog box. This procedure opens the DNS Suffix And NetBIOS Computer Name dialog box, shown in Figure 2-32.

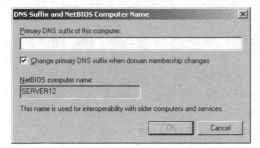

FIGURE 2-32 Manually configuring a DNS suffix

Configuring a Connection-Specific DNS Suffix

Besides being assigned a primary DNS suffix, a computer can also be assigned a *connection-specific suffix* from a DHCP server or from a manual configuration. This type of suffix is associated with a particular network connection only. From a DHCP server, the connection-specific suffix is assigned through the 015 DNS Domain Name option. You can assign a connection-specific suffix manually for any particular network connection in the DNS tab of the Advanced TCP/IP Settings dialog box, as shown in Figure 2-33.

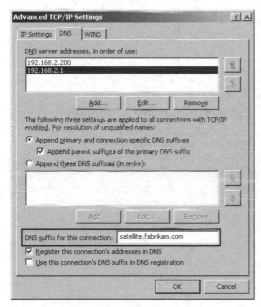

FIGURE 2-33 Assigning a connection-specific DNS suffix

A connection-specific suffix is useful if a computer has two network adapters and you want to distinguish the two routes to that computer by name. For example, in Figure 2-34, a file server named FileSrv1 is connected to two subnets through two separate adapters. The first adapter, assigned the address 10.1.1.11 /16, is connected to Subnet 1 by a Gigabit Ethernet connection. This connection is assigned a connection-specific DNS suffix of public.nwtraders.com. The second adapter, assigned the address 10.2.2.22 /16, is connected to Subnet 2 by a 100 Mbps Ethernet connection. This second connection is assigned a connection-specific DNS suffix of backup.nwtraders.com.

Computers on both subnets can connect to FileSrv1 through either adapter. However, when users specify the address *filesrv1.public.nwtraders.com*, their connections are resolved and then routed to FileSrv1 through the faster Gigabit Ethernet link. When they specify *filesrv1.backup.nwtraders.com*, their connections are resolved and then routed to FileSrv1 through the slower backup link.

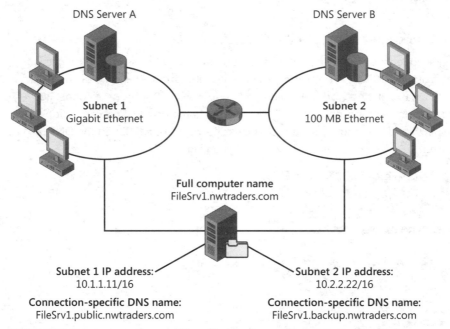

FIGURE 2-34 Using connection-specific suffixes to name different routes to a file server

Configuring a Suffix Search List

For DNS clients, you can configure a DNS domain suffix search list that extends or revises their DNS search capabilities. By adding suffixes to the list, you can search for single-tag, unqualified computer names in more than one specified DNS domain. Then, if a DNS query fails, the DNS Client service can use this list to append other name suffix endings to your original name and repeat DNS queries to the DNS server for these alternate FQDNs.

Default DNS Suffix Searches

By default, the DNS Client service first attaches the primary DNS suffix of the local computer to the single-tag name. If the query fails to resolve this name, the DNS Client service then adds any connection-specific suffix that you have assigned to a network adapter. Finally, if these queries are also unsuccessful, the DNS Client service by default then performs what is called DNS *devolution*. First, it adds the parent suffix of the primary DNS suffix. If there are more parent suffixes, those too are searched, down to the forest root domain name.

For example, suppose the full computer name of a multihomed computer is computer1.tokyo .asia.microsoft.com in an Active Directory forest named microsoft.com. The network adapters on Computer1 have been assigned the connection-specific suffixes subnet1.tokyo.asia.microsoft.com and subnet2.tokyo.asia.microsoft.com, respectively. If on this same computer, you type **\\Computer2** into the Run box and then press Enter, the local DNS Client service first tries to resolve the name Computer2 by performing a query for the name computer2.tokyo.asia .microsoft.com. If this query is unsuccessful, the DNS Client service queries for the names computer2.subnet1.tokyo.asia.microsoft.com and computer2.subnet2.tokyo.asia.microsoft.com. If this last query does not succeed in resolving the name, the DNS Client performs DNS devolution: it performs queries for the names computer2.asia.microsoft.com and finally computer2.microsoft.com.

> **NOTE** **DNS DEVOLUTION IS PERFORMED ONLY IN INHERITED NAMESPACES**
>
> If the domain name of a DNS client's forest is not a subset of the client's own domain name, the DNS client does not perform devolution. For example, if a forest is named corp.contoso.com and contains a domain brazil.sa.contoso.com, DNS clients in brazil.sa.contoso.com will not search in any parent domains such as sa.contoso.com, corp.contoso.com, or contoso.com. This behavior happens because the root domain includes the tag "corp," and the child domain does not.

DNS Devolution Levels

A new feature in Windows Server 2008 R2 and Windows 7 is the ability to specify for DNS clients the devolution level. A *devolution level* is the number of tags left in a domain name to serve as a limit or stopping point for parent domain searching. In the previous example, the client Computer1 in the domain tokyo.asia.microsoft.com eventually used devolution to search for the name Computer2 appended by the three-tag parent domain name asia.microsoft.com and finally the two-tag grandparent domain name microsoft.com. However, if you had set the devolution level to 3, Computer1 would have stopped searching after appending the three-tag name, asia.microsoft.com.

You can configure DNS devolution levels by using Group Policy setting named Primary DNS Suffix Devolution Level. You can find this policy setting in a GPO by navigating to Computer Configuration\Administrative Templates\Network\DNS Client.

EXAM TIP

Because devolution levels are new to Windows Server 2008 R2 and Windows 7, you should expect to see a question about them on the 70-642 exam.

Custom DNS Suffix Search Lists

You can customize suffix searches by creating a DNS suffix search list in the Advanced TCP/IP Settings dialog box, as shown in Figure 2-35.

The Append These DNS Suffixes option lets you specify a list of DNS suffixes to add to unqualified names. If you enter a DNS suffix search list, the DNS Client service adds those DNS suffixes in order and does not try any other domain names. For example, if the suffixes appearing in the search list in Figure 2-35 are configured and you submit the unqualified, single-label query "coffee," the DNS Client service first queries for coffee.lucernepublishing.com and then for coffee.eu.lucernepublishing.com.

You can also configure a DNS suffix search list through Group Policy. You can find this setting in a GPO by navigating to Computer Configuration\Policies\Administrative Templates\Network\DNS Client and then configuring the policy setting named DNS Suffix Search List.

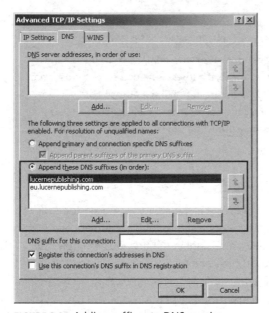

FIGURE 2-35 Adding suffixes to DNS queries

Configuring Dynamic Update Settings

When configured to do so, DNS servers running on Windows Server 2008 and Windows Server 2008 R2 can accept dynamic registration and updates of the A (host), AAAA (IPv6 host), and PTR (pointer) resource records. The registration and updates themselves must be performed either by a DNS client or by a DHCP server (on behalf of a DNS client).

> **NOTE WHAT ARE HOST AND POINTER RECORDS?**
>
> A *host record* in a forward lookup zone is a record that returns the address of a computer when you query using its name. It is the most important resource record type. A *pointer record* provides the opposite service: it is found only in a reverse lookup zone and returns the name of a computer when you query by using its IP address. For more information about zone types and resource records, see Chapter 3.

Dynamic updates for particular clients can occur only when those clients are configured with a primary or connection-specific DNS suffix that matches the zone name hosted by the preferred DNS server. For example, for the record of a computer named Client1 to be dynamically updated in the lucernepublishing.com zone, the FQDN of that computer must be client1.lucernepublishing.com, and the client must specify as its preferred DNS server the IP address of a DNS server hosting a primary zone named lucernepublishing.com.

Default Client Update Behavior

Figure 2-36 shows the default DNS registration settings for a DNS client, which are found on the DNS tab of the Advanced TCP/IP Settings dialog box.

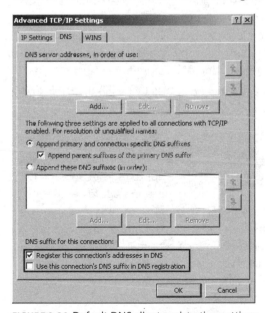

FIGURE 2-36 Default DNS client registration settings

UPDATE BEHAVIOR FOR HOST RECORDS

The setting named Register This Connection's Addresses In DNS, when enabled, configures a client to attempt to register both A and AAAA records with its preferred DNS server. For these Host record registrations to succeed, a number of conditions must be met. First, a primary DNS suffix must also be assigned to the local computer, either manually or through Active Directory membership. Second, the preferred DNS server specified for the client must host a primary zone that matches the name of the client's primary DNS suffix. Finally, the primary zone hosted at the preferred DNS server must be configured to allow the type of dynamic updates that the client can perform: either secure updates (only from domain members) or both secure and nonsecure updates (from either domain members or non–domain-joined computers).

> *NOTE* **AUTOMATIC ADDRESSING AND AUTOMATIC DNS UPDATES**
>
> **DNS clients never attempt to register IPv4 APIPA addresses or IPv6 link-local addresses with a DNS server.**

The setting named Use This Connection's DNS Suffix In DNS Registration configures the local computer to attempt to register the A and AAAA records for any connection-specific DNS suffixes that are assigned to the associated network connection. Note that the connection-specific DNS suffix does not actually have to appear in the DNS Suffix For This Connection text box on the same tab; the connection-specific suffix can instead be inherited from a DHCP server (specifically from the 015 DNS Domain Name option). Enabling this setting therefore configures a DHCP client that has been assigned a DNS domain name from DHCP to register an A and AAAA record with its preferred DNS server. For these registrations to succeed, the DNS domain name inherited from the DHCP server must match the name of a primary zone hosted on the preferred DNS server and the primary zone hosted at the preferred DNS server must be configured to allow the type of dynamic updates that the client can perform. Note also that if a client is already configured with a primary DNS suffix that matches this connection-specific DNS suffix, enabling this setting does not force the registration of any additional Host records.

For all host records, you can attempt to force a registration in DNS by typing the command Ipconfig /registerdns at an elevated command prompt.

UPDATE BEHAVIOR FOR POINTER RECORDS

For statically addressed clients, the update behavior for PTR records is the same as that for Host (A or AAAA) records: Statically addressed DNS clients always attempt to register and update their Pointer records in a DNS server when the Register This Connection's Addresses In DNS setting is enabled. You can attempt to force a registration in DNS of PTR records for a statically addressed client by typing **Ipconfig /registerdns** at an elevated command prompt on the client. For the registration to succeed, however, some conditions must be met. First, the DNS client must be configured with an appropriate primary DNS suffix, and then the client's preferred DNS server must be hosting appropriately configured forward and reverse lookup zones.

The PTR record update behavior of DHCP clients differs from that of statically addressed clients, and the PTR update behavior of DHCP clients in a workgroup environment differs from the behavior of those in an Active Directory environment. The following section explains the PTR update behavior of DHCP clients in these two environments.

In a workgroup environment, DHCP clients have their PTR records updated by the DHCP server. To force an update, you can run the command Ipconfig /renew. For this registration to succeed, a number of conditions must be met. First, the DNS client must be configured with the address of the DNS server as the preferred DNS server. Second, the DNS client must have the Register This Connection's Addresses In DNS setting enabled. Third, both the DNS client and server must be configured with an appropriate DNS suffix, either specified manually as a primary DNS suffix or (in the case of the DNS client) assigned automatically from the DHCP server. Finally, the DNS server must host appropriately configured forward and reverse lookup zones.

In an Active Directory environment, DHCP clients update their own PTR records. To force an update, you can run either the Ipconfig /registerdns or the Ipconfig /renew commands. For such an update to succeed, the Use This Connection's DNS Suffix In DNS Registration setting must be enabled. (To enable this setting, you must first enable the Register This Connection's Addresses In DNS setting.) Finally, for a PTR record to be updated successfully in an AD DS environment, the client's preferred DNS server must host appropriately configured forward and reverse lookup zones.

NOTE   USING GROUP POLICY TO REGISTER CONNECTION-SPECIFIC NAMES

You can use Group Policy to force computers on a network to register connection-specific DNS names. In a GPO, navigate to Computer Configuration\Policies\Administrative Templates \Network\DNS Client. Search for the policy setting named Register DNS Records With Connection-Specific DNS Suffix and configure the setting as Enabled.

EXAM TIP

To force a DNS client to attempt dynamic registration of its resource records, type `ipconfig /registerdns` at a command prompt.

 Quick Check

- By default, does a client with a domain name assigned by DHCP (and not Active Directory membership) attempt to register its address in DNS?

Quick Check Answer

- No.

Viewing and Clearing the DNS Client Cache

The *DNS client cache,* also known as the DNS resolver cache, is maintained on all DNS clients. DNS clients check this resolver cache before they attempt to query a DNS server. New entries are added to the resolver cache whenever a DNS client receives a query response from a DNS server.

To view the DNS client cache, type **ipconfig /displaydns** at a command prompt. The output of this command includes any entries loaded from the local Hosts file, as well as any recently obtained resource records for name queries resolved by the system.

To clear the DNS client cache, you can type **ipconfig /flushdns** at the command prompt. Alternatively, you can restart the DNS Client service by using the Services console, which is an administrative tool accessible through the Start menu.

EXAM TIP

For the exam, remember that you sometimes need to run Ipconfig /flushdns on your computer before you can see the benefit of having fixed a DNS problem elsewhere on the network. For example, if a Windows client has cached a negative response from a DNS server to a recent query, the client will continue to receive a negative response even if the DNS server can now resolve the query. To fix such a problem, flush the DNS client cache by executing Ipconfig /flushdns on the Windows computer. This command forces the Windows client to contact the DNS server again instead of just responding with the cached negative response.

PRACTICE Managing the DNS Client Cache

In this practice, you use the Ipconfig command with the /flushdns and /displaydns switches to clear and display the DNS client cache.

EXERCISE Exploring the DNS Resolver (Client) Cache

In this exercise, you observe the behavior of the DNS client cache.

1. Log on to Nwtraders from Boston as a domain administrator.

2. At a command prompt, type **ipconfig /flushdns**. At the command prompt, a message appears indicating that the DNS Resolver Cache has been flushed.

3. At a command prompt, type **ipconfig /displaydns**. You receive a message indicating that the DNS Resolver Cache could not be displayed.

4. At the command prompt, type **ping dcsrv1**. You receive a response from the IPv6 address of Dcrsv1. Note that the primary DNS suffix of the local computer, nwtraders.msft, has been appended to the name "dcsrv1." This DNS suffix was assigned to Boston when Boston joined the Nwtraders domain.

5. At the command prompt, type **ipconfig /displaydns**. Beneath the same heading of dcsrv1.nwtraders.msft, two new records appear in the cache: an A (Host) Record and an AAAA Record. Note that the A record is associated with Dcsrv1's IPv4 address and the AAAA record is associated with Dcrv1's IPv6 address.

6. At the command prompt, type **ipconfig /flushdns**.

7. At the command prompt, type **ipconfig /displaydns**. The output reveals that the two new records have been flushed from the cache.

8. Close all open windows.

Lesson Summary

- When a client performs a DNS query, the client first directs that query toward the address specified as the client's preferred DNS server. If the preferred DNS server is unavailable, a DNS client then contacts an alternate DNS server, if one is specified. You can configure a DNS client with a prioritized list of as many DNS server addresses you choose, either by using DHCP to assign the list or by manually specifying the addresses.

- In DNS, the computer name is called a host name. This is a single-tag name that you can discover by typing the command **hostname** at a command prompt.

- DNS client settings affect a computer's ability to resolve DNS names successfully and to have the client's own name resolved by other querying computers.

- A client can take the fullest advantage of DNS name resolution services when it is configured with a primary DNS suffix. The primary DNS suffix enables a client to automatically register its own host record in the DNS zone whose name corresponds to the primary DNS suffix name. The client also appends the primary DNS suffix to DNS queries that do not already include a suffix. A connection-specific suffix applies only to connections through a specific network adapter.

- You can configure a DNS client to specify a list of DNS suffixes to add to unqualified names. This list is known as a DNS suffix search list.

- DNS clients can register their own records in DNS only when the clients are configured with a primary or connection-specific DNS suffix that matches the zone name hosted by the preferred DNS server. By default, DNS clients assigned static addresses attempt to register both host and pointer records. DNS clients that are also DHCP clients attempt to register only host records.

Lesson Review

You can use the following questions to test your knowledge of the information in Lesson 3, "Configuring DNS Client Settings." The questions are also available on the companion CD if you prefer to review them in electronic form.

> **NOTE** **ANSWERS**
>
> Answers to these questions and explanations of why each answer choice is correct or incorrect are located in the "Answers" section at the end of the book.

1. You are a network administrator for an organization whose network is composed of two Active Directory domains, east.cpandl.com and west.cpandl.com. Users in each domain can already connect to resources in the opposing domain by specifying an FQDN, such as client1.west.cpandl.com. You now want users in the east.cpandl.com domain also to be able to connect to computers in the west.cpandl.com domain by specifying those computers with a single name tag in a UNC path, such as \\WestSrv1. What can you do to enable this functionality?

   A. Use conditional forwarding to configure the DNS server in the east.cpandl.com domain to forward queries for names in the west.cpandl.com domain to the DNS servers in the west.cpandl.com domain.

   B. Use Group Policy in the east.cpandl.com domain to configure network clients with a DNS suffix search list. Add the domain suffix west.cpandl.com to the list.

   C. On the clients in the east.cpandl.com domain, configure TCP/IP properties of the local area connection to use the connection's DNS suffix in DNS registration.

   D. You do not need to do anything. The DNS suffix of the opposing will automatically be appended to single-tag name queries.

2. A computer named ClientA is not registering its DNS record with a DNS server. ClientA is configured with a static IP address and with the IP address of the DNS server authoritative for nwtraders.com domain. The TCP/IP properties for the local area connection on ClientA have been left at the default settings. What can you do to ensure that ClientA registers its own record with the DNS server?

   A. Configure a connection-specific suffix.

   B. Enable the option to use the connection's DNS suffix in DNS registration.

   C. Enable the option to register the connection's addresses in DNS.

   D. Configure a primary DNS suffix.

3. You work as a network administrator in a branch office for a large multinational corporation named Fabrikam.com. The name of the Active Directory Domain Services domain for the network in your local branch is Dublin.ie.fabrikam.com. You have noticed that when users within your local domain try to connect to other computers by specifying a single name such as Server1, the network is very slow to respond when no such host can be found. What can you do to reduce the latency of negative network responses to single name queries?

   A. Configure a custom DNS suffix search list consisting of Dublin.ie.fabrikam.com, ie.fabrikam.com, and fabrikam.com.

   B. Use Group Policy to set the devolution level on the network to 3.

   C. Configure clients to append parent suffixes of the primary DNS suffix in to resolve unqualified names.

   D. Configure clients in your domain with a connection-specific suffix.

Chapter Review

To further practice and reinforce the skills you learned in this chapter, you can

- Review the chapter summary.
- Review the list of key terms introduced in this chapter.
- Complete the case scenarios. These scenarios set up a real-world situation involving the topics of this chapter and ask you to create solutions.
- Complete the suggested practices.
- Take a practice test.

Chapter Summary

- DNS is the preferred name resolution service in Windows networks. However, because of the way DNS is designed, it requires configuration. When DNS is not available, Windows Server 2008 R2 and Windows 7 use LLMNR to resolve computer names to IP addresses. When LLMNR is unavailable or unable to resolve a computer name, NetBIOS name resolution is used.

- DNS provides a hierarchical name structure. In DNS, an FQDN is a domain name that has been stated unambiguously to indicate its location relative to the root of the DNS domain tree. An example of an FQDN is Client1.east.fabrikam.com.

- When a DNS client queries for a name, it first checks its local cache for the answer. If it doesn't find the answer, the DNS client queries its preferred DNS server. If the DNS server doesn't know the answer, it will attempt to resolve the query by performing iterative queries against the DNS namespace, beginning with the root server.

- In most Windows networks, DNS servers are hosted on Active Directory domain controllers. You can install a DNS server together with a domain controller by running Dcpromo.exe. To install a DNS server without a domain controller, use the Add Roles Wizard to add the DNS Server role.

- DNS client settings affect a computer's ability to resolve DNS names successfully and to have the client's own name resolved by other querying computers.

Key Terms

Do you know what these key terms mean? You can check your answers by looking up the terms in the glossary at the end of the book.

- Authoritative server
- Domain Name System (DNS)
- dynamic updates
- forwarder
- forwarding
- fully qualified domain name (FQDN)
- host name
- HOSTS
- Link Local Multicast Name Resolution (LLMNR)
- Lmhosts
- name resolution
- NetBIOS
- primary DNS suffix
- recursion
- resolver
- Resource record
- root hints
- Time to Live (TTL)
- WINS server
- zone

Case Scenarios

In the following case scenarios, you will apply what you've learned about DNS clients and servers. You can find answers to these questions in the "Answers" section at the end of this book.

Case Scenario 1: Troubleshooting DNS Clients

You work as a network administrator for a company named Contoso Pharmaceuticals. You have recently deployed a number of Windows 7 clients in a research workgroup. The workgroup is isolated on its own subnet, which is physically connected to the larger corporate network.

You have deployed a DHCP server in the research workgroup to assign these computers an IP address, a default gateway, a DNS server, and the DNS domain name of contoso.com. The preferred DNS server address assigned to the clients belongs to a DNS server hosting a primary zone for the contoso.com domain. The zone is configured to accept both secure and nonsecure dynamic updates.

1. None of the clients in the research workgroup is successfully registering DNS records with the DNS server. Which TCP/IP setting can you enable to ensure that these dynamic registrations occur?

2. Certain network computers running Windows XP are configured as WINS clients, yet they are unable to browse to the research subnet by using the My Network Places icon. Which setting can you configure on the Windows 7 clients to enable them to be seen by the Windows XP clients? Assume that the default settings have been left for all options not assigned by DHCP.

Case Scenario 2: Deploying a DNS Server

You work as a network support specialist for a company named Fabrikam.com. You are planning to deploy a new DNS server in a branch office to improve name resolution response times.

1. There are no administrators at the branch office. You want to deploy a DNS server that will not require any administration but that will help resolve the queries of computers on the Internet. What kind of DNS server should you deploy?

2. You also want the new DNS server to be able to resolve names on the internal Fabrikam.com network at the main office. How can you achieve this without hosting a zone named Fabrikam.com on the branch office network?

Suggested Practices

To help you successfully master the exam objectives presented in this chapter, complete the following tasks.

Configure a DNS Server

Use this practice to deploy DNS servers manually (without Dcpromo) and configure conditional forwarding.

- **Practice** In a test network, deploy two DNS servers outside of an Active Directory environment. Configure zones for each server with domain names of your choice. Configure both servers with conditional forwarding so that each server forwards queries to the other server when appropriate. Test the configuration.

Configure Name Resolution for Client Computers

Perform this practice to become more familiar with client update behavior. To prepare for this practice, you need to enable dynamic updates in the primary zones hosted on each DNS server.

- **Practice** Using the same test described in the previous practice, configure a DNS client to register its own host records with one of the DNS servers without specifying a primary DNS suffix for the client computer.

Take a Practice Test

The practice tests on this book's companion CD offer many options. For example, you can test yourself on just one exam objective, or you can test yourself on all the 70-642 certification exam content. You can set up the test so that it closely simulates the experience of taking a certification exam, or you can set it up in study mode so that you can look at the correct answers and explanations after you answer each question.

> **MORE INFO   PRACTICE TESTS**
>
> For details about all the practice test options available, see the "How to Use the Practice Tests" section in this book's Introduction.

CHAPTER 3

Configuring a DNS Zone Infrastructure

Deploying a DNS server is a fairly simple procedure, especially on a domain controller. But to manage and troubleshoot DNS, you need to understand zones in more detail.

Zones are the databases in which DNS data is stored. A DNS zone infrastructure essentially consists of the various servers and hosted zones that communicate with one another in a way that ensures consistent name resolution. This chapter introduces you to the types of zones that make up a DNS infrastructure, the options for zone replications and transfers among them, and the configurable settings within zones that you need to understand in order to manage DNS effectively on your network.

Exam objectives in this chapter:

- Configure DNS zones.
- Configure DNS records.
- Configure DNS replication.

Lessons in this chapter:

- Lesson 1: Creating and Configuring Zones **176**
- Lesson 2: Configuring Zone Replication, Transfers, and Delegations **204**
- Lesson 3: Implementing DNSSEC **223**

Before You Begin

To complete the lessons in this chapter, you must have the following:

- Two networked computers running Windows Server 2008 R2.
- The first computer must be a domain controller named Dcsrv1 in a domain named nwtraders.msft. Dcsrv1 must be assigned the static address 192.168.0.1/24 with the DNS server specified as the same address. Dcsrv1 includes the server roles Active Directory Domain Services and DNS Server.
- The second computer must be named Boston.nwtraders.msft and must be assigned the address 192.168.0.2/24. Its DNS server must be specified as 192.168.0.1. Finally, Boston must be joined to the Nwtraders.msft domain.

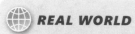
DNS Manager is the main administration tool for DNS servers, but if you need to manage DNS for your job, it's a good idea to become familiar with some other DNS tools as well. Of all the alternate tools available, the Dnscmd command-line tool is the most important and the most powerful. By typing *dnscmd* at a command prompt, you can see all 40 or so of its subcommands. Some of the most important of these include dnscmd /clearcache, which clears the server cache; dnscmd /enumdirectorypartitions, which shows the application directory partitions available on the local server; and dnscmd /info (which provides a basic overview of the DNS server configuration).

If your network includes Active Directory–integrated zones, you should also review tools for managing Active Directory replication. If you want to test replication on a domain controller, type *dcdiag /test:replications*. If you want to show replication partners, type *repadmin /showrepl*. Finally, if you want to force replication with another domain controller, use the Active Directory Sites and Services console to browse to the NTDS settings beneath your server, right-click the connection object in the details pane, and click Replicate Now.

Lesson 1: Creating and Configuring Zones

A *zone* is a database that contains authoritative information about a portion of the DNS namespace. When you install a DNS server with a domain controller, the DNS zone used to support the Active Directory domain is created automatically. However, if you install a DNS server at any other time, either on a domain controller, domain member server, or stand-alone server, you have to create and configure zones manually.

This lesson describes the steps required to create and configure a zone, as well as the underlying concepts you need to understand to configure a zone properly.

> **After this lesson, you will be able to:**
> - Create and configure DNS zones.
> - Create and configure resource records.
>
> **Estimated lesson time: 120 minutes**

Creating Zones

A *DNS zone* is a database containing records that associate names with addresses for a defined portion of a DNS namespace. Although a DNS server can use cached information from other servers to answer queries for names, it is only through a locally hosted zone that a DNS server can answer queries authoritatively. For any portion of a DNS namespace represented by a domain name such as "proseware.com," there can be only one authoritative source of zone data.

To create a new zone on a DNS server, you can use the New Zone Wizard in DNS Manager. To launch this wizard, right-click the server icon in the DNS Manager console tree, and then choose New Zone, as shown in Figure 3-1.

The New Zone Wizard includes the following configuration pages:

- Zone Type
- Active Directory Zone Replication Scope
- Forward or Reverse Lookup Zone
- Zone Name
- Dynamic Update

The sections that follow describe the configuration concepts related to these five wizard pages.

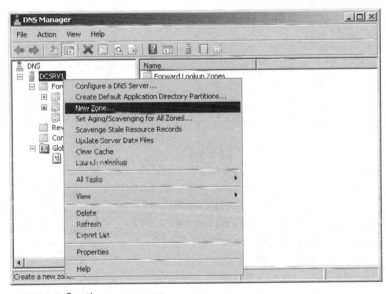

FIGURE 3-1 Creating a new zone

Choosing a Zone Type

The Zone Type page of the New Zone Wizard, shown in Figure 3-2, enables you to create your choice of a primary zone, a secondary zone, or a stub zone. If you are creating a primary or stub zone on a domain controller, you also have the option to store zone data in Active Directory.

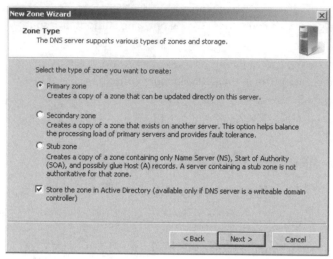

FIGURE 3-2 Choosing a zone type

PRIMARY ZONES

A *primary zone* is the main type of DNS zone. A primary zone provides original read-write source data that allows the local DNS server to answer DNS queries authoritatively about a portion of a DNS namespace.

When the local DNS server hosts a primary zone, the DNS server is the primary source for information about this zone, and the server stores the master copy of zone data in a local file or in Active Directory Domain Services (AD DS). When the zone is stored in a file instead of Active Directory, by default the primary zone file is named *zone_name*.dns, and this file is located in the %systemroot%\System32\Dns folder on the server.

SECONDARY ZONES

A *secondary zone* provides an authoritative, read-only copy of a primary zone or another secondary zone. Secondary zones provide a means to offload DNS query traffic in areas of the network where a zone is heavily queried and used. Additionally, if the zone server hosting a primary zone is unavailable, a secondary zone can provide name resolution for the namespace until the primary server becomes available again.

The source zones from which secondary zones acquire their information are called *masters*, and the data copy procedures through which this information is regularly updated are called *zone transfers*. A master can be a primary zone or other secondary zone. You can specify the master of a secondary zone when the secondary zone is created through the New Zone Wizard. Because a secondary zone is merely a copy of a primary zone that is hosted on another server, it cannot be stored in AD DS.

STUB ZONES

A *stub zone* is similar to a secondary zone, but it contains only those resource records necessary to identify the authoritative DNS servers for the master zone. Stub zones are often used to enable a parent zone like proseware.com to keep an updated list of the name servers available in a delegated child zone, such as east.proseware.com. They can also be used to improve name resolution and simplify DNS administration.

STORING THE ZONE IN ACTIVE DIRECTORY

When you create a new primary or stub zone on a domain controller, the Zone Type page gives you the option to store the zone in Active Directory. In Active Directory–integrated zones, zone data is automatically replicated through Active Directory in a manner determined by the settings you choose on the Active Directory Zone Replication Scope page. In most cases, this option eliminates the need to configure zone transfers to secondary servers.

Integrating your DNS zone with Active Directory has several advantages. First, because Active Directory performs zone replication, you do not need to configure a separate mechanism for DNS zone transfers between primary and secondary servers. Fault tolerance, along with improved performance from the availability of multiple read/write primary servers, is automatically supplied by the presence of multimaster replication on your network. Second, Active Directory allows for single properties of resource records to be updated and replicated among DNS servers. Avoiding the transfer of many and complete resource records decreases the load on network resources during zone transfers. Finally, Active Directory–integrated zones also provide the optional benefit of requiring security for dynamic updates, an option you can configure on the Dynamic Update page.

> *NOTE* **READ-ONLY DOMAIN CONTROLLERS AND ACTIVE DIRECTORY–INTEGRATED ZONES**
> For traditional domain controllers, the copy of the zone is a read-write copy. For read-only domain controllers (RODCs), the copy of the zone will be read-only.

STANDARD ZONES

By default, on the Zone Type page, the option to store the zone in Active Directory is selected when you are creating the zone on a domain controller. However, you can clear this check box and instead create what is called a standard zone. A standard zone is also the only option for a new zone when you are creating the zone on a server that is not a domain controller; in this case the check box on this page cannot be selected.

As opposed to an Active Directory–integrated zone, a *standard zone* stores its data in a text file on the local DNS server. Also unlike Active Directory–integrated zones, with standard zones, you can configure only a single read-write (primary) copy of zone data. All other copies of the zone (secondary zones) are read-only.

The standard zone model implies a single point of failure for the writable version of the zone. If the primary zone is unavailable to the network, no changes to the zone can be made. However, queries for names in the zone can continue uninterrupted as long as secondary zones are available.

Choosing an Active Directory Zone Replication Scope

On the Active Directory Zone Replication Scope page of the New Scope Wizard, you can choose which domain controllers in your network will store the zone. This page, shown in Figure 3-3, appears only when you have configured the zone to be stored in Active Directory. Note that the choice of where you store the zone determines the domain controllers among which the zone data will be replicated.

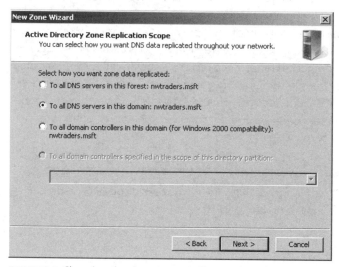

FIGURE 3-3 Choosing the domain controllers to store the zone

You have four choices:

- Store the zone in all domain controllers that are also DNS servers in the entire Active Directory forest.

- Store the zone in all domain controllers that are also DNS servers in the local Active Directory domain.

- Store the zone in all domain controllers in the local Active Directory domain (used for compatibility with Windows 2000).

- Store the zone in all domain controllers specified in the scope of a custom Active Directory directory partition.

These options are described in more detail in Lesson 2, "Configuring Zone Replication, Transfers, and Delegations."

Creating a Forward or Reverse Lookup Zone

On the Forward Or Reverse Lookup Zone page of the New Zone Wizard, you determine whether the new zone you are creating should act as a forward or reverse lookup zone. This page is shown in Figure 3-4.

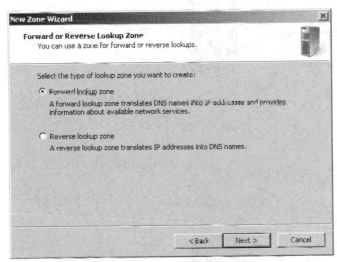

FIGURE 3-4 Choosing a forward or reverse lookup zone

In *forward lookup zones*, DNS servers map fully qualified domain names (FQDNs) to IP addresses. In *reverse lookup zones*, DNS servers map IP addresses to FQDNs. Forward lookup zones thus answer queries to resolve FQDNs to IP addresses, and reverse lookup zones answer queries to resolve IP addresses to FQDNs. Note that forward lookup zones adopt the name of the DNS domain name for whose names you want to provide resolution service, such as "proseware.com." Reverse lookup zones are named by a reverse order of the network ID octets in the address space for which you want to provide reverse name resolution service *plus* the final tag "in-addr.arpa." For example, if you want to provide reverse name resolution service for the subnet 192.168.1.0/24, the name of the reverse lookup zone will be "1.168.192.in-addr.arpa." Within a forward lookup zone, a single database entry or record that maps a host name to an IPv4 address is known as a *host* or an *A* record. (For an IPv6 address, the host record is also known as *AAAA*, or a "quad A" record.) In a reverse lookup zone, a single database entry that maps an address host ID to a host name is known as *pointer* or *PTR* record.

A forward lookup zone is illustrated in Figure 3-5, and a reverse lookup zone is illustrated in Figure 3-6.

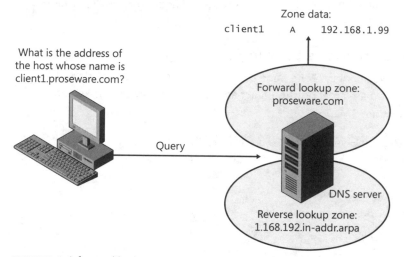

FIGURE 3-5 A forward lookup zone

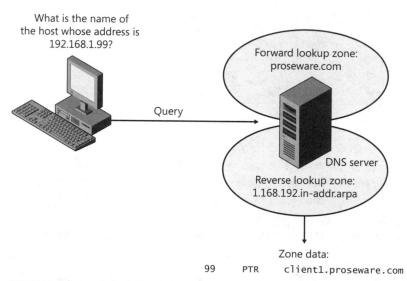

FIGURE 3-6 A reverse lookup zone

Choosing a Zone Name

The Zone Name page of the New Zone Wizard enables you to choose a name for the forward lookup zone you are creating. (Reverse lookup zones have specific names corresponding to the IP address range for which they are authoritative.) The Zone Name page is shown in Figure 3-7.

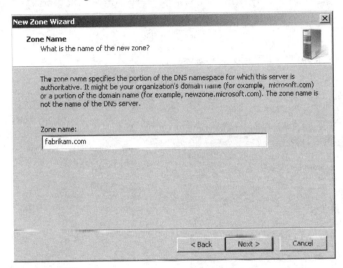

FIGURE 3-7 Choosing a zone name

In general, If the zone you are creating is going to be providing name resolution for an Active Directory domain, you want the zone to match the name of that Active Directory domain. For example, if your organization includes two Active Directory domains named proseware.com and east.proseware.com, your name resolution infrastructure should include two zones with names that match those Active Directory domains.

If you are creating a zone for a DNS namespace outside of an Active Directory environment, you should supply the name of your organization's Internet domain name, such as fabrikam.com.

Configuring Dynamic Update Settings

DNS client computers can register and dynamically update their resource records with a DNS server. By default, DNS clients that are configured with static IP addresses attempt to update host (A or AAAA) and pointer (PTR) records, and DNS clients that are DHCP clients attempt to update only host records. In a workgroup environment, the DHCP server updates the pointer record on behalf of the DHCP client whenever the IP configuration is renewed.

For dynamic DNS updates to succeed, the zone in which the client attempts to register or update a record must be configured to accept dynamic updates. Two types of dynamic updates are allowed:

- **Secure updates**   Allow registrations only from Active Directory domain member computers and updates only from the same computer that originally performed the registration

- **Nonsecure updates**   Allow updates from any computer

The Dynamic Update page of the New Zone Wizard enables you to specify whether the zone you are creating should accept secure, nonsecure, or no dynamic updates. The Dynamic Update page is shown in Figure 3-8.

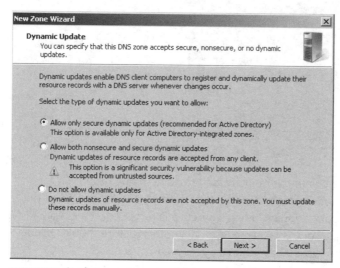

FIGURE 3-8 Configuring dynamic updates on a zone

DYNAMIC UPDATES AND DNS RECORD SECURITY

If you look at the security properties of a resource record, you can see that various users and groups are assigned permissions to the record, just as with any resource in Windows. These security permissions are used for secure dynamic updates. When only secure dynamic updates are allowed in a zone, the user listed as the owner of the resource record (in the advanced security settings) is the only user that can update that record.

The owner of a resource in Windows by default is the user who created that resource. For this reason, when a computer first registers in DNS by creating an A record, that computer becomes the owner of the record.

NOTE   USER ACCOUNTS FOR COMPUTERS IN AD DS

Every computer in AD DS gets a user account corresponding to its computer name plus the "$" symbol, such as Client1$ or Server1$.

EXAM TIP

To manually force a DNS client to perform a dynamic update, use the `Ipconfig/registerdns` command.

 Quick Check

- What are the server requirements for storing a zone in Active Directory?

Quick Check Answer

- The DNS server needs to be a domain controller.

Examining Built-in Resource Records

When you create a new zone, two types of records required for the zone are automatically created. First, a new zone always includes a Start of Authority (SOA) record that defines basic properties for the zone. All new zones also include at least one NS record signifying the name of the server or servers authoritative for the zone. Figure 3-9 shows a new zone populated by these two records.

The following section describes the functions and features of these two resource records.

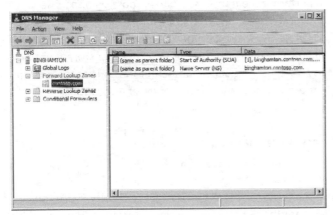

FIGURE 3-9 A new zone always includes at least an SOA and an NS record.

Start of Authority (SOA) Records

When a DNS server loads a zone, it uses the SOA resource record to determine basic and authoritative properties for the zone. These settings also determine how often zone transfers are performed between primary and secondary servers.

If you double-click the SOA record, you open the Start Of Authority (SOA) tab of the zone properties dialog box, shown in Figure 3-10.

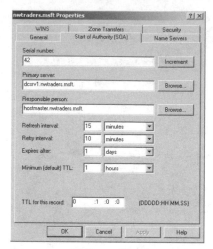

FIGURE 3-10 SOA record settings

On this tab, you can modify the following settings:

- **Serial Number**   The Serial Number text box on the Start Of Authority (SOA) tab contains the revision number of the zone file. This number increases each time a resource record changes in the zone or when you manually increment the value in this tab by clicking Increment.

    When zones are configured to perform zone transfers to one or more secondary servers, the secondary servers query the master server intermittently for the serial number of the zone. This query is called the *SOA query*. If, through the SOA query, the serial number of the master zone is determined to be equivalent to the serial number stored on the secondary, no transfer is made. However, if the serial number for the zone at the master server is greater than that at the requesting secondary server, the secondary server initiates a transfer.

> **NOTE**   **FORCING A ZONE TRANSFER ON THE MASTER**
>
> When you click the Increment button, you force a zone transfer.

- **Primary Server**   The Primary Server text box on the Start Of Authority (SOA) tab contains the full computer name for the primary DNS server of the zone. This name must end with a period.

- **Responsible Person** When this text box is configured, it contains the name of a responsible person (RP) resource record that specifies a domain mailbox name for a zone administrator. The name of the record entered into this field should always end with a period. The name "hostmaster" is used in this field by default.

- **Refresh Interval** The value you configure in the Refresh Interval text box determines how long a secondary DNS server waits before querying the master server for a zone renewal. When the refresh interval expires, the secondary DNS server requests a copy of the current SOA resource record for the zone from its master server source, which then answers this SOA query. The secondary DNS server then compares the serial number of the source server's current SOA resource record (as indicated in the master's response) with the serial number of its own local SOA resource record. If they are different, the secondary DNS server requests a zone transfer from the primary DNS server. The default value for this setting is 15 minutes.

EXAM TIP

Increasing the refresh interval decreases zone transfer traffic.

- **Retry Interval** The value you configure in the Retry Interval text box determines how long a secondary server waits before retrying a failed zone transfer. Normally, this time is less than the refresh interval. The default value is 10 minutes.

- **Expires After** The value you configure in the Expires After text box determines the length of time that a secondary server, without any contact with its master server, continues to answer queries from DNS clients. After this time elapses, the data is considered unreliable. The default value is one day.

- **Minimum (Default) TTL** The value you configure in the Minimum (Default) TTL text box determines the default Time to Live (TTL) that is applied to all resource records in the zone. The default value is one hour.

  TTL values are not relevant for resource records within their authoritative zones. Instead, the TTL refers to the cache life of a resource record in nonauthoritative servers. A DNS server that has cached a resource record from a previous query discards the record when that record's TTL has expired.

- **TTL For This Record** The value you configure in this text box determines the TTL of the present SOA resource record. This value overrides the default value setting in the preceding field.

  After you create it, an SOA resource record is represented textually in a standard zone file in the manner shown in this example:

```
@ IN SOA computer1.domain1.local. hostmaster.domain1.local. (
    5099    ; serial number
    3600    ; refresh (1 hour)
    600     ; retry (10 mins)
    86400   ; expire (1 day)
    60  )   ; minimum TTL (1 min)
```

Name Server Records

A name server (NS) record specifies a server that is authoritative for a given zone. When you create a zone in Windows Server 2008 or Windows Server 2008 R2, every server hosting a primary copy of an Active Directory–integrated zone will have its own NS record appear in the new zone by default. If you are creating a standard primary zone, an NS record for the local server appears in the zone by default. However, you need to manually add NS records for servers hosting secondary zones on a primary copy of the zone.

Creating an NS record requires a procedure that is different from the one used for creating other resource record types. To add an NS record, double-click any existing NS record in DNS Manager. This step opens the Name Servers tab of the zone properties dialog box, shown in Figure 3-11. On the Name Servers tab, click the Add button to add the FQDN and IP address of the server hosting the secondary zone of the local primary zone. When you click OK after adding the new server, a new NS record pointing to that server appears in DNS Manager.

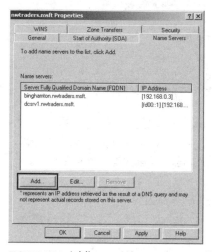

FIGURE 3-11 Adding an NS record to specify a server hosting a secondary zone

> **NOTE   ENABLING TRANSFERS TO SECONDARY ZONES**
>
> A secondary zone will not be recognized as a valid name server until it contains a valid copy of zone data. For the secondary zone to obtain this data, you must first enable zone transfers to that server by using the Zone Transfers tab in the Zone Properties dialog box. This tab is discussed in more detail in Lesson 2.

After you create the record, a line such as the following appears in the standard zone file:

```
@ NS  dns1.lucernepublishing.com.
```

In this record, the "@" symbol represents the zone defined by the SOA record in the same zone file. The complete entry, then, effectively maps the lucernepublishing.com domain to a DNS server named dns1.lucernepublishing.com.

Creating Resource Records

Beyond the SOA and NS records, some other resource records are also created automatically. For example, if you choose to install a new DNS server when promoting a server to a domain controller, many SRV records for AD DS services are automatically created in the locally hosted zone. In addition, through dynamic updates, many DNS clients automatically register host (A or AAAA) and pointer (PTR) records in a zone by default.

Even though many resource records are created automatically, in a production environment, you usually need to create some resource records manually as well. Such records might include mail exchanger (MX) records for mail servers, alias (CNAME) records for web servers or application servers, and host records for servers or clients that cannot perform their own updates.

To add a resource record for a zone manually, right-click the zone icon in the DNS Manager console, and then choose the type of resource record you want to create from the shortcut menu. Figure 3-12 demonstrates the creation of a new MX record.

After you make your selection from the shortcut menu, a new dialog box appears in which you can specify the name of the record and the computer associated with it. Figure 3-13 shows the New Resource Record dialog box that appears for the creation of a new MX record. Note that only host records associate the name of a computer with the actual IP address of the computer. Most record types associate the name of a service or alias with the original host record. As a result, the MX record shown in Figure 3-13 relies on the presence in the zone of a host record named SRV12.nwtraders.msft.

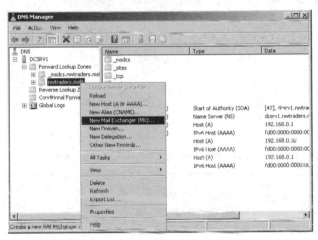

FIGURE 3-12 Creating a new resource record

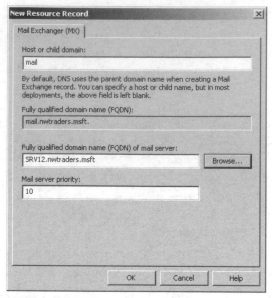

FIGURE 3-13 Defining a new MX record

Record Types

The most common resource records you need to create manually include the following:

- Host (A or AAAA)
- Alias (CNAME)
- Mail exchanger (MX)
- Pointer (PTR)
- Service location (SRV)

HOST RESOURCE RECORDS

For most networks, host (A or AAAA) resource records make up the majority of resource records in a zone database. These records are used in a zone to associate computer names (host names) to IP addresses.

After you create them in the DNS Manager console, an A resource record that maps the host name server1.lucernepublishing.com to the IPv4 address 192.168.0.99 and an AAAA resource record that maps the same name to the IPv6 address fd00:0:0:5::8 would be represented textually within the standard zone file lucernepublishing.com.dns in the following way:

```
;
;   Zone records
;

server1                 A                   192.168.0.99
                        AAAA                fd00:0:0:5::8
```

Even when dynamic updates are enabled for a particular zone, in some scenarios it might be necessary to add host records manually to that zone. For example, in Figure 3-14, a company named Contoso, Ltd., uses the domain name contoso.com for both its public namespace and its internal Active Directory domain. In this case, the public web server named www.contoso.com is located outside the Active Directory domain and performs updates only on the public DNS server authoritative for contoso.com. Internal clients, however, point their DNS requests toward internal DNS servers. Because the A record for www.contoso.com is not updated dynamically on these internal DNS servers, the record must be added manually for internal clients to resolve the name and connect to the public web server.

Another case in which you might need to add host records manually is when you have a UNIX server on your network. For example, in Figure 3-15, a company named Fabrikam, Inc., uses a single Active Directory domain named fabrikam.com for its private network. The network also includes a UNIX server named App1.fabrikam.com that runs an application critical to the company's daily operations. Because UNIX servers often do not perform dynamic updates (or especially secure dynamic updates) with Microsoft DNS servers, you might need to add a host record manually for App1 on the DNS server hosting the fabrikam.com zone. Otherwise, users will not be able to connect to the application server when they specify it by FQDN.

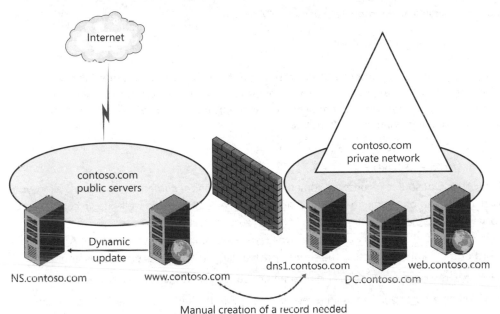

FIGURE 3-14 Adding a host record for a public web server

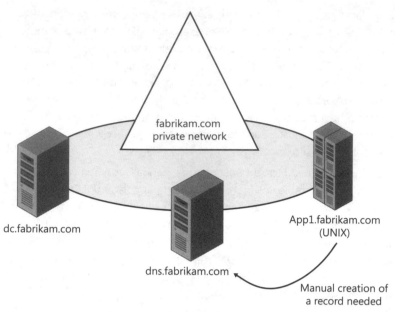

FIGURE 3-15 Adding a host record for a private UNIX server

ALIAS RESOURCE RECORDS

Alias (CNAME) resource records are sometimes called *canonical names*. These records allow you to use more than one name to point to a single host. For example, the well-known server names (ftp, www) are typically registered using CNAME resource records. These records map the host name specific to a given service (such as ftp.lucernepublishing.com) to the actual A resource record of the computer hosting the service (such as server-boston.lucernepublishing.com).

CNAME resource records are also recommended for use in the following scenarios:

- When a host specified in an A resource record in the same zone needs to be renamed
- When a generic name for a well-known server such as www needs to resolve to a group of individual computers (each with individual A resource records) that provide the same service (for example, a group of redundant web servers)

After you create it in the DNS Manager console, a CNAME resource record that maps the alias ftp.lucernepublishing.com to the host name ftp1.lucernepublishing.com would be represented textually within the lucernepublishing.com.dns standard zone file as follows:

```
ftp            CNAME      ftp1.lucernepublishing.com.
```

MAIL EXCHANGER RESOURCE RECORDS

The mail exchanger (MX) resource record is used by SMTP (mail) agents to locate other SMTP servers in a remote domain, typically for the purpose of routing mail to that domain. An MX record maps the domain name found in an email address (such as joe@lucernepublishing.com) to a particular server hosting the mail server in that domain.

Multiple MX records are also often used to specify a preferred SMTP server and a backup SMTP server. Each MX record is assigned a Mail Server Priority value, with the lower values representing higher preference. The DNS server responds to the original query by returning all the MX records matching the domain name. Finally, the SMTP agent that has queried the DNS server looks at the MX records it has received and then contacts the server whose record is assigned the lowest Mail Server Priority value. If the server assigned the lowest value is unavailable, the server assigned the next lowest value is contacted.

When two or more MX records are assigned the lowest preference value, DNS round robin can be used to balance the workload evenly among the SMTP servers corresponding to those MX records. For example, if you create three MX records in DNS Manager for mailserver1, mailserver2, and mailserver3, and then assign these records preference values of 10, 10, and 20, respectively, the workload would be split evenly between mailserver1 and mailserver2. Mailserver3 would be used as a backup. These resource records would be represented textually within the lucernepublishing.com.dns zone file as follows:

```
@       MX      10      mailserver1.lucernepublishing.com.
@       MX      10      mailserver2.lucernepublishing.com.
@       MX      20      mailserver3.lucernepublishing.com.
```

> **NOTE   WHAT DOES THE @ SYMBOL MEAN?**
>
> In this example, the @ symbol represents the local domain name contained in an email address.

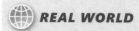

REAL WORLD

J.C. Mackin

In theory as well as in Microsoft exams, the Mail Server Priority value you set for MX records takes precedence over round-robin distribution in DNS. It doesn't always work that way in reality, however.

At first, everything works according to plan. An SMTP agent queries a DNS server for an MX record corresponding to a particular domain name, and the DNS server responds with a list of all matching MX records. The order of that list rotates from response to response if round robin is left enabled on the DNS server. So far, so good, but what happens after that point is inconsistent. The SMTP agent is then supposed to scan through the response list and contact the server whose MX record is weighted with the lowest preference value. In reality, this happens only sometimes. Reports are common of SMTP agents ignoring the preference values in MX records and contacting merely the first server in the DNS response list.

The take-away? If you want to use preference values to set load balancing and specify a backup mail server, go ahead. Know, however, that this configuration is only approximate, and that your mail server workload will be distributed in a way that is hard to predict accurately.

POINTER RESOURCE RECORDS

The pointer (PTR) resource record is used in reverse lookup zones only to support reverse lookups, which perform queries to resolve IP addresses to host names or FQDNs. Reverse lookups are performed in zones rooted in the in-addr.arpa domain. PTR resource records can be added to zones manually or automatically.

After you create it in the DNS Manager console, a PTR resource record that maps the IP address 192.168.0.99 to the host name server1.lucernepublishing.com would be represented textually within a zone file as follows:

```
99              PTR     server1.lucernepublishing.com.
```

NOTE WHY IS THE PTR RECORD NAMED 99?

In a reverse lookup zone, the host ID portion of an IPv4 address is equivalent to a host name. The 99 therefore represents the name assigned to the host within the 0.168.192.in-addr.arpa zone. This zone corresponds to the 192.168.0.0 subnet.

SERVICE RESOURCE RECORDS

Service location (SRV) resource records are used to specify the location of specific services in a domain. Client applications that are SRV-aware can use DNS to retrieve the SRV resource records for given application servers.

Active Directory Directory Service (AD DS) is an example of an SRV-aware application. The Netlogon service uses SRV records to locate domain controllers in a domain by searching the domain for the Lightweight Directory Access Protocol (LDAP) service. (LDAP is the protocol used to query AD DS.)

If a computer needs to locate a domain controller in the lucernepublishing.com domain, the DNS client sends an SRV query for the name:

```
_ldap._tcp.lucernepublishing.com.
```

The DNS server then responds to the client with all records matching the query.

Although SRV resource records for AD DS are created automatically, you might need to create SRV records manually for other services or if some records have been accidentally deleted. The following example shows the textual representation of two SRV records that have been configured manually in the DNS Manager console:

```
_ldap._tcp    SRV    0  0 389     dc1.lucernepublishing.com.
              SRV    10 0 389     dc2.lucernepublishing.com.
```

In the example, an LDAP server (domain controller) with a priority of 0 (highest) is mapped to port 389 at the host dc1.lucernepublishing.com. A second domain controller with a lower priority of 10 is mapped to port 389 at the host dc2.lucernepublishing.com. Both entries have a *0* value in the weight field, which means that no load balancing has been configured among servers with equal priority.

Enabling DNS to Use WINS Resolution

You can use the WINS tab in the properties of a zone to specify a WINS server that the DNS Server service can contact to look up names not found through DNS queries. When you specify a WINS server on the WINS tab in the properties of a forward lookup zone, a special WINS resource record pointing to that WINS server is added to the zone. When you specify a WINS server on the WINS tab in a reverse lookup zone, a special WINS-R resource record pointing to that WINS server is added to the zone.

For example, if a DNS client queries for the name ClientZ.contoso.com and the preferred DNS server cannot find the answer through any of its usual sources (local zone data, cache, queries to other servers), the server then queries the WINS server specified in the WINS record for the name "CLIENTZ." If the WINS server responds with an answer to the query, the DNS server returns this response to the original client.

EXAM TIP

For the 70-642 exam, you need to understand the function of the WINS and WINS-R records in a DNS zone.

Aging and Scavenging

Aging in DNS refers to the process of using time stamps to track the age of dynamically registered resource records. *Scavenging* refers to the process of deleting outdated resource records on which time stamps have been placed. Scavenging can occur only when aging is enabled. Together, aging and scavenging provide a mechanism to remove stale resource records, which can accumulate in zone data over time. Both aging and scavenging are disabled by default.

Enabling Aging

To enable aging for a zone, you have to enable this feature either at the server level or at the zone level.

To enable aging at the server level, first open the Server Aging/Scavenging Properties dialog box by right-clicking the server icon in the DNS Manager console tree and then choosing Set Aging/Scavenging For All Zones, as shown in Figure 3-16. Next, in the Server Aging/Scavenging Properties dialog box that opens, select the Scavenge Stale Resource Records check box. Although this setting enables aging and scavenging for all new zones at the server level, it does not automatically enable aging or scavenging on existing Active Directory–integrated zones at the server level. To do that, click OK, and then, in the Server Aging/Scavenging Confirmation dialog box that appears, enable the option to apply these settings to existing Active Directory–integrated zones, as shown in Figure 3-17.

To enable aging and scavenging at the zone level, open the properties of the zone and then, in the General tab, click Aging, as shown in Figure 3-18. Then, in the Zone Aging/Scavenging Properties dialog box that opens, select the Scavenge Stale Resource Records check box, as shown in Figure 3-19.

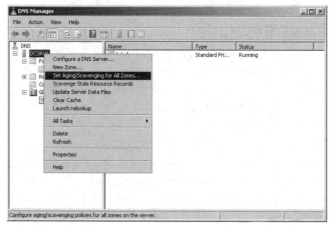

FIGURE 3-16 Enabling aging at the server level

FIGURE 3-17 Enabling aging on Active Directory–integrated zones

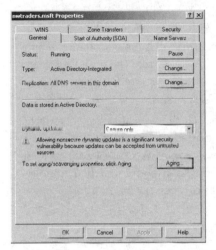

FIGURE 3-18 Accessing aging properties for a zone

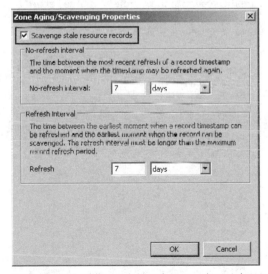

FIGURE 3-19 Enabling aging and scavenging at the zone level

Time Stamping

The DNS server performs aging and scavenging by using time stamp values set on resource records in a zone. Active Directory–integrated zones perform time stamping for dynamically registered records by default, even before aging and scavenging are enabled. However, primary standard zones place time stamps on dynamically registered records in the zone only after aging is enabled. Manually created resource records for all zone types are assigned a time stamp of *0*; this value indicates that they will not be aged.

Modifying Zone Aging/Scavenging Properties

The Zone Aging/Scavenging Properties dialog box enables you to modify two key settings related to aging and scavenging: the no-refresh interval and the refresh interval.

- **Modifying the no-refresh interval**   The *no-refresh interval* is the period after a time stamp during which a zone or server rejects a time stamp refresh. The no-refresh feature prevents the server from processing unnecessary refreshes and reduces unnecessary zone transfer traffic. The default no-refresh interval is 7 days.

- **Modifying the refresh interval**   The *refresh interval* is the time after the no-refresh interval during which time stamp refreshes are accepted and resource records are not scavenged. After the no-refresh and refresh intervals expire, records can be scavenged from the zone. The default refresh interval is 7 days. Consequently, when aging is enabled, dynamically registered resource records can be scavenged after 14 days by default.

Performing Scavenging

Scavenging in a zone is performed either automatically or manually. For scavenging to be performed automatically, you must enable automatic scavenging of stale resource records on the Advanced tab of the DNS server properties dialog box, as shown in Figure 3-20.

FIGURE 3-20 Enabling automatic scavenging on a DNS server

When this feature is not enabled, you can perform manual scavenging in zones by right-clicking the server icon in the DNS Manager console tree and then choosing Scavenge Stale Resource Records, as shown in Figure 3-21.

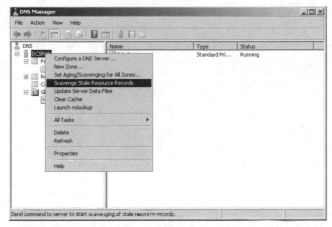

FIGURE 3-21 Performing manual scavenging for zones

✔ **Quick Check**
- What kind of zones do not automatically perform time stamping on dynamically created resource records?

Quick Check Answer
- Standard zones

Using a GlobalNames Zone

Windows Server 2008 and Windows Server 2008 R2 include a new feature that enables all DNS clients in an Active Directory forest to use single-label name tags such as "Mail" to connect to specific server resources located anywhere in the forest. This feature can be useful when the default DNS suffix search list for DNS clients would not enable users to connect quickly (or connect at all) to a resource by using a single-label name.

To support this functionality, the DNS Server role in Windows Server 2008 and Windows Server 2008 R2 includes capability for a GlobalNames zone. The GlobalNames zone does not exist by default, but by deploying a zone with this name you can provide access to selected resources through single-label names without relying on WINS. These single-label names typically refer to records for important, well-known, and widely used servers—servers that are already assigned static IP addresses.

Figure 3-22 shows a GlobalNames zone with a record for a server with a single-label name of "Mail."

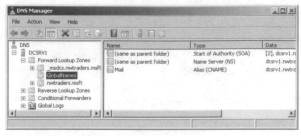

FIGURE 3-22 The GlobalNames zone

Deploying a GlobalNames Zone

The GlobalNames zone is compatible only with DNS servers running Windows Server 2008 and Windows Server 2008 R2. Therefore, it cannot replicate to servers running earlier versions of Windows Server.

There are three basic steps in deploying a GlobalNames zone.

1. Enable GlobalNames zone support. You can perform this step before or after you create the zone, but you must perform it on every DNS server to which the GlobalNames zone will be replicated.

    At an elevated command prompt, type the following:

    ```
    dnscmd . /config /enableglobalnamessupport 1
    ```

    In this case the "." is used to represent the local server. If you want to enable GlobalNames zone support on a remote server, substitute the "." for the DNS server name.

2. Create the GlobalNames zone. The next step in deploying a GlobalNames zone is to create the zone on a DNS server that is a domain controller running Windows Server 2008 or Windows Server 2008 R2. The GlobalNames zone is not a special zone type; rather, it is simply an Active Directory–integrated forward lookup zone that is called GlobalNames. When you create the zone, make sure to select the option to replicate zone data to all DNS servers in the forest. (This option appears on the Active Directory Zone Replication Scope page of the New Zone Wizard.)

3. Populate the GlobalNames zone. For each server for which you want to be able to provide single-label name resolution, create an alias (CNAME) resource record in the GlobalNames zone. The name you give each CNAME record represents the single-label name that users will use to connect to the resource. Note that each CNAME record points to a host record in another zone.

EXAM TIP

Expect to see a question about the GlobalNames zone on the 70-642 exam.

Quick Check

- Why would you use a GlobalNames zone?

Quick Check Answer

- To facilitate the resolution of single-label computer names in a large network.

PRACTICE **Deploying a GlobalNames Zone**

In this practice, you will create the GlobalNames Zone to enable connectivity to a specific single-label name throughout an Active Directory forest.

EXERCISE 1 Enabling the GlobalNames Zone

In this exercise, you will enable the GlobalNames zone on Dcsrv1. In a production environment, you would need to perform this step on every DNS server in the forest.

1. Log on to Nwtraders from Dcsrv1 as a domain administrator.
2. Open an elevated command prompt.
3. At the command prompt, type **dnscmd . /config /enableglobalnamessupport 1**. Note the space in this command after the "." You receive an output message indicating that the Registry property was successfully reset.

EXERCISE 2 Creating the GlobalNames Zone

In this exercise, you will create a new DNS forward lookup zone named GlobalNames on Dcsrv1.

1. While you are logged on to Nwtraders from Dcsrv1 as a domain administrator, open DNS Manager.
2. In the DNS Manager console tree, right-click the Forward Lookup Zones container, and then choose New Zone.
3. On the Welcome page of the New Zone Wizard, read the text, and then click Next.
4. On the Zone Type page, read all the text on the page. Leave the default selections of Primary and Store The Zone In Active Directory, and then click Next.
5. On the Active Directory Zone Replication Scope page, select To All DNS Servers In This Forest, and then click Next.
6. On the Zone Name page, type **GlobalNames**, and then click Next.
7. On the Dynamic Update page, select the Do Not Allow Dynamic Updates option, and then click Next. You should choose the option because dynamic updates are not supported with the GlobalNames zone.
8. After the Completing The New Zone Wizard page, read the text, and then click Finish. In the DNS Manager console tree, the new GlobalNames zone appears.

EXERCISE 3 Adding Records to the GlobalNames Zone

In this exercise, you will add records to the GlobalNames zone so that you can later test its functionality.

1. While you are still logged on to Nwtraders from Dcsrv1 as a domain administrator, in the DNS Manager console tree, select and then right-click the GlobalNames zone, and then choose New Alias (CNAME).

2. In the New Resource Record dialog box, in the Alias Name text box, type **mail**.

3. In the Fully Qualified Domain Name (FQDN) For Target Host text box, type **dcsrv1.nwtraders.msft**, and then click OK. A new alias (CNAME) record with the name "mail" now appears in the GlobalNames zone.

EXERCISE 4 Testing the GlobalNames Zone

In this exercise, you will attempt to resolve the name of the new record you have created. The GlobalNames zone is used to resolve single-name tags anywhere in an Active Directory forest.

1. Log on to Nwtraders from Boston as a domain administrator.

2. Open an elevated command prompt.

3. At the command prompt, type **ping mail**. Boston translates the name "mail" to dcsrv1.nwtraders.msft and then pings the address of that server. You know that this name has been resolved from the GlobalNames zone because there is no record in the Nwtraders.msft zone for a host or an alias named "mail."

4. Log off both Dcsrv1 and Boston.

Lesson Summary

- A DNS zone is a database containing records that associate names with addresses for a defined portion of a DNS namespace. To create a new zone on a DNS server, you can use the New Zone Wizard in DNS Manager. The New Zone Wizard enables you to choose a zone type, specify a forward or reverse lookup zone, set the zone replication scope, name the zone, and configure options for dynamic updates.

- A primary zone provides original read-write source data that allows the local DNS server to answer DNS queries authoritatively about a portion of a DNS namespace. A secondary zone provides an authoritative, read-only copy of a primary zone or another secondary zone. A stub zone is similar to a secondary zone, but it contains only those resource records necessary to identify the authoritative DNS servers for the master zone.

- When you create a new primary or stub zone on a domain controller, the Zone Type page gives you the option to store the zone in Active Directory. There are several advantages to integrating your DNS zone with Active Directory, including ease of management, the availability of multiple primary zones, and improved security.

- When you do not store a zone in Active Directory, the zone is called a standard zone, and zone data is stored in text files on the DNS server.

- When you create a new zone, two types of records required for the zone are automatically created: an SOA record and at least one NS record. The SOA record defines basic properties for the zone. NS records determine which servers hold authoritative information for the zone.

- Aging in DNS refers to the process of using time stamps to track the age of dynamically registered resource records. Scavenging refers to the process of deleting outdated resource records on which time stamps have been placed.

Lesson Review

You can use the following questions to test your knowledge of the information in Lesson 1, "Creating and Configuring Zones." The questions are also available on the companion CD if you prefer to review them in electronic form.

> **NOTE ANSWERS**
>
> Answers to these questions and explanations of why each answer choice is correct or incorrect are located in the "Answers" section at the end of the book.

1. You want to prevent a certain host (A) record from being scavenged. The record belongs to a portable computer named LaptopA that connects to the network only infrequently. LaptopA obtains its address from a DHCP server on the network. Which of the following steps would best enable you to achieve this goal?

   A. Disable scavenging on the zone in which the record has been created.

   B. Disable scavenging on the server with which the computer registers its record.

   C. Assign the computer a static address.

   D. Create a record for LaptopA manually.

2. You are a network administrator for a company named Fabrikam, Inc. A DNS server for the network is located on a member server named Dns1 in the Fabrikam.com Active Directory domain. Dns1 provides name resolution for the Fabrikam.com domain only.

   Occasionally, you see DNS records for unauthorized computers in the Fabrikam.com zone. These computers do not have accounts in the Fabrikam.com Active Directory domain.

   What steps should you take to prevent unauthorized computers from registering host records with the DNS server? (Choose three. Each answer represents part of the solution.)

   A. Promote DNS1 to a domain controller.

   B. Choose the option to store the zone in Active Directory.

   C. Clear the option to store the zone in Active Directory.

   D. Configure the zone not to accept dynamic updates.

   E. Configure the zone to accept secure and nonsecure dynamic updates.

   F. Configure the zone to accept secure updates only.

3. You work for Contoso.com as a network administrator. In your network, you use three servers to distribute the email workload. The contoso.com zone file shows the following data for the three mail servers.

```
@       MX      10      mailserver1.contoso.com.
@       MX      10      mailserver2.contoso.com.
@       MX      10      mailserver3.contoso.com.
```

You want to configure mail servers so that mailserver1 and mailserver2 share the email workload and mailserver3 is used as a backup. What should you do?

A. Create a second, identical MX record for both mailserver1 and mailserver2. Enable round robin on the DNS server.

B. Create a second, identical MX record for both mailserver1 and mailserver2. Disable round robin on the DNS server.

C. Replace the value *10* with *1* in the mailserver3 MX record.

D. Replace the value *10* with *20* in the mailserver3 MX record.

Lesson 2: Configuring Zone Replication, Transfers, and Delegations

To deploy DNS in a medium-to-large sized organization, you need to do more than configure DNS on an individual server. You also have to design DNS in a way that keeps the processing workload and administration workload distributed in a sensible way. For all but the smallest organizations, achieving these goals requires you to deploy more than one DNS server.

To manage your DNS data well and preserve data consistency among multiple servers, you need to understand zone replication, transfers, and delegations.

After this lesson, you will be able to:

- Configure a zone replication scope appropriate to your network.
- Create a new directory partition and enlist a server in that partition.
- Understand the benefits of a secondary zone.
- Implement a secondary zone.
- Understand the benefits of zone delegations.
- Understand the benefits of stub zones.
- Implement a stub zone.
- Enable zone transfers to secondary and stub zones.

Estimated lesson time: 90 minutes

Configuring Zone Replication for Active Directory–Integrated Zones

You can install Active Directory–integrated zones only on domain controllers on which the DNS Server role is installed. Active Directory–integrated zones are generally preferable to standard zones because they offer multimaster data replication, simpler configuration, and improved security and efficiency. With Active Directory–integrated storage, DNS clients can send updates to any Active Directory–integrated DNS server. These updates are then copied to other Active Directory–integrated DNS servers by means of Active Directory replication.

Replication and Application Directory Partitions

DNS data for any particular zone can be replicated among domain controllers in a number of ways, depending on the application directory partition on which the DNS zone data is stored.

DOMAINDNSZONES AND FORESTDNSZONES

A *partition* is a data structure in Active Directory that distinguishes data for different replication purposes. By default, domain controllers include two application directory partitions reserved for DNS data: DomainDnsZones and ForestDnsZones. The DomainDnsZones partition is replicated among all domain controllers that are also DNS servers in a particular domain, and the ForestDnsZones partition is replicated among all domain controllers that are also DNS servers in every domain in an Active Directory forest.

Each of these application directory partitions is designated by a DNS subdomain and an FQDN. For example, in an Active Directory domain named east.nwtraders.msft and whose root domain in the Active Directory forest is nwtraders.msft, the built-in DNS application partition directories are specified by these FQDNs: DomainDnsZones.east.nwtraders.msft and ForestDnsZones.nwtraders.msft.

You can see evidence of these partitions when you browse DNS Manager, as shown in Figure 3-23. Note that the ForestDnsZones name is located in the nwtraders.msft zone. Note also that each zone includes a DomainDnsZones name that points to the partition that is replicated only within each local domain.

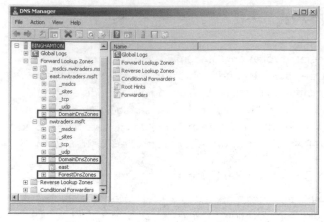

FIGURE 3-23 You can see evidence of the built-in directory partitions for DNS within an Active Directory–integrated zone.

CUSTOM APPLICATION DIRECTORY PARTITIONS

In addition to the two application directory partition types DomainDnsZones and ForestDnsZones, you can create a custom (user-defined) application directory partition with a name of your own choosing. You can then configure a zone to be stored in this new structure that you created. By default, the new application directory partition exists only on the server on which you created the partition, but you can enlist other servers in the partition so that replication of its data content are copied to those particular servers you choose.

The replication pattern displayed by these three application data partition types—DomainDnsZones, ForestDnsZones, and custom—is illustrated in Figure 3-24.

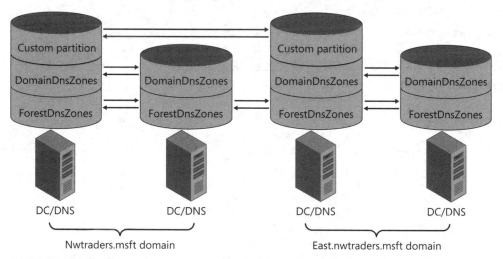

FIGURE 3-24 Replication patterns among application directory partitions

STORING DNS DATA IN THE DOMAIN PARTITION

The final storage option for an Active Directory–integrated zone is to store the zone in the domain partition along with all remaining data for a domain. In this configuration, the DNS data does not replicate merely to domain controllers that are also DNS servers; it replicates to all domain controllers in general in the local domain. This option is not ideal because it generates unnecessary replication traffic. However, you need to use it if you want your DNS data to be replicated to computers running Windows 2000 Server.

Choosing Zone Replication Scope

The partition in which a zone is stored effectively determines the replication scope for that zone. Replication scope is set when an Active Directory–integrated zone is first created. When you use Dcpromo to promote a server to a domain controller in a new domain, the new Active Directory–integrated zone created for the domain is stored automatically in the DomainDnsZones partition. However, when you create a new zone by using the New Zone Wizard instead, you are given an opportunity on the Active Directory Zone Replication Scope page to choose the partition in which to store the zone, as shown in Figure 3-25.

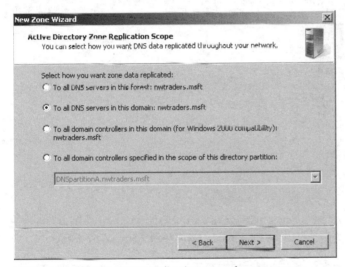

FIGURE 3-25 Choosing zone replication scope for a new zone

The four options presented on the Active Directory Zone Replication Scope page are the following:

- **To All DNS Servers In This Forest** This option stores the new zone in the ForestDnsZones partition. Every domain controller in the entire forest and on which the DNS Server role is installed will receive a copy of the zone.

- **To All DNS Servers In This Domain** This option stores the new zone in the Domain-DnsZones partition. Every domain controller in the local domain and on which the DNS Server role is installed will receive a copy of the zone.

- **To All Domain Controllers In This Domain (For Windows 2000 Compatibility)** This option stores the zone in the domain partition. Every domain controller in the local domain will receive a copy of the zone, regardless of whether the DNS Server role is installed on that domain controller. This setting is required for compatibility with Windows 2000 Server domain controllers because Windows 2000 Server does not support directory partitions.

- **To All Domain Controllers Specified In The Scope Of This Directory Partition** This option stores the zone in the user-created application directory partition specified in the associated drop-down list box. For a domain controller to fall within the scope of such a directory partition, you must manually enlist that domain controller in the partition.

After a new zone is created, you can choose to change the replication scope for the zone at any time. To do so, on the General tab of the properties of the zone, click the Change button associated with replication, as shown in Figure 3-26.

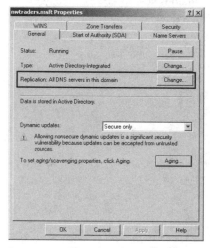

FIGURE 3-26 Changing the replication scope of an existing zone

This step opens the Change Zone Replication Scope dialog box, which, as shown in Figure 3-27, provides the same zone replication scope options that the New Zone Wizard does.

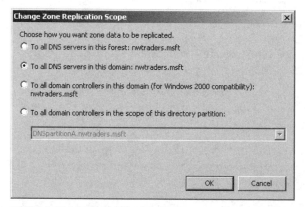

FIGURE 3-27 Modifying the replication scope for an existing zone

When deciding which replication scope to choose, consider that the broader the replication scope, the greater the network traffic caused by replication. For example, if you choose to have Active Directory–integrated DNS zone data replicated to all DNS servers in the forest, this setting produces greater network traffic than does replicating the DNS zone data to all DNS servers in the local domain only. On the other hand, replicating zone data to all DNS servers in a forest can improve forest-wide name resolution performance and increase fault tolerance.

> **NOTE RE-CREATING DOMAINDNSZONES AND FORESTDNSZONES**
>
> If either of the default application directory partitions is deleted or damaged, you can re-create them in DNS Manager by right-clicking the server node and choosing Create Default Application Directory Partitions.

Creating Custom Application Directory Partitions

You can create your own custom application directory partitions for use with DNS and then enlist selected domain controllers in your network to host replicas of this partition.

To accomplish this task, first create the partition by typing the following command:

```
dnscmd servername /createdirectorypartition FQDN
```

Then enlist other DNS servers in the partition by typing the following command:

```
dnscmd servername /enlistdirectorypartition FQDN
```

For example, to create an application directory partition named DNSpartitionA on a computer named Server1 in the Active Directory domain contoso.com, type the following command:

```
dnscmd server1 /createdirectorypartition DNSpartitionA.contoso.com
```

> **NOTE USE A DOT (".") FOR THE LOCAL SERVER NAME**
>
> You can substitute a "." for the server name if you are executing the command on the same server on which you want to create the partition.

To enlist a computer named Server2 in the application directory partition, type the following command:

```
dnscmd server2 /enlistdirectorypartition DNSpartitionA.contoso.com
```

> **NOTE WHO CAN CREATE A CUSTOM APPLICATION DIRECTORY PARTITION?**
>
> You must be a member of the Enterprise Admins group to create an application directory partition.

After you create a new application directory partition, that partition will appear as an option in the drop-down list box both on the Active Directory Zone Replication Scope page of the New Zone Wizard and in the Change Zone Replication Scope dialog box. To store a zone in the new partition, choose To All Domain Controllers Specified In The Scope Of This Directory Partition and then select the partition in the drop-down list box.

Using Zone Transfers

When all your DNS servers are located on domain controllers, you will normally want to use Active Directory replication to keep zone data consistent among all DNS servers. However, this option is not available when you install a DNS server on a computer that is not a domain controller. In such cases, you cannot store the zone in Active Directory and instead must use a standard zone that stores data in a local text file on each DNS server. If your organization requires multiple DNS servers, the source data can be copied to read-only secondary zones hosted on other servers. To keep data consistent and up to date between a primary and any secondary zones, you need to configure zone transfers.

Zone transfers are essentially pull operations initiated on secondary zones that copy zone data from a master zone, which itself can be a primary or another secondary. In fact, the master zone for a secondary zone need not even be another standard zone—you can configure a secondary zone for an Active Directory–integrated primary zone. This arrangement might be suitable, for example, if you have two sites, one in New York and one in Los Angeles, each with its own Active Directory domain. In each domain, you might want to provide name resolution for the opposite domain without installing a new domain controller and managing replication traffic between the two sites. Such an infrastructure is illustrated in Figure 3-28.

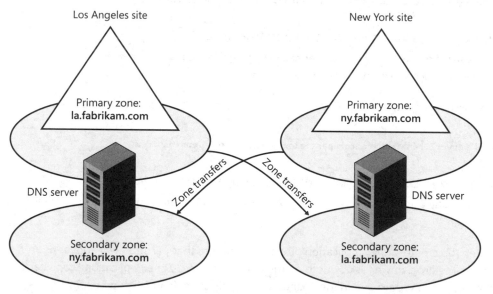

FIGURE 3-28 A DNS infrastructure with zone transfers between sites

Zone Transfer Initiation

Any of three events can trigger zone transfers on secondary zones:

- When the refresh interval of the primary zone's SOA resource record expires
- When a server hosting a secondary zone boots up
- When a change occurs in the configuration of the primary zone and this primary zone is configured to notify a secondary zone of zone updates

In the first two cases, the secondary server initiates a query to find out whether any updates in the zone have occurred. This information is determined by comparing the serial number (specified in the SOA record) of the secondary zone to the serial number of the master zone. If the master zone has a higher serial number, the secondary zone initiates a transfer from the master.

Enabling Zone Transfers

By default, zone transfers are disabled from any zone, and you must enable them on the Zone Transfers tab of the zone properties dialog box, as shown in Figure 3-29. After you have selected the option to allow zone transfers from the zone, you have a choice of three suboptions:

- **To Any Server** This option is the least secure. Because a zone transfer is essentially a copy of zone data, this setting allows anyone with network access to the DNS server to discover the complete contents of the zone, including all server and computer names along with their IP addresses. This option should therefore be used only in private networks with a high degree of security.

- **Only To Servers Listed On The Name Servers Tab** This option restricts zone transfers only to secondary DNS servers that have an NS record in the zone and are therefore already authoritative for zone data.

- **Only To The Following Servers** This option allows you to specify a list of secondary servers to which you will allow zone transfers. The secondary servers do not need to be identified by an NS record in the zone.

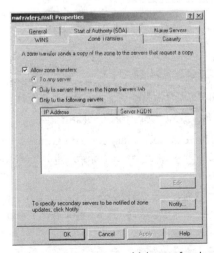

FIGURE 3-29 A zone on which transfers have been enabled

Configuring Notifications

The Zone Transfers tab also allows you to configure notification to secondary servers whenever a change occurs at the primary zone. Zone transfers are pull operations and cannot be initiated from the master to push new data to secondary zones. However, when a modification occurs in zone data, you can configure a primary zone to send a notification to any specified servers hosting secondary zones. When the secondary zone receives this notification, it initiates a zone transfer.

To configure notifications, click Notify on the Zone Transfers tab when zone transfers are enabled. This action opens the Notify dialog box, shown in Figure 3-30, in which you can specify secondary servers that should be notified whenever a zone update occurs at the local master server. By default, when zone transfers are enabled, all servers listed on the Name Servers tab are automatically notified of zone changes.

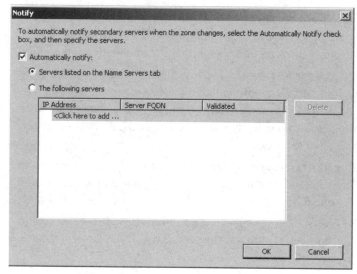

FIGURE 3-30 Notify dialog box

Manually Updating a Secondary Zone

By right-clicking a secondary zone in the DNS Manager console tree, you can use the shortcut menu to perform the following secondary zone update operations:

- **Reload**   This operation reloads the secondary zone from the local storage.

- **Transfer From Master**   The server hosting the local secondary zone determines whether the serial number in the secondary zone's SOA resource record has expired and then pulls a zone transfer from the master server.

- **Transfer New Copy Of Zone From Master**   This operation performs a zone transfer from the secondary zone's master server regardless of the serial number in the secondary zone's SOA resource record.

Understanding Zone Delegations

To delegate a zone is to create a new zone for a subdomain within a DNS namespace and relinquish authority of that new zone. For example, the organization VeriSign manages the top-level domain "com" and creates new zones for subdomains such as microsoft.com. These child zones are then managed by the private organizations that have purchased the associated portion of the public DNS namespace. Delegations also appear within a single organization. For example, a company owning the domain contoso.com can delegate subdomains such as asia.contoso.com and eu.contoso.com to its various regional offices.

When to Delegate Zones

DNS delegations are automatically used to separate parent and child AD DS domains in a single forest. For example, if your organization originally includes a single AD DS domain northwindtraders.com and then creates a second child AD DS domain named ny.northwindtraders.com, the DNS namespace of the new child AD DS domain will automatically be configured as a new DNS zone and delegated subdomain of the parent zone. The authoritative DNS data for all computers in the child domain will be stored on DNS servers in that new AD DS domain.

Outside of an AD DS infrastructure, you should consider delegating a zone within your network whenever any of the following conditions are present:

- You need to delegate management of a DNS domain to a branch or department within your organization.
- You need to distribute the load of maintaining one large DNS database among multiple name servers to improve name resolution performance and fault tolerance.
- You need hosts and host names to be structured according to branch or departmental affiliation within your organization.

Above all, when choosing how to structure zones, you should use a plan that reflects the structure of your organization.

How Delegations Work

For a delegation to be implemented, the parent zone must contain an NS record and an associated A record (called a *glue record*) pointing to each authoritative server of the delegated domain. These records are necessary both to transfer authority to the new name servers and to provide referrals to other servers querying for names in the delegated namespace.

Figure 3-31 illustrates how DNS queries are handled with delegated subdomains. In the figure, a local DNS server named ns.contoso.com is authoritative for the domain contoso.com and has a configured delegation for the subdomain asia.contoso.com. If a client queries this local DNS server for the FQDN "hk4.asia.contoso.com", the server consults the locally stored NS and A records that are configured for the delegation to determine that the authoritative name server for the asia.contoso.com domain is ns1.asia.contoso.com, and that this server's IP address is 192.168.3.5. The local DNS server then queries ns1.asia.contoso.com for the name "hk4.asia.contoso.com". After the remote DNS server receives the query, it consults its locally stored database and responds to the querying DNS server with the IP address of the host hk4.asia.contoso.com, which is 192.168.3.10. The local DNS server then responds to the original querying client with the information requested.

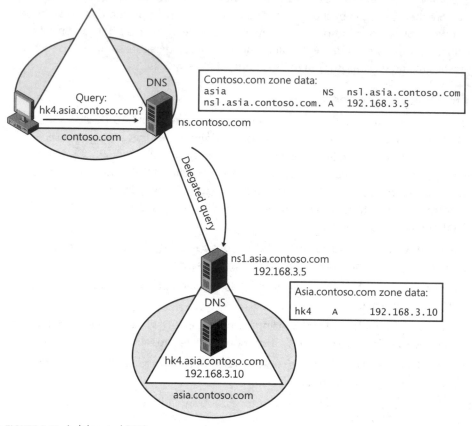

FIGURE 3-31 A delegated DNS query

Creating a Zone Delegation

To create a zone delegation, the domain to be delegated must already be created on a remote server that is authoritative for the DNS subdomain. Then, run the New Delegation Wizard on the server hosting the parent zone by right-clicking the parent zone folder in the DNS console and selecting New Delegation, as shown in Figure 3-32.

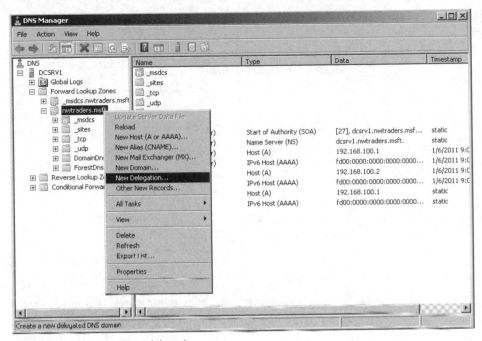

FIGURE 3-32 Creating a new delegation

To complete the New Delegation Wizard, you will need to specify the name of the delegated subdomain and the name of at least one name server that will be authoritative for the new zone. After you run the wizard, a new folder will appear in the DNS console tree representing the newly delegated subdomain.

Implementing Stub Zones

As you learned earlier, a stub zone is a copy of a zone that contains only the most basic records in the master zone. The purpose of a stub zone is to enable the local DNS server to forward queries to the name servers authoritative for the master zone. In this way, a stub zone is functionally similar to a zone delegation. However, because stub zones can initiate and receive zone transfers from the master (delegated) zone, stub zones provide the added benefit of informing parent zones of updates in the NS records of child zones.

An example of a stub zone is shown in Figure 3-33.

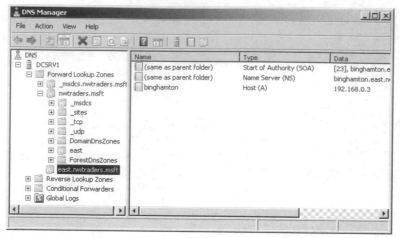

FIGURE 3-33 East.nwtraders.msft is a stub zone of a child zone hosted on remote server.

You can use stub zones to do the following:

- **Keep delegated zone information current**   In a delegation scenario, a stub zone helps a parent zone stay up-to-date about the authoritative name servers for a delegated (child) subdomain.

- **Improve name resolution**   Stub zones enable a DNS server to perform recursion using the stub zone's list of name servers without having to query the Internet or an internal server within the local DNS namespace. When stub zones are deployed for this reason, they are deployed not between parent and child zones but rather across domains in a large Active Directory forest or DNS namespace.

Stub Zone Example

Suppose that you are an administrator for the DNS server named Dns1.contoso.com, which is authoritative for the zone Contoso.com. Your company includes a child Active Directory domain, India.contoso.com, for which a delegation has been performed. When the delegation is originally performed, the child zone (which is Active Directory–integrated) contains only two authoritative DNS servers: 192.168.2.1 and 192.168.2.2. Later, administrators of the India. contoso.com domain deploy additional domain controllers and install the DNS Server role on these new domain controllers. However, these same administrators do not notify you of the addition of more authoritative DNS servers in their domain. As a result, Dns1.contoso.com is not configured with the records of the new DNS servers authoritative for India.contoso.com and continues to query only the two DNS servers that were defined in the original delegation.

You can remedy this problem by configuring Dns1.contoso.com to host a stub zone for India.contoso.com. As a result of this new stub zone, Dns1 learns through zone transfers about the new name servers authoritative for the India.contoso.com child zone. Dns1 is thus able to direct queries for names within the India.contoso.com namespace to all of that child zone's authoritative DNS servers.

This example is illustrated in Figure 3-34.

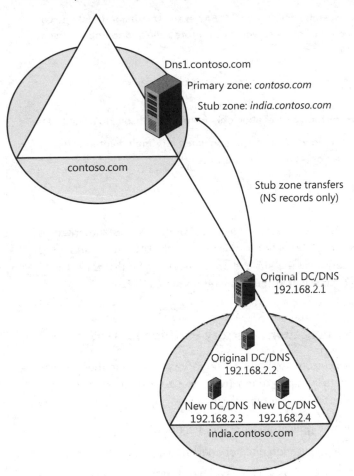

FIGURE 3-34 Stub zones enable a parent domain to keep an updated list of name servers in a child domain.

Other Uses for Stub Zones

Another use for stub zones is to facilitate name resolution across domains in a manner that avoids searching the DNS namespace for a common parent server. Stub zones can thus replace secondary zones in situations where achieving DNS connectivity across domains is important but providing data redundancy for the master zone is not. Also note that stub zones improve name resolution and eliminate the burden on network resources that would otherwise result from large zone transfers.

Quick Check

1. True or False: You can perform a delegation only from a parent zone to a child zone.

2. Why does a stub zone improve name resolution when it is implemented across domains in a large forest or other DNS namespace?

Quick Check Answers

1. True.

2. A stub zone provides a DNS server with the names of servers that are authoritative for a given zone. When this information is stored locally, the DNS server does not need to query other servers to find the authoritative servers for that zone. The process of resolving a name in that zone is therefore more efficient.

PRACTICE **Creating an Application Directory Partition for DNS**

In this practice, you will create a custom application directory partition and then modify the Nwtraders.msft zone to store data in that partition. (Note that zone data can be stored only in directory partitions for Active Directory–integrated zones.)

EXERCISE 1 Creating the New Application Directory Partition

In this exercise, you will create an application directory partition on Dcsrv1.

1. Log on to Nwtraders from Dcsrv1 as a domain administrator.

2. At an elevated command prompt, type the following:

   `dnscmd . /createdirectorypartition DNSpartitionA.nwtraders.msft`

   This command creates an application directory partition that will replicate in Active Directory only to domain controllers that you enlist in the partition. You do not need to enlist the local server in the partition.

EXERCISE 2 Storing Zone Data in the New Application Directory Partition

In this exercise, you will modify the properties of the Nwtraders.msft zone so that its data is stored in the new application directory partition you have just created.

1. While you are logged on to Nwtraders from Dcsrv1 as a domain administrator, open DNS Manager.

2. In the DNS Manager console tree, expand the Forward Lookup Zones folder, select and then right-click the Nwtraders.msft zone, and then choose Properties.

3. On the General tab of the Nwtraders.msft Properties dialog box, click the Change button for replication. This button is directly to the right of the text Replication: All DNS Servers In This Domain.

4. In the Change Zone Replication Scope dialog box that opens, select To All Domain Controllers In The Scope Of This Directory Partition.

5. In the associated drop-down list box, select DNSpartitionA.nwtraders.msft, and then click OK.

6. In the Nwtraders.msft Properties dialog box, click OK. The Nwtraders.msft zone data is now stored in the new application directory partition you created on Dcsrv1. Other domain controllers that are DNS servers in the Nwtraders.msft forest will receive a copy of the Nwtraders.msft primary zone only if you later enlist those servers in the new partition by using the following command:

```
dnscmd <server name> /enlistdirectorypartition DNSpartitionA.nwtraders.msft
```

PRACTICE Deploying a Secondary Zone

In this practice, you will create a secondary DNS zone for Nwtraders.msft on the Boston server. Because the Boston server is not a domain controller, it cannot host an Active Directory–integrated copy of the Nwtraders.msft primary zone. In a production environment, you might choose to install a secondary zone when you want to install a DNS server without installing a domain controller.

EXERCISE 1 Adding the DNS Server Role

In this exercise, you will install the DNS server role on the Boston server.

1. Log on to Nwtraders from Boston as a domain administrator.

2. If the Initial Configuration Tasks window appears, click Add Roles. Otherwise, open Server Manager and click Add Roles in the details pane.

3. On the Before You Begin page of the Add Roles Wizard, click Next.

4. On the Select Server Roles page, select the DNS Server check box, and then click Next.

5. On the DNS Server page, read all the text, and then click Next.

6. On the Confirm Installation Selections page, click Install.

7. After the installation completes, on the Installation Results page, click Close.

EXERCISE 2 Creating the Secondary Zone

In this exercise, you will create a secondary zone named Nwtraders.msft on Boston.nwtraders.msft.

1. While you are still logged on to Nwtraders from Boston as a domain administrator, open DNS Manager.

2. Expand the DNS Manager console tree.

3. In the DNS Manager console tree, select and then right-click the Forward Lookup Zones folder, and then choose New Zone. The Welcome page of the New Zone Wizard appears. Click Next.

4. On the Zone Type page, read all the text, and then select Secondary Zone. Note that the option to store the zone in Active Directory is dimmed. This choice is unavailable because the local computer is not a domain controller. Click Next.

5. On the Zone Name page, in the Zone Name text box, type **nwtraders.msft**. Click Next.

6. On the Master DNS Servers page, read the text on the page.

7. In the Master Servers area, type **192.168.0.1**, and then press Enter.

8. Wait about 30 seconds for the name DCSRV1 to appear beneath the Server FQDN heading in the Master Servers area. Click Next.

9. On the Completing The New Zone Wizard page, click Finish. The new zone now appears in DNS Manager.

10. In the DNS Manager console tree, select the Nwtraders.msft forward lookup zone. An error message that appears in the details pane indicates that the zone is not loaded by the DNS server. The problem is that you have not enabled zone transfers in the properties of the primary zone on Dcsrv1.

EXERCISE 3 Enabling Zone Transfers to the Secondary Zone

In this exercise, you will enable zone transfers to the Boston computer from Dcsrv1.

1. Log on to Nwtraders from Dcsrv1 as a domain administrator.

2. Open DNS Manager.

3. Expand the DNS Manager console tree.

4. Right-click the Nwtraders.msft forward lookup zone, and then choose Properties.

5. In the Nwtraders.msft Properties dialog box, click the Zone Transfers tab.

6. On the Zone Transfers tab, select the Allow Zone Transfers check box.

7. Verify that To Any Server is selected, and then click OK.

EXERCISE 4 Transferring the Zone Data

In this exercise, you will load the zone data from the primary zone to the secondary zone. You will perform this exercise while logged on to Nwtraders from the Boston computer as a domain administrator.

1. On Boston, in the DNS Manager console tree, right-click the Nwtraders.msft forward lookup zone, and then choose Transfer From Master. If you see an error, wait 15 seconds, and then press F5 or select Refresh from the Action menu.

2. The Nwtraders.msft zone data eventually appears in the details pane of DNS Manager. Note that the application directory partition DNSpartitionA appears above DomainDNSZones and ForestDNSZones.

EXERCISE 5   Creating an NS Record for the Server Hosting the Secondary Zone

In this exercise, you will create an NS record for the Boston DNS server in the primary zone. Note that you cannot create an NS record for a secondary zone server from within the secondary zone itself because a secondary zone is a read-only copy of the zone.

You perform this exercise while logged on to Nwtraders from Dcsrv1 as a domain administrator.

1. On Dcrsv1, in the DNS Manager console tree, select the Nwtraders.msft zone. In the details pane, note that the only name server (NS) record included in the zone points to dcsrv1.nwtraders.msft. The fact that there is only one such NS record means that even if the DNS domain were connected to a larger DNS namespace, information about names in the Nwtraders.msft domain will always originate from Dcsrv1.

2. In the detail pane, double-click the NS record. The Nwtraders.msft Properties dialog box opens, and the Name Servers tab is selected.

3. Click the Add button.

4. In the New Name Server Record dialog box, in the Server Fully Qualified Domain Name (FQDN) text box, type **boston.nwtraders.msft**, and then click Resolve. The name is resolved to an IPv6 address and an IPv4 address.

5. In the New Name Server Record dialog box, click OK.

6. In the Nwtraders.msft Properties dialog box, click the Zone Transfers tab.

7. Select Only To Servers Listed On The Name Servers Tab. This setting provides security for the zone by restricting copies (transfers) of the zone data to only authorized servers.

8. In the Nwtraders.msft Properties dialog box, click OK. In the details pane of DNS Manager, a new NS record appears that points to boston.nwtraders.msft.

9. Close all windows and log off both servers.

Lesson Summary

- Zone replication refers to the synchronization of zone data for Active Directory–integrated zones. Zone transfers refer to the synchronization of zone data between any master and a secondary standard zone.

- A partition is a data structure in Active Directory that distinguishes data for different replication purposes. By default, domain controllers include two application directory partitions reserved for DNS data: DomainDnsZones and ForestDnsZones. The DomainDnsZones partition is replicated among all domain controllers that are also DNS servers in a particular domain, and the ForestDnsZones partition is replicated among all domain controllers that are also DNS servers in every domain in an Active Directory forest.

- You can also create a user-defined directory partition with a name of your choice. You can then configure a zone to be stored in this new structure that you have created.

- The partition in which a zone is stored effectively determines the replication scope for that zone.

- Zone transfers are essentially pull operations initiated on secondary zones that copy zone data from a master zone, which itself can be a primary zone or another secondary zone. By default, zone transfers are disabled from any zone and you must enable them on the Zone Transfers tab of the zone properties dialog box.

- A delegation is a subdomain of a parent zone that has been created as a new, separately administered zone and for which minimal records still appear in the parent zone. A delegation enables a parent zone to direct queries intended for the subdomain to the authoritative servers of that subdomain.

- You can use stub zones to keep delegated zone information current or to improve name resolution across domains in a large DNS namespace.

Lesson Review

You can use the following questions to test your knowledge of the information in Lesson 2. The questions are also available on the companion CD if you prefer to review them in electronic form.

> **NOTE ANSWERS**
>
> Answers to these questions and explanations of why each answer choice is correct or incorrect are located in the "Answers" section at the end of the book.

1. You are a network administrator for a large company named Northwind Traders that has many branch offices worldwide. You work at the New York office, which has its own Active Directory domain, ny.us.nwtraders.msft.

   Recently you have noticed that when users in the New York office want to connect to resources located in the uk.eu.nwtraders.msft domain, name resolution for computer names in the remote domain is very slow. You want to improve name resolution response times for names within uk.eu.nwtraders.msft domain by keeping an updated list of remote name servers authoritative for that domain name. You also want to minimize zone transfer traffic. What should you do?

   A. Create a stub zone of the uk.eu.nwtraders.msft domain on the DNS servers at the New York office.

   B. Configure conditional forwarding so that queries for names within the uk.eu .nwtraders.msft domain are automatically forwarded to the name servers in that domain.

   C. Create a secondary zone of the uk.eu.nwtraders.msft domain on the DNS servers at the New York office.

   D. Perform a delegation of the uk.eu.nwtraders.msft domain on the DNS servers at the New York office.

2. You recently migrated a DNS zone named Contoso.com to a domain controller running Windows Server 2008 R2. You have selected the option to store the zone in Active Directory, but you find that the zone does not appear on a domain controller named DC2000 that is running Windows 2000 Server in the same domain. DC2000 is already configured with the DNS server component.

   You want the zone to appear on the DC2000 domain controller in the Contoso.com domain. What should you do?

   A. Choose the option to store the zone in all DNS servers in the forest.

   B. Choose the option to store the zone in all DNS servers in the domain.

   C. Choose the option to store the zone in all domain controllers in the domain.

   D. Create a new directory partition, and then choose the option to store the zone in the new partition.

3. The server ns1.contoso.com acts as the DNS server in the contoso.com domain. You create a new secondary zone for the domain on a server named ns2.contoso.com and specify ns1.contoso.com as the master. However, whenever you attempt to populate the zone in DNS Manager by selecting Transfer From Master from the Action menu, you see only a red "x" mark on the zone folder, and no data appears.

   You want to populate the secondary zone with data from the master zone. What should you do?

   A. Select Reload from the Action menu in DNS Manager.

   B. Select Transfer New Copy Of Zone From Master from the Action menu in DNS Manager.

   C. Configure ns1.contoso.com to allow zone transfers.

   D. Configure ns1.contoso.com to perform notifications, and add ns2.contoso.com to the list of servers to notify.

Lesson 3: Implementing DNSSEC

DNS does not strongly validate the source of the information received through its queries. As a result, attackers can use methods such as DNS cache poisoning to provide forged data to DNS clients and trick these clients into visiting spoofed sites or addresses.

DNSSEC was created to stop the threat of forged DNS data. DNSSEC is an optional DNS server feature that provides digital signatures for its records and validates the signatures received from other DNSSEC-enabled servers. In Windows networks, DNSSEC is used as a server-to-server protocol that validates responses on behalf of Windows 7 clients.

Support for the latest version of DNSSEC is new to Windows Server 2008 R2 and Windows 7.

Understanding Public Key Cryptography in DNSSEC

DNSSEC validates information by using public key cryptography. To understand DNSSEC, therefore, you need to review some basic concepts related to this technology, such as key pairs, digital signatures, and trust relationships.

Understanding Key Pairs

Public key cryptography provides *asymmetric encryption*, which means that separate keys are used to encrypt and decrypt data. These separate keys amount to a unique *key pair* generated by each organization that wants to send or receive encrypted data with the public. One of these two keys, the *public key*, is validated and shared freely with the world, but the *private key* is kept secret. Either key may be used to encrypt or decrypt data. However, as illustrated in Figure 3-35, data encrypted by the public key can be decrypted only by the corresponding private key, and data encrypted by the private key can be decrypted only by the corresponding public key.

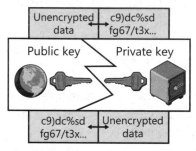

FIGURE 3-35 A key pair is used to encrypt and decrypt data.

In Windows Server 2008 R2, key pairs are generated by using the Dnscmd command in a manner described in the section "Generating Key Pairs" later in this lesson. After you run the command, public keys needed for DNSSEC are made available to the world in DNS zones and are stored in a resource record type called a DNSKEY. The private keys are stored in the local certificate store on the server on which the command is run, but you can export these private keys to a disk or another safe location.

Understanding Digital Signatures

A *digital signature* is a version of some unit of data, such as a specific file, that an organization has encrypted with its private key. This signature is then delivered to another party along with the original unencrypted version of the same data. The receiving party decrypts the encrypted data by using the sender's validated public key and compares the result to the original unencrypted data. If the two data sets match, the data is authenticated as truly originating from that organization. The signature check also effectively ensures that the data is unmodified from the original version that was signed. In this way, digital signatures use public key cryptography to prove that information is unspoofed and unchanged.

The procedure of creating and validating a digital signature is illustrated by an example shown in Figure 3-36. In the figure, Contoso.com creates a signature of a file by encrypting the file with its private key. The original file and the signature are then sent to another party, Nwtraders.com, who needs to verify that the file is authentic and unchanged. Nwtraders.com uses the validated public key for Contoso.com to decrypt the signature. If the decrypted signature matches the original file exactly, the file is effectively authenticated.

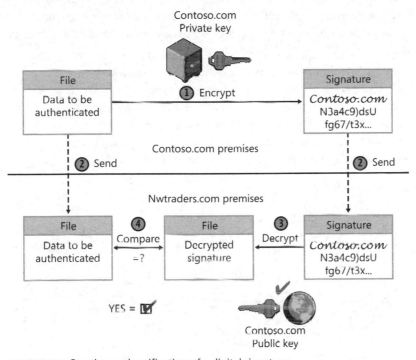

FIGURE 3-36 Creation and verification of a digital signature

Understanding DNSSEC Trust Relationships

DNSSEC in Windows Server 2008 R2 allows a DNS server to validate DNS data on behalf of its Windows 7 clients. When a DNSSEC-enabled DNS server receives a query that it cannot answer immediately, it first contacts other DNS servers to obtain the queried-for data and then verifies the digital signatures associated with that data before responding to the client.

However, a digital signature alone is not sufficient to authenticate data to other DNS servers. A spoofing DNS server could use its own private key to sign false records and present public keys claiming to belong to another source. In order for the data to be truly validated, therefore, the public key itself needs to be validated by other DNS servers through a trust relationship, either directly or indirectly.

Trust anchors are used with DNSSEC to establish trust relationships between DNS servers. A *trust anchor* is a public key for a remote DNS server that is trusted and able to provide DNSSEC responses.

When you configure a local DNS server with a trust anchor for a remote DNS server, the local DNS server is able to validate the DNS information for the zone(s) for which that remote server is authoritative. In addition, through a chain of trust relationships, the local server is also able to validate the data from any delegated DNS subdomains that also can provide DNSSEC responses.

Figure 3-37 illustrates how trust anchors extend DNSSEC validation. The DNS server authoritative for nwtraders.com is configured with a trust anchor for the DNS server authoritative for contoso.com. This latter DNS server has two delegated subdomains, one of which, asia.contoso.com, is also configured with DNSSEC. As a result of these configured trust relationships, the DNS server at nwtraders.com is able to provide DNSSEC validation to its clients for queries related to both the contoso.com domain and the asia.constoso.com domain. Validated responses are not possible, however, for the uk.contoso.com domain.

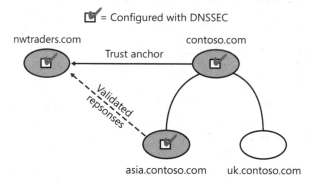

FIGURE 3-37 Trust anchors extend DNSSEC validation to remote domains and their DNSSEC-compatible subdomains.

Understanding DNSSEC Name Resolution

In Microsoft's implementation of DNSSEC, a client does not validate DNS responses received from its local server. Instead, Windows 7 clients request DNSSEC from their local Windows Server 2008 R2 server, which then uses DNSSEC to validate only the responses obtained from other servers.

Windows 7 clients can be configured to request DNSSEC through the Name Resolution Policy Table (NRPT) in Group Policy. The NRPT allows you to specify the DNS query suffixes, prefixes, FQDNs, or reverse lookup subnets for which a Windows 7 or Windows Server 2008 R2 client will request DNSSEC. (Note that you can also use the NRPT to enforce IPsec between the local DNS client and the local DNS server; this configuration essentially authenticates the local DNS server and prevents man-in-the-middle attacks.)

The next series of figures illustrates an example of a name resolution procedure with DNSSEC. In Figure 3-38, a Windows 7 client named client1.nwtraders.com needs to query its DNS server for the name www.ny.contoso.com. DNSSEC in this example validates four elements in a row: the zone delegation from contoso.com to ny.contoso.com, the Key Signing Key from ny.contoso.com, the Zone Signing Key from ny.contoso.com, and finally the host record for www.ny.contoso.com.

In step 1, the client first checks its NRPT to determine whether this query should be performed with a request for DNSSEC. The NRPT includes an entry for the suffix contoso.com, so in step 2, the client queries the local server at ns1.nwtraders.com for the name www.ny.contoso.com with a request for DNSSEC validation.

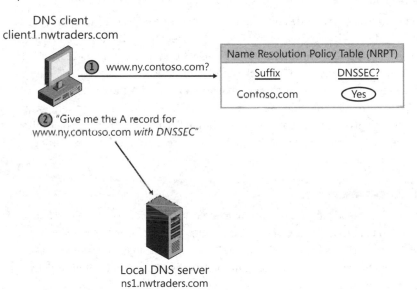

FIGURE 3-38 DNSSEC validation begins when a Windows 7 client checks its NRPT before querying the local DNS server.

In Figure 3-39, the local DNS server at ns1.nwtraders.com confirms in step 3 that it has a trust anchor for contoso.com, which is a parent DNS domain of the target domain ny.contoso.com. Then, in step 4, the local DNS server forwards the query to the server authoritative for contoso.com, the address of which has been configured as a conditional forwarder for that domain.

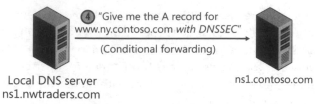

FIGURE 3-39 DNSSEC requires the local DNS server to have a trust anchor configured for the queried-for domain or parent domain.

In step 5, shown in Figure 3-40, ns1.contoso.com responds to ns1.nwtraders.com with information about the DNS server authoritative for the delegated subdomain ny.contoso.com. As with a normal DNS query, this information is contained in the NS and A records.

In addition, ns1.contoso.com provides two additional records for DNSSEC whose purpose is to validate the DNS delegation: a Delegation Signer (DS) record and a Resource Record Signature (RRSIG) record. DS records appear in parent DNS domains and include a SHA-1 or SHA-256 hash of the public key used in a delegated subdomain that is also DNSSEC-compatible. In this case, the DS record includes a hash of a particular public key called a Key Signing Key (KSK) from ny.contoso.com. (This hash will later be used to authenticate the KSK obtained directly from the ny.contoso.com domain.) The RRSIG record is a digital signature of this latter DS record. It is signed by contoso.com to enable others to verify that the DS record is authentic and unchanged.

NOTE **WHAT ARE THE KSK AND ZSK?**

Zones that are digitally signed typically use two separate key pairs and, therefore, two public keys. The KSK is updated rarely and is stored in other zones as a DS record or trust anchor. The second public key is called a Zone Signing Key (ZSK). The ZSK is updated frequently and is stored only in the native zone. The KSK is used to validate the ZSK, and the ZSK is used to validate the records in a zone.

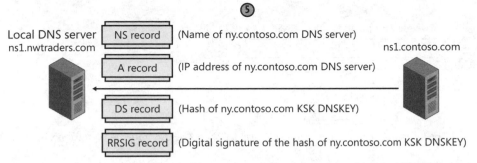

FIGURE 3-40 DNS servers configured with DNSSEC validate delegations with DS and RRSIG records.

Figure 3-41 shows the procedure for verifying the digital signature of the DS record obtained in step 5. In step 6, the public key stored as a trust anchor on ns1.nwtraders.com is used to decrypt the RRSIG record obtained with the DS record. Then, in step 7, this decrypted RRSIG record is compared to the DS record. If the two are identical, the DS record is validated.

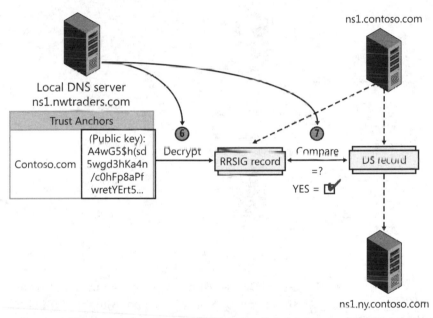

FIGURE 3-41 The trust anchor is used to validate the digital signature of the DS record.

After the DS record is validated, the local DNS server contacts the server authoritative for the ny.contoso.com domain. As shown in step 8 of Figure 3-42, the local DNS server requests the KSK for ny.contoso.com, a hash of which is contained in the just-validated DS record. In step 9, ns1.ny.contoso.com provides the requested KSK in a DNSKEY record. (DNSKEY records always contain public keys.)

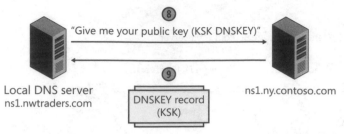

FIGURE 3-42 The local DNS server obtains a public key in a DNSKEY record from the target zone.

Figure 3-43 shows the process of validating the public key obtained in step 9. In step 10, the local DNS server applies the same SHA-1 or SHA-256 hashing algorithm to the just-obtained KSK from ns1.ny.contoso.com. In step 11, the local DNS server compares the hash of the DNSKEY generated by the procedure in step 10 to the DS record obtained in step 5 from ns1.contoso.com. If the two hashes match, the KSK from ny.contoso.com is validated.

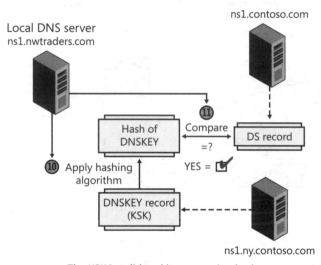

FIGURE 3-43 The KSK is validated by comparing hashes.

Figure 3-44 shows how, in step 12, the local DNS server next contacts ns1.ny.contoso.com to request its ZSK public key. In step 13, the remote DNS server responds with the ZSK and an accompanying RRSIG record, or digital signature.

Figure 3-45 illustrates the process of verifying the digital signature for the ZSK obtained in this last step. In step 14, the KSK obtained and validated in steps 9–11 is now used to unlock the digital signature of the ZSK. The decrypted digital signature in step 15 is then compared to the DNSKEY record that includes the ZSK. If the two match, the ZSK is validated.

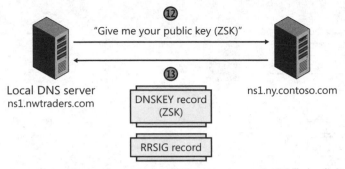

FIGURE 3-44 The local server obtains the remote zone's ZSK and a digital signature used to validate it.

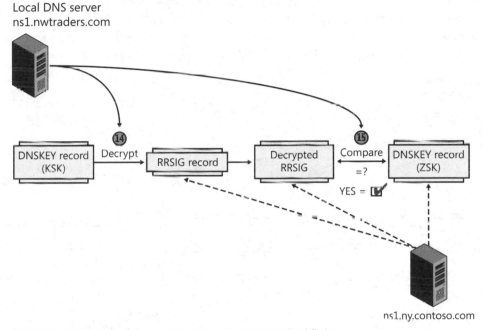

FIGURE 3-45 The KSK public key is used to validate the ZSK public key.

Now that the ZSK has been obtained, the local DNS server in step 16 can query ns1.ny .contoso.com for the name www.ny.contoso.com with DNSSEC, as shown in Figure 3-46. In step 17, the response is received in the form of an A record and accompanying digital signature in an RRSIG record. Note that even if the DNS responded with many matching A records, still only one RRSIG record would be included in the response because an RRSIG record is a digital signature of the *set of* DNS resource records that can match a query.

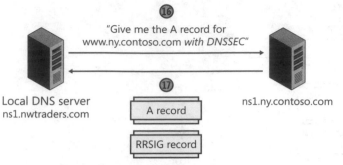

FIGURE 3-46 A DNSSEC-enabled DNS server responds to queries with a digital signature.

Next, in Figure 3-47, the local DNS server can validate the A record received in step 17, which is the response to the original query. In step 18, the now-validated ZSK public key is used to decrypt the RRSIG of the A record received in step 17. Then, in step 19, this decrypted RRSIG is compared to the A record received in step 17. If the two match, the A record is validated.

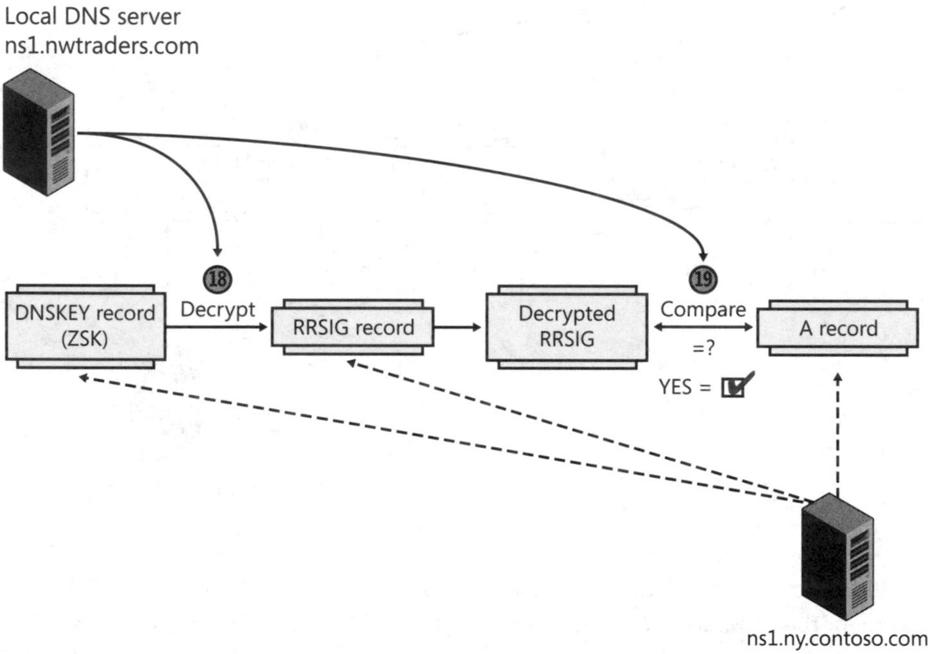

FIGURE 3-47 The digital signature of the A record is checked by using the validated ZSK from the remote zone.

Step 19 marks the end of the validation process. Now that the client's original query has been answered for the local DNS server with DNSSEC validation, that local DNS server in step 20 finally responds to the DNS client with an A record for www.ny.contoso.com. This step is shown in Figure 3-48.

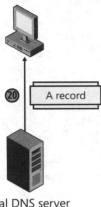

Local DNS server
ns1.nwtraders.com

FIGURE 3-48 After DNSSEC validation, the DNS server responds to the client with an A record.

NOTE **WHAT IS A NEXT SECURE (NSEC) RECORD?**

The earlier description of DNSSEC name validation applies to queried-for names that have a matching A record in the authoritative DNS server. If the queried-for name had no matching A record, however, the authoritative server would have responded with an NSEC record and accompanying RRSIG. An NSEC record is used with DNSSEC to prove that a queried-for name does not exist in a zone.

As a zone is signed, all the records in the zone are ordered alphabetically, and the record corresponding to the name of the zone is placed at the end of the list. Then, an NSEC record is created for every gap between successive records. For example, in a zone named Contoso.com containing only three records, named Boston, Phoenix, and the domain name record "Contoso.com," three NSEC records would be created: the first to prove the absence of names between Boston and Phoenix, the second to prove the absence of names between Phoenix and "Contoso.com," and the third to prove the absence of names between "Contoso.com" and Boston.

When the server receives a query for a name that doesn't exist in the zone, it responds with the NSEC record that shows that no name exists in the corresponding alphabetical range.

✔ **Quick Check**

- What is the name of the record that contains a hash of the public key in a delegated subdomain?

Quick Check Answer

- A DS record

Configuring DNSSEC

For DNSSEC to work, DNSSEC has to be configured on the local DNS server that receives the client's original query and on every remote DNS server that the local DNS server contacts to resolve the query. In addition, the DNS client needs to be configured through Group Policy to request DNSSEC for the specific name queried.

> **NOTE DNSSEC IN WINDOWS SERVER 2008 AND WINDOWS SERVER 2008 R2**
>
> Windows Server 2003 and Windows Server 2008 implementations of DNSSEC are not inter-operable with the Windows Server 2008 R2 or Windows 7 implementation. In Windows Server 2003 and Windows Server 2008, DNSSEC is implemented on secondary zones as described in RFC 2535, which is now obsolete. DNSSEC on Windows Server 2008 R2 and Windows 7 are based on RFC 4033, RFC 4034, and RFC 4035.

Configuring DNSSEC in Windows Server 2008 R2

Configuring DNSSEC on a DNS server requires you to prepare the zone to be signed; devise a roll-over mechanism for your keys; create the keys; sign the zone; and, finally, configure trust anchors.

PREPARING A ZONE FOR DNSSEC

The first step in preparing a zone for DNSSEC is to back up the current zone data. To back up a zone, type the following command at an elevated command prompt:

dnscmd /ZoneExport *<zone name>* *<zone file name>*

This command exports the zone data to a file in the %windir%\System32\DNS directory.

Next, disable dynamic updates for the zone because DNSSEC works only with static zones. (If you make a change to a zone, you have to resign the zone.)

Finally, make the zone a standard zone. Although DNSSEC is compatible with AD-integrated zones, the process of signing a zone requires that the zone data be stored in a zone file. There-fore, if your zone is AD-integrated, you should temporarily configure it as a standard zone. After you have signed the zone, you can reconfigure it as an AD-integrated zone.

CHOOSING A KEY ROLLOVER MECHANISM

DNSSEC keys do not have a permanent lifetime, so you need to plan a method to regularly generate new keys, resign the zone, and distribute the new keys for trust anchors and delega-tions. This process of updating keys and digital signatures is also called *key rollover*. Note that to facilitate rollover, DNSSEC allows multiple ZSKs and KSKs in a zone at the same time. When other DNS servers detect multiple public keys in the zone, each public key is used to attempt the validation of signatures.

The following two methods can be used for key rollover:

- **Prepublished rollover**   With this method, you introduce a new, second key to the zone before using it. After introducing the second key, you resign the zone with the old key to account for the presence of a new record (the new DNSKEY) in the zone. Then, when the old zone data has expired from remote server caches, you resign the zone with the new key. Resigning a zone with a single new key automatically deletes the old signatures in the zone. This type of rollover method is typically best suited for the ZSK.

- **Double signature rollover**   With this method, you add a new, second key to the zone and resign the zone with both the old and new keys at the same time. Then, when the old zone data has expired from remote server caches and any necessary updates are made at parent domain servers or remote servers using the key as a trust anchor, you resign the zone again with only the new key. This type of rollover method is typically best suited for the KSK.

> **MORE INFO   PERFORMING KEY ROLLOVERS**
>
> For more information about performing a key rollover, search for the "DNSSEC Deployment Guide" on the Microsoft website.

GENERATING KEY PAIRS

The purpose of using two keys with a zone is to give a long validity period to one key (KSK) that is distributed to other zones in trust anchors and delegations. If you used a long validity period with the same key to sign the zone records, however, security could be compromised. The presence of a KSK allows the key that is signing the zone (the ZSK) to be frequently updated without burdening administrators with the frequent task of distributing new keys to other zones. Note that the use of the KSK is recommended but is not required. When a single key is used both to sign the zone records and act as a trust anchor on remote servers, that key is a ZSK.

Use the following procedures to generate the KSK and ZSK key pairs. Once created, the keys are stored in a self-signed certificate in the local computer certificate store, in the MS-DNSSEC container.

To generate a KSK, follow these steps:

1. Open an elevated command prompt.
2. Type the following command:

```
DnsCmd /OfflineSign /GenKey /Alg rsasha1 /Flags KSK /Length <length> /Zone <zone
name> /SSCert /FriendlyName KSK-<zone name>
```

To generate a ZSK, follow these steps:

1. Open an elevated command prompt.
2. Type the following command:

```
DnsCmd /OfflineSign /GenKey /Alg rsasha1 /Length <length> /Zone <zone name> /
SSCert/FriendlyName ZSK-<zone name>
```

Table 3-1 describes the switches and options used with key generation and the Dnscmd. The values are listed in the table in the order in which you would type them in a command.

TABLE 3-1 Dnscmd Values for DNSSEC Key Generation

VALUE	DESCRIPTION
/OfflineSign	Required. Used with the GenKey, DeleteKey, ImportKey, or SignZone commands to modify certificates and keys or to sign a zone file.
/GenKey	Required. Generates a self-signed certificate with a private key.
/Alg	Required. Used with rsasha1 to specify the algorithm of the signing key. Currently, only RSA/SHA-1 is supported.
rsasha1	Required. Specifies the RSA/SHA-1 algorithm is used for the signing key.
/Flags	Used with KSK to specify the flags in DNSKEY. Currently, only KSK is supported, which indicates that the Zone Key bit and the Secure Entry Point bit are turned on. If /flags is not specified, only the Zone Key bit is turned on, which indicates a zone signing key.
KSK	Specifies that the KSK flag in DNSKEY is set.
/Length	Required. Used with *<length>* to specify the number of bits used in the key.
<length>	Required. Numerical value of bits used in the key. The allowed values for length are from 512 bits through 4096 bits, in 64 bit increments.
/Zone	Required. Used with *<zone name>* to specify the fully qualified domain name (FQDN) of the zone.
<zone name>	Required. The FQDN of the zone.
/SSCert	Required. Specifies that the key will be stored in a self-signed certificate.
/FriendlyName	Used with KSK-*<zone name>* or ZSK-*<zone name>* to specify the friendly name of the self-signed certificate.
KSK-*<zone name>*	Specifies the friendly name of the self-signed certificate used with a KSK.
ZSK-*<zone name>*	Specifies the friendly name of the self-signed certificate used with a ZSK.
/ValidFrom	Optional. Used with *<validfromtime>* to specify the start time for the validity period of the certificate. If not specified, the default will be Current time minus 1 hour.

VALUE	DESCRIPTION
<validfromtime>	Optional. Specifies the local start time for the validity period of the certificate. The required format is *YYYYMMDDHHMMSS*.
/ValidTo	Optional. Used with *<validtotime>* to specify the end time for the validity period of the certificate. If not specified, the certificate will be valid for 5 years.
<validtotime>	Optional. Specifies the local end time for the validity period of the certificate. The required format is *YYYYMMDDHHMMSS*.

After you generate the keys, you may choose to back up the associated certificates using the Certificates snap-in. In the console tree, navigate to Certificates\MS-DNSSEC\Certificates. Then, in the details pane, right-click each certificate and choose Export from the shortcut menu, as shown in Figure 3-49. When exporting, note that the certificate labeled "257" corresponds to the KSK, and the certificate labeled "256" corresponds to the ZSK.

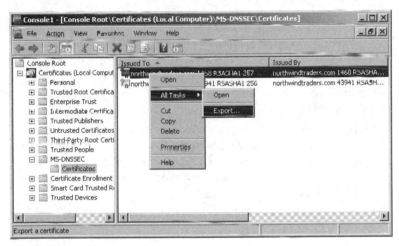

FIGURE 3-49 Backing up a KSK

SIGNING A ZONE FILE

After the keys are generated, you can sign a zone file. If the zone is Active Directory–integrated, you should first export the zone to a file. To sign a zone file, open an elevated command prompt and browse to the %windir%\System32\DNS directory.

Type the following command, and then press Enter:

```
DnsCmd /OfflineSign /SignZone /input <input zone file> /output <output zone file>
/zone <zone name> /signkey /ValidTo <validtodate> /ValidFrom <validfromdate> /cert
/friendlyname ksk-<zone name> /signkey /cert /friendlyname zsk-<zone name>
```

Table 3-2 describes the particular values used in signing a file with the Dnscmd command.

TABLE 3-2 Dnscmd Values for Zone Signing

VALUE	DESCRIPTION
/SignZone	Required. Used to sign a zone file.
/input	Required. Used with *<input filename>* to designate the zone file to be signed.
<input filename>	Required. The name of the zone file to be signed.
/output	Required. Used with *<output filename>* to designate the name of the zone file after it has been signed.
<output filename>	Required. The file name of the signed zone.
/Zone	Required. Used with *<zone name>* to specify the fully qualified domain name (FQDN) of the zone.
<zone name>	Required. The FQDN of the zone.
/Signkey	Required. Specifies the key that will be used to sign the zone.
/ValidFrom	Optional. Used with *<validfromdate>* to specify the start time of the validity period of RRSIG records created using this key. If not specified, the validity period will start 1 hour prior to the current UTC time.
<validfromdate>	Optional. Specifies the UTC start time of the validity period in YYYYMMDDHHMMSS format.
/ValidTo	Optional. Used with *<validtodate>* to specify the end time of the validity period of RRSIG records created using this key. If not specified, the validity period will end 30 days from the start of the validity period for zone signing keys, or 13 months from the start of the validity period for key signing keys.
<validtodate>	Optional. Specifies the UTC end time of the validity period in YYYYMMDDHHMMSS format.
/Cert	Required. Specifies that keys are stored in a certificate.

CONFIGURE TRUST ANCHORS

A validating DNS server must be configured with one or more trust anchors from a remote zone in order to perform validation. Note that it is not necessary to configure a trust anchor for a locally-hosted zone (a zone for which the DNS server is authoritative).

If the DNS server is running on a domain controller, trust anchors are stored in AD DS and are replicated to all domain controllers in the forest. On stand-alone DNS servers, trust anchors are stored in a file named TrustAnchors.dns in %windir%\System32\DNS.

To add a trust anchor, perform the following steps:

1. In the DNS console tree, right-click the name of the DNS server and then click Properties.

2. On the Trust Anchors tab, click the Add button shown in Figure 3-50.

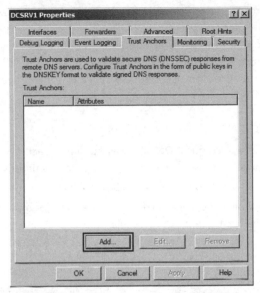

FIGURE 3-50 Adding a trust anchor to a DNS server

3. In the New Trust Anchor dialog box, shown in Figure 3-51, type the name of the signed zone in the Name text box. Do not change the settings for Protocol (DNSSEC) or Algorithm (RSA/SHA-1).

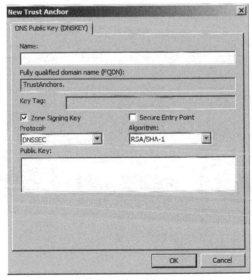

FIGURE 3-51 Configuring a new trust anchor

4. Paste the public key of the signed zone into the Public Key text box. Both the Zone Signing Key and Secure Entry Point check boxes must be selected if the remote anchor is a KSK, which is the typical configuration. However, some zones might use only a single key with the zone and not use a KSK. If the remote zone provides the ZSK as a trust anchor, you should select only the Zone Signing Key check box and leave the Secure Entry Point check box cleared.

Configuring Clients for DNSSEC

You use Group Policy to configure DNS clients to request DNSSEC validation for specific queries. To locate the DNSSEC configuration settings in a GPO, navigate to Computer Configuration \Policies\Windows Settings\Name Resolution Policy, as shown in Figure 3-52.

You can then use this Name Resolution Policy section in a GPO to create rules for the NRPT. The purpose of the NRPT is to provide special instructions for particular DNS client queries. These special instructions can relate to either DNSSEC or DirectAccess, which is a new IPv6-based VPN technology covered in Chapter 7, "Connecting to Networks."

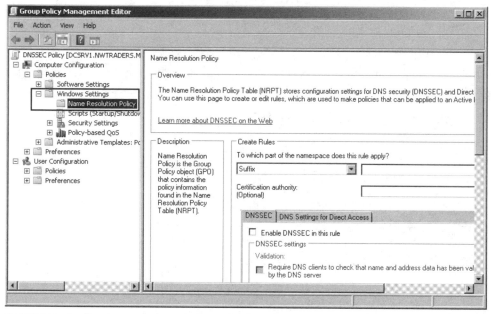

FIGURE 3-52 Configuring a name resolution policy for DNSSEC

To create a name resolution policy rule that enables DNSSEC for a given query, use the Create Rules area in the details pane to specify a name or portion of a name that will match the DNS query. First, in the drop-down list beneath To Which Part Of The Namespace Does This Rule Apply, choose Suffix, Prefix, FQDN, Subnet (IPv4), Subnet (IPv6), or Any, as shown in Figure 3-53.

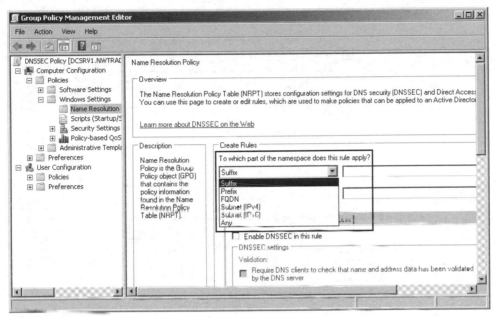

FIGURE 3-53 Choosing at least a portion of a name to match a DNS query

Then, in the text box to the right of the drop-down list, type in the name or portion of a name that represents the query you want to match, and click Enable DNSSEC In This Rule. By itself, this step enables DNS clients merely to receive DNSSEC data. If in addition you want to *require* DNS clients to request DNSSEC validation, click Require DNS Clients To Check That Name And Address Data Has Been Validated. Finally, you can also enforce IPSec authentication or encryption for the specified query by clicking Use IPsec In Communication Between DNS Client And DNS Server. These configuration settings are all indicated in Figure 3-54. After choosing the desired settings, click Create to create the rule.

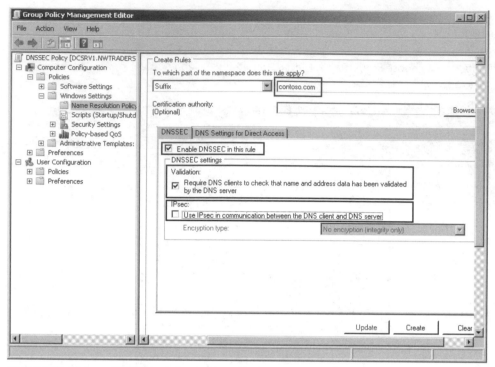

FIGURE 3-54 Adding a DNSSEC rule for the domain contoso.com

After you create the rule, a new entry is added to the NRPT, as shown in Figure 3-55. (The NRPT is visible when you scroll down the details pane in Name Resolution Policy.) Be sure to click Apply to apply the new rule to the policy.

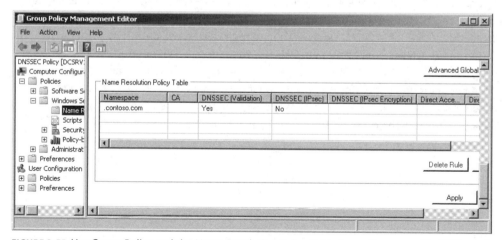

FIGURE 3-55 Use Group Policy and the Name Resolution Policy Table to configure specific DNS queries for DNSSEC.

In this practice, you create and sign a new zone and then configure clients in the domain to request DNSSEC.

EXERCISE 1   Creating a New Static Zone

In this exercise, you will create a new zone whose data is stored in a text file instead of AD DS. The zone will not allow any dynamic updates. You will then create resource records for the Dcsrv1 and Boston computers.

1. Log on to Nwtraders.msft from Dcsrv1 as a domain administrator.

2. Open the DNS console by clicking Start, Administrative Tools, DNS.

3. In the DNS console tree, right-click the Forward Lookup Zones container, and then click New Zone. The New Zone Wizard opens.

4. Click Next on the first page of the New Zone Wizard.

5. On the Zone Type page, clear the Store The Zone In Active Directory check box, and then click Next.

6. On the Zone Name page, type **northwindtraders.com**, and then click Next.

7. On the Zone File page, click Next.

8. On the Dynamic Update page, verify that Do Not Allow Dynamic Updates is selected, and then click Next.

9. On the last page of the New Zone Wizard, click Finish.

10. In the DNS console tree, navigate to and select the Northwindtraders.com container.

11. Right-click the Northwindtraders.com container and then choose New Host (A Or AAAA) from the shortcut menu.

12. In the New Host dialog box, type **dcsrv1** in the Name box and **192.168.0.1** in the IP Address text box, and then click Add Host.

13. In the DNS message box, click OK.

14. In the New Host dialog box, type **boston** in the Name box and **192.168.0.2** in the IP Address text box, and then click Add Host.

15. In the DNS message box, click OK.

16. Click Done to close the New Host dialog box.

EXERCISE 2 Signing Zone Data

In this exercise, you will create the KSK and ZSK keys used to sign the zone. You will then create a signed version of the zone file and re-create the zone using the new signed DNS file.

1. While you are logged on to Nwtraders.msft from Dcsrv1 as a domain administrator, open an elevated command prompt.

2. At the elevated command prompt, type **cd \windows\system32\dns**.

3. Generate the KSK by typing the following command:
dnscmd /OfflineSign /GenKey /Alg rsasha1 /Flags KSK /Length 1024 /Zone northwindtraders.com /SSCert /FriendlyName KSK-northwindtraders.com.

4. Generate the ZSK by typing the following command:
dnscmd /OfflineSign /GenKey /Alg rsasha1 /Length 1024 /Zone northwindtraders.com /SSCert /FriendlyName ZSK-northwindtraders.com.

   The new keys are stored in the Local Computer certificate store for the computer account, in the MS-DNSSEC container. The next step is to use the keys to create a signed version of the zone file, northwindtraders.com.dns. You will call the new version signed.northwindtraders.com.dns.

5. Leave the command prompt open, and then open the DNS console. In the DNS console tree, right-click the northwindtraders.com folder and then click Update Server Data File. You should perform this step to ensure that the newest records have been added to the file.

6. Switch back to the command prompt and type the following command:
dnscmd /OfflineSign /SignZone /Input northwindtraders.com.dns /Output signed.northwindtraders.com.dns /Zone northwindtraders.com /SignKey /Cert /FriendlyName KSK-northwindtraders.com /SignKey /Cert /FriendlyName ZSK-northwindtraders.com.

   You now need to recreate the zone using the new zone file.

7. At the command prompt, type **dnscmd /ZoneDelete northwindtraders.com /f**.

8. At the command prompt, type **dnscmd /ZoneAdd northwindtraders.com /Primary /File signed.northwindtraders.com.dns /Load**.

9. In the DNS console tree, right-click the northwindtraders.com folder, and then click Refresh.

   In the details pane, you can see new RRSIG, DNSKEY, and NSEC records. The RRSIG records are the signatures of hashes of all other records in the zone: A, NS, SOA, DNSKEY, and NSEC.

EXERCISE 3 Configuring DNS Clients to Request DNS

DNS clients do not receive DNSSEC information unless they request it. You now need to create and apply a Group Policy object that configures DNS clients to request DNSSEC information from the DNS server.

1. While you are logged on to Nwtraders.msft from Dcsrv1 as a domain administrator, open the Group Policy Management console by clicking Start, Administrative Tools, and Group Policy Management.

2. In the Group Policy Management console tree, open the Domains container, right-click the Nwtraders.msft icon, and then click Create A GPO In This Domain, And Link It Here.

3. In the New GPO dialog box, type **DNSSEC Policy** in the Name box, and then click OK.

4. In the Group Policy Management console tree, right-click DNSSEC Policy, and then click Edit. The Group Policy Management Editor opens.

5. In the Group Policy Management Editor console tree, navigate to Computer Configuration \Policies\Windows Settings\Name Resolution Policy.

6. In the details pane, in the Create Rules area, ensure that Suffix is selected beneath To Which Part Of The Namespace Does This Rule Apply? Then, In the text box to the right of Suffix, type **northwindtraders.com**.

   To properly configure DNSSEC, you would normally type in this text box the suffix of a remote domain. We are specifying the local suffix here only as a simplified example for our limited test environment.

7. On the DNSSEC tab, click Enable DNSSEC In This Rule.

8. In the DNSSEC Settings area, beneath Validation, click the option to require DNS clients to check that name and address data has been validated by the DNS server.

9. Click Create, and then click Apply. A new entry appears in the Name Resolution Policy Table lower in the pane.

10. Close the Group Policy Management Editor.

11. Switch to the Boston computer. At a command prompt on Boston, type **gpupdate**.

12. On a command prompt on Boston, type **ping dcsrv1.northwindtraders.com**.

   The name is successfully resolved and authenticated, and Dcsrv1 responds to the ping. You can use a protocol analyzer such as Network Monitor to verify that Boston has received RRSIG and NSEC records along with the A record that resolves the name Dcsrv1.northwindtraders.com. The frame containing an RRSIG from such a capture is shown in Figure 3-56.

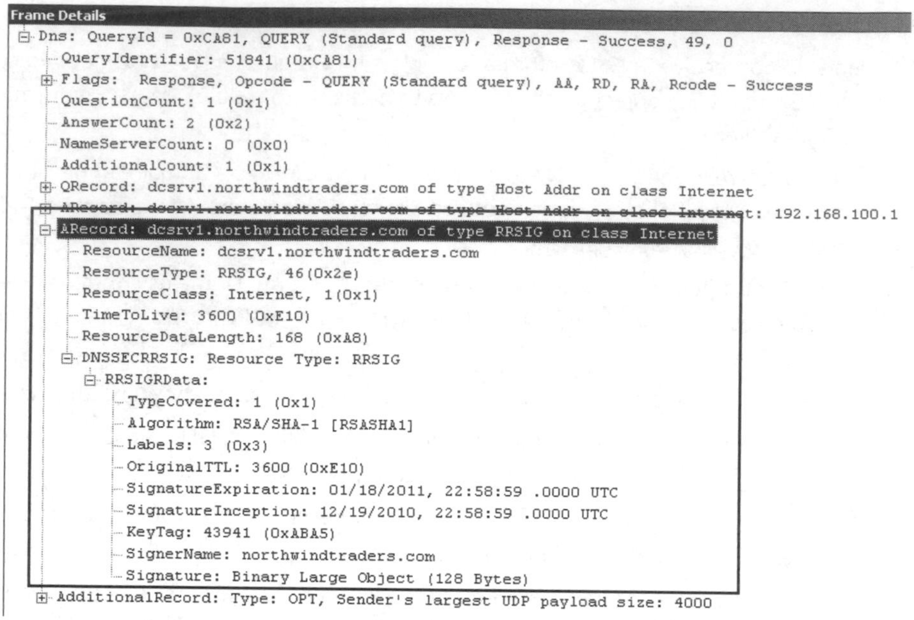

```
Frame Details
─ Dns: QueryId = 0xCA81, QUERY (Standard query), Response - Success, 49, 0
  ── QueryIdentifier: 51841 (0xCA81)
  ┼─ Flags:  Response, Opcode - QUERY (Standard query), AA, RD, RA, Rcode - Success
  ── QuestionCount: 1 (0x1)
  ── AnswerCount: 2 (0x2)
  ── NameServerCount: 0 (0x0)
  ── AdditionalCount: 1 (0x1)
  ┼─ QRecord: dcsrv1.northwindtraders.com of type Host Addr on class Internet
  ┼─ ARecord: dcsrv1.northwindtraders.com of type Host Addr on class Internet: 192.168.100.1
  ┼─ ARecord: dcsrv1.northwindtraders.com of type RRSIG on class Internet
    ── ResourceName: dcsrv1.northwindtraders.com
    ── ResourceType: RRSIG, 46(0x2e)
    ── ResourceClass: Internet, 1(0x1)
    ── TimeToLive: 3600 (0xE10)
    ── ResourceDataLength: 168 (0xA8)
    ─ DNSSECRRSIG: Resource Type: RRSIG
      ─ RRSIGRData:
        ── TypeCovered: 1 (0x1)
        ── Algorithm: RSA/SHA-1 [RSASHA1]
        ── Labels: 3 (0x3)
        ── OriginalTTL: 3600 (0xE10)
        ── SignatureExpiration: 01/18/2011, 22:58:59 .0000 UTC
        ── SignatureInception: 12/19/2010, 22:58:59 .0000 UTC
        ── KeyTag: 43941 (0xABA5)
        ── SignerName: northwindtraders.com
        ── Signature: Binary Large Object (128 Bytes)
  ┼─ AdditionalRecord: Type: OPT, Sender's largest UDP payload size: 4000
```

FIGURE 3-56 Boston receives a resource record signature (RRSIG) along with the Host record.

Lesson Summary

- DNSSEC enables a DNS server to digitally sign the resource records in its zones. DNSSEC also enables DNS servers to validate the digital signatures of resource records received from other servers.

- Trust anchors are public keys from other zones that are used to validate digitally signed records originating from those zones and from delegated subdomains that are also DNSSEC-compatible. A DNS server configured with DNSSEC must have configured at least one trust anchor from a remote zone.

- You use Group Policy to configure DNS clients to request DNSSEC validation. In Group Policy, you specify queries in the Name Resolution Policy Table for which clients request DNSSEC validation.

- You use the Dnscmd utility to create the keys needed for DNSSEC and to sign the zone with these keys.

- It is recommended that you use two key pairs with your zone: the first, a frequently updated zone signing key (ZSK) to sign the zone; and a second, a rarely updated key signing key (KSK) that is stored on other servers and that validates the ZSK.

Lesson Review

You can use the following questions to test your knowledge of the information in Lesson 3, "Implementing DNSSEC." The questions are also available on the companion CD if you prefer to review them in electronic form.

> **NOTE ANSWERS**
>
> Answers to these questions and explanations of why each answer choice is correct or incorrect are located in the "Answers" section at the end of the book.

1. You work for an organization named Fabrikam.com whose network includes 10 servers running Windows Server 2008, 60 clients running Windows Vista Professional, and 40 clients running Windows 7 Professional. You need to implement the latest version of DNSSEC so that your clients can receive validated DNS responses. Which of the following steps do you need to take? (Choose all that apply.)

    A. Upgrade the DNS server to Windows Server 2008 R2.

    B. Configure a trust anchor for the public root domain.

    C. Upgrade all clients to Windows 7.

    D. Configure a trust anchor for every top-level domain.

2. You are a network administrator for Contoso.com, whose network includes 25 servers running Windows Server 2008 R2 and 300 clients running Windows 7 Professional. Contoso.com is in the process of implementing DNSSEC so that its local DNS server can validate responses received from a remote DNS server in a partner organization named Northwindtraders.com.

    Both the Contoso.com domain and the Northwindtraders.com domain have made a single zone-signing key (ZSK) and a single key-signing key (KSK) available in their respective DNS zones. You want to validate responses from Northwindtraders.com and minimize administrative effort in the future. What should you do?

    A. Inform the administrator at Northwindtraders.com to configure the ZSK from Contoso.com as a trust anchor.

    B. Inform the administrator at Northwindtraders.com to configure the KSK from Contoso.com as a trust anchor.

    C. Import the ZSK from Northwindtraders.com and configure it as a trust anchor.

    D. Import the KSK from Northwindtraders.com and configure it as a trust anchor.

3. You are an administrator for northwindtraders.com. You want to configure the clients in the northwindtraders.com domain to request DNSSEC validation whenever they query for a name in the fabrikam.com domain. What should you do?

   A. Use Name Resolution Policy to create and enforce a rule that enables DNSSEC for the FQDN "fabrikam.com."

   B. Use Name Resolution Policy to create and enforce a rule that enables DNSSEC for the suffix "fabrikam.com."

   C. Import the trust anchor for the fabrikam.com domain to all your DNS servers.

   D. Export the trust anchor for the northwindtraders.com domain to the fabrikam.com DNS servers, and configure conditional forwarding to the fabrikam.com domain.

Chapter Review

To further practice and reinforce the skills you learned in this chapter, you can perform the following tasks:

- Review the chapter summary.
- Review the list of key terms introduced in this chapter.
- Complete the case scenarios. The scenarios set up real-world situations involving the topics of this chapter and ask you to create solutions.
- Complete the suggested practices.
- Take a practice test.

Chapter Summary

- A zone is a database that contains authoritative information about a portion of the DNS namespace. Zones are created on DNS servers. Primary zones provide the original read-write source data for a zone. Secondary zones are read-only copies of a zone. Stub zones contain only the names of servers containing primary or secondary zones.

- When you create a zone on a domain controller, you have the option to store the zone in Active Directory. This option offers a number of benefits, including reduced administration, improved security for dynamic updates, and multiple primary servers. If you do not store a zone in Active Directory, the zone is known as a standard zone, and the zone file is a text file. In standard zones, there is only one copy of the primary zone.

- Aging and scavenging provide a mechanism for removing stale resource records in a zone.

- The GlobalNames zone enables the resolution of single-label names in a multidomain forest.

- An application directory partition is a type of data structure used by DNS to store data for Active Directory–integrated zones. By default, every domain controller includes application directory partitions called DomainDnsZones and ForestDnsZones. These partitions are replicated among all domain controllers in the domain and the forest, respectively. You can also create custom application directory partitions and enlist chosen servers in the partition. You can choose to store a zone in any of these partitions. This decision affects what is called "the replication scope of the zone."

- Zone transfers keep DNS data consistent between secondary zones and a master zone, which is usually a primary zone.

- DNSSEC is a means for a DNS server to generate digital signatures for records in its zone and to validate the digital signatures of records from remote zones. With DNSSEC, you use the Dnscmd utility both to create the keys needed to sign the zone and to sign the zone. The latest version of DNSSEC requires Windows Server 2008 R2 and Windows 7.

Key Terms

Do you know what these key terms mean? You can check your answers by looking up the terms in the glossary at the end of the book.

- aging
- application directory partition
- key pair
- key rollover
- key signing key (KSK)
- master zone
- Name Resolution Policy Table (NRPT)
- primary zone
- private key
- public key
- replication
- scavenging
- secondary zone
- stub zone
- trust anchor
- zone
- zone signing key (ZSK)
- zone transfers

Case Scenarios

In the following case scenarios, you will apply what you've learned about configuring DNS zones and zone transfers. You can find answers to these questions in the "Answers" section at the end of this book.

Case Scenario 1: Managing Outdated Zone Data

You work as a domain administrator for Fabrikam, Inc. Your responsibilities include managing the Active Directory and network infrastructure, including DNS. The DNS servers for the Fabrikam.com domain are all installed on domain controllers.

1. Recently you have noticed that some records in the Fabrikam.com zone refer to computers that were removed from the network several months ago. What is the best way to remove these stale records?

2. What is the best way to prevent such data from accumulating in the future?

3. You want to allow records to remain in the zone for 21 days without being scavenged. However, you want to prevent time stamps from being refreshed for the first seven days after each record is first created in the zone. How should you configure the No-Refresh and the Refresh intervals?

Case Scenario 2: Configuring Zone Transfers

You are a network administrator for City Power & Light, whose network is composed of a single Active Directory domain, Cpandl.com. The Cpandl.com zone is stored in Active Directory.

At the company headquarters, the Cpandl.com domain controllers host the DNS zones for the domain. The Cpandl.com network also includes several branch offices.

1. The Rochester office does not include a DNS server. You want to improve name resolution of computer names in the Cpandl.com domain, but you don't want to host a domain controller at the Rochester site. Minimizing zone transfer traffic is not a priority. What should you do?

2. You want zone transfers to the Rochester office to occur whenever a change occurs in the zone data. How can you enable this functionality?

Suggested Practices

To help you successfully master the exam objectives presented in this chapter, complete the following tasks.

Configure a DNS Infrastructure

The following practices will deepen your understanding of DNS replication within multi-domain forests. They both require three computers, but you can still perform these practices easily by using virtual machine software such as Hyper-V or VirtualBox.

- **Practice 1** Using virtual machines, create an Active Directory forest with two domain controllers in a domain named Contoso.com, and one domain controller in a child domain called East.contoso.com. Choose the option to store both DNS zones in all DNS servers in the forest. View the zone data and then add a record manually to each zone. Force replication by using Active Directory Sites and Services.

- **Practice 2** Using the same three-computer network, create a custom application directory partition on the domain controller in the East.contoso.com domain. Configure the zone to store its data in the newly created partition. Enlist only one of the domain controllers in the Contoso.com domain in the partition. Reboot each computer and then verify that the zone data is stored on only two of the three servers.

Take a Practice Test

The practice tests on this book's companion CD offer many options. For example, you can test yourself on just one exam objective, or you can test yourself on all the 70-642 certification exam content. You can set up the test so that it closely simulates the experience of taking a certification exam, or you can set it up in study mode so that you can look at the correct answers and explanations after you answer each question.

> **MORE INFO** **PRACTICE TESTS**
>
> For details about all the practice test options available, see the "How to Use the Practice Tests" section in this book's Introduction.

CHAPTER 4

Creating a DHCP Infrastructure

Dynamic Host Configuration Protocol (DHCP) allows you to assign IP addresses, subnet masks, and other configuration information to client computers on a local network. When a DHCP server is available, computers that are configured to obtain an IP address automatically request and receive their IP configuration from that DHCP server upon starting.

This chapter introduces you to DHCP concepts as well as to the steps you need to take to deploy and configure a DHCP server on your network.

Exam objectives in this chapter:

- Configure Dynamic Host Configuration Protocol (DHCP).

Lessons in this chapter:

- Lesson 1: Installing a DHCP Server **254**
- Lesson 2: Configuring a DHCP Server **270**

Before You Begin

To complete the lessons in this chapter, you must have the following in place:

- Two networked computers running Windows Server 2008 R2.
- The first computer must be a domain controller named Dcsrv1 in a domain named nwtraders.msft. Dcsrv1 must be assigned the static address 192.168.0.1/24, with the DNS server specified as the same address. Dcsrv1 includes the server roles Active Directory Domain Services (AD DS) and DNS Server.
- The second computer must be named Boston.nwtraders.msft and must be assigned the address 192.168.0.2/24. Its DNS server must be specified as 192.168.0.1. Finally, Boston must be joined to the Nwtraders.msft Active Directory domain.

Lesson 1: Installing a DHCP Server

Every computer needs an address to communicate on an IP network, and this address can be provided either manually or automatically. For IPv4, the great majority of devices on a network receive their configurations automatically through a DHCP server. DHCP servers can also assign IPv6 addresses, but this arrangement is not as common because by default, IPv6 hosts configure their own addresses.

The actual procedure of installing and configuring a DHCP server is simple, but you still need to understand DHCP concepts in order to implement and manage DHCP on your network. This lesson introduces you not only to the initial configuration steps required to deploy a DHCP server but also to these basic DHCP concepts.

After this lesson, you will be able to:
- Deploy a DHCP server.
- Configure a server DHCP scope.
- Configure DHCP scope options.

Estimated lesson time: 45 minutes

Understanding DHCP Address Assignment

The function of a DHCP server is to assign IP addresses to computers. More specifically, when a computer without an IPv4 address is configured to obtain an address automatically, that computer, upon starting, broadcasts DHCP Discover packets on the network. These DHCP Discover messages are then transmitted through all neighboring cables, hubs, and switches. If a DHCP server lies within broadcast range of the computer, that server receives the message and responds by providing the client computer with an IPv4 address configuration. This configuration includes at least an IPv4 address, a subnet mask, and usually other settings as well (such as a default gateway and DNS server).

The actual negotiation between a DHCP client and a DHCP server occurs in four stages, illustrated in Figure 4-1 and described in the list that follows, which corresponds to the stages in the figure.

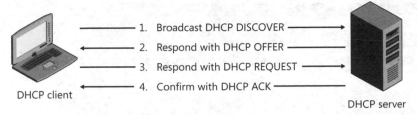

FIGURE 4-1 The DHCP address assignment process

1. Broadcast DHCP Discover

   In this first stage, the client broadcasts a DHCP Discover message to the local network to identify any available DHCP servers. This broadcast reaches only as far as the nearest router (unless the router is configured to forward it).

2. Respond with DHCP Offer

   If a DHCP server is connected to the local network and can provide the DHCP client with an IP address assignment, it broadcasts a DHCP Offer message for the DHCP client. The DHCP Offer message contains a list of DHCP configuration parameters and an available IP address from the DHCP scope. If the DHCP server has an IP address reservation that matches the DHCP client's MAC address, it offers the reserved IP address to the DHCP client.

3. Respond with DHCP Request

   In the third stage of DHCP negotiation, the DHCP client responds to the DHCP Offer message and requests the IP address contained in this DHCP Offer message. Alternatively, the DHCP client might request the IP address that was previously assigned.

4. Confirm with DHCP Ack

   If the IP address requested by the DHCP client is still available, the DHCP server responds with a DHCP Ack (acknowledgement) message. The client can now use the IP address.

Figure 4-2 shows a specific Network Monitor capture of this four-message DHCP exchange. The first frame shows that a client with no IP address (0.0.0.0) has sent out a Discover message to the broadcast address at 255.255.255.255. The second frame shows that the DHCP server at address 192.168.100.1 has responded with its own broadcast, an Offer message. This Offer message is selected in Network Monitor, and the Frame details pane shows that this Offer message includes an offer of an address of 192.168.100.20. The third frame shows that the client, still without an address, responds to the offer with a Request message. Though the contents of the message are not shown, the client has requested the same address offered: 192.168.100.20. The fourth frame shows the final Ack message broadcast from the DHCP server at 192.168.100.1. After this point, the server can communicate with the client directly by sending packets directly to 192.168.100.20.

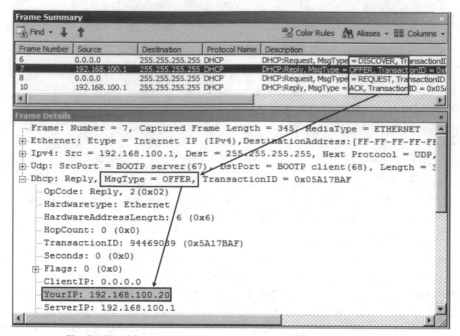

FIGURE 4-2 The DHCP address assignment process shown in Network Monitor

Understanding Address Leases

Every DHCP server maintains a database of addresses that the server can distribute to clients. When a DHCP server assigns a computer an address, it assigns that address in the form of a lease that lasts six or eight days by default (depending on the method used to configure the server). The DHCP server keeps track of leased addresses so that no address is assigned to two clients.

To prevent an IP address from being indefinitely assigned to a client that has disconnected from the network, DHCP servers reclaim addresses at the end of the DHCP lease period. Halfway through a DHCP lease, the DHCP client submits a lease renewal request to the DHCP server. If the DHCP server is online, the DHCP server typically accepts the renewal, and the lease period restarts. If the DHCP server is not available, the DHCP client tries to renew the DHCP lease again after half the remaining lease period has passed. If the DHCP server is not available when 87.5 percent of the lease time has elapsed, the DHCP client attempts to locate a new DHCP server and possibly acquire a different IP address.

If an administrator runs the command Ipconfig /release, the client sends a DHCP Release message to the DHCP server that assigned the IP address. The DHCP server then marks the IP address as available and can reassign it to a different DHCP client. If the DHCP client does not request a DHCP release, the DHCP server will not assign the IP address to a different client until the DHCP lease expires. For this reason, it's important to use a shorter DHCP lease period (for example, six hours instead of six days) on networks where clients frequently connect and disconnect—such as in wireless networks.

Understanding DHCP Scopes

Before your DHCP server can provide IP address leases to clients, a range of IP addresses must be defined at the DHCP server. This range, known as a *scope*, defines a single physical subnet on your network to which DHCP services are offered. So, for example, if you have two subnets defined by the address ranges 10.0.1.0/24 and 192.168.10.0/24, your DHCP server should be directly connected to each subnet (unless a DHCP Relay Agent is used) and must define a scope for each of these subnets and associated address ranges. Scopes also provide the principal method for the server to manage the distribution and assignment of IP addresses and options to clients on the network.

Understanding DHCP Options

DHCP options provide clients with additional configuration parameters, such as DNS or WINS server addresses, along with an address lease. For example, when the TCP/IP properties of a client computer have been configured to obtain a DNS server address automatically, that computer relies on DHCP options configured at the DHCP server to acquire a DNS server address (or list of addresses).

More than 60 standard DHCP options are available. For an IPv4 configuration, the most common of these include the following:

- **003 Router** A preferred list of IPv4 addresses for routers on the same subnet as DHCP clients. The client can then contact these routers as needed to forward IPv4 packets destined for remote hosts.

- **006 DNS Servers** The IP addresses for DNS name servers that DHCP clients can contact and use to resolve a domain host name query.

- **015 DNS Domain Name** An option that specifies the domain name that DHCP clients should use when resolving unqualified names during DNS domain name resolution. This option also allows clients to perform dynamic DNS updates.

- **044 WINS/NBNS Servers** The IPv4 addresses of primary and secondary WINS servers for the DHCP client to use.

- **046 WINS/NBT Node Type** A preferred NetBIOS name resolution method for the DHCP client to use—such as b-node (0x1) for broadcast only, or h-node (0x8) for a hybrid of point-to-point and broadcast methods.

- **051 Lease** An option that assigns a special lease duration only to remote access clients. This option relies on user class information advertised by this client type.

DHCP options are usually assigned to an entire scope, but they can also be assigned at the server level and apply to all leases within all scopes defined for a DHCP server installation. Finally, they can also be assigned on a per-computer basis at the reservation level.

EXAM TIP
You need to understand these six DHCP options for the 70-642 exam.

Adding the DHCP Server Role

To install and configure a DHCP server on a computer running Windows Server 2008 or Windows Server 2008 R2, first deploy a server on the physical subnet for which you want to provide addressing. Be sure to assign the server a static IP address that will be compatible with the address range planned for the local subnet. For example, if you want to assign computers addresses in the range of 10.1.1.0/24, you could assign the DHCP server the address 10.1.1.2/24.

After you have assigned the server a static address, use the Add Roles Wizard to add the DHCP Server role on the computer. You can launch the Add Roles Wizard in the Initial Configuration Tasks window or in Server Manager.

When you select the DHCP Server role check box on the Select Server Roles page of the Add Roles Wizard, shown in Figure 4-3, the wizard presents you with the following configuration pages:

- Select Network Connection Bindings
- Specify IPv4 DNS Server Settings
- Specify IPv4 WINS Server Settings
- Add Or Edit DHCP Scopes
- Configure DHCPv6 Stateless Mode
- Specify IPv6 DNS Server Settings
- Authorize DHCP Server

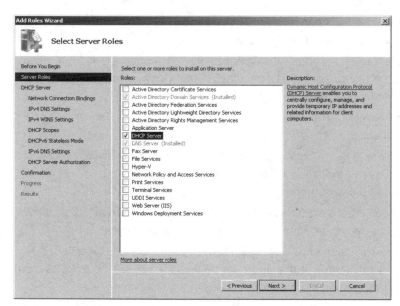

FIGURE 4-3 Selecting the DHCP Server role

The sections that follow describe the configuration options presented on these seven wizard pages.

Selecting Network Connection Bindings

On the Select Network Connection Bindings page of the Add Roles Wizard, shown in Figure 4-4, you specify the network adapter or adapters that the DHCP server will use to service clients. If your DHCP server is multihomed, this page gives you an opportunity to limit DHCP service to one network only. Remember also that the IP address tied to the adapter must be a manually assigned address and that the addresses you assign to clients from the server must be on the same logical subnet as this statically assigned address (unless you are using a DHCP Relay Agent to provide service to a remote subnet).

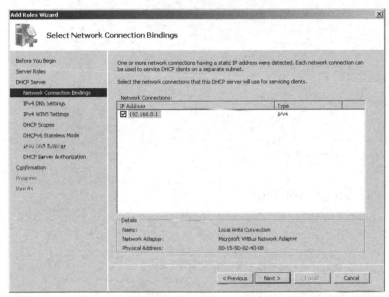

FIGURE 4-4 The Select Network Connection Bindings page

Specifying IPv4 DNS Server Settings

The Specify IPv4 DNS Server Settings page of the Add Roles Wizard, shown in Figure 4-5, essentially provides you an opportunity to configure the 015 DNS Domain Names and the 006 DNS Servers options for all scopes that you will create on the DHCP server.

The 015 DNS Domain Names option enables you to set a DNS suffix for the client connections obtaining an address lease from the DHCP server. This DNS suffix is specified by the value that you supply in the Parent Domain text box on the Specify IPv4 DNS Server Settings page.

The 006 DNS Servers option enables you to configure a DNS server address list for the client connections obtaining an address lease from the DHCP server. Although the option itself does not limit the number of addresses you can specify, the Specify IPv4 DNS Server Settings page allows you to configure only two. The value you specify in the Preferred DNS Server IPv4 Address corresponds to the first address in the DNS server list, and the Alternate DNS Server IPv4 Address value corresponds to the second DNS server address in the list assigned to each DHCP client.

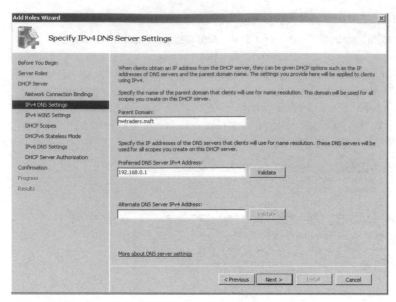

FIGURE 4-5 The Specify IPv4 DNS Server Settings page

Specifying IPv4 WINS Server Settings

Shown in Figure 4-6, the Specify IPv4 WINS Server Settings page enables you to configure the 044 WINS/NBNS Server option, in which you can assign a WINS server list to clients. To configure this option, select WINS Is Required For Applications On This Network, and then specify a preferred and (optionally) an alternate WINS server address.

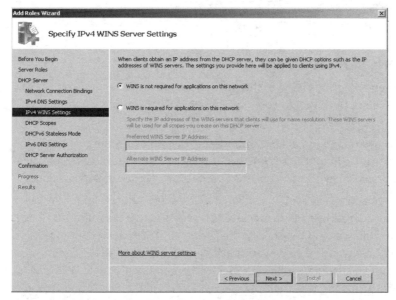

FIGURE 4-6 The Specify IPv4 WINS Server Settings page

Adding DHCP Scopes

The Add Or Edit DHCP Scopes page, shown in Figure 4-7, enables you to define or edit scopes on the DHCP server.

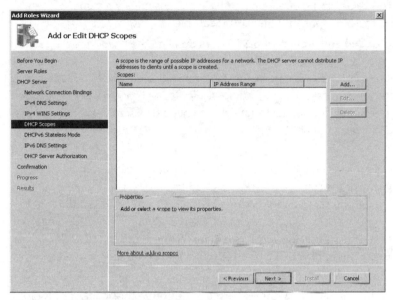

FIGURE 4-7 The Add Or Edit DHCP Scopes page

As explained earlier in the chapter, a scope is an administrative grouping of IP addresses for computers on a subnet that use the DHCP service. Each subnet can have only a single DHCP scope with a single continuous range of IP addresses.

To add a new scope, click the Add button. This opens the Add Scope dialog box, shown in Figure 4-8.

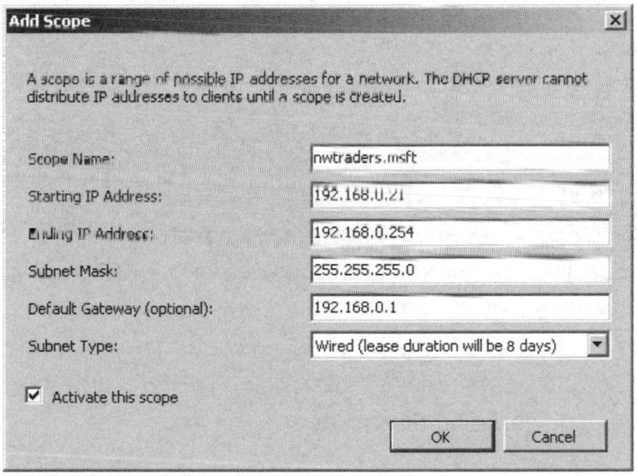

FIGURE 4-8 The Add Scope dialog box

The process of creating a scope is the most important aspect of configuring a DHCP server. The following list describes the features that you can configure for a scope by using this dialog box.

- **Scope Name** This value has no effect on DHCP clients. It is merely a name you can use to label the scope as it appears in the DHCP console.

- **Starting IP Address and Ending IP Address** When defining the IP address range of a scope, you should use the consecutive addresses that make up the subnet for which you are enabling the DHCP service. However, you should also be sure to exclude from this defined range any statically assigned addresses for existing or planned servers on your network. For example, on the same subnet, you need to assign a static IP address to the local DHCP server, a router (default gateway), and any DNS servers, WINS servers, and domain controllers.

  To exclude these addresses, you can simply choose to limit the scope range so that it does not include any of the static addresses assigned to servers. For example, in the subnet 192.168.0.0/24, you can keep the addresses 192.168.0.1 through 192.168.0.20 for your statically addressed servers, such as your DHCP server, DNS server, WINS server, and router, and other servers whose addresses should not change. You can then define the addresses 192.168.0.21 through 192.168.0.254 as the range for the subnet's DHCP scope.

- **Subnet Mask** The subnet mask that you choose here is the subnet mask that will be assigned to DHCP clients that receive an address lease through this scope. Be sure to choose the same subnet mask as the one configured for the DHCP server itself.

- **Default Gateway (optional)** This field effectively enables you to configure the 003 Router option, which assigns a default gateway address to the DHCP clients that receive an address lease through this scope.

- **Subnet Type** This setting essentially allows you to assign one of two lease durations to the scope. By default, the scope is set to the Wired subnet type, which configures a lease duration of eight days. The alternative setting is Wireless, for which the lease duration is eight hours.

- **Activate This Scope** A scope will lease out addresses only if it is activated. By default, this option to activate the new scope is enabled.

Configuring DHCPv6 Stateless Mode

DHCPv6 refers to DHCP for IPv6, and stateless mode refers to the default addressing mode for IPv6 hosts. Addresses in stateless mode are configured without the help of a DHCP server, although options can still be obtained from the DHCP server. When an IPv6 host is configured to obtain an address automatically, instead of using a DHCP server, the host in stateless mode self-configures an address compatible with the local subnet by exchanging Router Solicitation and Router Advertisement messages with a neighboring IPv6 router.

However, on the Configure DHCPv6 Stateless Mode page, shown in Figure 4-9, you can disable stateless mode on the DHCP server and enable it to respond to IPv6 hosts that have been enabled for stateful addressing. When stateful addressing is then enabled on IPv6 hosts, the hosts request an address and potentially other IPv6 configuration options (such as DNS server addresses) from a DHCP server by using the DHCPv6 protocol.

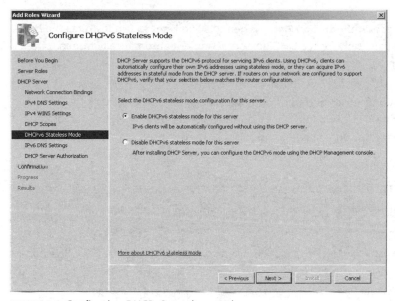

FIGURE 4-9 Configuring DHCPv6 stateless mode

If you choose to disable stateless addressing on the DHCP server on the Configure DHCPv6 Stateless Mode page, you will later need to create a scope for an IPv6 address range by using the DHCP console. To do so, right-click the IPv6 node in the DHCP console tree, choose New Scope as shown in Figure 4-10, and then follow the prompts in the New Scope Wizard.

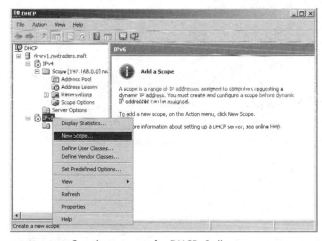

FIGURE 4-10 Creating a scope for DHCPv6 clients

CONFIGURING CLIENTS FOR STATEFUL OR STATELESS IPV6 ADDRESSING

By default, IPv6 hosts perform stateless address autoconfiguration automatically, which means that they assign themselves addresses from routers when possible and obtain other configuration information from a DHCPv6 server. However, neighboring routers that send out Router Advertisement messages can set the following flags that affect autoconfiguration settings for IPv6 hosts.

- **Managed Address Configuration Flag**   When this flag is set to 1, it instructs the host to obtain an address only from a DHCPv6 server and not automatically from a router. Setting the flag to 0 instructs the host to autoconfigure its own IPv6 address with the help of Router Advertisement messages and not to use a DHCPv6 server.

- **Other Stateful Configuration Flag**   When this flag is set to 1, it instructs the host to obtain configuration information other than the address from a DHCPv6 server and not from neighboring routers. When the flag is set to 0, it instructs the host not to obtain configuration information from a DHCPv6 server.

NOTE ENABLING STATEFUL ADDRESSING DIRECTLY ON IPV6 HOSTS

To enable stateful addressing on an IPv6 host, type the following command:

`netsh interface ipv6 set interface interface_name managedaddress=enabled`

To enable the IPv6 host to obtain DHCP options from a DHCPv6 server, type the following command:

`netsh interface ipv6 set interface interface_name otherstateful=enabled`

EXAM TIP

You need to understand the basics of stateful and stateless addressing on the 70-642 exam, including how the flags affect IPv6 host behavior.

MORE INFO   DHCPV6 ADDRESSING

For more information about DHCPv6 addressing, visit *http://technet.microsoft.com* and search for DHCPv6.

Configuring IPv6 DNS Server Settings

After the DHCPv6 Stateless Mode page in the Add Roles Wizard, the next page is the Configure IPv6 DNS Server Settings page. This page appears only when you have left the default (stateless) option configured for DHCPv6.

You can use the Configure IPv6 DNS Server Settings page to specify a DNS server address for IPv6 clients enabled for configuration of DHCP options. This page resembles the Specify IPv4 DNS Server Settings page except that you must specify a DNS server by its IPv6 address.

Authorizing DHCP Server

The page that follows the Configure IPv6 DNS Server Settings page is the Authorize DHCP Server page, shown in Figure 4-11. This page gives you an opportunity to authorize a DHCP server for use in an Active Directory domain.

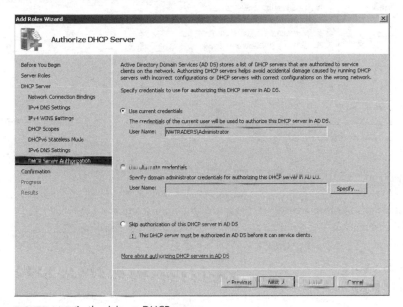

FIGURE 4-11 Authorizing a DHCP server

In Active Directory domain environments, a DHCP server will not issue IP addresses to clients unless the server is authorized. (In fact, the DHCP Server service will shut down if the server is not authorized.) Requiring servers to be authorized reduces the risk that a user will accidentally or intentionally create a DHCP server that assigns invalid IP address configurations to DHCP clients, which might prevent the clients from accessing network resources.

If a server requires authorization, you will see a red arrow pointing downward next to the IPv4 or IPv6 icon in the DHCP console, as shown in Figure 4-12.

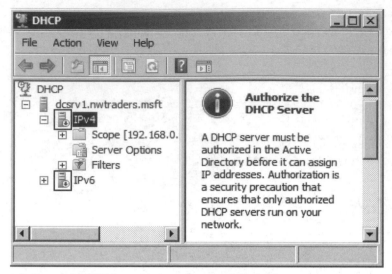

FIGURE 4-12 A DHCP Server that needs to be authorized

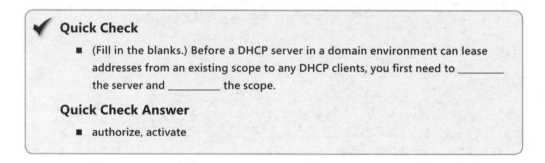

✔ Quick Check
- (Fill in the blanks.) Before a DHCP server in a domain environment can lease addresses from an existing scope to any DHCP clients, you first need to _____ the server and _____ the scope.

Quick Check Answer
- authorize, activate

PRACTICE Deploying a DHCP Server

In this practice, you will use the Add Roles Wizard to add the DHCP Server role and configure a scope for IPv4 on Dcsrv1. You will then configure the Boston computer as a DHCP client and observe the output.

EXERCISE 1 Adding the DHCP Server Role

In this exercise, you will add the DHCP Server role on Dcsrv1.

1. Log on to Nwtraders from Dcsrv1 as a domain administrator.
2. In the Initial Configuration Tasks window (or Server Manager), click Add Roles. The Add Roles Wizard opens.
3. On the Before You Begin page, click Next.
4. On the Select Server Roles page, select the DHCP Server check box.
5. On the Select Server Roles page, click Next.

6. On the DHCP Server page, read all of the text on the page, and then click Next.

7. On the Select Network Connection Bindings page, read all of the text on the page. Then, verify that the check box next to 192.168.0.1 is selected and click Next.

8. On the Specify IPv4 DNS Server Settings page, read all of the text on the page. Then, verify that nwtraders.msft is specified as the parent domain. Next, specify **192.168.0.1** as the preferred DNS server IPv4 address. (Do not leave the default of 127.0.0.1.) Click Next.

9. On the Specify IPv4 WINS Server Settings page, read all of the text on the page. Then, leave the selection specifying that WINS is not required for applications on the network and click Next.

10. On the Add Or Edit DHCP Scopes page, read all of the text on the page, and then click Add. The Add Scope dialog box appears.

11. Use the following information to complete the fields in the Add Scope dialog box:

    Scope Name: **Nwtraders.msft IPv4**

    Starting IP Address: **192.168.0.20**

    Ending IP Address: **192.168.0.254**

    Subnet Type: Wired (lease duration will be 8 days)

    Activate this scope: Checked

    Subnet Mask: **255.255.255.0**

    Default Gateway (optional): **192.168.0.1**

12. After you have entered the appropriate values in the Add Scope dialog box, click OK.

13. On the Add Or Edit DHCP Scopes page, click Next.

14. On the Configure DHCPv6 Stateless Mode page, read all of the text on the page. Then, leave the Enable DHCPv6 Stateless Mode For This Server option selected and click Next.

> **NOTE STATELESS VERSUS STATEFUL MODE**
>
> DHCPv6 stateless mode clients use DHCPv6 to obtain only configuration options and not an IPv6 address. Stateless clients configure an IPv6 address through a non–DHCPv6-based mechanism, such as by exchanging Router Solicitation and Router Advertisement messages with neighboring routers. In the DHCPv6 stateful mode, clients acquire both the IPv6 address as well as other network configuration parameters through DHCPv6.

15. On the Specify IPv6 DNS Server Settings page, read all of the text on the page. Then, verify that nwtraders.msft is specified as the parent domain. Next, specify **fd00::1** as the preferred DNS server IPv6 address (do not leave the default of ::1). Verify that fec0:0:0:ffff::1 is specified as the alternate DNS server IPv6 address. Click Next.

16. On the Authorize DHCP Server page, read all of the text on the page. Then, verify that the Use Current Credentials option is selected and click Next.

17. On the Confirm Installation Selections page, review the selections, and then click Install. When the installation completes, the Installation Results page appears.

18. On the Installation Results page, click Close.

EXERCISE 2 Enabling DHCP on the Client

In this exercise, you will configure the Boston computer as a DHCP client for IPv4.

1. Log on to Nwtraders from Boston as a domain administrator.

2. Open an elevated command prompt.

3. At the command prompt, type the following:

    ```
    netsh interface ipv4 set address "local area connection" dhcp
    ```

    (Note that if the local area connection has been assigned a number such as "Local Area Connection 2," you should specify that name in the Netsh commands instead.)

4. After the command completes successfully and the prompt reappears, type the following:

    ```
    netsh interface ipv4 set dnsserver "local area connection" dhcp
    ```

5. After the command completes successfully and the prompt reappears, type **ipconfig /all**. The Ipconfig output shows that DHCP is enabled and that Boston has received a new IP address, 192.168.0.20.

6. Log off both computers.

Lesson Summary

- When a computer without an IPv4 address is configured to obtain an address automatically, the computer, upon starting, broadcasts DHCP Discover packets on the network. If a DHCP server lies within broadcast range of the computer, that server will receive the message and respond by providing the client computer with an IPv4 address configuration. This configuration includes at least an IPv4 address and a subnet mask and usually other settings as well (such as a default gateway and DNS server).

- When a DHCP server assigns a computer an address, it assigns that address in the form of a lease. The DHCP server keeps track of leased addresses so that no address is assigned to two clients.

- Before your DHCP server can provide IP address leases to clients, a range of IP addresses must be defined at the DHCP server. This range, known as a scope, defines a single physical subnet on your network to which DHCP services are offered.

- DHCP options provide clients with additional configuration parameters, such as DNS or WINS server addresses, along with an address lease.

- To deploy a DHCP server, use the Add Roles Wizard to add the DHCP Server role. The Add Roles Wizard guides you through an initial DHCP configuration and enables you to select network bindings, specify DNS and WINS server addresses, add DHCP scopes, configure DHCPv6 stateless mode, and specify IPv6 DNS server settings.

Lesson Review

You can use the following questions to test your knowledge of the information in Lesson 1, "Installing a DHCP Server." The questions are also available on the companion CD if you prefer to review them in electronic form.

> **NOTE   ANSWERS**
>
> Answers to these questions and explanations of why each answer choice is correct or incorrect are located in the "Answers" section at the end of the book.

1. After you deploy a DHCP server for the 192.168.1.0/24 subnet, you find that none of the DHCP clients can communicate beyond the local subnet. Statically assigned computers can successfully communicate beyond the local subnet.

   How can you configure the DHCP server to enable DHCP clients to communicate beyond the local subnet?

   A. Configure the 003 Router option.

   B. Configure the 006 DNS Servers option.

   C. Configure the 015 Domain Name option.

   D. Configure the 044 WINS/NBNS Servers option.

2. You want to deploy a DHCP server on a computer named Dhcp1.nwtraders.msft. You configured this server with a static address of 10.10.0.5/24 and specified a DNS server address of 10.10.1.1. You then create a scope with the range 10.10.1.0/24. You activate the scope and authorize the server, but the server does not successfully lease any addresses to computers on the local subnet. When you verify the addresses of the clients on the subnet, you find that they are all assigned addresses in the 169.254.0.0/16 range.

   You want the DHCP server to lease addresses to client computers on the local subnet only. Which of the following actions will most likely fix the problem?

   A. Configure the clients as DHCP clients.

   B. Enable the DHCP client service on Dhcp1.

   C. Change the address of Dhcp1 and redeploy the DHCP server.

   D. Run the command Ipconfig /registerdns on Dhcp1.

3. You want your DHCPv6 clients to self-configure their IPv6 addresses, but you want them to obtain DHCPv6 options through the DHCPv6 server on the local subnet. What should you do?

   A. Configure the DHCPv6 server for stateless mode.

   B. Configure the DHCPv6 server for stateful mode.

   C. Set the Managed Address Configuration Flag to 1.

   D. Set the Other Stateful Address Configuration Flag to 0.

Lesson 2: Configuring a DHCP Server

Although using the Add Roles Wizard enables you to deploy a DHCP server with basic installation options, you can use the main DHCP management tool, the DHCP console, to finish the configuration.

This lesson describes the key features of a DHCP server that you can configure after deployment by using the DHCP console.

> **After this lesson, you will be able to:**
> - Create scope reservations.
> - Create scope exclusions.
> - Configure DHCP scope options.
>
> **Estimated lesson time: 50 minutes**

Performing Post-Installation Tasks

After you add the DHCP Server role, you can perform further configuration tasks by using the DHCP console. These tasks include configuring exclusions, creating address reservations, adjusting the lease duration of a scope, and configuring additional scope or server options. Each of these tasks is described in the sections that follow.

Creating Address Exclusions

An *exclusion range* is a set of one or more IP addresses that is included within the range of a defined scope but that you do not want to lease to DHCP clients. Exclusion ranges ensure that the DHCP server does not assign addresses that are already assigned manually to servers or other computers.

For example, you might define a new scope whose address range is 192.168.0.10–192.168.0.254. Within the subnet serviced by the DHCP server, however, you might have a number of preexisting servers whose static addresses might lie within this range—for example, between 192.168.0.200 and 192.168.0.210. Or you might have servers with isolated static addresses, such as 192.168.0.99. By setting an exclusion for these addresses, you specify that DHCP clients are never offered these addresses when they request a lease from the server.

To add an exclusion range, in the DHCP console tree, navigate to DHCP\<*server node*>\IPv4\Scope\Address Pool. Right-click the Address Pool folder, and then choose New Exclusion Range, as shown in Figure 4-13.

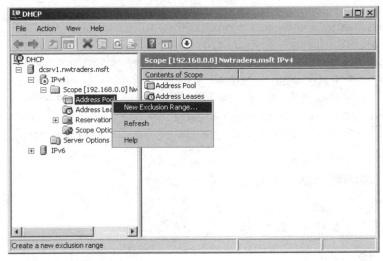

FIGURE 4-13 Adding exclusions

Then, in the Add Exclusion dialog box that opens, configure the range of addresses that you want to exclude from the address range within the scope you have defined. If you want to exclude a single address, specify the Start IP Address and the End IP Address as the same address. The Add Exclusion dialog box is shown in Figure 4-14.

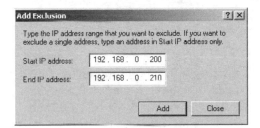

FIGURE 4-14 Adding an exclusion range

If you have more than one contiguous range of addresses that you need to exclude or separate individual addresses, such as 192.168.0.25 and 192.168.0.200, that need to be excluded, you need to create more than one exclusion range to exclude all of the necessary addresses.

Creating Reservations

You use a *reservation* to create a permanent address lease assignment by the DHCP server by associating an IP address with a MAC address. Reservations ensure that a specified hardware device on the subnet can always use the same IP address without relying on a manually configured address. For example, if you have defined the range 192.168.0.11–192.168.0.254 as your DHCP scope, you can then reserve the IP address 192.168.0.100 within that scope for the network adapter whose hardware address is 00-b0-d0-01-18-86. Every time the computer that is hosting this adapter starts up, the server recognizes the adapter's MAC address and leases the address 192.168.0.100.

The advantage of a reservation, compared to a manually configured address, is that it is centrally managed and less likely to be configured incorrectly. The disadvantage of a reservation is that its address is assigned late in the startup process and depends on the presence of a DHCP server, which is unsuitable for certain infrastructure servers, such as DNS servers. However, some servers, such as application servers, print servers, and even some domain controllers, benefit from a permanent address, but you do not need to configure this address manually.

To create a reservation, in the DHCP console tree, navigate to DHCP\<*server node*>\IPv4 \Scope\Reservations. Right-click the Reservations folder, and then choose New Reservation, as shown in Figure 4-15.

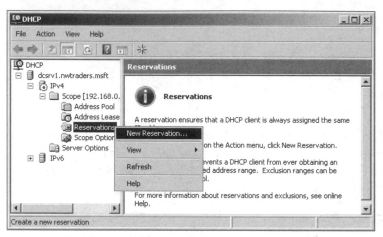

FIGURE 4-15 Creating an address reservation

Then, in the New Reservation dialog box that opens, specify a name, IP address, and MAC address for the reservation. For the reservation configured in Figure 4-16, the DHCP server will recognize DHCP requests originating from the hardware address 00-15-5D-02-40-08 and will then assign the IP address 192.168.0.30 to that MAC address.

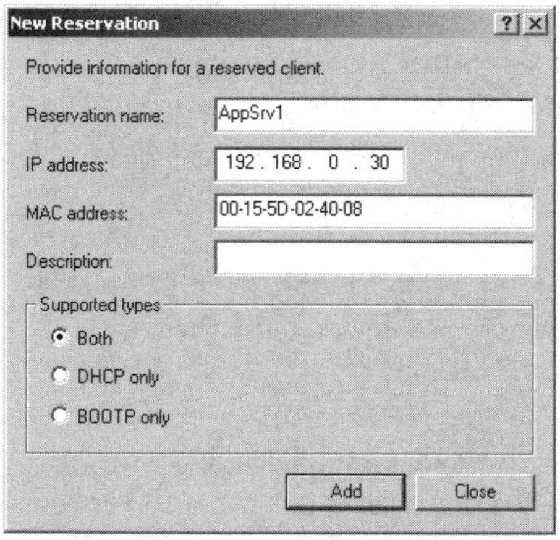

FIGURE 4-16 Creating an address reservation

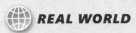
Adjusting Lease Durations

You can modify the lease duration to be used for assigning IP address leases. For most local area networks (LANs), the default value of six days is acceptable but can be further increased if computers seldom move or change locations. In cases where addresses are sparse and in cases where users connect for brief periods of time, you should shorten the lease duration. Be especially careful with configuring unlimited lease times. You can configure these in small networks when addresses are abundant, but you should use this setting with caution.

To adjust the length of a lease duration, open the properties of the scope whose lease duration you want to adjust. You can adjust the lease duration on the General tab in the Lease Duration For DHCP Clients area, shown in Figure 4-17.

NOTE DELETING LEASES

In the DHCP console, the Address Leases node displays which IP addresses are currently leased to which clients. If you want to end the lease for a given address or client, you can simply delete that lease by right-clicking the lease and then choosing Delete. Normally, if you want to end the lease of any particular computer, you can use the Ipconfig /release command on that computer. However, by using the DHCP console, you can end the leases of many clients at once. This option is useful, for example, if you want many clients to obtain a new address (because of new exclusions or reservations affecting those clients). Another case in which deleting many leases is useful is when you want to assign a newly defined DHCP option to many clients. By deleting the address leases, the DHCP clients will be forced to renew their leases and obtain the new addresses or new options.

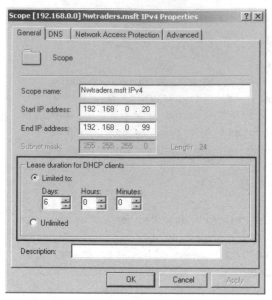

FIGURE 4-17 Adjusting the lease duration for a scope

Configuring Additional DHCP Options

You can assign options at the server level, the scope level, and the reservation level. Options defined at the server level are inherited by all scopes configured on the server. Options defined at the scope level are inherited by all leases and reservations within the scope. Options defined at the reservation level apply to that reservation only. At all three levels, the DHCP options available are the same.

EXAM TIP

You need to understand this concept of options inheritance for the 70-642 exam. For example, if you want an option to apply to all scopes, leases, and reservations, you should define the option at the server level. To do so, right-click the Server Options folder in the DHCP console tree, and then choose Configure Options.

Although the Add Roles Wizard enables you to define a small number of server and scope options, the full range of DHCP options can be configured in the DHCP console. To see the built-in options that you can configure, in the DHCP console, navigate to DHCP\<*server node*>\IPv4\Scope\Scope Options. Right-click the Scope Options folder, and then choose Configure Options, as shown in Figure 4-18.

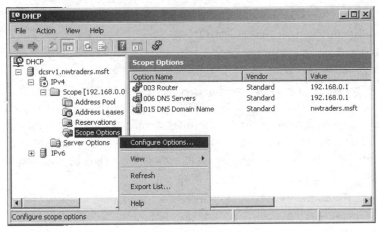

FIGURE 4-18 Configuring options for an existing scope

Then use the Scope Options dialog box to choose an option for the scope, as shown in Figure 4-19.

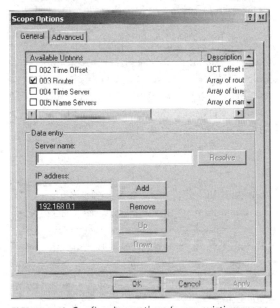

FIGURE 4-19 Configuring options for an existing scope

> **NOTE BROWSE THE DHCP OPTIONS**
>
> On the 70-642 exam, you won't be tested on any DHCP options beyond those covered in the section entitled "Understanding DHCP Options" in Lesson 1 of this chapter. However, browsing the long list of options made available through the DHCP console helps you get a feel for what DHCP options are and how you might use them in a production environment.

Understanding DHCP Options Classes

An *options class* is a client category that enables the DHCP server to assign options only to particular clients within a scope. When an options class is added to the server, clients of that class can be provided class-specific options. Options classes can be of two types:

- **Vendor classes** These are used to assign vendor-specific options to DHCP clients identified as a vendor type. For example, you can configure clients that can be identified as running Windows 2000 to enable or disable NetBIOS. A vendor class is generally not configurable in the sense that the class identification is built into the software of the client. An administrator typically does not need to populate the class by enabling a setting on the client.

- **User classes** These are used to assign options to any set of clients identified as sharing a common need for similar DHCP options configuration. These classes are configurable. Administrators can create new user classes, which they then populate by configuring a setting on clients they choose.

> **NOTE** **WHAT IS THE DEFAULT USER CLASS?**
>
> The Default User class is a class to which all DHCP clients belong and the class in which all options are created by default. If you want an option to apply to all DHCP clients, regardless of their class identification, leave the option configured for the Default User class. Note, however, that particular options assigned through the Default User class can be overridden by options defined in other classes. For example, if the Default User class defines both a WINS server and DNS server address, and a custom user class named Special WINS defines only a WINS server, a client assigned to special WINS will obtain the WINS server address from special WINS and the DNS server address from the Default User class.

Implementing User Classes

User classes enable you to apply a particular configuration of DHCP options to any subset of DHCP clients you define. To implement a user class, you first define the class at the DHCP server by assigning an ID and a set of options for the class. Then you assign selected client computers to that class by using the Ipconfig /setclassid command. When these clients subsequently communicate with DHCP servers, they announce their class ID and inherit the options of that class along with the options of the default user class. If no class ID is manually configured in this way, the client inherits the options merely of the default user class.

A custom user class is helpful when you need to assign distinct options to distinct sets of client computers. For example, your network might require certain clients to be assigned a special default gateway that allows them to bypass the company firewall. In this example, you could configure options to distribute the unique default gateway to the security-exempt class.

To create a custom or new user class, begin by right-clicking the IPv4 icon in the DHCP console and choosing Define User Classes, as shown in Figure 4-20.

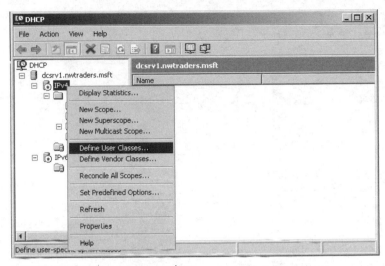

FIGURE 4-20 Creating a new user class

This step opens the DHCP User Classes dialog box. In this dialog box, shown in Figure 4-21, you can see that three user classes are predefined: Default Routing And Remote Access Class, Default Network Access Protection Class, and Default BOOTP Class. Beyond these three, the Default User Class is the implicit class to which all clients belong by default.

You can create a new user class by clicking the Add button in the DHCP User Classes dialog box. This step opens the New Class dialog box, shown in Figure 4-22. In this dialog box, you merely need to name the class and then set an ID string of your choice for the class. (Use the ASCII field to define the string.)

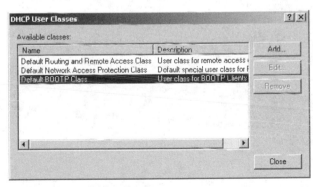

FIGURE 4-21 Available user classes

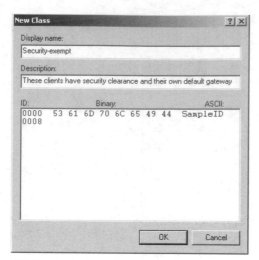

FIGURE 4-22 Defining a new user class

After defining a new class and specifying an ID string for that class, the new user class appears in the User Class drop-down list box on the Advanced tab of the Scope Options dialog box, as shown in Figure 4-23. You can then select that user class and define a set of options that will be assigned only to members of the class.

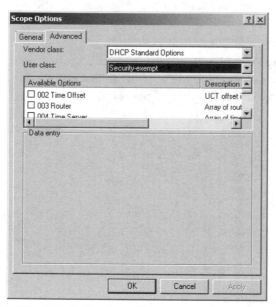

FIGURE 4-23 Configuring options for a custom user class

Finally, you need to populate the class. For the desired computers to inherit the options of the new class, you need to set the class ID of appropriate client computers to match the ID you have defined for that class at the DHCP server. You can do this by executing the Ipconfig /setclassid command at a command prompt at each client computer.

For example, to configure a connection named "Local Area Connection" with the class ID named "SampleID," type the following command:

```
ipconfig /setclassid "local area connection" SampleID
```

After you run this command on a DHCP client, the client will inherit the options defined for that class in addition to the options defined for the default user class. If the two options conflict, such as with the definition of a default gateway, the option defined for the more specific class takes precedence over the setting defined for the Default User class.

Controlling DHCP Access Through MAC Filtering

Windows Server 2008 R2 has a new feature called MAC filtering that allows you to restrict access to DHCP service by MAC address. MAC filtering is configured in the DHCP console in the Filters node, which includes an Allow folder and a Deny folder, as shown in Figure 4-24.

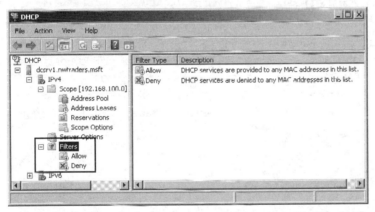

FIGURE 4-24 The Filters node allows you to restrict access to DHCP by MAC address.

The Allow folder acts as a whitelist. If you add a single MAC address to the Allow folder and enable the filter, all clients not listed are denied DHCP service. The Deny folder is a block list. Clients whose MAC addresses you add to this folder are explicitly denied DHCP service as soon as the filter is enabled.

You can easily add multiple MAC addresses to the Allow or Deny filter by using active leases. Select the Address Leases folder in the DHCP console tree, and then in the details pane, right-click the leases owned by the MAC addresses you want to filter. On the shortcut menu, point to Filters, and then select Allow or Deny. Figure 4-25 shows this procedure of using active leases to add MAC addresses to an Allow filter.

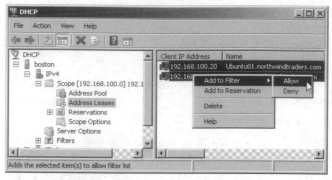

FIGURE 4-25 Adding computers to an Allow filter in DHCP

After you add computers to a filter, you still need to enable the Allow or Deny filter to change the default behavior of the DHCP server. You can enable (or disable) a filter by right-clicking the Allow or Deny folder in the DHCP console tree and then clicking Enable (or Disable). Alternatively, you can adjust these settings on the Filters tab of the IPv4 node properties dialog box.

DHCP Delay Configuration

The Delay Configuration setting is another feature new to DHCP in Windows Server 2008 R2. When you configure a delay on the Advanced tab of the Scope Properties dialog box (shown in Figure 4-26), you instruct the DHCP server to wait a specified number of milliseconds before responding to client requests for DHCP service. This feature is useful when you have two DHCP servers on the network and want to use one as a backup. In this scenario, you should configure the delay on your backup DHCP server so that the preferred server has a chance to respond first.

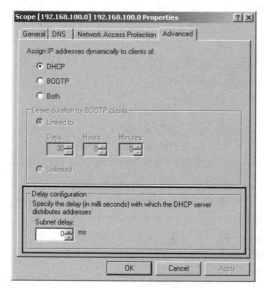

FIGURE 4-26 Configuring a delayed response from the DHCP server

Using the DHCP Split-Scope Configuration Wizard

It is recommended for fault tolerance that you deploy a backup DHCP server along with your primary DHCP server. To help you implement this two-DHCP server scenario, Windows Server 2008 R2 includes a wizard that configures two DHCP servers with identical configurations that split an address range. Prepare for the wizard by configuring the first DHCP server with the full address range and all desired options and settings. Then, add the DHCP server role to the second server, but don't add any scopes. On the first server, right-click the Scope folder in the DHCP console, point to Advanced, and then select Split-Scope, as shown in Figure 4-27.

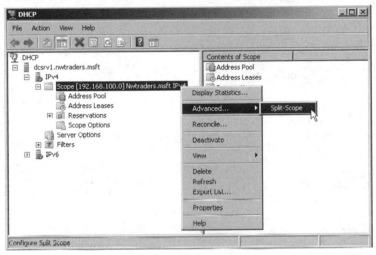

FIGURE 4-27 Starting the Split-Scope Configuration Wizard

The wizard asks you to specify the second DHCP server, and then it lets you distribute the addresses within the range as you choose, with a default of an 80/20 split, as shown in Figure 4-28.

The next page of the wizard allows you to configure a response delay for either server. It is recommended that you configure a response delay for the server with the smaller number of addresses available for lease.

After you complete the wizard, the new scope is automatically created on the second DHCP server, with all of the options, reservations, filters, and settings you configured on the first.

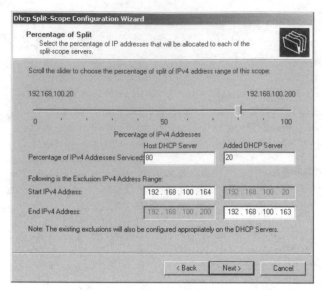

FIGURE 4-28 Splitting the address range in the DHCP Split-Scope Configuration Wizard

Configuring DHCP to Perform Dynamic DNS Updates for Clients

By default, whenever a DHCP server provides an address lease to a client running Windows 2000 or later, that DHCP server automatically attempts to register a pointer (PTR) record for the client in a reverse lookup zone on the DNS server. However, DHCP servers do not register host (A) records on behalf of clients by default. This is not a problem whenever clients running Windows 2000 or later are configured with a primary DNS suffix (such as in AD DS environments), because such DHCP clients can register their own host (A) records directly with the DNS server.

However, for computers not running Windows or Windows NT, and for all computers in workgroup environments, DHCP clients do not automatically register host (A) records in DNS. In these cases, you might want to change the DHCP server's default DNS update behavior so that it can perform more types of updates on behalf of its clients. To modify a DHCP server's DNS update behavior, use the DNS tab of a scope's Properties dialog box in the DHCP console. This DNS tab is shown with its default settings in Figure 4-29.

The default setting of Dynamically Update DNS A And PTR Records Only If Requested By The DHCP Clients essentially updates only a PTR record for DHCP clients running Windows 2000 and later. If you instead select Always Dynamically Update DNS A And PTR Records, the DHCP server will also update an A record for DHCP clients running Windows 2000 and later, provided that the DHCP client has received a lease specifying DHCP option 015 with a DNS domain name. The option Discard A And PTR Records When Lease Is Deleted, which is selected by default, removes the A and PTR records from the DNS database when the DHCP leases expire.

Next, you can also select the option to dynamically update DNS A and PTR records for DHCP clients that do not request updates. This option configures the DHCP server to perform DNS registration of A and PTR records for clients such as Windows NT clients and many Linux clients that do not request DNS updates.

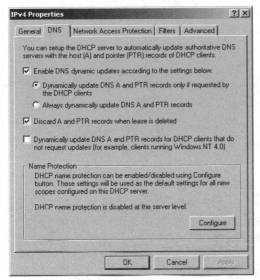

FIGURE 4-29 Default DNS update settings for a DHCP server

REAL WORLD

J.C. Mackin

The settings on the DNS tab are confusing, if not outright misleading. For example, the default setting claims to dynamically update A records if requested. However, I've never seen a single case where a DHCP server has registered an A record for a client when this setting is enabled. Also, the setting "Always dynamically update A and PTR records" sounds like an absolute rule, but this setting applies only to clients running Windows 2000 or later, not to Linux boxes or Macs, for example.

I've also made the mistake of applying dynamic update settings to the IPv4 node instead of to individual scopes. Bad idea. You are better off applying settings on a per-scope basis if you want to get the dynamic update behavior you expect.

Overall, dynamic update settings in DHCP seem temperamental and susceptible to unexpected behavior. Don't assume that enabling certain options will result in the behavior you are looking for, so be sure to test your configuration.

Configuring Name Protection

Windows Server 2008 R2 offers a new Name Protection feature for dynamic updates that you can configure by clicking the Configure button on the DNS tab. The Name Protection dialog box that opens is shown in Figure 4-30.

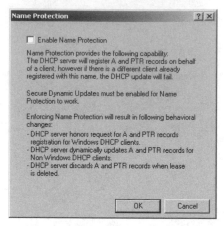

FIGURE 4-30 Configuring Name Protection for dynamic updates

Name Protection addresses a problem in which registrations for clients not running Windows can overwrite each other's resource records, even in zones where secure dynamic updates are enabled. With name protection, clients not running Windows are registered with additional resource records called DHCID records that effectively associate computer IDs with A records. As a result of this procedure, the DHCP server can perform DNS registrations on behalf of its clients only as long as no other computer, including non-Windows clients, has been registered in that DNS zone with the same name.

> **MORE INFO   NAME PROTECTION**
>
> For more information about the new feature of DHCP name protection in Windows Server 2008 R2, visit *http://technet.microsoft.com* and do a search for "Configuring Name Protection" and "DHCP Step-by-Step Guide: Demonstrate DHCP Name Protection in a Test Lab."

Using the DnsUpdateProxy Security Group

As mentioned previously, you can configure a DHCP server so that it dynamically registers both A and PTR resource records on behalf of DHCP clients. This configuration, however, can occasionally lead to problems in zones in which only secure dynamic updates are allowed. For example, if the DHCP server fails and is replaced by a backup DHCP server, the backup DHCP server will be unable to update any resource records that the original DHCP registered. As another example, if a DHCP server has registered a resource record on behalf of a client running an older version of Windows, and then the client computer is upgraded, the client will no longer be able to update its DNS record.

You can prevent these types of problems by adding the DHCP server to the built-in security group called DnsUpdateProxy in AD DS. When members of DnsUpdateProxy create resource records, the resource records have no security information. These records can therefore be updated by any computer, even in zones requiring secure updates. However, as soon as the first DHCP server or client that is not a member of the DnsUpdateProxy group modifies such a record, that server or client then becomes its owner. After that point, only the owner can update the record in zones requiring secure updates.

Installing and Configuring DHCP on a Server Core Installation

To configure a DHCP server on a Server Core installation of Windows Server 2008 or Windows Server 2008 R2, first install the DHCP Server role by typing the following command:

```
start /w ocsetup DHCPServerCore
```

Even though this command installs the DHCP Server role, it does not automatically start the DHCP Server service or configure the service to start automatically by default upon starting. To start the service for the first time, use the following command:

```
net start dhcpserver
```

To configure the DHCP service to start automatically, type the following command. (Be sure to include the space after the equal sign.)

```
sc config dhcpserver start= auto
```

After the DHCP Server role is installed on the Server Core installation, you will need to configure it. To add scopes and configure the server, you can simply connect to the server from the DHCP console on a computer running a full installation of Windows Server 2008 or Windows Server 2008 R2, or even Windows 7 with the Remote Server Administration Tools installed. You can then add scopes and perform all configurations remotely as if the server were local. Alternatively, you can create and configure scopes on the Server Core installation itself by using the Netsh utility at the command prompt.

If you want to configure a Server Core installation as a DHCP client for IPv4, type the following command, where "*local area connection*" is the name of the connection on the network:

```
netsh interface ipv4 set address "local area connection" dhcp
```

To configure the server to obtain a DNS server address through DHCP, type the following:

```
netsh interface ipv4 set dnsserver "local area connection" dhcp
```

Note that these two final commands need to be executed only if the setting has been changed from the default. As with all installations of Windows, a Server Core installation of Windows Server 2008 or Windows Server 2008 R2 is a full DHCP client by default.

Quick Check

- When you configure DHCP options for the Default User class, which clients are assigned these options?

Quick Check Answer

- All clients, except when a client is assigned a class-specific option that conflicts with an option defined for the Default User class. In this case, the class-specific option takes precedence.

PRACTICE **Creating an Exclusion Range**

In this practice, you will create an exclusion range on Dcsrv1 that prevents the DHCP server from leasing a particular set of addresses.

EXERCISE Creating an Exclusion Range

In this exercise, you will create an exclusion range on Dcsrv1 for the address range 192.168.0.200–192.168.0.210.

1. Log on to Nwtraders from Dcsrv1 as a domain administrator.

2. Open the DHCP console by clicking Start, pointing to Administrative Tools, and then choosing DHCP.

3. In the DHCP console tree, navigate to DHCP \dcsrv1.nwtraders.msft\IPv4\Scope [192.168.0.0.] Nwtraders.msft IPv4\Address Pool.

4. Right-click the Address Pool folder, and then choose New Exclusion Range. The Add Exclusion dialog box opens.

5. In the Add Exclusion dialog box, type **192.168.0.200** and **192.168.0.210** in the Start IP Address and End IP Address boxes, respectively.

6. Click Add, and then click Close. In the details pane, you can see that the address range you have configured is now listed. The icon next to the range includes a red X, and the description associated with the range is IP Addresses Excluded From Distribution.

7. Log off Dcsrv1.

Lesson Summary

- After you deploy a DHCP server, you might want to perform additional configuration by using the DHCP console. For example, you can create exclusion ranges, create reservations, adjust the lease duration, and configure additional options.

- An exclusion is an address within a scope's address range that cannot be leased to DHCP clients. You can use exclusions to make a scope's address range compatible with static addresses already assigned to computers on a network.

- A DHCP reservation is a particular address that a DHCP server assigns to a computer owning a particular MAC address.

- An options class is a client category that enables the DHCP server to assign options only to particular clients within a scope. Vendor classes are used to assign vendor-specific options to DHCP clients identified as a vendor type. User classes are used to assign options to any set of clients identified as sharing a common need for similar DHCP options configuration.

- The Default User class is a class to which all DHCP clients belong and the class in which all options are created by default.

- You can create a custom user class when you need to assign distinct options to distinct sets of client computers. After you create a custom user class and assign options to it, you can assign a client to a class by using the Ipconfig /setclassid command.

Lesson Review

You can use the following questions to test your knowledge of the information in Lesson 2, "Configuring a DHCP Server." The questions are also available on the companion CD if you prefer to review them in electronic form.

NOTE ANSWERS

Answers to these questions and explanations of why each answer choice is correct or incorrect are located in the "Answers" section at the end of the book.

1. You are deploying a DHCP server on your network to supply addresses in the 192.168.1.0/24 range. You have 200 DHCP client computers on the local subnet.

   The subnet includes a DNS server on the network with a statically assigned address of 192.168.1.100. How can you create a scope on the DHCP server that does not conflict with the existing DNS server address?

   A. Use the 006 DNS Servers option to assign to clients the address of the DNS server.

   B. Create a reservation that assigns the address 192.168.1.100 to the DNS server.

   C. Configure two address ranges in the DHCP scope that avoids the address 192.168.1.100.

   D. Create an exclusion for the address 192.168.1.100.

2. Which of the following commands should you run to install a DHCP server on a Server Core installation of Windows Server 2008 R2?

   A. sc config dhcpserver start= auto

   B. start /w ocsetup DHCPServerCore

   C. net start DHCPServer

   D. servermanagercmd -install dhcp

3. You are a network administrator for Contoso.com. Your network includes a single subnet of 200 computers, including 40 clients that are not running Windows. All computers are members of the Contoso.com Active Directory domain, which includes a DHCP server running Windows Server 2008 R2.

   You have noticed that certain Linux clients on your network are overwriting the DNS records of other clients that are not running Windows. What should you do to resolve this problem?

   A. Configure name protection on the DHCP server.

   B. Disable the option on the DHCP server to dynamically update A and PTR records for clients that do not request updates.

   C. Configure the DNS zone to allow nonsecure and secure dynamic updates.

   D. Add the DHCP server to the DnsUpdateProxy security group.

Chapter Review

To further practice and reinforce the skills you learned in this chapter, you can

- Review the chapter summary.
- Review the list of key terms introduced in this chapter.
- Complete the case scenario. This scenario sets up a real-world situation involving the topics of this chapter and asks you to create solutions.
- Complete the suggested practices.
- Take a practice test.

Chapter Summary

- DHCP servers provide clients with IP addresses. DHCP clients are those that have been configured to receive an address automatically. When such clients have no address, they send a network broadcast requesting the service of a DHCP server. If a DHCP server lies within broadcast range, it will answer the request and provide the client with an address from an address range you configure.
- Each range of contiguous addresses that can be assigned to DHCP clients is known as a scope.
- Addresses are leased to clients for a finite amount of time. The DHCP server keeps track of leased addresses in a local database.
- DHCP options are configuration settings that a DHCP server can assign to clients—settings such as a default gateway address and DNS server address.
- You can deploy a DHCP server by using the Add Roles Wizard to add the DHCP Server role. When you choose this role, the Add Roles Wizard gives you an opportunity to configure the basic features of a DHCP server. These features include a DHCP scope and basic DHCP options.

- You can also configure a DHCP server by using the DHCP console after you run the Add Roles Wizard. You can use the DHCP console to add new scopes, create exclusion ranges, create reservations, adjust the lease duration, and configure additional options.

Key Terms

Do you know what these key terms mean? You can check your answers by looking up the terms in the glossary at the end of the book.

- Default User class
- exclusion
- lease
- option
- options class
- reservation
- user class
- vendor class

Case Scenarios

In the following case scenarios, you will apply what you've learned about DHCP in this chapter. You can find answers to these questions in the "Answers" section at the end of this book.

Case Scenario 1: Deploying a New DHCP Server

You have just deployed a new DHCP server in your organization, whose network consists of a single subnet. After you finish running the Add Roles Wizard, you find that although all company computers can communicate with each other, only the computers with static addresses can communicate with the Internet. You confirm that the problem is not related to name resolution.

1. What configuration change can you make in the new scope that will enable the clients to communicate beyond the local subnet?
2. What step can you take in the DHCP console to force this configuration change to take effect?

Case Scenario 2: Configuring DHCP Options

Your network includes a DHCP server connected to both a wired subnet and a wireless subnet. The DHCP server uses a separate scope to provide addressing for each of the two subnets. For the wired subnet, the DHCP leases addresses in the range 192.168.10.0/24, and for the wireless subnet the DHCP server leases addresses in the range 192.168.20.0/24. These two subnets share many configuration options, including the same DNS domain name, the same DNS server list, and the same WINS server.

1. At what level should you configure the DHCP options specifying a domain name, DNS server, and WINS server?

2. You want to configure a special connection-specific DNS suffix for 30 of the 200 DCHP clients on the wired subnet. How can you best achieve this by using DHCP options?

Suggested Practice

To help you successfully master the exam objectives presented in this chapter, complete the following task.

Configure DHCP

This practice helps solidify your understanding of DHCP server concepts on your home network. If you do not have a home network, you can perform these exercises in a virtual environment instead.

- **Practice** Remove DHCP services from any devices on your network, and then deploy a new DHCP server on a server running Windows Server 2008 R2 on your home network. On the DHCP server, configure a scope with options for a DNS server and a default gateway. Run the **Ipconfig /release** and **Ipconfig /renew** commands on every client to ensure that they obtain addresses from the new DHCP server.

  Using the DHCP console, create a new user class with a name and class ID of your choice. Configure a special DHCP option for the class, such as an extended DNS server list or a WINS server address. Use the **Ipconfig /setclassid** command to assign the class ID to a client. Use **Ipconfig /renew** to obtain a new address lease on the same client and observe the effects.

  Create a DHCP reservation for another client on your network. In the reservation, specify a particular address in the middle of the IP address range of the scope. Then, configure DHCP options for the reservation. Use **Ipconfig /renew** to observe how the client is assigned the address specified and the option defined in the reservation.

Take a Practice Test

The practice tests on this book's companion CD offer many options. For example, you can test yourself on just one exam objective, or you can test yourself on all the 70-642 certification exam content. You can set up the test so that it closely simulates the experience of taking a certification exam, or you can set it up in study mode so that you can look at the correct answers and explanations after you answer each question.

> **MORE INFO** **PRACTICE TESTS**
>
> For details about all the practice test options available, see the "How to Use the Practice Tests" section in this book's Introduction.

CHAPTER 5

Configuring IP Routing

IP networks, including home networks, enterprise intranets, and the Internet, consist of a series of interconnected routers. *Routers* forward traffic to computers, to other routers, and finally to a destination computer. At the most basic, client computers send all communications through a single router known as the *default gateway*. If you connect multiple routers to a single subnet, however, you might need to configure more complex routing for computers on the subnet. Additionally, computers running Windows Server 2008 R2 can act as routers.

Exam objectives in this chapter:

- Configure routing.

Lessons in this chapter:

- Lesson 1: Routing   **292**

Before You Begin

To complete the lessons in this chapter, you should:

- Be familiar with Windows networking.
- Be comfortable with basic network configuration, including configuring IP settings.
- Have three virtual machines running Windows Server 2008 R2.

 REAL WORLD

Tony Northrup

For the exam, it's important to understand how to configure Windows Server 2008 R2 as a router. In the real world, you almost never use computers as routers. Hardware-based routers offer better performance with a lower purchase cost and cheaper maintenance. More importantly, they offer much better reliability. Because routers are designed to be only routers (whereas Windows Server 2008 R2 is designed to be everything from a web server to a mail server), much less can go wrong.

Although you might never configure a computer as a router, the understanding of IP routing that you will gain from this chapter will be immensely valuable when troubleshooting routers in the real world.

Lesson 1: Routing

This lesson provides an overview of routing concepts, describes how to troubleshoot routing problems using PathPing and Tracert, and then shows you how to configure static routing.

> **After this lesson, you will be able to:**
> - Describe routing concepts.
> - Use PathPing and Tracert to examine network routes.
> - Describe and configure routing protocols.
> - Use static routing to configure access to networks that cannot be reached through a default gateway.
>
> **Estimated lesson time: 45 minutes**

Routing Overview

Figure 5-1 shows a typical enterprise intranet consisting of three locations, each with four routers. As you can see, any of the example computers can communicate with any other computer by forwarding communications between routers.

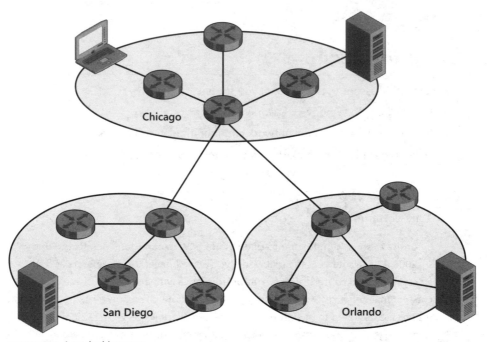

FIGURE 5-1 A typical intranet

As you know from earlier chapters, every computer must have a unique IP address. A router has an IP address, too, and must have a unique IP address assigned to every network interface. Figure 5-2 shows the Chicago network from Figure 5-1 with more detail, showing sample IP addresses for every router interface. In this example, all networks are class C with a subnet mask of 255.255.255.0.

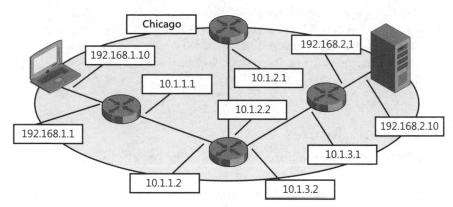

FIGURE 5-2 A routed network with IP addresses

On the network shown in Figure 5-2, imagine that the mobile computer on the left needs to connect to the server on the right. In this example, the mobile computer has the IP address 192.168.1.10. The router on the same subnet has the IP address 192.168.1.1 and would be configured as the default gateway on the mobile computer. To communicate from the mobile computer to the server, the process would be:

1. The mobile computer sends a packet with a source IP address of 192.168.1.10 and a destination IP address of 192.168.2.10. The mobile computer compares the destination IP address to the network ID of the local subnet and determines that the packet must be sent to a remote network. Because remote networks are always accessed through routers, the mobile computer forwards the packet to the default gateway with the IP address 192.168.1.1. *Gateway* is just another term for router.

2. When the default gateway receives the packet, it checks the destination address, 192.168.2.10. It examines its *routing table* (an index of destination networks and the interface or router used to access it) and determines that the next *hop* (a term for a router in a path) is the router with the IP address 10.1.1.2. So it forwards the packet to 10.1.1.2.

3. When the router with IP address 10.1.1.2 receives the packet, it also checks the destination IP address, 192.168.2.10, and determines that the next hop toward the destination is the router with the IP address 10.1.3.1.

4. When the router with IP address 10.1.3.1 receives the packet, it checks the destination IP address, 192.168.2.10, and determines that it has a network interface that is directly connected to the destination network. So it forwards the packet directly to the server by sending it on the server's local area network.

   If the server responds to the client, the packet flows back through each of the routers to the client.

Examining Network Routes

You can use the PathPing and Tracert commands to determine how packets travel between your computer and a destination. Both tools provide similar results: PathPing provides a more detailed and reliable analysis of network performance and Tracert provides a quicker response. The following demonstrates how PathPing displays a route to the *www.microsoft.com* destination:

```
Tracing route to www.microsoft.com [10.46.19.190]
over a maximum of 30 hops:
  0  d820.hsd1.nh.contoso.com. [192.168.1.199]
  1  c-3-0-ubr01.winchendon.ma.boston.contoso.com [10.165.8.1]
  2  ge-1-2-ur01.winchendon.ma.boston.contoso.com [10.87.148.129]
  3  ge-1-1-ur01.gardner.ma.boston.contoso.com [10.87.144.225]
  4  vlan99.csw4.NewYork1.Fabrikam.com [10.68.16.254]
  5  ae-94-94.ebr4.NewYork1.Fabrikam.com [10.69.134.125]
  6  ae-2.ebr4.SanJose1.Fabrikam.com [10.69.135.185]
  7  ae-64-64.csw1.SanJose1.Fabrikam.com [10.69.134.242]
  8  ge-2-0-0-51.gar1.SanJose1.Fabrikam.com [10.68.123.2]
  9    *        *        *
Computing statistics for 450 seconds...
            Source to Here   This Node/Link
Hop  RTT    Lost/Sent = Pct  Lost/Sent = Pct  Address
  0                                            d820.hsd1.nh.contoso.com. [192.168.1.199]
                              0/ 100 =  0%    |
  1   10ms    0/ 100 =  0%   0/ 100 =  0%  c-3-0-ubr01.winchendon.ma.boston.contoso.com
[10.165.8.1]
                              0/ 100 =  0%    |
  2   11ms    0/ 100 =  0%   0/ 100 =  0%  ge-1-2-ur01.winchendon.ma.boston.contoso.com
[10.87.148.129]
                              0/ 100 =  0%    |
  3   13ms    0/ 100 =  0%   0/ 100 =  0%  ge-1-1-ur01.gardner.ma.boston.contoso.com
[10.87.144.225]
                              0/ 100 =  0%    |
```

```
14    40ms      0/ 100 =   0%      0/ 100 =   0%  vlan99.csw4.NewYork1.Fabrikam.com
[10.68.16.254]
                                   0/ 100 =   0%   |
 15    40ms      0/ 100 =   0%      0/ 100 =   0%  ae-94-94.ebr4.NewYork1.Fabrikam.com
[10.69.134.125]
                                   0/ 100 =   0%   |
 16   107ms      0/ 100 =   0%      0/ 100 =   0%  ae-2.ebr4.SanJose1.Fabrikam.com
[10.69.135.185]
                                   0/ 100 =   0%   |
 17   108ms      0/ 100 =   0%      0/ 100 =   0%  ae-64-64.csw1.SanJose1.Fabrikam.com
[10.69.134.242]
                                   0/ 100 =   0%   |
 18   104ms      0/ 100 =   0%      0/ 100 =   0%  ge-2-0-0-51.gar1.SanJose1.Fabrikam.com
[10.68.123.2]
```

```
Trace complete.
```

Notice that PathPing shows the data in two sections. The first section shows the route from the source to the destination. The second section takes longer to generate and shows the latency in milliseconds (ms) to each router.

In this example, the last line of the first section shows three asterisk (*) symbols. This occurs when a node does not respond to the Internet Control Message Protocol (ICMP) requests. Servers are often configured to not respond to ICMP, so they will not appear in the list, even though they might be online and responding to other requests.

By default, Windows Server 2008 R2 does not respond to ICMP requests. This improves security, but can make troubleshooting difficult. To enable Windows Server 2008 R2 to respond to ICMP requests, run the following command at an administrative command prompt:

```
netsh advfirewall firewall add rule name="ICMP Allow incoming V4 echo request"
protocol=icmpv4:8,any dir=in action=allow
```

Routing Protocols

Although you can manually configure each router with a list of destination networks and the next hop for each network, routing protocols simplify configuration and allow routers to automatically adjust when network conditions change (for example, if a router or network connection fails).

When a router is connected to a network and the router has a routing protocol enabled, the routing protocol announces a list of networks to which it is directly connected. The router also listens for announcements from neighboring routers so that it can learn how to reach specific remote networks. This is illustrated in Figure 5-3.

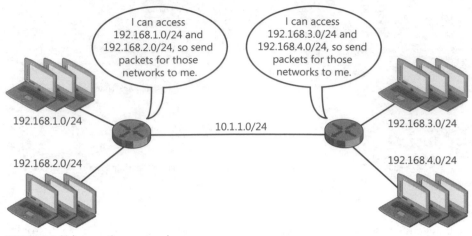

FIGURE 5-3 Using routing protocols

 EXAM TIP

For the exam, know what routing protocols do and when they should be used. You don't
need to understand the details of how they function, however.

Windows Server 2008 R2 (as well as earlier versions of Windows) supports Routing Internet
Protocol (RIP) version 2, a popular routing protocol. Windows Server 2008 R2 can also forward
multicast communications between subnets using the Internet Group Management Protocol
(IGMP) routing protocol. The sections that follow describe how to enable routing and how to
configure RIP and IGMP.

> **NOTE OSPF**
>
> Earlier versions of Windows supported the Open Shortest Path First (OSPF) routing protocol,
> which has been removed from Windows Server 2008 and Windows Server 2008R2.

Installing Routing and Remote Access Services

To install Routing And Remote Access Services, which includes tools for configuring Windows
Server 2008 R2 as a router, follow these steps:

1. Launch Server Manager.
2. In the left pane, select Roles, and then, in the right pane, click Add Roles.
3. If the Before You Begin page appears, click Next.

4. On the Select Server Roles page, select the Network Policy And Access Services check box, and then click Next.

5. On the Network Policy And Access Services page, click Next.

6. On the Select Role Services page, select the Routing And Remote Access Services check box. The wizard automatically selects the Remote Access Service and Routing check boxes. Click Next.

7. On the Confirmation page, click Install.

8. After the Add Roles Wizard completes the installation, click Close.

9. In the console tree of Server Manager, expand Roles, expand Network Policy And Access Services, and then select Routing And Remote Access. Right-click Routing And Remote Access, and then choose Configure And Enable Routing And Remote Access. The Routing And Remote Access Server Setup Wizard appears.

10. On the Welcome To The Routing And Remote Access Server Setup Wizard page, click Next.

11. On the Configuration page, select Custom Configuration, and then click Next.

12. On the Custom Configuration page, select the LAN Routing check box, and then click Next.

13. On the Completing The Routing And Remote Access Server Setup Wizard page, click Finish.

14. If the Routing And Remote Access dialog box appears, click Start Service.

Now you can configure RIP, as described in the following section, or use graphical tools to configure static routes, as discussed later in this lesson.

Configuring RIP

When you enable RIP, you allow Windows Server 2008 R2 to advertise routes to neighboring routers and to automatically detect neighboring routers and remote networks. To enable RIP, follow these steps:

1. In Server Manager, right-click Roles\Network Policy And Access Services\Routing And Remote Access\IPv4\General, and then choose New Routing Protocol.

2. In the New Routing Protocol dialog box, select RIP Version 2 For Internet Protocol, and then click OK.

3. Right-click Roles\Network Policy And Access Services\Routing And Remote Access \IPv4\RIP, and then choose New Interface.

4. In the New Interface For RIP Version 2 For Internet Protocol dialog box, select the interface you want to advertise with RIP. Then click OK. The RIP Properties dialog box appears.

5. Configure RIP settings to match those of neighboring routers. The default settings will work in most environments. You can adjust settings using the four tabs of the RIP Properties dialog box:

- **General** Select whether RIP v1 or RIP v2 is used and whether authentication is required.

- **Security** Choose whether to filter router advertisements. Because a routing protocol could be used to advertise a route to a malicious computer, RIP could be used as part of a man-in-the-middle attack. Therefore, you should restrict the advertised routes that will be accepted whenever possible.

- **Neighbors** Manually list the neighbors that the computer will communicate with.

- **Advanced** Configure announcement intervals and time-outs, as well as other infrequently used settings.

6. Click OK.

RIP is now enabled on the selected interface. Repeat this process for every interface that will have routing enabled.

Configuring an IGMP Proxy

IGMP multicasting transmits communications from one server to many clients. Instead of transmitting separate packets to each individual client, one packet is transmitted to all the clients simultaneously. Originally intended for streaming media, such as live video broadcasts across the Internet, IGMP is more commonly used in enterprise environments to deploy an operating system across the network to dozens of computers simultaneously.

Routers have to be specially configured to forward IGMP multicasts; otherwise, they will block the multicasts from being forwarded. If you use IGMP multicasting across subnets and configure a computer running Windows Server 2008 R2 as a router, you need to configure the IGMP Router And Proxy routing protocol to forward IGMP communications between subnets.

To configure the IGMP routing protocol, add the Network Policy And Access Services server role, configure Routing And Remote Access for LAN Routing, and then follow these steps:

1. In Server Manager, right-click Roles\Network Policy And Access Services\Routing And Remote Access\IPv4\General, and then click New Routing Protocol. The New Routing Protocol dialog box appears.

2. Select IGMP Router And Proxy, and then click OK. Routing And Remote Access adds the IPv4\IGMP node.

3. Right-click IGMP, and then click New Interface. The New Interface For IGMP Router And Proxy dialog box appears.

4. Select the network interface connected to the network that is transmitting IGMP communications, and then click OK. The IGMP Properties dialog box appears.

5. Verify that Enable IGMP Router is selected. You should configure the interface receiving IGMP communications as the IGMP Router, and the interface forwarding IGMP communications as the IGMP proxy. In other words, the IGMP Router is closest to the server, and the IGMP Proxy is closest to the clients. Click OK.

6. Right-click IGMP, and then click New Interface. The New Interface For IGMP Router And Proxy dialog box appears.

7. Select the network interface connected to the network that is receiving IGMP communications, and then click OK. The IGMP Properties dialog box appears.

8. Select IGMP Proxy, and then click OK.

Now, the computer will forward IGMP communications from the IGMP Router interface to the IGMP Proxy interface.

Demand-Dial Routing

Although most network connections stay active at all times, dial-up and virtual private network (VPN) connections can be connected only when a specified route is required. If you use a computer running Windows Server 2008 R2 as a router, you can configure it to establish a dial-up or VPN connection when clients attempt to communicate across a specified route (called *demand-dial routing*).

To configure demand-dial routing, add the Network Policy And Access Services server role, configure Routing And Remote Access for demand-dial routing, and then follow these steps:

1. In Server Manager, right-click Roles\Network Policy And Access Services\Routing And Remote Access, and then click Properties. Verify that LAN And Demand-Dial Routing is selected for either or both IPv4 Router and IPv6 Router. Click OK.

2. Right-click Network Interfaces, and then click New Demand-Dial Interface. The Demand-Dial Interface Wizard appears.

3. On the Welcome To The Demand-dial Interface Wizard page, click Next.

4. On the Interface Name page, type a name, and then click Next.

5. On the Connection Type page, click the type of connection you are creating, and then click Next. The next pages to appear in the wizard will vary depending on the type of connection you are creating. However, you will need to specify the remote server's location and select connection options, such as the VPN protocol to use.

6. On the Static Routes For Remote Networks page, click Add to configure the route for the demand-dial interface. The Static Route dialog box appears.

7. Select the type of network and then specify the destination, network mask, and metric. Any communications that match the destination and network mask and do not have an alternate route available with a lower metric will be sent across the demand-dial interface. Click OK.

8. Repeat steps 6 and 7 to add other routes to the demand-dial interface. Then, click Next. Other pages might appear, depending on the type of connection you are creating.

9. Click Finish.

Now, demand-dial routing will establish a connection each time any packet matches the routes you configured, and it will forward the packets across the connection. The connection will remain connected until the time-out period (5 minutes by default) expires. To test your newly configured interface by manually establishing a connection, right-click the interface, and then click Connect.

The default settings such as the time-out period are rarely useful, however. Computers tend to transmit packets regularly to determine whether a connection is still active, check for updates, and announce their presence on a network. As a result, these communications keep demand-dial interfaces active even if they are not required by an application. You can use demand-dial filters to configure which communications cause Routing And Remote Access to establish a connection by following these steps:

1. In the Routing and Remote Access snap-in, select the Network Interfaces node. In the details pane, right-click your demand-dial interface and select either Set IP Demand-Dial Filters or Set IPv6 Demand-Dial Filters.

   The Set Demand-Dial Filters dialog box appears. This dialog box can be configured in two ways: to establish a connection for any communications except those you explicitly configure, and to establish a connection only when Routing And Remote Access detects specified communications. To select the Only For The Following Traffic option, first add a filter.

2. Click New. The Add IP Filter dialog box appears.

3. Configure the source and destination networks for the filter. You can also configure specific protocols, such as TCP port 80, that the filter will match. Leave Source Port or Destination Port empty to match any port number. Click OK.

4. Repeat steps 2 and 3 to add more filters. Then, click OK.

You can further configure when Routing and Remote Access establishes connections by right-clicking the demand-dial interface and selecting Dial-Out Hours. The Dial-Out Hours dialog box allows you to configure when connections can be established. When you want the connection to remain connected permanently, right-click the interface and click Properties. Then, on the Options tab, select Persistent Connection and click OK.

Static Routing

On most networks, client computers need to be configured with a single default gateway that handles all communications to and from the subnet. Sometimes, for redundancy, network administrators might place two default gateways on a single subnet. Whether you use single or multiple default gateways, you do not need to configure static routing—just configure the default gateways using standard network configuration techniques such as Dynamic Host Configuration Protocol (DHCP).

EXAM TIP

For the exam, know that a router's IP address must always be on the same subnet as the computer.

If a computer needs to use different routers to communicate with different remote networks, you need to configure static routing. For example, in the network shown in Figure 5-4, the client computer would have a default gateway of 192.168.1.1 (because that leads to the Internet, where most IP address destinations reside). However, an administrator would need to configure a static route for the 192.168.2.0/24 subnet that uses the gateway at 192.168.1.2.

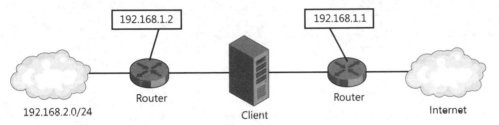

FIGURE 5-4 A network that requires static routing

Typically, you would do this configuration using the command-line tool Route. For the example shown in Figure 5-4, you could allow it to access the 192.168.2.0/24 network by running the following command:

```
route -p add 192.168.2.0 MASK 255.255.255.0 192.168.1.2
```

After running the command, the computer would route traffic destined for the 192.168.2.0/24 subnet through the router at 192.168.1.2. All other communications would be sent through the default gateway. The next section provides more information about using the Route command to configure static routing, and the section that follows it describes how to use Routing and Remote Access to configure static routes using graphical tools.

NOTE ON-DEMAND NETWORK CONNECTIONS

Dial-up networks and VPNs change a client's routing configuration automatically. Depending on how the connection is configured, dial-up networks either change the default gateway so that all traffic travels through the on-demand connection, or they establish temporary routes so that just the traffic destined for the private network is sent through the on-demand connection. Either way, you shouldn't have to manually configure the routing.

Configuring Static Routing with the Route Command

You can use the Route command to examine and configure static routing from a command prompt. To view the routing table, run the Route Print command. Output resembles the code on the following page.

```
==============================================================================
Interface List
 28 ........................... ContosoVPN
  7 ...00 15 c5 08 82 f3 ...... Broadcom NetXtreme 57xx Gigabit Controller
  8 ...00 13 02 1e e6 59 ...... Intel(R) PRO/Wireless 3945ABG Network Connection
  1 ........................... Software Loopback Interface 1
 16 ...00 00 00 00 00 00 00 e0  isatap.hsd1.nh.comcast.net.
 13 ...00 00 00 00 00 00 00 e0  6TO4 Adapter
 18 ...00 00 00 00 00 00 00 e0  Microsoft 6to4 Adapter
  9 ...02 00 54 55 4e 01 ...... Teredo Tunneling Pseudo-Interface
 30 ...00 00 00 00 00 00 00 e0  Microsoft ISATAP Adapter #2
 19 ...00 00 00 00 00 00 00 e0  isatap.hsd1.nh.comcast.net.
==============================================================================

IPv4 Route Table
==============================================================================
Active Routes:
Network Destination        Netmask          Gateway       Interface  Metric
          0.0.0.0          0.0.0.0      192.168.1.1   192.168.1.198     25
          0.0.0.0          0.0.0.0      192.168.1.1   192.168.1.199     10
         10.0.0.0        255.0.0.0          On-link   192.168.2.102     21
   10.255.255.255  255.255.255.255          On-link   192.168.2.102    266
   71.121.128.170  255.255.255.255      192.168.1.1   192.168.1.199     11
        127.0.0.0        255.0.0.0          On-link       127.0.0.1    306
        127.0.0.1  255.255.255.255          On-link       127.0.0.1    306
  127.255.255.255  255.255.255.255          On-link       127.0.0.1    306
      192.168.1.0    255.255.255.0          On-link   192.168.1.198    281
      192.168.1.0    255.255.255.0          On-link   192.168.1.199    266
    192.168.1.198  255.255.255.255          On-link   192.168.1.198    281
    192.168.1.199  255.255.255.255          On-link   192.168.1.199    266
    192.168.1.255  255.255.255.255          On-link   192.168.1.198    281
    192.168.1.255  255.255.255.255          On-link   192.168.1.199    266
      192.168.2.0    255.255.255.0      192.168.1.2   192.168.1.198     26
      192.168.2.0    255.255.255.0      192.168.1.2   192.168.1.199     11
      192.168.2.0    255.255.255.0    192.168.2.100   192.168.2.102     11
    192.168.2.102  255.255.255.255          On-link   192.168.2.102    266
        224.0.0.0        240.0.0.0          On-link       127.0.0.1    306
        224.0.0.0        240.0.0.0          On-link   192.168.1.198    281
        224.0.0.0        240.0.0.0          On-link   192.168.1.199    266
  255.255.255.255  255.255.255.255          On-link       127.0.0.1    306
  255.255.255.255  255.255.255.255          On-link   192.168.1.198    281
  255.255.255.255  255.255.255.255          On-link   192.168.1.199    266
  255.255.255.255  255.255.255.255          On-link   192.168.2.102    266
==============================================================================
Persistent Routes:
  Network Address          Netmask  Gateway Address  Metric
         10.0.0.0        255.0.0.0          On-link      11
      192.168.2.0    255.255.255.0      192.168.1.2       1
==============================================================================
```

```
IPv6 Route Table
===========================================================================
Active Routes:
 If Metric Network Destination       Gateway
  9    18 ::/0                       On-link
  1   306 ::1/128                    On-link
  9    18 2001::/32                  On-link
  9   266 2001:0:4137:9e66:2020:7c1:e7c0:b11e/128
                                     On-link
  8   281 fe80::/64                  On-link
  9   266 fe80::/64                  On-link
 19   266 fe80::5efe:192.168.1.198/128
                                     On-link
 19   266 fe80::5efe:192.168.1.199/128
                                     On-link
 30   266 fe80::5efe:192.168.2.102/128
                                     On-link
  8   281 fe80::462:7ed4:795b:1c9f/128
                                     On-link
  9   266 fe80::2020:7c1:e7c0:b11e/128
                                     On-link
  1   306 ff00::/8                   On-link
  9   266 ff00::/8                   On-link
  8   281 ff00::/8                   On-link
---------------------------------------------------------------------------
Persistent Routes:
  None
```

The routing table lists destination networks and the interface or router used to access it. Windows maintains separate routing tables for IPv4 and IPv6.

Although the routing table is complex, looking for specific details makes it easier to interpret. Most networks exclusively use IPv4, which means you should focus on the IPv4 Route Table section. Within that section, for example, focus on the following information:

- Routes with a Netmask of 0.0.0.0 show the default gateway.

- The Persistent Routes section displays any static routes to remote networks that have been added.

- Routes with a Netmask of 255.255.255.255 identify an interface and can be ignored.

- A network destination of 127.0.0.0 or 127.0.0.1 shows a loopback interface, which you can ignore.

- A network destination of 224.0.0.0 is a multicast address. Multicasting is rarely used

For example, consider the following line from the Route Print output:

```
10.0.0.0        255.0.0.0       On-link     192.168.2.102       21
```

This output indicates that the computer is configured to send traffic destined for the 10.0.0.0/8 network (a network of 10.0.0.0 with a subnet mask of 255.0.0.0) to the router at 192.168.2.102, rather than to the default gateway.

The following line of output shows that the default gateway is configured to be 192.168.1.1 (for the interface with the IP address 192.168.1.198). You can tell it's the default gateway because the subnet mask is set to 0.0.0.0, which would match all destination networks—assuming no more specific route exists.

```
0.0.0.0          0.0.0.0      192.168.1.1    192.168.1.198      25
```

Examining just the previous two static routes, you can determine that a connection to the IP address 10.12.55.32 would be sent to the router at 192.168.2.102. However, a connection to the IP address 172.18.39.75 would be routed through 192.168.1.1—the default gateway.

> **MORE INFO** **ROUTERS ON THE LOCAL NETWORK**
>
> Routers must always be on the same subnet as a computer. For example, a computer with the IP address 192.168.1.10 and a subnet mask of 255.255.255.0 could have a router with the IP address 192.168.1.1. However, a router with the IP address 192.168.2.1 would be invalid, because the router is on a different subnet—and to communicate with a remote subnet, a computer needs to send the packets to a router.

To add static routes from the command line, use the Route Add command. For example, if a neighboring router with the IP address 192.168.1.2 provides access to the network 10.2.2.0/24 (which would have a network mask of 255.255.255.0), you would run the following command to add a static route to the network:

```
route -p add 10.2.2.0 MASK 255.255.255.0 192.168.1.2
```

When using the Route Add command, the –p parameter makes a route persistent. If a route is not persistent, it will be removed the next time you restart the computer. Nonpersistent routes are primarily useful for temporary troubleshooting; for example, you might add a nonpersistent route as a workaround when the primary router fails or when you are testing a new router.

 Quick Check

1. When are static routes required?
2. What command would you use to configure a static route?

Quick Check Answers

1. Static routes are required when multiple gateways are connected to the local network, and one or more of them does not act as a default gateway.
2. You would use the *route add* command.

Configuring Static Routing with Routing and Remote Access

After installing Routing And Remote Access Services, you can view the IP routing table by right-clicking Roles\Network Policy And Access Services\Routing And Remote Access\IPv4 \Static Routes, and then choosing Show IP Routing Table. As shown in Figure 5-5, Routing And Remote Access displays the static routing table (which does not include any dynamic routes added from RIP).

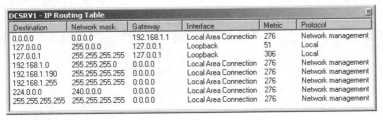

Destination	Network mask	Gateway	Interface	Metric	Protocol
0.0.0.0	0.0.0.0	192.168.1.1	Local Area Connection	276	Network management
127.0.0.0	255.0.0.0	127.0.0.1	Loopback	51	Local
127.0.0.1	255.255.255.255	127.0.0.1	Loopback	306	Local
192.168.1.0	255.255.255.0	0.0.0.0	Local Area Connection	276	Network management
192.168.1.190	255.255.255.255	0.0.0.0	Local Area Connection	276	Network management
192.168.1.255	255.255.255.255	0.0.0.0	Local Area Connection	276	Network management
224.0.0.0	240.0.0.0	0.0.0.0	Local Area Connection	276	Network management
255.255.255.255	255.255.255.255	0.0.0.0	Local Area Connection	276	Network management

DCSRV1 - IP Routing Table

FIGURE 5-5 The static routing table

To add static routes, follow these steps:

1. In Server Manager, right-click Roles\Network Policy And Access Services\Routing And Remote Access\IPv4\Static Routes, and then choose New Static Route.

2. In the IPv4 Static Route dialog box, select the network interface that will be used to forward traffic to the remote network. In the Destination text box, type the network ID of the destination network. In the Network Mask text box, type the subnet mask of the destination network. In the Gateway text box, type the IP address of the router to which packets for the destination network should be forwarded. Adjust the Metric only if you have multiple paths to the same destination network and want the computer to prefer one gateway over the others; in this case, configure the preferred routes with lower metrics. Figure 5-6 illustrates how to configure a static route. Click OK.

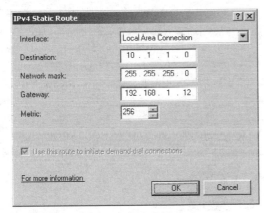

FIGURE 5-6 Adding a static route

Routing And Remote Access adds the static route, which is displayed in the details pane.

To remove static routes, right-click the route and then choose Delete.

Analyzing and Configuring Routing

In this practice, you examine real-world network routes and then use the Route command to configure static routes on a computer.

EXERCISE 1   Using PathPing and Tracert

In this exercise, you use PathPing and Tracert to examine the list of routers used to connect your computer to the web server at *www.microsoft.com*.

1. Log on to any computer (even a computer running an earlier version of Windows) with an Internet connection.

2. At a command prompt, run the command **pathping www.microsoft.com**.

3. While PathPing is computing statistics, open a second command prompt and run the command **tracert www.microsoft.com**.

4. In the Tracert window, examine the router names and IP addresses. The list shows every router used to carry communications from your computer to the web server at *www.microsoft.com*. Notice the latency time for each hop; routers that are farther away probably have higher latency because packets must travel a farther distance, and through more routers, before reaching the router. Notice that the last several lines of the Tracert output show the message Request Timed Out. This message is generated because the web server at *www.microsoft.com* is configured to not reply to ICMP messages.

5. When PathPing has completed computing statistics, examine the output. The router names and IP addresses should match those displayed by Tracert. The latency information is more detailed and accurate than Tracert, however, because the data was computed over a longer period of time.

EXERCISE 2   Configuring Static Routes

In this exercise, you will follow the steps to configure your network as shown in Figure 5-7. Then you will configure Dcsrv1 with a static route to forward traffic to the 192.168.112.0/24 subnet through Boston. Before changing the network configuration, use your virtual machine software to take a snapshot of all three virtual machines. After the exercise, revert your virtual machines to the snapshot state you created before reconfiguring the network settings.

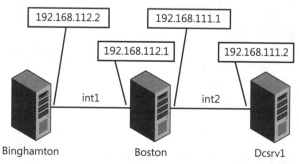

FIGURE 5-7 A practice routing architecture

Follow these steps to configure the three virtual machines with the necessary configurations for routing between two subnets:

1. Using your virtual machine software, create a snapshot of three virtual machines running Windows Server 2008 R2: Binghamton, Boston, and Dcsrv1. After the exercise, you can restore this snapshot to return the three computers to their original state. If you do not have three virtual machines, create them by following the instructions in the Introduction of this book.

2. Using your virtual machine software, create two new virtual machine networks named **int1** and **int2**. Both networks should be internal networks not connected to the Internet or any physical network. They do not need Network Address Translation (NAT) or DHCP.

3. Using your virtual machine software, shut down all virtual machines. Then, configure the following virtual networks and virtual network adapters:

   - **Binghamton**   One network adapter, connected to the int1 internal network.

   - **Boston**   Two network adapters. Connect the first network adapter to the int1 network. Connect the second network adapter to the new internal network named int2.

   - **Dcsrv1**   One network adapter connected to the int2 internal network.

> **MORE INFO**   **CONFIGURING VIRTUAL MACHINES FOR MULTIPLE NETWORKS**
>
> For a demonstration of how to do this using the VirtualBox virtual machine software, watch the video "Configure Virtual Machine Network Adapters using VirtualBox" at http://www.youtube.com/watch?v=NBFtjAzMmUM.

4. Start the three virtual machines and log on to Windows. Then, configure the following IPv4 settings, which do not use DNS servers:

   - **Binghamton**   Configure the network adapter with the static IP address 192.168.112.2, a network mask of 255.255.255.0, and a default gateway of 192.168.112.1.

   - **Boston**   Configure the network adapter attached to int1 (probably Local Area Connection) with the IP address 192.168.112.1, a network mask of 255.255.255.0, and no default gateway. Configure the network adapter attached to int2 (probably Local Area Connection 2) with the IP address 192.168.111.1, a network mask of 255.255.255.0, and no default gateway.

   - **Dcsrv1**   Configure the network adapter with the static IP address 192.168.111.2, a network mask of 255.255.255.0, and no default gateway.

5. To enable you to test the connections between computers, run the following command at an administrative command prompt on Binghamton, Boston, and Dcsrv1:

```
netsh advfirewall firewall add rule name="ICMP Allow incoming V4 echo request" _
    protocol=icmpv4:8,any dir=in action=allow
```

6. On Boston, verify that you can communicate with Binghamton and Dcsrv1 by running the following commands:

```
ping 192.168.112.2
ping 192.168.111.2
```

   If the virtual machines do not respond to the ping requests, try swapping the IP configuration between Boston's two network adapters. If the virtual machines still do not respond to the ping requests, verify the network configuration in your virtual machine software.

7. On Binghamton, run the following commands to ping Boston's two network addresses:

```
ping 192.168.112.1
ping 192.168.111.1
```

   The first request, for Boston's local network adapter, will succeed. The second request, for Boston's remote network adapter, will fail. Even though the computers can communicate, Boston is not yet configured to act as a router. Therefore, it will not forward packets from int1 to int2.

8. Now, configure Boston to act as a router. Configure Routing and Remote Access on Boston by following these steps:

   a. Launch Server Manager.

   b. In the left pane, select Roles, and then, in the right pane, click Add Roles.

   c. If the Before You Begin page appears, click Next.

   d. On the Select Server Roles page, select the Network Policy And Access Services check box, and then click Next.

   e. On the Network Policy And Access Services page, click Next.

   f. On the Select Role Services page, select the Routing And Remote Access Services check box. The wizard automatically selects the Remote Access Service and Routing check boxes. Click Next.

   g. On the Confirmation page, click Install.

   h. After the Add Roles Wizard completes the installation, click Close.

   i. In the console tree of Server Manager, expand Roles, expand Network Policy And Access Services, and then select Routing And Remote Access. Right-click Routing And Remote Access, and then choose Configure And Enable Routing And Remote Access. The Routing And Remote Access Server Setup Wizard appears.

   j. On the Welcome To The Routing And Remote Access Server Setup Wizard page, click Next.

   k. On the Configuration page, select Custom Configuration, and then click Next.

   l. On the Custom Configuration page, select the LAN Routing check box, and then click Next.

m. On the Completing The Routing And Remote Access Server Setup Wizard page, click Finish.

n. If the Routing And Remote Access dialog box appears, click Start Service. Now, Boston will forward requests between its two network adapters.

9. On Binghamton, run the following command to ping Boston's remote network address:

   `ping 192.168.111.1`

   The ping request will succeed even though the IP address is not on the local network, because Binghamton has Boston configured as a default gateway. Therefore, requests for any subnet that do not match 192.168.112.0 with a network mask of 255.255.255.0 (192.168.112.0/24) will be forwarded to Boston's local IP address, 192.168.112.1. Boston will then forward the request, and any responses, to the appropriate subnet.

10. On Dcsrv1, run the following command to ping Binghamton:

    `ping 192.168.112.2`

    The ping transmit will fail because Dcsrv1 does not have a route to the 192.168.112.2 network; recall that you did not configure it with a default gateway.

11. On Binghamton, run the following command to ping Dcsrv1:

    `ping 192.168.111.2`

    The ping request will fail even though Binghamton has Boston configured as a default gateway. Because Dcsrv1 does not have a route to the 192.168.112.2 network, it cannot respond to the ICMP ping requests that Boston forwards to it.

12. On Dcsrv1, run the following command at an administrative command prompt to add a static route to the 192.168.112.2 network through Boston's IP address, 192.168.111.1:

    `route add 192.168.112.0 MASK 255.255.255.0 192.168.111.1`

    Because you did not use the –p parameter, the route will disappear if you restart Dcsrv1.

13. Now, run the following command and verify that the static route was added correctly:

    `route print`

14. On Dcsrv1, run the following command again to ping Binghamton:

    `ping 192.168.112.2`

    This time, Binghamton will respond because Dcsrv1 has a route to the 192.168.112.0/24 network through Boston. Because ping requires two-way communications, this response also verifies that Binghamton can communicate to Dcsrv1.

15. You can now return all virtual machines to their original network configuration and restore the snapshot you created at the beginning of the exercise.

Lesson Summary

- Routing allows routers to forward traffic between each other to allow clients and servers on different subnets to communicate.

- PathPing and Tracert allow you to identify the routers between a source and destination. Both tools are also useful for identifying routing problems.

- Routers use routing protocols to communicate available routes, as well as to communicate changes such as failed links. Windows Server 2008 R2 supports RIP v2, which you can enable by installing the Routing and Remote Access Services role service.

- You can use static routing to allow computers with multiple routers connected to their subnet to forward traffic with different destinations to the correct router.

Lesson Review

You can use the following questions to test your knowledge of the information in Lesson 1, "Routing." The questions are also available on the companion CD if you prefer to review them in electronic form.

> **NOTE ANSWERS**
>
> Answers to these questions and explanations of why each answer choice is correct or incorrect are located in the "Answers" section at the end of the book.

1. Currently, client computers on the 192.168.1.0/24 subnet are configured with the default gateway 192.168.1.1. You connect a second router to both the 192.168.1.0/24 subnet and the 192.168.2.0/24 subnet. You would like clients on the 192.168.1.0/24 subnet to connect to the 192.168.2.0/24 subnet using the new router, which has the IP address 192.168.1.2. What command should you run?

   A. route add 192.168.2.0 MASK 255.255.255.0 192.168.1.1

   B. route add 192.168.2.0 MASK 255.255.255.0 192.168.1.2

   C. route add 192.168.1.2 MASK 255.255.255.0 192.168.2.0

   D. route add 192.168.1.1 MASK 255.255.255.0 192.168.2.0

2. You are experiencing intermittent connectivity problems accessing an internal website on a remote network. You would like to view a list of routers that packets travel through between the client and the server. Which tools can you use? (Choose all that apply.)

   A. PathPing

   B. Ping

   C. Ipconfig

   D. Tracert

3. You configure a computer running Windows Server 2008 R2 with two network interfaces. Each of the interfaces is connected to different subnets. One of those subnets has four other routers connected to it, and each router provides access to different subnets. You would like the computer running Windows Server 2008 R2 to automatically identify the routers and determine which remote subnets are available using each router. What should you do?

   A. Enable NAT on the interface.

   B. Enable OSPF on the interface.

   C. Enable RIP on the interface.

   D. Add a static route to the interface.

Chapter Review

To further practice and reinforce the skills you learned in this chapter, you can perform the following tasks:

- Review the chapter summary.
- Review the list of key terms introduced in this chapter.
- Complete the case scenarios. These scenarios set up real-world situations involving the topics of this chapter and ask you to create a solution.
- Complete the suggested practices.
- Take a practice test.

Chapter Summary

- Routing allows communications to be forwarded between subnets. On most networks, configuring computers with a default gateway is sufficient. On more complex networks with multiple routers that provide access to different remote networks, you need to configure static routing.
- By installing the Routing and Remote Access Services role service, you can use Windows Server 2008 R2 as a router, including the RIP version 2 routing protocol.

Key Terms

Do you know what these key terms mean? You can check your answers by looking up the terms in the glossary at the end of the book.

- gateway
- hop
- router
- routing table

Case Scenarios

In the following case scenarios, you will apply what you've learned about how to plan and configure routing. You can find answers to these questions in the "Answers" section at the end of this book.

Case Scenario 1: Adding a Second Default Gateway

You are a systems administrator for City Power & Light. Recently, the default gateway for the subnet used by your customer support staff failed. The network was offline for several hours until the default gateway was replaced.

Network engineering has since added a second default gateway. Now you need to configure client computers to connect through the second default gateway if the first default gateway is unavailable.

Answer the following question for your manager:

- How can you configure the client computers to use the second default gateway?

Case Scenario 2: Adding a New Subnet

You are a systems administrator working for Humongous Insurance. Recently, network administration added a new subnet, 192.168.2.0/24, that will be used for internal servers. Although client computers on the 192.168.1.0/24 subnet can access the new subnet through their default gateway of 192.168.1.1, the route is less than ideal because traffic must pass through two routers instead of just one. This network is illustrated in Figure 5-8.

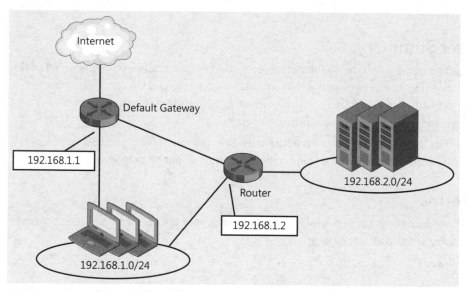

FIGURE 5-8 A sample network architecture

Answer the following questions for your manager:

1. Is there any way client computers on the 192.168.1.0/24 subnet can send traffic for the 192.168.2.0/24 subnet through the new router while sending traffic destined for every other network through the current default gateway?

2. What command should we run on the client computers?

Suggested Practices

To help you successfully master the exam objectives presented in this chapter, complete the following tasks.

- **Practice 1**   Use PathPing to check the path to several of your favorite websites. Which websites are near and which are far? Can you determine from the names of the routers where communications move from one Internet service provider (ISP) to another?

- **Practice 2**   Run the **route print** command at a command prompt. Examine each line until you understand the purpose of every route.

- **Practice 3**   If you have access to multiple routers and computers, connect two or more routers to a single subnet. Use static routing, configured using both command-line and graphical tools, to configure appropriate routes for each network.

- **Practice 4**   Repeat Practice 3, but configure IPv6 routing.

Take a Practice Test

The practice tests on this book's companion CD offer many options. For example, you can test yourself on just the content covered in this chapter, or you can test yourself on all the 70-642 certification exam content. You can set up the test so that it closely simulates the experience of taking a certification exam, or you can set it up in study mode so that you can look at the correct answers and explanations after you answer each question.

> **MORE INFO**   **PRACTICE TESTS**
>
> For details about all the practice test options available, see "How to Use the Practice Tests" in this book's Introduction.

CHAPTER 6

Protecting Network Traffic with IPsec

Internet Protocol Security (IPsec) protects networks by securing IP packets through encryption and through the enforcement of trusted communication. You can use IPsec to secure communication between two hosts or to secure traffic across the Internet in virtual private network (VPN) scenarios.

You can manage IPsec through Local Security Policy, Group Policy, or command-line tools.

Exam objectives in this chapter:
- Configure Windows Firewall with Advanced Security.
- Gather network data.

Lessons in this chapter:
- Lesson 1: Configuring IPsec **316**

Before You Begin

To complete the lessons in this chapter, you must have the following:

- A Windows Server 2008 R2 domain controller named dcsrv1.nwtraders.msft.
- A computer named boston.nwtraders.msft that is running Windows Server 2008 R2 and that is a member of the Nwtraders domain (file sharing must be enabled on this computer).
- A computer named binghamton.nwtraders.msft that is running Windows Server 2008 R2 and that is a member of the Nwtraders domain. Binghamton can obtain its IPv4 address via DHCP, or you can assign it a static address such as 192.168.0.3. You can manually assign Binghamton an IPv6 address such as fd00::3, and specify the DNS server in IPv6 as fd00::1.
- A basic understanding of Windows networking and Group Policy.

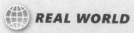

REAL WORLD

J.C. Mackin

Windows Server 2008 and Windows Server 2008 R2 have introduced a few modest but noteworthy enhancements to IPsec. The most important of these changes is the addition of Connection Security Rules, which facilitate implementing IPsec for authenticated communication on a network. Connection Security Rules aren't heavily tested on the 70-642 exam, but they are a useful addition to your real-world expertise.

Connection Security Rules first appeared as an option for individual computers in Windows Vista, but beginning with Windows Server 2008, you now have the option of enforcing Connection Security Rules through a Group Policy object (GPO), which is in the Windows Firewall with Advanced Security node.

By default, Connection Security Rules do not encrypt data but only provide protection against spoofed data, altered data, and replay attacks. I would recommend leaving Connection Security Rules to perform these default functions and instead using IPsec Policies when you need encryption. The biggest advantage of Connection Security Rules is their simplicity, and when you create custom rules with expanded functionality, you negate the main benefit of the feature.

Lesson 1: Configuring IPsec

Internet Protocol Security (IPsec) is a means to protect network data by ensuring its authenticity, its confidentiality, or both. In Windows Server 2008 or Windows Server 2008 R2 networks, you typically implement IPsec through Group Policy, either through IPsec Policies or through Connection Security Rules.

> **After this lesson, you will be able to:**
> - Deploy IPsec on a network through Group Policy.
>
> **Estimated lesson time: 70 minutes**

What Is IPsec?

IPsec is essentially a way to provide security for data sent between two computers on an IP network. IPsec is not just a Windows feature but also an industry-wide standard developed by the Internet Engineering Task Force (IETF) and implemented on many types of operating systems and devices.

IPsec protects data between two IP addresses by providing the following services:

- **Data authentication** IPsec provides data authentication in the form of data origin authentication, data integrity, and anti-replay protection.

    - **Data origin authentication** You can configure IPsec to ensure that each packet you receive from a trusted party in fact originates from that party and is not spoofed.

    - **Data integrity** You can use IPsec to ensure that data is not altered in transit.

    - **Anti-replay protection** You can configure IPsec to verify that each packet received is unique and not duplicated.

- **Encryption** You can use IPsec to encrypt network data so that the data is unreadable if captured in transit.

In Windows Vista, Windows 7, Windows Server 2008 and Windows Server 2008 R2, IPsec is enforced either by IPsec Policies or Connection Security Rules. IPsec Policies by default attempt to negotiate both authentication and encryption services. Connection Security Rules by default attempt to negotiate only authentication services. However, you can configure IPsec Policies and Connection Security Rules to provide any combination of data protection services.

> **NOTE IPSEC BEYOND WINDOWS**
> Because IPsec is an interoperable standard, it can be implemented to secure communications between computers running Windows and computers not running Windows.

IPsec Policies

IPsec Policies define how a computer or group of computers handles IPsec communications. You can assign an IPsec Policy either to an individual computer by using Local Security Policy or to a group of computers by using Group Policy. Although you may define many IPsec Policies for use on a computer or network, only one policy is ever assigned to a computer at any given time.

Figure 6-1 shows a Group Policy object (GPO) in which an IPsec Policy is assigned.

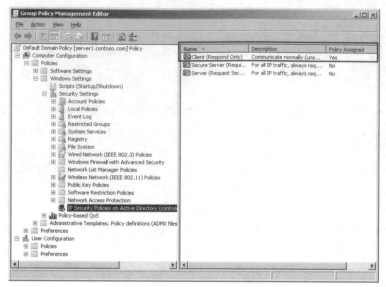

FIGURE 6-1 IPsec Policies in a GPO

Every IPsec Policy is composed of one or more IPsec Policy *rules* that determine when and how IP traffic should be protected. Each policy rule, in turn, is associated with one IP filter list and one filter action.

IP filter lists contain a set of one or more *IP filters* that capture IP traffic for an IPsec Policy. IP filters define a source or destination address, address range, computer name, TCP/UDP port, or server type (DNS, WINS, DHCP, or default gateway). If traffic leaving or arriving at a computer on which a policy is assigned matches a filter in one of the assigned policy's policy rules, the filter action associated with that rule is applied. Possible filter actions for a rule include block, permit, or negotiate security. Note that when matching a source or destination address, the most specific IPsec filter always takes precedence.

> **NOTE   HOW IS SECURITY NEGOTIATED?**
>
> Negotiate Security is a general option for a filter action, but you can then specifically choose the way security is negotiated for that filter action. For example, should encryption or merely authentication (data integrity) be negotiated? What is the order of preference for encryption technologies or hashing algorithms? Is it okay to fall back to unsecured communications if no common protocol for security can be agreed upon? Because there are so many ways that you can choose to negotiate security for a filter action, it is possible to define many distinct rules for which the Negotiate Security option has been selected. Remember also that you can successfully negotiate security only when both ends of an IPsec connection can agree on the particular services and algorithms used to protect the data.

IPSEC POLICY EXAMPLE

Figure 6-2 illustrates an IPsec Policy and how that policy is composed of rules, filters, and filter actions. In the illustrated example, the IPsec Policy is made up of three rules. The first rule has priority because it defines traffic the most specifically—both by type (Telnet or Post Office Protocol 3 [POP3]) and by address (from 192.168.3.32 or 192.168.3.200). The second rule is the next most specific, defining traffic by type only (Telnet or POP3). The third rule is the least specific because it applies to all traffic and therefore has the lowest priority. As a result of the IPsec policy composed of these three rules, a computer to which this policy is assigned will attempt to authenticate (but not encrypt) all data aside from Telnet traffic and POP3 traffic. Telnet traffic and POP3 traffic by default are blocked unless they originate from 192.168.3.32 (for Telnet) or 192.168.3.200 (for POP3), in which case the traffic is allowed if encryption can be successfully negotiated.

IPsec Policy

	IP Filter Lists	Filter Actions
Policy Rule #1	Filter #1. Telnet Traffic from 192.168.3.32 Filter #2: POP3 Traffic from 192.168.3.200	Negotiate Security (Require Encryption)
Policy Rule #2	Filter #1: All Telnet Traffic Filter #2: All POP3 Traffic	Block
Policy Rule #3	Filter #1: All Traffic	Negotiate Security (Request Authentication)

Less specific/Lower priority ↓

FIGURE 6-2 IPsec Policies, rules, filters, and filter actions

 Quick Check

1. Does every IPsec Policy rule have an IP filter list?
2. In terms of its function within an IPsec Policy, what does a filter action do?

Quick Check Answers

1. Yes, even if the list has only one IP filter.
2. A filter action determines whether the traffic captured by an IP filter in a given policy rule is permitted, blocked, encrypted, or authenticated.

Connection Security Rules

You can also use Connection Security Rules to configure IPsec settings for connections between computers. Like IPsec Policies, Connection Security Rules evaluate network traffic and then block, allow, or negotiate security for messages based on the criteria you establish. The main advantage of using Connection Security Rules is that they are simpler to configure.

A Connection Security Rule first authenticates the computers defined in the rule before the computers begin communication. It then secures the information sent between these two authenticated computers. If you have configured a Connection Security Rule that requires security for a given connection and the two computers in question cannot authenticate each other, the connection is blocked.

By default, Connection Security Rules provide only data authentication security (data origin authentication, data integrity, and anti-replay security). For this reason, Connection Security Rules are typically said to only *authenticate* connections. However, you can also configure data encryption for Connection Security Rules so that the connections in question are truly *secured* and not merely authenticated.

You configure Connection Security Rules for any one computer in the Windows Firewall with Advanced Security (WFAS) console or the WFAS node in Server Manager. If you want to enforce specific WFAS settings for multiple clients on a network, you should use Group Policy. Figure 6-3 shows a GPO that defines Connection Security Rules for many computers on a network.

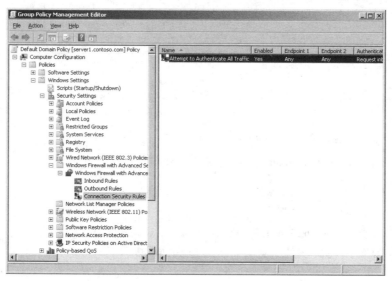

FIGURE 6-3 Defining Connection Security Rules in Group Policy

NOTE **EXPORTING CONNECTION SECURITY RULES**

By using the Export Policy and Import Policy functions in the WFAS console, you can create one set of Connection Security Rules and export them to other computers or GPOs.

Security Associations

After two computers negotiate an IPsec connection, whether through IPsec Policies or Connection Security Rules, the data sent between those computers is secured in what is known as a *Security Association (SA)*. Security for an SA is provided by the two IPsec protocols—Authentication Header (AH) and Encapsulating Security Payload (ESP). These protocols provide data and identity protection for each IP packet in an SA. AH provides data origin authentication, data integrity, and anti-replay protection for the entire IP packet. ESP provides data encryption, data origin authentication, data integrity, and anti-replay protection for the ESP payload. To secure data within any SA, you can use either AH alone, ESP alone, or AH and ESP together.

EXAM TIP

You need to know the basic difference between AH and ESP for the 70-642 exam. If you need encryption, use ESP. If you just need to authenticate the data origin or verify data integrity, use AH.

How IPsec Connections Are Established

To establish SAs dynamically between IPsec peers, the Internet Key Exchange (IKE) protocol is used. IKE establishes a mutually agreeable policy that defines the SA—a policy that includes its security services, protection mechanisms, and cryptographic keys between communicating peers. In establishing the SA, IKE also provides the keying and negotiation for the IPsec security protocols AH and ESP.

To ensure successful and secure communication, IKE performs a two-phase negotiation operation, each with its own SAs. Phase 1 negotiation is known as *main mode* negotiation, and Phase 2 is known as *quick mode* negotiation. The IKE main mode SAs are used to secure the second IKE negotiation phase. As a result of the second IKE negotiation phase, quick mode SAs are created. These quick mode SAs are the ones used to protect application traffic.

You can summarize the steps for establishing an IPsec connection in the following way:

1. Set up a main mode SA.

   You can see this step in Figure 6-4, which shows a network capture of an IPsec connection being established between two computers, Boston and Binghamton. In the first 10 packets of the capture, you can see that the description of the IKE packets refer to "Main Mode." In addition, Kerberos is used for authentication in setting up the main mode SA.

2. Agree upon the terms of communication and encryption algorithm.

   You can see this exchange in Figure 6-4 after authentication is complete in main mode SA. After the main mode is negotiated, the terms of communication and encryption for the quick mode are established in a two-packet exchange between the two computers.

3. Create a quick mode SA.

You can see this exchange in Figure 6-4 by looking for the description "Quick Mode" in IKE packet descriptions. In the quick mode SA, the terms of communication and encryption for the subsequent data stream are established.

4. Send data.

You can see this exchange in Figure 6-4 by the protocol name "ESP." ESP is the protocol used to encrypt traffic in IPsec. As a result, you can see only the sequence information about the data stream. All other information contained in the packets is protected.

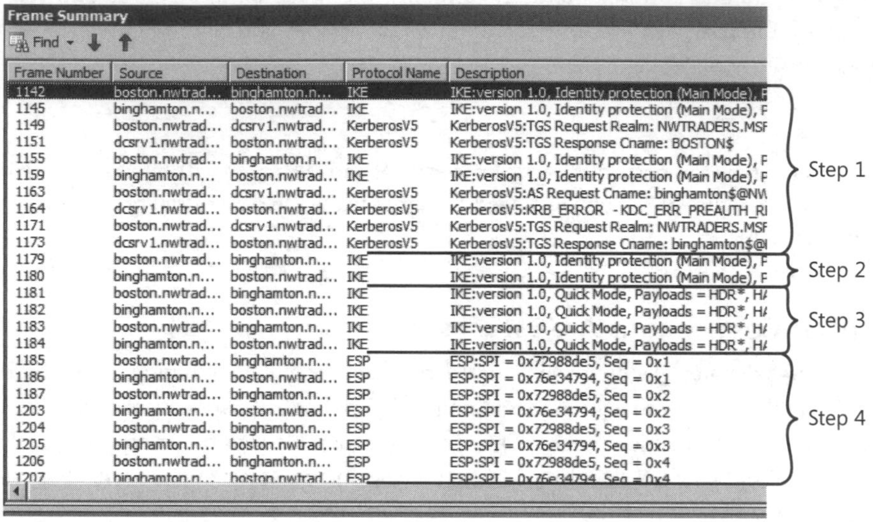

FIGURE 6-4 A network capture of IPsec encryption

Using IPsec in Tunnel Mode

IPsec by default operates in *transport mode*, which is used to provide end-to-end security between computers. Transport mode is also used in most IPsec-based VPNs, for which the Layer Two Tunneling Protocol (L2TP) is used to tunnel the IPsec connection through the public network.

However, when a particular VPN gateway is not compatible with L2TP/IPsec VPNs, you can use IPsec in *tunnel mode* instead. With tunnel mode, an entire IP packet is protected and then encapsulated with an additional, unprotected IP header. The IP addresses of the outer IP header represent the tunnel endpoints, and the IP addresses of the inner IP header represent the ultimate source and destination addresses.

> **NOTE TUNNEL MODE IS RARELY USED**
>
> IPsec tunnel mode is supported as an advanced feature. It is used in some gateway-to-gateway tunneling scenarios to provide interoperability with routers, gateways, or end-systems that do not support L2TP/IPsec or Point-to-Point Tunneling Protocol (PPTP) connections. IPsec tunnels are not supported for remote access VPN scenarios. For remote access VPNs, use L2TP/IPsec or PPTP. These VPNs are discussed in Chapter 7, "Connecting to Networks."

An illustration of an IPsec tunnel is shown in Figure 6-5.

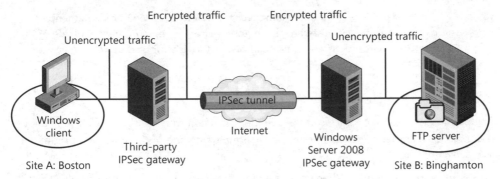

FIGURE 6-5 Gateway-to-gateway tunneling between sites

 EXAM TIP

You need to understand the basics of IPsec tunnel mode for the 70-642 exam.

Authentication Methods for IPsec

An essential concept in implementing IPsec is that IPsec requires a shared authentication mechanism between communicating computers. You can use any of these three methods to authenticate the hosts communicating through IPsec:

- **Kerberos (Active Directory)** Because Kerberos is the default authentication protocol in an Active Directory environment, the easiest way to configure authentication for IPsec is to implement IPsec within a single Active Directory forest. When the two IPsec endpoints can be authenticated by Active Directory, the security foundation for IPsec requires no configuration beyond joining the hosts to the domain. Note that if your network environment includes a Kerberos realm outside of Active Directory, you can also use this Kerberos realm to provide authentication for IPsec communications.

- **Certificates** If you need to implement IPsec in a production environment in which Kerberos authentication is not available, you should use a certificate infrastructure to authenticate the IPsec peers. In this solution, each host must obtain and install a computer certificate from a public or private certification authority (CA). The computer certificates do not need to originate from the same CA, but each host must trust the CA that has issued the certificate to the communicating peer.

- **Preshared key** A preshared key is a password shared by peers and used both to encrypt and decrypt data. In IPsec, you can also specify a preshared key on endpoints to enable encryption between hosts. Although this authentication method enables IPsec SAs to be established, preshared keys do not provide the same level of authentication that certificates and Kerberos do. In addition, preshared keys for IPsec are stored in plaintext on each computer or in Active Directory, which reduces the security of this solution. For these reasons, it is recommended that you use preshared keys only in nonproduction environments such as test networks.

Assigning a Predefined IPsec Policy

In Group Policy, three IPsec Policies are predefined. You can thus configure an IPsec Policy for a domain or an organizational unit (OU) by assigning any one of the following predefined policies:

- **Client (Respond Only)**   When you assign this policy to a computer through a GPO, that computer will never initiate a request to establish an IPsec communications channel with another computer. However, any computer to which you assign the Client policy will negotiate and establish IPsec communications when requested by another computer. You typically assign this policy to intranet computers that need to communicate with secured servers but that do not need to protect all traffic.

- **Server (Request Security)**   You should assign this policy to computers for which encryption is preferred but not required. With this policy, the computer accepts unsecured traffic but always attempts to secure additional communications by requesting security from the original sender. This policy allows the entire communication to be unsecured if the other computer is not IPsec-enabled. For example, communication to specific servers can be secure while allowing the server to communicate in an unsecured manner to accommodate a mixture of clients (some of which support IPsec and some of which do not).

- **Secure Server (Require Security)**   You should assign this policy to intranet servers that require secure communications, such as a server that transmits highly sensitive data.

To assign an IPsec Policy within a GPO, select the IP Security Policies node, right-click the chosen policy in the details pane, and then choose Assign from the shortcut menu, as shown in Figure 6-6.

You can assign only one IPsec Policy to a computer at a time. If you assign a second IPsec Policy to a computer, the first IPsec Policy automatically becomes unassigned. If Group Policy assigns an IPsec Policy to a computer, the computer ignores any IPsec Policy assigned in its Local Security Policy.

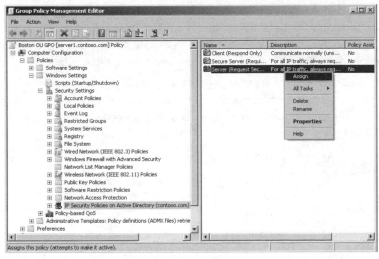

FIGURE 6-6 Assigning an IPsec Policy in a GPO

Creating a New IPsec Policy

To create a new custom IPsec Policy, first open Local Security Policy or a GPO. In the console tree below Security Settings, right-click the IP Security Policies node, and then choose Create IP Security Policy, as shown in Figure 6-7. (You can find Security Settings in a GPO in the Computer Configuration\Policies\Windows Settings container.) This procedure launches the IP Security Policy Wizard.

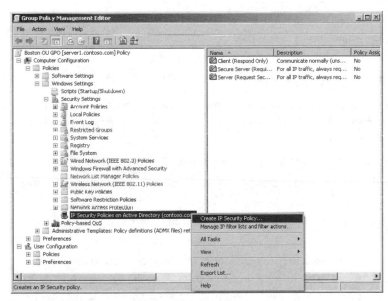

FIGURE 6-7 Creating a new IPsec Policy in a GPO

The IP Security Policy Wizard simply gives you an opportunity to create an "empty" policy, to name that IPsec Policy, and to enable the Default Response Rule. (The Default Response Rule is read only by versions of Windows earlier than Windows Vista. For those operating systems the rule provides a default action for an IPsec Policy when no other IPsec Policy filters apply.)

After you have created the IPsec Policy, you can configure the policy through its properties. In the properties, you can add rules to the policy by clicking the Add button in the Rules tab in the Properties dialog box for the policy, as shown in Figure 6-8. This procedure launches the Create IP Security Rule Wizard.

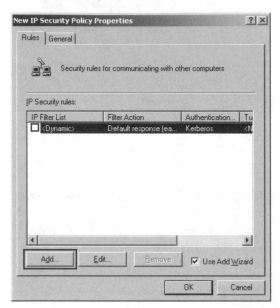

FIGURE 6-8 Launching the Create IP Security Rule Wizard

Using the Create IP Security Rule Wizard

The bulk of IPsec Policy configuration involves creating and configuring IPsec rules for that policy. To create and configure these rules, use the Create IP Security Rule Wizard (also known simply as the Security Rule Wizard).

The following list describes the five main pages of the Create IP Security Rule Wizard.

- **Tunnel Endpoint page**   Configure this page only when you want to use IPsec in tunnel mode.

- **Network Type page**   Use this page if you want to limit the rule to either the local area network or remote access connections.

- **IP Filter List page**   Use this page to specify the set of IP filters you want to attach to the rule. In Group Policy, two IP filter lists are predefined for IPsec Policy rules: All ICMP Traffic and All IP Traffic. To create a new IP filter list, click the Add button on the IP Filter List page, as shown in Figure 6-9. This procedure opens the IP Filter List dialog box.

Internet Control Message Protocol (ICMP) is a messaging feature of IP that allows Ping and Tracert to function. ICMP traffic typically refers to Ping and Tracert traffic.

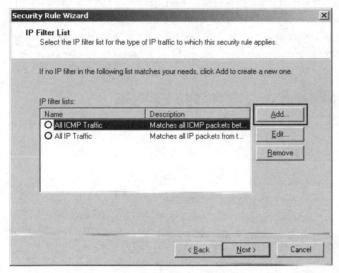

FIGURE 6-9 Creating a new IP filter list to attach to an IPsec Policy rule

To create a new IP filter to add to the new IP filter list you are creating, click the Add button in the IP Filter List dialog box, as shown in Figure 6-10. This procedure, in turn, launches the IP Filter Wizard.

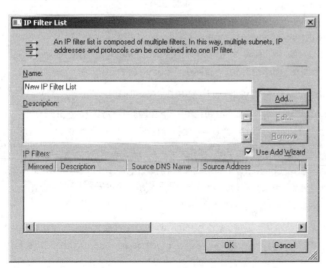

FIGURE 6-10 Creating a new IP filter to add to an IP filter list

Use the IP Filter Wizard to define IP traffic according to source and destination. You can specify a source and destination according to IP address, DNS name, server function (such as any DHCP server, DNS server, WINS server, or default gateway), and IP protocol type (including TCP/UDP port number).

You can also use the IP Filter Wizard to create a "mirrored" filter. A *mirrored filter* matches the source and destination with the exact opposite addresses so that, for example, you can easily configure a filter that captures POP3 traffic sent *to and from* the local address. To configure your filter as a mirrored filter, leave the Mirrored check box selected on the first page of the IP Filter Wizard, as shown in Figure 6-11.

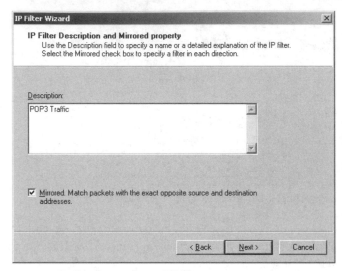

FIGURE 6-11 Creating a mirrored IP filter

- **Filter Action page** After you have attached the desired IP filter list to the rule, you can specify a filter action for the rule in the Security Rule Wizard. In Group Policy, the following three IP filters are predefined for IPsec Policy rules:

  - **Permit** Permits the IP packets to pass through unsecured.

  - **Request Security (Optional)** Permits the IP packets to pass through unsecured but requests that clients negotiate security (preferably encryption).

  - **Require Security** Triggers the local computer to request secure communications from the client source of the IP packets. If security methods (including encryption) cannot be established, the local computer will stop communicating with that client.

To create a new filter action, click the Add button on the Filter Action page of the Security Rule Wizard, as shown in Figure 6-12. This procedure launches the Filter Action Wizard.

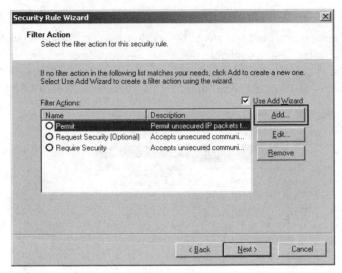

FIGURE 6-12 Creating a new filter action

- **Authentication Method page** Security can be negotiated only after the IPsec clients are authenticated. By default, IPsec rules rely on Active Directory directory service and the Kerberos protocol to authenticate clients. However, you can also specify a certificate infrastructure or a preshared key as a means to authenticate IPsec clients. To select the authentication method for IPsec, you can use the Authentication Method page of the Security Rule Wizard, as shown in Figure 6-13. (Note that this page does not appear if you select Permit on the Filter Action page.)

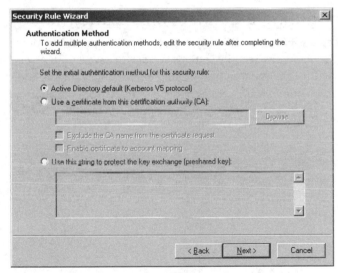

FIGURE 6-13 Specifying an authentication method for a new IPsec Policy rule

Managing IP Filter Lists and Filter Actions

The IP filters, IP filter lists, and filter actions you create for an IPsec rule can be shared with other IPsec rules. You can also create and configure these features outside of the Security Rule Wizard. To do so, right-click the IP Security Policies node in Local Security Policy or a GPO, and then choose Manage IP Filter Lists And Filter Actions, as shown in Figure 6-14.

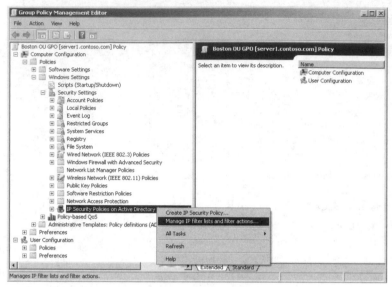

FIGURE 6-14 Managing IP filter lists and filter actions

Creating and Configuring a Connection Security Rule

To create a Connection Security Rule in a GPO, first browse to and expand Computer Configuration\Policies\Windows Settings\Security Settings\Windows Firewall With Advanced Security\Windows Firewall With Advanced Security – LDAP://*address*. Beneath this node, select and right-click the Connection Security Rules node, and then, from the shortcut menu, choose New Rule.

This procedure, which launches the New Connection Security Rule Wizard, is shown in Figure 6-15.

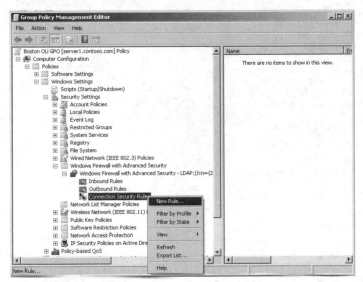

FIGURE 6-15 Creating a new Connection Security Rule

Using the New Connection Security Rule Wizard

The specific pages you see when you use the New Connection Security Rule Wizard depend on the type of rule you choose to create on the first page. The following sections describe the seven pages and associated rules you find when creating a custom rule.

RULE TYPE PAGE

As shown in Figure 6-16, the Rule Type page allows you to create any of five rule types—Isolation, Authentication Exemption, Server-To-Server, Tunnel, and Custom.

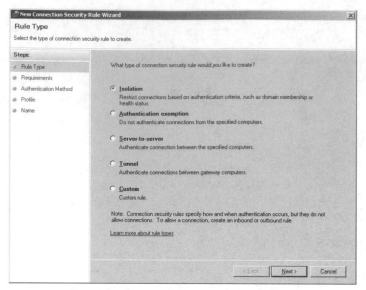

FIGURE 6-16 Choosing a Connection Security Rule type

- **Isolation rule** This is a general rule used to authenticate all traffic for select network *profiles* (network location types). When the network location defined for the local computer in Network and Sharing Center corresponds to one of the profiles selected for the rule, the local computer attempts to negotiate security as defined in the rule. The three profiles defined are Domain, Private, and Public.

EXAM TIP

You can use an Isolation rule to configure "domain isolation." This term simply means that you can use Connection Security Rules to block traffic from computers originating from outside the local Active Directory domain.

- **Authentication Exemption rule** You can use this rule type to exempt specific computers or a group or range of IP addresses (computers) from being required to authenticate themselves, regardless of other Connection Security Rules. You commonly use this rule type to grant access to infrastructure computers that the local computer must communicate with before authentication can be performed. It is also used for other computers that cannot use the form of authentication you configured for this policy and profile.

To create an authentication exemption rule, you need only to specify the computers by name or IP address and then name the rule.

- **Server-To-Server rule**   This rule type allows you to authenticate the communications between IP addresses or sets of addresses, including specific computers and subnets.

- **Tunnel rule**   Use this rule type to configure IPsec tunnel mode for VPN gateways.

- **Custom rule**   Use this rule type to create a rule that requires special settings or a combination of features from the various rule types.

ENDPOINTS PAGE

Use this page to specify the remote computers with which you want to negotiate an IPsec connection. You can specify endpoints by IP address, but you can you also use the Customize button to limit the application of the rule only to specific interface types, such as LAN, remote access, or wireless connections.

REQUIREMENTS PAGE

Use this page to specify whether authenticated communication should be required or merely requested. As a third option, you can require authentication for inbound connections but only request them for outbound connections. Finally, you can also choose not to authenticate the connection type described in the rule.

AUTHENTICATION METHOD PAGE

This page allows you to specify the method by which computer endpoints are authenticated. The first option is Default. When you choose this option, the authentication method that the connection uses is the one specified for the profile on the IPsec Settings tab in the properties of the Windows Firewall with Advanced Security node. (By default, this authentication method is set to Kerberos V5 for computers in an Active Directory Domain Services, or AD DS, domain. Kerberos V5 is built into AD DS domains and requires no further configuration for IPsec.) The other authentication options you can choose on this page override the default settings. These options include Kerberos V5 authentication for both computers and users, Kerberos V5 authentication for computers only, and the Advanced authentication option. The Advanced option allows you to configure an order of preference for various authentication methods, including Kerberos V5, NTLMv2, a computer certificate from a specified certification authority, and a preshared key.

PROTOCOLS AND PORTS PAGE

This page allows you to specify the type of traffic to which the rule should apply. You can specify traffic by protocol type (for example, TCP, UDP, or IPv6), by protocol number, or by ports used at either communication endpoint.

PROFILE PAGE

The Profile page allows you to limit the local network location types to which the rule will apply. The profiles you can enable for the rule are Domain, Private, and Public.

NAME PAGE

The Name page allows you to name the new Connection Security Rule and (optionally) to provide a description.

Configuring IPsec Settings for Connection Security Rules

You can define IPsec Settings in the WFAS node of a GPO or in the WFAS console. To access these settings in either location, first open the properties of the Windows Firewall with Advanced Security node, as shown in Figure 6-17.

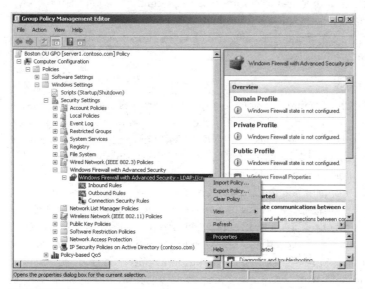

FIGURE 6-17 Opening Windows Firewall properties

Then, in the properties dialog box that opens, click the IPsec Settings tab, as shown in Figure 6-18.

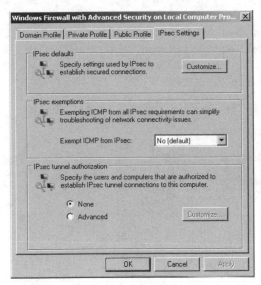

FIGURE 6-18 Configuring IPsec settings

Through this tab, you can configure three aspects of IPsec: IPsec defaults, ICMP exemptions from IPsec, and IPsec tunnel authorization.

- **IPsec defaults** Clicking the Customize button opens the Customize IPsec Settings dialog box, as shown in Figure 6-19. From this dialog box, you can set new default parameters for key negotiation (exchange), for data protection, and for the authentication method.

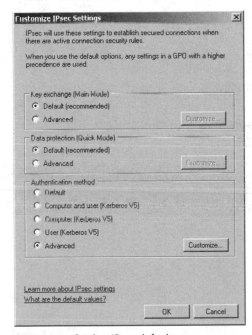

FIGURE 6-19 Setting IPsec defaults

For example, to configure data encryption for Connection Security Rules, first select Advanced in the Data Protection area, and then click Customize. This procedure opens the Customize Data Protection Settings dialog box, as shown in Figure 6-20. Next, in this dialog box, select the Require Encryption For All Connection Security Rules That Use These Settings check box, and then click OK.

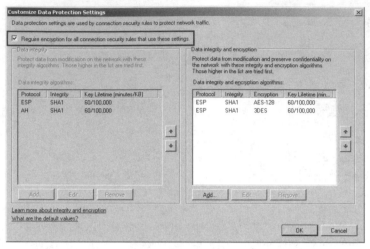

FIGURE 6-20 Requiring encryption for Connection Security Rules

- **Exempt ICMP from IPsec** Use this setting in the IPsec Settings tab to prevent ICMP (Ping and Tracert) messages from being authenticated, encrypted, or both. Keeping ICMP messages unprotected allows you to perform basic network troubleshooting when IPsec cannot be successfully negotiated.

- **IPsec Tunnel Authorization** Use this area to specify users or computers authorized to initiate a tunnel connection *to* the local computer. Connections initiated by the local computer are not affected by this setting.

<table>
<tr><td>PRACTICE</td><td>**Deploying IPsec Through IPsec Policies and Connection Security Rules**</td></tr>
</table>

In the first stage of this practice, you will install Telnet services and then configure an IPsec Policy to encrypt Telnet traffic between Boston.nwtraders.msft and Binghamton.nwtraders.msft. In the second stage, you will create a Connection Security Rule that authenticates all network traffic between the same two computers.

EXERCISE 1 Installing Telnet Services

In this exercise, you install Telnet services on both Boston and Binghamton computers. You then set the Telnet service startup type to Automatic and start the service. Finally, you add Domain Admins to the TelnetClients group in Local Users and Groups.

1. Log on to Nwtraders from Boston as a domain administrator.

2. In the Initial Configuration Tasks or Server Manager window, click Add Features. (To see the Add Features option in Server Manager, you need to select the Features node.) The Select Features page of the Add Features Wizard opens.

3. In the list of features, select both the Telnet Client and Telnet Server check boxes, and then click Next.

4. On the Confirm Installation Selections page of the Add Features Wizard, click Install.

5. After the installation has completed, click Close on the Installation Results page.

6. Open the Services console by clicking Start, pointing to Administrative Tools, and then choosing Services.

7. In the Services console, locate and then double-click Telnet to open its properties.

8. In the Telnet Properties dialog box, change the Startup Type to Automatic, and then click Apply.

9. In the Service Status area, click Start.

10. When the Service Status has changed to Started, click OK to close the Telnet Properties dialog box, and then close the Services console.

11. In the Search Programs And Files box of the Start menu, type **lusrmgr.msc**, and then press Enter.

12. In the Local Users And Groups console tree, select the Groups folder.

13. In the details pane, double-click TelnetClients.

14. In the TelnetClients Properties dialog box, click the Add button.

15. In the Select Users, Computers, Or Groups dialog box, in the Enter The Object Names To Select text box, type **Domain Admins**, and then click OK.

16. In the TelnetClients Properties dialog box, click OK.

17. Log off Boston.

18. Log on to Nwtraders from Binghamton, and then perform steps 2 through 17 on Binghamton.

EXERCISE 2   Creating an IPsec Policy

In this exercise, you will create a GPO and an IPsec Policy that you will later configure to encrypt Telnet traffic in the Nwtraders.msft domain.

1. Log on to Nwtraders from Dcsrv1 as a domain administrator.
2. Open the Group Policy Management (GPM) console by clicking Start, pointing to Administrative Tools, and then choosing Group Policy Management.
3. In the GPM console tree, expand the Forest container, expand the Domains container, and then select the Nwtraders.msft node.
4. Right-click the Nwtraders.msft node and choose Create A GPO In This Domain, And Link It Here.
5. In the New GPO box, type **IPsec GPO**, and then click OK.
6. In the GPM console tree, right-click the IPsec GPO, and then, from the shortcut menu, choose Edit.
7. In the Group Policy Management Editor window, navigate to Computer Configuration, Policies, Windows Settings, Security Settings, and IP Security Policies On Active Directory.
8. Right-click the IP Security Policies On Active Directory node, and then choose Create IP Security Policy on the shortcut menu. The IP Security Policy Wizard opens.
9. Click Next.
10. On the IP Security Policy Name page, type **Nwtraders IPsec-Telnet Policy**.
11. In the Description field, type **This IPsec policy encrypts Telnet traffic**.
12. Click Next.
13. On the Requests For Secure Communications Page, read all of the text on the page, and then click Next.
14. Click Finish. The Nwtraders IPsec-Telnet Policy Properties dialog box appears.
15. Leave all windows open and continue to Exercise 3.

EXERCISE 3   Creating an IPsec Policy Rule and Filter

In this exercise, you will configure the newly created Nwtraders IPsec-Telnet Policy with rules that require high security for Telnet traffic. In the process, you will run the Security Rule Wizard, the IP Filter Wizard, and the Filter Action Wizard.

1. While you are still logged on to Dcsrv1, in the Nwtraders IPsec-Telnet Policy Properties dialog box, click Add. The Create IP Security Rule Wizard opens. (This wizard is also called the Security Rule Wizard.)
2. Read all the text on the first page, and then click Next.
3. On the Tunnel Endpoint page, read all the text on the page, and then click Next.
4. On the Network Type page, read all the text on the page, and then click Next.
5. On the IP Filter List page, read all the text on the page, and then click the Add button. The IP Filter List dialog box opens.

6. In the Name text box, type **Encrypt Telnet filter list**, and then click Add. The IP Filter Wizard opens.

7. Click Next.

8. On the IP Filter Description And Mirrored Property page, read all the text on the page, and then click Next.

9. On the IP Traffic Source page, leave the default selection of Any IP Address, and then click Next.

10. On the IP Traffic Destination page, leave the default of Any IP Address, and then click Next.

11. On the IP Protocol Type page, select TCP from the Select A Protocol Type drop-down list box, and then click Next. Telnet runs on TCP port 23, so you need to specify both TCP and the appropriate port.

12. On the IP Protocol Port page, select To This Port, and then type **23** in the accompanying text box. (Leave From Any Port selected.)

13. Click Next, and then click Finish to close the IP Filter Wizard.

14. In the IP Filter List dialog box, click OK. The IP Filter List page of the Security Rule Wizard reappears.

15. In the IP Filter Lists area, select the Encrypt Telnet Filter List option button, and then click Next.

16. On the Filter Action page, read all the text on the page, and then click Add. The Filter Action Wizard opens. Leave this wizard open and continue to Exercise 4.

EXERCISE 4 Using the Filter Action Wizard

In this exercise, you use the Filter Action Wizard to configure a custom filter action to apply to Telnet traffic. Although the default filter actions available in Group Policy are usually adequate for creating IPsec rules, it is a good idea to configure higher security for Telnet. In addition, you should be familiar with the IP Security Filter Action Wizard for the 70-642 exam.

1. On the Welcome To The IP Security Filter Action Wizard page, read all the text on the page, and then click Next.

2. On the Filter Action Name page, in the Name text box, type **Require High Authentication and Encryption**.

3. In the Description field, type **Require AH authentication and 3DES encryption**.

4. Click Next.

5. On the Filter Action General Options page, ensure that Negotiate Security is selected, and then click Next.

6. On the Communicating With Computers That Do Not Support IPsec page, ensure that Do Not Allow Unsecured Communication is selected, and then click Next.

7. On the IP Traffic Security page, select Custom, and then click Settings.

8. In the Custom Security Method Settings dialog box, select the Data And Address Integrity Without Encryption (AH) check box.

9. In the Session Key Settings area, select both Generate A New Key Every check boxes.

10. Ensure that the Data Integrity And Encryption (ESP) check box is selected, verify that 3DES is the selected encryption algorithm, and then click OK.

11. On the IP Traffic Security page, click Next.

12. On the Completing The IP Security Filter Action Wizard page, click Finish.

13. On the Filter Action page of the Security Rule Wizard, in the list of Filter Actions, select Require High Authentication And Encryption, and then click Next.

14. On the Authentication Method page of the Security Rule Wizard, leave the default as Active Directory Default (Kerberos V5 Protocol), and then click Next. The Completing The Security Rule Wizard page appears.

15. Click Finish.

16. In the Nwtraders IPsec-Telnet Policy Properties dialog box, click OK.

17. In the Group Policy Management Editor, right-click the Nwtraders IPsec Policy, and then, from the shortcut menu, choose Assign.

18. Log on to Boston and Binghamton as a domain administrator, and run the **Gpupdate** command at a command prompt on each computer.

EXERCISE 5 Testing the New IPsec Policy

In this exercise, you will initiate a Telnet session from Boston to Binghamton. You will then verify that data authentication and encryption are applied to the Telnet session.

1. On Boston, open a command prompt.

2. At the command prompt, type **telnet Binghamton**. A Telnet session to the Telnet server on Binghamton begins.

3. On Boston, from the Start menu, point to Administrative Tools, and then choose Windows Firewall With Advanced Security.

4. In the WFAS console tree, expand the Monitoring node and expand the Security Associations node.

5. Beneath the Security Associations node, select the Main Mode folder, and then the Quick Mode folder. You will see that an entry appears in the details pane when you select each folder. These entries each represent an SA. Spend a few moments browsing the information displayed about these SAs. If the quick mode SA disappears, type a command such as **dir** at the Telnet prompt to reestablish it.

    Question: How do you know that the quick mode SA is securing Telnet traffic in particular?

    Answer: Because the remote port is specified as port 23.

6. At the Telnet prompt, type **exit**. You now want to unlink the IPsec GPO so that it does not interfere with the next practice.

7. On Dcsrv1, open the GPM console.

8. In the GPM console tree, right-click the GPO named IPsec GPO, and then click to de-select Link Enabled.

9. Verify that the Link Enabled status of IPsec GPO is now set to No in the details pane of the console.

10. At a command prompt on both Boston and Binghamton, run the **Gpupdate** command.

EXERCISE 6 Implementing IPsec Through Connection Security Rules

In this exercise, you will configure Connection Security Rules in the domain so that all IP traffic between those clients is authenticated.

1. If you have not already done so, log on to Nwtraders from Dcsrv1 as a domain administrator.

2. In the GPM console tree, beneath the Domains container, right-click the Nwtraders.msft node, and then click Create A GPO In This Domain, And Link It Here.

3. In the New GPO dialog box, type **Connection Security Rule GPO**, and then click OK.

4. In the GPM console tree, right-click the Connection Security Rule GPO, and then, from the shortcut menu, choose Edit.

5. In the Group Policy Management Editor window, expand Computer Configuration, Policies, Windows Settings, Security Settings, Windows Firewall With Advanced Security, and then Windows Firewall With Advanced Security - LDAP.//*address*. This last object in the GPO is known as the "WFAS node."

6. Beneath the WFAS node, select Connection Security Rules.

7. Right-click the Connection Security Rules node, and then, from the shortcut menu, choose New Rule. The New Connection Security Rule Wizard appears.

8. On the Rule Type page, read all of the text on the page, and then, leaving the default selection of Isolation, click Next.

9. On the Requirements page, read all the text on the page, and then click Next.

10. On the Authentication Method page, leave the default selection, and then click Next.

11. On the Profile page, leave the default selections, and then click Next.

12. On the Name page, type **Request Data Authentication**, and then click Finish.

13. On both Boston and Binghamton, run the **Gpupdate** command at a command prompt.

14. From the Start Menu of Binghamton, type **\\Boston** in Search Programs And Files, and then press Enter. A blank window appears in Windows Explorer, but the address box shows that a connection to Boston has been established.

15. Open the WFAS console on Binghamton.

16. In the WFAS console tree, expand the Monitoring node and expand the Security Associations node.

17. Beneath the Security Associations node, select the Main Mode folder, and then the Quick Mode folder. You will now see that at least one SA appears in the details pane when each folder is selected. Spend a few moments browsing the information displayed about these SAs.

    Question: Which SA reveals that ESP encryption is None?

    Answer: The quick mode SA.

    Question: Can you configure a Connection Security Rule that encrypts only Telnet traffic?

    Answer: Yes, by configuring a custom rule.

    You will now unlink the Connection Security Rule GPO you just created so that it does not interfere with any other practices in this book.

18. On DCSrv1, open the GPM console.

19. In the GPM console tree, right-click the GPO named Connection Security Rule GPO, and then click to deselect Link Enabled.

20. Verify in the details pane of the GPM console that the Link Enabled status of Connection Security Rule GPO is now set to No.

21. Shut down all three computers, or run the Gpupdate command on all three computers.

Lesson Summary

- IPsec allows you to protect network traffic by providing data authentication or encryption, or both. Security in IPsec is provided by two protocols, Authentication Header (AH) and Encapsulating Security Payload (ESP). AH provides data origin authentication, data integrity, and anti-replay protection for the entire IP packet. ESP provides data encryption, data origin authentication, data integrity, and anti-replay protection for the ESP payload.

- In Windows Server 2008 and Windows Server 2008 R2 networks, you can implement IPsec either through IPsec Policies or through Connection Security Rules.

- IPsec by default operates in transport mode, which is used to provide end-to-end security between computers. Transport mode is also used in most IPsec-based virtual public networks (VPNs), for which the L2TP protocol is used to tunnel the IPsec connection through the public network. However, when a particular VPN gateway is not compatible with L2TP /IPsec VPNs, you can use IPsec in tunnel mode instead.

- IPsec Policies, which are deployed through Local Computer Policy or a GPO, are made up of a set of IPsec rules. Each IPsec rule in turn comprises one IP filter list and one filter action. The filter list defines the type of traffic to which the filter action is applied. Filter actions are allow, block, and negotiate security (authenticate, encrypt, or both).

- Connection Security Rules provide a simplified means of configuring IPsec. By default, Connection Security Rules do not encrypt data but only ensure data integrity. You can configure Connection Security Rules in the Windows Firewall with Advanced Security console on an individual computer or enforce them through a GPO.

Lesson Review

You can use the following questions to test your knowledge of the information in Lesson 1, "Configuring IPsec." The questions are also available on the companion CD if you prefer to review them in electronic form.

> **NOTE ANSWERS**
>
> Answers to these questions and explanations of why each answer choice is correct or incorrect are located in the "Answers" section at the end of the book.

1. You want to require network communications to be encrypted in the Nwtraders.com domain. What should you do?

    A. Use IPsec with Authentication Header (AH).

    B. Use IPsec with Encapsulating Security Payload (ESP).

    C. Use a server-to-server type connection security rule.

    D. Use a tunnel-type connection security rule.

2. You want to enforce IPsec communications between the Nwtraders.com domain and the Contoso.com domain. Both domains belong to the same Active Directory forest. Which authentication method should you choose for IPsec?

    A. Kerberos

    B. Certificates

    C. Preshared key

    D. NTLM

3. You want all traffic sent among domain computers to be encrypted. You begin by creating a new GPO and linking it to the domain. Which is the next configuration step you should take in this new GPO to help you achieve your goal?

    A. Create an Isolation Connection Security Rule with the option to request authentication for inbound and outbound connections. Leave all other default selections.

    B. Create an Isolation Connection Security Rule with the option to require authentication for inbound and outbound connections. Leave all other default selections.

    C. Create an IPsec policy including a rule with an IP filter action of Permit.

    D. Create an IPsec policy including a rule with an IP filter action of Request Security.

Chapter Review

To further practice and reinforce the skills you learned in this chapter, you can perform the following tasks:

- Review the chapter summary.
- Review the list of key terms introduced in this chapter.
- Complete the case scenario. This scenario sets up a real-world situation involving the topics of this chapter and asks you to create solutions.
- Complete the suggested practices.
- Take a practice test.

Chapter Summary

- IPsec allows you to protect network traffic by providing data authentication or encryption, or both.
- In Windows Server 2008 and Windows Serer 2008 R2 networks, you can implement IPsec either through IPsec policies or through Connection Security Rules. As a means to deploy IPsec, IPsec policies are more powerful but are also more difficult to configure than Connection Security Rules are.

Key Terms

Do you know what these key terms mean? You can check your answers by looking up the terms in the glossary at the end of the book.

- Authentication Header (AH)
- Encapsulating Security Payload (ESP)
- Internet Control Message Protocol (ICMP)
- Internet Protocol Security (IPsec)
- Kerberos
- Preshared Key
- Security Association (SA)
- Transport mode
- Tunnel mode

Case Scenario

In the following case scenario, you will apply what you've learned about IPsec in this chapter. You can find answers to these questions in the "Answers" section at the end of this book.

Case Scenario: Implementing IPsec

You are a network administrator for a company whose network consists of a single Active Directory domain, Contoso.com. Recently, you have decided to implement mandatory IPsec-based data authentication to all finance servers.

1. What authentication method should you use for IPsec?
2. After you implement the new mandatory policy, users complain that they cannot connect to the finance servers. You want to allow users to communicate with the finance servers, but you do not want to affect communications with other computers and servers that do not require security. Which predefined IPsec policy should you assign to computers outside of the finance servers?

Suggested Practices

To help you successfully master the exam objectives presented in this chapter, complete the following tasks.

Deploy IPsec

- **Practice**   In an Active Directory domain, configure and assign an IPsec policy that requires the securest methods of authentication and encryption. Make a note of any disruptions or difficulty in network communication. Then, unassign the IPsec policy and deploy a Connection Security Rule through Group Policy that also requires the securest methods of authentication and encryption. Again, make a note of any disruptions or difficulty in network communication.

Watch a Webcast

- **Practice**   Watch the Webcast, "Deploying Internet Protocol Security (IPsec) with Windows Vista," by Chris Avis, available on the companion CD in the Webcasts folder. (You can find this Webcast also by browsing to *http://msevents.microsoft.com* and searching for Event ID 1032327282.)

Take a Practice Test

The practice tests on this book's companion CD offer many options. For example, you can test yourself on just one exam objective, or you can test yourself on all the 70-642 certification exam content. You can set up the test so that it closely simulates the experience of taking a certification exam, or you can set it up in study mode so that you can look at the correct answers and explanations after you answer each question.

> **MORE INFO** **PRACTICE TESTS**
>
> For details about all the practice test options available, see the "How to Use the Practice Tests" section in this book's Introduction.

CHAPTER 7

Connecting to Networks

Many employees need to stay productive while away from their desks. If their work requires them to connect to internal email servers, file servers, and databases, you will need to provide a way for them to connect to their intranet from remote networks. This chapter describes five common scenarios that Windows Server 2008 R2 supports:

- **Network Address Translation (NAT)**   A technology that allows multiple computers on a local area network (LAN) to connect to the Internet using a single IP address.

- **Wireless networking**   Commonly known as wi-fi, most mobile computers and other devices can connect to a local area network (LAN) using radio signals.

- **Dial-up connections**   A remote access technology that uses the telephone circuits and modems to connect to the intranet.

- **Virtual Private Network (VPN) connections**   A remote access technology that tunnels encrypted traffic across the Internet to a VPN server, which forwards the communications to the intranet.

- **DirectAccess**   A new remote access technology that transparently connects users to the intranet anytime they have an Internet connection.

Exam objectives in this chapter:

- Configure Network Policy Server (NPS).
- Configure remote access.
- Configure DirectAccess.

Lessons in this chapter:

- Lesson 1: Configuring Network Policy Server   **349**
- Lesson 2: Configuring Network Address Translation   **372**
- Lesson 3: Connecting to Remote Networks   **382**
- Lesson 4: Configuring DirectAccess   **405**

Before You Begin

To complete the lessons in this chapter, you should be familiar with Windows networking and be comfortable with the following tasks:

- Adding roles to a computer running Windows Server 2008 R2
- Configuring Active Directory domain controllers and joining computers to a domain
- Configuring a basic network, including configuring IP settings
- Configuring a public key infrastructure (PKI)
- Configuring DNS and DHCP servers
- Configuring IPv6

You will also need the following nonproduction hardware connected to test networks:

- A computer or virtual machine running Windows Server 2008 R2 named Dcsrv1 that is a domain controller in the Nwtraders.msft domain. This computer must have two interfaces:
  - An interface connected to the Internet, with a public Internet IP address.
  - An interface connected to a private intranet.

> **NOTE COMPUTER AND DOMAIN NAMES**
>
> The computer and domain names you use will not affect these practices. The practices in this chapter, however, refer to these computer names for simplicity.

- A wireless access point that supports WPA-EAP authentication and a computer with a wireless network adapter that is a member of the Nwtraders.msft domain. If you do not have wireless hardware, you can watch the author complete the Lesson 1 practice at *http://www.vistaclues.com/wpa/*. In the practice, the wireless computer will be referred to by the computer name Hartford in these exercises; however, you can substitute any computer name. Hartford can be running Windows Vista, Windows 7, Windows Server 2008, or Windows Server 2008 R2. Hartford needs both a wired and a wireless network adapter.
- A computer or virtual machine named Boston that is connected to the same private network as Dcsrv1.

> **NOTE NETWORK CONFIGURATION**
>
> Both computers need to be connected to the private interface. If you are using two physical computers, you can connect them with a crossover Ethernet cable. If you are using two virtual machines, create a virtual network and connect one virtual network interface on each computer to the virtual network. Do not enable a Dynamic Host Configuration Protocol (DHCP) server on the internal network.

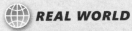
Because private IP addresses are private, different organizations can use the same IP address. Of course, this means that private IP addresses aren't routable on the public Internet—hence the need for NAT.

Here's the problem: when two companies merge, they need to connect their private networks. If these companies use the same private IP address ranges, one of them is going to have to renumber the network. Renumbering networks is a huge task, requiring updating DHCP servers, updating DNS records, updating servers with static IP addresses, and refreshing client IP settings. And, perhaps worst of all, the work needs to happen after hours to minimize downtime—meaning you'll have several late nights changing IP settings and testing everything afterward.

To minimize the chance of private IP address conflicts, pick random networks from within the private ranges. For example, the network 10.252.83.0/24 is much less likely to be used than the network 192.168.1.0/24, because people tend to choose networks at the beginning of the address ranges.

Lesson 1: Configuring Network Policy Server

Windows Server 2008 R2 can authenticate clients when they connect to wired or wireless networks by using Network Policy Server (NPS). With NPS, you have control over which computers can join your network, providing an additional layer of security for intranet resources and making it more difficult for uninvited guests to use your Internet connection. This lesson provides an overview of NPS and network authentication using wireless technologies as the primary example.

MORE INFO   **WIRELESS NETWORKS**

For a more detailed discussion of wireless networks, read Chapter 10, "IEEE 802.11 Wireless Networks," of *Windows Server 2008 Networking and Network Access Protection (NAP)* (Microsoft Press, 2008), by Joseph Davies and Tony Northrup.

After this lesson, you will be able to:

- Describe wireless authentication standards.
- Choose between infrastructure and ad hoc wireless networking.
- Configure a public key infrastructure (PKI) to enable wireless authentication using certificates.
- Configure Windows Server 2008 R2 as a RADIUS server to provide centralized, Active Directory–integrated authentication for wireless clients.
- Configure wired network security.
- Use NPS templates to quickly and consistently configure NPS.

Estimated lesson time: 90 minutes

Wireless Security Standards

Wireless access points can require clients to authenticate before connecting to the network. This authentication also allows the wireless access point and the client to establish a private key that they can use to encrypt wireless communications. Windows wireless clients support all common wireless security standards:

- **No security**   To grant guests easy access, you can choose to allow clients to connect to a wireless access point without authentication (or encryption). To provide some level of protection, some wireless access points detect new clients and require the user to open a web browser and acknowledge a usage agreement before the router grants the user access to the Internet. Unfortunately, any communications sent across an unprotected wireless network can be intercepted by attackers who can receive the wireless signal (which typically broadcasts several hundred feet). If you allow users to connect to unprotected wireless networks, provide encryption at other layers whenever possible. For example, use Secure Sockets Layer (SSL) to protect communications with your email server, require users to connect using DirectAccess (discussed in Lesson 4) or an encrypted VPN, or require IPsec communications with encryption.

- **Wired Equivalent Protection (WEP)**   WEP, available using either 64-bit or 128-bit encryption, was the original wireless security standard. Unfortunately, WEP has significant vulnerabilities because of weaknesses in the cryptography design. Potential attackers can download freely available tools on the Internet and use the tools to crack the key required to connect to the WEP network—often within a few minutes. Therefore, neither 64-bit nor 128-bit WEP can protect you against even unsophisticated attackers. However, WEP is sufficient to deter casual users who might connect to an otherwise unprotected wireless network. WEP is almost universally supported by wireless clients (including devices that do not run Windows, such as printers) and requires no additional infrastructure beyond the wireless access point. When connecting to a WEP network, users must enter a key or passphrase (though this process can be automated).

- **Wi-Fi Protected Access (WPA)**   Like WEP, WPA provides wireless authentication and encryption. WPA can offer significantly stronger cryptography than WEP, depending on how it is configured. WPA is not as universally supported as WEP, however, so if you have wireless clients that are not running Windows or wireless devices that do not support WEP, you might need to upgrade them to support WPA. Computers running Windows support WPA-PSK and WPA-EAP.

  - **WPA-PSK (for preshared key)**   Also known as WPA-Personal, WPA-PSK uses a static key, similar to WEP. Unfortunately, this static key means WPA-PSK can be cracked using brute force techniques. Additionally, static keys are extremely difficult to manage in enterprise environments; if a single computer configured with the key is compromised, you would need to change the key on every wireless access point. For that reason, WPA-PSK should be avoided.

    > **MORE INFO   CHOOSING A PRESHARED KEY**
    >
    > If you must use WPA-PSK, use a long, complex password as the preshared key. When attackers attempt to crack a WPA-PSK network, they will start with a precomputed rainbow table, which allows cracking tools to identify whether a WPA-PSK network is protected by a common value (such as a word in the dictionary) in a matter of minutes. If your preshared key isn't a common value, it probably won't appear in the rainbow table, and the attacker will have to resort to brute force methods, which can take much longer—typically hours, days, or weeks instead of seconds or minutes.

  - **WPA-EAP (Extensible Authentication Protocol)**   WPA-EAP (also known as *WPA-Enterprise*) passes authentication requests to a back-end server, such as a computer running Windows Server 2008 R2 and RADIUS. Network Policy Server (NPS) provides RADIUS authentication on Windows servers. NPS can pass authentication requests to a domain controller, allowing WPA-EAP protected wireless networks to authenticate domain computers without requiring users to type a key. WPA-EAP enables very flexible authentication, and Windows enables users to use a smart card to connect to a network protected by WPA-Enterprise. WPA-EAP does not use a static key, so it's easier to manage because you don't need to change the key if an attacker discovers it; and multiple wireless access points can use a single, central server for authentication. Additionally, it is much harder to crack than WEP or WPA-PSK.

- **WPA2**   WPA2 (also known as *IEEE 802.11i*) is an updated version of WPA, offering improved security and better protection from attacks. Like WPA, WPA2 is available as both WPA2-PSK and WPA2-EAP.

Windows Vista, Windows 7, Windows Server 2003, and Windows Server 2008 include built-in support for WEP, WPA, and WPA2. Windows XP can support both WPA and WPA2 by installing updates available from Microsoft.com. Recent versions of Linux, Mac OS, and mobile operating systems are capable of supporting WEP, WPA, and WPA2. Network devices, such as printers that connect to your wireless network, might not support WPA or WPA2. When selecting a wireless security standard, choose the first standard on this list that all clients can support:

- WPA2-EAP
- WPA-EAP
- WPA2-PSK
- WPA-PSK
- 128-bit WEP
- 64-bit WEP

If all clients cannot support WPA-EAP or WPA2-EAP, consider upgrading those clients before deploying a wireless network.

Infrastructure and Ad Hoc Wireless Networks

Wireless networks can operate in two modes:

- **Infrastructure mode** A wireless access point acts as a central hub to wireless clients, forwarding traffic to the wired network and between wireless clients. All communications travel to and from the wireless access point. The vast majority of wireless networks in business environments are of the infrastructure type.

- **Ad hoc mode** Ad hoc wireless networks are established between two or more wireless clients without using a wireless access point. Wireless communications occur directly between wireless clients, with no central hub. For business environments, ad hoc wireless networks are primarily used when short-term mobile networking is required. For example, in a meeting room without wired networking, a Windows 7 user could connect a video projector to a computer, establish an ad hoc wireless network, and then share the video with other computers that connected to the ad hoc wireless network. Similarly, if a hotel offers only wired networking, you could connect a Windows 7 computer to the wired network, share the wired connection using Internet Connection Sharing (ICS, described in Lesson 2), and then create an ad hoc wireless network so that other users could connect to the Internet.

Because servers rarely participate in ad hoc wireless networks, this book does not discuss them in depth.

Configuring the Public Key Infrastructure

WEP and WPA-PSK rely on static keys for wireless authentication, and, as a result, they are both not secure and unmanageable in enterprise environments. For better security and manageability, you will need to use WPA-EAP. The most straightforward approach to deploying WPA-EAP is to use a PKI to deploy certificates to both your RADIUS server and all wireless client computers.

To create a PKI and enable autoenrollment so that domain member computers have the necessary certificates to support WPA-EAP wireless authentication, follow these steps:

1. Add the Active Directory Certificate Services role to a server in your domain (the default settings work well for test environments).

2. In the Group Policy Management Console, edit the Group Policy object (GPO) used to apply wireless settings (or the Default Domain Policy). In the Group Policy Management Editor, select Computer Configuration\Policies\Windows Settings\Security Settings \Public Key Policies.

3. In the details pane, right-click Certificate Services Client – Auto-Enrollment, and then choose Properties.

4. In the Certificate Services Client – Auto-Enrollment Properties dialog box, from the Configuration Model drop-down list, select Enabled. Optionally, select the check boxes for other options related to autoenrollment, and then click OK.

Authenticating Wireless Networks by Using Windows Server 2008 R2

Windows wireless clients can authenticate using the following modes:

- **Computer or user**   Windows authenticates prior to logon by using computer credentials. After logon, Windows submits user credentials. In environments that use virtual LANs (VLANs), the computer's access to network resources can be limited until user credentials are provided (for example, the computer might be able to access only Active Directory domain controllers).

- **Computer only**   Windows authenticates to the wireless network prior to displaying the Windows logon screen. Windows can then connect to Active Directory domain controllers and other network resources before the user logs on. No user authentication is required.

- **User only**   Windows authenticates to the wireless network after the user logs on. Unless wireless Single Sign On is enabled (described later in this section), users cannot authenticate to the domain before connecting to the wireless network, however. Therefore, users can log on only when domain logon credentials have been cached locally. Additionally, domain logon operations (including processing Group Policy updates and logon scripts) will fail, resulting in Windows event log errors.

- **Guest**   Windows joins the network as a guest without authenticating.

Windows Vista, Windows 7, Windows Server 2008, and Windows Server 2008 R2 support wireless Single Sign On, which allows administrators to configure user authentication to the wireless network before the user logs on. This overcomes the weaknesses of user-only authentication. To enable wireless Single Sign On, use the Wireless Network (IEEE 802.11) Policies Group Policy extension or run the **netsh wlan** command with appropriate parameters.

Configuring the RADIUS Server for Wireless Networks

You can use a computer running Windows Server 2008 or Windows Server 2008 R2 to authenticate wireless users by configuring the computer as a RADIUS server and configuring your wireless access points to send authentication requests to the RADIUS server. This architecture is shown in Figure 7-1.

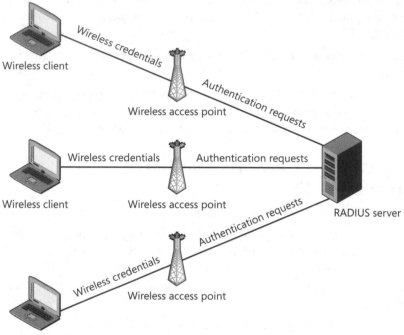

FIGURE 7-1 Wireless authentication to a RADIUS server

Different editions of Windows Server 2008 R2 offer different RADIUS server capabilities. Windows Web Server 2008 R2 does not include NPS. Windows Server 2008 R2 Standard supports NPS with a maximum of 50 RADIUS clients and 2 remote RADIUS server groups. Windows Server 2008 R2 Standard also does not support defining groups of RADIUS clients by specifying an IP address range. Windows Server 2008 R2 Enterprise and Windows Server 2008 R2 Datacenter support NPS without restrictions.

To configure Windows Server 2008 R2 as a RADIUS server, first add the Network Policy And Access Services role (if it is not yet installed) by following these steps. If the server role is already installed, you can simply add the Routing And Remote Access Services role service by right-clicking Network Policy And Access Services in Server Manager, and then choosing Add Role Services.

1. Click Start, and then choose Server Manager.

2. In the console tree, select Roles, and then in the details pane, click Add Roles.

3. If the Before You Begin page appears, click Next.

4. On the Select Server Roles page, select the Network Policy And Access Services check box, and then click Next.

5. On the Network Policy And Access Services page, click Next.

6. On the Select Role Services page, select the Network Policy Server check box. Then, select the Routing And Remote Access Services check box. The Remote Access Service and Routing check boxes are automatically selected. Click Next.

7. On the Confirmation page, click Install.

8. After the Add Roles Wizard completes the installation, click Close.

Next, configure the Network Policy Server to allow your wireless access point as a RADIUS client.

1. In Server Manager, select Roles, Network Policy And Access Services, and NPS. If this node does not appear, close and reopen Server Manager.

2. In the details pane, under Standard Configuration, select RADIUS Server For 802.1X Wireless Or Wired Connections. Then, click Configure 802.1X. The Configure 802.1X Wizard appears.

3. On the Select 802.1X Connections Type page, select Secure Wireless Connections, and then click Next.

4. On the Specify 802.1X Switches page, you will configure your wireless access points as valid RADIUS clients. Follow these steps for each wireless access point, and then click Next:

   a. Click Add.

   b. In the New RADIUS Client dialog box, in the Friendly Name box, type a name that identifies that specific wireless access point.

   c. In the Address box, type the host name or IP address that identifies the wireless access point.

   d. In the Shared Secret section, select Manual and type a shared secret. Alternatively, you can automatically create a complex secret by selecting the Generate option button and then clicking the Generate button that appears. Also, write the shared secret down for later use.

   e. Click OK.

5. On the Configure An Authentication Method page, from the Type drop-down list, select one of the following authentication methods, and then click Next:

   - **Microsoft: Protected EAP (PEAP)** This authentication method requires you to install a computer certificate on the RADIUS server and a computer certificate or user certificate on all wireless client computers. All client computers must trust the certification authority (CA) that issued the computer certificate installed on the RADIUS server, and the RADIUS server must trust the CA that issued the certificates that the client computers provide. The best way to do this is to use an enterprise PKI (such as the Active Directory Certificate Services role in Windows Server 2008 R2). PEAP is compatible with the 802.1X Network Access Protection (NAP) enforcement method, as described in Chapter 8, "Configuring Windows Firewall and Network Access Protection."

- **Microsoft: Smart Card Or Other Certificate** Essentially the same authentication method as PEAP, this authentication technique relies on users providing a certificate using a smart card. When you select this authentication method, Windows wireless clients prompt users to connect a smart card when they attempt to connect to the wireless network.

- **Microsoft: Secured Password (EAP-MSCHAP v2)** This authentication method requires computer certificates to be installed on all RADIUS servers and requires all client computers to trust the CA that issued the computer certificate installed on the RADIUS server. Clients authenticate using domain credentials.

6. On the Specify User Groups page, click Add. Specify the group you want to grant wireless access to, and then click OK. Click Next.

7. On the Configure A Virtual LAN (VLAN) page, you can click the Configure button to specify VLAN configuration settings. This is required only if you want to limit wireless users to specific network resources, and you have created a VLAN using your network infrastructure. Click Next.

8. On the Completing New IEEE 802.1X Secure Wired And Wireless Connections And RADIUS Clients page, click Finish.

9. In Server Manager, right-click Roles\Network Policy And Access Services\NPS, and then choose Register Server In Active Directory. Click OK twice.

RADIUS authentication messages use UDP port 1812, and RADIUS accounting messages use UDP port 1813.

 Quick Check

1. What is the strongest form of wireless network security supported by Windows 7 and Windows Server 2008 R2?

2. Which server role is required to support authenticating wireless users to Active Directory?

Quick Check Answers

1. WPA2.

2. You must add the Network Policy And Access Services role to configure the server as a RADIUS server.

Configuring RADIUS Proxies

If you have existing RADIUS servers and you need a layer of abstraction between the access points and the RADIUS servers, or if you need to submit requests to different RADIUS servers based on specific criteria, you can configure Windows Server 2008 or Windows Server 2008 R2 as a RADIUS proxy. Figure 7-2 illustrates a typical use.

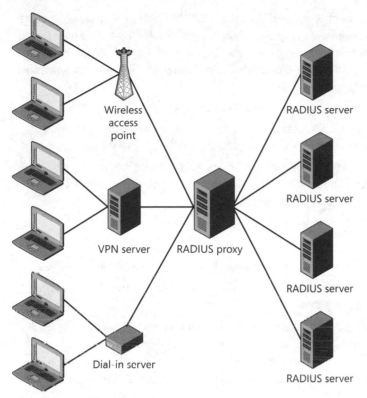

FIGURE 7-2 Sample RADIUS proxy architecture

The most common use of a RADIUS proxy is to submit requests to organization-specific RADIUS servers based on the realm identified in the RADIUS request. In this way, different organizations can manage their own RADIUS servers (and thus manage the user accounts that each RADIUS server authenticates). For example, if your organization has two domains that do not trust each other, you could have your wireless access points (or your VPN servers, as discussed in Lesson 3) submit requests to your RADIUS proxy. The RADIUS proxy could then determine which domain's RADIUS server to forward the request to. You can also use a RADIUS proxy to load-balance requests across multiple RADIUS servers if one RADIUS server is unable to handle the load.

To configure a computer running Windows Server 2008 or Windows Server 2008 R2 as a RADIUS proxy, follow these conceptual steps:

1. Create a RADIUS server proxy group.

2. Create a connection request policy that forwards authentication requests to the remote RADIUS server group and define it at a higher priority than the default Use Windows Authentication For All Users connection request policy.

After you configure the connection request policy, the RADIUS proxy might send requests that match specific criteria to any server in a group. Therefore, you must create a separate group for each set of RADIUS servers that will receive unique authentication requests. RADIUS server groups can consist of a single RADIUS server, or they can have many RADIUS servers (assuming the RADIUS servers authenticate the same users).

At a detailed level, follow these steps to create a RADIUS server proxy group:

1. Add the Network Policy And Access Services role as described in the section "Configuring the RADIUS Server for Wireless Networks" earlier in this lesson.

2. In Server Manager, right-click Roles\Network Policy And Access Services\NPS\RADIUS Clients And Servers\Remote RADIUS Server Groups, and then choose New. The New Remote RADIUS Server Group dialog box appears.

3. Type a name for the RADIUS server group.

4. Click the Add button. The Add RADIUS Server dialog box appears.

5. On the Address tab, type the host name or IP address of the RADIUS server.

6. On the Authentication/Accounting tab, type the shared secret in the Shared Secret and Confirm Shared Secret boxes.

7. On the Load Balancing tab, leave the default settings if you are not performing load balancing or if all servers should receive the same number of requests. If you are load balancing among servers with different capacities (for example, if one RADIUS server can handle twice as many requests as the next), adjust the Priority and Weight appropriately.

8. Click OK.

9. Repeat steps 4–8 to add RADIUS servers to the group.

Repeat steps 1–9 for every RADIUS server group. Then follow these steps to create a connection request policy:

1. In Server Manager, right-click Roles\Network Policy And Access Services\NPS\Policies \Connection Request Policies, and then choose New. The Specify Connection Request Policy Name And Connection Type Wizard appears.

2. Type a name for the policy. In the Type Of Network Access Server list, select the access server type. If your access server provides a specific type number, click Vendor Specific, and then type the number. Click Next.

3. On the Specify Conditions page, click Add. Select the condition you want to use to distinguish which RADIUS server group receives the authentication request. To distinguish using the realm name, select User Name. Click Add.

4. Provide any additional information requested for the condition you selected, and then click OK.

5. Repeat steps 3 and 4 to add criteria. Then, click Next.

6. On the Specify Connection Request Forwarding page, select Forward Requests To The Following Remote RADIUS Server Group For Authentication. Then, select the RADIUS server group from the drop-down list. Click Next.

7. On the Configure Settings page, you can add rules to overwrite any existing attributes, or you can add attributes that might not exist in the original request. For example, you could change the realm name of an authentication request before forwarding it to a RADIUS server. This step is optional and is required only when you know that a destination RADIUS server has specific requirements that the original RADIUS request does not meet. Click Next.

8. On the Completing Connection Request Policy Wizard page, click Finish.

9. In Server Manager, right-click the new policy, and then choose Move Up to move the policy above any lower-priority policies, if necessary.

Repeat steps 1–9 to define unique criteria that will forward different requests to each RADIUS group, and your configuration of the RADIUS proxy is complete.

Monitoring RADIUS Server Logons

Like any authentication mechanism, it's important to monitor logons to wireless networks. The Windows Server 2008 R2 RADIUS server provides several mechanisms. The most straightforward is the Security event log, viewable using the standard Event Viewer snap-in. Additionally, you can examine the RADIUS log file, which is formatted for compatibility with reporting software. For debugging or detailed troubleshooting, you can enable trace logging. The sections that follow describe each of these reporting mechanisms.

USING EVENT VIEWER

If a wireless user attempts to authenticate to a wireless access point using WPA-EAP, and the wireless access point is configured to use a computer running Windows Server 2008 R2 as the RADIUS server, the Network Policy Server service adds an event to the Security event log. Figure 7-3 shows a sample event. Events have a Task Category of Network Policy Server. Successful authentication attempts appear as Audit Success, and failed authentication attempts appear as Audit Failure.

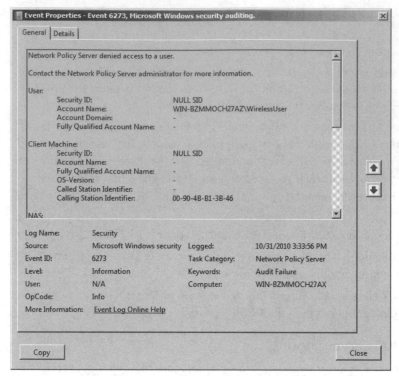

FIGURE 7-3 A failed authentication attempt logged to the Security event log

RADIUS LOGGING

RADIUS is a standards-based authentication mechanism, and it also has a standards-based log file. By default, the RADIUS log (also known as the IAS log) is stored in %SystemRoot% \system32\LogFiles, with the filename IN<*date*>.log. However, you can also configure RADIUS logging to a database server.

By default, RADIUS will stop authenticating users if it cannot log the authentications, so your RADIUS server is only as reliable as your database server. If you choose to log to a database server, there are three ways you can ensure that the RADIUS server continues working when the database goes offline:

- Log to a database, but failover to a text log file if the database is unavailable.
- Simultaneously log to both a database and a text file.
- Continue authenticating users if the database fails.

Typically, you will not directly analyze the RADIUS log data. Instead, you will parse the file with software specifically designed to analyze RADIUS logs, including security auditing software and accounting software used for usage-based billing. Table 7-1 shows the first several fields in the RADIUS log file format. The remaining fields can vary depending on the wireless access point being used.

TABLE 7-1 RADIUS Log Fields

FIELD	DESCRIPTION
Server name	The computer name registered to the RADIUS server
Service	Always the value *IAS*
Date	The date, in the format *MM/DD/YYYY*
Time	The time, in the format *hh:mm:ss*

ENABLING TRACE LOGGING ON THE SERVER

You can also enable extremely detailed trace logging, which is useful primarily when working with Microsoft support. To enable trace logging, run the following command:

```
netsh ras set tr * en
```

This will cause the network policy server to generate a log file named %SystemRoot% \Tracing\IASNAP.log. You can submit this log file to Microsoft support for detailed analysis.

> **MORE INFO NAP LOGGING**
>
> These log files should provide you with most of the information you need for both auditing and troubleshooting. If you need even more detailed information, read "The Definitive Guide to NAP Logging" at *http://blogs.technet.com/wincat/archive/2007/10/29 /the-definitive-guide-to-nap-logging.aspx*.

Connecting to Wireless Networks

You can use Group Policy settings to configure computers to automatically connect to protected wireless networks without requiring the user to manually connect:

1. From a domain controller, open the Group Policy Management console from the Administrative Tools folder. Right-click the GPO that applies to the computers you want to apply the policy to, and then click Edit.

2. In the Group Policy Management Editor console, right-click Computer Configuration \Policies\Windows Settings\Security Settings\Wireless Network (IEEE 802.11) Policies, and then choose Create A New Wireless Network Policy For Windows Vista And Later Releases.

> **NOTE WINDOWS XP AND WINDOWS VISTA POLICIES**
>
> You can create either Windows Vista or Windows XP policies. Windows Vista policies are automatically applied to wireless clients running Windows Vista, Windows 7, and Windows Server 2008. Windows XP policies apply to clients running Windows XP with SP2 and Windows Server 2003. If no Windows Vista policy exists, computers running Windows Vista, Windows 7, and Windows Server 2008 will apply the Windows XP policy.

3. On the General tab, click Add, and then click Infrastructure. You can also use this dialog box to configure ad hoc networks, although enterprises rarely use preconfigured ad hoc networks.

4. In the New Profile Properties dialog box, on the Connection tab, type a name for the wireless network in the Profile Name box. Then, type the Service Set Identifier (SSID) in the Network Name box and click Add.

5. In the New Profile Properties dialog box, click the Security tab. In the Authentication list, select the wireless authentication technique and network authentication method for that SSID, as shown in Figure 7-4.

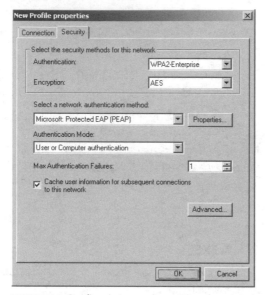

FIGURE 7-4 Configuring security settings for a wireless network using Group Policy

6. While still on the Security tab of the New Profile Properties dialog box, click Advanced. Optionally, select the Enable Single Sign On For This Network check box. Click OK.

7. Click OK again to return to the New Wireless Network Policy Properties dialog box.

8. In the New Profile Properties dialog box, click OK.

9. In the New Wireless Network Policy Properties dialog box, click OK.

Deploying Wireless Networks with WPA-EAP

Deploying a wireless network with WPA-EAP requires combining several technologies: wireless access points, Active Directory users and groups, a PKI, RADIUS, and Group Policy settings. Although deploying a protected wireless network can be complex, after you understand the individual components and how they fit together, the process is reasonably straightforward.

To deploy a protected wireless network, follow these high-level steps:

1. Deploy certificates (preferably, using Active Directory Certificate Services).

2. Create groups for users and computers that will have wireless access and add members to those groups.

3. Configure RADIUS servers using NPS.

4. Deploy wireless access points and configure them to forward authentication requests to your RADIUS server.

5. Configure wireless clients using Group Policy settings.

6. Allow the client computers to apply the Group Policy and either manually or automatically connect them to the wireless network.

Wired Network Security

It seems obvious why wireless networks require authentication; users outside of your offices could connect to your network, use your Internet connection, and possibly access internal resources. In the past, network administrators relied on physical security to protect their wired networks. By guarding the entrances to a building, they prevented attackers from connecting a network cable to the wired network.

However, for larger businesses, physical security is insufficient to protect internal networks. After all, businesses regularly allow people who do not require network access into their facilities, including delivery people, maintenance staff, and cleaning services. Additionally, an attacker could sneak into your building and find an empty office or meeting room to gain access to your physical network.

Just as you can use the IEEE 802.11 standards to help protect wireless networks, you can use the IEEE 802.1X standards to help protect wired networks. Once you enable wired network security, users or computers must authenticate when connecting to a network.

802.1X relies on a similar authentication architecture as wireless network security; however, it uses wired network switches instead of wireless access points. When a client computer connects to a wired network, the network switch (which must support IEEE 802.1X) connects it to a virtual local area network (VLAN) that is allowed to communicate with only those servers required for authentication, such as the RADIUS server and the domain controller. The client must then authenticate to the RADIUS server, which can be a computer running Windows Server 2008 R2, before gaining access to the entire network.

You can configure wired network policies for clients running Windows Vista, Windows 7, Windows Server 2008, and Windows Server 2008 R2 using Group Policy by following these steps:

1. From a domain controller, open the Group Policy Management console from the Administrative Tools folder. Right-click the GPO that applies to the computers you want to apply the policy to, and then click Edit.

2. In the Group Policy Management Editor console, right-click Computer Configuration, Policies, Windows Settings, Security Settings, Wired Network (IEEE 802.3) Policies, and then choose Create A New Wired Network Policy For Windows Vista And Later Releases.

3. On the General tab, shown in Figure 7-5, name your policy. You can configure two settings for Windows 7 clients:

■ **Don't Allow Shared User Credentials For Network Authentication** Select this check box to prevent client computers from caching user credentials and using those credentials to automatically log on to the network when a user is not logged on. Although this will be inconvenient for users, it might be important in environments where a single computer is shared by users with different network access levels.

■ **Enable Block Period** Select this check box to set the block period time when you want to prevent users from immediately attempting to reauthenticate if authentication fails.

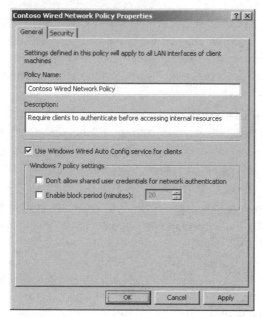

FIGURE 7-5 Configuring security settings for a wired network using Group Policy

4. On the Security tab, select the authentication method, which is identical to those used for wireless networks.

5. While still on the Security tab of the New Profile Properties dialog box, click Advanced. Optionally, select the Enable Single Sign On For This Network check box and choose whether to authenticate before or after user logon.

6. Click OK to close all dialog boxes.

MORE INFO **WIRED NETWORK SECURITY**

For more information about wired network security, read Lesson 2, "Configuring Network Access Protection," in Chapter 8.

Using NPS Templates

You can use NPS templates, a feature new to Windows Server 2008 R2, to reduce repetitive NPS configuration tasks. Templates store a group of NPS configuration settings that you can reuse on the same or a different computer.

You can create the following types of templates:

- **Shared Secrets**   Stores RADIUS shared secrets, allowing you to configure them without typing the shared secret at different computers. You can generate a complex shared secret when creating a shared secret template.

- **RADIUS Clients**   Allows you to quickly configure the same RADIUS clients on different servers. You can generate a complex shared secret when creating a RADIUS clients template.

- **Remote RADIUS Servers**   Stores remote RADIUS servers. You can specify existing shared secret templates for authentication and accounting.

- **Health Policies**   Configures health policies, which must be added to the Health Policies condition of your network policy before they are enforced. Create any system health validators (SHVs) prior to creating the health policy template. For more information about health policies, refer to Chapter 8.

- **Remediation Server Groups**   Configures remediation server groups, which are groups of servers that unauthenticated clients can access. Typically, remediation server groups are used to install updates or change settings to bring the client computer into compliance.

- **IP Filters**   Configures IPv4 or IPV6 filters to configure which networks can connect.

To create a template, follow these steps:

1. In the NPS console, expand Templates Management, right-click a template type, and then click New.

2. Complete the dialog box or wizard. Each template type prompts you for different information.

You can import and export templates by right-clicking Templates Management in the NPS console and then clicking Import Templates From A Computer, Import Templates From A File, or Export Templates To A File.

You can apply templates using the same dialog boxes you use to configure NPS settings. For example, to add remote RADIUS servers from a template, right-click Radius Clients And Servers \Remote RADIUS Server Groups, and then click New. In the Add RADIUS Server dialog box, click the Select An Existing Remote RADIUS Servers Template list, and select your template. Similarly, to add RADIUS clients from a template, open the New RADIUS Client dialog box, select the Select An Existing Template check box, and then select your template.

Configuring WPA-EAP Authentication for a Wireless Access Point

In this practice, you enable WPA-EAP wireless authentication using Windows Server 2008 R2, a wireless access point, and a wireless client. After you connect the client to the network, you will examine the event log on the RADIUS server.

This practice assumes you have a computer named DCSRV1 running Windows Server 2008 R2 and configured as a domain controller for the nwtraders.msft domain. You also need a computer named HARTFORD with wireless networking capabilities running Windows Vista, Windows 7, Windows Server 2008, or Windows Server 2008 R2 that is a member of the domain. Finally, you need a wireless access point (WAP).

If you do not have the hardware to complete this exercise on your own, you can watch the author complete the practice at *http://www.vistaclues.com/wpa/*.

EXERCISE 1   Installing and Configuring NPS

In this exercise, you configure Dcsrv1 as a RADIUS server.

1. If you haven't already, use Server Manager to add the Active Directory Domain Services and Active Directory Certificate Services roles to the domain controller. Use the default settings for the Active Directory Certificate Services role.

2. In Server Manager, use the Roles\Active Directory Domain Services\Active Directory Users And Computers\nwtraders.msft\Users node to create a universal group named **Wireless Users**. Then, create a user account named **WirelessUser**, with a complex password. Add the WirelessUser account to the Domain Users and Wireless Users groups. Copy the WirelessUser account to a second account named **WirelessUser2**. Then, add the computer account for your client computer to the Wireless Users group.

3. In the left pane of Server Manager, click Roles, and then in the details pane, click Add Roles.

4. If the Before You Begin page appears, click Next.

5. On the Select Server Roles page, select the Network Policy And Access Services check box, and then click Next.

> *NOTE*   **ADDING A ROLE SERVICE**
>
> If the Network Policy And Access Services role is already installed, close the wizard, expand Roles in Server Manager, right-click Network Policy And Access Services, and then click Add Role Services.

6. On the Network Policy And Access Services page, click Next.

7. On the Role Services page, select the Network Policy Server check box. Then, select the Routing And Remote Access Services check box. The Remote Access Service and Routing check boxes are automatically selected. Click Next.

8. On the Confirmation page, click Install.

9. After the Add Roles Wizard completes the installation, click Close.

   Next, configure the network policy server to allow your wireless access point as a RADIUS client.

10. In Server Manager, click Roles\Network Policy And Access Services\NPS. If this node does not appear, close and reopen Server Manager.

11. In the details pane, under Standard Configuration, select RADIUS Server For 802.1X Wireless Or Wired Connections. Then, click Configure 802.1X. The Configure 802.1X Wizard appears.

12. On the Select 802.1X Connections Type page, select Secure Wireless Connections. Click Next.

13. On the Specify 802.1X Switches page, you will configure your wireless access points as valid RADIUS clients. Follow these steps for each wireless access point, and then click Next:

    a. Click Add.

    b. In the New RADIUS client dialog box, in the Friendly Name box, type a name that identifies that specific wireless access point.

    c. In the Address box, type the host name or IP address that identifies the wireless access point.

    d. In the Shared Secret group, click the Generate option button. Then, click the Generate button. Copy the shared secret to your clipboard by selecting it and then pressing Ctrl+C. Also, write the key down for later use.

    e. Click OK.

14. On the Configure An Authentication Method page, click the Type list, and then select Microsoft: Protected EAP. Click Next.

15. On the Specify User Groups page, click Add. In the Select Group dialog box, type **Wireless Users,** and then click OK. Click Next.

16. On the Configure A Virtual LAN (VLAN) page, click Next. If you wanted to quarantine wireless clients to a specific VLAN, you could click Configure on this page, and then provide the details for the VLAN.

17. On the Completing New IEEE 802.1X Secure Wired And Wireless Connections And RADIUS Clients page, click Finish.

18. In Server Manager, right-click Roles\Network Policy And Access Services\NPS, and then click Register Server In Active Directory. Click OK twice.

Now, use Server Manager to examine the configuration of your new policy:

1. In Server Manager, expand Roles, expand Network Policy And Access Services, expand NPS, and then click Radius Clients. Notice that your wireless access point is listed in the details pane. Double-click the wireless access point to view the configuration settings. Click OK.

2. Select the Network Policy And Access Services\NPS\Policies\Network Policies node. In the details pane, notice that the Secure Wireless Connections policy is enabled with the Access Type set to Grant Access. Double-click Secure Wireless Connections to view its settings. In the Secure Wireless Connection Properties dialog box, select the Conditions tab and notice that the Wireless Users group is listed as a condition of type Windows Groups. Click the Add button, examine the other types of conditions you can add, and then click Cancel.

3. Select the Network Policy And Access Services\NPS\Accounting node. Notice that Windows Server 2008 saves the log file to the %SystemRoot%\system32\LogFiles\ folder by default. Click Change Log File Properties and make note of the different types of events that are logged. Click OK.

EXERCISE 2   Configuring the Wireless Access Point

In this exercise, you configure your wireless access point to use WPA-EAP authentication. Because different wireless access points use different configuration tools, the steps will vary depending on the hardware you use.

1. Open the administrative tool you use to manage your wireless access point. This is often a webpage accessed by typing the wireless access point's IP address into the address bar of your web browser.

2. Configure the wireless access point with an SSID of **Contoso**.

3. Set the wireless security setting to WPA-EAP (which might be listed as WPA-Enterprise) or, if supported, WPA2-EAP.

4. Set the RADIUS server IP address to your Windows Server 2008 computer's IP address.

5. For the shared secret, specify the shared secret that you generated in the Configure 802.1X Wizard.

Note that many wireless access points allow you to configure multiple RADIUS servers. Although not necessary for this practice, in production environments, you should always configure at least two RADIUS servers for redundancy. If you had only a single RADIUS server, wireless clients would be unable to connect if the RADIUS server was offline.

EXERCISE 3   Configuring Wireless Network Group Policy Settings

In this exercise, you configure Group Policy settings to allow clients to connect to the wireless network.

1. From Dcsrv1, open the Group Policy Management console from the Administrative Tools folder.

2. In the console tree, expand Forest, expand Domains, and expand your domain. Right-click Default Domain Policy, and then choose Edit.

3. In the Group Policy Management Editor console, right-click Default Domain Policy \Computer Configuration\Policies\Windows Settings\Security Settings\Wireless Network (IEEE 802.11) Policies, and then choose Create A New Wireless Network Policy For Windows Vista And Later Releases.

4. On the General tab, click Add, and then click Infrastructure.

5. In the New Profile Properties dialog box, on the Connection tab, type **Contoso** in the Profile Name box. Then, type **CONTOSO** in the Network Name box, and click Add.

6. In the New Profile Properties dialog box, click the Security tab and verify that Microsoft: Protected EAP Security is selected. Then, click Advanced. In the Advanced Security Settings dialog box, select the Enable Single Sign On For This Network check box. Click OK twice.

7. In the New Wireless Network Policy Properties dialog box, click OK.

8. In the Group Policy Management Console, select Default Domain Policy\Computer Configuration\Policies\Windows Settings\Security Settings\Public Key Policies.

9. In the details pane, right-click Certificate Services Client – Auto-Enrollment, and then click Properties.

10. In the Certificate Services Client – Auto-Enrollment Properties dialog box, click the Configuration Model list, and then click Enabled. Select both available check boxes, and then click OK.

11. In the details pane, right-click Certificate Path Validation Settings, and then click Properties.

12. In the Certificate Path Validation Settings Properties dialog box, select the Define These Policy Settings check box, and then click OK

EXERCISE 4   Connecting to the Wireless Access Point

In this exercise, you connect the Boston client computer to the WPA-EAP protected wireless net-work. You can use any Windows 7 or Windows Server 2008 computer that has a wireless network adapter. Technically, you could use a Windows XP or Windows Vista wireless computer, too, but the steps would be different.

1. Connect the Boston client computer to a wired network. Then, run **gpupdate /force** to update the Group Policy settings.

2. From Network And Sharing Center, click Connect To A Network.

3. Click the Contoso wireless network, and then click Connect.

4. After the client computer connects to the wireless network, click Close. The authentication was automatic because the client computer has the computer certificate installed.

5. In the Set Network Location dialog box, click Work. Provide administrative credentials if required, and then click OK.

6. Click Close.

7. Open Internet Explorer to verify that you can access network resources.

8. Restart the computer and log back on using the WirelessUser2 account. Notice that the computer automatically connected to the wireless network using computer authentica-tion. This network access allowed the computer to connect to the domain controller and authenticate using the WirelessUser2 account, even though that account did not have previously cached credentials.

EXERCISE 5 Viewing the Security Event Log

In this exercise, you view the log entries generated during your authentication attempt.

1. On Dcsrv1, use Server Manager to browse to Diagnostics\Event Viewer\Windows Logs \Security.

2. Browse through the recent events to identify the successful authentication from the client computer and the user account.

3. Using Windows Explorer, open the %SystemRoot%\system32\LogFiles folder, and then double-click the IN<*date*>.log file. Examine the RADIUS log file and note the lines that correspond to your recent authentication attempts.

Lesson Summary

- Private wireless networks should always be protected with security. WEP is compatible with almost every wireless device, but a competent attacker can easily break the security. WPA-EAP (also known as WPA-Enterprise) provides very strong security and easy manageability.

- Most wireless networks, especially those that provide access to an internal network or to the Internet, operate in infrastructure mode. In infrastructure mode, all wireless communications travel to and from a central wireless access point. For peer-to-peer networking without an infrastructure, you can also create ad hoc wireless networks.

- You can use a PKI to issue certificates to client computers and your RADIUS servers. These certificates provide a manageable and scalable authentication mechanism well suited to enterprise environments. Windows Server 2008 includes the Active Directory Certificate Services role, which provides an Active Directory-integrated PKI. Using Group Policy settings, you can provide client computers with computer and user certificates using autoenrollment.

- Typically, wireless access points aren't able to store a list of authorized users. Instead, the wireless access points submit requests to a central authentication server, known as a RADIUS server. Using NPS, Windows Server 2008 can provide a RADIUS server that authenticates credentials based on client certificates or user credentials.

- You can use NPS and Group Policy to require clients to authenticate to wired networks, much as they are typically required to authenticate to wireless networks.

- If you need to configure multiple, similar NPS policies, create NPS templates. Templates store groups of settings for shared secrets, RADIUS clients, remote RADIUS servers, health policies, remediation server groups, and IP filters.

Lesson Review

You can use the following questions to test your knowledge of the information in Lesson 1, "Configuring Network Policy Server." The questions are also available on the companion CD if you prefer to review them in electronic form.

> **NOTE** **ANSWERS**
>
> Answers to these questions and explanations of why each answer choice is correct or incorrect are located in the "Answers" section at the end of the book.

1. You are a systems administrator at an enterprise help desk. A user calls to complain that she is unable to connect to the wireless network. After discussing her problem, you discover that the wireless access point is rejecting her credentials. You examine the wireless access point configuration and determine that it is submitting authentication requests to a RADIUS service running on Windows Server 2008 R2. How can you determine the exact cause of the authentication failures?

   A. Examine the Security event log on the wireless client.

   B. Examine the System event log on the wireless client.

   C. Examine the Security event log on the computer running Windows Server 2008 R2.

   D. Examine the System event log on the computer running Windows Server 2008 R2

2. To improve productivity for employees during meetings, your organization has decided to provide authentication and encrypted wireless network access throughout your facilities. The organization is not willing to sacrifice security, however, and requires the most secure authentication mechanisms available. You have recently upgraded all client computers to either Windows XP (with the latest service pack) or Windows Vista. Which wireless security standard should you use?

   A. 128-bit WEP

   B. WPA-PSK

   C. 64-bit WEP

   D. WPA-EAP

3. You are planning wireless security for your organization. All computers are members of an Active Directory domain. Your wireless security standards require encryption and authentication, require users to authenticate to the wireless network without typing a password, and do not allow you to use static security keys. Which of these wireless security standards meets your requirements?

   A. WEP

   B. WPA-EAP

   C. WPA-PSK

   D. WPA2-PSK

Lesson 2: Configuring Network Address Translation

Today, the vast majority of intranets use private IP addressing. Private IP addresses are not routable on the public Internet, however. Therefore, to allow hosts with private IP addresses to communicate on the Internet, you need a NAT server to forward traffic to the Internet while translating private IP addresses to public IP addresses.

This lesson describes how to configure a computer running Windows Server 2008 R2 as a NAT server.

> **After this lesson, you will be able to:**
>
> - Describe the purpose of Network Address Translation.
> - Configure Internet Connection Sharing to act as a NAT server with minimal configuration.
> - Configure NAT using Routing And Remote Access to provide additional configuration options.
> - Troubleshoot NAT problems.
>
> **Estimated lesson time: 35 minutes**

Network Address Translation Concepts

The Internet was designed to provide every computer with a unique, public IP address. In recent years, however, the Internet has grown much larger than was ever anticipated. As a result, not enough public IP addresses are available.

> **NOTE IPV6 AND NAT**
>
> Because of the larger address space and improved private addressing design, IPv6 does not require NAT. Therefore, this lesson applies only to IPv4 networks.

As a result of the IP address shortage, Internet service providers (ISPs) typically assign a small number of public IP addresses to each organization with an Internet connection. For example, if an organization with 1000 computers purchases an Internet connection from the ISP, the ISP might assign the organization a total of four public IP addresses. Obviously, most of the organization's 1000 computers will need to share a public IP address.

Network Address Translation (NAT) allows one computer (or another type of network host, such as a router) with a public IP address to provide Internet access to hundreds or thousands of hosts on an internal network. The hosts on the internal network must have private IP addresses (as defined in Request for Comments [RFC] 1918) in one of the following address ranges:

- 192.168.0.0–192.168.255.255
- 172.16.0.0–172.31.255.255
- 10.0.0.0–10.255.255.255

Figure 7-6 illustrates how a NAT server can be placed on the boundary between the public Internet and a private intranet, translating the private IP addresses in outgoing connections into public IP addresses.

Although most recent versions of Windows can be used as a NAT server, most organizations choose dedicated network hardware to perform NAT. Many routers have NAT capabilities built-in, allowing you to configure NAT without purchasing additional hardware. If the NAT server ever goes offline, all clients will be unable to access the public Internet. Because of this, uptime is extremely important for a NAT server. Servers tend to have more downtime than dedicated network hardware because of the requirement to restart the server after installing updates, the higher risk of hardware failures (because of the more complex hardware configuration), and the higher risk of software failures (because of the instability that server applications can introduce).

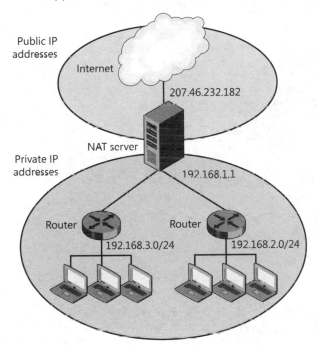

FIGURE 7-6 NAT architecture

Windows Server 2008 and Windows Server 2008 R2 include two NAT services:

- **Internet Connection Sharing (ICS)**   Primarily intended for home and small offices. ICS configuration can be performed with only a few clicks, but its configuration options are extremely limited.

- **Routing And Remote Access Services**   Intended for organizations with a routed intranet (meaning an intranet with multiple subnets).

The sections that follow describe each of these NAT technologies.

Configuring Internet Connection Sharing

Figure 7-7 shows a typical ICS architecture. The ICS computer has a public IP address (or an IP address that provides access to a remote network) on the external network interface. The internal network interface always has the IP address 192.168.137.1. Enabling ICS automatically enables a DHCP service that assigns clients IP addresses in the range 192.168.137.0/24. This DHCP service is not compatible with either the DHCP Server role or the DHCP relay agent feature of Routing And Remote Access.

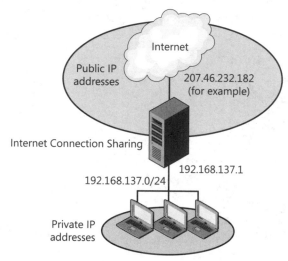

FIGURE 7-7 ICS architecture

Follow these steps to configure NAT using Internet Connection Sharing:

1. Configure the NAT server with two interfaces:

   - An interface connected to the Internet, with a public Internet IP address
   - An interface connected to your private intranet, with a static, private IP address

2. If you have previously enabled Routing And Remote Access, disable it before continuing.

3. Click Start, right-click Network, and then choose Properties. The Network And Sharing Center appears.

4. Click the network interface that connects to the Internet, and then click Properties.

5. Click the Sharing tab and select the Allow Other Network Users To Connect Through This Computer's Internet Connection check box.

6. If you want users on the Internet to access any servers on your intranet (such as a web or an email server that has only a private IP address), click the Settings button. For each internal service, follow these steps:

- If the service appears in the Services list, select its check box. In the Service Settings dialog box, type the internal name or IP address of the server and click OK.

- If the service does not appear on the list or if it uses a nonstandard port number, click Add. Type a description for the service and the internal name or IP address of the server. Then, in both the External Port Number For This Service and Internal Port Number For This Service boxes, type the port number used by the server. Select either TCP or UDP, and then click OK.

> **NOTE** **USING DIFFERENT INTERNAL AND EXTERNAL PORT NUMBERS**
>
> The only time you should specify an internal port number that is distinct from the external port number is when you want users on the Internet to use a different port number to connect to a server. For example, web servers typically use port 80 by default. If you have an internal web server using TCP port 81, you could provide an external port number of 80 and an internal port number of 81. Then, users on the Internet could access the server using the default port 80. If you have two web servers on your intranet, each using TCP port 80, you can assign the external TCP port number 80 to only one of the servers. For the second server, you should assign a different external port number, such as 8080, but leave the internal port number set to 80.

7. Click OK repeatedly to close all dialog boxes.

Enabling ICS does not change the configuration of the Internet network interface, but it does assign the IP address 192.168.137.1 to the intranet network interface. Additionally, the computer will now respond to DHCP requests on the intranet interface only and assign clients IP addresses in the range 192.168.137.0/24. All clients will have 192.168.137.1 (the private IP address of the ICS computer) as both their default gateway and the preferred DNS server address.

You can also share a VPN or dial-up connection. This allows a single computer to connect to a remote network and to forward traffic from other computers on the intranet. Sharing a VPN or dial-up connection works best when you allow other users to use the connection from that computer, because that computer can automatically connect when users on other computers attempt to access the connection. To enable ICS for a remote access connection, follow these steps:

1. Click Start, right-click Network, and then choose Properties.

2. In the Network And Sharing Center, click Change Adapter Settings.

3. In the Network Connections window, right-click the remote access connection, and then choose Properties.

4. Click the Sharing tab. Then, select the Allow Other Network Users To Connect Through This Computer's Internet Connection check box. If prompted, click OK.

5. Optionally, select the Establish A Dial-Up Connection Whenever A Computer On My Network Attempts To Access The Internet check box. This automatically establishes a remote access connection if a computer on the intranet sends any traffic that would need to be forwarded to the remote network. Realistically, computers automatically access different Internet services regularly enough that this ensures the connection stays online permanently even when no user is logged on.

6. Optionally, click the Settings button to configure internal services that should be accessible from the remote network.

7. Click OK.

Configuring Network Address Translation by Using Routing And Remote Access

Using Routing And Remote Access, you can enable full-featured NAT capabilities. The specific reasons to use Routing And Remote Access instead of ICS include:

- You can use internal networks other than 192.168.137.0/24.

- You can route to multiple internal networks.

- You can use a different DHCP server, including the DHCP Server role built into Windows Server 2008 R2.

- ICS cannot be enabled on a computer that uses any Routing And Remote Access component, including a DHCP relay agent.

Enabling NAT

Follow these steps to configure NAT by using Routing And Remote Access Services on a Windows Server 2008 computer:

1. Configure the NAT server with two interfaces:
   - An interface connected to the Internet, with a public Internet IP address
   - An interface connected to your private intranet, with a static, private IP address

2. In Server Manager, select the Roles object, and then click Add Roles. Add the Network Policy And Access Services role, with the Routing And Remote Access Services role service.

3. In Server Manager, right-click Roles\Network Policy And Access Services\Routing And Remote Access, and then choose Configure And Enable Routing And Remote Access.

4. On the Welcome To The Routing And Remote Access Server Setup Wizard page, click Next.

5. On the Configuration page, select Network Address Translation (NAT), and then click Next.

6. On the NAT Internet Connection page, select the interface that connects the server to the Internet. Then click Next.

7. On the Completing The Routing And Remote Access Server Setup Wizard page, click Finish.

8. Click OK when prompted.

The server is ready to forward packets from the internal network to the Internet.

Enabling DHCP

When you enable NAT, you can use any DHCP server. Typically, however, if you want to use a Windows Server 2008 R2 computer as a DHCP server, you should add the DHCP Server role instead, as described in Chapter 4, "Creating a DHCP Infrastructure." The DHCP Server role provides a very full-featured DHCP server.

NAT does include a very limited, but functional, DHCP server capable of providing IP address configuration to DHCP clients on a single subnet. To configure the NAT DHCP server, follow these steps:

1. In Server Manager, right-click Roles\Network Policy And Access Services\Routing And Remote Access\IPv4\NAT, and then choose Properties.

2. On the Address Assignment tab, select the Automatically Assign IP Addresses By Using The DHCP Allocator check box, as shown in Figure 7-8.

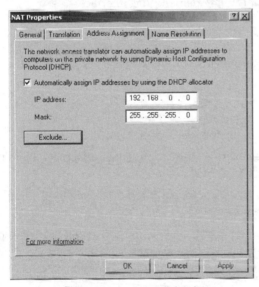

FIGURE 7-8 The NAT Properties dialog box

3. Type the private network address and subnet mask.

4. If you need to exclude specific addresses that are statically assigned to existing servers (other than the NAT server's private IP address), click the Exclude button and use the Exclude Reserved Addresses dialog box to list the addresses that will not be assigned to DHCP clients. Click OK.

5. Click OK.

You can view statistics for the DHCP server by right-clicking the Roles\Network Policy And Access Services\Routing And Remote Access\IPv4\NAT node in Server Manager and then choosing Show DHCP Allocator Information.

Enabling Forwarding of DNS Requests

To connect to the Internet, NAT clients need to be able to resolve DNS requests. You can provide this using the DNS Server role, as described in Chapter 3, "Configuring a DNS Zone Infrastructure."

For small networks not requiring a DNS server, you can configure NAT to forward DNS requests to the DNS server configured on the NAT server. Typically, this is the DNS server at your ISP. To configure forwarding of DNS requests, follow these steps:

1. In Server Manager, right-click Roles\Network Policy And Access Services\Routing And Remote Access\IPv4\NAT, and then choose Properties.

2. On the Name Resolution tab, select the Clients Using Domain Name System (DNS) check box.

3. If the NAT server must connect to a VPN or dial-up connection for network access, select the Connect To The Public Network When A Name Needs To Be Resolved check box, and then select the appropriate demand-dial interface.

4. Click OK.

You can view statistics for the DNS server by right-clicking the Roles\Network Policy And Access Services\Routing And Remote Access\IPv4\NAT node in Server Manager and then choosing Show DNS Proxy Information.

Configuring Client Computers

To configure the client computers, perform the following tasks:

- For computers on the same LAN as the NAT server's intranet interface, configure the default gateway as the NAT server's intranet IP address.

- For other intranet LANs, configure routers to forward traffic destined for the Internet to the NAT server's intranet IP address.

- Ensure that all clients can resolve Internet DNS names. The NAT server is often also configured as a DNS server, although this is not always the case. For more information about configuring DNS servers, refer to Chapter 2, "Configuring Name Resolution."

Troubleshooting Network Address Translation

By default, the Routing And Remote Access Services NAT component logs NAT errors to the System event log, which you can view in Server Manager at Diagnostics\Event Viewer \Windows Logs\System. All events will have a source of SharedAccess_NAT.

You can configure NAT to perform logging of warnings, perform verbose logging, or disable logging entirely. To configure NAT logging, in Server Manager, right-click the Roles \Network Policy And Access Services\Routing And Remote Access\IPv4\NAT node, and then choose Properties. On the General tab, select the desired logging level, and then click OK.

PRACTICE **Configuring NAT**

In this practice, you will configure two computers. In the first practice, you will configure a computer running Windows Server 2008 R2 as a NAT server. In the second practice, you will configure a second computer (which can be any operating system, although instructions are provided for Windows 7 or Windows Server 2008 R2) to connect to the Internet through the NAT server.

These are the exact steps you would go through to configure NAT in scenarios such as:

- Using a computer running Windows Server 2008 R2 to provide Internet access for a small business.
- Configuring NAT for a regional office that has only a single public IP address.

EXERCISE 1 **Configuring a NAT Server**

In this exercise, you configure Dcsrv1 as a NAT server to forward requests from an internal IP network to the Internet.

1. On Dcsrv1, add the Network Policy And Access Services role, with the Routing And Remote Access Services role service.

2. In Server Manager, right-click Roles\Network Policy And Access Services\Routing And Remote Access, and then choose Disable Routing And Remote Access (if necessary). Then, confirm the dialog box that appears. Disabling routing and remote access allows you to reconfigure it as if it were a newly configured computer.

3. In Server Manager, right-click Roles\Network Policy And Access Services\Routing And Remote Access, and then choose Configure And Enable Routing And Remote Access.

4. On the Welcome To The Routing And Remote Access Server Setup Wizard page, click Next.

5. On the Configuration page, select Network Address Translation, and then click Next.

6. On the NAT Internet Connection page, select the interface that connects the server to the Internet. If you are unsure, open Network And Sharing Center, click each network adapter, and check for Internet connectivity. Click Next.

7. On the Completing The Routing And Remote Access Server Setup Wizard page, click Finish.

8. Click OK when prompted.

9. In Server Manager, right-click Roles\Network Policy And Access Services\Routing And Remote Access\IPv4\NAT, and then choose Properties.

10. On the Address Assignment tab, select the Automatically Assign IP Addresses By Using The DHCP Allocator check box.

11. Type Dcsrv1's private network address, such as 10.0.0.1, and subnet mask, such as 255.255.255.0.

    If this computer were not a domain controller, and thus already acting as a DNS server, you would also need to click the Name Resolution tab and select the Clients Using Domain Name System (DNS) check box to allow clients to use Dcsrv1 as a DNS server.

12. Click OK.

EXERCISE 2   Configuring a NAT Client and Testing the Connection

In this exercise, you configure Boston as a NAT client, and then verify that the client can connect to the Internet.

1. Start the Boston computer and verify that it is connected to the private network and the network interface is configured to use DHCP.

2. If necessary, run **ipconfig /release** and **ipconfig /renew** at a command prompt to retrieve an IP address from the NAT DHCP server.

3. At a command prompt, run **ipconfig /all** to verify that the computer has an IP address in the 10.0.0.0/24 network and has 10.0.0.1 configured as both the default gateway and DNS server.

4. Open Internet Explorer and verify that you can connect to *http://www.microsoft.com*.

Lesson Summary

- If you have more computers than public IP addresses, you will need to assign hosts private IP addresses. To allow hosts with private IP addresses to communicate on the Internet, deploy a NAT server, with network interfaces attached both to the public Internet and to your private intranet.

- ICS allows you to enable NAT on a server with just a few clicks. However, configuration options are very limited. For example, the internal interface must have the IP address 192.168.137.1. Additionally, you cannot use the DHCP Server role built into Windows Server 2008; instead, you must use the DHCP server component built into ICS.

- Routing And Remote Access provides a much more flexible NAT server than is available with ICS. Although configuration is slightly more complex than configuring ICS, you can start the configuration wizard by right-clicking Roles\Network Policy And Access Services\Routing And Remote Access in Server Manager and then choosing Configure And Enable Routing And Remote Access. After it's configured, you can choose to use the built-in DHCP server or add the DHCP Server role.

Lesson Review

You can use the following questions to test your knowledge of the information in Lesson 2, "Configuring Network Address Translation." The questions are also available on the companion CD if you prefer to review them in electronic form.

> **NOTE ANSWERS**
>
> Answers to these questions and explanations of why each answer choice is correct or incorrect are located in the "Answers" section at the end of the book.

1. How does enabling ICS change the IP settings on a computer? (Choose all that apply.)

   A. The IP address of the internal network adapter is changed to 192.168.137.1.

   B. The IP address of the external network adapter is changed to 192.168.137.1.

   C. DHCP services are enabled on the internal network adapter.

   D. DHCP services are enabled on the external network adapter.

2. Which of the following scenarios are not likely to work with NAT without additional configuration?

   A. Clients on the Internet accessing a web server on the intranet using HTTP

   B. Clients on the intranet downloading email from an Exchange server on the Internet

   C. Clients on the intranet streaming video using a TCP connection from a server on the Internet

   D. Clients on the intranet accessing a web server on the Internet using HTTPS

3. You are an administrator for a small business with a single server. All computers on the network need to share a single Internet connection. You configure a Windows Server 2008 computer with two network adapters. You connect one network adapter directly to the DSL modem provided by your ISP. You connect the second network adapter to a Layer 2-switch that all other computers are connected to. Then, you enable ICS on the Internet network adapter. What is the IP address of the internal network adapter?

   A. The public IP address provided by your ISP

   B. The DNS server address provided by your ISP

   C. 192.168.137.1

   D. 192.168.0.0

Lesson 3: Connecting to Remote Networks

Public wireless networks allow users to connect to the Internet. Although that connection is sufficient to allow users to catch up on the news, check a flight, or read a weather forecast, business users typically need access to their company's or organization's intranet resources. To allow your users to connect to internal servers so that they can exchange documents, synchronize files, and read email, you need to configure remote access.

Remote access typically takes one of two forms: dial-up connections or VPNs. Dial-up connections allow users to connect from anywhere with a phone line. However, dial-up connections offer poor performance, and maintaining dial-up servers can be costly. VPNs require both the client and server to have an active Internet connection. VPNs can offer much better performance, and costs scale much better than they do for dial-up connections.

This lesson provides an overview of remote access technologies and step-by-step instructions for configuring remote access clients and servers.

After this lesson, you will be able to:

- Decide whether dial-up connections, VPN connections, or a combination of both best meet your remote access requirements.
- Configure a Windows Server 2008 R2 computer to act as a dial-up server, a RADIUS server for a separate dial-up server, or a dial-up client.
- Configure a Windows Server 2008 R2 computer to act as a VPN server or a VPN client.

Estimated lesson time: 45 minutes

Remote Access Overview

You can provide remote network access to users with either dial-up connections or VPNs. Dial-up connections provide a high level of privacy and do not require an Internet connection, but performance might be too low to meet your requirements. VPNs can be used any time a user has an Internet connection, but they require you to expose your internal network infrastructure to authentication requests from the Internet (and, potentially, attacks).

The sections that follow provide an overview of dial-up and VPN connections.

Dial-Up Connections

The traditional (and now largely outdated) remote access technique is to use a dial-up connection. With a dial-up connection, a client computer uses a modem to connect to a remote access server over a phone line. Figure 7-9 illustrates how connections are established, with each client requiring a separate physical circuit to the server.

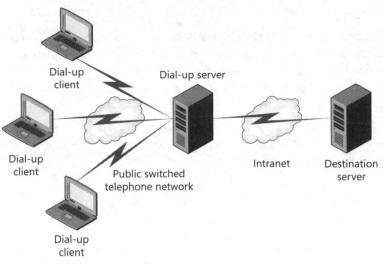

Dial-up client

Dial-up client

Dial-up client

Dial-up server

Public switched telephone network

Intranet

Destination server

FIGURE 7-9 The architecture of dial-up remote access connections

Dial-up connections offer the following advantages:

- **No Internet connection required**   Dial-up connections use a standard analog phone line to establish a network connection directly to your internal network. This means you do not need to expose your internal network to authentication requests from the Internet, as you do with a VPN. In fact, you do not need to connect your internal network to the Internet at all—a common requirement for high-security networks.

- **Minimal privacy risks**   Although dial-up connections lack encryption, the traffic crosses the public switched telephone network (PSTN), which many security experts consider to offer better privacy than the public Internet.

- **Predictable performance**   Dial-up connections offer consistent, predictable performance because the connection is dedicated to a single client.

However, dial-up connections have the following drawbacks:

- **High cost for scalability**   When planning to allow employees dial-up access, you need to have as many incoming phone lines and modems available as users who will simultaneously access the dial-up network. To support hundreds or thousands of users, the monthly costs of the telephone circuits can be very expensive, as can be the one-time costs of the modems required.

- **Poor bandwidth**   Modems for traditional analog phone lines are technically rated for 56 Kbps of bandwidth, but typically, usable bandwidth is between 20 Kbps and 25 Kbps. That bandwidth makes simple tasks such as browsing the web tedious and makes tasks such as listening to streaming video or audio impossible. Digital phone lines, such as Integrated Services Digital Network (ISDN) circuits, can offer true 128 Kbps bandwidth, but at a much higher cost.

Virtual Private Networks

Whereas dial-up connections use the PSTN to carry traffic to your internal network, VPNs traverse the public Internet. Because your organization probably already has an Internet connection, you might not need to purchase any additional bandwidth (unless you determine that your current bandwidth will not meet the needs of the users simultaneously connected using a VPN).

Figure 7-10 illustrates how connections are established, with each client requiring a separate Internet connection but the VPN server requiring only a single connection to the Internet (instead of a separate physical circuit per dial-up client).

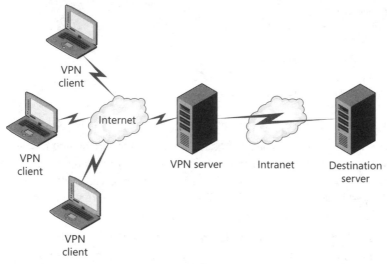

FIGURE 7-10 The architecture of VPN connections

VPNs offer the following advantages:

- **Higher bandwidth potential** Theoretically, VPN bandwidth can be as high as the client or VPN server's Internet connection (whichever is slower). In practice, because other services will probably use both connections and many other factors can limit bandwidth on the Internet, performance will be somewhat lower than the theoretical maximum. If the client has a broadband connection, however, bandwidth is likely to be much higher than it would be for a dial-up connection.

- **Minimal costs** Both the VPN server and the client need to be connected to the Internet. However, your organization probably has an existing Internet connection, and many home or traveling users have Internet access. Therefore, there are no connection costs associated with using a VPN, regardless of the number of incoming connections. If the number of incoming VPN connections requires more bandwidth than you have, you might need to purchase additional bandwidth from your ISP. However, this cost is likely to be far less than purchasing a similar number of telephone circuits and modems for dial-up connections.

However, VPNs have the following drawbacks:

- **Internet connection required** You must connect the VPN server, and thus your internal network, to the Internet and allow incoming VPN traffic through any firewalls. Additionally, users must have an Internet connection to use a VPN. Organizations typically take one of two approaches:

    - Work with an ISP to arrange Internet access for all users, using either a dial-up connection or a broadband connection such as a cable modem or DSL.

    - Require employees to find their own ISPs. Many users currently have an Internet connection at home, and traveling users can often connect to the Internet using public hotspots or wireless broadband services.

- **Poor latency** Even if the bandwidth is high, VPN connections often seem slow because of high latency. *Latency* is the delay that occurs when a packet travels from a client to a server. As Figure 7-10 shows, packets in a VPN have to travel across the Internet to the VPN server, across the intranet to the destination server, and back. The latency on a VPN connection can often be several times greater than the latency on a dial-up connection.

- **Poor efficiency with dial-up connections** Although it's possible to dial up to the Internet and then connect to a VPN, the added overhead of the VPN, and the latency added by the Internet, offer even worse performance than using a dial-up connection directly to a remote access server. If users will be using a dial-up connection to access the Internet, they will receive much better performance dialing directly to your intranet.

Configuring Dial-Up Connections

The sections that follow describe how to configure a computer running Windows Server 2008 as either a dial-up server (as described in the following section, "Configuring the Dial-Up Server") or a RADIUS server for a separate dial-up server (as described in the section "Configuring the RADIUS Server for Dial-Up Connections").

Configuring the Dial-Up Server

To configure a server to accept incoming dial-up connections, first connect the modem hardware to the server and connect the modems to the telephone circuits. Then, add the Network Policy And Access Services role, as described in the previous lesson.

> **NOTE CONFIGURING A DIAL-UP SERVER WITHOUT A PHYSICAL MODEM**
> For the purpose of experimentation, you can add a fake modem using the Add Hardware Wizard in Control Panel. Choose to manually select the hardware, and then select Standard 56000 Bps Modem in the Add Hardware Wizard.

Next, configure the Routing And Remote Access Service to accept dial-up connections by following these steps.

1. In Server Manager, right-click Roles\Network Policy And Access Services\Routing And Remote Access, and then choose Configure And Enable Routing And Remote Access. The Routing And Remote Access Server Setup Wizard appears.

2. On the Welcome To The Routing And Remote Access Server Setup Wizard page, click Next.

3. On the Configuration page, select Remote Access. Then, click Next.

4. On the Remote Access page, select the Dial-Up check box, and then click Next.

5. On the Network Selection page, select the network you want users to connect to after they dial in. Then, click Next.

6. On the IP Address Assignment page, select Automatically if there is already a DHCP server on the network. If you want the dial-up server to assign IP addresses from a pool not already assigned to a DHCP server, click From A Specified Range Of Addresses. Click Next.

7. If the Address Range Assignment page appears, click New, type an IP address range, and then click OK. Add as many address ranges as required. Click Next.

8. On the Managing Multiple Remote Access Servers page, you will choose how dial-up users are authenticated. If you have a separate RADIUS server, select Yes, Set Up This Server To Work With A RADIUS Server. If you want Routing And Remote Access to perform the authentication (which is fine for Active Directory domain authentication), select No, Use Routing And Remote Access To Authenticate Connection Requests. Then, click Next.

9. Click Finish. If prompted, click OK.

Next, you need to enable demand-dial routing on the server by following these steps:

1. In Server Manager, right-click Roles\Network Policy And Access Services\Routing And Remote Access, and then choose Properties.

2. On the General tab of the Routing And Remote Access Properties dialog box, do one or both of the following:

   - To allow IPv4 dial-up clients (the most common scenario), select the IPv4 Router check box, and then select LAN And Demand-Dial Routing. Then, select the IPv4 Remote Access Server check box.

   - To allow IPv6 dial-up clients, select the IPv6 Router check box, and then select LAN And Demand-Dial Routing. Then, select the IPv6 Remote Access Server check box.

3. If you are allowing IPv4 dial-up connections, click the IPv4 tab. Verify that the Enable IPv4 Forwarding check box is selected. If you want to assign IP addresses to clients using an existing DHCP sever, leave Dynamic Host Configuration Protocol selected. If you want the dial-up server to assign IP addresses from an address pool without having to install the DHCP server role, select Static Address Pool. Then, click the Add button to add the IP address ranges to assign addresses from. These IP address ranges should not overlap with other IP address ranges currently in use or assigned to an existing DHCP server.

4. If you are allowing IPv6 dial-up connections, click the IPv6 tab. Verify that Enable IPv6 Forwarding and Enable Default Route Advertisement are selected to allow the dial-up server to act as an IPv6 router. In the IPv6 Prefix Assignment box, type an IPv6 network prefix to be assigned to dial-up clients. If you are unsure of the network prefix, consult network administration.

5. On the PPP tab, notice that you can disable multilink connections (which allow users to dial up using multiple modems and phone lines to increase bandwidth). You can also disable link control protocol (LCP) extensions or software compression if you have a compatibility problem, although such compatibility problems are rare.

6. On the Logging tab, notice that errors and warnings are logged by default. You can choose to enable more detailed logging by clicking Log All Events and selecting Log Additional Routing And Remote Access Information, or you can click Do Not Log Any Events to disable logging entirely.

7. Click OK.

8. If prompted to restart the router, click Yes. Restarting the router will disconnect any users.

Next, verify that the modems are configured to accept dial-up connections by following these steps:

1. In Server Manager, right-click Roles\Network Policy And Access Services\Routing And Remote Access\Ports, and then choose Properties.

2. In the Ports Properties dialog box, select your modem, and then click Configure. If your modem does not appear, use the Add Hardware Wizard (available from within Control Panel) to add it first.

3. In the Configure Device dialog box, as shown in Figure 7-11, select the Remote Access Connections check box. In the Phone Number For This Device box, type the phone number assigned to that modem. Click OK.

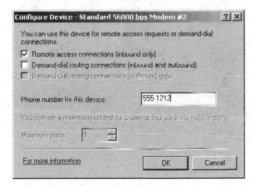

FIGURE 7-11 Configuring a modem to accept incoming connections

4. Repeat steps 2–3 for each modem you want to use to accept incoming dial-up connections.

5. In the Ports Properties dialog box, click OK.

The dial-up server is ready to accept dial-up connections. To view the status of all modems, select the Roles\Network Policy And Access Services\Routing And Remote Access\Ports node. To view the currently connected users, select the Roles\Network Policy And Access Services \Routing And Remote Access\Remote Access Clients node.

Configuring the RADIUS Server for Dial-Up Connections

Dial-up servers function exactly like wireless access points or any other access point and can submit RADIUS requests to the computer running Windows Server 2008 R2. Although users can dial directly into a modem attached to a dial-in server, most organizations that require more than one or two dial-up connections use dedicated hardware known as a modem bank. *Modem banks* accept dial-up connections and submit authentication requests to a RADIUS server in much the same way as a wireless access point.

Some organizations have an ISP manage the modem bank and accept the dial-up connections. In this scenario, the ISP can typically configure its modem bank to send authentication requests to a RADIUS server (such as a computer running Windows Server 2008 R2) on your internal network. In this way, users can log on to the dial-up connection using their Active Directory credentials, rather than being required to supply a separate set of credentials for the ISP. This also allows you to add and remove users without contacting the ISP. Figure 7-12 illustrates this scenario. In this case, have the ISP provide the realm name it is using for the modem bank.

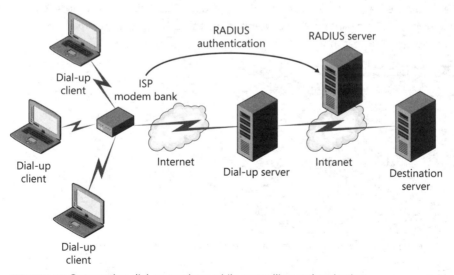

FIGURE 7-12 Outsourcing dial-up modems while controlling authentication

To configure a computer running Windows Server 2008 R2 to act as a RADIUS server for a modem bank or other dial-up server, follow these steps:

1. If you haven't already, create a user group for users who will be granted dial-up access. Then, configure the server with a static IP address.

2. In Server Manager, expand Roles, expand Network Policy And Access Services, and then select NPS.

3. In the details pane, under Standard Configuration, select RADIUS Server For Dial-Up Or VPN Connections. Then, click Configure VPN Or Dial-Up. The Configure VPN Or Dial-Up Wizard appears.

4. On the Select Dial-Up Or Virtual Private Network Connections Type page, select Dial-Up Connections. Optionally, type a name. Click Next.

5. On the Specify Dial-Up Or VPN Server page, you will configure your modem banks as valid RADIUS clients. Follow these steps for each modem bank, and then click Next:

   a. Click Add.

   b. In the New RADIUS client dialog box, in the Friendly Name box, type a name that identifies that specific modem bank.

   c. In the Address box, type the host name or IP address that identifies the modem bank.

   d. In the Shared Secret group, click the Generate option button to have a complex shared secret automatically generated. Alternatively, you can click Manual and type your own shared secret twice. Write the key down for later use; you'll need to enter it when configuring your modem bank.

   e. Click OK.

6. On the Configure Authentication Methods page, select the authentication method you want to use. Click Next.

7. On the Specify User Groups page, click Add. In the Select Group dialog box, type the name of the group you created for users who are allowed to connect using dial-up, and then click OK. Click Next.

8. On the Specify IP Filters page, as shown in Figure 7-13, click the Input Filters button or the Output Filters button to filter traffic going to or from remote access clients (using either IPv4 or IPv6). Typically, this is not required for intranet scenarios. However, to limit security risks, you might use this capability to prevent dial-up users from accessing specific IP addresses or networks containing highly confidential resources. Alternatively, you could limit dial-up users to accessing only specific resources by selecting the Permit Only The Packets Listed Below option on the Inbound Filters or Outbound Filters dialog box and then listing those networks that dial-up users are allowed to access. Click Next.

FIGURE 7-13 The Specify IP Filters page

9. On the Specify Encryption Settings page, select the check boxes for the encryption levels that you want to support. Click Next.

10. On the Specify A Realm Name page, type the realm name provided by your ISP if your ISP is managing the modem bank. Otherwise, leave the Realm Name box blank. Click Next.

11. On the Completing New Dial-Up Or Virtual Private Network Connections And RADIUS Clients page, click Finish.

Configure the modem bank to submit RADIUS requests to your server with the shared secret you selected.

Configuring the Dial-Up Client

From a computer running Windows Vista, Windows 7, or Windows Server 2008, you can manually create a dial-up connection by following these steps:

1. From Network And Sharing Center, click Setup A New Connection Or Network.

2. On the Choose A Connection Option page, select Set Up A Dial-Up Connection, and then click Next.

3. On the Set Up A Dial-Up Connection page, type the dial-up phone number (including a 1, a 9, or another dialing prefix that might be required by the phone system). Then, type the user name and password. If multiple users on the computer will use the same connection and you have administrative credentials, select the Allow Other People To Use This Connection check box. Click Connect. Windows will immediately attempt to connect.

4. After Windows is connected, click Close.

Configuring VPN Connections

Windows Server 2008 and Windows Vista support three VPN technologies:

- **Point-to-Point Tunneling Protocol (PPTP)** A Microsoft VPN technology that is now widely supported by non-Microsoft operating systems. PPTP uses Point-to-Point Protocol (PPP) authentication methods for user-level authentication and Microsoft Point-to-Point Encryption (MPPE) for data encryption. PPTP does not require a client certificate when using PEAP-MS-CHAP v2, EAP-MS-CHAP v2, or MS-CHAP v2 for authentication.

- **Layer Two Tunneling Protocol (L2TP)** An open standards VPN technology that is widely supported by both Microsoft and non-Microsoft operating systems. L2TP uses PPP authentication methods for user-level authentication and IPsec for computer-level peer authentication, data authentication, data integrity, and data encryption. L2TP requires both the VPN clients and servers to have computer certificates. Most organizations implement this using Active Directory Certificate Services, exactly as you configured in Lesson 2, "Configuring Network Address Translation." L2TP is the only VPN technology that can be used across the IPv6 Internet.

- **Secure Socket Tunneling Protocol (SSTP)** SSTP uses PPP authentication methods for user-level authentication and Hypertext Transfer Protocol (HTTP) encapsulation over a Secure Sockets Layer (SSL) channel for data authentication, data integrity, and data encryption. Using HTTP encapsulation allows SSTP to traverse many firewalls, NATs, and proxy servers that would cause PPTP and L2TP to fail. SSTP is supported only by Windows Server 2008 and Windows Server 2008 R2 (as a VPN server or client) and Windows Vista with Service Pack 1 and Windows 7 (as a VPN client). SSTP requires that the VPN server has a computer certificate installed and that clients trust the CA that issued the computer certificate. Most organizations implement this using Active Directory Certificate Services, exactly as you configured it in Lesson 2, "Configuring Network Address Translation" (except that autoenrollment of client computers is not required).

By default, a Windows Server 2008 VPN server supports each of these three VPN technologies simultaneously, although you can selectively disable them. The sections that follow describe how to configure VPN servers and clients.

Configuring the VPN Server

Configuring a VPN server is very similar to configuring a dial-up server. First, configure the VPN server with at least two network adapters. Connect one network adapter to the public Internet—this interface will accept incoming VPN connections and should have a static IP address. Connect the second network adapter to your intranet—this interface will forward traffic between the VPN and your network resources. Then, add the Network Policy And Access Services role.

Next, you need to enable demand-dial routing on the server by following these steps:

1. In Server Manager, right-click Roles\Network Policy And Access Services\Routing And Remote Access, and then choose Configure And Enable Routing And Remote Access.

2. On the Welcome To The Routing And Remote Access Server Setup Wizard page, click Next.

3. On the Configuration page, select Remote Access, and then click Next.

4. On the Remote Access page, select the VPN check box, and then click Next.

5. On the VPN Connection page, select the network adapter that connects the server to the Internet. Then, click Next.

6. On the Network Selection page, select the interface that connects the server to the internal network.

7. On the IP Address Assignment page, select Automatically if there is already a DHCP server on the network. If you want the VPN Server to assign IP addresses from a pool not already assigned to a DHCP server, select From A Specified Range Of Addresses. Click Next.

8. If the Address Range Assignment page appears, click New, type an IP address range, and then click OK. Add as many address ranges as required. Click Next.

9. On the Managing Multiple Remote Access Servers page, you will choose how VPN users are authenticated. If you have a separate RADIUS server, select Yes. If you want Routing And Remote Access to perform the authentication (which is fine for Active Directory domain authentication), select No. Then, click Next.

10. Click Finish. If prompted, click OK.

Now you can click the Roles\Network Policy And Access Services\Routing And Remote Access \Ports node to view the list of VPN ports available to accept incoming VPN connections. By default, Windows Server 2008 creates 128 ports for each of the three VPN technologies. Each

VPN connection requires a single port. To add or remove ports, right-click Ports, and then click Properties. In the Ports Properties dialog box, click the port type you want to adjust, and then click Configure.

When you configure a computer as a VPN server, Windows Server 2008 automatically configures a DHCP relay agent. If the VPN server is a DHCP client at the time the Routing And Remote Access Server Setup Wizard is run, the wizard automatically configures the DHCP Relay Agent with the IPv4 address of a DHCP server. If you need to change the IP address later, edit the DHCP relay agent properties using the Roles\Network Policy And Access Services\Routing And Remote Access\IPv4\DHCP Relay Agent node. For more information about DHCP, refer to Chapter 4.

Configuring VPN Packet Filters

After configuring the VPN server to accept incoming VPN connections, you will no longer be able to ping the VPN server on the Internet interface, because the Routing And Remote Access Server Setup Wizard creates filters to block all incoming traffic except incoming VPN connections. If you are running a web server, an email server, or other services on the VPN server, you must manually add packet filters and exceptions for Windows Firewall to allow the traffic to and from the other services.

To change the inbound filters, follow these steps:

1. In Server Manager, select either Roles\Network Policy And Access Services\Routing And Remote Access\IPv4\General (for IPv4 traffic) or Roles\Network Policy And Access Services\Routing And Remote Access\IPv6\General (for IPv6 traffic).

2. In the details pane, right-click your Internet interface, and then choose Properties. The properties dialog box for the network interface appears.

3. On the General tab, click the Inbound Filters button.

4. In the Inbound Filters dialog box, as shown in Figure 7-14, update, add, or remove filters as necessary. Then, click OK.

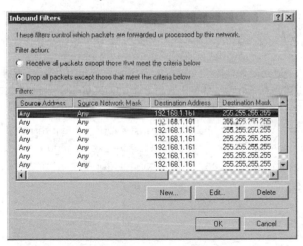

FIGURE 7-14 Configuring inbound filters

5. On the General tab, you can also click the Outbound Filters button to configure outbound packet filtering.

6. Click OK again.

Configuring the VPN Client

First, grant VPN users remote access. In Active Directory domain environments, you can do this by editing the user's properties, clicking the Dial-In tab, and then selecting Allow Access.

To connect a VPN client to your VPN server, follow these steps:

1. On the VPN client computer, from Network And Sharing Center, click Set Up A New Connection Or Network. The Set Up A Connection Or Network wizard appears.

2. On the Choose A Connection Option page, select Connect To A Workplace, and then click Next.

3. If the Do You Want To Use A Connection That You Already Have page appears, click No, Create A New Connection, and then click Next.

4. On the How Do You Want To Connect page, click Use My Internet Connection (VPN).

5. On the Type The Internet Address To Connect To page, type the IP address of your VPN server's network adapter that is connected to your external network. Then, click Next.

6. On the Type Your User Name And Password page, type the user name, password, and domain. Select the Remember This Password check box. Then, click Connect.

7. After the connection is established, click Close.

8. On the Set Network Location page, choose the network profile type for the VPN. Typically, this should be Work.

9. When prompted, click Close.

In the future, you can connect to the VPN either from Network And Sharing Center or by clicking the networking icon in the system tray.

Configuring VPN Reconnect

Windows 7 and Windows Server 2008 R2 VPN clients support VPN Reconnect to automatically re-establish a VPN connection when it is lost because of intermittent network connectivity or when users switch between wired and wireless networks. This provides for users a more consistent, lower-maintenance VPN connection that feels persistent, even when the underlying network is unstable.

To use VPN Reconnect, both the VPN client and server must support the Internet Key Exchange version 2 (IKEv2) VPN protocol, as described in RFC 4306. To configure a Windows 7 or Windows Server 2008 R2 client to use IKEv2 and VPN Reconnect for an existing VPN connection, follow these steps.

1. In Network and Sharing Center, click Change Adapter Settings.

2. Right-click the VPN connection and then click Properties.

3. On the Security tab, click the Type Of VPN list, and then click IKEv2.

4. Click OK.

Typically, no additional configuration is required on the VPN server; just verify that EAP-MSCHAPv2 authentication is allowed, which it will be by default.

If the computer is disconnected from the Internet after the user manually establishes the VPN connection, the VPN connection will switch to a state of dormant instead of disconnecting like a standard VPN connection. If the computer later connects to the Internet, even through a different network, VPN Reconnect will automatically re-establish the existing VPN session without prompting the user for credentials.

Troubleshooting VPN Connection Problems

Windows Server 2008 adds VPN connection events to the System event log. As shown in Figure 7-15, these events have a Source of RemoteAccess and provide a description of any authentication errors.

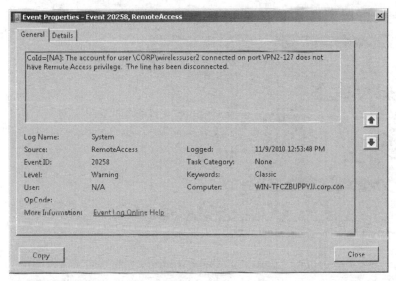

FIGURE 7-15 A VPN connection error

Configuring Connection Restrictions

Whether you configure dial-up, VPN, or wireless connections, you can configure network policies to control access based on time of day, day of week, user name, domain, or dozens of other factors. Network policies can also be used to restrict wireless access—for example, to disable wireless networks after hours when attackers are more likely to be connecting than legitimate users.

To configure an existing network policy, follow these steps:

1. Click Start, and then click Server Manager.
2. In Server Manager, select Roles\Policies\Network Policies.
3. In the details pane, double-click the policy that you want to update.
4. The properties dialog box for the connection appears.
5. Select the Conditions tab. This tab shows the default conditions that the wizard creates when you initially configured the server.
6. Click the Add button.
7. On the Select Condition tab, you can create conditions that must be matched before the policy applies to the connection. Select one of the following conditions, and then click Add. The most commonly used conditions (not including conditions related to NAP, which are discussed in Chapter 8) are:

   - **Windows Groups, Machine Groups, and User Groups**   Requires the computer or user to belong to a specified group.

   - **Day And Time Restrictions**   Restricts connections based on day of week or time of day, as shown in Figure 7-16. This is useful if you allow dial-up connections only after hours. You can also configure day and time restrictions using the Constraints tab.

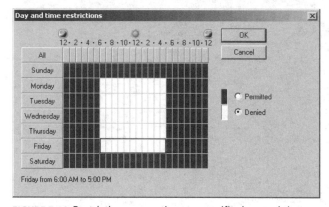

FIGURE 7-16 Restricting connections to specific days and times

   - **Access Client IPv4 Address and Access Client IPv6 Address**   Controls access based on the IP address of the client when the Windows Server 2008 computer is acting as a VPN server. This condition is primarily useful for remote access VPN connections.

   - **Client IPv4 Address and Client IPv6 Address**   Controls access based on the IP address of the client when the Windows Server 2008 computer is acting as a RADIUS server. This condition is primarily useful for remote access VPN connections.

   - **NAS IPv4 Address and NAS IPv6 Address**   Controls access based on the IP address of the wireless access point (or other network access server).

- **Authentication Type, Allowed EAP Types, Framed Protocol, Service Type, and Tunnel Type** Requires specific protocols or authentication methods. This condition is primarily useful for remote access VPN connections. You can also configure authentication method restrictions using the Constraints tab.

- **Calling Station ID** When caller ID exists for a dial-up connection, allows you to accept connections only from a specific phone number. This is primarily useful for demand-dial routing connections, although you can use it for dial-up remote access connections if you know in advance all phone numbers in use by clients.

- **NAS Port Type** Policy applied only when the Network Access Server (NAS) port type matches. Use this condition to restrict access to modems, wireless access points, or VPN connections. You can also configure NAS port type restrictions using the Constraints tab.

8. In the Constraints tab, you can set an idle time-out (which disconnects idle sessions, primarily for use with dial-up connections) or a session time-out (which ends a session after a specified amount of time, regardless of whether the connection is idle). You can also configure the Called Station ID, which identifies the phone number of the dial-up server (as opposed to the Calling Station ID condition, which identifies the phone number of the dial-up client). Additionally, although they are also available as conditions, you can configure authentication methods, day and time restrictions, and NAS port type constraints. Click OK.

9. On the Settings tab, you can configure NAP settings (described in Chapter 8) and RADIUS attributes (which might be required by specific RADIUS clients but are not typically used). For dial-up connections, click Multilink And Bandwidth Allocation Protocol (BAP) to configure whether clients with access to multiple modems and multiple phone lines can establish multiple dial-up connections for increased bandwidth as well as at what bandwidth threshold you disconnect any unused circuits. To configure packet filtering for this connection type, click IP Filters. Click Encryption to configure encryption requirements. Click IP settings to specify whether the client may request an IP address (typically, you will not change the default setting of Server Settings Determine IP Address Assignment).

10. Click OK.

Testing Connectivity

After users are connected, most want to immediately verify connectivity. The most straightforward and reliable way to check connectivity is to attempt to connect to an internal resource. For example, the user could open a web browser and attempt to open an internal webpage. If the webpage opens, it shows that connectivity is in place, name resolution is occurring correctly, and internal services are accessible.

If application layer services are not available, begin by examining the current configuration. Then, use IP troubleshooting tools to isolate which components are working correctly and which are not.

Ipconfig

Ipconfig is a command-line tool for displaying the current IP address configuration. To quickly retrieve a list of IP addresses and default gateways for each network adapter (including dial-up and VPN connections), run the following command:

```
ipconfig
```

Ipconfig displays output that resembles the following:

```
Windows IP Configuration

PPP adapter VPN Connection:
   Connection-specific DNS Suffix  . :
   IPv4 Address. . . . . . . . . . . : 192.168.2.103
   Subnet Mask . . . . . . . . . . . : 255.255.255.255
   Default Gateway . . . . . . . . . :

Ethernet adapter Local Area Connection:
   Connection-specific DNS Suffix   . : hsd1.nh.contoso.com.
   IPv4 Address. . . . . . . . . . . : 192.168.1.197
   Subnet Mask . . . . . . . . . . . : 255.255.255.0
   Default Gateway . . . . . . . . . : 192.168.1.1

Wireless LAN adapter Wireless Network Connection:
   Connection-specific DNS Suffix   . : hsd1.nh.contoso.com.
   Link-local IPv6 Address . . . . . : fe80::462:7ed4:795b:1c9f%8
   IPv4 Address. . . . . . . . . . . : 192.168.1.142
   Subnet Mask . . . . . . . . . . . : 255.255.255.0
   Default Gateway . . . . . . . . . : 192.168.1.1
```

For more detailed configuration information, including DNS and DHCP servers, run the following command:

```
ipconfig /all
```

Ipconfig displays output that resembles the following:

```
Windows IP Configuration

   Host Name . . . . . . . . . . . . : ClientComputer
   Primary Dns Suffix  . . . . . . . :
   Node Type . . . . . . . . . . . . : Hybrid
   IP Routing Enabled. . . . . . . . : No
   WINS Proxy Enabled. . . . . . . . : No
   DNS Suffix Search List. . . . . . : hsd1.nh.contoso.com.

PPP adapter VPN Connection:

   Connection-specific DNS Suffix  . :
   Description . . . . . . . . . . . : VPN Connection
   Physical Address. . . . . . . . . :
   DHCP Enabled. . . . . . . . . . . : No
```

```
    Autoconfiguration Enabled . . . . : Yes
    IPv4 Address. . . . . . . . . . . : 192.168.2.103(Preferred)
    Subnet Mask . . . . . . . . . . . : 255.255.255.255
    Default Gateway . . . . . . . . . :
    DNS Servers . . . . . . . . . . . : 10.100.100.201
                                        10.100.100.204
    Primary WINS Server . . . . . . . : 10.100.100.201
    Secondary WINS Server . . . . . . : 10.100.100.204
    NetBIOS over Tcpip. . . . . . . . : Enabled

Ethernet adapter Local Area Connection:

    Connection-specific DNS Suffix  . : hsd1.nh.contoso.com.
    Description . . . . . . . . . . . : 57xx Gigabit Controller
    Physical Address. . . . . . . . . : 00-15-C5-08-82-F3
    DHCP Enabled. . . . . . . . . . . : Yes
    Autoconfiguration Enabled . . . . : Yes
    IPv4 Address. . . . . . . . . . . : 192.168.1.197(Preferred)
    Subnet Mask . . . . . . . . . . . : 255.255.255.0
    Lease Obtained. . . . . . . . . . : Tuesday, November 06, 2007 6:16:30 AM
    Lease Expires . . . . . . . . . . : Wednesday, November 07, 2007 6:16:29 AM
    Default Gateway . . . . . . . . . : 192.168.1.1
    DHCP Server . . . . . . . . . . . : 192.168.1.1
    DNS Servers . . . . . . . . . . . : 192.168.1.1
    NetBIOS over Tcpip. . . . . . . . : Enabled

Wireless LAN adapter Wireless Network Connection:

    Connection-specific DNS Suffix  . : hsd1.nh.contoso.com.
    Description . . . . . . . . . . . : Wireless 3945ABG Network Connection
    Physical Address. . . . . . . . . : 00-13-02-1E-E6-59
    DHCP Enabled. . . . . . . . . . . : Yes
    Autoconfiguration Enabled . . . . : Yes
    Link-local IPv6 Address . . . . . : fe80::462:7ed4:795b:1c9f%8(Preferred)
    IPv4 Address. . . . . . . . . . . : 192.168.1.142(Preferred)
    Subnet Mask . . . . . . . . . . . : 255.255.255.0
    Lease Obtained. . . . . . . . . . : Tuesday, November 06, 2007 6:19:17 AM
    Lease Expires . . . . . . . . . . : Wednesday, November 07, 2007 6:19:16 AM
    Default Gateway . . . . . . . . . : 192.168.1.1
    DHCP Server . . . . . . . . . . . : 192.168.1.1
    DHCPv6 IAID . . . . . . . . . . . : 184554242
    DNS Servers . . . . . . . . . . . : 192.168.1.1
    NetBIOS over Tcpip. . . . . . . . : Enabled

Tunnel adapter Local Area Connection*:

    Media State . . . . . . . . . . . : Media disconnected
    Connection-specific DNS Suffix  . :
    Description . . . . . . . . . . . : isatap.hsd1.nh.contoso.com.
    Physical Address. . . . . . . . . : 00-00-00-00-00-00-00-E0
    DHCP Enabled. . . . . . . . . . . : No
    Autoconfiguration Enabled . . . . : Yes
```

If you establish a connection but fail to retrieve an IP address from a DHCP server (a scenario that is more common on LANs than on VPNs), run the following commands to give up your current DHCP-assigned IP addresses and attempt to retrieve new addresses:

```
ipconfig /release
ipconfig /renew
```

Ping

The Ping tool uses Internet Control Message Protocol (ICMP) to contact remote hosts and show how long it took to receive a response from the remote host. Typically, you ping your default gateway, DNS server, or another server that you know responds to pings. For example:

```
ping 192.168.1.1
```

The output follows:

```
Pinging 192.168.1.1 with 32 bytes of data:
Reply from 192.168.1.1: bytes=32 time<1ms TTL=64
Reply from 192.168.1.1: bytes=32 time<1ms TTL=64
Reply from 192.168.1.1: bytes=32 time<1ms TTL=64
Reply from 192.168.1.1: bytes=32 time<1ms TTL=64

Ping statistics for 192.168.1.1:
    Packets: Sent = 4, Received = 4, Lost = 0 (0% loss),
Approximate round trip times in milli-seconds:
    Minimum = 0ms, Maximum = 0ms, Average = 0ms
```

This output reveals that the host with an IP address of 192.168.1.1 is responding to network communications. The following output demonstrates that a host could not be reached, which might be a sign that the network has failed or that the remote host is offline:

```
ping 192.168.1.2
```

The output follows:

```
Pinging 192.168.1.2 with 32 bytes of data:
Request timed out.
Request timed out.
Request timed out.
Request timed out.
Ping statistics for 192.168.1.2:
    Packets: Sent = 4, Received = 0, Lost = 4 (100% loss),
```

If a host responds to pings, you know that host is at least connected to the network and online. If a host doesn't respond to pings, it could be any of the following:

- The host you are pinging is configured to drop ICMP communications, which is true of Windows Server 2008 R2 by default.

- A firewall between the client and the host you are pinging is configured to drop ICMP communications.

- The host you are pinging is offline.

- The client is not connected to the network, or the client's network settings are misconfigured.
- The network has a problem, such as a routing error.

Familiarize yourself with hosts on your network that respond to pings so that you can ping those specific hosts and be sure that failure to respond to a ping is not caused by firewall configuration.

Tracert

Tracert performs Ping tests for every router between the client and destination host. This allows you to identify the path packets take, to isolate possible routing problems, and to determine the source of performance problems. For example:

```
tracert www.microsoft.com

Tracing route to www.microsoft.com [10.46.19.254]
over a maximum of 30 hops:

  1    22 ms    24 ms     7 ms  c-3-0-ubr01.winchendon.contoso.com [10.165.8.1]
  2     7 ms    19 ms    18 ms  ge-1-2-ur01.winchendon.contoso.com [10.87.148.129]
  3    13 ms     9 ms     9 ms  ge-1-1-ur01.gardner.contoso.com [10.87.144.225]
  4    10 ms    17 ms     9 ms  te-9-1-ur01.sterling.contoso.com [10.87.144.217]
  5     8 ms     8 ms     8 ms  tc-9-2-ur01.marlboro.contoso.com [10.87.144.77]
  6    17 ms    17 ms    14 ms  te-8-1-ur01.natick.contoso.com [10.87.144.197]
  7    23 ms    38 ms    35 ms  te-8-3-ar02.woburn.contoso.com [10.87.145.9]
  8    23 ms    16 ms    18 ms  po-12-ar02.needham.contoso.com [10.87.146.45]
  9    16 ms    19 ms    13 ms  po-11-ar01.needham.contoso.com [10.87.146.37]
 10    13 ms    11 ms    14 ms  po-10-ar01.springfield.contoso.com [10.87.146.22]
 11    23 ms    15 ms    14 ms  po-11-ar01.chartford.contoso.com [10.87.146.26]
 12     *         *       16 ms  edge1.NewYork2.Fabricam.com [10.71.186.10]
 13    17 ms    17 ms    15 ms  edge1.NewYork2.Fabricam.com [10.71.186.9]
 14    22 ms    18 ms    16 ms  bbr2.NewYork1.Fabricam.com [10.68.16.130]
 15   109 ms   103 ms    98 ms  SanJose1.Fabricam.com [10.159.1.130]
 16    92 ms    91 ms   105 ms  SanJose1.Fabricam.com [10.68.18.62]
 17    90 ms    91 ms    91 ms  www.microsoft.com [10.68.123.2]
```

> **NOTE PREVENTING TRACERT FROM PERFORMING DNS LOOKUPS**
> To improve Tracert performance, add the -d parameter before the IP address.

Each host that Tracert displays is a router that forwards packets between your computer and the destination. Typically, the first host will be your default gateway, and the last host will be the destination.

Tracert pings each host three times and reports the number of milliseconds the host took to respond. Typically, hosts farther down the list take longer to respond because they are farther away from your computer. An asterisk indicates that a host failed to respond. The last host will always be the target computer you specify. If that computer is offline or does not respond to ICMP requests, Tracert will display a series of Request Timed Out messages.

As an alternative to Tracert, you can use PathPing. The PathPing tool functions similarly but spends several minutes performing performance testing for more accurate latency information.

PRACTICE **Establishing a Remote Access VPN Connection**

In this practice, you configure a VPN server, and then connect to the VPN server from a client computer.

EXERCISE 1 Configuring a VPN Server

In this exercise, you configure Dcsrv1 as a VPN server to accept incoming connections. Dcsrv1 must have two network adapters: one network adapter that is connected to your internal network (or the public Internet) and a second, private network adapter. You will connect Boston, the VPN client, to the private network adapter and verify VPN connectivity by establishing a VPN connection and connecting to resources on the Internet.

This practice assumes that you have completed Practice 1 in the previous lesson. If you have not completed that practice, add the Network Policy And Access Services role before completing this practice with the Routing And Remote Access Services role service.

1. Using Server Manager on Dcsrv1, create a group named "VPN Users." Then, create a user account named **VPNUser** with a complex password. Add the VPNUser account to the Domain Users and VPN Users groups.

   Next, you need to enable demand-dial routing on the server by following these steps:

2. In Server Manager, right-click Roles\Network Policy And Access Services\Routing And Remote Access, and then choose Disable Routing And Remote Access (if necessary). Then, confirm the dialog box that appears. Disabling routing and remote access allows you to reconfigure it as if it were a newly configured computer.

3. Right-click Roles\Network Policy And Access Services\Routing And Remote Access, and then choose Configure And Enable Routing And Remote Access.

4. On the Welcome To The Routing And Remote Access Server Setup Wizard page, click Next.

5. On the Configuration page, select Remote Access, and then click Next.

6. On the Remote Access page, select VPN, and then click Next.

7. On the VPN Connection page, select the network adapter that connects the server to the Internet. Click Next.

8. On the Network Selection page, select the interface that connects the server to the internal network.

9. On the IP Address Assignment page, select Automatically, and then click Next. If you do not have a DHCP server, click From A Specified Range Of Addresses, click Next, complete the Address Range Assignment page, and click Next again.

10. On the Managing Multiple Remote Access Servers page, select No, and then click Next.

11. On the Completing The Routing And Remote Access Server Setup Wizard page, click Finish.

12. In the Routing And Remote Access dialog box, click OK.

13. Click the Roles\Network Policy And Access Services\Routing And Remote Access\Ports node to view the list of VPN ports available to accept incoming VPN connections.

EXERCISE 2 Configuring a VPN Client

In this exercise, you configure Boston as a VPN client.

1. On the Boston VPN client computer, open Network And Sharing Center.

2. Click Set Up A New Connection Or Network.

3. On the Choose A Connection Option page, click Connect To A Workplace, and then click Next.

4. If the Do You Want To Use A Connection That You Already Have page appears, click No, Create A New Connection, and then click Next.

5. On the How Do You Want To Connect page, click Use My Internet Connection.

6. On the Type The Internet Address To Connect To page, type the IP address of your VPN server's network adapter that is connected to your external network. Click Next.

7. On the Type Your User Name And Password page, type the user name, password, and domain. Select the Remember This Password check box. Then, click Connect.

8. After the connection is established, click Close.

9. On the Set Network Location page, click Work.

10. When prompted, click Close.

11. Open a command prompt and ping the internal interface on the VPN server—the IP address you did not connect directly to. The server should reply to the Ping request, indicating that you have successfully established a VPN connection and that the VPN server is routing communications correctly.

12. On the VPN server, in Server Manager, click Roles\Network Policy And Access Services \Routing And Remote Access\Remote Access Clients. Notice that the details pane shows the single VPN connection. Right-click the connection, and then click Disconnect. Notice that the client displays the Network Connections dialog box, prompting the user to reconnect.

You can also disconnect a VPN connection from the client from Network And Sharing Center or by clicking the networking icon in the system tray.

Lesson Summary

- Dial-up connections provide remote connectivity to your internal network without requiring you to connect to the Internet. VPN connections use the Internet to tunnel encryption communications from the client to the internal network.

- Windows Server 2008 can act as either a dial-up server or a RADIUS server to authenticate a separate dial-up server. To configure a Windows Server 2008 computer to accept dial-up connections, you must connect one or more modems to it.

- Windows Server 2008 can act as a VPN server and accept PPTP, L2TP, and SSTP connections. PPTP provides simple Windows authentication. L2TP, which is based on IPsec, requires client certificates for authentication and thus requires you to implement a PKI. SSTP is supported by Windows Vista with Service Pack 1, Windows 7, Windows Server 2008, and Windows Server 2008 R2, and it provides VPN connectivity across proxy servers and firewalls.

Lesson Review

You can use the following questions to test your knowledge of the information in Lesson 3, "Connecting to Remote Networks." The questions are also available on the companion CD if you prefer to review them in electronic form.

> **NOTE ANSWERS**
>
> Answers to these questions and explanations of why each answer choice is correct or incorrect are located in the "Answers" section at the end of the book.

1. You are a systems engineer for a paper sales company. Frequently, your sales staff travels overnight and needs to connect to resources on your protected intranet. After discussions with some of the sales staff, you discover that they frequently use their mobile computers to connect to the Internet using wireless networks. At other times, hotels offer Ethernet connections with Internet access. Frequently, however, they have access only to a phone line that they can use to establish a dial-up connection. At any given time, 100 salespeople might need to connect, and at most 30 would need dial-up connections. Your organization is near the end of its fiscal year, and capital budget is tight. Therefore, you need to minimize up-front costs. What is the best way to configure remote access for the sales staff while using existing Active Directory user credentials? (Choose all that apply. Each answer forms part of the complete solution.)

   A. Connect a Windows Server 2008 computer to both the public Internet and your intranet. Then, configure it to accept incoming VPN connections.

   B. Connect a Windows Server 2008 computer to the public Internet. Then, configure it as a RADIUS server. Configure the client computers to submit RADIUS authentication requests to the server when they connect to remote networks.

C. Configure a Windows Server 2008 computer to accept dial-up connections. Lease a circuit from your local telecommunications provider for 30 PSTN connections. Purchase a modem bank capable of accepting 30 simultaneous connections and connect it to the Windows Server 2008 computer.

D. Establish an agreement with an ISP to provide dial-up access to your users. Then, configure a Windows Server 2008 computer as a RADIUS server. Have the ISP configure its modem bank to submit authentication requests to the RADIUS server.

2. You are a systems engineer evaluating remote access technologies. Which of the following statements comparing dial-up connections to VPN connections are true? (Choose all that apply.)

A. VPN connections typically provide better performance than dial-up connections. However, dial-up connections are adequate for common tasks, including email and streaming video.

B. VPN connections require an existing Internet connection, while dial-up connections can completely bypass the Internet.

C. Data sent across a VPN connection can be intercepted and interpreted by an attacker who has access to the ISP's infrastructure, whereas dial-up connections provide a much higher level of security by using the PSTN.

D. Both VPN and dial-up connections can authenticate to the same, central RADIUS server. That RADIUS server can be hosted on a computer running Windows Server 2008.

3. You are a systems administrator for a large fabric manufacturing company. You need to allow sales people to connect to your VPN server while traveling. Many sales people have complained that they are unable to connect at times, and you have isolated the problem as being caused by firewalls that do not allow PPTP or L2TP traffic through. You would like to recommend that the sales staff use SSTP VPN connections. Which operating systems support SSTP VPN connections? (Choose all that apply.)

A. Windows XP Professional

B. Windows 2000 Professional

C. Windows Vista with Service Pack 1

D. Windows Server 2008 R2

Lesson 4: Configuring DirectAccess

For years, administrators used VPNs to connect mobile users with Internet access to an intranet. VPNs can be frustrating for both users and administrators, however. The biggest challenge with a VPN is staying connected, because users have to manually initiate a connection.

For users, this means they have to think about whether a network resource, such as their email, is on the Internet or their intranet. If a resource is on the intranet, they have to initiate a VPN connection, provide their credentials, and wait for the connection to be established. Often, users do not bother, and they miss opportunities to be productive because internal resources are too time-consuming to access.

For administrators, making internal resources readily accessible to users often involves creating externally accessible versions of those resources. For example, users might use Microsoft Outlook when connected to their internal network, but resort to Outlook Web Access when connected to the Internet. That requires additional server hardware and management time. Additionally, users with traditional VPN connections are sporadically and unpredictably connected, making the computers more difficult for administrators to manage.

DirectAccess can keep mobile users connected to your intranet any time they have an Internet connection. The connection is automatic and entirely transparent to users, eliminating the need for users to manually initiate a connection or think about where network resources are located. Administration is simplified, the need for duplicate external resources is lessened, and computers are more regularly available for remote management.

DirectAccess was introduced with Windows 7 and Windows Server 2008 R2, so clients on earlier operating systems will need to continue to use a traditional VPN. Additionally, DirectAccess configures clients with globally routable IPv6 addresses. Therefore, you will need to use transition technologies, such as 6to4, Teredo, and ISATAP, to allow connections across the IPv4 Internet and portions of your intranet that do not yet support IPv6.

This lesson provides an overview of DirectAccess and walks you through basic configuration. However, DirectAccess is a complex feature and this lesson cannot cover it in complete detail. For more information, refer to the DirectAccess Design, Deployment, and Troubleshooting Guides at *http://www.microsoft.com/downloads/en/details.aspx?FamilyID=647222d1-a41e-4cdb-ba34-f057fbc7198f.*

After this lesson, you will be able to:

- List the different DirectAccess connection types.
- Describe how to use IPv6 transition technologies to allow DirectAccess to work on IPv4 networks.
- Explain how the Name Resolution Policy Table (NRPT) allows DirectAccess clients to identify whether hosts are on the intranet or Internet.
- Describe the purpose of the Network Location Server (NLS).
- Configure a firewall to allow DirectAccess communications.

Estimated lesson time: 45 minutes

DirectAccess Connection Types

You can choose from two different DirectAccess connection types: end-to-edge protection and end-to-end protection. Most environments will start with end-to-edge protection because it is the easiest to setup. Over time, you should strive to migrate to full end-to-end protection for the ultimate in communications security.

- **End-to-edge protection** DirectAccess clients connect to the DirectAccess server using IPsec. The connection between the DirectAccess client and DirectAccess server is authenticated and encrypted, providing communications security where it is needed the most—across the public Internet. Communications across the intranet are not protected by IPsec, which allows you to communicate with servers that do not support IPv6. Application servers can be running earlier versions of Windows, but they must still support IPv6.

- **End-to-end protection** DirectAccess clients connect directly to application servers using IPsec. IPsec authenticates both the client and the application server and encrypts all communications as they travel across both the Internet and the intranet. The DirectAccess server acts much like a router, forwarding traffic without having access to the unencrypted contents. This provides the highest level of security, but it requires that application servers run Windows Server 2008 or Windows Server 2008 R2 and use both IPv6 and IPsec.

Figure 7-17 shows end-to-end protection, whereas Figure 7-18 shows end-to-edge protection. The solid lines show IPsec-protected traffic, and the dotted lines show unprotected traffic.

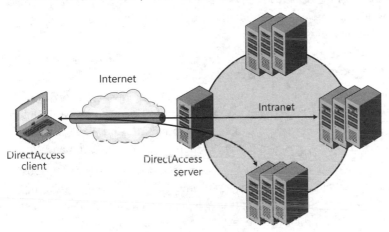

FIGURE 7-17 DirectAccess end-to-end protection

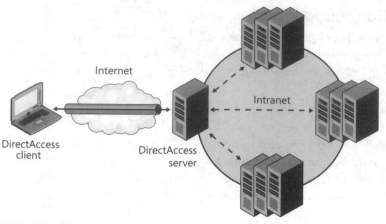

FIGURE 7-18 DirectAccess end-to-edge protection

By default, whichever connection type you choose, DirectAccess only routes traffic destined for the intranet through the DirectAccess connection. Internet traffic is sent directly to the Internet, just as it would if DirectAccess were not enabled. You can choose to route all Internet traffic through the DirectAccess connection, a common behavior for VPNs. However, this architecture can dramatically decrease the performance of Internet applications.

DirectAccess distinguishes intranet and Internet traffic by examining the IPv6 address at the network layer and the host name at the application layer. If the IPv6 address matches the intranet's IPv6 address space, or the destination server host name matches a name in the Name Resolution Policy Table (NRPT), the packets are routed through DirectAccess. The DirectAccess setup wizard automatically configures the NRPT for you.

Using DirectAccess on IPv4 Networks

From the smallest home network to the biggest enterprise, the vast majority of networks use IPv4 and connect to the IPv4 Internet. In fact, very few can accomplish anything across the Internet using only IPv6. However, all recent versions of operating systems running Windows clients and servers support IPv6 by default. Not all network applications support IPv6, but many do.

Because your clients and servers support IPv6, but the Internet they communicate across probably does not, you will need to use IPv6 transition technologies to allow IPv6 to work across the IPv4 Internet. The technology that clients use depends on how they're connected to the Internet. From most to least preferred, the technologies are the following:

- **6to4** For clients with public IPv4 address
- **Teredo** For clients located behind a NAT device
- **IP-HTTPS (Internet Protocol over Secure Hypertext Transfer Protocol)** For clients that block Teredo communications but allow HTTPS, such as a web proxy server

Additionally, to allow IPv6 communications across an IPv4 intranet, IPv6 computers can use ISATAP.

Although recent versions of Windows support IPv6, and many new applications support it, many operating systems and applications still do not support IPv6. Larger organizations, in particular, might not be able to update their intranet infrastructure to IPv6 because they might require new network equipment or computer operating system updates.

DirectAccess and Name Resolution

Traditionally, clients resolve DNS host names using the DNS servers configured for their network adapter by their DHCP server. Therefore, when connected to an intranet, clients send name resolution requests to their intranet DNS server. When connected to the Internet, clients send name resolution requests to the ISP DNS server.

DirectAccess clients, however, are connected to both the Internet and intranet at the same time, with the same interface. Windows 7 and Windows Server 2008 R2 include the NRPT, which provides a new way to identify which DNS servers to send requests to. Now, clients can choose different DNS servers based on the namespace of the request. Clients still use the standard DNS servers configured for each network adapter if a name does not appear in the NRPT, which would be the case for most Internet hostnames.

DirectAccess clients must still connect to the DirectAccess server while connected only to the Internet. Therefore, the DirectAccess server needs a host name that clients on the Internet can resolve (such as directaccess.contoso.com). If the NRPT indicates that the host name is on the intranet (for example, if all contoso.com addresses are considered part of the intranet), you will need to create an NRPT exception for the public DNS name. Similarly, you must create exceptions for the NLS and public CRL distribution points.

DirectAccess setup uses Group Policy settings to create an NRPT rule for your intranet namespaces, such as internal.contoso.com, so that all requests for a particular namespace go to your internal DNS server's IPv6 address. For that reason, having separate internal and external namespaces simplifies configuration. DirectAccess then creates an exception to that rule, allowing the NLS to be identified using public DNS servers.

DirectAccess NRPT rules are applied only when clients are disconnected from the intranet. You can view the active NRPT rules by running **netsh namespace show effectivepolicy** at a command prompt. You can view the NRPT rules configured by Group Policy by running the **netsh namespace show policy** command.

> **NOTE** **MITIGATING MAN-IN-THE-MIDDLE ATTACKS**
>
> To reduce the risk of an attacker intercepting DNS requests and providing a malicious IP address for a DirectAccess server, enable IPsec protection for DNS messages.

The Network Location Server

If DirectAccess clients are not connected to the intranet, they will attempt to establish a DirectAccess connection. To determine whether they are connected to the intranet, they attempt to establish an HTTPS connection to a server that is accessible only from the intranet: the Network Location Server (NLS). If they can connect to the NLS, they disable DirectAccess, including the DirectAccess NRPT rules.

The DirectAccess server can also act as the NLS server, but Microsoft best practices recommend using a separate, highly available NLS server. If the NLS server is offline, the DirectAccess client will assume that it is not connected to the intranet, which means it will activate the DirectAccess NRPT and attempt to connect to the DirectAccess server. This errant behavior could cause the client to be unable to access intranet resources. Even though an enterprise could technically use a single NLS server, to ensure clients operate reliably, consider adding NLS servers to each branch office.

DirectAccess setup automatically configures clients with the URL of the NLS. If you need to update it manually, you can edit the Computer Configuration\Policies\Administrative Templates \Network\Network Connectivity Status Indicator\Domain Location Determination URL Group Policy setting. The NLS can be any type of web server, including Internet Information Services (IIS), but the client must trust the SSL certificate. The NLS server should accept anonymous requests; it should not attempt to authenticate clients.

If DirectAccess clients are able to connect to the NLS, they must then verify that the NLS SSL certificate has not been revoked. In order to verify this, they must be able to download a certificate revocation list (CRL)—a component of the PKI. If you use an SSL certificate from a public certification authority, they typically host the CRL for you.

DirectAccess Requirements

DirectAccess requires the following:

- **A DirectAccess server running Windows Server 2008 R2 that is a member of a domain (but not a domain controller)**   It must have a computer certificate for IPsec authentication and a Secure Sockets Layer (SSL) certificate for IP-HTTPS. The server must have two network adapters: one connected to the Internet (and not behind NAT), and one connected to the intranet. The domain controller must be reachable from the DirectAccess server across the intranet connection, and it must not be accessible across the Internet connection. The Internet adapter must have two consecutive public IPv4 addresses. The addresses must be alphabetically consecutive. For example, 131.10.12.3 and 131.10.12.4 would work, but 131.10.12.9 and 131.10.12.10 would not work because 131.10.12.10 would be alphabetically sorted between 131.10.12.1 and 131.10.12.2.

- **DirectAccess clients must be domain members and must run Windows 7 Enterprise, Windows 7 Ultimate, or Windows Server 2008 R2**   They must have computer certificates for IPsec security authentication.

- **An Active Directory domain with at least one domain controller running Windows Server 2008 with Service Pack 2 or Windows Server 2008 R2**   Windows Server 2008 R2 domain or forest functional levels are not required. DirectAccess Setup updates Group Policy settings to configure DirectAccess clients and servers.

- **A NLS with IIS and an SSL certificate**   As described in the previous section, the DirectAccess server can also act as the NLS.

- **A PKI to issue computer security certificates to support IPsec**   The PKI must have a publically accessible certificate revocation list (CRL), which can be accomplished by configuring Active Directory Certificate Services to publish a CRL to an Internet Information Services (IIS)–based web server. To avoid hosting a public CRL, you can purchase an SSL certificate for your DirectAccess server from a public certification authority.

- **A DNS server running Windows Server 2008 R2, Windows Server 2008 with the Q958194 hotfix (*http://go.microsoft.com/fwlink/?Linkid=159951*), Windows Server 2008 SP2 or later, or a third-party DNS server that supports DNS message exchanges over the Intra-Site Automatic Tunnel Addressing Protocol (ISATAP)**   Typically, this requirement is fulfilled by a domain controller.

- **Application servers and network infrastructure to support IPv6 communications (which can include IPv6 translation technologies)**

At first glance, DirectAccess might seem complex to configure. Whereas many enterprises already have most of the requirements in place, DirectAccess is actually more accessible to small and mid-sized organizations. Enterprises tend to have client computers running earlier versions of Windows and servers running operating systems that will not be accessible from DirectAccess. Smaller organizations, however, are often more able to quickly upgrade their clients and servers.

 REAL WORLD

Tony Northrup

In the real world, enterprises upgrade their computers and networks slowly. Though the benefits of DirectAccess can be tremendous, it will probably be several years (at least) before we start to see DirectAccess and other transparent tunneling technologies overtaking traditional VPN connections. Even after VPNs had been commonly used for more than a decade, I was still designing remote access solutions for enterprises that primarily relied on dial-up—either because the infrastructure was not in place or because they simply didn't trust the new technology.

A decade from now, the idea of manually establishing a VPN connection will seem as arcane as using a dial-up seems today. Take the time to understand DirectAccess now, because it's the future—just not the *immediate* future.

DirectAccess Limitations

DirectAccess uses IPv6 for all communications, which prevents users from accessing IPv4-only resources. Whereas most modern networking equipment and operating systems support IPv6, many environments still have applications that only work with IPv4. Some of the applications that will not be available by default with DirectAccess include:

- Applications running on Windows Server 2000 or prior versions of Windows
- System services running on Windows Server 2003 or Windows XP, such as file sharing or Internet Information Services (IIS)
- Applications that support only IPv4, such as Office Communications Server (OCS)

If your DirectAccess clients need to access any resources of this type, you will need to use an IPv6/IPv4 translation technology, such as NAT64/DNS64.

Firewall Configuration

Most enterprises use a firewall to help protect their internal network from the Internet. Firewalls examine incoming and outgoing communications, and drop any communications that have not specifically been allowed. To allow DirectAccess clients on the Internet to communicate with your DirectAccess server across a firewall, you need to create firewall rules to allow specific packet types.

If your DirectAccess server is connected to the IPv4 Internet, allow the following types of packets:

- **Protocol 41, inbound and outbound** Required to allow IPv6 communications tunneled within IPv4 packets. Clients set the Protocol field to 41 for IPv4 packets that contain an IPv6 payload.
- **UDP destination port 3544, inbound** Allows clients to send Teredo communications to the DirectAccess server.
- **UDP source port 3544, outbound** Allows the DirectAccess server to respond to Teredo communications.
- **TCP destination port 443, inbound** Allows clients to send HTTPS communications to the DirectAccess server. DirectAccess uses HTTPS to allow connections across client-side firewalls that only allow web communications.
- **TCP source port 443, outbound** Allows the DirectAccess server to respond to HTTPS communications.

If your DirectAccess server is connected to the IPv6 Internet, allow the following types of packets:

- **Protocol 50, inbound and outbound** Required to allow Encapsulating Security Payload (ESP) communications.
- **UDP destination port 500 inbound** Allows clients to send Internet Key Exchange (IKE) and Authenticated Internet Protocol (AuthIP) communications to the DirectAccess server, which are required to negotiate IPsec security settings.

- **UDP source port 500 outbound**   Allows DirectAccess servers to respond to Internet Key Exchange (IKE) and Authenticated Internet Protocol (AuthIP) communications.

- **UDP destination port 4500 inbound**   Allows clients to send NAT-Traversal (NAT-T) communications to the DirectAccess server, which are required for translated IPv6 clients on the IPv6 Internet.

- **UDP source port 4500 outbound**   Allows DirectAccess servers to respond to NAT-T communications.

- **ICMPv6, inbound and outbound**   Required for DirectAccess.

Running the DirectAccess Setup Wizard

Once you have met all the DirectAccess infrastructure requirements, you can add the DirectAccess Management Console and run the DirectAccess setup wizard. This process is very straightforward; configuring the prerequisites will consume the bulk of the time you spend setting up DirectAccess.

First, install the DirectAccess Management Console by following these steps:

1. In Server Manager, right-click Features, and then click Add Features.

2. On the Select Features page of the Add Features Wizard, select DirectAccess Management Console. Click Next.

3. Click Install, and then click Close.

With the DirectAccess Management Console installed, you can run the DirectAccess Setup Wizard by following these steps:

1. In Server Manager, click Features\DirectAccess. In the details pane, click Checklist: Before You Configure DirectAccess. Verify that you have fulfilled every DirectAccess requirement.

2. In Server Manager, click Features\DirectAccess\Setup. If you have not met all the prerequisites, DirectAccess will warn you now. Go back and fix any problems that appear and click the Retry button to re-verify your settings before continuing.

3. In the console tree, click Setup. In the details pane, in the Step 1 group, click Configure.

4. In the DirectAccess Client Setup wizard, click Add. In the Select Group dialog box, select the security group you created for DirectAccess clients, click OK, and then click Finish.

5. Click Configure for Step 2. In the DirectAccess Server Setup wizard, on the Connectivity page, select the correct adapters for the Internet and your internal network if the DirectAccess Server Setup wizard did not automatically select them. Click Next.

6. On the Certificate Components page, for Select The Root Certificate To Which Remote Client Certificates Must Chain, click Browse. In the list of certificates, click your domain's root certificate, and then click OK.

7. For Select The Certificate That Will Be Used To Secure Remote Client Connectivity Over HTTPS, click Browse. In the list of certificates, click the certificate that DirectAccess will use for IP-HTTPS, and then click OK. Click Finish.

8. Click Configure for Step 3. On the Location page, click Network Location Server Is Run On A Highly Available Server, type the URL of the NLS, click Validate, and then click Next.

9. On the DNS and Domain Controller page, click Next.

10. On the Management page, click Finish.

11. Click Configure for Step 4. On the DirectAccess Application Server Setup page, click Finish.

12. Click Save, and then click Finish.

13. In the DirectAccess Review dialog box, click Apply.

14. In the DirectAccess Policy Configuration message box, click OK.

Before DirectAccess can accept connections, it needs to apply the updated IPv6 settings. You can do this by restarting the IP Helper service (IPHlpSvc) or by simply restarting the computer.

DirectAccess clients receive all their settings from Group Policy. Before they can connect using DirectAccess, you will need to refresh Group Policy (which you can do by running **GPUpdate** at an administrative command prompt) and then restarting the IP Helper service. Alternatively, you can simply wait for users to restart their computers.

PRACTICE **Configuring DirectAccess**

Before beginning this practice, you must configure three virtual machines:

- **Boston**   Boston will act as the DirectAccess server. Configure it with the DNS Server and Web Server (IIS) server roles. Connect Boston to two virtual machine networks: an intranet with private IP addresses, and a network that will simulate the public Internet.

- **DCSRV1**   DCSRV1 will be the domain controller. Configure it with the Active Directory Domain Services, Active Directory Certificate Services, DNS Server, DHCP Server, and Web Server (IIS) server roles. Remove the Network Policy And Access Services server role if necessary. Connect Boston to the intranet network.

- **Binghamton**   The DirectAccess client. Connect Binghamton to the simulated Internet virtual machine network and join the domain.

Initially, connect all three computers to the same local area network. Later, you will connect Binghamton to a different network segment that simulates the Internet.

Configuring a working DirectAccess environment requires more network and computer resources than most readers have available. However, if you have Internet access with multiple consecutive public IP addresses and six computers or virtual machines which can be connected to different networks, follow the steps in "Test Lab Guide: Demonstrate DirectAccess" at *http://www.microsoft.com/downloads/en/confirmation.aspx?FamilyID=8D47ED5F-D217-4D84-B698-F39360D82FAC* for additional experience configuring DirectAccess.

EXERCISE 1 Watching DirectAccess Configuration Videos

In this exercise, you watch a series of videos that demonstrate configuring DirectAccess. Although this book typically provides hands-on practices, many readers will be unable to meet the DirectAccess infrastructure requirements.

1. To understand the user experience when DirectAccess is deployed, watch "How Do I: DirectAccess" at *http://technet.microsoft.com/en-us/windows/dd572177.aspx*.

2. Watch the five DirectAccess screencasts available at *http://technet.microsoft.com /en-us/edge/directaccess-configuration-windows-7-demo-screencast-1-of-5.aspx*. This provides a high-level overview of the configuration requirements, but does not demonstrate configuring every aspect of the infrastructure.

3. Watch all videos in the DirectAccess Configuration playlist on YouTube at *http://www.youtube.com/view_play_list?p=6D83BDDB312391E2*. These videos provide the most detailed, step-by-step guidance for configuring the entire DirectAccess infrastructure.

EXERCISE 2 Configuring DirectAccess Infrastructure

In this exercise, you configure Dcsrv1 to provide the infrastructure required for a DirectAccess server. In the real world, each of these roles (domain controller, certificate server, DNS server, and Web server) might be performed by different servers.

1. On Dcsrv1, use Server Manager to create a global security group named DA_Clients. Members of this group will have privileges to connect using DirectAccess.

2. Add Binghamton to the DA_Clients group.

3. Use Server manager to add a DNS A record for the network location service, nls.nwtraders.msft. Specify Dcsrv1's intranet IP address.

4. Add a second DNS A record for the DirectAccess server's Internet IP address, da.contoso.com. Specify the first of Boston's Internet IP address.

5. Configure permissions for the Web Server certificate template, which the DirectAccess server and network location server will request to allow clients to establish HTTPS connections. Follow these steps:

   a. Click Start, type **certtmpl.msc**, and then press Enter.

   b. Right-click the Web Server template and then click Properties.

   c. Click the Security tab, and then click Authenticated Users.

   d. In Permissions For Authenticated Users, under Allow, click Enroll. This allows any authenticated user to request a Web server certificate. In a production environment, you would probably create a security group containing just the computer accounts of your DirectAccess and network location servers.

   e. Click OK, and close the Certificate Templates console.

6. Configure Windows Firewall to allow inbound and outbound ICMPv6 Echo Request messages. Follow these steps:

   a. Open the Group Policy Management console.

   b. Right-click Domains\nwtraders.msft\Domain Controllers\Default Domain Policy, and then click Edit. In the real world, you would create a new Group Policy Object for DirectAccess servers.

   c. Select the Computer Configuration\Policies\Windows Settings\Security Settings \Windows Firewall with Advanced Security\Windows Firewall with Advanced Security \Inbound Rules node.

   d. In the console tree, right-click Inbound Rules, and then click New Rule.

   e. On the Rule Type page, click Custom, and then click Next.

   f. On the Program page, click Next.

   g. On the Protocols and Ports page, for Protocol type, select ICMPv6, and then click Customize.

   h. In the Customize ICMP Settings dialog box, click Specific ICMP types, select Echo Request, and then click OK. Click Next.

   i. On the Scope page, click Next.

   j. On the Action page, click Allow The Connection, and then click Next.

   k. On the Profile page, click Next.

   l. On the Name page, for Name, type **Inbound ICMPv6 Echo Requests**, and then click Finish.

   m. In the console tree of the Group Policy Management Editor, right-click Outbound Rules, and then click New Rule.

   n. On the Rule Type page, click Custom, and then click Next.

   o. On the Program page, click Next.

   p. On the Protocols and Ports page, for Protocol type, select ICMPv6, and then click Customize.

   q. In the Customize ICMP Settings dialog box, click Specific ICMP types, select Echo Request, and then click OK. Click Next.

   r. On the Scope page, click Next.

   s. On the Action page, click Allow The Connection, and then click Next.

   t. On the Profile page, click Next.

   u. On the Name page, for Name, type **Outbound ICMPv6 Echo Requests**, and then click Finish.

   v. Open an administrative command prompt and run **Gpupdate** to apply the latest Group Policy settings.

7. Configure the DNS Server service to remove the ISATAP name from its default global block list. At a Command Prompt window, type **dnscmd /config /globalqueryblocklist wpad**, and then press Enter.

8. Configure the enterprise root CA with additional certificate revocation list (CRL) distribution settings that allow DirectAccess clients to check the CRL of certificates when connected to the Internet. Follow these steps:

   a. In Server Manager, right-click the Active Directory Certificate Services\nwtraders node, and then click Properties.

   b. Click the Extensions tab, and then click Add. In Location, type **http://boston. nwtraders.msft/crld/**. In Variable, click <CAName>, and then click Insert. In Variable, click <CRLNameSuffix>, and then click Insert. In Variable, click <DeltaCR-LAllowed>, and then click Insert. In Location, type **.crl** at the end of the Location string, and then click OK.

   c. Select the Include In CRLs and Include In The CDP Extension Of Issued Certificates check boxes.

   d. Click Add again. In Location, type **\\boston\crldist$**. In Variable, click <CAName>, and then click Insert. In Variable, click <CRLNameSuffix>, and then click Insert. In Variable, click <DeltaCRLAllowed>, and then click Insert. In Location, type **.crl** at the end of the string, and then click OK. Select the Publish CRLs To This Location and Publish Delta CRLs To This Location check boxes, and then click OK.

   e. Click Yes to restart Active Directory Certificate Services.

9. Obtain a web server certificate so that clients can connect to nls.nwtraders.msft using HTTPS.

   a. Click Start, type **mmc**, and then press Enter.

   b. In the blank MMC console, click File, and then click Add/Remove Snap-in.

   c. Click Certificates, click Add, click Computer Account, click Next, select Local Computer, click Finish, and then click OK.

   d. In the console tree of the Certificates snap-in, right-click Certificates (Local Computer)\Personal\Certificates, point to All Tasks, and then click Request New Certificate.

   e. Click Next twice. On the Request Certificates page, select the Web Server check box, and then click More Information Is Required To Enroll For This Certificate.

   f. On the Subject tab of the Certificate Properties dialog box, in Subject Name, for Type, select Common Name. In Value, type **nls.nwtraders.msft**, and then click Add. Click OK.

   g. Returning to the Certificate Enrollment page, click Enroll, and then click Finish.

10. Configure IIS to use the certificate.

   a. In Server Manager, click Roles\Web Server (IIS)\Internet Information Services (IIS) Manager.

   b. In the details pane, right-click Dcsrv1\Sites\Default Web Site, and then click Editing Bindings.

   c. In the Site Bindings dialog box, click Add. Set the Type to Https, and select the Web server certificate. Click OK.

   d. Click Close.

EXERCISE 3   Configuring DirectAccess Server

In this exercise, you configure Boston as a DirectAccess server to forward requests from the Internet to an internal IP network.

1. Create the web-based CRL distribution point by following these steps:

   a. In Server Manager, select Roles\Web Server (IIS)\Internet Information Services (IIS) Manager.

   b. In the details pane, right-click Boston\Sites\Default Web Site, and then click Add Virtual Directory.

   c. In the Alias box, type **CRLD**.

   d. In Physical Path, click the ellipsis button (...). With the C drive selected, click Make New Folder. Type **CRLDist**, and then click OK twice.

   e. Now, enable directory browsing for the virtual directory, which is required for DirectAccess clients to access the CRL. In the contents pane, double-click Directory Browsing. In the Actions pane, click Enable.

   f. Select CRLD in the contents pane. Then, double-click Configuration Editor. Click the Section list, and then click system.webServer\security\requestFiltering. In the contents pane, double-click allowDoubleEscaping to change it from False to True. In the Actions pane, click Apply.

2. Obtain a Web server certificate so that clients can connect to da.nwtraders.msft using HTTPS.

   a. Click Start, type **mmc**, and then press Enter.

   b. In the blank MMC console, click File, and then click Add/Remove Snap-in.

   c. Click Certificates, click Add, click Computer account, click Next, select Local computer, click Finish, and then click OK.

   d. In the console tree of the Certificates snap-in, right-click Certificates (Local Computer) \Personal\Certificates, point to All Tasks, and then click Request New Certificate.

   e. Click Next twice. On the Request Certificates page, select the Web Server check box, and then click More Information Is Required To Enroll For This Certificate.

   f. On the Subject tab of the Certificate Properties dialog box, in Subject name, for Type, select Common Name. In Value, type **da.nwtraders.msft**, and then click Add. Click OK.

g. Returning to the Certificate Enrollment page, click Enroll, and then click Finish.

h. In the Certificates snap-in, select the Certificates (Local Computer)\Personal \Certificates node. In the details pane, right-click the new Web server certificate, and then click Properties. In Friendly Name, type **IP-HTTPS Certificate**, and then click OK.

3. Next, configure IIS to use the certificate.

a. In Server Manager, click Roles\Web Server (IIS)\Internet Information Services (IIS) Manager.

b. In the details pane, right-click Boston\Sites\Default Web Site, and then click Editing Bindings.

c. In the Site Bindings dialog box, click Add. Set the Type to Https, and select the IP-HTTPS certificate. Click OK.

d. Click Close.

4. In this step, you will configure permissions on the CRL distribution point file share by following these steps:

a. Open Windows Explorer. Right-click the C:\CRLDist folder, and then click Properties.

b. Click the Sharing tab, and then click Advanced Sharing.

c. Select the Share This Folder check box. Change the Share Name to **CRLDist$**.

d. Click Permissions. In the Permissions For CRLDist$ dialog box, click Add, and then click Object Types. Select the Computers check box, and click OK. In the Enter The Object Names To Select box, type **DCSRV1**, and then click OK.

e. In the Permissions For CRLDist$ dialog box, select the Allow Full Control check box. Click OK three times.

5. Now you will publish the CRL by following these steps:

a. In Server Manager, right-click Roles\Active Directory Certificate Services \nwtraders-dcsrv1\Revoked Certificates, click All Tasks, and then click Publish. If you receive an error, verify that you entered the share name (\\boston\crldist$\) correctly.

b. Click New CRL, and then click OK.

c. In Windows Explorer, type **\\boston\crldist$** in the address bar, and press Enter. Verify that you see two CRL files; if you do not, double-check the previous steps to verify that you correctly configured the CRL.

6. Now, you are ready to install the DirectAccess Management Console by following these steps:

a. In Server Manager, right-click Features, and then click Add Features.

b. On the Select Features page of the Add Features Wizard, select DirectAccess Management Console. Click Next.

c. Click Install, and then click Close.

7. To run the DirectAccess Setup Wizard, follow these steps:

   a. In Server Manager, click Features\DirectAccess. In the details pane, click Checklist: Before You Configure DirectAccess. Verify that you have fulfilled every DirectAccess requirement.

   b. In Server Manager, click Features\DirectAccess\Setup. If you have not met all the pre-requisites, DirectAccess will warn you now. Go back and fix any problems that appear and click the Retry button to re-verify your settings before continuing.

   c. In the console tree, click Setup. In the details pane, in the Step 1 group, click Configure.

   d. In the DirectAccess Client Setup wizard, click Add. In the Select Group dialog box, type **DA_Clients**, click OK, and then click Finish.

   e. Click Configure for step 2. In the DirectAccess Server Setup wizard, on the Connectivity page, select the correct adapters for the Internet and your internal network if the DirectAccess Server Setup wizard did not automatically select them. Click Next.

   f. On the Certificate Components page, for Select The Root Certificate To Which Remote Client Certificates Must Chain, click Browse. In the list of certificates, click the nwtraders.msft root certificate, and then click OK.

   g. For Select The Certificate That Will Be Used To Secure Remote Client Connectivity Over HTTPS, click Browse. In the list of certificates, click the certificate named IP-HTTPS Certificate, and then click OK. Click Finish.

   h. Click Configure for step 3. On the Location page, click Network Location Server Is Run On A Highly Available Server, type **https://nls.nwtraders.msft**, click Validate, and then click Next.

   i. On the DNS And Domain Controller page, note the entry for the name dcsrv1. nswtraders.msft This IPv6 address is assigned to DC1 and is composed of a 6to4 network prefix (such as 2002:836b:2:1::/64) and an ISATAP-based interface identifier (such as ::0:5efe:10.0.0.1). Click Next.

   J. On the Management page, click Finish.

   k. Click Configure for step 4. On the DirectAccess Application Server Setup page, click Finish.

   l. Click Save, and then click Finish.

   m. In the DirectAccess Review dialog box, click Apply.

   n. In the DirectAccess Policy Configuration message box, click OK.

8. On DCSRV1, open an administrative command prompt. Then, run the commands **net stop iphlpsvc** and **net start iphlpsvc**. This refreshes DCSRV1's IPv6 settings.

EXERCISE 4 Configuring a DirectAccess Client

In this exercise, you configure Binghamton to act as a DirectAccess client, which is as easy as refreshing the Group Policy and restarting one service. Then, you will connect Binghamton to a NAT-protected network and test connectivity through Boston to the domain controller.

1. On Binghamton, open an administrative command prompt. Then, run three commands: **gpupdate**, **net stop iphlpsvc**, and **net start iphlpsvc**. This refreshes Binghamton's Group Policy and IPv6 settings. This is sufficient to configure Binghamton as a DirectAccess client. Alternatively, you could simply restart Binghamton.

2. Connect Binghamton to the Internet subnet. Assign it the IP address **131.107.10.9**, with the DNS server **131.107.10.1**, and no default gateway. Figure 7-19 shows how you should connect the virtual machines to the network. Wait until the network icon in the notification area of the desktop displays a connected network. Then, open Internet Explorer and connect to *http://dcsrv1.nwtraders.msft*. The page should load exactly as if you were connected directly to the intranet, even though it would be inaccessible to other clients on the Internet. Close Internet Explorer.

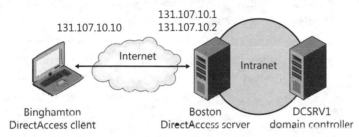

FIGURE 7-19 Using DirectAccess from the Internet

3. Now, use your virtual machine software to create a new private subnet with a NAT device connected to it. Bridge the NAT device to the Internet subnet. If your virtual machine software cannot provide NAT, you can configure another virtual machine with Internet Connection Services (ICS) as described in Lesson 2, and then connect it to both the private network and the Internet subnet. Figure 7-20 shows how you should connect the virtual machines to the network. Wait until the network icon in the notification area of the desktop displays a connected network. Then, open Internet Explorer and connect to *http://dcsrv1.nwtraders.msft*. The page should load exactly as if you were connected directly to the intranet, even though it would be inaccessible to other clients on the Internet. In this configuration, DirectAccess is using IP-HTTPS to tunnel IPv6 traffic through the NAT device because the NAT device does not forward Teredo communications.

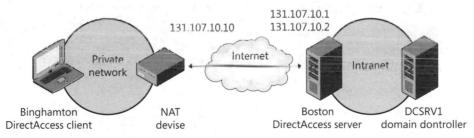

FIGURE 7-20 Using DirectAccess from a private network

Lesson Summary

- DirectAccess provides Windows 7 client computers with transparent connectivity to the intranet any time they have an Internet connection.

- DirectAccess uses IPv6 and IPsec for communications. As a result, you will need applications and server operating systems that support IPv6. To allow communications across the IPv4 Internet, you will need to use IPv6 transition technologies including 6to4, Teredo, IP-HTTPS, and ISATAP.

- DirectAccess requires several infrastructure components that are available as part of Windows Server 2008 R2. DirectAccess requires an Active Directory domain with at least one domain controller and DNS server running Windows Server 2008 with Service Pack 2 or Windows Server 2008 R2. Additionally, you will need a PKI, such as Certificate Services, with a publically accessible CRL to issue IPsec and SSL certificates.

- Clients attempt to connect to the NLS to determine whether they are directly connected to the intranet. If they are not, they use the NRPT to determine whether resources are accessible on the Internet or intranet.

- The DirectAccess setup wizard configures the Group Policy settings that clients and servers need to connect.

Lesson Review

You can use the following questions to test your knowledge of the information in Lesson 4, "Configuring DirectAccess." The questions are also available on the companion CD if you prefer to review them in electronic form.

> **NOTE   ANSWERS**
>
> Answers to these questions and explanations of why each answer choice is correct or incorrect are located in the "Answers" section at the end of the book.

1. You need to ensure that any Windows 7 client can connect to your intranet using DirectAccess. Many users will connect to public hotspots, such as hotels and airports, that support only HTTP and HTTPS communications. Which technology will DirectAccess use to connect those clients to the DirectAccess server? (Choose all that apply.)

   A. Teredo

   B. ISATAP

   C. IP-HTTPS

   D. 6-to-4

2. Which of the following infrastructure components does DirectAccess require? (Choose all that apply.)

   A. An Active Directory domain at the Windows Server 2008 functional level.

   B. Two consecutive public IP addresses.

   C. A public key infrastructure that distributes computer certificates to clients.

   D. The Active Directory Domain Services role installed on the DirectAccess server.

3. You have successfully configured a DirectAccess server. After refreshing Group Policy on a client computer, which service do you need to restart on client computers before they can connect to DirectAccess?

   A. Network Connections

   B. IPsec Policy Agent

   C. Workstation

   D. IP Helper

Chapter Review

To further practice and reinforce the skills you learned in this chapter, you can perform the following tasks:

- Review the chapter summary.
- Review the list of key terms introduced in this chapter.
- Complete the case scenarios. These scenarios set up real-world situations involving the topics of this chapter and ask you to create a solution.
- Complete the suggested practices.
- Take a practice test.

Chapter Summary

- NAT allows clients on an intranet with private IP addresses to access the Internet. NAT works like a router, but replaces the client computer's private source IP address with its own public IP address. When the NAT server receives return packets, it identifies which connection the packet is associated with, replaces the destination IP address with the client's private IP address, and forwards the packet to the client computer on the intranet. You can configure a Windows Server 2008 computer as a NAT server, however, most organizations choose to use a router, firewall, or dedicated network device.

- Wireless connectivity is now a requirement for many organizations. To minimize the inherent security risks, use WPA-EAP security. When a wireless access point is configured to use WPA-EAP security, it must forward authentication requests to a RADIUS server. You can configure Windows Server 2008 as a RADIUS server, and authenticate users with either domain credentials or client computer certificates. If you have existing RADIUS servers, you can configure Windows Server 2008 as a RADIUS proxy, and forward RADIUS requests to the appropriate RADIUS server based on criteria such as the realm of the RADIUS request.

- When away from the office, users can access internal resources using either a dial-up or a VPN connection. Windows Server 2008 can act as either a dial-up server, a VPN server, or a RADIUS server that authenticates requests from other dial-up or VPN servers.

Key Terms

Do you know what these key terms mean? You can check your answers by looking up the terms in the glossary at the end of the book.

- latency
- Wired Equivalent Protection (WEP)
- Wi-Fi Protected Access (WPA)

Case Scenarios

In the following case scenarios, you will apply what you've learned about how to connect computers to networks. You can find answers to these questions in the "Answers" section at the end of this book.

Case Scenario 1: Connecting a Branch Office to the Internet

You are a systems administrator for City Power & Light. Because your organization acquired a large block of public IP addresses from the Internet Assigned Numbers Authority (IANA) in the early 1980s, all of your hosts are configured with routed public IP addresses.

Because of recent changes to government regulations, your organization needs to open a small branch office. Currently, all of your IP addresses are routed to the headquarters, and you do not have any public IP address blocks available to assign to the branch office. However, after contacting a local ISP in the area, you learn that the DSL connection you plan to use includes one public IP address. You plan to deploy at least 50 computers to the office. You do not plan to host any servers at the office, and the only incoming connection from the Internet you plan to use is a VPN connection.

QUESTIONS

Your manager asks you to come by his office to discuss connectivity for the branch office. Answer the following questions for your manager:

1. Can we, and should we, get a block of public IP addresses for the branch office?

2. If we use private addresses on the intranet, how will client computers communicate on the Internet?

3. If we choose to use NAT, what technology should we use to implement it?

Case Scenario 2: Planning Remote Access

You are a systems administrator working for Humongous Insurance. Although your organization's sales staff has always traveled with laptops, they have traditionally called their administrative assistants at your headquarters when they needed to access internal resources. Even sales staff who used mobile computers lacked a way to connect to your intranet.

Recently, the IT department has been posting a great deal of valuable information on your intranet, and your sales staff has requested the ability to connect to that information while they travel. You do have an Internet connection at your headquarters, and several servers are currently connected to both the public Internet and your intranet. Your manager asks you to interview key people and then come to her office to answer her questions about your design choices.

INTERVIEWS

The following is a list of company personnel interviewed and their statements:

- **Salesperson** "I don't normally take my laptop to customer sites, but I do use my computer in my hotel room. The phone always has a data connection with a picture of a computer, and sometimes they have a network cable there, too. I've seen signs at some front desks showing that they had a wireless network available."

- **Sales Manager** "My sales staff aren't the most technically sophisticated group, overall. Many of them still insist on using Windows XP. However, we do have several team members who are very competent with their computers and use Windows 7. For example, while I'm on a customer premises, I often hop on their wireless network to check my personal email. In fact, I have my admin forward my work email to my personal email so that I can more easily check it while I'm traveling."

QUESTIONS

1. Which remote access technologies should we use?

2. If we use a VPN server, how will we configure it? I want to make sure users don't have to remember a separate user name and password.

3. I'm guessing that we need to support about 50 dial-in users simultaneously. What are our options for making that happen?

4. If one of our sales staff connects to a wireless network, can that person connect to a VPN or DirectAccess from there?

Suggested Practices

To help you successfully master the exam objectives presented in this chapter, complete the following tasks.

Configure Wireless Access

For this task, you should complete at least Practice 1. For more experience about real-world wireless security risks, complete Practice 2.

- **Practice 1** Configure a Windows Server 2008 computer as a RADIUS server for a wireless network. First, configure the RADIUS server to authenticate users with domain credentials and use a client computer to connect to the wireless network. Next, configure the RADIUS server to authenticate users with certificates. Change the SSID of the wireless network (so that the wireless client will see it as a new network) and connect to the wireless network. Examine the event logs and view the information that Windows Server 2008 recorded about the authentication.

- **Practice 2** Configure a wireless access point to use 64-bit WEP security. Using the Internet, identify software tools used for cracking WEP security. Attempt to connect to the wireless access point using only the cracking tools you can find freely available on the Internet.

Configure Remote Access

For this task, you should complete all six practices.

- **Practice 1** Connect a modem to a computer running Windows Server 2008, and connect the modem to a phone line. From a different phone line, dial in to the computer running Windows Server 2008 and verify that you can connect to network resources.

- **Practice 2** Configure a computer running Windows 98, Windows 2000 Professional, or Windows XP to connect to both a dial-up server and a VPN server.

- **Practice 3** Configure filters on a Windows Server 2008 VPN server so that the sever replies to ping requests on the Internet interface.

- **Practice 4** Without connecting to a VPN, use Tracert to determine the path between a client computer and a server on the Internet (such as *http://www.microsoft.com*). Next, connect to a VPN (preferably at a different location) and perform the Tracert command again. Notice how the route changes.

- **Practice 5** Connect a Windows Vista or Windows Server 2008 VPN client to a network with a very restrictive firewall. Attempt to establish a VPN connection using either PPTP or L2TP; if the firewall is genuinely restrictive, it will block the connection. Next, attempt the same VPN connection using SSTP. Does it work?

- **Practice 6** Establish a VPN connection. Then, run Network Monitor (available at *http://www.microsoft.com*) and capture the VPN communications. Examine the communications and verify that the traffic is encrypted.

Configure Network Authentication

For this task, you should complete Practice 1. For more experience about real-world security risks, complete Practice 2.

- **Practice 1** Configure a Windows Server 2008 computer as a VPN server. Experiment with the different authentication protocols. Test connectivity using both PPTP and L2TP.

- **Practice 2** Use the Internet to find tools that can crack MS-CHAP protected credentials. Attempt to capture and crack credentials by intercepting network communications, as if you were attacking your own network.

Configure DirectAccess

Configuring DirectAccess in a lab environment can be a challenge because of the large number of infrastructure components required. If at all possible, complete both these practices to gain real-world experience working with DirectAccess.

- **Practice 1** Follow the steps in the DirectAccess Step-by-Step Guide, available at *http://www.microsoft.com/downloads/en/details.aspx?displaylang=en&FamilyID=8d47ed5f-d217-4d84-b698-f39360d82fac*, to configure a working DirectAccess infrastructure.

- **Practice 2** Configure a DirectAccess server at your work environment, and test it using your own Windows 7 computer.

Take a Practice Test

The practice tests on this book's companion CD offer many options. For example, you can test yourself on just the content covered in this chapter, or you can test yourself on all the 70-642 certification exam content. You can set up the test so that it closely simulates the experience of taking a certification exam, or you can set it up in study mode so that you can look at the correct answers and explanations after you answer each question.

> **MORE INFO PRACTICE TESTS**
>
> For details about all the practice test options available, see "How to Use the Practice Tests" in this book's Introduction.

CHAPTER 8

Configuring Windows Firewall and Network Access Protection

B y their nature, networks can allow healthy computers to communicate with unhealthy computers and malicious tools to attack legitimate applications. This can result in costly security compromises, such as a worm that spreads rapidly through an internal network or a sophisticated attacker who steals confidential data across the network.

Windows Server 2008 R2 supports two technologies that are useful for improving network security: Windows Firewall and Network Access Protection (NAP). Windows Firewall can filter incoming and outgoing traffic, using complex criteria to distinguish between legitimate and potentially malicious communications. NAP requires computers to complete a health check before allowing unrestricted access to your network and facilitates resolving problems with computers that do not meet health requirements.

This lesson describes how to plan and implement Windows Firewall and NAP using Windows Server 2008 R2.

Exam objectives in this chapter:

- Configure Windows Firewall with Advanced Security.
- Configure Network Access Protection (NAP).

Lessons in this chapter:

- Lesson 1: Configuring Windows Firewall   **430**
- Lesson 2: Configuring Network Access Protection   **444**

Before You Begin

To complete the lessons in this chapter, you should be familiar with Windows networking and be comfortable with the following tasks:

- Adding roles to a computer running Windows Server 2008 R2
- Configuring Active Directory domain controllers and joining computers to a domain
- Configuring a basic network, including configuring IP settings

You will also need the following nonproduction hardware connected to test networks:

- A computer named Dcsrv1 that is a domain controller in the Nwtraders.msft domain. This computer must have at least one network interface that you can connect to either the Internet or a private network.

> **NOTE COMPUTER AND DOMAIN NAMES**
>
> The computer and domain names you use will not affect these exercises. The practices in this chapter refer to these computer names for simplicity, however.

- A computer named Hartford that is running Windows 7 Professional, Enterprise, or Ultimate, and is a member of the Nwtraders.msft domain. You must use Windows 7 because Windows Server 2008 R2 does not support the Windows Security Health Validator.

 REAL WORLD

Tony Northrup

Instead of absolutes, security can be measured only in degrees of risk. Although NAP can't prevent a determined, skilled attacker from connecting to your network, NAP can improve your network security by helping keep computers up to date and ensuring that legitimate users do not accidentally connect to your internal network without meeting your security requirements.

When evaluating NAP as a way to protect against malicious attackers, remember that NAP trusts the System Health Agent (SHA) to report on the health of the client. The SHA is also running on the client computer. So it's a bit like airport security merely asking people if they are carrying any banned substances—people without any malicious intent would happily volunteer anything they accidentally brought. People with malicious intent would simply lie.

It's not *quite* as easy as simply lying, because the SHA signs the Statement of Health (SoH) to help prove that the health report is genuine. Additional security measures, such as requiring IPsec connection security, can help further reduce the opportunity for attackers. Nonetheless, with some time and effort, it's entirely possible that someone will create a malicious SHA that impersonates a legitimate SHA.

Lesson 1: Configuring Windows Firewall

Windows Firewall filters incoming traffic to help block unwanted network traffic. Optionally, Windows Firewall can also filter outgoing traffic to help limit the risk of malware. Although Windows Firewall's default settings will work well with components built into Windows, they might prevent other applications from functioning correctly. Windows Firewall's default settings can also be significantly improved to provide even stronger protection by requiring authorization or limiting the scope of allowed connections.

After this lesson, you will be able to:

- Describe the purpose of firewalls.
- List the three firewall profiles and how each is used.
- Create a firewall rule to allow inbound traffic.
- Create a firewall rule to allow outbound traffic and enable outbound filtering.
- Configure the scope of a firewall rule to limit communications to specific subnets.
- Configure firewall rules to require IPsec connection security and, optionally, limit authorization to specific users and computers.
- Use Group Policy settings to configure firewall rules in an Active Directory domain environment.
- Enable Windows Firewall logging so that you can isolate problems related to firewall rules.
- Identify network communications used by a specific application so that you can create rules for the application.

Estimated lesson time: 45 minutes

Why Firewalls Are Important

In networking, *firewalls* analyze communications and drop packets that haven't been specifically allowed. This is an important task, because connecting to the Internet means any of the millions of other Internet-connected computers can attack you. A successful compromise can crash a service or computer, compromise confidential data, or even allow the attacker to take complete control of the remote computer. In the case of *worms*, automated software attacks computers across the Internet, gains elevated privileges, copies itself to the compromised computer, and then begins attacking other computers (typically at random).

The purpose of a firewall is to drop unwanted traffic, such as traffic from worms, while allowing legitimate traffic, such as authorized file sharing. The more precisely you use firewall rules to identify legitimate traffic, the less you risk exposure to unwanted traffic from worms.

Firewall Profiles

When you create firewall rules to allow or block traffic, you can separately apply them to the Domain, Private, and Public profiles. These profiles enable mobile computers to allow incoming connections while connected to a domain network (for example, to allow incoming Remote Desktop connections) but block connection attempts on less secure networks (such as public wireless hotspots).

The firewall profiles are:

- **Domain** Applies when a computer is connected to its Active Directory domain. Specifically, any time a member computer's domain controller is accessible, this profile will be applied.

- **Private**   Applies when a computer is connected to a private network location. By default, no networks are considered private—users must specifically mark a network location, such as their home office network, as private.

- **Public**   The default profile applied to all networks when a domain controller is not available. For example, the Public profile is applied when users connect to Wi-Fi hotspots at airports or coffee shops. By default, the Public profile allows outgoing connections but blocks all incoming traffic that is not part of an existing connection.

Most servers are always connected to a domain environment. To ensure consistent operation even when a domain controller is not available, configure the same firewall rules for all three profiles when configuring a server.

Filtering Inbound Traffic

By default, Windows Firewall (as well as most other firewalls) blocks any inbound traffic that hasn't been specifically allowed. By default, the Public profile allows absolutely no incoming connections—this provides excellent security when connecting to public hotspots or other untrusted networks. The Domain and Private profiles allow some incoming connections, such as connections for file and printer sharing.

If you install or enable a Windows feature that requires incoming connections, Windows will automatically enable the required firewall rules. Therefore, you do not need to manually adjust the firewall rules. Figure 8-1 shows the default inbound firewall rules for a Windows Server 2008 R2 computer configured as a domain controller. As you can see, rules exist to allow each of the protocols required for a domain controller.

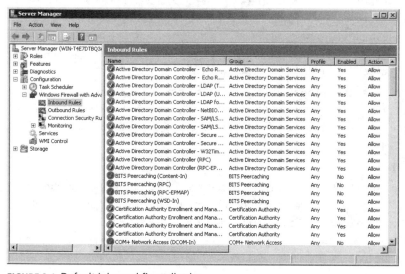

FIGURE 8-1 Default inbound firewall rules

If you install an application that does not automatically enable the required firewall rules, you will need to create the rules manually. You can create firewall rules by using the stand-alone Windows Firewall With Advanced Security console, or you can apply the rules with Group Policy by using the same interface at Computer Configuration\Policies\Windows Settings\Security Settings\Windows Firewall With Advanced Security\Windows Firewall With Advanced Security.

To create an inbound filter, follow these steps:

1. In the Windows Firewall With Advanced Security snap-in, right-click Inbound Rules, and then choose New Rule. The New Inbound Rule Wizard appears.

2. On the Rule Type page, select one of the following options, and then click Next:

   - **Program** A rule that allows or blocks connections for a specific executable file, regardless of the port numbers it might use. You should use the Program rule type whenever possible. The only time it's not possible to use the Program rule type is when a service does not have its own executable.

   - **Port** A rule that allows or blocks communications for a specific TCP or UDP port number, regardless of the program generating the traffic.

   - **Predefined** A rule that controls connections for a Windows component, such as Active Directory Domain Services, File And Printer Sharing, or Remote Desktop. Typically, Windows enables these rules automatically.

   - **Custom** A rule that can combine program and port information.

3. Complete the page or pages that appear after you select one of the rule types. The page or pages you see will vary depending on the rule type you selected. Click Next.

4. On the Action page, select one of the following options, and then click Next.

   - **Allow The Connection** Allows any connection that matches the criteria you specified on the previous pages.

   - **Allow The Connection If It Is Secure** Allows connections that match the criteria you specified on the previous pages only if those connections are protected with IPsec. Optionally, you can select the Require The Connections To Be Encrypted check box, which requires encryption in addition to authentication. Selecting the Override Block Rules check box configures the rule to take precedence over other rules that might prevent a client from connecting. If you select this rule type, the wizard will also prompt you to select users and computers that are authorized to establish this type of connection.

   - **Block The Connection** Drops any connection attempt that matches the criteria you specified on the previous pages. Because inbound connections are blocked by default, you rarely need to create this rule type. However, you might use this action for an outbound rule if you specifically want to prevent an application from initiating outgoing connections.

5. On the Profile page, choose which profiles to apply the rule to. For most servers, you should apply the rule to all three profiles, because servers are usually continually connected to a single network. For mobile computers in domain environments, you typically need to apply firewall rules only to the Domain profile. If you do not have an Active Directory domain or if users need to use the firewall rule when connected to their home networks, apply the rule to the Private profile. Avoid creating firewall rules on mobile computers for the Public profile, because an attacker on an unprotected network might be able to exploit a vulnerability exposed by the firewall rule. Click Next.

6. On the Name page, type a name for the rule, and then click Finish.

The inbound rule takes effect immediately, allowing incoming connections that match the criteria you specified.

Filtering Outbound Traffic

By default, Windows Firewall allows all outbound traffic. Allowing outbound traffic is much less risky than allowing inbound traffic. However, outbound traffic still carries some risk:

- If malware infects a computer, it might send outbound traffic containing confidential data (such as content from a Microsoft SQL Server database, email messages from a Microsoft Exchange server, or a list of passwords).

- Worms and viruses seek to replicate themselves. If they successfully infect a computer, they will attempt to send outbound traffic to infect other computers. After one computer on an intranet is infected, network attacks can allow malware to rapidly infect computers on an intranet.

- Users might use unapproved applications to send data to Internet resources and either knowingly or unknowingly transmit confidential data.

By default, all versions of Windows (including Windows Server 2008 R2) do not filter outbound traffic. However, Windows Server 2008 R2 does include outbound filters for core networking services, enabling you to quickly enable outbound filtering while retaining basic network functionality. By default, outbound rules are enabled for:

- Dynamic Host Configuration Protocol (DHCP) requests
- DNS requests
- Group Policy communications
- Internet Group Management Protocol (IGMP)
- IPv6 and related protocols

Blocking outbound communications by default will prevent many built-in Windows features, and all third-party applications you might install, from communicating on the network. For example, Windows Update will no longer be able to retrieve updates, Windows will no longer be able to activate across the Internet, and the computer will be unable to send Simple Network Management Protocol (SNMP) alerts to a management host.

If you do enable outbound filtering, you must be prepared to test every application to verify that it runs correctly. Most applications are not designed to support outbound filtering and will require you to both identify the firewall rules that need to be created and then create those rules.

To create an outbound filter, follow these steps:

1. In Windows Firewall With Advanced Security (which you can access in Server Manager under Configuration), right-click Outbound Rules, and then choose New Rule. The New Outbound Rule Wizard appears.

2. On the Rule Type page, select a rule type (as described in the section "Filtering Inbound Traffic" earlier in this lesson), and then click Next.

3. On the Program page, click This Program Path. In the text box, type the path to the application's executable file. Click Next.

4. On the Action page, select an action type (as described in the section "Filtering Inbound Traffic" earlier in this lesson), and then click Next.

5. On the Profile page, select the check boxes for the profiles that you want to apply the rule to, and then click Next.

6. On the Name page, type a name for the rule, and then click Finish.

The outbound rule takes effect immediately, allowing outgoing packets that match the criteria you specified.

To block outbound connections by default, first create and enable any outbound firewall rules so that applications do not immediately stop functioning. Then, follow these steps:

1. In Server Manager, right-click Configuration\Windows Firewall With Advanced Security, and then choose Properties.

2. Click the Domain Profile, Private Profile, or Public Profile tab.

3. From the Outbound Connections drop-down list, select Block. If necessary, return to the previous step to block outbound traffic for other profiles. Then click OK.

You will need to perform extensive testing to verify that all required applications function correctly when outbound connections are blocked by default. This testing should include background processes, such as Automatic Updates.

Configuring Scope

One of the most powerful ways to increase computer security is to configure firewall scope. Using *scope*, you can allow connections from your internal network and block connections from external networks. Scope can be used in the following ways:

- For a server that is connected to the Internet, you can allow anyone on the Internet to connect to public services (such as the web server) while allowing only users on your internal network to access private servers (such as Remote Desktop).

- For internal servers, you can allow connections only from the specific subnets that contain potential users. When planning such scope limitations, remember to include remote access subnets.

- For outgoing connections, you can allow an application to connect to servers only on specific internal subnets. For example, you might allow SNMP traps to be sent to only your SNMP management servers. Similarly, you might allow a network backup application to connect to only your backup servers.

- For mobile computers, you can allow specific communications (such as Remote Desktop) from only the subnets you use for management.

To configure the scope of a rule, follow these steps:

1. In the Windows Firewall With Advanced Security snap-in, select Inbound Rules or Outbound Rules.

2. In the details pane, right-click the rule you want to configure, and then choose Properties.

3. Click the Scope tab. In the Remote IP Address group, select These IP Addresses.

4. In the Remote IP Address group, click Add.

> **NOTE CONFIGURING SCOPE FOR LOCAL IP ADDRESSES**
> The only time you would want to configure the scope using the Local IP Address group is when the computer is configured with multiple IP addresses, and you do not want to accept connections on all IP addresses.

5. In the IP Address dialog box, select one of the following three options, and then click OK:

   - **This IP Address Or Subnet**   Type an IP address (such as 192.168.1.22) or a subnet using Classless Inter Domain Routing (CIDR) notation (such as 192.168.1.0/24) that should be allowed to use the firewall rule.

   - **This IP Address Range**   Using the From and To boxes, type the first and last IP address that should be allowed to use the firewall rule.

   - **Predefined Set Of Computers**   Select a host from the list: Default Gateway, WINS Servers, DHCP Servers, DNS Servers, and Local Subnet.

6. Repeat steps 4 and 5 for any additional IP addresses that should be allowed to use the firewall rule, and then click OK.

Authorizing Connections

If you are using IPsec connection security in an Active Directory environment, you can also require the remote computer or user to be authorized before a connection can be established.

For example, imagine that your organization had a custom accounting application that used TCP port 1073, but the application had no access control mechanism—any user who connected to the network service could access confidential accounting data. Using Windows Firewall connection authorization, you could limit inbound connections to users who are members of the Accounting group—adding access control to the application without writing any additional code.

Most network applications do have access control built in, however. For example, you can configure Internet Information Server (a web server installed as part of the Application

Server role) to authenticate users and allow only authorized users to connect to a web application. Similarly, if you share a folder on the network, you can use file permissions and share permissions to restrict who can access the folder. Application-layer authorization should always be your first layer of security; however, connection authorization using Windows Firewall can provide an additional layer of security. Using multiple layers of security—a technique known as *defense-in-depth*—reduces risk by providing protection even when one layer has a vulnerability.

To configure connection authorization for a firewall rule, follow these steps:

1. In Server Manager, select Configuration\Windows Firewall With Advanced Security\Inbound Rules or Configuration\Windows Firewall With Advanced Security\Outbound Rules.

2. In the details pane, right-click the rule you want to configure, and then choose Properties.

3. Click the General tab. Select Allow Only Secure Connections. Because the authorization relies on IPsec, you can configure authorization only on secure connections.

4. Click the Users And Computers tab for an inbound rule or the Computers tab for an outbound rule. Select the proper options based on the rule you selected:

   - **To allow connections only from specific computers**   Select the Only Allow Connections From These Computers check box for an inbound rule or the Only Allow Connections To These Computers check box for an outbound rule.

   - **To allow connections only from specific users**   If you are editing an inbound rule, select the Only Allow Connections From These Users check box. You can use this option only for inbound connections.

5. Click Add and select the groups containing the users or computers you want to authorize. Figure 8-2 shows how the Users And Computers tab appears after you have configured connections for an inbound rule. Click OK.

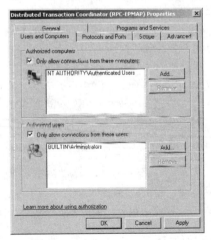

FIGURE 8-2 The Users And Computers tab

6. Click OK again.

Any future connections that match the firewall rule will require IPsec for the connection to be established. Additionally, if the authenticated computer or user is not on the list of authorized computers and users that you specified, the connection will be immediately dropped.

Configuring Firewall Settings with Group Policy

You can configure Windows Firewall locally, by using Server Manager or the Windows Firewall With Advanced Security console in the Administrative Tools folder; or globally, by using the Computer Configuration\Policies\Windows Settings\Security Settings\Windows Firewall With Advanced Security\Windows Firewall With Advanced Security node of a Group Policy Object (GPO). Typically, you edit server-specific policies (such as configuring the range of IP addresses a DNS server accepts queries from) by using local tools, and you configure policies that apply to groups of computers (including IPsec connection security policies) by using GPOs.

You can use Group Policy to manage Windows Firewall settings for computers running Windows Vista, Windows 7, Windows Server 2008, and Windows Server 2008 R2 by using two nodes:

- **Computer Configuration\Policies\Windows Settings\Security Settings\Windows Firewall With Advanced Security\Windows Firewall With Advanced Security** This node applies settings only to computers running Windows Vista, Windows 7, Windows Server 2008, and Windows Server 2008 R2 and provides exactly the same interface as the same node in Server Manager. You should always use this node when configuring computers running these recent versions of Windows because it provides for more detailed configuration of firewall rules.

- **Computer Configuration\Policies\Administrative Templates\Network\Network Connections \Windows Firewall** This node applies settings to computers running Windows XP, Windows Server 2003, Windows Vista, Windows 7, Windows Server 2008, and Windows Server 2008 R2. This tool is less flexible than the Windows Firewall With Advanced Security console; however, settings apply to all versions of Windows that support Windows Firewall. If you are not using the new IPsec features in recent versions of Windows, you can use this node to configure all your clients.

For best results, create one GPO for Windows 7, Windows Vista, Windows Server 2008 R2, and Windows Server 2008, and create a second GPO for Windows Server 2003 and Windows XP. Then, use WMI filters to target the GPOs to computers running only the appropriate version of Windows.

> **MORE INFO CREATING WMI FILTERS**
>
> For more information about creating WMI filters, read Microsoft Knowledge Base article 555253, "HOWTO: Leverage Group Policies with WMI Filters," at *http://support.microsoft.com /kb/555253*.

Enabling Logging for Windows Firewall

If you are ever unsure about whether Windows Firewall is blocking or allowing traffic, you should enable logging, re-create the problem you're having, and then examine the log files. To enable logging, follow these steps:

1. In the console tree of the Windows Firewall With Advanced Security snap-in, right-click Windows Firewall With Advanced Security, and then choose Properties. The Windows Firewall With Advanced Security Properties dialog box appears.

2. Select the Domain Profile, Private Profile, or Public Profile tab.

3. In the Logging group, click the Customize button. The Customize Logging Settings dialog box appears.

4. To log packets that Windows Firewall drops, from the Log Dropped Packets drop-down list, select Yes. To log connections that Windows Firewall allows, from the Log Successful Connections drop-down list, select Yes.

5. Click OK.

By default, Windows Firewall writes log entries to %SystemRoot%\System32\LogFiles\Firewall \Pfirewall.log and stores only the last 4 KB of data. In most production environments, this log will be almost constantly written to, which can cause a performance impact. For that reason, you should enable logging only when actively troubleshooting a problem and then immediately disable logging when you're finished.

Identifying Network Communications

The documentation included with network applications often does not clearly identify the communication protocols the application uses. Fortunately, creating Program firewall rules allows any communications required by that particular program.

If you prefer to use Port firewall rules, or if you need to configure a network firewall that can identify communications based only on port number and the application's documentation does not list the firewall requirements, you can examine the application's behavior to determine the port numbers in use.

The simplest tool to use is Netstat. On the server, run the application, and then run the following command to examine which ports are listening for active connections:

```
netstat -a -b
```

Any rows in the output with a State of LISTENING are attempting to receive incoming connections on the port number specified in the Local Address column. The executable name listed after the row is the executable that is listening for the connection. For example, the following output demonstrates that RpcSs, running under the SvcHost.exe process (which runs many services), is listening for connections on TCP port 135.

```
Active Connections

   Proto  Local Address          Foreign Address        State
   TCP    0.0.0.0:135            Dcsrv1:0               LISTENING
   RpcSs
   [svchost.exe]
```

Similarly, the following output demonstrates that the DNS service (Dns.exe) is listening for connections on TCP port 53:

```
Active Connections

   Proto  Local Address          Foreign Address        State
   TCP    0.0.0.0:53             Dcsrv1:0               LISTENING
   [dns.exe]
```

Although Windows Firewall has existing rules in place for these services (because they are built into Windows), the same technique would allow you to identify the port numbers used by any third-party application.

PRACTICE   **Configuring Windows Firewall**

In this practice, you configure both inbound and outbound filtering. These are common tasks that occur when you install new applications in almost any network environment, from small businesses to large enterprises.

EXERCISE 1   Configuring Inbound Filtering

In this exercise, you will install the Telnet Server feature, which configures Windows Server 2008 R2 to accept incoming connections on TCP port 23. Then, you will examine the incoming firewall rule that applies to the Telnet Server and adjust the rule configuration.

1. In the console tree of Server Manager, select Features. In the details pane, click Add Features. The Add Features Wizard appears.

2. On the Select Features page, select the Telnet Server check box. Click Next.

3. On the Confirm Installation Selections page, click Install.

4. On the Installation Results page, click Close.

5. In Server Manager, select Configuration\Services. Then, in the details pane, right-click the Telnet Server service and choose Properties. From the Startup Type drop-down list, select Manual. Click the Apply button. Then, click the Start button to start the telnet server. Click OK.

6. On a client computer, open a command prompt and run the following command (where *ip_address* is the telnet server's IP address):

   ```
   telnet ip_address
   ```

   The telnet server should prompt you for a user name. This proves that the client was able to establish a TCP connection to port 23.

7. Press Ctrl+] to exit the telnet session. Type **quit** and press Enter to close telnet.

8. On the telnet server, in Server Manager, select Configuration\Windows Firewall With Advanced Security\Inbound Rules. In the details pane, right-click the Telnet Server rule, and then choose Properties.

> **NOTE AUTOMATICALLY ENABLING REQUIRED RULES**
>
> Notice that the Telnet Server rule is enabled; the Add Features Wizard automatically enabled the rule when it installed the Telnet Server feature.

9. Click the Programs And Services tab. Notice that the default rule is configured to allow communications for %SystemRoot%\system32\TlntSvr.exe, which is the executable file for the telnet server service. Click the Settings button and verify that Telnet is selected. Click Cancel twice.

10. In Server Manager, right-click the Telnet Server rule, and then choose Disable Rule.

11. On the telnet client computer, run the same Telnet command again. This time the command should fail because Windows Firewall is no longer allowing incoming telnet requests.

12. Use Server Manager to remove the Telnet Server feature and restart the computer if necessary.

EXERCISE 2   Configuring Outbound Filtering

In this exercise, you configure Windows Server 2008 R2 to block outbound requests by default. Then, you test it by attempting to visit a website with Internet Explorer. Next, you create an outbound rule to allow requests from Internet Explorer and verify that the outbound rule works correctly. Finally, you return your computer to its original state.

1. Open Internet Explorer and visit *http://www.microsoft.com*. If an Internet Explorer Enhanced Security Configuration dialog box appears, you can click Close to dismiss it.

2. In Server Manager, right-click Configuration\Windows Firewall With Advanced Security, and then choose Properties.

3. Click the Domain Profile tab. From the Outbound Connections drop-down list, select Block. Repeat this step for the Private Profile and Public Profile tabs. Then click OK.

4. Open Internet Explorer and attempt to visit *http://support.microsoft.com*. You should be unable to visit the website because outbound filtering is blocking Internet Explorer's outgoing HTTP queries.

5. In Server Manager, within Configuration\Windows Firewall With Advanced Security, right-click Outbound Rules, and then choose New Rule. The New Outbound Rule Wizard appears.

6. On the Rule Type page, select Program. Then, click Next.

7. On the Program page, select This Program Path. In the box, type **%ProgramFiles% \Internet Explorer\iexplore.exe** (the path to the Internet Explorer executable file). Click Next.

8. On the Action page, select Allow The Connection. Then, click Next.

9. On the Profile page, accept the default selection of applying the rule to all three profiles. Click Next.

10. On the Name page, type **Allow Internet Explorer outgoing communications**. Then click Finish.

11. In Internet Explorer, attempt to visit *http://support.microsoft.com* again. This time the connection succeeds because you created an outbound filter specifically for Internet Explorer.

12. In Server Manager, disable outbound filtering by right-clicking Configuration\Windows Firewall With Advanced Security, and then choosing Properties. On the Domain Profile tab, click the Outbound Connections list, and then click Allow (Default). Repeat this step for the Private Profile and Public Profile tabs. Click OK.

Lesson Summary

- Firewalls are designed to drop unwanted communications (such as packets generated by a worm) while still allowing legitimate communications (such as packets generated by a network management tool).

- Windows Vista, Windows 7, Windows Server 2008, and Windows Server 2008 R2 support three firewall profiles: Domain, Private, and Public. The Domain profile applies whenever a computer can communicate with its domain controller. The Private profile must be manually applied to a network. The Public profile applies any time a domain controller is not available, and a network has not been configured as Private.

- Use the Windows Firewall With Advanced Security snap-in to create an inbound firewall rule that allows a server application to receive incoming connections.

- Use the Windows Firewall With Advanced Security snap-in to create an outbound firewall rule that allows a client application to establish outgoing connections. You need to create outbound firewall rules only when you configure outbound connections to be blocked by default.

- You can edit the properties of a firewall rule to configure the scope, which limits the subnets an application can communicate with. Configuring scope can greatly reduce the risk of attacks from untrusted networks.

- If you use IPsec in your environment, you can configure firewall rules to allow only secure connections and to allow only connections for authorized users and computers.

- Group Policy is the most effective way to configure firewall settings for all computers in a domain. Using Group Policy, you can quickly improve the security of a large number of computers and control which applications are allowed to communicate on the network.

- Windows Firewall logging identifies connections that Windows Firewall allows or blocks. This information is very useful when troubleshooting a connectivity problem that might be caused by Windows Firewall.

- If an application must accept incoming connections but the developers have not documented the communication ports that the application uses, you can use the Netstat tool to identify which ports the application listens on. With this information, you can then create Port firewall rules.

Lesson Review

You can use the following questions to test your knowledge of the information in Lesson 1, "Configuring Windows Firewall." The questions are also available on the companion CD if you prefer to review them in electronic form.

> **NOTE ANSWERS**
>
> Answers to these questions and explanations of why each answer choice is correct or incorrect are located in the "Answers" section at the end of the book.

1. You need to install an internally developed automation tool on a computer running Windows Server 2008 R2. The tool acts as a network client and needs to connect to a server on your intranet using TCP port 88 and to a server on the Internet using TCP port 290. Additionally, a client component you install on your workstation running Windows 7 will connect to the computer running Windows Server 2008 R2 using TCP port 39. Windows Firewall is currently configured with the default settings on both computers. Which of the following changes do you need to make to allow the application to work?

   A. On the computer running Windows Server 2008 R2, add a firewall rule to allow outbound connections on TCP port 290.

   B. On the computer running Windows Server 2008 R2, add a firewall rule to allow inbound connections on TCP port 39.

   C. On the computer running Windows Server 2008 R2, add a firewall rule to allow inbound connections on TCP port 290.

   D. On your workstation, add a firewall rule to allow outbound connections on TCP port 39.

2. You have recently installed an internal server application on a computer running Windows Server 2008 R2 that accepts incoming connections on TCP port 1036. The application does not include any access control capability. How can you configure the inbound firewall rule properties to allow connections only from authorized users in your domain? (Choose all that apply. Each answer forms part of the complete solution.)

   A. On the General tab, click Allow Only Secure Connections.

   B. On the Advanced tab, click These Profiles, and then select Domain.

   C. On the Users And Computers tab, select Only Allow Connections From These Users. Then, add the Domain Users group.

   D. On the Scope tab, in the Local IP Address group, select These IP Addresses. Then, add each of your internal networks.

3. You need to use Group Policy settings to configure firewall settings on your client computers running Windows XP and Windows 7. You would like to configure firewall rules using only the Windows Firewall node rather than the Windows Firewall With Advanced Security node. Which of the following features are *not* available when using the Windows Firewall node in Group Policy settings?

A. Filtering UDP traffic

B. Allowing a specific executable to accept incoming connections on any port number

C. Dropping connections not originating from a specific subnet

D. Requiring IPsec authentication for a connection

Lesson 2: Configuring Network Access Protection

Consider this common scenario: an enterprise has thousands of computers on a private network. Perimeter firewalls protect the network from Internet threats, including network attacks from worms. Suddenly, someone creates a worm that can exploit a vulnerability in computers running Windows that do not have the latest security updates installed. The worm spreads quickly across the Internet, but the private network's perimeter firewalls protect the vulnerable computers on the internal network. A traveling salesperson then returns to the office with his mobile computer. While on his trip, he connected his computer to the wireless network at the hotel, where another guest's computer transmitted a worm across the network. When he connects to the private network, the worm immediately begins spreading to the vulnerable computers, completely bypassing the perimeter security. In a few hours, most of the computers on the internal network are infected.

This exact scenario has happened to many organizations and resulted in countless financial losses. NAP can prevent this scenario. When computers connect to your local area network (LAN), they must meet specific health requirements, such as having recent updates installed. If they can't meet those health requirements, they can be quarantined to a network where they can download updates, install antivirus software, and obtain more information about how to meet the requirements of the LAN. This lesson describes NAP and how you can deploy it on your network.

After this lesson, you will be able to:

- Describe how NAP works to protect your network.
- Plan a NAP deployment while minimizing the impact on users.
- Install and configure the Network Policy Service.
- Configure NAP enforcement.
- Configure various NAP components.
- Examine NAP log files.

Estimated lesson time: 90 minutes

Network Access Protection Concepts

As shown in Figure 8-3, NAP is designed to connect hosts to different network resources depending on their current health state. This division of network resources can be implemented using virtual LANs (VLANs, as Figure 8-3 illustrates), IP filters, IP subnet assignment, static routes, or IPsec enforcement.

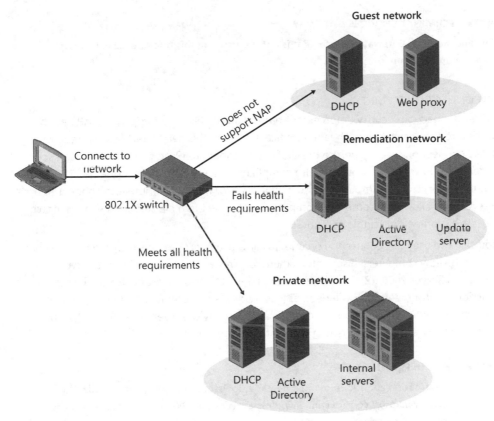

FIGURE 8-3 A typical NAP VLAN architecture

If you choose to provide a remediation network (rather than simply denying network access), you might need additional infrastructure servers for it. For example, if you configure an Active Directory domain controller on the remediation network, you should use a read-only domain controller to limit the risk if the domain controller is attacked. Similarly, you should provide separate DHCP and DNS servers from your infrastructure servers to reduce the risk that a noncompliant computer might spread malware to the production server.

Enforcement Types

For NAP to work, a network component must enforce NAP by either allowing or denying network access. The sections that follow describe the different NAP enforcement types you can use: IPsec connection security, 802.1X access points, VPN servers, DHCP servers, and Remote Desktop Gateways (RD Gateway).

> **NOTE** **TERMINAL SERVICES GATEWAY**
>
> Terminal Services Gateway enforcement is not discussed in this book because it is not covered on the exam.

IPSEC CONNECTION SECURITY

The IPsec connection security enforcement type requires clients to perform a NAP health check before they can receive a health certificate. In turn, this health certificate is required for IPsec connection security before the client can connect to IPsec-protected hosts. IPsec enforcement allows you to require health compliance on a per-IP address or a per-TCP/UDP port number basis. For example, you could allow noncompliant computers to connect to a web server but allow only compliant computers to connect to a file server—even if the two services are running on a single computer.

You can also use IPsec connection security to allow healthy computers to communicate only with other healthy computers. IPsec enforcement requires a CA running Windows Server 2008 (or Windows Server 2008 R2) Certificate Services and NAP to support health certificates. In production environments, you will need at least two CAs for redundancy. Other public key infrastructures (PKIs) will not work. IPsec enforcement provides a very high level of security, but it can protect only computers that are configured to support IPsec.

> **MORE INFO** **DEPLOYING A PKI**
>
> For more information about deploying a new Windows-based PKI in your organization, see *http://www.microsoft.com/pki* and *Windows Server 2008 PKI and Certificate Security* by Brian Komar (Microsoft Press, 2008).

802.1X ACCESS POINTS

The 802.1X access points enforcement type uses Ethernet switches or wireless access points that support 802.1X authentication. Compliant computers are granted full network access, and noncompliant computers are connected to a remediation network or completely prevented from connecting to the network. If a computer falls out of compliance after connecting to the 802.1X network, the 802.1X network access device can change the computer's network access. This provides some assurance of compliance for desktop computers, which might remain connected to the network indefinitely.

802.1X enforcement uses one of two methods to control which level of access compliant, noncompliant, and unauthenticated computers receive:

- **An access control list (ACL)** A set of Internet Protocol version 4 (IPv4) or Internet Protocol version 6 (IPv6) packet filters configured on the 802.1X access point. The 802.1X access point applies the ACL to the connection and drops all packets that are not allowed by the ACL. Typically, you apply an ACL to noncompliant computer connections and allow compliant computers to connect without an ACL (thus granting them unlimited network access). ACLs allow you to prevent noncompliant computers from connecting to one another, thus limiting the ability of a worm to spread, even among noncompliant computers.

- **A virtual local area network (VLAN)** A group of ports on the switch that are grouped together to create a separate network. VLANs cannot communicate with one another unless you connect them using a router. VLANs are identified using a VLAN identifier, which must be configured on the switch itself. You can then use NAP to specify in which VLAN the compliant, noncompliant, and unauthenticated computers are placed. When you place noncompliant computers into a VLAN, they can communicate with one another. This can allow a noncompliant computer infected with a worm to attack, and possibly infect, other noncompliant computers. Another disadvantage of using VLANs is that the client's network configuration must change when transitioning from being a non-compliant NAP client to being a compliant NAP client (for example, if they are able to successfully apply updates). Changing the network configuration during system startup and user logon can cause Group Policy updates or other boot processes to fail.

Your 802.1X access points may support ACLs, VLANs, or both. If they support both and you're already using either ACLs or VLANs for other purposes, use the same technique for 802.1X enforcement. If your 802.1X access point supports both ACLs and VLANs and you are not currently using either, use ACLs for 802.1X enforcement so that you can take advantage of their ability to limit network access between noncompliant clients.

VPN SERVERS

The VPN servers type enforces NAP for remote access connections using a VPN server running Windows Server 2008 or Windows Server 2008 R2 and Routing and Remote Access (other VPN servers do not support NAP). With VPN server enforcement enabled, only compliant client computers are granted unlimited network access. The VPN server can apply a set of packet filters to connections for noncompliant computers, limiting their access to a remediation server group that you define. You can also define IPv4 and IPv6 packet filters, exactly as you would when configuring a standard VPN connection.

> **MORE INFO** **CONFIGURING VPN CONNECTIONS**
>
> For more information about configuring VPN connections, refer to Chapter 7, "Connecting to Networks."

DHCP SERVERS

The DHCP servers enforcement type uses a computer running Windows Server 2008 or Windows Server 2008 R2 and the Dynamic Host Configuration Protocol (DHCP) Server service that provides IP addresses to intranet clients. Only compliant computers receive an IP address that grants full network access; noncompliant computers are granted an IP address with a subnet mask of 255.255.255.255 and no default gateway.

Additionally, noncompliant hosts receive a list of *host routes* (routes that direct traffic to a single IP address) for network resources in a remediation server group that you can use to allow the client to apply any updates required to become compliant. This IP configuration prevents noncompliant computers from communicating with network resources other than those you configure as part of a remediation server group.

If the health state of a NAP client changes (for example, if Windows Firewall is disabled), the NAP client performs a new health evaluation using a DHCP renewal. This allows clients that become noncompliant after successfully authenticating to the network to be blocked from further network access. If you change the health policy on NAP servers, the changes will not be enforced until the client's DHCP lease is renewed.

Although 802.1X network access devices and VPN servers are capable of disconnecting computers from the network and IPsec enforcement can allow connections only from healthy computers, DHCP server enforcement points can be bypassed by an attacker who manually configures an IP address. Nonetheless, DHCP server enforcement can reduce the risk from nonmalicious users who might attempt to connect to your network with a noncompliant computer.

REMOTE DESKTOP GATEWAYS

If you use RD Gateway (called Terminal Services Gateway in Windows Server 2008) to allow users to control their desktops from remote computers across the Internet, you can use the RD Gateway enforcement type to block access using RD Gateway unless the client computer passes a health check. RD Gateway enforcement does not provide remediation.

System Health Agents and System Health Validators

NAP health validation takes place between two components:

- **System Health Agents (SHAs)** The client components that create a Statement of Health (SoH) containing a description of the health of the client computer. Windows 7, Windows Vista, Windows Server 2008, Windows Server 2008 R2, and Windows XP with Service Pack 3 include an SHA that monitors Windows Security Center settings. Microsoft and third-party developers can create custom SHAs that provide more complex reporting.

- **System Health Validators (SHVs)** The server components that analyze the SoH generated by the SHA and create an SoH Response (SoHR). The NAP health policy server uses the SoHR to determine the level of access the client computer should have and whether any remediation is necessary. Windows Server 2008 and Windows Server 2008 R2 include an SHV that corresponds to the SHA built into Windows 7, Windows Vista, and Windows XP with Service Pack 3.

The NAP connection process is as follows:

1. The NAP client connects to a network that requires NAP.

2. Each SHA on the NAP client validates its system health and generates an SoH. The NAP client combines the SoHs from multiple SHAs into a System Statement of Health (SSoH), which includes version information for the NAP client and the set of SoHs for the installed SHAs.

3. The NAP client sends the SSoH to the NAP health policy server through the NAP enforcement point.

4. The NAP health policy server uses its installed SHVs and the health requirement policies that you have configured to determine whether the NAP client meets health requirements. Each SHV produces a Statement of Health Response (SoHR), which can contain remediation instructions (such as the version number of an antivirus signature file) if the client doesn't meet that SHV's health requirements.

5. The NAP health policy server combines the SoHRs from the multiple SHVs into a System Statement of Health Response (SSoHR).

6. The NAP health policy server sends the SSoHR back to the NAP client through the NAP enforcement point. The NAP enforcement point can now connect a compliant computer to the network or connect a noncompliant computer to a remediation network.

7. Each SHA on the NAP client processes the SoHR created by the corresponding SHV. If possible, any noncompliant SHAs can attempt to come into compliance (for example, by downloading updated antivirus signatures).

8. If any noncompliant SHAs were able to meet the requirements specified by the SHV, the entire process starts over again—hopefully with a successful result.

 Quick Check

1. Which NAP enforcement types do not require support from your network infrastructure?

2. Which versions of Windows can act as NAP clients?

Quick Check Answers

1. IPsec connection security, DHCP, VPN, and Remote Desktop Gateway enforcement do not require support from your network infrastructure. They can be implemented using only Windows Server 2008 R2. The 802.1X type provides very powerful enforcement, but requires a network infrastructure that supports 802.1X.

2. Windows XP with Service Pack 3, Windows Vista, Windows 7, Windows Server 2008, and Windows Server 2008 R2.

Planning a NAP Deployment

NAP has the potential to prevent legitimate users from accessing the network. Any security mechanism that reduces productivity will be quickly removed, so you must carefully plan a NAP deployment to minimize user impact.

Typically, a NAP deployment occurs in three phases:

- **Testing**   Test the NAP using examples of each different operating system, client computer configuration, and enforcement points in your environment.
- **Monitoring**   Deploy NAP in a monitoring-only mode that notifies administrators if a computer fails to meet health requirements but does not prevent the user from connecting to the network. This allows you to identify computers that are not meeting health requirements and to bring them into compliance. You could bring computers into compliance manually or by using automated tools, such as Microsoft System Center Configuration Manager 2007. For more information, read the section entitled "Configuring NAP for Monitoring Only" later in this chapter.
- **Limited access**   If, during the monitoring phase, you reach a point where almost all of your computers are compliant, you can enable NAP enforcement to prevent noncompliant computers from connecting to your production network. Users can then use resources on the remediation network to bring their computers into compliance, if necessary. Typically, you will need to configure exceptions for computers that are not NAP-compliant.

Installing and Configuring the Network Policy Server

NAP depends on a Windows Server 2008 or Windows Server 2008 R2 NAP health policy server, which acts as a RADIUS server, to evaluate the health of client computers. If you have existing RADIUS servers that are running Windows Server 2003 or Windows 2000 Server and Internet Authentication Service (IAS), you can upgrade them to Windows Server 2008 or Windows Server 2008 R2 and configure them as NAP health policy servers. If you have RADIUS servers running any other operating system, you will need to configure new Windows Server 2008 or Windows Server 2008 R2 NAP health policy servers, configure the health policy, and then migrate your existing RADIUS clients to the NAP health policy servers.

Typically, you will need to deploy at least two NAP health policy servers for fault tolerance. If you have only a single NAP health policy server, clients will be unable to connect to the network if it is offline. As described in Chapter 7, you can use connection request policies to allow a single RADIUS server to act as a NAP health policy server and authenticate requests from other RADIUS clients.

Installing NAP

To install NAP, follow these steps:

1. In the console tree of Server Manager, select Roles. In the details pane, click Add Roles. The Add Roles Wizard appears.
2. If the Before You Begin page appears, click Next.

3. On the Select Server Roles page, select the Network Policy And Access Services check box. Click Next.

4. On the Network Policy And Access Services page, click Next.

5. On the Select Role Services page, select the Network Policy Server check box. Click Next.

6. On the Confirmation page, click Install.

7. On the Results page, click Close.

This installs the core NPS service, which is sufficient for using the Windows Server 2008 computer as a RADIUS server for 802.1X, VPN, or DHCP enforcement.

Using the Configure NAP Wizard

After installing the Network Policy And Access Services role, follow these steps to configure NAP:

1. In Server Manager, select Roles\Network Policy And Access Services\NPS. You might need to close and reopen Server Manager if you recently installed the Network Policy And Access Services role.

2. In the details pane, select Network Access Protection, and then click Configure NAP. The Configure NAP Wizard appears.

3. On the Select Network Connection Method For Use With NAP page, choose your enforcement method. Then, click Next.

4. On the next page (whose title depends on the previously selected network connection method), you need to add any HRA servers (other than the local computer) and RADIUS clients, for example:

   - If you are using 802.1X enforcement, add the IP address of each switch.
   - If you are using VPN enforcement, add the IP address of each VPN server.
   - If you are configuring DHCP servers, add each of your NAP-capable DHCP servers.

   Click Add for each host and configure a friendly name, address, and shared secret. Then click OK. After you have configured any external HRA servers and RADIUS clients, click Next.

5. Depending on the network method you chose, you might be presented with additional page options, such as DHCP scopes or RD gateway redirection options. Configure these options appropriately.

6. On the Configure User Groups And Machines page, click the Add buttons to allow computers or groups to connect. Click Next.

7. The pages that follow vary depending on your NAP enforcement method:

   - For the 802.1X or VPN enforcement methods, you use the Configure An Authentication Method page (shown in Figure 8-4) to specify the NAP health policy server certificate and the EAP types to use for user or computer-level authentication.
   - For the 802.1X enforcement method, you use the Configure Traffic Controls page to configure the unlimited VLAN and the restricted network VLAN.

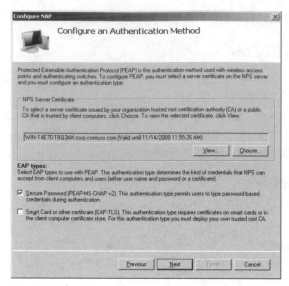

FIGURE 8-4 Configuring an 802.1X enforcement authentication method

8. On the Define NAP Health Policy page, you can select from the installed SHVs. By default, only the Windows Security Health Validator is installed. As shown in Figure 8-5, you should leave autoremediation enabled for enforcement types that support it to allow client computers to automatically change settings to meet health requirements. During initial production deployments, select Allow Full Network Access To NAP-Ineligible Client Computers to configure NAP in monitoring-only mode. Noncompliant computers will generate an event in the event log, allowing you to fix noncompliant computers before they are prevented from connecting to the network. Click Next.

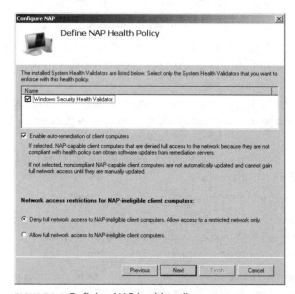

FIGURE 8-5 Defining NAP health policy

9. On the Completing NAP Enforcement Policy And RADIUS Client Configuration page, click Finish.

The Configure NAP Wizard creates the following policies:

- A connection request policy with the name specified on the Select Network Connection Method For Use With NAP page
- Compliant and noncompliant health policies, based on the name specified on the Select Network Connection Method For Use With NAP page
- Compliant and noncompliant network policies, based on the same name as the health policies

Configuring NAP Enforcement

After you have installed and configured NAP, you must perform additional steps to enable NAP enforcement. The steps you follow vary depending on whether you are using IPsec, 802.1X, DHCP, VPN, or RD Gateway enforcement. The sections that follow describe how to configure each of these enforcement types at a high level, cross-referencing other sections in this lesson that have more detailed instructions.

Configuring IPsec Enforcement

Configuring IPsec enforcement requires the following high-level steps:

1. Install the Health Registration Authority (HRA) role service and the Active Directory Certificate Services role (if it's not already present).
2. Use the Configure NAP Wizard to configure the connection request policy, network policy, and NAP health policy, as described earlier in this chapter in the section titled "Using the Configure NAP Wizard." Although you can configure these elements individually, using the wizard is much easier.
3. Configure HRA, as described in the sections that follow.
4. Enable the NAP IPsec Relying Party enforcement client and start the NAP service on NAP-capable client computers, as described later in this chapter in the sections entitled "Configuring Client Computers for IPsec Enforcement" and "Configuring NAP Clients."
5. Require IPsec connection security using health certificates for computers that should communicate only with other healthy computers, as described in the sections that follow.

The following sections describe these steps in more detail.

STEP 1: INSTALLING THE HRA ROLE SERVICE

If you plan to use IPsec enforcement, you will also need to install the HRA role service. In production environments, you should always configure at least two HRAs for fault tolerance. Large networks might require additional HRAs to meet the performance requirements.

Installing the HRA role service configures the following:

- **A certification authority (if one does not already exist)** HRA requires a certification authority running Windows Server 2008 or Windows Server 2008 R2 Certificate Services, which can be an existing CA or a new CA. For a Windows Server 2003–based CA, you must manually create a System Health Authentication certificate template so that members of the IPsec exemption group can autoenroll a long-lived health certificate.

> ***MORE INFO*** **CONFIGURING A CA FOR IPSEC NAP ENFORCEMENT**
>
> For more information about configuring a Windows Server 2003–based CA, read "Step By Step Guide: Demonstrate IPsec NAP Enforcement in a Test Lab" at *http://download.microsoft.com/download/d/2/2/d22daf01-a6d4-486c-8239-04db487e6413/NAPIPsec_StepByStep.doc*.

- **A web application** The Add Role Services Wizard creates a web application named DomainHRA under the default website in Internet Information Services (IIS).

You can install the HRA role service using the Add Roles Wizard by selecting the Health Registration Authority check box on the Select Role Services page and following the prompts that appear, or you can install the role service after installing the Network Policy And Access Services role by following these steps:

1. In Server Manager, right-click Roles\Network Policy and Access Services, and then choose Add Role Services. The Add Role Services Wizard appears.

2. On the Select Role Services page, select the Health Registration Authority check box. When prompted, click Add Required Role Services. Click Next.

3. On the Choose The Certification Authority To Use With The Health Registration Authority page, choose to install a CA, use the local CA, specify a remote CA, or defer the decision until later. Then, click Next.

4. On the Choose Authentication Requirements For The Health Registration Authority page, select Yes if all client computers are members of a trusted domain. If some computers are not members of a domain, you can select No—but you must accept slightly weaker security. Click Next.

5. If the Server Authentication Certificate page appears, you can select an SSL certificate to encrypt communications with the HRA server using one of the following three options. After you select an option, click Next.

   - **Choose An Existing Certificate For SSL Encryption** If you have an SSL certificate, select this option, and then select the certificate you want to use. If your certificate does not appear in the list, click Import.

   - **Create A Self-Signed Certificate For SSL Encryption** Clients do not trust self-signed certificates by default, which means you will need to manually configure the certificate on every client computer. For this reason, it is not a practical option in most circumstances.

- **Don't Use SSL Or Choose A Certificate For SSL Encryption Later** If you are installing Certificate Services as part of this wizard, select this option so that you can manually add an SSL certificate after you have completed the Certificate Services installation.

> **NOTE** **INSTALLING AN SSL CERTIFICATE AFTER COMPLETING THE WIZARD**
>
> You can install an SSL certificate later using the Internet Information Services Manager. Right-click Sites\Default Web Site, and then choose Edit Bindings. In the Site Bindings dialog box, click Add and create an HTTPS binding with your SSL certificate.

6. If you are installing the Windows Server 2008 Certificate Services role at this time, the Active Directory Certificate Services page appears. If it does not appear, skip to step 15. On this page, click Next.

7. On the Role Services page, click Next.

8. On the Setup Type page, select whether to configure an enterprise or stand-alone CA. In Active Directory environments, configuring an Enterprise CA is much easier because you can automatically issue certificates to client computers. Click Next.

9. On the CA Type page, select Root CA if this is your first CA. If you have an existing PKI, select Subordinate CA. The remainder of these steps apply to configuring a root CA; some pages are different if you configure a subordinate CA. Click Next.

10. On the Private Key page, click Next.

11. On the Cryptography page, click Next.

12. On the CA Name page, you can type a new common name for the CA. This name must be the name clients will use to connect to the server. The default will typically work. Click Next.

13. On the Validity Period page, click Next.

14. On the Certificate Database page, click Next.

15. If you are installing IIS role services at this time, the Web Server page appears. If it does not appear, skip to step 17. Otherwise, Click Next.

16. On the Role Services page, click Next.

17. On the Confirmation page, click Install.

18. On the Results page, click Close.

STEP 2: CONFIGURING THE NAP WIZARD

Follow the steps in "Using The Configure NAP Wizard" and, on the Select Network Connection Method For Use With NAP page, select IPsec With Health Registration Authority. Completing the wizard creates the following:

- A connection request policy named NAP IPsec With HRA (at Roles\Network Policy And Access Server\NPS\Policies\Connection Request Policies in Server Manager). This connection request policy configures the local server to process NAP IPsec requests using the HRA.

- A health policy named NAP IPsec With HRA Compliant (at Roles\Network Policy And Access Server\NPS\Policies\Health Policies in Server Manager). This health policy applies to compliant computers that pass all SHV checks.

- A network policy named NAP IPsec With HRA Compliant (at Roles\Network Policy And Access Server\NPS\Policies\Network Policies in Server Manager). This network policy grants access to compliant computers.

- A health policy named NAP IPsec With HRA Noncompliant (at Roles\Network Policy And Access Server\NPS\Policies\Heath Policies in Server Manager). This health policy applies to noncompliant computers that fail one or more SHV checks.

- A network policy named NAP IPsec With HRA Noncompliant (at Roles\Network Policy And Access Server\NPS\Policies\Network Policies in Server Manager). This network policy grants limited network access to noncompliant computers. Specifically, non-compliant computers will be able to access only remediation servers. You should never set the Access Permission to Deny Access, because doing so prevents the health check from being performed.

STEP 3: CONFIGURING HRA

Now you can configure HRA settings using Server Manager by selecting the Roles\Network Policy And Access Services\NPS\Health Registration Authority node. Before you can use IPsec enforcement, you must configure a CA (such as Windows Server 2008 R2 Certificate Services) that will issue health certificates. If you didn't configure the CA while installing HRA, you can install it afterward.

To configure the CA that will be used to issue health certificates for IPsec enforcements, follow these steps:

1. In Server Manager, right-click Roles\Network Policy And Access services\Health Registration Authority\Certification Authority, and then choose Add Certification Authority.

2. In the Add Certification Authority dialog box, click Browse to select an enterprise CA. Select the appropriate server, and then click OK. Alternatively, you can type the fully qualified domain name (FQDN) of your CA. Figure 8-6 shows the Add Certification Authority dialog box with an enterprise CA selected.

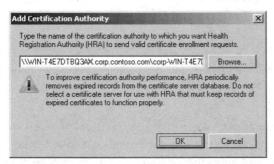

FIGURE 8-6 Selecting a CA for IPsec enforcement

3. Click OK.

4. Right-click Roles\Network Policy And Access Services\Health Registration Authority \Certification Authority, and then click Properties. The Certification Authorities Properties dialog box appears.

5. If you are using an enterprise CA, select Use Enterprise Certification Authority. Then click OK.

The CA appears in the details pane when you select the Roles\Network Policy And Access Services\Health Registration Authority\Certification Authority node in Server Manager. You can repeat the previous steps to add CAs, which allows for fault tolerance. If you have only a single CA and it goes offline, clients will be unable to undergo a NAP health check. If you have NAP enforcement enabled, this means clients will be unable to connect to the network.

You can also configure the mechanisms used for IPsec enforcement using the Roles\Network Policy And Access Services\Health Registration Authority\Certification Authority node in Server Manager. However, the default settings are typically sufficient.

STEP 4: CONFIGURING CLIENT COMPUTERS FOR IPSEC ENFORCEMENT

After configuring the NPS server for IPsec enforcement, you must configure client computers for IPsec enforcement. First, configure clients to use IPsec, as described in Chapter 6, "Protecting Network Traffic with IPsec." Then, configure the client by following these steps:

1. Use the Group Policy Management Editor to open the GPO you want to use to apply the NAP enforcement client settings.

2. Right-click the Computer Configuration\Policies\Windows Settings\Security Settings \Network Access Protection\NAP Client Configuration\Health Registration Settings\Trusted Server Groups node, and then choose New. The New Trusted Server Group Wizard appears.

3. On the Group Name page, type a name that describes the group of HRA servers you will use for IPsec enforcement. Click Next.

4. On the Add Servers page, type the URL for each HRA. If you have an SSL certificate (that clients trust) installed on the server, type the URL as **https://<*servername*>**, where <*servername*> matches the common name on the SSL certificate. If you do not have an SSL certificate, clear the Require Server Verification check box and type the URL as **https://<*servername*>**. Click Add and repeat the process for any additional HRAs. NAP clients always start with the first HRA and continue through the list until an HRA can be contacted. Click Finish.

Now that you have configured clients to trust your HRAs, you should enable IPsec enforcement.

1. Select the Computer Configuration\Policies\Windows Settings\Security Settings\Network Access Protection\NAP Client Configuration\Enforcement Clients node.

2. In the details pane, double-click IPsec Relying Party.

3. In the IPsec Relying Party Properties dialog box, select the Enable This Enforcement Client check box. Then, click OK.

Additionally, follow the steps described in the section "Configuring NAP Clients" later in this chapter.

STEP 5: CONFIGURING IPSEC CONNECTION SECURITY RULES

Next, configure any servers that should be accessed only by compliant computers to require IPsec for inbound (but not outbound) connections. Note that this will prevent network communications from all computers that are not NAP-compliant or NAP-capable. In the Windows Firewall With Advanced Security snap-in (which you can access within the Configuration node of Server Manager), follow these steps:

1. Click Connection Security Rules. Then, right-click Connection Security Rules, and then choose New Rule. The New Connection Security Rule Wizard page appears.

2. On the Rule Type page, select Isolation. Then, click Next.

3. On the Requirements page, select Require Authentication For Inbound Connections And Request Authentication For Outbound Connections. Click Next.

4. On the Authentication Method page, select Advanced. Then, click Customize. In the First Authentication Group, click Add. In the Add First Authentication Method dialog box, shown in Figure 8-7, click Computer Certificate From This Certification Authority (CA). Click Browse and select the CA used to generate the certificate for your HRA. Click OK. Select the Accept Only Health Certificates and Enable Certificate To Account Mapping check boxes and then click OK. When you return to the wizard, click Next.

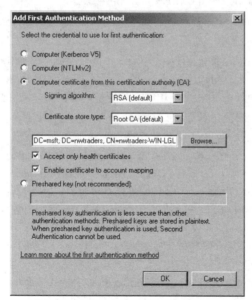

FIGURE 8-7 Requiring health certificates for a server

5. On the Profile page, click Next.

6. On the Name page, type a name, and then click Finish.

After the policy is applied to computers, only clients with a valid health certificate will be able to communicate. For this reason, you can't require health certificates for your HRA server, or clients would be unable to retrieve their health certificates.

For the HRA server, remediation servers, and any other computer that should be accessible by either noncompliant or non-NAP–capable computers, configure an IPsec connection security rule to request, but not require, security for inbound connections. For more information, read Chapter 6.

For NAP clients running Windows XP SP3, you will need to configure the equivalent policies using the IP Security Polices snap-in, available in Group Policy at Computer Configuration \Policies \Windows Settings\IP Security Policies. To configure a Windows XP SP3–based NAP client to use its health certificate for IPsec authentication, you must set the HKEY_LOCAL_MACHINE\ SYSTEM\CurrentControlSet\Services\PolicyAgent\Oakley \IKEFlags registry value to 0x1c.

Configuring 802.1X Enforcement

Configuring 802.1X enforcement requires the following high-level steps:

1. Use the Configure NAP Wizard to configure the connection request policy, network policy, and NAP health policy, as described in the section of this chapter entitled "Using the Configure NAP Wizard." Although you can configure these elements individually, using the wizard is much easier. On the Virtual LAN (VLAN) Configuration page, you will need to specify the ACLs or VLANs for both compliant and noncompliant NAP clients, as shown in Figure 8-8. Refer to your switch documentation for information about which RADIUS attributes to use to specify the VLAN or ACL.

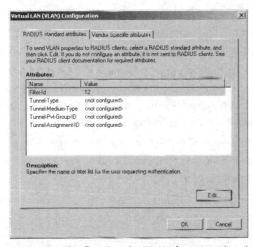

FIGURE 8-8 Configuring the VLAN for unrestricted network access

2. Configure your 802.1X authenticating switches to perform Protected Extensible Authentication Protocol (PEAP)-based authentication (either PEAP-MS-CHAP v2 or PEAP-TLS) and submit RADIUS requests to your NAP server. Additionally, configure a reauthentication interval to require authenticated client computers that remain connected to the network to be reauthenticated regularly. Microsoft suggests a reauthentication interval of four hours. Refer to your switch documentation for instructions.

3. If you plan to use certificates for authentication (using either PEAP-TLS or EAP-TLS), deploy a PKI such as the Certificate Services role and distribute certificates to client computers using a mechanism such as Active Directory autoenrollment. For more information, refer to Chapter 7. If you plan to use PEAP-MS-CHAP v2 domain authentication, use a PKI to issue server certificates to the NAP server.

4. Create NAP exemptions for computers that cannot complete a NAP health evaluation by creating a network policy that grants wireless or wired access and uses the Windows Groups condition set to the security group for the exempted computers but does not use the Health Policy condition. For more information, read "Configuring Network Policies" later in this lesson.

5. Enable the NAP EAP Quarantine Enforcement Client and start the NAP service on NAP-capable client computers. For more information, read "Configuring NAP Clients" later in this lesson.

Configuring DHCP Enforcement

Configuring DHCP enforcement requires the following high-level steps:

1. Use the Configure NAP Wizard to configure the connection request policy, network policy, and NAP health policy, as described in the section of this chapter entitled "Using the Configure NAP Wizard." Although you can configure these elements individually, it's much easier to use the wizard.

2. Configure remediation servers to define the computers that noncompliant clients can access. For more information, read "Configuring Remediation" later in this lesson.

3. Configure a DHCP server. For more information, refer to Chapter 4, "Creating a DHCP Infrastructure." NPS must be installed on the DHCP server. If your DHCP and primary NPS servers are different computers, configure NPS on the remote DHCP NPS server as a RADIUS proxy to forward connection requests to the primary NPS server. For more information about configuring RADIUS proxies, refer to Chapter 7.

4. In the DHCP console, enable NAP for individual scopes or for all scopes on the DHCP server, as described in the sections that follow.

5. Enable the NAP DHCP Quarantine Enforcement Client and start the NAP service on NAP-capable client computers. For more information, read "Configuring NAP Clients" later in this chapter.

ENABLING NAP ON ALL DHCP SCOPES

To enable NAP for all DHCP scopes on a DHCP server, follow these steps:

1. In Server Manager, right-click Roles\DHCP Server\<Computer Name>\IPv4, and then choose Properties.

2. In the Network Access Protection tab (as shown in Figure 8-9), click Enable On All Scopes. Confirm your choice, and then select one of the following options:

- **Full Access** Enables NAP for monitoring only. Noncompliant clients will be granted full network access.

- **Restricted Access** Enables NAP enforcement. Noncompliant clients will be assigned an IP address configuration that grants access only to servers listed in the remediation server group.

- **Drop Client Packet** Ignores DHCP requests from noncompliant clients. Windows clients will then automatically assign themselves an Automatic Private IP Addressing (APIPA) address in the 169.254.0.0/16 network, where they will be able to communicate only with other APIPA computers.

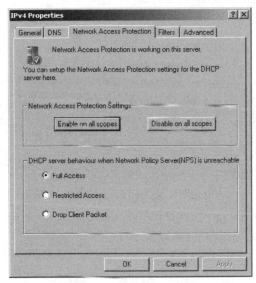

FIGURE 8-9 Configuring NAP on a DHCP server

3. Click OK.

ENABLING NAP ON A SINGLE DHCP SCOPE

To enable NAP for a single DHCP scope, follow these steps:

1. In Server Manager, right-click Roles\DHCP Server\<*Computer Name*>\IPv4\<*Scope Name*>, and then choose Properties.

2. In the Network Access Protection tab, select Enable For This Scope. Then, click OK.

Repeat these steps for each scope that you want to protect using NAP. For more information, read Chapter 4.

Configuring VPN Enforcement

Configuring VPN enforcement requires the following high-level steps:

1. Use the Configure NAP Wizard to configure the connection request policy, network policy, and NAP health policy, as described in the section of this chapter entitled "Using the Configure NAP Wizard." Although you can configure these elements individually, it is much easier to use the wizard.

2. Configure remediation servers to define the computers that noncompliant clients can access. For more information, read "Configuring Remediation" later in this lesson.

3. Configure your VPN servers to perform PEAP-based authentication (either PEAP-MS-CHAP v2 or PEAP-TLS) and submit RADIUS requests to your NAP server. For more information, refer to Chapter 7.

4. If you plan to use certificates for authentication (using either PEAP-TLS or EAP-TLS), deploy a PKI such as the Certificate Services role and distribute certificates to client computers using a mechanism such as Active Directory autoenrollment. For more information, refer to Chapter 7. If you plan to use PEAP-MS-CHAP v2 domain authentication, use a PKI to issue server certificates to the NAP server.

5. Enable the NAP Remote Access Quarantine Enforcement Client and start the NAP service on NAP-capable client computers. For more information, read "Configuring NAP Clients" later in this chapter.

Configuring RD Gateway Enforcement

Configuring RD Gateway enforcement requires the following high-level steps:

1. Use the Configure NAP Wizard to configure the connection request policy, network policy, and NAP health policy, as described in the section of this chapter entitled "Using the Configure NAP Wizard." Although you can configure these elements individually, it is much easier to use the wizard.

2. If you plan to use certificates for authentication (using either PEAP-TLS or EAP-TLS), deploy a PKI such as the Certificate Services role and distribute certificates to client computers using a mechanism such as Active Directory autoenrollment. For more information, refer to Chapter 7. If you plan to use PEAP-MS-CHAP v2 domain authentication, use a PKI to issue server certificates to the NAP server.

3. Enable NAP health policy checks on your RD Gateway server using the RD Gateway Manager snap-in. In Server Manager, right-click Roles\Remote Desktop Services\RD Gateway Manager\<computer_name>, and then click Properties. On the RD CAP Store tab, verify that the Request Clients To Send A Statement Of Health check box is selected, which it is by default. If NPS is running on a different server, select the Central Server Running NPS check box, and then select your NPS server.

4. On NAP-capable client computers, enable the NAP RD Gateway Enforcement Client and the EAP Enforcement Client. Then, start the NAP service. For more information, read "Configuring NAP Clients" later in this chapter.

Configuring NAP Components

Depending on the NAP enforcement type and your organization's specific requirements, you will need to configure SHVs, NAP client settings, and health requirement policies. Additionally, during the initial deployment phase, you will need to configure NAP for monitoring only. The sections that follow describe these tasks in detail.

Configuring NAP Clients

After configuring the NPS server, you must configure client computers for NAP. The easiest way to do this is to use GPO settings in the Computer Configuration\Policies\Windows Settings \Security Settings\Network Access Protection\NAP Client Configuration node. You can con-figure client NAP settings using the three subnodes:

- **Enforcement Clients**   You must enable one policy to configure clients to use that enforcement type.

- **User Interface Settings**   Configure the User Interface Settings policy to provide customized text (and, optionally, an image) that users will see as part of the NAP client interface.

- **Health Registration Settings**   Use the Request Policy subnode to configure cryp-tographic settings for NAP clients (the default settings are typically fine). Use the Trusted Server Group subnode to configure an HRA for IPsec NAP clients to use.

Additionally, you must start the Network Access Protection Agent service on all client com-puters. You can do this manually, but it is easiest to use Group Policy settings. In your GPO, select the Computer Configuration\Policies\Windows Settings\Security Settings\System Services node. Then, double-click the Network Access Protection Agent service. Define the policy in the proper-ties dialog box, and set it to start automatically, as shown in Figure 8-10.

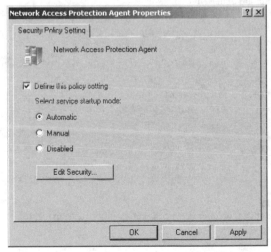

FIGURE 8-10 Starting the Network Access Protection Agent service automatically

Finally, to allow managed clients to use the default Windows SHV, you must enable Security Center by enabling the Computer Configuration\Policies\Administrative Templates\Windows Components\Security Center\Turn On Security Center policy.

> **NOTE CONFIGURING A WORKING NAP ENVIRONMENT**
>
> NAP configuration is complex, and this lesson has shown you many ways to configure NAP. Be sure to complete the practice at the end of this lesson to complete a NAP implementation from start to finish.

You can quickly verify a client's configuration by running the following command at a command prompt:

```
netsh nap client show state
```

The following output shows a client that has the Network Access Protection Agent service started and only the IPsec enforcement agent enabled:

```
Client state:
-------------------------------------------------------
Name                    = Network Access Protection Client
Description             = Microsoft Network Access Protection Client
Protocol version        = 1.0
Status                  = Enabled
Restriction state       = Not restricted
Troubleshooting URL     =
Restriction start time  =


Enforcement client state:
-------------------------------------------------------
Id                      = 79617
Name                    = DHCP Quarantine Enforcement Client
Description             = Provides DHCP based enforcement for NAP
Version                 = 1.0
Vendor name             = Microsoft Corporation
Registration date       =
Initialized             = No


Id                      = 79618
Name                    = Remote Access Quarantine Enforcement Client
Description             = Provides the quarantine enforcement for RAS Client
Version                 = 1.0
Vendor name             = Microsoft Corporation
Registration date       =
Initialized             = No


Id                      = 79619
Name                    = IPSec Relying Party
Description             = Provides IPSec based enforcement for Network Access Protection
Version                 = 1.0
Vendor name             = Microsoft Corporation
Registration date       =
Initialized             = Yes
```

```
Id                      = 79621
Name                    = TS Gateway Quarantine Enforcement Client
Description             = Provides TS Gateway enforcement for NAP
Version                 = 1.0
Vendor name             = Microsoft Corporation
Registration date       =
Initialized             = No


Id                      = 79623
Name                    = EAP Quarantine Enforcement Client
Description             = Provides EAP based enforcement for NAP
Version                 = 1.0
Vendor name             = Microsoft Corporation
Registration date       =
Initialized             = No

System health agent (SHA) state:
----------------------------------------------------
Id                      = 79744
Name                    = Windows Security Health Agent

Description             = The Windows Security Health Agent checks the compliance of a
computer with an administrator-defined policy.

Version                 = 1.0

Vendor name             = Microsoft Corporation

Registration date       =
Initialized             = Yes
Failure category        = None
Remediation state       = Success
Remediation percentage = 0
Fixup Message           = (3237937214) - The Windows Security Health Agent has finished
updating its security state.

Compliance results      =
Remediation results     =

Ok.
```

If applying Group Policy settings is not convenient, you can use the SHA ID numbers to
enable a NAP client at the command line (or from within a script). For example, to enable the
DHCP Quarantine enforcement client (which has an ID of 79617), run the following command:

```
netsh nap client set enforcement 79617 enable
```

Configuring a Health Requirement Policy

Health requirement policies determine which clients must meet health requirements, what those health requirements are, and what happens if a client cannot comply. A health requirement policy is a combination of the following:

- **Connection request policy** Determines whether a request should be processed by NPS.
- **System health validators** Define which health checks a client must meet to be considered compliant. For example, with the default Windows SHV, you can configure whether not having a firewall enabled makes a client noncompliant.
- **Remediation server group** A group of servers that noncompliant clients can access. These servers should provide clients with DNS and Active Directory services, as well as access to resources that will allow the client to become compliant, such as an update server.
- **Health policy** Defines health requirements using SHV settings. Separate health policies must exist for both compliant and noncompliant clients.
- **Network policy** Defines the level of network access clients get based on which health policy they match. You also use network policies to define the remediation servers that clients with limited access can connect to. As shown in Figure 8-11, you can specify network policy conditions that cause the network policy to apply to a client based on matching a specific health policy, operating system, or whether the client supports NAP.

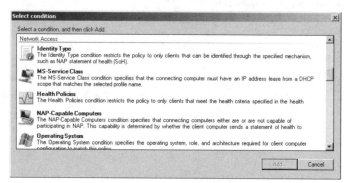

FIGURE 8-11 Configuring conditions for a network policy

CONFIGURING SHVS

Windows Server 2008 R2 includes only the Windows Security Health Validator SHV. Either Microsoft or third parties can supply additional SHVs that you would need to install on every NPS server.

After installing SHVs, configure the defaults (including the Windows SHV, described in the next section, "Configuring the Windows Security Health Validator") by following these steps:

1. In Server Manager, select the Roles\Network Policy And Access Services\NPS\Network Access Protection\System Health Validators node.

2. In the details pane, right-click the SHV, and then choose Properties.

3. First, configure the error code resolution settings, as shown in Figure 8-12. In Server Manager, right-click Roles\Network Policy And Access Services\NPS\Network Access Protection\System Health Validators\<*SHV_Name*>\Error Codes, and then click Properties. For each of the five settings, you can define whether clients are compliant or noncompliant. Leave these set to Noncompliant for best security. However, if you experience a problem with clients receiving an error code when they should be compliant (for example, if an SHV or SHA needs to contact external services and cannot because of intermittent connectivity problems), you can change the error code resolution to Compliant. This could allow clients who would otherwise fail a health check to connect to your network, however.

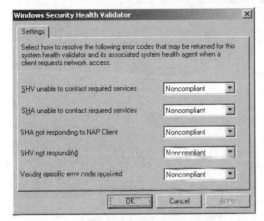

FIGURE 8-12 Configuring SHV error code resolution

4. Select the Roles\Network Policy And Access Services\NPS\Network Access Protection \System Health Validators\<*SHV_Name*>\Settings node in Server Manager to configure settings specific to that SHV, and then click OK. This dialog box is different for every SHV.

CONFIGURING THE WINDOWS SECURITY HEALTH VALIDATOR

By default, Windows Server 2008 R2 includes a single SHV: the Windows SHV. The Windows SHV performs many of the same checks as the Security Center:

- Verifies that a firewall (such as Windows Firewall) is enabled for all network connections. Windows XP, Windows Vista, and Windows 7 include Windows Firewall, which fulfills this requirement.

- Verifies that antivirus software is present and that the signatures are up to date. Because Windows does not include antivirus software, this check will cause Windows computers to fail by default.

- For Windows Vista and Windows 7 computers, verifies that antispyware software is present and the signatures are up to date. Windows Vista and Windows 7 include Windows Defender, which fulfills this requirement. You can also install Windows Defender on Windows XP computers, but the Windows Security Health Validator does not support checking antispyware software for computers running Windows XP.

- Automatic Updating is enabled.

Additionally, you can restrict access for clients that do not have all recent security updates installed and establish what level of security updates are required: Critical Only, Important And Above, Moderate And Above, Low And Above, or All. Figure 8-13 shows the Windows Security Health Validator properties with its default settings. The Windows XP node applies only to Windows XP clients with Service Pack 3 installed.

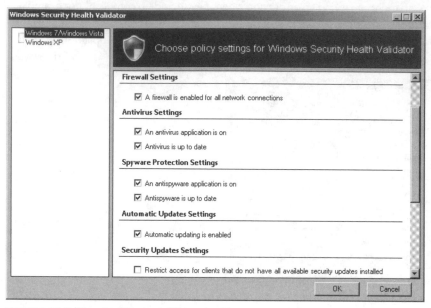

FIGURE 8-13 Editing the Windows SHV properties

To configure the Windows SHV, select NPS\Network Access Protection\System Health Validators\Windows Security Health Validator\Settings in the Network Policy And Access Services snap-in. Then, in the details pane, double-click Default Configuration. Alternatively, you can create additional configurations by clicking New in the Actions pane.

CONFIGURING REMEDIATION

Although NPS is designed to improve security by preventing noncompliant computers from connecting to your network, when it does detect a problem, it prevents legitimate users from their jobs. Therefore, you need resources so that those users can quickly and easily bring their computers into compliance and once again be productive.

To provide assistance to users of noncompliant computers when requiring NAP health enforcement, you can configure a remediation server group and troubleshooting URL that will be available to users if they fail the compliance check. The remediation server group is used only for DHCP and VPN enforcement types; 802.1X and IPsec enforcement use different technologies to limit network access. Remediation servers are not required if you are using reporting mode, because computers that fail the health check will still be allowed to connect to the network.

Although your exact remediation servers will vary depending on the requirements of your SHVs (the remediation servers should allow a noncompliant computer to enter compliance), remediation servers typically consist of the following:

- DHCP servers to provide IP configuration
- DNS servers, and optionally WINS servers, to provide name resolution
- Active Directory domain controllers, preferably configured as read-only, to minimize security risks
- Internet proxy servers so that noncompliant NAP clients can access the Internet
- HRAs so that noncompliant NAP clients can obtain a health certificate for the IPsec enforcement method
- A troubleshooting URL server, which provides a webpage users can access to view more information about the problem
- Antivirus update servers to retrieve updated antivirus signatures (if required by the health policy)
- Antispyware update servers to retrieve updated antispyware signatures (if required by the health policy)
- Software update servers

To configure these settings, follow these steps.

1. In Server Manager, select Roles\Network Policy And Access Services\NPS\Policies \Network Policies.

2. In the details pane, double-click the compliance policy that applies to noncompliant computers.

3. In the properties dialog box, click the Settings tab. In the Settings list, select NAP Enforcement. Then, click the Configure button.

4. In the Remediation Servers And Troubleshooting URL dialog box, do one or both of the following:

   - Use the Remediation Server Group list to select a remediation server group. If you haven't created a remediation server group, click the New Group button. Name the group, and then click the Add button to add each server that should be accessible to clients who fail the compliance check. One remediation server group might be enough, but you can create separate remediation server groups for noncompliant NAP clients and non-NAP–capable clients. Click OK.

NOTE **UPDATING THE REMEDIATION SERVER GROUP**
You can update your remediation server group later using Server Manager by selecting the Roles\Network Policy And Access Services\NPS\Network Access Protection\Remediation Server Groups node.

- In the Troubleshooting URL group, type the internal URL to a webpage that provides users with more information about why they can't connect to the network, how they can bring their computers into compliance, and whom they can call for assistance. A noncompliant computer visits this URL when a user clicks More Information in the Network Access Protection dialog box, which appears when a user attempts to troubleshoot a failed connection, as shown in Figure 8-14. On the webpage, you should provide information that the user can employ either to determine how to update the computer so that it is compliant or to troubleshoot network access. This URL is also visible when a user runs the **netsh nap client show state** command. The web server you specify in the URL should be part of the Remediation Server Group list so that the client computer can access it.

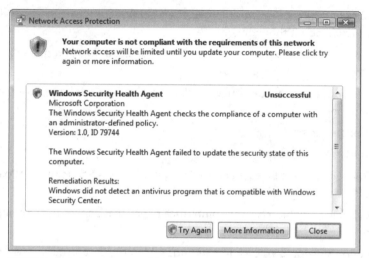

FIGURE 8-14 Information provided to a noncompliant NAP client

5. Click OK.

CONFIGURING NETWORK POLICIES

Network policies determine whether a connection request matches specific conditions (such as a health policy or a client operating system, or whether a computer is NAP-capable). They then grant full or limited network access to the client.

To add a network policy, follow these steps:

1. In Server Manager, right-click Roles\Network Policy And Access Services\NPS\Policies \Network Policies, and then choose New. The New Network Policy Wizard appears.

2. On the Specify Network Policy Name And Connection Type page, type a policy name, and then select a network access server type. For IPsec enforcement, select Health Registration Authority. For 802.1X or VPN enforcement, select Remote Access Server. If you plan to use the Health Credential Authorization Protocol (HCAP) to integrate with Cisco Network Access Control, select HCAP Server. Click Next.

3. On the Specify Conditions page, click the Add button to create any conditions you require, as shown in Figure 8-15, and then click Next. The most useful conditions for NAP are the following:

   - **Health Policies** Specifies that a client must meet the conditions specified in a health policy.

   - **NAP-Capable Computers** Allows you to match either computers that support NAP or computers that do not support NAP.

   - **Operating System** Allows you to apply the network policy to NAP-capable computers with specific operating system version numbers or computer architectures (such as 32-bit or 64-bit computers). This condition is not used as frequently as Health Policies and NAP-Capable Computers.

   - **Policy Expiration** Use this to apply different conditions based on the current date and time. For example, if you are creating a temporary policy that applies only for the next week, you would add the Policy Expiration condition. You should create a second network policy to apply after the Policy Expiration condition expires.

   - **Windows Groups, Machine Groups, And User Groups** These conditions determine the computer or user's Active Directory group membership.

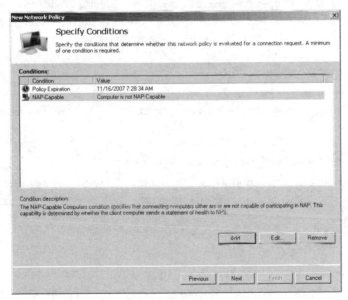

FIGURE 8-15 Specifying network policy conditions

4. On the Specify Access Permission page, select Access Granted. You should never select Access Denied for NPS policies because doing so prevents the health check from occurring. Click Next.

5. On the Configure Authentication Methods page, click Next. For NAP, authentication methods are selected in the Connection Request Policy.

6. On the Configure Constraints page, click Next. NAP rarely uses constraints, although you could use the Day And Time Restrictions constraints to apply the network policy at only specific times.

7. On the Configure Settings page, select NAP Enforcement. Then, select one of the following options and click Next:

   - **Allow Full Network Access**   Grants full access. Use this option if you are creating a network policy for healthy computers.

   - **Allow Full Network Access For A Limited Time**   Grants full access up to a specific date and then restricts access to the selected Remediation Server Group. Use this option during the initial NAP deployment if you want to offer a grace period for noncompliant computers. When selecting this option, click the Configure button to select a remediation server group and specify a troubleshooting URL. If you select this option when using VPN enforcement, VPN clients are disconnected when the expiration time is reached.

   - **Allow Limited Access**   Limits access to the servers specified in the selected remediation server group. Use this option when creating a network policy for noncompliant computers. When selecting this option, click the Configure button to select a remediation server group and specify a troubleshooting URL.

   > *NOTE*   **THE EXTENDED STATE SETTING**
   > This page also includes the Extended State setting. This setting is used only if you are using HCAP with Cisco Network Admission Control. Otherwise, leave this setting as the default.

8. On the Completing New Network Policy Wizard page, click Finish.

9. Right-click the network policy and choose Move Up or Move Down to prioritize it. Higher network policies are evaluated first, and the first network policy with criteria that match a client is applied.

Configuring NAP for Monitoring Only

During your initial NAP deployment, you should allow noncompliant computers to connect to all network resources, even if they fail the NAP health check. To do this, modify the non-compliant health policy to allow full network access by following these steps.

1. In Server Manager, select Roles\Network Policy And Access Services\NPS\Policies \Network Policies. In the details pane, double-click the noncompliant policy. For example, if you specified "NAP IPsec with HRA" as the name on the Select Network Connection Method For Use With NAP page of the NAP Wizard, the network policy for noncompliant NAP clients would have the name "NAP IPsec with HRA Noncompliant."

2. Click the Settings tab, and then select NAP Enforcement.

3. In the network policy properties dialog box, in the details pane, select Allow Full Network Access, and then click OK.

To re-enable NAP enforcement, change the setting to Allow Limited Access.

 REAL WORLD

Tony Northrup

Security risks have an annual cost, which is the potential damage if something bad happens, multiplied by the chance that it'll happen within a year. Countermeasures such as NAP reduce some security risks, which saves companies money. All countermeasures, including NAP, carry their own costs, though, and those costs must not exceed the money saved by reducing risk.

NAP might not actually cost you any cash; if you've already deployed the necessary infrastructure, you don't have to buy anything new. It still has the potential to cost your organization dearly, however. For example, imagine staying up late one night to enable NAP and prevent noncompliant computers from connecting to your network. The next morning, the president of your company has an important presentation in front of investors, but she can't access the network because her laptop is non compliant. Not properly impressing the investors could have a significant negative consequence for your company.

In the real world, the costs will be less dramatic and more nagging. An administrative assistant will log on from home to file his expense report and discover that he hasn't installed the latest updates. A salesperson will attempt to connect to your VPN to send an urgent technical question to an engineer, but she'll give up when the remediation server directs her to update her antivirus definitions. Little amounts of lost productivity and missed opportunities add up in a way that you can't calculate.

When implementing any countermeasure, including NAP, do so gracefully and slowly. All countermeasures include some inconvenience, and that inconvenience has a cost. Always remember that the primary goal of information technology is to make employees more productive.

NAP Logging

NAP logging allows you to identify noncompliant computers. This is particularly important during the initial stages of a NAP deployment, when you will be using NAP only to gather information about the compliance level of the computers on your network. Using NAP logging, you can identify computers that are not compliant and resolve the problem before you enable NAP enforcement and prevent the computer from connecting to your network. NAP logging also enables you to identify computers that would be unable to connect to the network if NAP enforcement were enabled.

To configure NAP logging, right-click Roles\Network Policy And Access Services\NPS, and then choose Properties. On the General tab, select or clear the Rejected Authentication Requests and Successful Authentication Requests check boxes, as shown in Figure 8-16.

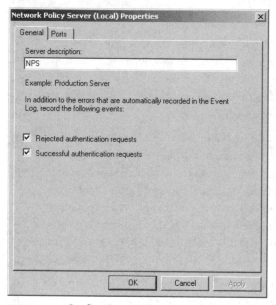

FIGURE 8-16 Configuring NPS logging

On the NAP server, you can use the Windows Logs\Security event log, available in Server Manager at Diagnostics\Event Viewer\Windows Logs\Security, to view NPS events. These events will reveal which NAP clients are not compliant. Figure 8-17 shows an event that indicates a computer that failed to pass the NAP health check. Figure 8-18 shows a computer that passed the NAP health check.

On clients running Windows Vista, Windows 7, Windows Server 2008, and Windows Server 2008 R2 NAP, use the Event Viewer console to examine the Applications and Services Logs \Microsoft\Windows\Network Access Protection\Operational log. On NAP clients running Windows XP With Service Pack 3, use the Event Viewer console to examine the System event log.

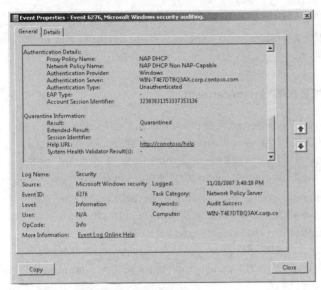

FIGURE 8-17 A failed NAP health check

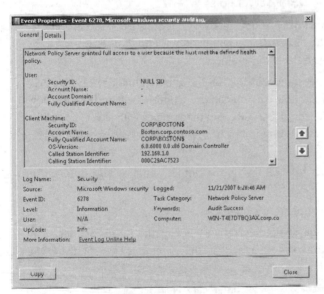

FIGURE 8-18 A successful NAP health check

Additionally, you can enable tracing for the Network Access Protection Agent service to gather extremely detailed information, which is typically required only when troubleshooting complex network problems. To enable tracing, run the following command:

```
netsh nap client set tracing enable level=verbose
```

The trace log files are stored in the %SystemRoot%\Tracing folder.

For more information about NAP logging, refer to Chapter 7. (NAP performs the same logging when used as a RADIUS server.)

Configuring DHCP NAP Enforcement

In this practice, you configure DHCP NAP enforcement and test it with both a compliant and noncompliant NAP client. Although DHCP NAP enforcement is the least secure, it is used as an example here because the configuration is the easiest to demonstrate. To prepare for the exam, you should configure each of the different NAP enforcement types in a lab environment.

Configuring NAP DHCP enforcement is a common scenario for networks with hardware that does not support 802.1X and where IPsec is not available. Although DHCP enforcement does not prevent knowledgeable attackers from connecting to your network, it does inform users who are unaware that their computers do not meet your security requirements of the problem. In production environments, you would typically implement NAP for monitoring only before enabling NAP enforcement.

EXERCISE 1   Adding the NPS and DHCP Server Roles

In this exercise, you add the Network Policy And Access Services and DHCP Server roles to Dcsrv1. If either of these roles already exists (for example, if you added one or both in a previous exercise), remove the roles before continuing.

1. Configure Dcsrv1 with a static IP address of 192.168.1.2, a subnet mask of 255.255.255.0, and a DNS server address of 192.168.1.2. You can use a different IP address for Dcsrv1 as long as you replace all instances of 192.168.1.2 in this practice with Dcsrv1's IP address. Start Hartford, and verify that it is a member of the domain and can communicate with Dcsrv1.

2. In Server Manager, on Dcsrv1, select Roles. In the details pane, click Add Roles. The Add Roles Wizard appears.

3. If the Before You Begin page appears, click Next.

4. On the Select Server Roles page, select the Network Policy And Access Services and DHCP Server check boxes. If the roles are already installed, remove them first, and then return to this step. Click Next.

5. On the Network Policy And Access Services page, click Next.

6. On the Select Role Services page, select the Network Policy Server check box. Click Next.

7. On the DHCP Server page, click Next.

8. On the Network Connection Bindings page, click Next.

9. On the IPv4 DNS Settings page, click Next.

10. On the IPv4 WINS Settings page, click Next.

11. On the DHCP Scopes page, click Add. Complete the Add Scope dialog box, as shown in Figure 8-19. Name the scope **NAP Clients**. Provide an IP address range of 192.168.1.10 to 192.168.1.100. If you are using a different IP address for Dcsrv1, specify an IP address range on the same subnet. In the Subnet Mask box, type **255.255.255.0**. In the Default Gateway box, type **192.168.1.1** (even though that IP address does not exist). In the Subnet Type list, select Wireless. Selecting Wireless simply specifies a shorter lease duration, which requires NAP clients to process any health policy updates more regularly. Click OK, and then click Next.

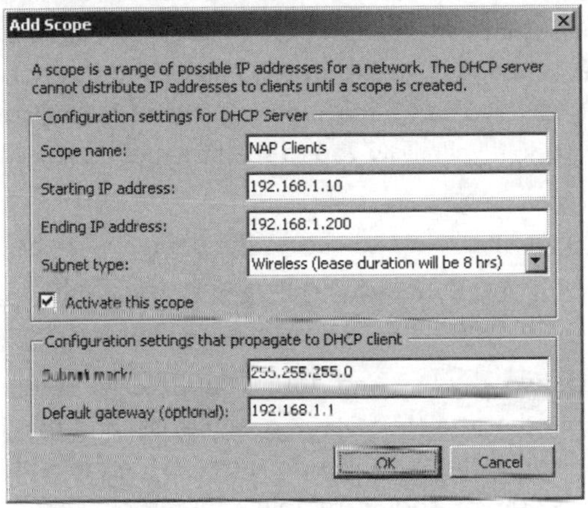

FIGURE 8-19 Configuring a DHCP scope

12. On the Configure DHCPv6 Stateless Mode page, click Next.

13. On the IPv6 DNS Settings page, click Next.

14. On the Authorize DHCP Server page, click Next.

15. On the Confirmation page, click Install.

16. On the Results page, click Close.

The DHCP and core NPS service are installed.

EXERCISE 2   Configuring NAP on the DHCP Server

In this exercise, you must configure NAP on the DHCP server to enforce health checks before assigning client computers an IP address that provides unlimited network access.

1. In Server Manager on Dcsrv1, select Roles\Network Policy And Access Services\NPS. If the node does not appear, close and re-open Server Manager.

2. In the details pane, under Standard Configuration, in the drop-down list, select Network Access Protection (NAP), and then click Configure NAP.

3. On the Select Network Connection Method For Use With NAP page, under Network Connection Method, select Dynamic Host Configuration Protocol (DHCP). Click Next.

4. On the Specify NAP Enforcement Servers Running DHCP Server page, click Add. In the New RADIUS Client dialog box, type **Dcsrv1** in the Friendly Name box and type Dcsrv1's IPv4 address (**192.168.1.2**) in the Address box. Click OK, and then click Next.

5. On the Specify DHCP Scopes page, click Next to apply NAP to all DHCP scopes.

6. On the Configure Machine Groups page, click Next to apply the policy to all users.

7. On the Specify A NAP Remediation Server Group And URL page, click New Group. In the New Remediation Server Group dialog box, type a Group Name of DHCP Remediation Servers. Then, click Add and provide a Friendly Name of NAP and Dcsrv1's IPv4 address (**192.168.1.2**). Click OK twice. Notice that you can also type a troubleshooting URL in this dialog box if you had set up a webpage for this purpose and added that server to the remediation server group. For now, type a troubleshooting URL of **http://contoso /help**. Although this URL will not work, it will allow you to see how the troubleshooting URL is used. Click Next.

8. On the Define NAP Health Policy page, click Next to accept the default settings.

9. On the Completing NAP Enforcement Policy And RADIUS Client Configuration page, click Finish.

10. In Server Manager, select Roles\Network Policy And Access Services\NPS\Policies \Connection Request Policies. Verify that the NAP DHCP policy exists and that it is the first policy listed. If other NAP connection request policies exist, remove them. Similarly, if other network policies exist, you should remove them, too.

Now you need to enable NAP enforcement on the DHCP server:

1. In Server Manager, select Roles\DHCP Server\<*Computer Name*>\IPv4. Then right-click the node, and choose Properties.

2. In the Network Access Protection tab, click Enable On All Scopes, and then click Yes. Then select Restricted Access, and click OK.

EXERCISE 3 Configuring NAP Client Group Policy Settings

After configuring the NPS server, you must configure client computers for NAP by following these steps:

1. Click Start, Administrative Tools, and then Group Policy Management. The Group Policy Management console appears.

2. Right-click Group Policy Management\Forest\Domains\<*Domain Name*>\Default Domain Policy, and then click Edit. The Group Policy Management Editor console appears.

3. Select the Computer Configuration\Policies\Windows Settings\Security Settings\Network Access Protection\NAP Client Configuration\Enforcement Clients node.

4. In the details pane, double-click DHCP Quarantine Enforcement Client. Select the Enable This Enforcement Client check box, and then click OK.

5. Select the Computer Configuration\Policies\Windows Settings\Security Settings\System Services node. Then, in the details pane, double-click Network Access Protection Agent. Select the Define This Policy Setting check box, and then select Automatic. Click OK.

6. Select the Computer Configuration\Policies\Administrative Templates\Windows Components\Security Center node. In the details pane, double-click Turn On Security Center. Select Enabled, and then click OK.

EXERCISE 4   Testing a Noncompliant Client

In this exercise, you connect a noncompliant computer to the network and determine whether it receives an IP address intended for compliant or noncompliant computers.

1. On Hartford, open a command prompt with administrative credentials and run the command **gpupdate /force**. This retrieves the updated Group Policy settings from the domain controller, verifying that the changes you made for NAP clients are applied correctly. Verify that the Network Access Protection Agent service is started.

2. On Hartford, run the command **netsh nap client show state** to verify that the DHCP Quarantine enforcement agent is enabled. If it is not, run the command **netsh nap client set enforcement /9617 enable** to manually enable it.

3. Disable any DHCP servers other than Dcsrv1. If you are using virtual machines, you can create a virtual network and connect both Dcsrv1 and Hartford to the virtual network.

4. Connect Hartford to the same network as Dcsrv1.

5. On Hartford, open a command prompt with administrative privileges. Then, run the following commands to retrieve new IP address settings from the DHCP server:

   ```
   ipconfig /release
   ipconfig /renew
   ```

6. The client computer should display a new IP address configuration, with an IP address of 192.168.1.10 and a subnet mask of 255.255.255.255. Because the subnet mask is invalid (it should be 255.255.255.0), this indicates that the client computer failed the NAP health check.

7. At a command prompt, run the command **route print**. In the IPv4 Route Table, you should see a route with a Network Destination of 192.168.1.2. This address corresponds to the remediation server you configured.

8. At a command prompt, run the command **ping 192.168.1.2** (the IP address of Dcsrv1). Dcsrv1 should respond to the ping, verifying that the remediation server is accessible.

9. At a command prompt, run the command **ping 192.168.1.1**. The command fails with a Transmit Failed error because there is no valid route to the destination.

10. Notice that a notification bubble appears in the system tray, indicating that there was a problem. Click the link to view the details of the error. Notice that the error specifies that Windows did not detect an antivirus program. Click the More Information button to attempt to open the *http://contoso/help* page. Click Close.

11. On Dcsrv1, check the System event log. Find the event indicating that the client computer failed the NAP health check. If you had implemented NAP in monitoring-only mode, this would be the only sign that a computer did not meet the health requirements.

EXERCISE 5   Updating a Health Policy

In this exercise, you change the health policy to allow the client computer to pass the health check.

1. On Dcsrv1, in Server Manager, select Roles\Network Policy And Access Services \NPS\Network Access Protection\System Health Validators\Windows Security Health Validator\Settings. In the details pane, double-click Default Configuration.

2. On the Windows 7/Windows Vista tab, clear the An Antivirus Application Is On check box. Then, clear the Automatic Updating Is Enabled check box. Click OK.

The Hartford client computer will be able to pass the remaining health validation tests.

EXERCISE 6   Testing a Compliant Client

In this exercise, you connect a compliant computer to the network and determine whether it receives an IP address intended for compliant or noncompliant computers.

1. On Hartford, open a command prompt with administrative privileges. Then, run the following commands to retrieve new IP address settings from the DHCP server:

```
ipconfig /release
ipconfig /renew
```

The client computer should display a new IP address configuration, with an IP address of 192.168.1.10, a subnet mask of 255.255.255.0 and a default gateway of 192.168.1.1. Because the subnet mask is now valid, it will be able to connect to other computers on the subnet (if any were available). A notification bubble will also appear, indicating that you have met the network's requirements.

2. On Hartford, open Event Viewer and view the Applications and Services Logs\Microsoft \Windows\Network Access Protection\Operational log. Examine the events for both the unsuccessful and successful NAP health checks.

3. On Dcsrv1, open Event Viewer and view the Windows Logs\Security log. Examine the events for both the unsuccessful and successful NAP health checks.

You can now remove NAP from Dcsrv1 and remove the DHCP enforcement client configuration from Hartford.

Lesson Summary

■ Network Access Protection (NAP) allows you to verify that computers meet specific health requirements before granting them unlimited access to your internal network. You can enforce NAP by using IPsec, 802.1X access points, VPN servers, or DHCP servers.

- When deploying NAP, plan to implement it in monitoring-only mode first. This will allow you to identify and fix noncompliant computers before preventing them from connecting to your network.
- You can use Server Manager to install and configure Network Policy Server.
- Although the Configure NAP Wizard performs much of the configuration, each of the different NAP enforcement methods requires customized configuration steps.
- Before NAP takes effect, you must configure NAP clients. Additionally, when using IPsec enforcement, you must configure a health requirement policy.
- By default, NAP adds events to the Security event log on the NAP server each time a computer passes or fails a NAP health check. You can use the Security event log for auditing and to identify noncompliant computers that require manual configuration to become compliant.

Lesson Review

You can use the following questions to test your knowledge of the information in Lesson 2, "Configuring Network Access Protection." The questions are also available on the companion CD if you prefer to review them in electronic form.

> **NOTE** **ANSWERS**
>
> Answers to these questions and explanations of why each answer choice is correct or incorrect are located in the "Answers" section at the end of the book.

1. You are currently configuring NAP enforcement in a lab environment. You need to create a network policy that prevents noncompliant computers from connecting to the network. How should you configure the network policy properties?

   A. On the Settings tab, set NAP Enforcement to Allow Limited Access.

   B. On the Overview tab, set Access Permission to Deny Access.

   C. On the Constraints tab, set the Session Timeout to 0.

   D. On the Settings tab, create an IP filter that drops all traffic.

2. You are a systems engineer developing NAP scenarios for future deployment within your organization. You want to configure a set of remediation servers that should be accessible for clients that do not support NAP. Which of the following do you need to do? (Choose all that apply.)

   A. Create a health policy and set it to Client Fails All SHV Checks.

   B. Create a network policy with a Condition type of NAP-Capable Computers.

   C. Create a remediation server group with the servers that should be accessible.

   D. Create a connection request policy with a Condition type of NAP-Capable Computers.

3. You are a systems administrator configuring NAP using DHCP enforcement. You plan to run NPS and DHCP on separate computers. Which of the following requirements do you need to fulfill? (Choose all that apply.)

   A. Configure a RADIUS proxy on the DHCP server.

   B. Install NPS on the DHCP server.

   C. Install HRA on the DHCP Server.

   D. Configure Certificate Services on the DHCP server.

Chapter Review

To further practice and reinforce the skills you learned in this chapter, you can perform the following tasks:

- Review the chapter summary.
- Review the list of key terms introduced in this chapter.
- Complete the case scenarios. These scenarios set up real-world situations involving the topics of this chapter and ask you to create a solution.
- Complete the suggested practices.
- Take a practice test.

Chapter Summary

- Windows Firewall is enabled by default to block most unwanted incoming connections. With additional configuration, you can limit the incoming connections that are allowed to specific subnets, user groups, or computer groups. Additionally, you can control which applications can initiate outgoing connections.
- Network Access Protection (NAP) is not enabled by default and requires complex planning and configuration to implement. After you deploy it, however, NAP provides network-level protection by allowing only clients that pass a health check to connect to your network.

Key Terms

Do you know what these key terms mean? You can check your answers by looking up the terms in the glossary at the end of the book.

- defense-in-depth
- firewall
- host route
- worm

Case Scenarios

In the following case scenarios, you will apply what you've learned about how to plan and deploy Windows Firewall and NAP. You can find answers to these questions in the "Answers" section at the end of this book.

Case Scenario 1: Evaluating Firewall Settings

You are a systems administrator for Fabrikam, Inc. Recently, your IT development department created a new client/server application that uses a web service. Your manager asks you to interview key people and then come to his office to answer his questions about the changes you will need to make to the Windows Firewall configuration.

INTERVIEWS

Following is a list of company personnel interviewed and their statements:

- **Developer** "It's a web service application, but it doesn't use IIS. Instead, it's its own service and listens for connections on TCP port 81. We need the server part of the application installed on Server1, and all client computers in the Accounting department should receive the client application. The client application just connects to the server on TCP port 81."

- **Lead systems engineer** "We use the default settings for Windows Firewall, so just let me know what I need to change."

QUESTIONS

Answer the following questions for your manager:

1. What type of firewall rule will you need to create to Windows Firewall on Server1?

2. What type of firewall rule will you need to create on the Windows Vista client computers in the Accounting department?

Case Scenario 2: Planning NAP

You are a systems administrator at Contoso, Ltd., an enterprise that manufactures large-scale farm equipment. Last night the news carried a story of corporate espionage—and your organization was the victim. According to the story, an employee of your biggest competitor gained access to your internal network six months ago, stole confidential plans for new equipment, and used them to improve their own designs. Last week, a disgruntled employee contacted the media and told the entire story.

Apparently, your competitor's employee waited patiently at a coffee shop near your offices. When he saw someone come in with a laptop and a Contoso badge, he waited for the employee to connect to the wireless network. He then exploited a known network vulnerability (which had been fixed several months earlier but had not been updated on the employee's computer) in the user's computer running Windows XP to install a tool that would automatically gather and forward documents from your company's internal network.

Your Chief Executive Officer (CEO) blames your Chief Security Officer (CSO), who in turn holds your Chief Information Officer (CIO) responsible. The CIO blames your manager, and your manager needs your help to create a plan to prevent this from happening again.

QUESTIONS

Answer the following questions for your manager:

1. Why would the attacker have been able to exploit a network vulnerability? How can that be prevented?

2. Is there some way we could have prevented the malware application from transmitting the confidential documents to a server on the Internet?

3. We can never guarantee that mobile computers will receive updates and won't be infected. After all, some of our staffers stay disconnected from the internal network for weeks at a time. So how can we keep these computers from connecting to our internal network and potentially doing damage?

4. If we suddenly turn on NAP, won't that cause problems for many of our client computers? How can we prevent that?

5. Which NAP enforcement method should we use?

Suggested Practices

To help you successfully master the exam objectives presented in this chapter, complete the following tasks.

Configure Firewall Settings

For this task, you should complete all four practices to gain real-world experience working with Windows Firewall.

- **Practice 1**   Configure outbound filtering to block requests by default. Then, create firewall rules to allow common applications, including Internet Explorer and Microsoft Office, to connect to the Internet. Verify that Windows Update can retrieve updates from Microsoft.

- **Practice 2**   Using a computer that is connected to the public Internet, enable firewall logging. Wait several hours, and then examine the firewall log. What types of requests were dropped? What might have happened if the firewall were not enabled?

- **Practice 3**   On your organization's production network, examine the inbound firewall rules. How can you adjust the scope of these rules to minimize security risks?

- **Practice 4**   Register for and watch the "Windows Vista Firewall And IPSec Enhancements" presentation by Steve Riley at *https://msevents.microsoft.com /CUI/Register.aspx?EventID=1032298288*.

Configure Network Access Protection

For this task, you should complete all six practices to gain experience using Network Access Protection in a variety of scenarios.

- **Practice 1** In a lab environment, deploy NAP using 802.1X, VPN, and IPsec. First, deploy NAP in monitoring-only mode. Then, switch to NAP enforcement.

- **Practice 2** Create a webpage that you could specify in the Troubleshooting URL, providing all the information the user of a noncompliant computer needs to remedy a problem and connect to the network.

- **Practice 3** Create a NAP test environment, including remediation servers. Using a noncompliant computer and any NAP enforcement technique, verify that you can bring the computer into compliance using just the resources provided by your remediation servers.

- **Practice 4** Watch the "Security and Policy Enforcement: Network Access Protection" presentation by Graziano Galante at *http://www.microsoft.com/emea/spotlight /sessionh .aspx?videoid=491*.

- **Practice 5** Watch the "NAP using DHCP in Windows Server 2008 R2" presentation by Kunal D. Mehta at *http://www.youtube.com/watch?v=iRtsj3BbwVs*.

- **Practice 6** Watch the "NAP Network Access Protection Demo" at *http://www.youtube.com /watch?v=DoO-x5MSsKw*.

Take a Practice Test

The practice tests on this book's companion CD offer many options. For example, you can test yourself on just the content covered in this chapter, or you can test yourself on all the 70-642 certification exam content. You can set up the test so that it closely simulates the experience of taking a certification exam, or you can set it up in study mode so that you can look at the correct answers and explanations after you answer each question.

> **MORE INFO** **PRACTICE TESTS**
>
> For details about all the practice test options available, see "How to Use the Practice Tests" in this book's Introduction.

CHAPTER 9

Managing Software Updates

Over the years, computers have become much easier to manage. Hardware and software are more reliable, operating systems are easier to use, and many management tasks (for example, defragmentation) are now completely automated. However, there remains one area that requires constant, ongoing maintenance: software updates.

Unfortunately, the penalty for not installing software updates can be severe. If computers do not have recent updates installed, it's much more likely that an attacker will exploit a software vulnerability. This in turn can lead to extended downtime, additional computers being compromised, and confidential information leaving your internal network.

To help you distribute updates throughout your organization while minimizing the management time required, Microsoft provides Windows Server Update Services (WSUS). WSUS allows you to download, approve (after you've tested the updates), and distribute updates throughout your organization—no matter how many client computers you manage.

The lessons in this chapter provide an overview of WSUS to enable you to plan an update infrastructure deployment, as well as detailed information about configuring WSUS.

Exam objectives in this chapter:

- Configure Windows Server Update Services (WSUS) server settings.

Lessons in this chapter:

- Lesson 1: Understanding Windows Server Update Services   **489**
- Lesson 2: Using Windows Server Update Services   **499**

Before You Begin

To complete the lessons in this chapter, you should be familiar with Windows networking and be comfortable with the following tasks:

- Adding roles to a computer running Windows Server 2008 R2
- Configuring Active Directory domain controllers and joining computers to a domain
- Basic network configuration, including configuring IP settings

You will also need the following nonproduction hardware, connected to test networks:

- A computer named Dcsrv1 that is a domain controller in the Nwtraders.msft domain

> **NOTE COMPUTER AND DOMAIN NAMES**
>
> The computer and domain names you use will not affect these exercises. The practices in this chapter refer to these computer names for simplicity, however.

- A computer named Boston that is a member of the Nwtraders.msft domain.

 REAL WORLD

Tony Northrup

Deploying updates can take a lot of time. You need to test the update against all applicable operating systems and the applications that you run on that operating system. When you deploy it, client computers often need to be restarted—which can interrupt user productivity. Additionally, any update can cause compatibility problems, even with proper testing. As you can see, deploying updates has a significant cost, but doesn't provide any new functionality.

The truth is that it's all too easy to fall behind when distributing security updates. If Microsoft releases a new security update and you do absolutely nothing with it, you'll *probably* be fine. After all, many vulnerabilities can be exploited only when multiple layers of protection are bypassed, and, even when exploited, the attacker might not be able to take any significant action on the compromised computer.

Several times a year, however, someone releases malicious software to exploit a known vulnerability for which an update already exists. These exploits can devastate organizations, costing millions of dollars in lost productivity. You can typically avoid these losses by installing a single update prior to the release of the malicious software, but you never know which update will be the important one.

The only way to be sure you're protected from the next big exploit is to promptly test and install all security updates. Adding Network Access Protection (NAP) to provide an additional layer of protection for unpatched computers helps, too.

Lesson 1: Understanding Windows Server Update Services

Before deploying Windows Server Update Services (WSUS), you must understand how both the client and server components should be configured for different environments. Without proper planning, updates can take too long to distribute, waste large amounts of your limited Internet and wide area network (WAN) bandwidth, or fail to install correctly. This lesson provides background and planning information for WSUS.

> **NOTE NEW FEATURES**
>
> If you are familiar with earlier versions of WSUS, WSUS 3.0 with Service Pack 2 provides a significant amount of new functionality. Most significantly, there is now a console to manage WSUS; you no longer need to manage it using a Web browser. Additionally, it supports BranchCache, more flexible reporting, and user interface improvements.

> **After this lesson, you will be able to:**
> - Describe the purpose of WSUS.
> - Configure the WSUS client.
> - Design a WSUS architecture to meet the needs of both small and large organizations.
> - List the client and server requirements for WSUS.
> - Describe the tools you can use to identify computers that are missing important updates.
>
> **Estimated lesson time: 15 minutes**

WSUS Overview

WSUS is a private version of the Microsoft Update service from which Windows computers automatically download updates. Because you can run WSUS on your own internal network and use it to distribute updates to your computers, you can use bandwidth more efficiently and maintain complete control over the updates installed on your client computer.

When you run WSUS, it connects to the Microsoft Update site, downloads information about available updates, and adds them to a list of updates that require administrative approval. After an administrator approves and prioritizes these updates (a process that you can entirely automate), WSUS automatically makes them available to Windows computers. The Windows Update client (when properly configured) then checks the WSUS server and automatically downloads and, optionally, installs approved updates. You can distribute WSUS across multiple servers and locations to scale from small business to enterprise needs.

Windows Update Client

The Windows Update client is the component of WSUS clients that retrieves software from the WSUS server, verifies the digital signature and the Secure Hash Algorithm (SHA1) hash, notifies the user that the update is available, and installs the software (if configured to do so). The Windows Update client installs updates at a scheduled time and can automatically restart the computer if necessary. If the computer is turned off at that time, the updates can be installed as soon as the computer is turned on. If the computer's hardware supports it, Windows Update can wake a computer from sleep and install the updates at the specified time.

> **NOTE WSUS CLIENT IN EARLIER VERSIONS OF WINDOWS**
>
> In Windows XP and Windows 2000, the client component of WSUS is called the Automatic Updates client.

Because Windows Update settings should be applied to all computers in your organization, Group Policy is typically the best way to distribute the settings. Windows Update settings are located at Computer Configuration\Policies\Administrative Templates\Windows Components\Windows Update. The Windows Update Group Policy settings are:

- **Specify Intranet Microsoft Update Service Location**   Specifies the location of your WSUS server.

- **Configure Automatic Updates**   Specifies whether client computers will receive security updates and other important downloads through the Windows Update service. You also use this setting to configure whether the user is prompted to install updates or the Windows Update client automatically installs them (and at what time of day the installation occurs).

- **Automatic Updates Detection Frequency**   Specifies how frequently the Windows Update client checks for new updates. By default, this is a random time between 17 and 22 hours.

- **Allow Non-Administrators To Receive Update Notifications**   Determines whether all users or only administrators will receive update notifications. Nonadministrators can install updates using the Windows Update client.

- **Allow Automatic Updates Immediate Installation**   Specifies whether Windows Update will immediately install updates that don't require the computer to be restarted.

- **Turn On Recommended Updates Via Automatic Updates**   Determines whether client computers install both critical and recommended updates, which might include updated drivers.

- **No Auto-Restart For Scheduled Automatic Updates Installations**   Specifies that to complete a scheduled installation, Windows Update will wait for the computer to be restarted by any user who is logged on instead of cause the computer to restart automatically.

- **Re-Prompt For Restart With Scheduled Installations** Specifies how often the Windows Update client prompts the user to restart. Depending on other configuration settings, users might have the option of delaying a scheduled restart. However, the Windows Update client will automatically remind them to restart based on the frequency configured in this setting.

- **Delay Restart For Scheduled Installations** Specifies how long the Windows Update client waits before automatically restarting.

- **Reschedule Automatic Updates Scheduled Installations** Specifies the amount of time for Windows Update to wait, following system startup, before continuing with a scheduled installation that was missed previously. If you don't specify this amount of time, a missed scheduled installation will occur one minute after the computer is next started.

- **Enable Client-Side Targeting** Specifies which group the computer is a member of. This option is useful only if you are using WSUS; you cannot use this option with Software Update Services (SUS), the predecessor to WSUS.

- **Enabling Windows Update Power Management To Automatically Wake Up The System To Install Scheduled Updates** If people in your organization tend to shut down their computers when they leave the office, enable this setting to configure computers with supported hardware to automatically start up and install an update at the scheduled time. Computers will not wake up unless there is an update to be installed. If the computer is on battery power, the computer will automatically return to sleep after two minutes.

- **Allow Signed Updates From An Intranet Microsoft Update Service Location** Specifies whether Windows XP with Service Pack 1 or later will install updates signed using a trusted certificate even if the certificate is not from Microsoft. This is not a commonly used setting.

- **Turn On Software Notifications** If you use Automatic Updates, you can choose to enable this setting to have Windows Vista or Windows 7 display information about optional updates to users. It's disabled by default, and typically should remain disabled.

Additionally, the following two settings are available at the same location under User Configuration (which you can use to specify per-user settings) in addition to Computer Configuration:

- **Do Not Display 'Install Updates And Shut Down' Option In Shut Down Windows Dialog Box** Specifies whether Windows XP with Service Pack 2 or later shows the Install Updates And Shut Down option.

- **Do Not Adjust Default Option To 'Install Updates And Shut Down' In Shut Down Windows Dialog Box** Specifies whether Windows XP with Service Pack 2 or later automatically changes the default shutdown option to Install Updates And Shut Down when Windows Update is waiting to install an update.

Finally, the last user setting is available only at User Configuration\Administrative Templates\Windows Components\Windows Update:

- **Remove Access To Use All Windows Update Features** When enabled, prevents a user from accessing the Windows Update interface.

WSUS Architecture

WSUS can scale from small organizations to multinational enterprises. In general, you need a single WSUS server for each regional office with more than 10 computers and a separate WSUS server for each different IT department that requires control over how updates are approved.

Typically, redundancy is not required for WSUS servers; however, you should back up the WSUS database and be prepared to repair or replace the server within a week of failure. If a WSUS server fails, there's no direct impact on users, and updates are rarely so time-critical that there would be any impact if it took even a few days to restore a WSUS server.

The sections that follow describe how to design WSUS architectures for different types of offices.

Organizations with One Office

If you have only one location, you can use a single WSUS server—regardless of the total number of client computers. The Windows Update client is designed to share bandwidth and wait when your network is busy, so network impact should be minimal.

Organizations with Multiple Offices

If you were to use a single WSUS server to support clients at multiple offices, each client computer would need to download updates across your WAN connection. Updates, especially service packs, can be several hundred megabytes. Because WAN connections tend to have lower bandwidth than LAN connections, downloading large updates across the WAN could affect overall WAN performance. If your WAN is low-bandwidth or highly busy, clients might not be able to retrieve updates promptly.

To allow clients to retrieve updates from your LAN, configure one WSUS server at each regional location and configure the WSUS servers to retrieve updates in a hierarchy from their parent servers. For best results, use a hierarchy that mirrors your WAN architecture while minimizing the number of levels in the hierarchy. Figure 9-1 illustrates a typical WAN architecture, and Figure 9-2 illustrates an efficient WSUS design for that architecture.

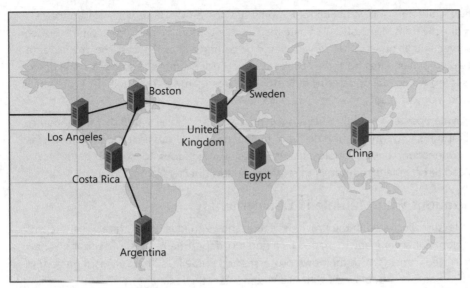

FIGURE 9-1 A typical WAN architecture

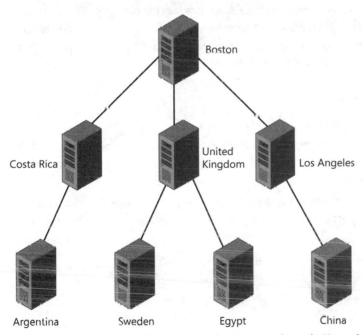

FIGURE 9-2 An efficient WSUS architecture for the WAN shown in Figure 9-1

In the architecture shown in Figure 9-2, only the Boston WSUS server would retrieve updates directly from Microsoft. All update management would be performed on the Boston WSUS server, and all other WSUS servers would be configured as replicas. The downstream servers would pull updates from the upstream servers; for example, Los Angeles (the downstream server) would pull updates from Boston (the upstream server). Similarly, Argentina is considered a downstream server to Costa Rica.

To provide updates for small offices that cannot support a local WSUS server, configure client computers to download updates from the nearest WSUS server. If the office has a fast Internet connection, consider deploying a WSUS replica that does not store updates locally and instead directs client computers to retrieve updates directly from Microsoft.

Organizations with Multiple IT Departments

The architecture illustrated in the previous section shows an ideal that is rarely realistic: an entire multinational company managed by a single IT department. Most organizations have separate IT departments, with their own processes and guidelines, that will insist on controlling which updates are deployed to the client computers they manage.

In organizations with distributed IT departments, you can design the WSUS architecture exactly as described in the previous section. The only difference is in the configuration—instead of configuring each WSUS server as a replica, configure the WSUS servers as autonomous, which allows for approvals and management at each specific server. The configuration steps required are described in Lesson 2, "Using Windows Server Update Services."

WSUS Requirements

When planning your WSUS deployment, keep the following requirements in mind:

- The WSUS server must establish HTTP connections to the Internet (specifically, to the Microsoft Update website). If the connection uses a proxy server, you must provide credentials (if required).
- Downstream WSUS servers must establish connections to upstream WSUS servers using HTTP (and TCP port 80) or, if you have an SSL certificate installed, HTTPS (and TCP port 443).
- Client computers must connect from your intranet by using either HTTP or HTTPS.
- The client computer operating system must be one of the following:
  - Windows 2000 with Service Pack 3 or Service Pack 4
  - Windows XP Professional
  - Windows Vista
  - Windows 7
  - Windows Server 2003
  - Windows Server 2008
  - Windows Server 2008 R2

- If client computers are disconnected from your network for an extended period of time (for example, if a professor leaves on sabbatical or an employee works from home for months and does not connect to the virtual private network [VPN]), the client will not be able to download updates. Consider configuring the computer to automatically install updates directly from Microsoft or, using NAP, to require computers to have updates before connecting to your intranet. DirectAccess can also help by automatically connecting the computer to your intranet every time it has Internet access. For more information about DirectAccess, read Chapter 7, "Connecting to Networks." For more information about NAP, read Chapter 8, "Configuring Windows Firewall and Network Access Protection."

Planning the WSUS Installation

During the WSUS installation process, you will need to make several critical decisions:

- **Update source** WSUS can retrieve updates either directly from Microsoft Update or from another WSUS server on your own network. Typically, you should choose the method that is most bandwidth-efficient. If two WSUS servers are connected by a high-speed local area network (LAN), have one of those servers retrieve updates from Microsoft Update and the second server retrieve updates from the first server. If you have WSUS servers in three remote offices that are linked using VPNs across the Internet, it would be more efficient for each to download updates directly from Microsoft—because the updates would need to cross the individual Internet connections anyway. Your WSUS architecture defines the exact arrangement, with downstream servers configured to retrieve updates from upstream servers.

- **Approval and configuration replication** If you have multiple WSUS servers and you configure servers to retrieve updates from one of your WSUS servers, you can choose to also synchronize approvals, settings, computers, and groups from the parent WSUS server. Essentially, this makes the child WSUS server a perfect replica. If you configure a server as a replica, you do not need to approve updates on the replica server. If you configure a server as autonomous, you must manually approve updates on the WSUS servers—which is useful for giving multiple IT departments independent control.

- **Update storage** WSUS can either copy updates from Microsoft and store them locally or direct client computers to download updates directly from Microsoft. If you choose to store updates locally, the WSUS server will require at least 6 GB of free disk space (although the actual amount can be much greater, depending on how many updates Microsoft releases and how many languages you require). Storing updates locally can greatly reduce your Internet bandwidth update by allowing clients to retrieve updates across the LAN.

- **Database** By default, WSUS will store the list of updates (including which updates you want to deploy and other settings) in a Windows Internal Database. The WSUS setup process requires at least 3 GB of free disk space to store the Windows Internal Database, although the actual size is typically closer to 1 GB. The Windows Internal Database works for most purposes, but you can also use an existing database server on the local computer or a remote computer. The database server must be running either full or express editions of Microsoft SQL Server 2005 with Service Pack 2 or SQL Server 2008.

- **Website selection** WSUS requires Internet Information Services (IIS) because client computers retrieve updates by using HTTP or HTTPS (if you have an SSL certificate, such as one purchased from a public certification authority or generated by a Windows Server 2008 certification authority). If you do not use IIS for any other purposes on the WSUS server, you can use the existing IIS default website. Otherwise, you can create a new website specifically for WSUS.

- **Languages** Many updates are language-specific. To minimize disk space usage, you should choose to download only languages that are required by client computers that will access the WSUS server. You should avoid selecting all languages, because the total storage space and bandwidth required will be very high.

- **Products** Microsoft Update can provide updates for a wide variety of products other than core Windows operating systems. For example, Microsoft Update distributes updates for Microsoft Exchange Server, SQL Server, and Microsoft Office. Select only the applications and operating systems used within your organization to minimize the disk space required.

EXAM TIP

When you need to protect network communications between WSUS clients and the WSUS server, install an SSL certificate on the server and configure IIS to require secure communications. When you need to protect network communications between WSUS and a SQL Server, use IPsec or just move the SQL Server database to the same computer as WSUS.

Auditing Updates

After deploying WSUS, some client computers might still be missing updates because the update installation fails, the client computer is misconfigured (or is not part of your Active Directory domain), or the client computer has been disconnected from your network for a long time. You can use several techniques to identify computers that are missing updates:

- **Windows Update console** You can use the Computers And Reports node to identify WSUS clients that have not installed approved updates.

- **Microsoft System Center Configuration Manager 2007 R3 (Configuration Manager 2007 R3)** Configuration Manager 2007 R3 is the latest version of Microsoft Systems Management Server (SMS). It can provide detailed information about the updates and applications installed on managed computers. Configuration Manager 2007 R3 is best suited to enterprises with an Active Directory domain. For more information about Configuration Manager 2007 R3, visit *http://www.microsoft.com/systemcenter/*.

- **Microsoft Baseline Security Analyzer (MBSA)** MBSA is an automated security auditing tool that identifies missing updates and configurations that might lead to security vulnerabilities. MBSA can scan entire networks, enabling you to identify unmanaged computers on your network. This provides a significant advantage over the Windows Update console, which can report only on clients that are configured to use the WSUS server. For more information about MBSA and to download the free tool, visit *http://www.microsoft.com/mbsa/.*

- **Network Access Protection (NAP)** NAP, when combined with the standard Windows System Health Validator (as described in Chapter 8), can verify that computers have recent updates installed each time they connect to your network. In monitoring-only mode, NAP adds an event to the event log that you can monitor, allowing you to identify out-of-date computers. If you enable NAP enforcement, client computers that do not meet your health requirements can be connected to a remediation network, where they must apply required updates before gaining access to the private network.

Lesson Summary

- WSUS allows you to store and distribute software updates from Microsoft across your internal network, reducing Internet bandwidth usage. Additionally, WSUS gives you complete control over when updates are deployed to client computers, allowing you to test updates prior to release.

- The Windows Update client retrieves updates from the WSUS server. Depending on how you have configured the Windows Update client, the client can notify the user that the update is available for installation or automatically install the update without interacting with the user. You can configure the Windows Update client by using Group Policy settings.

- A single WSUS server is sufficient for most organizations that have a single location. Typically, you will want to deploy a separate WSUS server to each office to minimize Internet and WAN usage. Additional WSUS servers can be configured as replicas (which copy their configuration from the upstream WSUS server) or can be autonomous (which allows separate IT departments to make their own decisions about when updates are deployed).

- Several types of problems can prevent WSUS clients from installing updates. To identify these updates, you can use the Update Services console, Configuration Manager 2007 R3, MBSA, and NAP.

Lesson Review

You can use the following questions to test your knowledge of the information in Lesson 1, "Understanding Windows Server Update Services." The questions are also available on the companion CD if you prefer to review them in electronic form.

> **NOTE ANSWERS**
>
> Answers to these questions and explanations of why each answer choice is correct or incorrect are located in the "Answers" section at the end of the book.

1. You are a systems engineer for an enterprise video production company. Your organization has six offices and a centralized IT department that manages all of the 1200 client computers. Each of the offices has about 200 computers. The WAN uses a hub-and-spoke architecture, with each of the five remote offices connected directly to the headquarters. How would you design the WSUS architecture?

   A. Deploy a WSUS server to each office. Configure the WSUS servers to be managed by each office's local IT support department.

   B. Deploy a WSUS server at the headquarters. Configure all client computers to retrieve updates directly from Microsoft.

   C. Deploy a WSUS server at the headquarters. Configure all client computers to retrieve updates directly from the WSUS server.

   D. Deploy a WSUS server to each office. Configure the WSUS servers at the remote offices to be replicas of the WSUS server at the headquarters.

2. You are a systems administrator configuring an update infrastructure for your organization. You need to use Group Policy settings to configure client computers to download updates and install them automatically without prompting the user. Which Group Policy setting should you enable and configure?

   A. Allow Automatic Updates Immediate Installation

   B. Configure Automatic Updates

   C. No Auto-Restart For Scheduled Automatic Updates

   D. Enable Client-Side Targeting

3. You are currently evaluating which of the computers in your environment will be able to download updates from WSUS. Which of the following operating systems can act as WSUS clients (even if they require a service pack)? (Choose all that apply.)

   A. Windows 95

   B. Windows 98

   C. Windows 2000 Professional

   D. Windows XP Professional

Lesson 2: Using Windows Server Update Services

With Windows Server 2008 R2, you can install WSUS by using Server Manager and manage it with the Update Services console. This newest version of WSUS includes a significant number of new features and user interface changes, and, even if you are familiar with earlier versions, you should complete this lesson so that you understand exactly how to manage the software.

> **After this lesson, you will be able to:**
> - Install WSUS on a computer running Windows Server 2008 R2.
> - Configure computer groups, approve updates, and view WSUS reports.
> - Troubleshoot both client and server problems installing updates.
> - Manually remove problematic updates from client computers.
>
> **Estimated lesson time: 40 minutes**

Installing Windows Server Update Services

Before installing WSUS, you should install the Microsoft Report Viewer Redistributable 2008, available at *http://www.microsoft.com/downloads/en/details.aspx?familyid=CC96C246-61E5-4D9E-BB5F-416D75A1B9EF*. The current version of WSUS at the time of this writing, WSUS 3.0 SP2, uses that redistributable component for the WSUS user interface.

You can install WSUS by either adding the Windows Server Update Services server role or by downloading WSUS directly from *http://www.microsoft.com/wsus*. If you install the server role, the Add Roles Wizard will prompt you to install the required components. Even if you add the server role, Server Manager downloads the latest version from Microsoft.

The WSUS installation process performs basic configuration, including configuring whether updates are retrieved from another WSUS server or directly from Microsoft, choosing which updates to synchronize, and beginning the update synchronization process. For detailed WSUS installation steps, complete Exercise 1 at the end of this lesson.

If your organization uses a firewall that filters outgoing Web requests based on the URL, you must ensure that WSUS servers have access to the following URLs:

- *http://windowsupdate.microsoft.com*
- *http://*.windowsupdate.microsoft.com*
- *https://*.windowsupdate.microsoft.com*
- *http://*.update.microsoft.com*
- *https://*.update.microsoft.com*
- *http://*.windowsupdate.com*

- *http://download.windowsupdate.com*
- *http://download.microsoft.com*
- *http://*.download.windowsupdate.com*
- *http://wustat.windows.com*
- *http://ntservicepack.microsoft.com*

Configuring Windows Server Update Services

After installing WSUS and beginning synchronization, configure WSUS by following these steps:

1. Fine-tune the WSUS configuration by editing WSUS options.
2. Configure computer groups to allow you to distribute updates to different sets of computers at different times.
3. Configure client computers to retrieve updates from your WSUS server.
4. After testing updates, approve or decline them.
5. View reports to verify that updates are being distributed successfully and identify any problems.

The sections that follow describe each of these steps in more detail.

Configuring WSUS Options

Though the setup wizard prompts you to configure the most important WSUS options, you can configure other options after the initial configuration by selecting the Options node in the Update Services console, as shown in Figure 9-3.

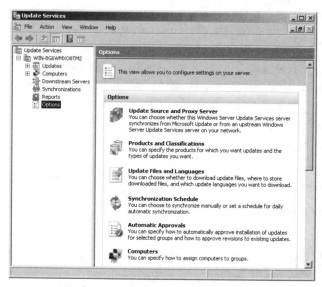

FIGURE 9-3 Configuring WSUS options

You can configure options in the following categories:

- **Update Source And Proxy Server**   Configure the upstream WSUS server or configure the WSUS server to retrieve updates from Microsoft. You configure this during installation and rarely need to change it unless you modify your WSUS architecture.

- **Products And Classifications**   Choose the Microsoft products that WSUS will download updates for. You should update these settings when you begin supporting a new product or stop supporting an existing product (such as an earlier version of Office).

- **Update Files And Languages**   Select where updates are stored and which languages to download updates for.

- **Synchronization Schedule**   Configure whether WSUS automatically synchronizes updates from the upstream server and how frequently.

- **Automatic Approvals**   Configure updates for automatic approval. For example, you can configure critical updates to be automatically approved. You should use this only if you have decided not to test updates for compatibility—a risky decision that can lead to compatibility problems with production computers.

- **Computers**   Choose whether to place computers into groups by using the Update Services console or Group Policy and registry settings. For more information, read the next section, "Configuring Computer Groups."

- **Server Cleanup Wizard**   Over time, WSUS will accumulate updates that are no longer required and computers that are no longer active. This wizard helps you remove these outdated and unnecessary updates and computers, freeing disk space (if you store updates locally) and reducing the size of the WSUS database.

- **Reporting Rollup**   By default, downstream servers push reporting information to upstream servers, aggregating reporting data. You can use this option to configure each server to manage its own reporting data.

- **E-Mail Notifications**   WSUS can send an email message when new updates are synchronized, informing administrators that they should be evaluated, tested, and approved. In addition to configuring those email notifications, you can use this option to send daily or weekly status reports.

- **Microsoft Update Improvement Program**   This is disabled by default; you can enable it to send Microsoft some high-level details about updates in your organization, including the number of computers and how many computers successfully or unsuccessfully install each update. Microsoft can use this information to improve the update process.

- **Personalization**   On this page, you can configure whether the server displays data from downstream servers in reports. You can also select which items are shown in the To Do list that appears when you select the WSUS server name in the Update Services console.

- **WSUS Server Configuration Wizard**   This allows you to reconfigure WSUS by using the wizard interface used for initial configuration. Typically, it's easier to configure the individual settings you need.

Configuring Computer Groups

In most environments, you will not deploy all updates to all clients at once. To give you control over when computers receive updates, WSUS 3.0 allows you to configure groups of computers and deploy updates to one or more groups. You might create additional groups for different models of computers or different organizations, depending entirely on the process you use for deploying updates. Typically, you will create computer groups for each stage of your update deployment process, which should resemble this scenario:

- **Testing** Deploy updates to computers in a lab environment. This will allow you to verify that the update distribution mechanism works properly. Then you can test your applications on a computer after the updates have been installed.

- **Pilot** After testing, you will deploy updates to a pilot group. Typically, the pilot group is a set of computers belonging to your IT department or another computer-savvy group that is able to identify and work around problems.

- **Production** If the pilot deployment goes well and there are no reported problems after a week or more, you can deploy updates to your production computers with less risk of compatibility problems.

You can configure computer groups in one of two ways:

- **Server-side Targeting** Best suited for small organizations, you add computers to computer groups manually by using the Update Services console.

- **Client-side Targeting** Better suited for larger organizations, you use Group Policy settings to configure computers as part of a computer group. Computers automatically add themselves to the correct computer group when they connect to the WSUS server.

Whichever approach you use, you must first use the Update Services console to create computer groups. By default, a single computer group exists: All Computers. To create additional groups, follow these steps:

1. In the Update Services console, expand Computers, and then right-click All Computers (or the computer group you want to nest the new computer group within). Choose Add Computer Group. The Add Computer Group dialog box appears.

2. Type a name for the computer group, and then click Add.

3. Repeat steps 2 and 3 to create as many computer groups as you need.

SERVER-SIDE TARGETING

To add computers to a group using server-side targeting, follow these steps:

1. In the console tree of the Update Services console, expand Computers, All Computers, and then select Unassigned Computers. In the details pane, right-click the computer you want to assign to a group (you can also select multiple computers by holding down Ctrl and clicking), and choose Change Membership.

2. In the Set Computer Group Membership dialog box, select the check box for each group that you want to assign the computer or computers to. Click OK.

The computers you selected will be moved to the specified computer groups.

CLIENT-SIDE TARGETING

You use Group Policy objects (GPOs) to add computers to computer groups when you enable client-side targeting. First, configure the WSUS server for client-side targeting by following these steps:

1. In the Update Services console, select Options. In the details pane, click Computers.
2. In the Computers dialog box, select Use Group Policy Or Registry Settings On Computers. Then, click OK.

Next, configure GPOs to place computers in the correct computer group. You will need to create separate GPOs for each computer group and configure each to apply only to the appropriate computers.

1. Open the GPO in the Group Policy Management Editor.
2. In the console tree, select the Computer Configuration\Policies\Administrative Templates\Windows Components\Windows Update node.
3. In the details pane, double-click the Enable Client-Side Targeting policy.
4. In the Enable Client-Side Targeting Properties dialog box, select Enabled. Then, type the name of the computer group you want to add the computer to and click OK.

After the client computers apply the Group Policy settings, restart the Windows Update services, and contact the WSUS server; they will place themselves in the specified group.

 Quick Check

1. What protocol do Windows Update clients use to retrieve updates from an update server?
2. Should an enterprise use client-side targeting or server-side targeting?

Quick Check Answers

1. HTTP.
2. Enterprises should use client-side targeting, which leverages Group Policy settings to configure which updates client computers retrieve.

Configuring Client Computers

The section "Windows Update Client" in Lesson 1 described the different Group Policy settings available to configure how clients retrieve updates. The following steps provide instructions for performing the minimal amount of configuration necessary (which is sufficient for many organizations) for WSUS clients to download updates from your WSUS server.

1. Open the GPO you want to use to distribute the configuration settings. In the Group Policy Management Editor, select the Computer Configuration\Policies\Administrative Templates\Windows Components\Windows Update node.

2. In the details pane, double-click Specify Intranet Microsoft Update Service Location. The Specify Intranet Microsoft Update Service Location Properties dialog box appears.

3. Select Enabled. In both the Set The Intranet Update Service For Detecting Updates box and the Set The Intranet Statistics Server box, type **http://WSUS_Computer_Name**. Click OK.

4. Double-click Configure Automatic Updates. The Configure Automatic Updates Properties dialog box appears.

5. Select Enabled. Configure the automatic update settings. For example, to have updates automatically installed, from the Configure Automatic Updating drop-down list, select 4 - Auto Download And Schedule The Install. Click OK.

With these Group Policy settings enabled, clients will retrieve and optionally install updates from your WSUS server.

Approving Updates

Unless you have configured automatic approval, updates are not approved by default. To manually approve updates, follow these steps:

1. In the Update Services console, expand Updates. Select one of the following options:

    - **All Updates**   Displays all updates. This is the most convenient option for approving updates.

    - **Critical Updates**   Displays only critical updates, which are high-priority updates, such as bug fixes, that are not security related.

    - **Security Updates**   Displays only updates that fix known security problems.

    - **WSUS Updates**   Displays updates related to the update process.

2. On the toolbar at the top of the details pane, from the Approval drop-down list, select Unapproved, as shown in Figure 9-4. You can also use this list to view updates that you have approved or declined.

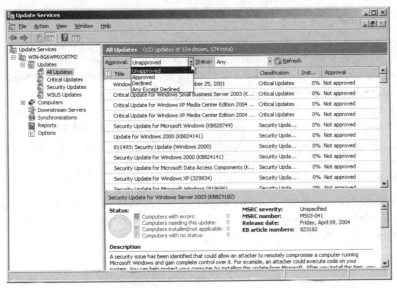

FIGURE 9-4 Viewing updates that require approval

3. From the Status drop-down list, select Any. Click Refresh to display the updates.

> **NOTE SORTING UPDATES**
>
> To sort updates so that newer updates appear first in the list, right-click the column headings, and then select the Release Date column. Then, click the Release Date column header to sort by that date.

4. Select the updates that you want to approve. You can select multiple updates by holding down Ctrl and clicking each update. Alternatively, you can select many updates by clicking the first update and then holding down Shift and clicking the last update. Press Ctrl+A to select all updates. Right-click the selected updates, and then choose either Approve (to distribute the update to clients the next time they check for updates) or Decline (to prevent the update from being distributed).

5. If the Approve Updates dialog box appears, select the computer group you want to apply the updates to, click the red circle, and then choose Approved For Install. Repeat to apply the update to multiple computer groups.

6. To define a deadline (after which an update must be installed and users will not be given the option of delaying the update), right-click the computer group, choose Deadline, and then select the deadline.

7. Click OK.

8. If a license agreement appears, click I Accept.

> **NOTE REMOVING UPDATES**
>
> If you've previously applied updates to computers, you can choose Approved For Removal to remove the update. Most updates do not support automated removal, however, and WSUS will report an error in the Approval Progress dialog box. To remove these updates, follow the instructions in "Removing Updates" later in this lesson.

The Approval Progress dialog box appears as WSUS applies the updates.

9. Examine any errors displayed in the Approval Progress dialog box, and then click Close.

Declining Updates

After approving necessary updates, you can decline updates that you do not want to install on computers. Declining updates does not directly affect client computers; it only helps you organize updates in the WSUS console.

To decline updates, follow these steps:

1. In the Update Services console, right-click the update you want to decline, and then choose Decline.

2. In the Decline Update dialog box, click Yes.

To review updates that have been declined, from the Approval drop-down list in the Windows Update console, select Declined. Then click Refresh.

Viewing Reports

You can view detailed information about updates, computers, and synchronization by using the Reports node in the Update Services console, as shown in Figure 9-5.

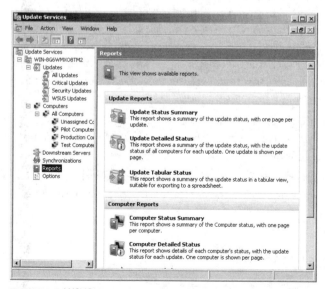

FIGURE 9-5 WSUS reports

WSUS provides the following reports:

- **Update Status Summary** As shown in Figure 9-6, this report displays detailed information about every update that you choose to report on, including the full description (provided by Microsoft), the computer groups the update has been approved for, and the number of computers the update has been installed on.

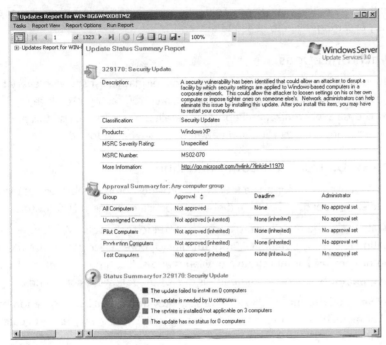

FIGURE 9-6 Update Status Summary report

- **Update Detailed Status** In addition to the information shown for the Update Status Summary report (which is shown on odd-numbered pages), this report shows the update status for all computers for each update on even-numbered pages, allowing you to determine exactly which computers have the update installed. This report is useful if you determine that a security exploit has been released and you need to quickly identify any computers that might be vulnerable because a critical update has not been applied.

- **Update Tabular Status** This report provides data similar to the previous two reports but uses a table format that can be exported to a spreadsheet.

- **Computer Status Summary** This report displays update information for every computer in your organization. It is useful if you are interested in auditing specific computers.

- **Computer Detailed Status** In addition to the information shown for the Computer Status Summary report, this report shows whether each update has been installed on each of your computers.

- **Computer Tabular Status**   This report provides data similar to the previous two reports but uses a table format that can be exported to a spreadsheet.
- **Synchronization Results**   This report displays the results of the last synchronization.

When you open a report, you can configure options to filter the information shown in the report. For example, for update reports, you can choose which products to display updates for. After configuring the options, click Run Report to display the report. The last page of the report displays a summary of settings used to generate the report.

Managing Synchronizations

The Synchronizations node in the Update Services console displays a list showing every time WSUS has retrieved a list of updates from the upstream server. You can right-click any synchronization and then choose Synchronization Report for detailed information. Use this node to verify that synchronizations are occurring and new updates are being found.

Administering WSUS from the Command Line

WSUS includes the WSUSUtil command-line tool, which provides some capabilities not offered by the WSUS console. The tool does not have the same capabilities as the WSUS console.

When you install WSUS, the setup wizard adds WSUSUtil to the \Tools subfolder within the WSUS installation folder (by default, C:\Program Files\Update Services\). To use the tool, open a command prompt with administrative privileges and select the tool's folder. Then, run **WSUSUtil <*command*>**, where <*command*> is one of the following commands:

- **ConfigureSSL**   Updates the WSUS server registry key after the IIS configuration has changed. For more information, read "Configuring WSUS to Use an SSL Certificate" later in this lesson.
- **HealthMonitoring**   Configures health monitoring values in the database by using the values you specify. For a list of health monitoring parameters, run **WSUSUtil HealthMonitoring /?**.
- **Export**   Exports update metadata to an export package file, which you can import on a downstream WSUS server to synchronize it without using a network connection. Typically, you would copy the export package file to an external hard disk, connect it to the downstream WSUS server, and then import it. This process reduces the bandwidth that would be required to transfer a large amount of updates.
- **Import**   Imports an export package file created with the Export command.
- **MoveContent**   Use this command to move WSUS files to a different location on the local computer.
- **ListFrontEndServers**   Lists the front-end servers related to this WSUS server.
- **DeleteFrontEndServer**   Deletes the specified front-end server from the WSUS database.
- **CheckHealth**   Adds an entry in the Application Event Log describing the health of the WSUS server.

- **Reset**   Checks that every update metadata row in the database has corresponding update files stored in the file system. When update files are missing or corrupted, this command causes WSUS to download them again.

- **ListInactiveApprovals**   Returns a list of update titles with approvals that are in a permanently inactive state because of a change in server language settings.

- **RemoveInactiveApprovals**   Removes approvals for updates that are in a permanently inactive state because of a change in WSUS server language settings.

- **UseCustomWebsite**   Changes the port number used by the WSUS web services from 80 to 8530 or vice versa.

Several of the commands require additional parameters. For detailed information about any command, run **WSUSUtil <command> /?**.

You can also configure WSUS by accessing the Application Programming Interfaces (APIs) using Windows PowerShell. First, install the WSUS console on the computer you will use to develop and run the script. With the WSUS console installed, you will be able to access the Microsoft.UpdateServices.Administration namespace. For detailed information about the APIs available, read "Microsoft.UpdateServices.Administration Namespace" at *http://msdn.microsoft.com/en-us/library/microsoft.updateservices.administration.aspx*.

Configuring WSUS to Use an SSL Certificate

If you want to encrypt communications between WSUS clients and your WSUS server, you can either require IPsec communications or add an SSL certificate to IIS. For information about configuring IPsec, refer to Chapter 6, "Protecting Network Traffic with IPsec."

The steps you follow to configure an SSL certificate for WSUS differ depending on whether you are using IIS 6 and Windows Server 2003 or IIS 7 and Windows Server 2008. At a high level, you must first require SSL on the WSUS virtual directories in IIS, and then use the WSUSUtil tool to configure a required WSUS registry setting.

If you are using IIS 6 and Windows Server 2003, follow these steps:

1. On the WSUS server, open Internet Information Services (IIS) Manager. Expand Web Sites, and then expand the website for the WSUS server.

2. Perform the following steps on the APIRemoting30, ClientWebService, DSSAuthWebService, ServerSyncWebService, and SimpleAuthWebService virtual directories that reside under the WSUS website:

   a. Right-click the website or virtual directory, and then click Properties.

   b. Click the Directory Security tab, and then click Edit in the Secure Communications section.

   c. Select Require Secure Channel (SSL), and then click OK.

   d. Click OK to close the properties for the virtual root.

3. Run the following command from <*WSUS_Installation_Folder*>\Tools: **WSUSUtil.exe configuressl <*intranet_WSUS_hostname*>**.

If you are using IIS 7 and Windows Server 2008 or IIS 7.5 and Windows Server 2008 R2, follow these steps:

1. On the WSUS server, open Internet Information Services (IIS) Manager. Expand Sites, and then expand the website for the WSUS server.

2. Perform the following steps on the APIRemoting30, ClientWebService, DSSAuthWebService, ServerSyncWebService, and SimpleAuthWebService virtual directories that reside under the WSUS website:

   a. In Features View, double-click SSL Settings.

   b. On the SSL Settings page, select Require SSL.

   c. In the Actions pane, click Apply.

3. Run the following command from *<WSUS_Installation_Folder>*\Tools: **WSUSUtil.exe configuressl *<intranet_WSUS_hostname>***.

Troubleshooting Problems Installing Updates

Occasionally, you might experience a problem installing an update. You can use the WSUS console to identify clients that have updates installed, as well as clients that have been unable to install updates. To gather more information about a specific failed installation, you can troubleshoot the problem at the client computer.

The sections that follow describe how to troubleshoot server-side and client-side problems.

Troubleshooting WSUS

WSUS creates three logs files that can be useful in troubleshooting. The default locations are:

- **The Application event log**   A log that stores events related to synchronization, Update Services console errors, and WSUS database errors with a source of Windows Server Update Services. Most events provide detailed information about the cause of the problem and guidance for further troubleshooting the problem. For additional help with specific errors, search for the error at *http://support.microsoft.com*. The Application event log should always be the first place you check when troubleshooting WSUS errors.

- **C:\Program Files\Update Services\LogFiles\Change.txt**   A text file that stores a record of every update installation, synchronization, and WSUS configuration change. The log entries aren't detailed, however. For example, if an administrator changes a configuration setting, WSUS records only "WSUS configuration has been changed" in the log file.

- **C:\Program Files\Update Services\LogFiles\SoftwareDistribution.txt**   An extremely detailed text log file used primarily for debugging purposes by Microsoft support.

Troubleshooting the Windows Update Client

To identify the source of the problem causing an update to fail, follow these steps:

1. Examine the %SystemRoot%\WindowsUpdate.log file to verify that the client is contacting the correct update server and to identify any error messages. For detailed information about how to read the WindowsUpdate.log file, refer to Microsoft Knowledge Base article 902093 at *http://support.microsoft.com/kb/902093/.*

2. Verify that the client can connect to the WSUS server by opening a web browser and visiting *http://<WSUSServerName>/iuident.cab.* Being prompted to download the file means that the client can reach the WSUS server and the problem is not a connectivity issue. Otherwise, you could have a name resolution or connectivity issue, or WSUS is not configured correctly.

3. If you use Group Policy to configure the Windows Update client, use the Resultant Set of Policy (RSOP) tool (Rsop.msc) to verify the configuration. Within RSOP, browse to the Computer Configuration\Administrative Templates\Windows Components\Windows Update node and verify the configuration settings.

If you have identified a problem and made a configuration change that you hope will resolve it, restart the Windows Update service on the client computer to make the change take effect and begin another update cycle. You can do this by using the Services console or by running the following two commands:

```
net stop wuauserv
net start wuauserv
```

Within 6 to 10 minutes, Windows Update will attempt to contact your update server.

To make Windows Update begin querying the WSUS server, run the following command:

```
wuauclt /a
```

Although the WindowsUpdate.log file provides the most detailed information and should typically be the first place you look when troubleshooting, you can view high-level Windows Update–related events in the System event log, with a source of WindowsUpdateClient. The Windows Update service adds events each time an update is downloaded or installed and when a computer needs to be restarted to apply an update. The Windows Update service also adds a Warning event (with Event ID 16) when it cannot connect to the automatic updates service, a sign that the client cannot reach your WSUS server.

Even more detailed information can be found in the Applications And Services Logs\Microsoft \Windows\WindowsUpdateClient\Operational log. The Windows Update service adds an event to this log each time it connects to or loses connectivity with a WSUS server; checks for updates (even if no updates are available), as shown in Figure 9-7; and experiences an error.

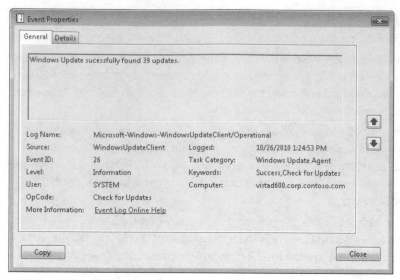

FIGURE 9-7 Verifying that the Windows Update client found available updates

To view which updates have been installed on a computer running Windows 7 or Windows Server 2008 R2, follow these steps:

1. Click Start, and then click Control Panel. Click the System And Security link, and then click the Windows Update link.

2. Click View Update History.

Windows Update displays the complete list of installed updates, as illustrated by Figure 9-8. You can double-click any update to view more detailed information.

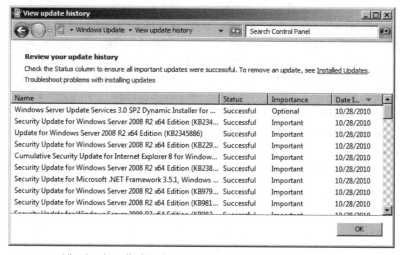

FIGURE 9-8 Viewing installed updates

Removing Updates

Occasionally, an update might cause a compatibility problem. If you experience a problem with an application or a Windows feature after installing an update, you can uninstall the update to determine whether the update is related to the problem.

To remove an update, follow these steps:

Use Windows Update to view the update history, as described in the section "Troubleshooting the Windows Update Client" earlier in this chapter. View the details of each update to identify the update that might be causing a problem. Make note of the Knowledge Base (KB) number for the update.

1. Click Start, and then click Control Panel.

2. Under Programs, click the Uninstall A Program link.

3. In the upper-left corner of the window, click the View Installed Updates link.

4. Select the update you want to remove by using the KB number you noted in the paragraph preceding step 1. Then click Uninstall.

5. Follow the prompts that appear, and restart the computer if required.

If removing the update does not resolve the problem, you should reapply the update. Then contact the application developer (in the case of a program incompatibility) or your Microsoft support representative to inform them of the incompatibility.

PRACTICE   Deploying Updates with WSUS

In this practice, you configure WSUS on a server, use Group Policy settings to configure client computers, and then approve and distribute updates.

EXERCISE 1   Installing WSUS

In this exercise, you add WSUS to a server that has Internet access. To minimize storage requirements, you configure the WSUS server to direct clients to retrieve updates directly from Microsoft.

1. On Dcsrv1, open Windows Internet Explorer to download and install the Microsoft Report Viewer Redistributable 2008, available at *http://www.microsoft.com/downloads /en/details.aspx?familyid=CC96C246-61E5-4D9E-BB5F-416D75A1B9EF*. This component is required for the WSUS user interface. If Internet Explorer prevents you from installing the redistributable, add download.microsoft.com to the list of trusted sites in Internet Explorer.

2. In Server Manager, select the Roles node. Then, right-click Roles and click Add Roles.

3. If the Before You Begin page appears, click Next.

4. On the Select Server Roles page, select Windows Server Update Services. If the Add Role Services Required For Windows Server Update Services dialog box appears, click Add Required Role Services. Click Next.

5. If the Web Server page appears, click Next twice.

6. On the Windows Server Update Services page, click Next.

7. On the Confirm Installation Services page, click Install. The Windows Server Update Services Setup Wizard appears.

   Unlike most server roles, the Add Roles Wizard downloads the latest version of WSUS from the Internet. Therefore, you must have Internet access. If the connection fails, verify that you can connect to the Internet and try again. Because Server Manager downloads the latest version of WSUS, the following steps (based on WSUS 3.0 SP2) might vary.

8. In the Windows Server Update Services Setup Wizard, on the Welcome page, click Next.

9. On the Select Update Services page, clear the Store Updates Locally check box. This will configure WSUS to direct client computers to download updates directly from Microsoft. In production environments, you should store updates locally so that they need to be downloaded only once. However, in a test environment, not storing updates locally reduces the storage and bandwidth requirements.

10. On the Database Options page, click Next.

11. On the Web Site Selection page, accept the default setting by clicking Next.

12. On the Ready To Install Windows Server Update Services 3.0 page, click Next.

13. On the final page, click Finish. The Windows Server Update Services Configuration Wizard appears.

14. On the Before You Begin page, click Next.

15. On the Join The Microsoft Update Improvement Program, click Next.

16. On the Choose Upstream Server page, leave the default setting selected. This will configure the server to synchronize directly from Microsoft Update. If you had an existing WSUS server on the same network, it would be more efficient to synchronize with that server. Click Next.

17. On the Specify Proxy Server page, click Next.

18. On the Connect To Upstream Server page, click Start Connecting. Wait several minutes until the download completes, and then click Next.

19. On the Choose Products page, browse the list of products for which updates are available. Notice that Office and Windows are selected by default. Select Microsoft\SQL Server, and then click Next.

20. On the Choose Classifications page, notice that some types of updates are not synchronized by default. Select all check boxes, and then click Next.

21. On the Set Sync Schedule page, click Synchronize Automatically. Then, click Next.

22. On the Finished page, click Finish.

23. Returning to the Add Roles Wizard, click Close.

EXERCISE 2 Configuring Client Computers to Retrieve Updates

In this exercise, you update Group Policy settings to configure client computers to retrieve updates from your WSUS server, rather than directly from Microsoft.

1. Open the GPO you want to use to distribute the configuration settings. In the Group Policy Management Editor, select the Computer Configuration\Policies\Administrative Templates\Windows Components\Windows Update node.

2. In the details pane, double-click Specify Intranet Microsoft Update Service Location. The Specify Intranet Microsoft Update Service Location Properties dialog box appears.

3. Select Enabled. In both the Set The Intranet Update Service For Detecting Updates box and the Set The Intranet Statistics Server box, type **http://Dcsrv1** (or the name of your WSUS server). Click OK.

4. Double-click Configure Automatic Updates. The Configure Automatic Updates Properties dialog box appears.

5. Select Enabled. Configure the automatic update settings. For example, to have updates automatically installed, from the Configure Automatic Updating drop-down list, select 4 - Auto Download And Schedule The Install. Click OK.

   Next, log on to Boston as a member of the Administrators group. Run the command **gpupdate /force** to cause the client computer to apply the updated Group Policy settings. Then restart the Windows Update service to cause Boston to immediately connect to the WSUS server.

EXERCISE 3 Approving Updates

In this exercise, you approve an update to be deployed to your client computer, Boston.

1. On Dcsrv1, in Server Manager, select Roles\Windows Server Update Services\Updates\All Updates.

2. On the toolbar at the top of the details pane, from the Approval drop-down list, select Unapproved.

3. From the Status drop-down list, select Any. Click Refresh to display the updates.

4. Select a recent update that would apply to Boston (your client computer). Right-click the selected updates, and then choose Approve.

> **NOTE** REMOVING THE UPDATE FOR TESTING PURPOSES
> If the update has already been applied to Boston, remove the update by using the Programs tool in Control Panel.

5. In the Approve Updates dialog box, select the All Computers computer group, and then click the red circle to choose Approved For Install. In a production environment, you would typically create several computer groups. Click OK.

6. If a license agreement appears, click I Accept. The Approval Progress dialog box appears as WSUS applies the updates.

7. Examine any errors displayed in the Approval Progress dialog box to verify that the update can be applied to Boston, and then click Close.

8. In the Update Services console, select the Computers\All Computers node. Then, select Any on the Status drop-down list, and click the Refresh button. The Boston client computer should appear on the list, having had sufficient time to connect to the WSUS server after refreshing Group Policy. If it has not appeared yet, wait another few minutes.

On the Boston client computer, restart the Windows Update service. Wait 15 minutes or more, and Windows Update should display a notification that an update is available. For detailed information, examine the System log on Boston for Windows Update events.

Lesson Summary

- After installing WSUS and synchronizing updates from the upstream server, you should configure computer groups to allow you to selectively distribute updates to clients. Next, approve or decline updates and wait for them to be distributed to clients. Use reports to verify that the update process is successful and identify any clients who have been unable to install important updates.

- If you experience problems with WSUS, examine the Application event log on the WSUS server. Although WSUS also creates two text-based log files, the Application event log contains the most useful troubleshooting information. If a client experiences problems connecting to the WSUS server or installing updates, begin troubleshooting by examining the %SystemRoot%\WindowsUpdate.log file.

- Although you can remove some updates using WSUS, you typically need to manually remove updates from client computers by using the Programs tool in Control Panel.

Lesson Review

You can use the following questions to test your knowledge of the information in Lesson 2, "Using Windows Server Update Services." The questions are also available on the companion CD if you prefer to review them in electronic form.

> **NOTE** **ANSWERS**
>
> Answers to these questions and explanations of why each answer choice is correct or incorrect are located in the "Answers" section at the end of the book.

1. Recently, you used MBSA to audit your client computers for the presence of specific security updates. You found several computers that did not have the updates installed. How can you determine why the update installation failed? (Choose all that apply.)

A. Examine the System log on the client computer.

B. Examine the Applications And Services Logs\Microsoft\Windows\Windows UpdateClient\Operational on the client computer.

C. Examine the System log on the WSUS server.

D. Examine the %SystemRoot%\WindowsUpdate.log file.

2. You have recently deployed WSUS, and you need to verify that updates are being distributed successfully. Which of the following pieces of information can you get from the Update Status Summary report?

   A. Which computer groups a particular update has been approved for

   B. Which computers have successfully installed an update

   C. Whether an update can be removed by using WSUS

   D. The number of computers that failed to install an update

3. You are in the process of deploying WSUS to your organization. Currently, you are configuring client computers to be members of different computer groups so that you can stagger update deployments. How can you configure the computer group for a computer? (Choose all that apply.)

   A. Enable the Configure Automatic Updates policy.

   B. Configure the Enable Client-Side Targeting Group Policy setting.

   C. In the Update Services console, right-click the computer, and then choose Change Membership.

   D. In the Update Services console, drag the computers to the appropriate computer group.

Chapter Review

To further practice and reinforce the skills you learned in this chapter, you can perform the following tasks:

- Review the chapter summary.
- Review the list of key terms introduced in this chapter.
- Complete the case scenarios. These scenarios set up real-world situations involving the topics of this chapter and ask you to create a solution.
- Complete the suggested practices.
- Take a practice test.

Chapter Summary

- WSUS gives you control over the approval and distribution of updates from Microsoft to your client computers. A WSUS server can copy updates from Microsoft and store them locally. Then client computers will download updates from your WSUS server instead of downloading them from Microsoft across the Internet. To support organizations with multiple offices, downstream WSUS servers can synchronize updates, approvals, and configuration settings from upstream WSUS servers, allowing you to design a hierarchy that can scale to any capacity.

- Installing WSUS also requires installing IIS, but WSUS can coexist with other IIS websites. After WSUS is installed, you can manage WSUS with the Windows Update console, available from the Administrative Tools menu on the WSUS server. First, you should begin synchronizing the WSUS server with updates from Microsoft. Then, create the different computer groups you will use to deploy updates selectively to different computers. Next, configure client computers to contact your local WSUS servers instead of the Microsoft Update servers on the Internet and add client computers to the appropriate computer groups.

Key Terms

Do you know what these key terms mean? You can check your answers by looking up the terms in the glossary at the end of the book.

- downstream server
- upstream server
- Windows Server Update Services (WSUS)

Case Scenarios

In the following case scenarios, you will apply what you've learned about how to design and configure a WSUS infrastructure. You can find answers to these questions in the "Answers" section at the end of this book.

Case Scenario 1: Planning a Basic WSUS Infrastructure

You are a systems engineer for City Power & Light. Currently, you have configured all client computers to download updates directly from Microsoft and automatically install them. However, after a recent service pack release, you notice that the bill from your Internet service provider (ISP) for Internet bandwidth jumped significantly after Microsoft released a large service pack to Windows Update (you pay per usage with your contract).

You'd like to use WSUS to reduce your bandwidth usage to your headquarters, where you have approximately 250 computers. Eventually, you'd like to begin testing updates before deploying them. However, you do not have the staff to perform the testing, so for the time being you want updates to be automatically approved and installed.

You go into your manager's office to discuss the ISP bill and how you can avoid it in the future. Answer the following questions for your manager:

1. How can WSUS reduce your bandwidth utilization?
2. How many WSUS servers will you need?
3. How can you configure WSUS to automatically approve updates?

Case Scenario 2: Planning a Complex WSUS Infrastructure

You are a systems engineer working for Northwind Traders, an international company with offices around the globe. Your headquarters are in London, and you have branch offices in New York, Mexico City, Tokyo, and Casablanca. All offices have high-speed Internet connections, and they are interconnected with VPNs using a full mesh architecture. In other words, each of the five offices is connected directly to the other four offices.

Currently, the London IT department manages both the London and New York offices. The Mexico City, Tokyo, and Casablanca offices each have their own IT departments. As you are beginning to deploy Windows Server 2008, you are evaluating WSUS and would like to create an architecture that will meet the needs of each of your five locations.

INTERVIEWS

Following is a list of company personnel interviewed and their statements:

- **Mexico City IT Manager** "I talked with the IT managers in Tokyo and Casablanca, and we each have unique technical requirements, languages, client operating systems, and testing procedures. Therefore, we need to be able to manage our own update approvals. However, we're open to synchronizing updates from a central server, if that's your preference."

- **Your Manager** "It doesn't matter to me whether you synchronize updates between offices or from the Internet. Because we're using a VPN, it all crosses the same Internet connection anyway. So it's up to you."

QUESTIONS

Answer the following questions for your manager:

1. How many WSUS servers do you need, and where will you locate them?
2. Which of the WSUS servers will be replicas, and which will be managed independently?

Suggested Practice

To help you successfully master the exam objectives presented in this chapter, complete the following tasks.

Configure Windows Server Update Services Server Settings

For this task, you should watch the videos listed in Practice 1. Then, complete at least Practices 2 and 4. If your organization currently uses WSUS, also complete Practice 3.

- **Practice 1** Watch two videos about WSUS: "What's new with WSUS Service Pack 3" at *http://www.youtube.com/watch?v=hK35ZDdqnK0*, and "WSUS Architectures" at *http://www.youtube.com/watch?v=GTgyVhaaVrw.*

- **Practice 2** Examine the WindowsUpdate.log file on your computer (or any production computer that has been running for a long time). When did failures occur and what caused them? Were the failed updates successfully installed later?

- **Practice 3** If your organization currently uses WSUS, view the different reports that are available to determine how many computers are up to date and which updates failed most often during installation.

- **Practice 4** Consider your organization's current network (including any remote offices) and the WAN connections. How would you design a WSUS infrastructure to most efficiently distribute updates? If you currently use WSUS, is the design optimal?

Take a Practice Test

The practice tests on this book's companion CD offer many options. For example, you can test yourself on just the content covered in this chapter, or you can test yourself on all the 70-642 certification exam content. You can set up the test so that it closely simulates the experience of taking a certification exam, or you can set it up in study mode so that you can look at the correct answers and explanations after you answer each question.

> **MORE INFO** **PRACTICE TESTS**
>
> For details about all the practice test options available, see "How to Use the Practice Tests" in this book's Introduction.

CHAPTER 10

Monitoring Computers

A solid understanding of how to monitor computers in your organization is vital for both quickly troubleshooting problems and responding to problems before they become critical. For troubleshooting problems, monitoring allows you to gather detailed information about a computer's state, such as the processor, memory, and disk utilization. Monitoring can also allow you to be proactive and identify warning signs that indicate an impending problem before the problem becomes serious.

This chapter describes three useful monitoring techniques: event monitoring, performance monitoring, and network monitoring.

Exam objectives in this chapter:

- Configure event logs.
- Configure performance monitoring.
- Gather network data.

Lessons in this chapter:

- Lesson 1: Monitoring Events   **523**
- Lesson 2: Monitoring Performance and Reliability   **539**
- Lesson 3: Using Network Monitor and Simple Network Management Protocol   **554**

Before You Begin

To complete the lessons in this chapter, you should be familiar with Windows networking and be comfortable with the following tasks:

- Adding roles to a computer running Windows Server 2008 R2
- Configuring Active Directory domain controllers and joining computers to a domain
- Basic network configuration, including configuring IP settings

You will also need the following nonproduction hardware, connected to test networks:

- A computer named Dcsrv1 that is a domain controller in the Nwtraders.msft domain. This computer must have at least one network interface that is connected to the Internet.

> **NOTE**   **COMPUTER AND DOMAIN NAMES**
>
> The computer and domain names you use will not affect these exercises. The practices in this chapter refer to these computer names for simplicity, however.

- A computer named Boston that is a member of the Nwtraders.msft domain.

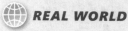

REAL WORLD

Tony Northrup

What Process Monitor (available at *http://technet.microsoft.com/en-us /sysinternals/bb896645.aspx*) is to troubleshooting application problems, Network Monitor is to troubleshooting network problems.

When errors occur, applications often present useless messages. For example, consider an email client that is unable to connect to a server. The email client is likely to show the user a message such as, "Unable to connect to server. Please contact your network administrator." If you use Network Monitor to capture the unsuccessful connection attempt, you can quickly determine whether the cause of the problem is connectivity, name resolution, authentication, or something else.

When I worked with the original version of Network Monitor, network administrators weren't as concerned about security. As a result, communications were rarely encrypted and Network Monitor could capture traffic in clear text. This made troubleshooting network problems easy—but it also made it easy to collect people's passwords on the network.

To address that privacy risk, most applications that transfer private data now provide some form of application-layer security (including email) and more organizations are using IPsec to encrypt data at the network layer. Encrypted packets appear as garbage in Network Monitor, which can interpret only the headers. If you need to troubleshoot a network problem and encryption is preventing you from interpreting the data, consider temporarily disabling IPsec or application-layer encryption until you have isolated the problem.

Lesson 1: Monitoring Events

Windows has always stored a great deal of important information in the event logs. Unfortunately, with versions of Windows released prior to Windows Vista, that information could be very hard to access. Event logs were always stored on the local computer, and finding important events among the vast quantity of informational events could be very difficult.

With Windows Vista, Windows 7, Windows Server 2003 R2, Windows Server 2008, and Windows Server 2008 R2, you can collect events from remote computers (including computers running Windows XP) and detect problems such as low disk space before they become more serious. Additionally, Windows now includes many more event logs to make it easier to troubleshoot problems with a specific Windows component or application. This lesson describes how to manage events in Windows Server 2008 R2 and Windows 7.

> **After this lesson, you will be able to:**
> - Describe how event forwarding works.
> - Configure computers to support event forwarding and create a subscription.
>
> **Estimated lesson time: 35 minutes**

Using Event Viewer

You can open Event Viewer from within Server Manager by selecting the Diagnostics \Event Viewer node. Alternatively, you can open the stand-alone version of Event Viewer from Administrative Tools on the Start menu.

The log files are contained in two subnodes: Windows Logs and Applications And Services Logs. Windows Logs contains four subnodes:

- **Application** Contains events generated by applications. Many applications do not generate events, however, and many of those applications store events in a custom event log located within Applications And Services Logs.
- **Security** Contains auditing events that Windows adds when a user accesses or attempts to access a resource that has been configured for auditing. For an overview of auditing, read "Audit Policy" at *http://technet.microsoft.com/library/cc766468.aspx*.
- **Setup** Contains events generated while installing and updating Windows and when installing or removing roles and features.
- **System** Contains core system events. Other system events are contained with Applications And Services Logs.
- **Forwarded Events** Contains events forwarded to this computer from other computers. Event forwarding is discussed later in this lesson.

To view each of these types of events, click the node, and then double-click an event.

The Applications And Services Logs node contains dozens of event logs, each for a specific feature of Windows. For example, the Directory Service subnode contains Active Directory Domain Controller events. Similarly, events generated by a DHCP server are visible within the Applications And Services Logs\Microsoft\Windows\DHCP-Server node.

EXAM TIP

You certainly should not attempt to memorize all the application and service logs. However, you should familiarize yourself with the list and remember to look within Applications And Services Logs when searching for detailed troubleshooting information about a specific Windows feature.

Filtering Events

During the troubleshooting process, you might decide to browse an event log looking for information about a specific application or Windows feature. The biggest challenge of using Event Viewer is the sheer number of events. Busy servers generate thousands of events every day, so browsing events to look for something useful is impractical.

A more efficient way to find meaningful events is to create a filter. To create a filter, follow these steps:

1. Select an event log, such as Windows Logs\System.

2. Right-click the log, and then click Filter Current Log.

3. Use the Filter Current Log dialog box to specify which events you want to view. You can configure the following settings:

    ■ **Logged**   Select a time range from this list to display only recent events.

    ■ **Event Level**   Events have one of five urgency levels assigned. From least to most urgent, the levels are: Verbose, Information, Warning, Error, and Critical.

    ■ **Event Logs**   Choose which event logs to search. When you create a filter, you can only search the current log. To search multiple logs, create a custom view instead, as discussed in the next section.

    ■ **Event Sources**   When a feature or application adds an event to the event log, it specifies a source. Typically, these have meaningful names; however, if you cannot find an event, consider searching for it by using the Find feature in Event Viewer, and then making note of the exact Source name.

    ■ **Event IDs**   If you already know which events you are looking for, specify the Event IDs in this box.

    ■ **Task Category**   The category of the task.

    ■ **Keywords**   A list of predefined keywords you can search for.

    ■ **User**   The active user when the event was generated. Many events do not have this field.

    ■ **Computers**   The computer the event was generated on.

4. Click OK.

Event Viewer will display the list of events that match your filter criteria. After you create a filter, you can save it as a custom view (described in the next section) so that you can easily recall it later by clicking Save Filter To Custom View in the actions pane.

Using Custom Views

Custom views are filters that can display events from multiple logs. When you create a custom view, Event Viewer saves it within the Custom Views node so that you can quickly view the same set of events. Windows Server 2008 R2 also includes custom views within the Server Roles node for standard roles such as Active Directory Certificate Services, DNS Server, and File Server.

Automatically Responding to Events

Windows 7 regularly runs background tasks to maintain the system and respond to events. For example, Windows starts a task to optimize the disk layout by using defragmentation every Wednesday at 01:00. Similarly, if a memory-related event appears in the event log, Windows responds to this event by launching the Memory Diagnostic tool. To view built-in events, open Server Manager and expand the Configuration\Task Scheduler\Task Scheduler Library\Microsoft \Windows node. Then, browse to each of the subnodes.

EXAM TIP

The 70-642 exam objectives don't include Task Scheduler, so we won't discuss it in detail in this book. However, you do need to know how to launch a task in response to an event. Exercise 1 at the end of this lesson walks you through the process of creating a task when a specific event appears, which should be all you need to know for the exam. However, for the real world and other Microsoft certifications, you should spend some time familiarizing yourself with the Task Scheduler capabilities and user interface.

One of the most useful ways to use Task Scheduler is to launch a task in response to a specific event type that appears in Event Viewer. You can respond to events in three ways:

- **Start A Program** Launches an application. Often, administrators write a script that carries out a series of tasks that they would otherwise need to manually perform, and automatically run that script when an event appears.

- **Send An E-mail** Sends an email by using the Simple Mail Transport Protocol (SMTP) server you specify. Often, administrators configure urgent events to be sent to a mobile device.

- **Display A Message** Displays a dialog box showing a message. This is typically useful only when a user needs to be notified of something happening on the computer.

To trigger a task when an event occurs, follow one of these three procedures:

- Find an example of the event in Event Viewer. Then, right-click the event and click Attach Task To This Event. A wizard will guide you through the process. Exercise 1 at the end of this lesson provides step-by-step instructions for this process.

- In Task Scheduler, click Create Basic Task in the actions pane. On the Trigger page of the wizard, select When A Specific Event Is Logged. Then, specify the Log, Source, and Event ID.

- Use the Schtasks command-line tool from a command prompt or a script. For example, to run a file named Respond.exe whenever event 177 is published in the System event log, run the following command:

```
SCHTASKS /Create /TN EventLog /TR respond.exe /SC ONEVENT /EC System /MO *[System/
EventID=177]
```

> **MORE INFO** **SCHEDULING TASKS AT THE COMMAND LINE**
>
> For complete details about using the Schtasks tool, read "Schtasks: Management Services" at *http://technet.microsoft.com/library/cc772785.aspx*.

Configuring Event Forwarding

With event forwarding, you can send events that match specific criteria to an administrative computer, allowing you to centralize event management. This allows you to view a single log and see the most important events from computers anywhere in your organization, rather than you needing to connect to the local event logs on individual computers. With event forwarding, the critical information in the event log becomes much more accessible.

Event forwarding uses Hypertext Transfer Protocol (HTTP) or HTTPS (Hypertext Transfer Protocol Secure) to send events from a forwarding computer to a collecting computer. Instead of using the standard TCP port numbers of 80 and 443, HTTP and HTTPS use ports 5985 and 5986, respectively. Because event forwarding uses the same protocols used to browse websites, it works through most firewalls and proxy servers. Whether event forwarding uses HTTP or HTTPS, it is encrypted.

Using event forwarding requires you to configure both the forwarding and collecting computers. On the forwarding computer, start the Windows Remote Management service. On the collecting computer, start both the Windows Remote Management service and the Windows Event Collector service.

Additionally, the forwarding computer must have a Windows Firewall exception for the HTTP protocol. As described later in this lesson, you might also need to create a Windows Firewall exception on the collecting computer, depending on the delivery optimization technique you choose. Only Windows Vista, Windows 7, Windows Server 2003 R2, Windows Server 2008, and Windows Server 2008 R2 can act as collecting computers. Only Windows XP with Service Pack 2, Windows Server 2003 with Service Pack 1 or 2, Windows Server 2003 R2, Windows Vista, Windows 7, Windows Server 2008, and Windows Server 2008 R2 can act as forwarding computers.

> **NOTE** **FORWARDING EVENTS FROM WINDOWS XP AND WINDOWS SERVER 2003**
>
> Before computers running Windows XP or Windows Server 2003 can act as forwarding computers, you must install WS-Management 1.1 and either Windows XP Service Pack 2 or Windows Sever 2003 Service Pack 1 or later. For more information, see *http://go.microsoft.com/fwlink/?Linkid=100895*.

The sections that follow describe step-by-step how to configure computers for event forwarding.

Configuring the Forwarding Computer

To configure a computer running Windows Vista, Windows 7, Windows Server 2008, or Windows Server 2008 R2 to forward events, follow these steps:

1. At a command prompt with administrative privileges, run the following command to configure the Windows Remote Management service:

   ```
   winrm quickconfig
   ```

   Windows displays a message similar to the following (other changes might be required, depending on how the operating system is configured):

   ```
   WinRM is not set up to allow remote access to this machine for management.
   The following changes must be made:

   Create a WinRM listener on HTTP://* to accept WS-Man requests to any IP on this
   machine.
   Enable the WinRM firewall exception.

   Make these changes [y/n]?
   ```

2. Type **Y**, and then press Enter.

   WinRM (the Windows Remote Management command-line tool) configures the computer to accept WS-Management requests from other computers. Depending on the current configuration, this might involve making the following changes:

   - On computers running Windows Vista and Windows 7, setting the Windows Remote Management (WS-Management) service to Automatic (Delayed Start) and starting the service. This service is already started on computers running Windows Server 2008 and Windows Server 2008 R2.

   - Configuring a Windows Remote Management HTTP listener.

   - Creating a Windows Firewall exception to allow incoming connections to the Windows Remote Management service using HTTP. This exception applies only to the Domain and Private profiles; traffic will still be blocked while the computer is connected to Public networks.

Next, you must add the computer account of the collector computer to the local Event Log Readers group on each of the forwarding computers. You can do this manually or automatically from a script or command prompt by running the following command:

```
net localgroup "Event Log Readers" <computer_name>$@<domain_name> /add
```

For example, to add the computer SERVER1 in the contoso.com domain, you would run the following command:

```
net localgroup "Event Log Readers" server1$@contoso.com /add
```

Configuring the Collecting Computer

To configure a computer running Windows Vista, Windows 7, Windows Server 2008, or Windows Server 2008 R2 to collect events, open a command prompt with administrative privileges. Then, run the following command to configure the Windows Event Collector service:

```
wecutil qc
```

In Windows Server 2008 and Windows Server 2008 R2, you can also simply select the Subscriptions node in the console tree of Event Viewer. Event Viewer will prompt you to configure the Windows Event Collector service to start automatically, as shown in Figure 10-1.

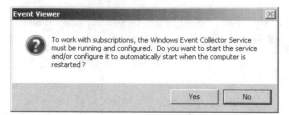

FIGURE 10-1 Event Viewer prompting the user to configure the computer as a collector

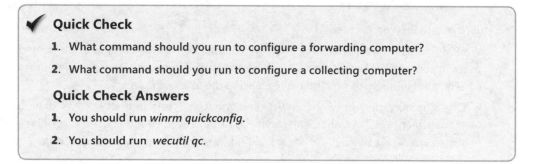

> ### ✔ Quick Check
>
> 1. What command should you run to configure a forwarding computer?
> 2. What command should you run to configure a collecting computer?
>
> ### Quick Check Answers
>
> 1. You should run *winrm quickconfig*.
> 2. You should run *wecutil qc*.

Creating an Event Subscription

To create a subscription on a collecting computer running Windows Server 2008 or Windows Server 2008 R2, follow these steps. (The steps on a computer running Windows Vista or Windows 7 are similar but slightly different.)

1. In Event Viewer (under the Diagnostics node in Server Manager), right-click Subscriptions, and then choose Create Subscription.

2. If the Event Viewer dialog box appears, click Yes to configure the Windows Event Collector service. The Subscription Properties dialog box appears, as shown in Figure 10-2.

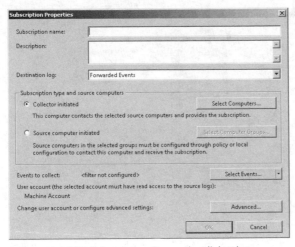

FIGURE 10-2 The Subscription Properties dialog box

3. In the Subscription Name box, type a name for the subscription. Optionally, type a description.

4. You can create two types of subscriptions:

   - **Collector initiated** The collecting computer contacts the source computers to retrieve events. Click the Select Computers button. In the Computers dialog box, click Add Domain Computers, choose the computers you want to monitor, and then click OK. Click the Test button to verify that the source computer is properly configured, and then click OK. If you have not run the winrm quickconfig command on the source computer, the connectivity test will fail. Click OK to return to the Subscription Properties dialog box.

   - **Source computer initiated** The forwarding computers contact the collecting computer. Select Source Computer Initiated, and then click Select Computer Groups. Click Add Domain Computers or Add Non-Domain Computers to add either type of computer. If you add nondomain computers, each needs to have a computer certificate installed. Click Add Certificates to add the certification authority (CA) that issued the certificate to the nondomain computer.

5. Click the Select Events button to open the Query Filter dialog box. Use this dialog box to define the criteria that forwarded events must match. (Figure 10-3 shows an example configuration.) Then click OK.

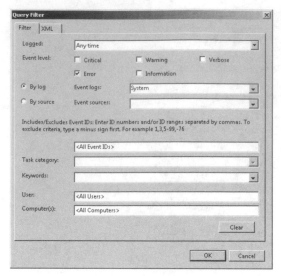

FIGURE 10-3 The Query Filter dialog box

6. Optionally, click the Advanced button to open the Advanced Subscription Settings dialog box. You can configure three types of subscriptions:

   - **Normal** This option ensures reliable delivery of events and does not attempt to conserve bandwidth. It is the appropriate choice unless you need tighter control over bandwidth usage or need forwarded events delivered as quickly as possible. It uses pull delivery mode (where the collecting computer contacts the forwarding computer) and downloads five events at a time unless 15 minutes pass, in which case it downloads any events that are available.

   - **Minimize Bandwidth** This option reduces the network bandwidth consumed by event delivery and is a good choice if you are using event forwarding across a wide area network (WAN) or on a large number of computers on a local area network (LAN). It uses push delivery mode (where the forwarding computer contacts the collecting computer) to forward events every six hours.

   - **Minimize Latency** This option ensures that events are delivered with minimal delay. It is an appropriate choice if you are collecting alerts or critical events. It uses push delivery mode and sets a batch time-out of 30 seconds.

   Additionally, if you use a collector-initiated subscription, you can use the Advanced Subscription Settings dialog box to configure the user account the subscription uses. Whether you use the default Machine Account setting or specify a user, you will need to ensure that the account is a member of the forwarding computer's Event Log Readers group.

7. In the Subscription Properties dialog box, click OK to create the subscription.

By default, normal event subscriptions check for new events every 15 minutes. You can decrease this interval to reduce the delay in retrieving events. However, there is no graphical interface for configuring the delay; you must use the command-line Wecutil tool that you initially used to configure the collecting computer.

To adjust the event subscription delay, first create your subscription using Event Viewer. Then run the following two commands at a command prompt with administrative privileges:

```
wecutil ss <subscription_name> /cm:custom
wecutil ss <subscription_name> /hi:<milliseconds_delay>
```

For example, if you created a subscription named "Disk Events" and you wanted the delay to be two minutes, you would run the following commands:

```
wecutil ss "Disk Events" /cm:custom
wecutil ss "Disk Events" /hi:12000
```

If you need to check the interval, run the following command:

```
wecutil gs "<subscription_name>"
```

For example, to verify that the interval for the "Disk Events" subscription is one minute, you would run the following command and look for the HeartbeatInterval value:

```
wecutil gs "Disk Events"
```

The Minimize Bandwidth and Minimize Latency options both batch a default number of items at a time. You can determine the value of this default by typing the following command at a command prompt:

```
winrm get winrm/config
```

Configuring Event Forwarding to Use HTTPS

Although standard HTTP transport uses encryption for forwarded events, you can configure event forwarding to use the encrypted HTTPS protocol. In addition to the configuration steps described in the section entitled "Configuring the Forwarding Computer" earlier in this chapter, you must do the following:

- Configure the computer with a computer certificate. You can do this automatically in Active Directory environments by using an enterprise CA.

- Create a Windows Firewall exception for the TCP port number. Standard HTTPS uses port 443, but Windows Server 2008 R2 uses TCP port 5986 by default. If you have configured Minimize Bandwidth or Minimize Latency Event Delivery Optimization for the subscription, you must also configure a computer certificate and an HTTPS Windows Firewall exception on the collecting computer.

- Run the following command at a command prompt with administrative privileges:

  ```
  winrm quickconfig -transport:https
  ```

On the collecting computer, you must view the Advanced Subscription Settings dialog box for the subscription and set the Protocol box to HTTPS, as shown in Figure 10-4. Additionally, the collecting computer must trust the CA that issued the computer certificate (which happens automatically if an enterprise CA issued the certificate and both the forwarding computer and the collecting computer are part of the same Active Directory domain).

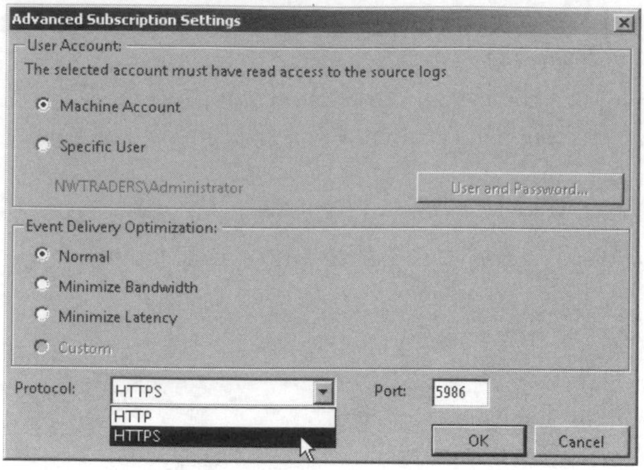

FIGURE 10-4 Changing the protocol to HTTPS

Troubleshooting Event Forwarding

If event forwarding doesn't seem to function properly, follow these steps to troubleshoot the problem:

1. Verify that you have waited long enough for the event to be forwarded. Forwarding events using the Normal setting can take up to 15 minutes. The delay might be longer if either the forwarding or the collection computer has recently restarted, because the Windows Remote Management service is set to start automatically, but with a delay so that it doesn't impact startup performance. The 15-minute counter doesn't start until after the Windows Remote Management service starts.

2. Check the Applications And Services Logs\Microsoft\Windows\Eventlog-ForwardingPlugin \Operational event log and verify that the subscription was created successfully. Event ID 100 indicates a new subscription whereas Event ID 103 indicates a subscription has been unsubscribed.

3. Verify that the subscription is Active. On the collecting computer, browse to Event Viewer \Subscriptions. The subscription status should be Active. If it is not, double-click it, and examine the status in the Subscription Properties box to determine the source of the problem.

4. Verify that the forwarding computer has the Windows Remote Management listener properly configured. From an elevated command prompt, run the following command:

   ```
   winrm enumerate winrm/config/Listener
   ```

   If the Windows Remote Management listener isn't configured, there will be no output. If it is properly configured for HTTP, the output will resemble the following:

   ```
   Listener
       Address = *
       Transport = HTTP
       Port = 5985
   ```

```
Hostname
Enabled = true
URLPrefix = wsman
CertificateThumbprint
ListeningOn = 127.0.0.1, 192.168.1.214, ::1, fe80::100:7f:ffe%9,
fe80::5efe:192.168.1.214%10
```

If the Windows Remote Management listener is properly configured for HTTPS, the output will resemble the following (note that the host name must match the name that the event collector uses to identify the computer):

```
Listener
Address = *
Transport = HTTPS
Port = 5986
Hostname = client.nwtraders.msft
Enabled = true
URLPrefix = wsman
CertificateThumbprint = 52 31 db a8 45 50 1f 29 d9 3e 16 f0 da 82 ae 94 18 8f
61 5c
ListeningOn = 127.0.0.1, 192.168.1.214, ::1, fe80::100:7f:ffe%9,
fe80::5efe:192.168.1.214%10
```

5. Verify that the collecting computer can connect to Windows Remote Management on the forwarding computer. From an elevated command prompt on the collecting computer, run the following command:

   winrm id –remote:<computer_name>.<domain_name>

   For example, if the forwarding computer is named client.nwtraders.msft, you would run the following command:

   winrm id –remote:client.nwtraders.msft

   ```
   IdentifyResponse
   ProtocolVersion = http://schemas.dmtf.org/wbem/wsman/1/wsman.xsd
   ProductVender = Microsoft Corporation
   ProductVersion = OS: 6.0.6000 SP: 0.0 Stack: 1.0
   ```

   If you receive the message "WS-Management could not connect to the specified destination," verify that the Windows Remote Management service is started on the forwarding computer and that no firewall is blocking connections between the two computers.

6. Verify that the user account you configured the subscription to use has privileges on the forwarding computer. If necessary, enable failure security auditing on the remote computer, wait for events to be forwarded, and then examine the Security event log for logon failures. Additionally, you can temporarily configure the subscription to use a Domain Admin account—if the subscription works with the Domain Admin account, the source of your problem is definitely related to authentication. Troubleshoot the authentication problem, and reconfigure the subscription to use the original user account.

7. If the subscription is configured to use Machine Account authentication, verify that the collecting computer's account is a member of the forwarding computer's Event Log Readers local group. If the subscription is configured to use a different user account, that account must be in the forwarding computer's Event Log Readers local group.

8. Verify that the following services are started on the forwarding computer:

   - Windows Remote Management (WS-Management)
   - Windows Event Collector

9. Verify that the Windows Event Collector service is started on the collecting computer.

10. Verify Windows firewall settings on the forwarding computer:

    - Verify that the Windows Remote Management (HTTP-In) firewall exception is enabled.
    - If you are using HTTPS instead of HTTP, verify that you have created and enabled a custom firewall exception for TCP port 5986.
    - Verify that the forwarding computer and the collecting computer are both connected to Private or Domain networks, rather than to Public networks. To verify the network profile, click Start, right-click Network, and then click Properties. In the Network And Sharing Center, the profile type will appear after the network name. If it shows Public Network, click the Customize button and change the profile type to Private.

11. In addition to the forwarding computer, verify that the Windows Remote Management (HTTP-In) firewall exception is enabled on the collecting computer.

12. Verify that a network firewall is not blocking traffic by testing connectivity. Because the forwarding computer must have HTTP and possibly HTTPS available, you can attempt to connect to it from the collecting computer by using Windows Internet Explorer— just type **http://computername:5985** (or **https://computername:5986** if you are using HTTPS) in the Address bar. If the firewall on the forwarding computer is correctly configured, you will receive an HTTP 404 error and Internet Explorer will display this message: "The webpage cannot be found". If Internet Explorer displays the message "Internet Explorer cannot display the webpage," the firewall exception on the forwarding computer has not been enabled.

13. Verify that the event query is valid by following these steps:

    a. View the subscription properties, and click the Select Events button.

    b. Select the XML tab, select the contents of the query, and press Ctrl+C to copy the contents to the clipboard.

    c. Open a second instance of Event Viewer. Right-click Event Viewer, and then click Connect To Another Computer. Select the forwarding computer, and then click OK.

    d. Right-click Custom Views, and then click Create Custom View.

    e. In the Create Custom View dialog box, select the XML tab. Select the Edit Query Manually check box, and click Yes when prompted.

    f. Click the query box, and press Ctrl+V to paste the query. Then, click OK.

The new custom view will appear and show the matching events. If any events have appeared since you created the event forwarder, they should have been forwarded. If there are no new events, the problem is your forwarding criteria. Try creating a custom view that matches the events you want to forward, and then importing that into a new subscription.

PRACTICE **Responding to and Collecting Events**

In this practice, you configure a computer running Windows Server 2008 R2, Boston, to forward events to the domain controller for the nwtraders.msft domain running Windows Server 2008 R2, Dcsrv1. In your environment, you can use different computer and domain names. Either computer can also be running Windows Vista, Windows 7, or Windows Server 2008.

EXERCISE 1   Configuring an Event to Trigger a Task

In this exercise, you use Event Viewer to configure a command to run each time the Service Control Manager adds an event with ID 7036 to the event log to indicate that a service stopped.

1. On Dcsrv1, use Notepad to create a file named Logservice.cmd in the C:\Windows\ folder. Add the following line to the file, save the file, and then close Notepad:

   ```
   echo Service Stopped >> %windir%\logs\servicelog.txt
   ```

   Echo is a command-line tool that writes text. When Windows runs the Logservice.cmd file, Windows adds the text "Service Stopped" to the C:\Windows\Logs\ServiceLog.txt file.

2. On Dcsrv1, in Event Viewer, select the Windows Logs\System node.

3. In the actions pane, click Filter Current Log. In the Filter Current Log dialog box, select the Information check box. In the Event Sources list, select the Service Control Manager check box. Click OK. Event Viewer displays only the events created by the Service Control Manager.

4. Find an event with Event ID 7036. Right-click the event and then click Attach Task To This Event. The Create Basic Task Wizard appears.

5. On the Create A Basic Task page, type **Respond To Stopped Event** in the Name box. Click Next.

6. On the When A Specific Event Is Logged page, notice that the Log, Source, and Event ID are already selected. Click Next.

7. On the Action page, notice that Start A Program is selected. Click Next.

8. On the Start A Program Page, in the Program/Script box, click the Browse button and select C:\Windows\logservice.cmd. Click Next.

9. On the Summary page, click Finish. When prompted, click OK.

10. Generate an event by stopping a service. In Server Manager, select the Configuration \Services node. In the details pane, right-click Background Intelligent Transfer Service, and then click Restart.

11. Open Explorer and browse to C:\Windows\Logs. Double-click the Servicelog.txt file, and notice that at least one service had been stopped.

   In practice, you would take additional actions when responding to events, such as automatically restarting the service or notifying an administrator of the stopped service.

EXERCISE 2 Configuring a Computer to Collect Events

In this exercise, you configure the computer Dcsrv1 to collect events.

1. Log on to Dcsrv1 using a domain account with administrative privileges.

2. At a command prompt, run the following command to configure the Windows Event Collector service:

   `wecutil qc`

3. When prompted to change the service startup mode to Delay-Start, type **Y**, and press Enter.

EXAM TIP

You could also change the service startup mode to Delay-Start by responding to the prompt that appears when you attempt to create the first subscription. However, the exam expects you to be familiar with the command-line tools for configuring computers for subscriptions.

EXERCISE 3 Configuring a Computer to Forward Events

In this exercise, you configure Boston to forward events to the collecting computer. To complete this exercise, you must have completed Exercise 1.

1. Log on to Boston using a domain account with administrative privileges.

2. At a command prompt, run the following command to configure the Windows Remote Management service:

   `winrm quickconfig`

3. When prompted to change the service startup mode, create the WinRM listener, enable the firewall exception, type **Y**, and press Enter.

4. Verify that the Windows Remote Management service is configured to automatically start by selecting the Configuration\Services node in Server Manager, selecting the Windows Remote Management (WS-Management) service, and verifying that it is started and that the Startup Type is set to Automatic (Delayed Start).

5. Run the following command at the command prompt to grant Dcsrv1 access to the event log. If your collecting computer has a different name or domain name, replace Dcsrv1 with the correct name and nwtraders.msft with the correct domain name.

   `net localgroup "Event Log Readers" Dcsrv1$@nwtraders.msft /add`

EXERCISE 4 Configuring an Event Subscription

In this exercise, you create an event subscription on Dcsrv1 to gather events from Boston. To complete this exercise, you must have completed Exercises 1 and 2.

1. Log on to Dcsrv1. In Server Manager, right-click Diagnostics\Event Viewer\Subscriptions, and then choose Create Subscription.

2. In the Event Viewer dialog box, click Yes to configure the Windows Event Collector service (if prompted). The Subscription Properties dialog box appears.

3. In the Subscription Name box, type **Kernel Events**.

4. Click the Select Computers button. In the Computers dialog box, click Add Domain Computers. Type **Boston**. Then click OK.

5. In the Computers dialog box, click Test. Click OK when Event Viewer verifies connectivity. Then click OK to close the Computers dialog box.

6. Click the Select Events button. In the Query Filter dialog box, select the Error, Critical, Warning, and Information check boxes. Select By Source. Then, from the Event Sources drop-down list, select the Kernel-General check box. Click OK.

7. Click the Advanced button to open the Advanced Subscription Settings dialog box. Note that it is configured to use the Machine Account by default. This will work because you added this computer's domain account to the forwarding computer's Event Log Readers local group. Also note that the subscription is configured by default to use Normal Event Delivery Optimization using the HTTP protocol. Click OK.

8. In the Subscription Properties dialog box, click OK.

Next, generate a Kernel event on Boston by following these steps:

1. Log on to Boston. Right-click the clock on the system tray, and then choose Adjust Date/Time.

2. In the Date And Time dialog box, click Change Date And Time.

3. Change the time, and then click OK twice.

4. While still using Boston, open Event Viewer and check the System log. You should see an Information event with a source of Kernel-General.

5. Using Dcsrv1, select the Forwarded Events event log (located below Windows Logs). If you don't immediately see the event, wait a few minutes—it might take up to 15 minutes for the event to appear.

Lesson Summary

- Event forwarding uses HTTP or HTTPS on nonstandard ports to send events that match a filter you create to a collecting computer. Using event forwarding, you can centralize event management and better track critical events that occur on client and server computers.

- To use event forwarding, you must configure both the collecting and forwarding computers. On the forwarding computer, run the command **winrm quickconfig**. On the collecting computer, run the command **wecutil qc**. Then you can configure the event subscription on the collecting computer.

Lesson Review

You can use the following questions to test your knowledge of the information in Lesson 1, "Monitoring Events." The questions are also available on the companion CD if you prefer to review them in electronic form.

> **NOTE ANSWERS**
>
> Answers to these questions and explanations of why each answer choice is correct or incorrect are located in the "Answers" section at the end of the book.

1. You are configuring a computer named Server to collect events from a computer named Client. Both computers are in the Nwtraders.msft domain. Which of the following commands would you run on the collecting computer?

   A. wecutil qc

   B. winrm quickconfig

   C. net localgroup "Event Log Readers" Server$@nwtraders.msft /add

   D. net localgroup "Event Log Readers" Client$@nwtraders.msft /add

2. You are configuring a computer named Server to collect events from a computer named Client. Both computers are in the Nwtraders.msft domain. Which of the following commands would you run on the forwarding computer? (Choose all that apply.)

   A. wecutil qc

   B. winrm quickconfig

   C. net localgroup "Event Log Readers" Server$@nwtraders.msft /add

   D. net localgroup "Event Log Readers" Client$@nwtraders.msft /add

3. You need to configure an event subscription to update every minute. Which tool should you use?

   A. Wecutil

   B. WinRM

   C. Net

   D. The Event Viewer console

Lesson 2: Monitoring Performance and Reliability

Performance and reliability monitoring is useful in several scenarios:

- Improving the performance of servers by identifying the performance bottleneck and then upgrading the bottlenecked resource.

- Identifying the source of critical performance problems that make services unusable or completely unavailable.

- Correlating events, such as application installations, with failures.

This lesson describes how to use three tools that provide performance and reliability monitoring: Performance Monitor, Reliability Monitor, and Data Collector Sets. It also describes how to configure virtual memory, which is a file that Windows Server 2008 R2 uses to store memory contents when Windows Server 2008 R2 lacks sufficient physical memory.

> **After this lesson, you will be able to:**
> - Use Performance Monitor to view real-time or recorded performance data.
> - Use Reliability Monitor to examine failures and software installations.
> - Use Data Collector Sets to record information about a computer's current state for later analysis.
> - Examine virtual memory utilization and configure page file location.
>
> **Estimated lesson time: 30 minutes**

Using Performance Monitor

Performance Monitor graphically shows real-time performance data, including processor utilization, network bandwidth usage, and thousands of other statistics. Figure 10-5 shows an example.

To use Performance Monitor, follow these steps:

1. In Server Manager, select Diagnostics\Performance\Monitoring Tools\Performance Monitor.

2. Add counters to the real-time graph by clicking the green plus button on the toolbar. You can also display data from other computers on the network.

Each line on the graph appears in a different color. To make it easier to view a specific line, select a counter and press Ctrl+H. The selected counter appears thick and black on the graph.

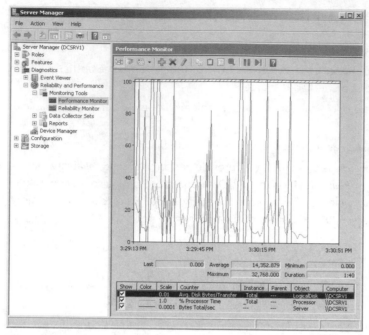

FIGURE 10-5 Performance Monitor showing real-time data

To change the appearance and refresh rate of the chart, right-click Performance Monitor, and then choose Properties. The five tabs of the Performance Monitor Properties dialog box provide access to different configuration options:

- **General** In the Graph Elements group, adjust the Sample Every box to change how frequently the graph updates. Use a longer interval to show a smoother, less jagged graph that is updated less frequently and uses less bandwidth. Adjust the Duration box to change how much data is displayed in the graph before Performance Monitor begins overwriting the graph on the left portion of the chart. A Duration of 3,600 displays one hour of data in the graph, and a Duration of 86,400 displays one full day.

- **Source** Choose whether to display current activity in real time or show log files that you have saved using a Data Collector Set. If you display a log file, you can use this tab to control the time range that is displayed in the Performance Monitor window.

- **Data** In the Counters list, select the counter you want to configure. Then adjust the Color, Width, and Style. Increase or decrease the Scale value to change the height of the graph for a counter. You can also adjust the scale for all counters by clicking the Graph tab and changing the Maximum and Minimum values in the Vertical Scale group.

- **Graph** By default, Performance Monitor begins overwriting graphed data on the left portion of the chart after the specified duration has been reached. When graphing data over a long period of time, it's typically easier to see the chart scroll from right to left, similar to the way that Task Manager shows data. To do this, in the Scroll Style group, select Scroll. Although the line chart shows the most information, you can select from the following chart types by clicking the Change Graph Type button on the toolbar or by pressing Ctr+G:

  - **Line** The default setting, this shows values over time as lines on the chart.

  - **Histogram bar** This shows a bar graph with the most recent values for each counter displayed. If you have a large number of values and you're primarily interested in the current value (rather than the value of each counter over time), this bar graph will be easier to read than the line chart.

  - **Report** This text report lists each current value.

- **Appearance** If you keep multiple Performance Monitor windows open simultaneously, you can make it easier to quickly distinguish between the windows by using this tab to change the color of the background or other elements.

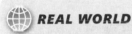

REAL WORLD

Tony Northrup

IT support often needs to troubleshoot performance problems in real-time. In the past, I would start by launching Task Manager, and if I needed more detailed information, I would start Performance Monitor.

Windows Vista and Windows Server 2008 introduced a new tool that fits nicely between Task Manager's simplicity and Performance Monitors complexity: Resource Monitor. Resource Monitor shows separate tabs for CPU, Memory, Disk, and Network. Each tab shows you exactly how much of that resource type every process is using and includes resource-specific graphs that give you a visual snapshot of the computer's current load. By selecting a process' check box, you can quickly identify exactly which files a process is accessing and which network hosts it is communicating with.

Resource Monitor is the quickest way to identify which process is burdening the process, network, memory, or disk. Like Task Manager, you can right-click a process to close it. Despite its usefulness, Resource Monitor isn't listed in the 70-642 exam objectives. Therefore, I won't cover it in this book. For the real world, though, you should definitely get to know the tool.

Using Reliability Monitor

Reliability Monitor tracks a computer's stability. Computers that have no errors and no new software installations are considered stable and can achieve the maximum system stability index of 10. The more installations and failures that occur on a computer, the lower the system stability index drops toward a minimum value of 0.

Reliability Monitor is useful for diagnosing intermittent and long-term problems. For example, if you were to install an application that caused the operating system to fail once a week, it would be very difficult to correlate the failures with the application installation. With Reliability Monitor, as shown in Figure 10-6, you can quickly browse both failures and the application installations over time. If recurring failures begin shortly after an application installation, the two might be related.

To open Reliability Monitor, right-click the Diagnostics\Performance\Monitoring Tools node in Server Manager and then click View System Reliability.

The chart at the top of Reliability Monitor shows one data point for each day. The rows below the chart show icons for successful and unsuccessful software installations, application failures, hardware failures, Windows failures, and other miscellaneous failures. Click a day to view the day's details in the System Stability Report below the chart.

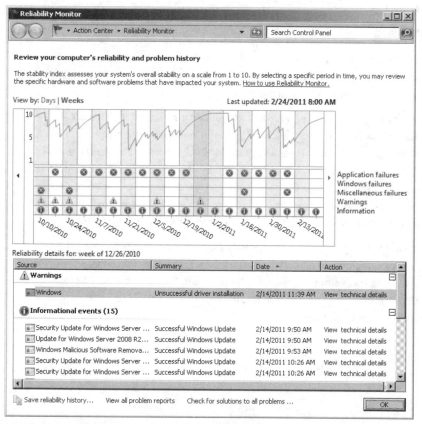

FIGURE 10-6 Reliability Monitor showing historical data

The Reliability Monitor displays data gathered by the Reliability Analysis Component (RAC), which is implemented using RACAgent.exe. Windows Server 2008 R2 includes a scheduled task that automatically runs RACAgent.exe once per hour. However, the hourly trigger is disabled by default. Additionally, you must enable Windows Management Instrumentation (WMI) reliability analysis by updating a registry value and restarting the computer.

To configure Windows Server 2008 R2 to automatically gather reliability data, follow these steps:

1. Use the Registry Editor to set the value HKEY_LOCAL_MACHINE\SOFTWARE\Microsoft\Reliability Analysis\WMI\WMIEnable to 1.

2. Restart the computer.

3. In Server Manager, select Configuration\Task Scheduler\Task Scheduler Library\Microsoft\Windows\RAC.

4. In the details pane, right-click RacTask, and then click Properties. The RacTask Properties dialog box appears.

5. Select the Triggers tab. Then, select One Time, and click the Edit button. Select the Enabled check box, and click OK twice.

6. In Server Manager, right-click RacTask, and then click Run.

   Running the task also causes the task to run automatically every hour thereafter. After the task completes running (which can take several minutes), you will be able to see data in Reliability Monitor.

Using Data Collector Sets

Data Collector Sets gather system information, including configuration settings and performance data, and store it in a data file. You can later use the data file to examine detailed performance data in Performance Monitor or view a report that summarizes the information.

The sections that follow describe how to create Data Collector Sets and how to view reports.

Using Built-in Data Collector Sets

Windows Server 2008 R2 includes several built-in Data Collector Sets located at Data Collector Sets\System:

- **Active Directory Diagnostics** Present only on domain controllers, this Data Collector Set logs kernel trace data, Active Directory trace data, performance counters, and Active Directory registry configuration.

- **System Performance** Logs processor, disk, memory, and network performance counters and kernel tracing. Use this Data Collector Set when troubleshooting a slow computer or intermittent performance problems.

- **System Diagnostics**   Logs all the information included in the System Performance Data Collector Set, plus detailed system information. Use this Data Collector Set when troubleshooting reliability problems such as problematic hardware, driver failures, or Stop errors (also known as blue screens). The report generated by the Data Collector Set provides a summary of error conditions on the system without requiring you to manually browse Event Viewer and Device Manager.

- **Wireless Diagnostics**   Present only on computers with wireless capabilities, this Data Collector Set logs the same information as the LAN Diagnostics Data Collector Set, plus information relevant to troubleshooting wireless network connections. Use this Data Collector Set only when troubleshooting network problems that occur when connected to a wireless network.

To use a Data Collector Set, right-click it, and then choose Start. The System Performance and System Diagnostics Data Collector Sets stop automatically after a minute, the Active Directory Diagnostics Data Collector Set stops automatically after five minutes, and the Wireless Diagnostics Data Collector Set runs until you stop it. If you are troubleshooting a network problem, you should attempt to reproduce the problem after starting the Data Collector Set. To manually stop a Data Collector Set, right-click it, and then click Stop.

After running a Data Collector Set, you can view a summary of the data gathered in the Reports node. To view the most recent report for a Data Collector Set, right-click the Data Collector Set, and then choose Latest Report. Reports are automatically named using the format *yyyymmdd-####*.

To minimize the performance impact of data logging, log the least amount of information required. For example, you should use System Performance instead of System Diagnostics whenever possible because System Performance includes fewer counters.

Creating a Data Collector Set

When you use Performance Monitor, you can see performance counters in real time. Data Collector Sets can record this data so that you can analyze it later in Performance Monitor.

If you either have a performance problem or you want to analyze and possibly improve the performance of a server, you can create a Data Collector Set to gather performance data. However, for the analysis to be useful, you should always create a baseline by logging performance data before you make any changes. Then you can compare the performance before and after your adjustments.

To create a custom Data Collector Set, follow these steps:

1. Right-click Data Collector Sets\User Defined, choose New, and then choose Data Collector Set. The Create New Data Collector Set Wizard appears.

2. On the How Would You Like To Create This New Data Collector Set page, type a name for the set. Make sure Create From A Template is selected. Then click Next.

3. On the Which Template Would You Like To Use page, as shown in Figure 10-7, choose from one of the standard templates (which can vary depending on the computer's configuration), and click Next:

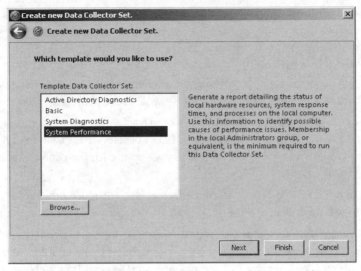

FIGURE 10-7 Creating a new Data Collector Set based on a template

The templates include the following:

- **Active Directory Diagnostics** Collects Active Directory configuration information and performance counters.

- **Basic** Logs all Processor performance counters, stores a copy of the HKLM \Software \Microsoft\Windows NT\CurrentVersion registry key, and performs a Windows Kernel trace.

- **System Diagnostics** Logs 13 useful performance counters (including processor, disk, memory, and network counters), stores a copy of dozens of important configuration settings, and performs a Windows Kernel trace. By default, System Diagnostics logs data for one minute, giving you a snapshot of the computer's status.

- **System Performance** Logs 14 useful performance counters (including the same counters logged by the System Diagnostics template) and performs a Windows Kernel trace. System Performance logs data for one minute.

4. On the Where Would You Like The Data To Be Saved page, click Next to accept the default location for the data (%SystemDrive%\perflogs\Admin\).

5. On the Create New Data Collector Set page, leave Run As set to <Default> to run it using the current user's credentials, or click the Change button to specify other administrative credentials. Select one of three options before clicking the Finish button:

- **Open Properties For This Data Collector Set** Immediately customize the Data Collector Set.

- **Start This Data Collector Set Now** Immediately begin logging data without customizing the Data Collector Set.

- **Save And Close** Close the Data Collector Set without starting it. You can edit the properties and start it at any time after saving it.

Custom Data Collector Sets are available under the User Defined node within Data Collector Sets.

Customizing a Data Collector Set

By default, a custom Data Collector Set logs only the data sources defined in the template you chose. To add your own data sources to a Data Collector Set, you must update it after creating it.

To add a data source to a Data Collector Set, right-click the Data Collector Set, choose New, and then choose Data Collector to open the Create New Data Collector Wizard. On the What Type Of Data Collector Would You Like To Create page, type a name for the Data Collector, select the type, and then click Next.

You can choose from the following types of Data Collectors (each of which provides different options in the Create New Data Collector Wizard):

- **Performance Counter Data Collector**   Logs data for any performance counter available when using the Performance Monitor console. You can add as many counters as you like to a Data Collector. You can assign a sample interval (15 seconds by default) to the Data Collector.

- **Event Trace Data Collector**   Stores events from an event trace provider that match a particular filter. Windows provides hundreds of event trace providers that are capable of logging even the minutest aspects of the computer's behavior. For best results, add every event trace provider that might relate to the problem you are troubleshooting.

- **Configuration Data Collector**   Stores a copy of specific registry keys, Windows Management Instrumentation (WMI) management paths, files, or the system state. After creating the Data Collector, edit the Data Collector's properties to add configuration data other than registry keys. If you are troubleshooting application problems or if you need to be aware of application settings, add the registry keys using a configuration Data Collector.

- **Performance Counter Alert**   Generates an alert when a performance counter is above or below a specified threshold. By viewing the Data Collector's properties after you create the Data Collector, you can log an entry in the Application event log or run a task when the alert is triggered.

You can add as many Data Collectors to a Data Collector Set as required. To edit a Data Collector, select the Data Collector Set within the Data Collector Sets\User Defined node. Then in the details pane, right-click the Data Collector, and choose Properties.

Saving Performance Data

After creating a Data Collector Set, you can gather the data specified in the Data Collector Set by right-clicking it and choosing Start. Depending on the settings configured on the Stop Condition tab of the Data Collector Set's properties dialog box, the logging might stop after a set amount of time or it might continue indefinitely. If it does not stop automatically, you can manually stop it by right-clicking it and clicking Stop.

Viewing Saved Performance Data in a Report

After using a Data Collector Set to gather information and then stopping the Data Collector Set, you can view a summary by right-clicking the Data Collector Set and then choosing Latest Report. As shown in Figure 10-8, the console selects the report generated when the Data Collector Set last ran. You can expand each section to find more detailed information.

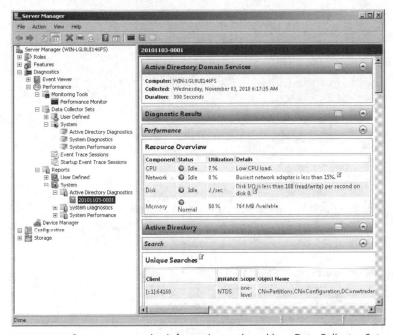

FIGURE 10-8 Reports summarize information gathered by a Data Collector Set.

If the Data Collector Set included performance counters, you can also view them using the Performance Monitor snap-in by right-clicking the report, choosing View, and then choosing Performance Monitor. Figure 10-9 shows performance data gathered using the standard Active Directory Diagnostics report.

Now Performance Monitor shows the logged data instead of real-time data. To narrow the time range shown, click and drag your cursor over the graph to select a time range. Then, right-click the graph and choose Zoom To, as shown in Figure 10-10. The horizontal bar beneath the graph illustrates the currently selected time range. Drag the left and right sides of the bar to expand the selected time range. Then, right-click the graph and choose Zoom To again to change the selection.

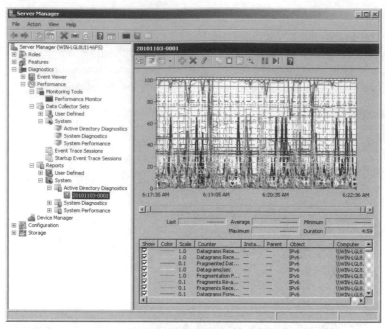

FIGURE 10-9 Active Directory Diagnostics performance data

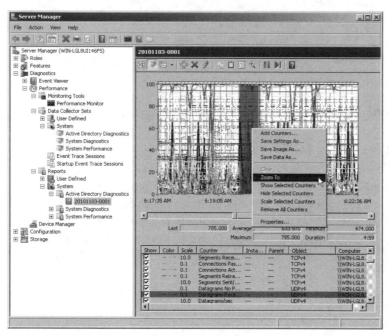

FIGURE 10-10 Using the Zoom To feature to analyze a narrow time span

Using Logman

Recent versions of Windows include the Logman command-line tool. You can use Logman to start data collector sets from a script or the command-line.

Although you can create data collector sets using the Logman tool, creating them using the Data Collector Sets console is easier. You can then run the data collector set by using the following command:

```
logman start "<Data Collector Set>"
```

After the data collector set has run, the report will be available in the typical location.

You can also use Logman to import and export data collector sets, which is useful when running a custom data collector set on a computer using a script. For example, after creating a new data collector set named Contoso Performance on your desktop computer, you could export it to an XML file by using the following command:

```
logman export "Contoso Performance" -xml "Contoso Performance Dataset.xml"
```

From a script, you could import and then run the data collector set by running the following commands:

```
logman export "Contoso Performance" -xml "Contoso Performance Dataset.xml"
```

```
logman start "Contoso Performance"
```

To view the complete set of Logman parameters, run **Logman /?** at a command prompt.

Configuring Virtual Memory

When Windows runs out of physical memory (also known as Random Access Memory, or RAM), it can move less-frequently accessed data to virtual memory. Virtual memory is stored in a file on the computer's hard disk known as the *page file*, or *paging file*. If a computer does not have enough memory for all the running applications, the page file can be the most frequently accessed file. As a result, you can often improve overall computer performance by optimizing the page file.

To determine whether the computer is low on available physical memory (and thus more likely to use virtual memory), open Task Manager by pressing Ctrl+Alt+Del and then view the Performance tab. Examine the Physical Memory group, as shown in Figure 10-11. If the Available memory is less than 10 percent of the Total memory, you are low enough on memory that paging could impact computer performance.

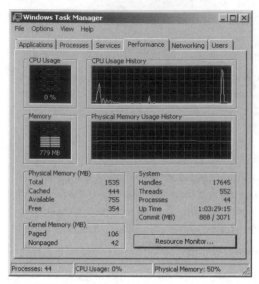

FIGURE 10-11 Task Manager showing total and available physical memory

To determine how frequently Windows is accessing a page file, monitor the Memory\Page Faults/Sec counter using Performance Monitor. A page fault occurs each time Windows reads from the page file. However, it can occur under other circumstances, too, which makes monitoring page file accesses difficult. Although occasional peaks are fine, if this counter stays high, the computer is probably accessing the page file often enough to impact performance. The practice at the end of this lesson shows you how to detect excessive paging by using a built-in data collector set.

If you determine that the computer is low on memory and accessing the paging file often, you should add more memory to the computer. If that is not an option, you might be able to improve performance by moving the paging file to a different disk that is either faster or less frequently accessed. For more information about identifying which disks in a computer offer better performance, read "How to Test Hard Disk Drive Performance" at *http://www.vistaclues.com/how-to-test-and-understand-hard-disk-drive-performance/*.

To change the default page file configuration, follow these steps:

1. Click Start, right-click Computer, and then click Properties.
2. Click Advanced System Settings.
3. In the System Properties dialog box, under Performance, click Settings.
4. In the Performance Options dialog box, on the Advanced tab, click Change.
5. The Virtual Memory dialog box, as shown in Figure 10-12, allows you to configure the size and location of the page file. By default, Windows automatically manages paging file size, and typically stores virtual memory on the system drive. To configure different settings, clear the Automatically Manage Paging File Size For All Drives check box.

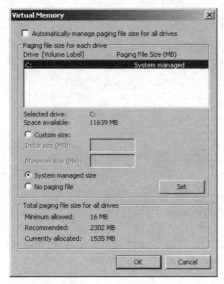

FIGURE 10-12 Manually configuring page file size

You should never create a separate partition for virtual memory, because a computer cannot access separate partitions on a single physical disk any faster than it can access a single partition on a physical disk. Additionally, creating multiple partitions makes managing free disk space more difficult. Whereas you can improve performance by putting virtual memory on a separate disk from application and system data, you will realize benefit only if the disk is at least as fast as the other disks. For better results, combine multiple disks into a RAID 0 array, which reads and writes data across all disks simultaneously.

PRACTICE **Running a Data Collector Set and Analyzing the Results**

In this practice, you run a standard Data Collector Set and then analyze the results.

1. On Dcsrv1, open Server Manager. Right-click Diagnostics\Reliability And Performance \Data Collector Sets\System\System Performance, and then choose Start.

   Wait one minute for the Data Collector Set to gather information about the system. When the minute has passed, the green icon will disappear from the System Performance node.

2. Right-click the System Performance node, and then choose Latest Report. Server Manager displays the report you just generated.

3. Examine the report. In particular, look for any warnings, such as the warning shown in Figure 10-13 that shows a report run on a system with insufficient memory.

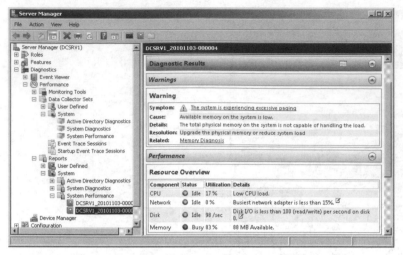

FIGURE 10-13 The report detects high paging due to insufficient memory.

4. Right-click the report, choose View, and then choose Performance Monitor.

5. Drag your cursor across the graph to select approximately 30 seconds out of the full minute of data that was collected. Then right-click the selected area and choose Zoom To.

6. Select each of the four performance counters and view the average, minimum, and maximum values for the time range.

Lesson Summary

- You can use Performance Monitor to view thousands of performance counters in real time. After running a Data Collector Set, you can also use Performance Monitor to analyze logged data.

- Reliability Monitor records application installations and different types of failures. You can use this tool to quickly view a computer's history, which is useful for correlating software installations with recurring problems.

- Data Collector Sets record configuration settings, performance data, and events. By creating your own Data Collector Set, you can quickly gather information about a computer's current state for later analysis.

- Windows Server 2008 R2 automatically configures virtual memory, which it uses to store information when there is not enough physical memory. However, you can manually configure the location of the virtual memory paging file, which might let you improve performance on computers with multiple hard disks.

Lesson Review

You can use the following questions to test your knowledge of the information in Lesson 2, "Monitoring Performance and Reliability." The questions are also available on the companion CD if you prefer to review them in electronic form.

> **NOTE ANSWERS**
>
> Answers to these questions and explanations of why each answer choice is correct or incorrect are located in the "Answers" section at the end of the book.

1. A computer running Windows Server 2008 R2 has been experiencing intermittent performance problems. You think the problems might be caused by an application that was installed last week. Which tool would you use to determine exactly when the application was installed?

   A. Performance Monitor

   B. Reliability Monitor

   C. Data Collector Sets

   D. Network Monitor

2. Users are complaining that email is very slow at peak usage times in the middle of the day. At night, performance seems adequate. You would like to determine what resources are limiting performance by recording performance data overnight and during the day, and then comparing them. Which tools should you use to accomplish this? (Choose all that apply.)

   A. Performance Monitor

   B. Reliability Monitor

   C. Data Collector Sets

   D. Network Monitor

3. Which of the following types of information might be stored in Reliability Monitor? (Choose all that apply.)

   A. A website configuration error

   B. An application that was uninstalled

   C. A service that was stopped

   D. A device driver that failed

Lesson 3: Using Network Monitor and Simple Network Management Protocol

Troubleshooting complex problems requires gaining insight into the inner workings of an application. When you are troubleshooting network problems, one of the best ways to gain insight is to capture and analyze the network communications using a protocol analyzer. Microsoft provides Network Monitor, a powerful protocol analyzer, as a free download.

This lesson explains how to use Network Monitor to record and analyze network traffic. It also describes how to configure computers running Windows Server 2008 R2 to be monitored using Simple Network Management Protocol (SNMP).

After this lesson, you will be able to:

- Download and install Network Monitor.
- Capture, filter, and analyze network communications.

Estimated lesson time: 30 minutes

Installing Network Monitor

Network Monitor is not included with Windows, but you can download it for free from the Microsoft Download Center at *http://www.microsoft.com/downloads*. After visiting that page, search for "Network Monitor." The installation is based on Windows Installer and uses a standard wizard interface.

The installation process adds the Network Monitor 3 Driver to each network adapter, as shown in Figure 10-14, including VPN and remote access adapters. You must install and enable this driver before Network Monitor can collect data from a network adapter.

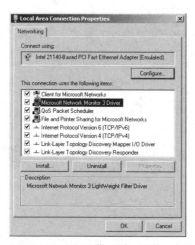

FIGURE 10-14 Installing the Network Monitor 3 Driver enables Network Monitor to collect data from a network adapter.

Capturing and Analyzing Network Communications

To start Network Monitor, follow these steps:

1. Click Start, All Programs, Microsoft Network Monitor 3.4 (or the current version), and then choose Microsoft Network Monitor.

2. If prompted, choose whether to automatically check for updates. On Windows Vista, Windows 7, Windows Server 2008, and Windows Server 2008 R2, this is unnecessary because Windows Update automatically retrieves updates for Network Monitor.

The sections that follow describe how to capture, analyze, and filter network communications.

Capturing Network Data

After you start Network Monitor, you can capture network traffic by following these steps:

1. On the Start Page tab, in the Select Networks pane, select the network adapters that you want to monitor, as shown in Figure 10-15.

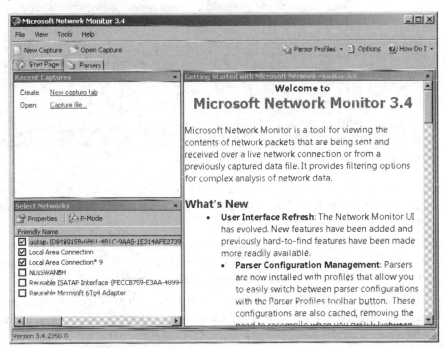

FIGURE 10-15 The Network Monitor window

2. After selecting the network adapters in the Select Networks pane, you can configure different options by selecting the network adapter and then clicking the Properties button. For wired network connections, you can enable P-Mode (promiscuous-mode) to capture frames sent to computers other than your own (which will not work in environments with Layer 2 switches). For wireless network connections, you can switch to Monitor Mode, which functions similarly to P-Mode for wireless connections.

3. Click New Capture on the toolbar. Network Monitor creates and selects a new capture tab.

4. On the toolbar, click the Start button. Network Monitor begins to capture network traffic and displays it in the Frame Summary pane, as shown in Figure 10-16.

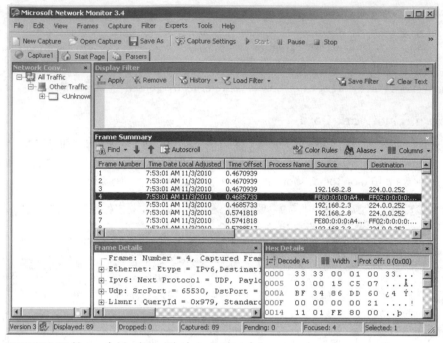

FIGURE 10-16 Network Monitor actively capturing data

5. If you are troubleshooting a network problem, you should re-create the problem while Network Monitor is capturing data. To stop capturing data, click the Stop button on the toolbar.

You can configure the size of the temporary capture file and where it is stored by clicking the Tools menu and then choosing Options. The Capture tab of the Options dialog box, shown in Figure 10-17, allows you to configure settings related to the temporary capture file.

Network Monitor can capture only traffic that the network adapter receives. Most modern networks connect wired computers to a Layer 2 switch, which sends a computer only the traffic that the computer needs to receive: broadcast messages and messages unicast to the computer's Media Access Control (MAC) address. Therefore, even if you have P-Mode enabled, Network Monitor will not be able to capture unicast communications sent between other computers.

Many Layer 2 switches can be configured with a *monitoring port*. The switch forwards all communications to the monitoring port. If you need to use Network Monitor to capture communications between two other hosts and your network uses a Layer 2 switch, you will need to enable the monitoring port and connect the computer running Network Monitor to that port.

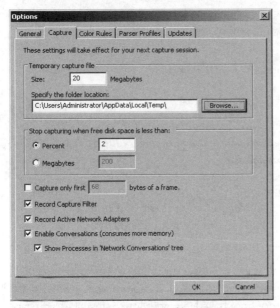

FIGURE 10-17 Configuring capture file settings

If your network uses hubs (a technology that predates Layer 2 switches), any computer can receive any other computer's communications if P-Mode is enabled. Therefore, if your computer is connected to a hub and one of the computers you are monitoring is connected to the same hub, you do not need to enable a monitoring port. This is also an important security concern: any user with a protocol analyzer, such as Network Monitor, can capture communications between other computers. For this reason, it's especially important to use encryption, such as that provided by IPsec (discussed in Chapter 8, "Configuring Windows Firewall and Network Access Protection").

Capturing Network Data by Using a Command Prompt

To capture network traffic from a command prompt, switch to the Network Monitor installation folder (C:\Program Files\Microsoft Network Monitor 3 by default) and run the following command:

```
NMCap /network * /capture /file filename.cap
```

This captures all traffic on all network interfaces and saves it to a file named *Filename*.cap. When you are finished capturing, press Ctrl+C. You can then analyze the capture file using Network Monitor by clicking the Open A Capture File button on the Start Page tab.

To use a filter capture, type the filter capture in quotation marks after the /capture parameter. For example, the following command captures only DNS traffic:

```
NMCap /network * /capture "DNS" /file filename.cap
```

To capture in P-Mode (capturing all traffic that is visible to the computer, not just broadcast traffic and traffic sent to or from the computer), use the /DisableLocalOnly parameter, as shown in the following example:

```
NMCap /network * /DisableLocalOnly /capture /file filename.cap
```

> **NOTE** **AUTOMATING THE CAPTURE OF NETWORK DATA**
>
> For more information about capturing with NMCap, read "NMCap: the Easy Way to Automate Capturing" at *http://blogs.technet.com/netmon/archive/2006/10/24 /nmcap-the-easy-way-to-automate-capturing.aspx*.

You can also use the /inputcapture parameter of NMCap to process an existing capture file. For example, to read an existing capture file named Capture1.cap and write a new capture file containing only HTTP packets, you would run the following command:

```
NMCap /InputCapture "Capture1.cap" /capture "HTTP" /file "HttpOnlyCapture.cap"
```

Because Network Monitor and NMCap require the Network Monitor driver to be installed, you cannot simply copy NMCap.exe to a computer that you need to capture from. If you need to quickly capture traffic on a computer that does not have Network Monitor installed, you can run Network Monitor OneClick, available for download at *http://www.microsoft.com/downloads /details.aspx?FamilyID=9F37302E-D491-4C69-B7CE-410C8784FD0C*. As shown in Figure 10-18, OneClick can capture traffic without requiring a complete Network Monitor installation. After completing the capture, OneClick automatically removes itself from the computer.

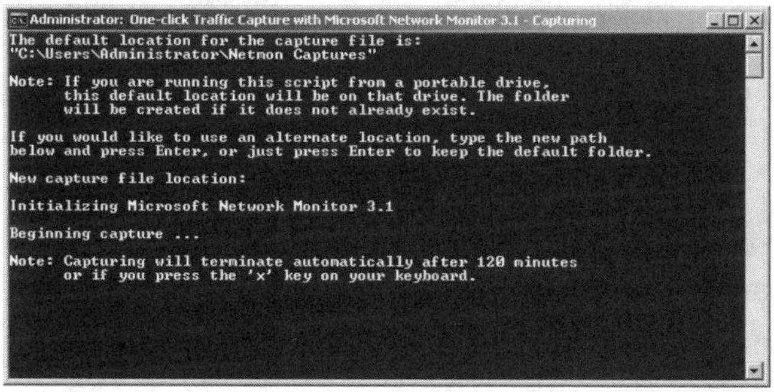

FIGURE 10-18 Capturing traffic with OneClick

Analyzing Network Data

After creating a capture, you can analyze the network data by using the same capture tab. Browse the captured data in the Frame Summary pane and select any frame to view the data. As shown in Figure 10-19, the Frame details pane summarizes the data in the frame, and the Hex details pane shows the raw data.

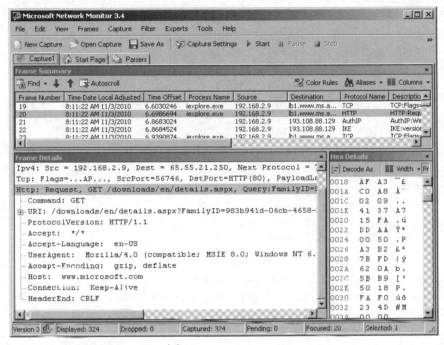

FIGURE 10-19 Examining captured data

NOTE **FRAMES AND PACKETS**

A frame isn't exactly like a packet, but it's similar. Technically, a frame includes Layer 2 data, such as the Ethernet header. Packets are Layer 3 units and start with the IP header.

Typically, the Frame details pane is much more useful than the Hex details pane because it shows frame data by layer. For example, Figure 10-20 shows just the Frame details pane. As you can see by examining the HTTP layer of the frame, that particular frame was requesting the file /downloads/ from the host www.microsoft.com. To provide more display area, you can right-click any frame in the Frame Summary pane and then choose View Selected Frame(s) In A New Window.

```
Frame Details
  Frame:
  + Ethernet: Etype = Internet IP (IPv4)
  + Ipv4: Next Protocol = TCP, Packet ID = 8187, Total IP Length = 505
  + Tcp: Flags=...PA..., SrcPort=56258, DstPort=HTTP(80), Len=465, Seq=3865462997 - 3865463462, Ack=1911
  - Http: Request, GET /downloads/
    - Request:
      - Command: GET
      + URI: /downloads/
      - ProtocolVersion: HTTP/1.1
      - Accept:  image/gif, image/x-xbitmap, image/jpeg, image/pjpeg, */*
      - Accept-Language:  en-us
      - UA-CPU:  x86
      - Accept-Encoding:  gzip, deflate
      - UserAgent:  Mozilla/4.0 (compatible; MSIE 7.0; Windows NT 6.0; SLCC1; .NET CLR 2.0.50727)
      - Host:  www.microsoft.com
      - Connection:  Keep-Alive
      - Cookie:  MUID=250628CBFD2A4A9B8F15E25F8950B06C; MC1=GUID=93b5a5ed54ce874c89781d66c7a918f0&HASH=
      - HeaderEnd: CRLF
```

FIGURE 10-20 Details of an HTTP request

Assigning Aliases

By default, Network Monitor displays IP addresses for the source and destination addresses. To make it easier to examine the frame summary, you can assign friendly aliases for different addresses. With a capture open, follow these steps to assign an alias:

1. In the Frame Summary pane, right-click either the Source or Destination column of a frame, and then click Create Alias For Source Address or Create Alias For Destination Address.

2. Enter the desired name in the Create New Alias box. Click OK.

After creating aliases, you can manage them by clicking the Aliases menu on the Frame Summary toolbar and then clicking Manage Aliases.

Filtering Network Data

A busy server can transfer hundreds of frames a second, making it difficult to isolate the specific frames you need to analyze. To narrow down the data, you can use a capture filter (which filters frames before they are captured) or a display filter (which filters frames after they are captured).

You must create capture filters before capturing data. If you want to filter data from an existing capture, create a display filter. To create a filter by using standard filters, in the Capture Filter or Display Filter pane, click the Load Filter button. Then choose Standard Filters and choose one of the built-in filters. Finally, click the Apply button. The most useful filters include:

- **BaseNetworkTShoot** This filter shows only frames that might be related to low-level network problems, including Internet Control Message Protocol (ICMP), Address Resolution Protocol (ARP), and Transmission Control Protocol (TCP) resets. Use this filter if you are experiencing general network problems and you want to try and identify the specific host causing the problems.

- **No-Broadcasts** Located within the Filter Out Noise group, this filter removes all broadcast frames.

- **DNS** The filters in the DNS group show only specific types of DNS traffic.

- **NameResolution** This filter shows all name resolution traffic, including DNS, NetBIOS name resolution, and ARP requests.

- **HttpWebpageSearch** Located within the HTTP group, this filter shows requests for specific webpages. This is useful for determining which computers on a network are requesting a specific page, particularly if the page you are searching for is a malformed path that might be involved in an attack against a web server (and thus might not be stored in the log files).

- **Capturing Machines IP Address** This filter shows only requests sent to or from the current computer.

- **IPv4Addresses** Located within the Addresses group, this filter shows only requests sent to or from specific IPv4 addresses.

- **IPv6Addresses** Located within the Addresses group, this filter shows only requests sent to or from specific IPv6 addresses.

- **IPv4SubNet** Located within the Addresses group, this filter shows only requests sent to or from a specific subnet.

Many of the standard filters require editing. For example, if you add the IPv4Addresses standard filter, you will need to change the sample IPv4 address to the IPv4 address that you want to filter for.

You can create more complex filters by combining multiple standard filters using binary operators. Separating two filters with the && operator requires frames to match both filters, whereas separating two filters with the || operator shows frames that match either filter. You can use parentheses to group multiple parameters. Prefix a parameter with an exclamation point to capture traffic that does not match the parameter. For example, the filter "!(tcp.port == 3389)" captures all traffic except Remote Desktop traffic (which uses TCP port 3389), which is useful when logging on to a computer remotely to capture traffic.

> **NOTE OTHER FILTER OPERATORS**
>
> You can also use the operators AND and OR instead of && and ||.

For example, if you were to capture traffic on a DNS server, the following filter would show all DNS traffic from the host at 192.168.10.123:

```
DNS && IPv4.SourceAddress == 192.168.10.123
```

The following filter would capture all web requests for the page named either Page1.htm or Page2.htm:

```
contains(Http.Request.URI,"Page1.htm") || contains(Http.Request.URI,"Page2.htm")
```

If you have an existing capture, you can create a display filter based on an existing frame by right-clicking the frame in the Frame Summary window and then choosing Add Cell To Display Filter. Then click Apply. Network Monitor will show only frames that match that exact description.

When creating custom filters, use the Verify button to check that your syntax is correct. The Display Filter pane will highlight any errors and allow you to correct them. For detailed information about creating custom filters, refer to the topic "Using Filters" in Network Monitor Help.

 EXAM TIP

For the exam, know how to create filters and how to capture network data at a command prompt by using NMCap.

Configuring SNMP

SNMP allows network management tools, such as Microsoft System Center Operations Manager or Microsoft System Center Essentials, to monitor computers and other network devices by querying them for information from across the network. Windows Server 2008 R2 does not include an application to monitor other network devices using SNMP. However, you can install the SNMP Services feature to allow the computer to be remotely monitored.

To install the SNMP Services feature, follow these steps:

1. In Server Manager, right-click Features, and then click Add Feature.

2. On the Select Features page, select SNMP Services. Click Next.

3. On the Installation Results page, click Close.

The SNMP Services feature includes two subfeatures:

- **SNMP Service** Installs the SNMP Service and sets it to start automatically, which provides core SNMP capabilities that would be required by SNMP management software.

- **SNMP WMI Provider** Enables WMI scripts and applications to access SNMP information. You need to install this subfeature only when you use WMI scripts or applications that use the WMI interfaces and need those specific capabilities.

SNMP includes basic security features to reduce the risk of unauthorized computers gathering SNMP data. Each SNMP computer must be configured with one or more community names, and the SNMP monitoring agent must submit a valid community name with each SNMP query. Additionally, you can configure trap destinations to which SNMP clients will send SNMP notifications.

To manage SNMP settings such as traps and the agent information (which describes who manages a particular device) on a single computer, follow these steps:

1. In Server Manager, select the Configuration\Services node.

2. Right-click SNMP Service, and then click Properties.

3. Select the Agent or Traps tabs, as shown in Figure 10-21, to configure SNMP settings. Click OK when you're finished.

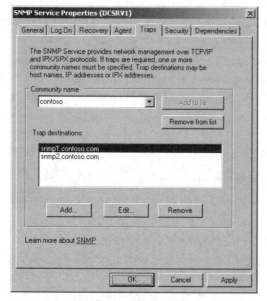

FIGURE 10-21 Configuring SNMP settings

To use Group Policy settings to manage SNMP settings such as traps, communities, and permitted managers that are allowed to submit queries, edit the three settings contained within the Computer Configuration\Policies\Administrative Templates\Network\SNMP node.

PRACTICE   Capturing and Analyzing Network Traffic

In this practice, you capture communications by using both graphical and command-line tools, and you work with both capture and display filters.

EXERCISE 1   Capturing Traffic by Using Graphical Tools

In this exercise, you must capture communications with Network Monitor. Then you use a display filter to view only the frames you are most interested in.

1. Download and install the latest version of Network Monitor.

2. Start Network Monitor by clicking Start, All Programs, Microsoft Network Monitor, and then click Microsoft Network Monitor.

3. If prompted, choose not to automatically check for updates.

4. On the Start Page tab, in the Select Networks pane, select only the network adapter that is connected to the Internet.

5. Click New Capture.

6. On the new capture tab that appears, click the Start button on the toolbar.

7. Open Internet Explorer and visit *http://www.microsoft.com*. After the page appears, return to Network Monitor and click the Stop button.

8. Use the Frame Summary pane to examine the captured data. You should see the following sequence (each step probably generated multiple frames):

   a. **ARP**   The computer might have generated an ARP request to identify the MAC address of its DNS server. If the DNS server is on another subnet, the computer would need to identify the MAC address of the default gateway. If no ARP requests were captured, the computer had previously cached the MAC address.

   b. **DNS**   The computer would need to identify the IP address associated with the host name www.microsoft.com.

   c. **TCP**   The computer establishes a TCP connection to the IP address that www.microsoft.com resolved to. This requires a total of three frames.

   d. **HTTP**   Using the newly established TCP connection to www.microsoft.com, the computer can now query the website for the "/" URI, which is the default page. After the first HTTP requests, several other DNS queries, TCP connections, and HTTP sessions were probably captured as the computer downloaded objects embedded in the www.microsoft.com website.

9. In the Display Filter pane, type the following, and then click Apply:
   HTTP && IPv4.SourceAddress == IpConfig .LocalIpv4Address

10. Browse the frames displayed in the Frame Summary pane to see every HTTP request required to open the default page at www.microsoft.com.

EXERCISE 2   Capturing Traffic at the Command Line

In this exercise, you must capture network communications at a command prompt by using a capture filter. Then you examine the communications by using Network Monitor.

1. Open a command prompt with administrative credentials, and run the following commands:

```
cd %ProgramFiles%\Microsoft Network Monitor 3
NMCap /network * /capture "DNS" /StopWhen /TimeAfter 2 min /file DNS.cap
```

2. Now open a second command prompt, and run the following commands:

```
ping www.contoso.com
nslookup www.fabrikam.com
```

3. Open Internet Explorer, and visit *http://www.microsoft.com*.

4. Wait two minutes for the NMCap capture to complete.

5. Open Network Monitor. On the Start Page tab, click Open A Capture File.

6. In the Open dialog box, select C:\Program Files\Microsoft Network Monitor 3\DNS.cap.

7. On the capture tab that appears, examine the Frame Summary pane. Notice that only DNS frames were captured—the HTTP requests associated with opening the website were not captured because they did not match the capture filter you specified. Select each frame and examine the Frame details pane to determine whether the frame is a query or a response and what host name each query was attempting to identify.

Lesson Summary

- Network Monitor is a free download available from *http://www.microsoft.com*.
- You can capture data by using either the graphical Network Monitor tool or the command-line NMCap tool. All analysis must be done using the graphical Network Monitor tool, however. Especially on a busy server, you will need to use filters to reduce the number of frames not related to the application you are examining. Capture filters are applied while data is captured, and display filters are applied after the data has been captured.

Lesson Review

You can use the following questions to test your knowledge of the information in Lesson 3, "Using Network Monitor and Simple Network Management Protocol." The questions are also available on the companion CD if you prefer to review them in electronic form.

> **NOTE   ANSWERS**
>
> Answers to these questions and explanations of why each answer choice is correct or incorrect are located in the "Answers" section at the end of the book.

1. You need to use Network Monitor to capture communications between two computers, HostA and HostB. You also have access to a third computer, HostC. In which of the following scenarios will you be able to capture the communications? (Choose all that apply.)

   A. You are running Network Monitor on HostA, but HostB does not have Network Monitor installed.

   B. You are running Network Monitor on HostC, with P-Mode enabled. HostA is connected to the same Layer 2 switch as HostC. HostB is connected to a different network.

   C. You are running Network Monitor on HostC, with P-Mode enabled. HostA is connected to the same hub as HostC. HostB is connected to a different network.

   D. You are running Network Monitor on HostC, with P-Mode enabled. HostA is connected to the same hub as HostB. HostC is connected to a Layer 2 switch.

2. You need to create a Network Monitor capture file from a command prompt. Which tool should you use?

   A. Netmon

   B. NMCap

   C. Nmconfig

   D. Nmwifi

3. A client computer with the IP address 192.168.10.12 is having a problem retrieving web-pages from a web server you manage. You use Network Monitor to capture network traffic while the client computer submits a request. However, you also capture hundreds of other requests. Which display filter should you use to view just the communications sent to and from the client computer?

   A. HTTP || IPv4.SourceAddress == 192.168.10.12

   B. HTTP && IPv4.SourceAddress == 192.168.10.12

   C. HTTP || IPv4.Address == 192.168.10.12

   D. HTTP && IPv4.Address == 192.168.10.12

Chapter Review

To further practice and reinforce the skills you learned in this chapter, you can perform the following tasks:

- Review the chapter summary.
- Review the list of key terms introduced in this chapter.
- Complete the case scenarios. These scenarios set up real-world situations involving the topics of this chapter and ask you to create a solution.
- Complete the suggested practices.
- Take a practice test.

Chapter Summary

- You can use event forwarding to centralize event management. Event forwarding uses HTTP or HTTPS to forward specific events from computers distributed throughout your organization to a central computer. To use event forwarding, you must configure both the forwarding and collecting computers. On the forwarding computer, run the command **winrm quickconfig**. On the collecting computer, run the command **wecutil qc**. Then you can configure the event subscription on the collecting computer.

- You can use Performance Monitor to analyze resource utilization on a computer, either in real time or by using data logged by a Data Collector Set. Reliability Monitor records application installations and different types of failures. You can use this tool to quickly view a computer's history, which is useful for correlating software installations with recurring problems. Data Collector Sets record configuration settings, performance data, and events. By creating your own Data Collector Set, you can quickly gather information about a computer's current state for later analysis.

- Network Monitor is a free protocol analyzer that can record and analyze network communications. To capture data from a command prompt, use the NMCap tool and then analyze the communications by using the graphical Network Monitor tool. Use filters to restrict which packets are captured and displayed.

Key Terms

Do you know what these key terms mean? You can check your answers by looking up the terms in the glossary at the end of the book.

- monitoring port
- P-Mode

Case Scenarios

In the following case scenarios, you will apply what you've learned about how to monitor computers. You can find answers to these questions in the "Answers" section at the end of this book.

Case Scenario 1: Troubleshooting a Network Performance Problem

You are a systems administrator at A. Datum Corporation. Recently, users have been complaining about intermittent performance problems when accessing a file server. Another systems administrator has been trying to isolate the problem but has failed. You discuss the problem with your manager and the system administrator who worked on the problem.

INTERVIEWS

Following is a list of company personnel interviewed and their statements:

- **Your Manager**   "David's had this ticket open for a week and hasn't made any progress, so I'm going to assign it to you. Talk to David, and then we'll meet again to discuss the best way to isolate the cause of the performance problems."

- **David, Systems Administrator** "What an awful ticket. When I get a complaint from a user, I connect to the server and run Task Manager, but the processor utilization is fine. So I don't know what the problem could be. I hope you have better luck than I did."

QUESTIONS

Now that you have talked with David, answer the following questions for your manager:

1. How can you analyze disk, network, processor, and memory resources both when the problem is occurring and when performance is normal?

2. If the problem is network related, how can you analyze the network traffic?

Case Scenario 2: Monitoring Computers for Low Disk Space

You are a systems administrator for Proseware, Inc. Recently, the CEO of your company called because he couldn't download his email. The help support technician identified the source of the problem as low disk space, helped the CEO clear sufficient free space, and resolved the problem.

The CEO would like your department to develop a proactive way to identify low disk space problems on computers so that you can free more disk space before the condition causes application failures.

Answer the following questions for your manager:

1. How can you monitor client computers for low disk space events?

2. Which client operating systems can you monitor?

Suggested Practices

To help you successfully master the exam objectives presented in this chapter, complete the following tasks.

Configure Event Logs

For this objective, you should complete both Practices 1 and 2.

- **Practice 1** Configure a forwarding computer to send events to a collecting computer by using each of the three bandwidth optimization techniques. Then use **Wecutil** to customize the event forwarding configuration by reducing the time required to forward events by half.

- **Practice 2** Examine the event logs on several production client computers in your organization. Identify several events that IT might want to be aware of. Then configure those computers to forward events to a central computer and monitor the central event log.

Configure Performance Monitoring

For this objective, you should complete all three practices to gain experience in troubleshooting performance and reliability problems.

- **Practice 1**   Run each standard Data Collector Set and analyze the report generated by each.

- **Practice 2**   On several production computers running Windows 7 or Windows Server 2008 R2 that have been online for more than a month, run Reliability Monitor. How stable are the computers? Can you identify the cause of any stability problems?

- **Practice 3**   Using several applications that your organization uses internally, create a Data Collector Set that gathers each of the application's configuration settings.

Gather Network Data

For this objective, you should complete all three practices.

- **Practice 1**   Have a friend (with the friend's permission) visit several websites and run network applications while you record the frames using Network Monitor. Then, analyze the frames and determine what applications your friend used. Can you determine which websites and webpages your friend visited? Are any passwords visible in the raw communications?

- **Practice 2**   Copy Network Monitor OneClick to a USB flash drive. Then connect the USB flash drive to a computer that does not have Network Monitor installed and capture network data to the USB flash drive. Return the USB flash drive to your own computer and analyze the .CAP file.

- **Practice 3**   Write a batch file that runs NMCap and captures data for five minutes. Then use Network Monitor to analyze the .CAP file.

Take a Practice Test

The practice tests on this book's companion CD offer many options. For example, you can test yourself on just the content covered in this chapter, or you can test yourself on all the 70-642 certification exam content. You can set up the test so that it closely simulates the experience of taking a certification exam, or you can set it up in study mode so that you can look at the correct answers and explanations after you answer each question.

> **MORE INFO**   **PRACTICE TESTS**
>
> For details about all the practice test options available, see "How to Use the Practice Tests" in this book's Introduction.

CHAPTER 11

Managing Files

Many types of documents, including financial spreadsheets, business plans, and sales presentations, must be shared on your network while remaining protected from unauthorized access. Windows Server 2008 R2 offers a suite of technologies to provide both availability and security for documents.

To control access, use NTFS file permissions and Encrypting File System (EFS). To provide redundancy, create a Distributed File System (DFS) namespace and use replication to copy files between multiple servers. You can use quotas to ensure that no single user consumes more than his or her share of disk space (which might prevent other users from saving files). Shadow copies and backups allow you to quickly recover from data corruption and hardware failures. This chapter describes how to use each of these technologies and explains the Windows Server 2008 R2 File Services server role.

Exam objectives in this chapter:

- Configure a file server.
- Configure Distributed File System (DFS).
- Manage file server resources.
- Configure backup and restore.

Lessons in this chapter:

- Lesson 1: Managing File Security   **570**
- Lesson 2: Sharing Folders   **585**
- Lesson 3: Backing Up and Restoring Files   **615**

Before You Begin

To complete the lessons in this chapter, you should be familiar with Windows networking and be comfortable with the following tasks:

- Adding roles to a computer running Windows Server 2008 R2
- Configuring Active Directory directory service domain controllers and joining computers to a domain
- Basic network configuration, including configuring IP settings

You will also need the following nonproduction hardware, connected to test networks:

- A computer named Dcsrv1 that is a domain controller in the Nwtraders.msft domain. This computer must have at least one network interface. Dcsrv1 must have at least two hard disks for this chapter, because Lesson 3, "Backing Up and Restoring Files," requires you to back up the system disk to a second hard disk.

> **NOTE COMPUTER AND DOMAIN NAMES**
>
> The computer and domain names you use will not affect these practices. The practices in this chapter refer to these computer names for simplicity, however.

- A computer named Boston that is a member of the Nwtraders.msft domain.

 REAL WORLD

Tony Northrup

Adding quotas can reduce disk performance, but you'll probably never notice it. According to a chat transcript, Ran Kalach at Microsoft feels that the performance impact should be 10 percent at most. Because the performance impact of quotas is so minimal, users should never notice this difference.

According to the same chat transcript, file screening should not have a noticeable impact. File screening checks file extensions only when new files are created or existing files are renamed—tasks that typically do not happen frequently.

Enabling EFS does have a performance impact because additional processing time is required for decryption when reading files. Although the exact impact varies widely depending on the type of file access and the processing capabilities of the computers, studies have found a performance decrease of 10 percent to 60 percent.

Lesson 1: Managing File Security

Much of an organization's most confidential data is stored in files and folders. Windows Server 2008 R2, along with most recent business versions of Windows, provide three technologies for controlling access to files, folders, and volumes: NTFS file permissions, EFS, and BitLocker.

The operating system uses NTFS file permissions to determine which users can read or change files and folders. NTFS file permissions work only when the operating system is running, however. To protect data when someone steals a hard drive or an entire computer, you must use encryption. EFS encrypts individual files and folders on a per-user basis, whereas BitLocker encrypts entire volumes and can help protect system files.

The sections that follow give more information about these three technologies.

After this lesson, you will be able to:

■ Use NTFS file permissions to control user access to files and folders.

■ Use EFS to protect files from offline attacks.

Estimated lesson time: 45 minutes

NTFS File Permissions

NTFS file permissions determine which users can view or update files. For example, you would use NTFS file permissions to grant your Human Resources group access to personnel files while preventing other users from accessing those files.

The default NTFS file permissions for user and system folders are designed to meet basic needs. These default permissions for different file types are:

■ **User files** Users have full control permissions over their own files. Administrators also have full control. Other users who are not administrators cannot read or write to a user's files.

■ **System files** Users can read, but not write to, the %SystemRoot% folder and subfolders. Administrators can add and update files. This allows administrators, but not users, to install updates and applications.

■ **Program files** Similar to the system files permissions, the %ProgramFiles% folder permissions are designed to allow users to run applications and allow only administrators to install applications. Users have read access, and administrators have full control.

Additionally, any new folders created in the root of a disk will grant administrators full control and users read access.

The default file and folder permissions work well for desktop environments. File servers, however, often require you to grant permissions to groups of users to allow collaboration. For example, you might want to create a folder that all Marketing users can read and update but that users outside the Marketing group cannot access. Administrators can assign users or groups any of the following permissions to a file or folder:

■ **List Folder Contents** Users can browse a folder but not necessarily open the files in it.

■ **Read** Users can view the contents of a folder and open files. If a user has Read but not Read & Execute permission for an executable file, the user will not be able to start the executable.

■ **Read & Execute** In addition to the Read permission, users can run applications.

■ **Write** Users can create files in a folder but not necessarily read them. This permission is useful for creating a folder in which several users can deliver files but not access each other's files or even see what other files exist.

■ **Modify** Users can read, edit, and delete files and folders.

■ **Full Control** Users can perform any action on the file or folder, including creating and deleting it as well as modifying its permissions.

To protect a file or folder with NTFS, follow these steps:

1. Open Windows Explorer (for example, by clicking Start and then choosing Computer).

2. Right-click the file or folder, and then choose Properties. The Properties dialog box for the file or folder appears.

3. Click the Security tab.

4. Click the Edit button. The Permissions dialog box appears.

5. If the user you want to configure access for does not appear in the Group Or User Names list, click Add. Type the user name, and then click OK.

6. Select the user you want to configure access for. Then, select the check boxes for the desired permissions in the Permissions For Users list, as shown in Figure 11-1. Denying access always overrides allowed access. For example, if Mary is a member of the Marketing group and you allow full control access for Mary and then deny full control access for the Marketing group, Mary's effective permissions will be to deny full control.

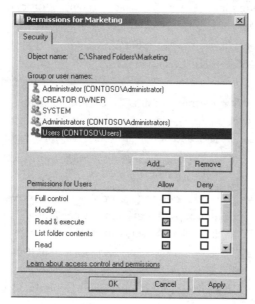

FIGURE 11-1 The Permissions dialog box

EXAM TIP

When taking the exam, expect questions where a user is granted access to a file but denied access through a group membership. Remember that although permission assignments are cumulative, denied access overrides all other permissions.

---

7. Repeat steps 5 and 6 to configure access for additional users.

8. Click OK twice.

Additionally, there are more than a dozen special permissions that you can assign to a user or group. To assign special permissions, click the Advanced button on the Security tab of the file or Administrator Properties dialog box, as shown in Figure 11-2.

To configure NTFS file permissions from a command prompt or script, use the icacls command. For complete usage information, type **icacls /?** at a command prompt.

NTFS file permissions are in effect whether users are logged on locally or accessing folders across the network.

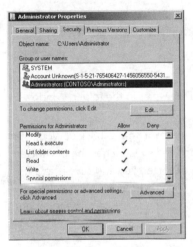

FIGURE 11-2 The Security tab

A user who does not have NTFS permissions to read a folder or file will not see it listed in the directory contents. This feature, known as Access-based Enumeration (ABE), was introduced with Windows Server 2003 Service Pack 1.

Encrypting File System

NTFS provides excellent protection for files and folders as long as Windows is running. However, an attacker who has physical access to a computer can start the computer from a different operating system (or simply reinstall Windows) or remove the hard disk and connect it to a different computer. Any of these very simple techniques would completely bypass NTFS security, granting the attacker full access to files and folders.

EFS protects files and folders by encrypting them on the disk. If an attacker bypasses the operating system to open a file, the file appears to be random, meaningless bytes. Windows controls access to the decryption key and provides it only to authorized users.

> **NOTE** **EFS SUPPORT**
>
> Windows 7, Windows Server 2008 R2, and earlier versions of Windows through Windows 2000 support EFS.

The sections that follow describe how to configure EFS. Another data encryption technology, BitLocker, encrypts entire volumes and helps prevent operating system files from being maliciously modified. BitLocker is described at the end of this lesson.

Protecting Files and Folders with EFS

To protect a file or folder with EFS, follow these steps:

1. Open Windows Explorer (for example, by clicking Start and then choosing Computer).
2. Right-click the file or folder, and then click Properties. The Properties dialog box appears.
3. On the General tab, click Advanced. The Advanced Attributes dialog box appears.
4. Select the Encrypt Contents To Secure Data check box.
5. Click OK twice.

If you encrypt a folder, Windows automatically encrypts all new files in the folder. Windows Explorer shows encrypted files in green.

The first time you encrypt a file or folder, Windows might prompt you to back up your file encryption key, as shown in Figure 11-3. Choosing to back up the key launches the Certificate Export Wizard, which prompts you to password-protect the exported key and save it to a file. Backing up the key is very important for stand-alone computers, because if the key is lost, the files are inaccessible. In Active Directory environments, you should use a data recovery agent (DRA), as described later in this section, to recover files.

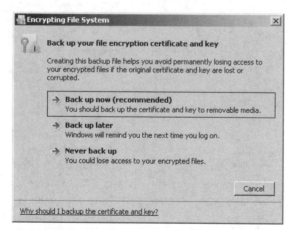

FIGURE 11-3 Prompting the user to back up the encryption key

Sharing Files Protected with EFS

If you need to share EFS-protected files with other users on your local computer or across the network, you need to add their encryption certificates to the file.

To share an EFS-protected file, follow these steps:

1. Open the Properties dialog box for an encrypted file.
2. On the General tab, click Advanced. The Advanced Attributes dialog box appears.
3. Click the Details button. The User Access dialog box appears, as shown in Figure 11-4.

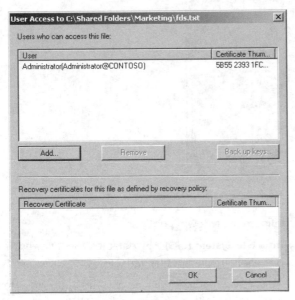

FIGURE 11-4 The User Access dialog box

4. Click the Add button. The Encrypting File System dialog box appears.
5. Select the user you want to grant access to, and then click OK.
6. Click OK three more times to close all open dialog boxes.

The user you selected will now be able to open the file when logged on locally.

Configuring EFS by Using Group Policy Settings

Users can selectively enable EFS on their own files and folders. However, most users are not aware of the need for encryption and will never enable EFS on their own. Rather than relying on users to configure their own data security, you should use Group Policy settings to ensure that domain member computers are configured to meet your organization's security needs.

Within the Group Policy Management Editor, you can configure EFS settings by right-clicking the Computer Configuration\Policies\Windows Settings\Security Settings\Public Key Policies \Encrypting File System node and then choosing Properties to open the Encrypting File System Properties dialog box, shown in Figure 11-5.

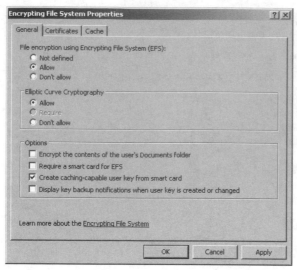

FIGURE 11-5 Defining EFS properties

This General tab allows you to configure the following options:

- **File Encryption Using Encrypting File System (EFS)**   By default, EFS is allowed. If you select Don't Allow, users will be unable to encrypt files with EFS.

- **Encrypt The Contents Of The User's Documents Folder**   Enable this option to automatically encrypt the user's Documents folder. Although many other folders might contain confidential information, encrypting the Documents folder significantly improves security, especially for mobile computers, which are at a higher risk of theft.

> **NOTE** **PREVENTING ATTACKERS FROM BYPASSING EFS**
> EFS protects files when the operating system is offline. Therefore, if someone steals an employee's laptop at an airport, the thief won't be able to access EFS-encrypted files—unless the user is currently logged on. If you enable EFS, you should also configure the desktop to automatically lock when not in use for a few minutes.

- **Require A Smart Card For EFS**   Select this check box to prevent the use of software certificates for EFS. Enable this when users have smart cards and you want to require the users to insert the smart cards to access encrypted files. This can add security, assuming the users do not always leave their smart cards in the computer.

- **Create Caching-Capable User Key From Smart Card**   If this and the previous option are enabled, users need to insert a smart card only the first time they access an encrypted file during their session. If this option is disabled, the smart card must be present every time the user accesses a file.

- **Display Key Backup Notifications When User Key Is Created Or Changed**   If enabled, Windows prompts the user to back up EFS keys when encryption keys are created or changed.

Use the Certificates tab to configure the template EFS uses when using a certification authority (CA) to generate certificates, as well as the strength of self-signed certificates. If you clear the Allow EFS To Generate Self-Signed Certificates When A Certification Authority Is Not Available check box, client computers will need to contact your CA the first time an EFS file is encrypted. This would prevent users who are disconnected from your network from enabling EFS for the first time. To allow EFS to retrieve a certificate from a CA instead of generating a self-signed certificate, you should configure a CA and enable autoenrollment. For detailed instructions, perform Practice 1 in this lesson.

Additionally, you should consider configuring the following EFS-related Group Policy settings:

- **Computer Configuration\Policies\Administrative Templates\Network\Offline Files \Encrypt The Offline Files Cache**   Enable this setting to encrypt Offline Files. Offline Files are discussed in Lesson 2, "Sharing Folders."

- **Computer Configuration\Policies\Administrative Templates\Windows Components \Search \Allow Indexing Of Encrypted Files**   If you index encrypted files, an attacker might be able to see the contents of an encrypted file by examining the index. Disabling indexing of encrypted files improves security but prevents users from searching those files.

Configuring a Data Recovery Agent

An encrypted file is inaccessible to anyone who lacks the decryption key, including system administrators and, if they lose their original keys, the users who encrypted the files. To enable recovery of encrypted files, EFS supports DRAs. DRAs can decrypt encrypted files by using the file properties dialog box, just as if they were the user that originally encrypted the files. In enterprise Active Directory environments, you can use Group Policy settings to configure one or more user accounts as DRAs for your entire organization.

To configure an enterprise DRA, follow these steps:

1. Configure an enterprise CA. For example, you can install the Windows Server 2008 Active Directory Certificate Services server role. The default settings work well.

2. Create a dedicated user account to act as the DRA. Although you could use an existing user account, the DRA has the ability to access any encrypted file—an almost unlimited power that must be carefully controlled in most organizations. Log on using the DRA account.

IMPORTANT   AVOID GIVING ONE PERSON TOO MUCH POWER

For the DRA user account, or any highly privileged account, have two people type half the account's password. Then have each user write down half of the password and give the password halves to different managers to protect. This requires at least two people to work together to access the DRA account—a security concept called *collusion*. Collusion greatly reduces the risk of malicious use by requiring attackers to trust each other and work together.

---

3. Open the Group Policy Object in the Group Policy Management Editor.

4. Right-click Computer Configuration\Policies\Windows Settings\Security Settings\Public Key Policies\Encrypting File System, and then choose Create Data Recovery Agent to set the current account as the DRA. Creating the DRA requires an enterprise CA; the command will fail if an enterprise CA is not available.

   The Group Policy Management Editor creates a file recovery certificate for the DRA account.

DRAs can automatically open encrypted files just like any other file—exactly as if they had encrypted it with their own user certificate. You can also add DRAs by right-clicking Computer Configuration\Policies\Windows Settings\Security Settings\Public Key Policies \Encrypting File System, choosing Add Data Recovery Agent, and completing the Add Recovery Agent Wizard.

BitLocker

EFS encrypts folders and files for individual users. You cannot use EFS to encrypt system files, however. Although system files do not contain confidential information, if an attacker were to modify system files, malicious software could be installed that monitored the user's actions, recorded passwords, or copied protected documents. To encrypt entire volumes and protect system files, use BitLocker Drive Encryption.

When you enable BitLocker protection for a volume, BitLocker encrypts every byte on the volume, including system files and the paging file. When you start the computer, BitLocker loads before Windows, acquires a decryption key, verifies the integrity of the system, and then transparently decrypts files on the volume until Windows shuts down. In this way, BitLocker provides protection that can be completely transparent to end users.

In addition to helping protect data, BitLocker also helps reduce the risk of an attacker altering system files. If BitLocker detects that a system file has unexpectedly changed or that the hard disk has been moved to a different computer, BitLocker prevents Windows from starting. This can help protect users from *rootkits*, which are a type of malware that runs beneath the operating system and are very difficult to detect or remove.

BitLocker does improve data security for servers that might be stolen (or have their hard disks stolen). However, security countermeasures always have drawbacks. Once enabled, BitLocker reduces disk performance because of the additional encryption and decryption that must occur. According to Microsoft, the performance impact is less than 10 percent. In April of 2007, Maximum PC performed independent performance testing and determined that hard drive performance dropped about 20 percent, and overall performance dropped about 10 percent. Your results will depend upon the performance of your computer and how frequently the disk is used.

Besides the potential performance impact, a corrupted or missing key can make your data unavailable. Before enabling BitLocker on a server, weigh the costs and benefits. Typically, you should enable BitLocker only when a server is managed locally, reliably backed up, not limited by disk performance, and not physically secure.

BitLocker Modes

BitLocker needs to retrieve a decryption key each time Windows starts. In most cases, BitLocker retrieves the key from a Trusted Platform Module (TPM) chip built-into the computer. TPM chips, which some newer computers have, can store keys and are very resistant to tampering.

To use BitLocker encryption on a computer without a compatible TPM, you will need to change a computer Group Policy setting by performing these steps:

1. In the Group Policy Object Editor, navigate to Computer Configuration\Administrative Templates\Windows Components\BitLocker Drive Encryption\Operating System Drives.

2. Enable the Require Additional Authentication At Startup setting. Then, select the Allow BitLocker Without A Compatible TPM check box.

3. Click OK.

You can configure BitLocker to retrieve and unlock this decryption key in several different ways:

- **TPM-only**   During startup, BitLocker automatically communicates with the TPM hardware to verify that the computer and critical operating system files have not been modified. If the TPM hardware has the key available and the system integrity is intact, BitLocker begins transparently decrypting the volume, and Windows starts without any interaction with the user.

- **External key without TPM**   If TPM hardware is not available, BitLocker can store decryption keys on an external key (usually a USB flash drive) instead of use a built-in TPM chip. Using BitLocker in this configuration can be risky, however, because if the user loses the USB flash drive, the encrypted volume is no longer accessible and the computer cannot start until a user types the recovery key. Windows does not make this option available by default.

- **TPM with external key**   BitLocker requires the user to provide an external key to start Windows. This technique is not transparent to users, but it helps protect data if someone steals a computer and Windows is not running. This provides protection from both hard-disk theft and stolen computers (assuming the computer was shut down or locked); however, it requires some effort from the user.

- **TPM with PIN**   In this mode, BitLocker requires the user to type a PIN before retrieving the key from the TPM. You cannot use a PIN without a TPM.

- **TPM with PIN and external key**   In this mode, BitLocker requires the user to provide an external key and to type a PIN. You cannot select this mode by using the BitLocker Setup Wizard. Instead, use the Manage-bde command-line tool. For example, to protect the C drive with both a PIN and a startup key located on the E:\ drive, you would run the command **manage-bde –protectors –add C: -TPMAndPINAndStartupKey –tsk E:**.

The only mode that is useful for most servers is TPM Only; the other techniques require someone to be physically at the server each time Windows starts, which is not practical because most servers are managed remotely, and to install updates, they regularly restart at scheduled times. BitLocker protects computers only at startup, so adding the protection of a PIN or USB flash drive is not as useful for mobile computers because the entire computer is often stolen while the operating system is running.

If the standard startup method fails because the decryption key is unavailable, the TPM chip is missing or damaged, the hard disk has been moved to a different computer, or because critical Windows files have been modified, BitLocker enters recovery mode. In recovery mode, the user needs to enter a 40-digit recovery key or insert a USB flash drive with a recovery key stored on it to regain access to the data. TPM-only mode provides protection from hard-disk theft with no user training necessary.

Managing TPM Hardware

BitLocker is designed to be primarily used with TPM hardware. If a computer has TPM hardware and it is disabled in the operating system, BitLocker setup will automatically enable the TPM hardware.

You can enable or disable TPM hardware and manage the keys contained within it by using the TPM Management snap-in, shown in Figure 11-6, which you must manually add to an MMC console. If the TPM Management console does not detect TPM hardware, check the BIOS settings to ensure it is enabled; computer manufacturers often disable it by default.

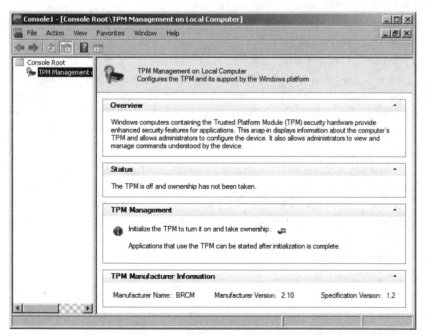

FIGURE 11-6 The TPM Console

Enabling BitLocker Encryption

Individual users can enable BitLocker from Control Panel, but most enterprises should use Active Directory Domain Services (AD DS) to manage keys.

> **MORE INFO   CONFIGURING AD DS TO BACK UP BITLOCKER**
>
> For detailed instructions about how to configure AD DS to back up BitLocker and TPM recovery information, read "Configuring Active Directory to Back up Windows BitLocker Drive Encryption and Trusted Platform Module Recovery Information" at *http://go.microsoft.com/fwlink/?LinkId=78953*.

To enable BitLocker from Control Panel, perform these steps:

1. Add the BitLocker feature. In Server Manager, right-click Features, and then click Add Features. The Add Features Wizard appears.

2. On the Select Features page, select BitLocker Drive Encryption. Click Next.

3. On the Confirm Installation Selections page, click Install.

4. On the Installation Results page, click Close. Click Yes to restart the computer.

5. After the computer restarts, the Resume Configuration Wizard appears. Click Close.

6. Perform a full backup of the computer. Even though BitLocker is very stable and corruption is unlikely, there is a possibility that you will be unable to access the protected volume once BitLocker is enabled.

7. Run a check of the integrity of the BitLocker volume. To check the integrity of a volume, right-click it in Explorer, and then click Properties. On the Tools tab, click Check Now. Select both check boxes, and then click Start.

8. Open Control Panel, and then click the System And Security link. Under BitLocker Drive Encryption, click the Protect Your Computer By Encrypting Data On Your Disk link.

9. On the BitLocker Drive Encryption page, click Turn On BitLocker.

10. When prompted, click Yes to start BitLocker setup.

11. If the Turn On The TPM Security Hardware page appears, click Next, and then click Restart.

12. On the Set BitLocker Startup Preferences page, select your authentication method. The choices available to you vary depending on whether the computer has TPM hardware. Additionally, the available choices can be controlled by the Group Policy settings contained within Computer Configuration\Administrative Templates\Windows Components\BitLocker Drive Encryption.

13. If you chose to require a startup key, the Save Your Startup Key page appears. Connect a USB flash drive, select it, and then click Save.

14. On the Save The Recovery Password page, choose the destination (a USB drive, a local or remote folder, or a printer) to save your recovery password. The recovery password is a small text file containing brief instructions, a drive label and password ID, and the 48-digit recovery password. Save the password and the recovery key on separate devices and store them in different locations. Click Next.

15. On the Encrypt The Volume page, select the Run BitLocker System Check check box, and click Continue. Then, click Restart Now. After Windows restarts, BitLocker verifies that the volume is ready to be encrypted.

16. BitLocker displays a special screen confirming that the key material was loaded. Now that this has been confirmed, BitLocker begins encrypting the C drive after Windows starts, and BitLocker is enabled.

BitLocker encrypts the drive in the background so that you can continue using the computer.

After enabling BitLocker, you can choose to turn off BitLocker from the Control Panel tool. You have two options:

- **Disable BitLocker Drive Encryption**   This option leaves the volume encrypted but stores the decryption key so that it is not protected. You can use this option to move a hard disk to another computer. Later, you can re-enable BitLocker without re-encrypting the entire volume.

- **Decrypt The Volume**   This option decrypts the volume, completely removing BitLocker.

> *NOTE* **BITLOCKER-TO-GO**
>
> Windows 7 and Windows Server 2008 R2 support BitLocker-To-Go, which encrypts removable flash drives by using a password. The feature is more useful for client computers than for server computers, however. For more information about BitLocker-To-Go, watch the overview video at *http://technet.microsoft.com/edge/bitlocker-drive-encryption-with-bitlocker-to-go-overview.aspx.*

PRACTICE   Encrypting and Recovering Files

In this practice, you create two user accounts: a user account that encrypts a file with EFS, and a DRA that accesses the encrypted file. Then, you encrypt a file, verify that other user accounts cannot access it, and finally recover the encrypted file by using the DRA.

EXERCISE 1   Configuring a DRA

In this exercise, you create accounts that represent a traditional EFS user and a DRA.

1. Add the Active Directory Certificate Services role by using the default settings to Dcsrv1 to configure it as an enterprise CA.

2. Create a domain user account named EFSUser and make the account a member of the Domain Admins group so that it can log on to the domain controller; users need standard-only user privileges to encrypt files on domain member computers. You will use the EFSUser account to create and encrypt a file.

3. Create two domain user accounts named DRA and NotDRA, and make the accounts a member of the Domain Admins group..

4. Log on using the DRA account. In Server Manager, right-click Features\Group Policy Management\Forest: nwtraders.msft\Domains\nwtraders.msft\Default Domain Policy, and then choose Edit. The Group Policy Management Editor appears.

5. In the console tree, select Computer Configuration\Policies\Windows Settings\Security Settings\Public Key Policies. In the details pane, double-click the Certificate Services Client – Auto-Enrollment policy. Set the Configuration Model to Enabled, and then click OK.

6. Right-click Computer Configuration\Policies\Windows Settings\Security Settings\Public Key Policies\Encrypting File System, and then choose Create Data Recovery Agent.

The account you are currently logged on with, DRA, is now configured as a DRA.

EXERCISE 2 Encrypting a File

In this exercise, you use the newly created EFSUser account to create an encrypted text file.

1. On Dcsrv1, log on using the EFSUser account.

2. Click Start, and then choose Documents.

3. In the Documents window, right-click Libraries\Documents\My Documents, and then choose Properties. Do not right-click the Documents shortcut listed in the Favorite Links pane; doing so will modify the shortcut and not the folder.

4. In the General tab of the Documents Properties dialog box, click Advanced. Select the Encrypt Contents To Secure Data check box, and then click OK three times.

5. Select the Libraries\Documents\My Documents folder. Right-click the details pane, choose New, and then choose Text Document. Name the document **Encrypted**. Notice that it appears in green in Windows Explorer because it is encrypted.

6. Open the encrypted document, and add the text "Hello, world." Save and close the document.

EXERCISE 3 Attempting to Access an Encrypted File

In this exercise, you use the Administrator account (which is not configured as a DRA) to simulate an attacker attempting to access a file that another user has encrypted.

1. On Dcsrv1, log on using the NotDRA account. This account has administrative privileges to Dcsrv1, but it is not configured as a DRA.

2. Click Start, and then choose Computer.

3. In the Computer window, browse to C:\Users\EFSUser\Documents.

4. Double-click the Encrypted document in the details pane. Notice that Notepad displays an Access Is Denied error. You would see this same error even if you reinstalled the operating system or connected the hard disk to a different computer.

EXERCISE 4   Recovering an Encrypted File

In this exercise, you use the DRA account to access the encrypted file and then remove the encryption from the file so that other users can access it.

1. On Dcsrv1, log on using the DRA account. This account is configured as a DRA.

2. Click Start, and then choose Computer.

3. In the Computer window, browse to C:\Users\EFSUser\My Documents. Respond to any User Account Control (UAC) prompts that appear.

4. Double-click the Encrypted document in the details pane. Notice that Notepad displays the file because the DRA account is configured as a DRA. Close Notepad.

5. In Windows Explorer, right-click the Encrypted file, and then choose Properties. On the General tab, click Advanced. Clear the Encrypt Contents To Secure Data check box, and then click OK twice. Respond to the UAC prompts that appear. DRA accounts can remove encryption, allowing other accounts to access previously encrypted files.

Lesson Summary

- NTFS file permissions control access to files when Windows is running, whether users access files locally or across the network. NTFS file permissions allow you to grant users and groups read access, write access, or full control access (which allows users to change permissions). If you deny a user NTFS file permissions, those deny permissions override any other assigned permissions. If a user does not have any NTFS file permissions assigned, that user is denied access.

- EFS encrypts files, which protects them when Windows is offline. Although encryption provides very strong security, users will be unable to access encrypted files if they lose the encryption key. To protect against this, use Active Directory Group Policy settings to configure a DRA that can recover encrypted files.

- BitLocker encrypts volumes and verifies the integrity of system files, which protects the files on the volume when Windows is offline, and it helps reduce the risks of malware that modifies system files.

Lesson Review

You can use the following questions to test your knowledge of the information in Lesson 1, "Managing File Security." The questions are also available on the companion CD if you prefer to review them in electronic form.

> **NOTE   ANSWERS**
>
> Answers to these questions and explanations of why each answer choice is correct or incorrect are located in the "Answers" section at the end of the book.

1. You create a folder named Marketing on a computer named FileServer and configure NTFS permissions to grant the Domain Users group Read permission and the Marketing group Modify permission. You share the folder and grant the Everyone group Reader permission. Mary, a user whose account is a member of both the Marketing group and the Domain Users group, logs on locally to the FileServer computer to access the Marketing folder. What effective permissions will Mary have?

   A. No access

   B. Read

   C. Write

   D. Full Control

2. You have a folder protected with EFS that contains a file you need to share across the network. You share the folder and assign NTFS and share permissions to allow the user to open the file. What should you do to allow the user to access the encrypted file without decreasing the security?

   A. Right-click the file, and then choose Properties. On the Security tab, add the user's account.

   B. Right-click the file, and then choose Properties. On the General tab, click Advanced. Click the Details button, and then add the user's account.

   C. Right-click the file, and then choose Properties. On the General tab, click Advanced. Clear the Encrypt Contents To Secure Data check box.

   D. Do nothing.

3. You are creating a shared folder on a computer running Windows Server 2008 R2. You need to allow the Management group to view, create, and modify files in the shared folders. You do not want members of the Management group to change permissions on files. Which permissions should you configure for the Management group? (Choose all that apply. Each answer forms part of the complete solution.)

   A. The Full Control share permission

   B. The Change share permission

   C. The Full Control NTFS permission

   D. The Modify NTFS permission

Lesson 2: Sharing Folders

One of the most common ways for users to collaborate is by storing documents in shared folders. Shared folders allow any user with access to your network and appropriate permissions to access files. Shared folders also allow documents to be centralized, where they are more easily managed than they would be if they were distributed to thousands of client computers.

Although all versions of Windows since Windows For Workgroups 3.11 have supported file sharing, Windows Server 2008 R2 includes the File Services server role, which provides a robust set of features for sharing folders and managing shared files. With the improved disk quota capability, Windows can notify users and administrators when individual users consume too much disk space. DFS provides a centralized directory structure for folders shared from multiple computers and is capable of automatically replicating files between folders for redundancy. Offline Files automatically copies shared files to mobile computers so that users can access the files while disconnected from the network.

After this lesson, you will be able to:

- Install the File Services server role.
- Use quotas to notify you when users consume more than an allotted amount of disk space.
- Share folders across the network.
- Use DFS to create a namespace of shared folders on multiple servers.
- Use Offline Files to grant mobile users access to copies of network files and folders while they are disconnected from the network.

Estimated lesson time: 70 minutes

Installing the File Services Server Role

Windows Server 2008 R2 can share folders without adding any server roles. However, adding the File Services server role adds useful management tools along with the ability to participate in DFS namespaces, configure quotas, generate storage reports, and other capabilities. To install the File Services server role, follow these steps:

1. In Server Manager, select and then right-click Roles. Choose Add Role. The Add Roles Wizard appears.
2. On the Before You Begin page, click Next.
3. On the Server Roles page, select the File Services check box. Click Next.
4. On the File Services page, click Next.
5. On the Select Role Services page, select from the following roles:
   - **File Server**   Although not required to share files, adding this core role service allows you to use the Share And Storage Management snap-in.
   - **Distributed File System**   Enables sharing files by using the DFS namespace and replicating files between DFS servers. If you select this role service, the wizard will prompt you to configure a namespace.

- **File Server Resources Manager**   Installs tools for generating storage reports, configuring quotas, and defining file screening policies. If you select this role service, the wizard will prompt you to enable storage monitoring on the local disks.

- **Services for Network File System**   Provides connectivity for UNIX client computers that use Network File System (NFS) for file sharing. Note that most modern UNIX operating systems can connect to standard Windows file shares, so this service is typically not required.

- **Windows Search Service**   Indexes files for faster searching when clients connect to shared folders. This role service is not intended for enterprise use. If you select this role service, the wizard will prompt you to enable indexing on the local disks.

- **Windows Server 2003 File Services**   Provides services compatible with computers running Windows Server 2003.

- **BranchCache for network files**   Caches shared files on servers at branch offices to reduce bandwidth usage on your Wide Area Network (WAN).

6. Respond to any roles service wizard pages that appear.

7. On the Confirmation page, click Install.

8. On the Results page, click Close.

You can access the File Services tools by using the Roles\File Services node in Server Manager. The sections that follow provide more information about these role services.

Quotas

When multiple users share a disk, whether locally or across the network, the disk will quickly become filled—usually because one or two users consume far more disk space than the rest of the users. Disk quotas make it easy to monitor users who consume more than a specified amount of disk space. Additionally, you can enforce quotas to prevent users from consuming more disk space (although this can cause applications to fail and is not typically recommended).

With Windows Server 2008 R2, you should use the Quota Management console to configure disk quotas. You can also configure quotas by using the DirQuota command-line tool. Additionally, you can configure disk quotas by using Group Policy settings or by using Windows Explorer. The sections that follow describe each of these techniques.

Configuring Disk Quotas by Using the Quota Management Console

After installing the File Server Resource Manager role service, you can manage disk quotas by using the Quota Management console. In Server Manager, you can access the snap-in at Roles\File Services\Share And Storage Management\File Server Resource Manager\Quota Management. The Quota Management console provides more flexible control over quotas and makes it easier to notify users or administrators that a user has exceeded a quota threshold, or to run an executable file that automatically clears up disk space.

CREATING QUOTA TEMPLATES

The Quota Management snap-in supports the use of quota templates. You can use a quota template to apply a set of quotas and response behavior to volumes. Windows Server 2008 R2 includes the following standard templates:

- **100 MB Limit**   Defines a *hard quota* (a quota that prevents the user from creating more files) of 100 MB per user, with email warnings sent to the user at 85 percent and 95 percent. At 100 percent of the quota, this template sends an email to the user and to administrators.

- **200 MB Limit Reports To User**   Defines a hard quota of 200 MB per user, with email warnings sent to the user at 85 percent and 95 percent. At 100 percent of the quota, this template sends an email to the user and to administrators and sends a report to the user.

- **200 MB Limit With 50 MB Extension**   Defines a 200-MB quota. When the 200-MB quota is reached, the computer sends an email to the user and administrators and then applies the 250 MB Extended Limit quota to grant the user additional capacity.

- **250 MB Extended Limit**   Primarily used with the previous quota template to provide the user an additional 50 MB of capacity. This template prevents the user from exceeding 250 MB.

- **Monitor 200 GB Volume Usage**   Provides email notifications when utilization reaches 70 percent, 80 percent, 90 percent, and 100 percent of the 200 GB soft quota.

- **Monitor 500 MB Share**   Provides email notifications when utilization reaches 80 percent, 100 percent, and 120 percent of the 500-MB soft quota.

These standard templates are provided as examples. To create your own quota templates, right-click Quota Templates in the Quota Management console, and then choose Create Quota Template. In the Create Quota Template dialog box, select a standard template you want to base your new template on, and then click Copy. Figure 11-7 demonstrates copying a quota template.

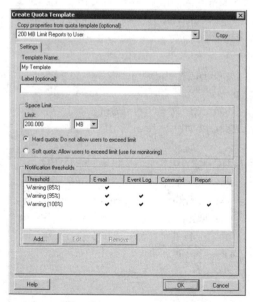

FIGURE 11-7 Creating a quota template

Thresholds define what happens when a user reaches a quota (or a percentage of a quota). To add a threshold, edit a quota template or a quota, and then click Add. The Add Threshold dialog box has four tabs:

- **E-mail Message** Sends an email notification to administrators or to the user. You can define the [AdmIn Email] variable and other email settings by right-clicking File Server Resource Manager and then choosing Configure Options.

- **Event Log** Logs an event to the event log, which is useful if you have management tools that process events.

- **Command** Runs a command or a script when a threshold is reached. You can use this to run a script that automatically compresses files, removes temporary files, or allocates more disk space for the user.

- **Report** Generates a report that you can send as an email message to administrators or the user. You can choose from a number of reports.

Use thresholds to notify users or administrators that a user has consumed a specific amount of disk space.

CREATING QUOTAS

To apply quotas consistently, you should always create a quota template first and then create a quota based on that template. To create a quota, follow these steps:

1. Select and right-click the Quotas node in Server Manager, and then choose Create Quota. The Create Quota dialog box appears, as shown in Figure 11-8.

FIGURE 11-8 Creating a quota

2. Click the Browse button to select a folder to apply the quota to, and then click OK.

3. To create a single quota for the specified folder and all subfolders, select Create Quote On Path. Select Auto Apply Template And Create Quotas On Existing And New Subfolders to apply a template to any new folders created within the parent folder you select.

4. Select the Derive Properties From This Quota Template option, and then select the quota template from the drop-down list. Otherwise, you can select the Define Custom Quota Properties option and then click the Custom Properties button to define a quota not based on an existing template.

5. Click Create.

The Quotas snap-in shows the newly created quota, which is immediately in effect.

Configuring Disk Quotas at a Command Prompt or Script

You can use the DirQuota command to configure quotas at the command prompt or from a script. For example, the following command applies the standard 200 MB Limit Reports To User template to the C:\Shared folder:

```
dirquota quota add /Path:C:\Shared /SourceTemplate:"200 MB Limit Reports To User"
```

To create a hard limit of 100 MB, run the following command:

```
dirquota quota add /Path:C:\Shared /Limit:100MB /Type:Hard
```

Although you can create multiple thresholds and notifications by using the DirQuota command, it is typically easier to create templates and use DirQuota to apply the templates. For complete usage information, type the command **DirQuota /?**.

Configuring Disk Quotas by Using Windows Explorer

Although you should always use the Quota Management console to configure quotas in Windows Server 2008 R2, the operating system continues to support quota management by using Windows Explorer, using the same interface as earlier versions of Windows. To configure disk quotas on a local computer by using Windows Explorer, follow these steps:

1. Open Windows Explorer (for example, by clicking Start and then choosing Computer).

2. Right-click the disk you want to configure quotas for, and then choose Properties. You cannot configure quotas for individual folders. The disk properties dialog box appears.

3. On the Quota tab, select the Enable Quota Management check box, as shown in Figure 11-9.

FIGURE 11-9 Enabling quota management

4. Select the Limit Disk Space To option. Specify the limit and warning levels. Windows does not notify users when they exceed either threshold. In fact, if you choose not to enforce quota limits, the only difference between the two thresholds is the event ID that is added to the System event log.

5. To add an event for the warning or limit levels, select the Log Event When A User Exceeds Their Quota Limit check box or the Log Event When A User Exceeds Their Warning Level check box. Events are added to the System event log with a source of NTFS. Event ID 36 indicates that a user reached the warning level, and event ID 37 indicates a user reached the quota limit. Use event triggers to send an email or run a program when these events are added so that systems administrators can address the problem. For more information about event triggers, read Chapter 10, "Monitoring Computers."

6. Select or clear the Deny Disk Space To Users Exceeding Quota Limit check box. If you select this check box, users will be unable to save or update files when they exceed their quota limit. For this reason, you should typically not select this option—the potential harm to user productivity is rarely worth it. Instead, create an event trigger that notifies IT when a user exceeds the quota limit so that IT can follow up with the user.

7. Click Quota Entries to view the current disk usage, as shown in Figure 11-10. In the Quota Entries window, double-click a user to configure a user-specific quota that differs from the default settings for the disk.

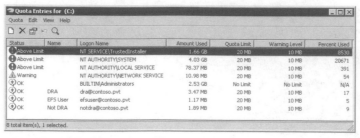

FIGURE 11-10 Viewing quota entries

8. Click OK to close the Quota Settings For *User Name* dialog box, close the Quota Entries For *Drive Letter* window, and then click OK again to close the Local Disk Properties dialog box. If prompted, click OK to enable system quotas.

Configuring Disk Quotas by Using Group Policy

You can also configure simple disk quotas by using Group Policy settings. In the Group Policy Management Editor, select the Computer Configuration\Policies\Administrative Templates \System\Disk Quotas node to define these policy settings:

- **Enable Disk Quotas**   You must enable this policy to use disk quotas.

- **Enforce Disk Quota Limit**   Equivalent to selecting the Deny Disk Space To Users Exceeding Quota Limit check box when configuring local disk quotas.

- **Default Quota Limit And Warning Level**   Defines the quota limit and warning levels, exactly as you can when configuring disk quotas using Windows Explorer.

- **Log Event When Quota Limit Exceeded**   Equivalent to selecting the Log Event When A User Exceeds Their Quota Limit check box in Windows Explorer.

- **Log Event When Quota Warning Level Exceeded**   Equivalent to selecting the Log Event When A User Exceeds Their Warning Level check box in Windows Explorer.

- **Apply Policy To Removable Media**   Defines whether quotas are applied to removable media. Typically, this policy should be disabled.

Folder Sharing

You can share folders across the network to allow other computers to access them, as if the computers were connected to a local disk.

Sharing Folders from Windows Explorer

The simplest way to share a folder is to right-click the folder in Windows Explorer, choose Share With, and then choose Specific People. As shown in Figure 11-11, the File Sharing dialog box appears and allows you to select the users who will have access to the folder. Click Share to create the shared folder, and then click Done.

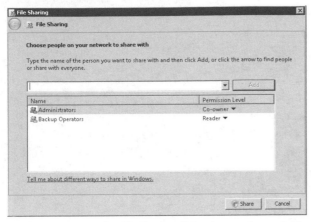

FIGURE 11-11 Using the File Sharing dialog box to share a folder

Using this interface you, can select either Read or Read/Write permissions. The following section describes a different technique for sharing folders that provides more permissions flexibility.

Sharing Folders by Using the Provision A Shared Folder Wizard

Using the Provision A Shared Folder Wizard, you can share folders, configure quotas, and specify security by following these steps:

1. In Server Manager, right-click Roles\File Services\Share And Storage Management, and then choose Provision Share. The Provision A Shared Folder Wizard appears.

2. On the Shared Folder Location page, click the Browse button to select the folder to share. Click OK. Click Next.

3. On the NTFS Permissions page, you can choose to edit the NTFS file system permissions for the shared folder. If you want to change the current permissions, select Yes, and then, if necessary, click Edit Permissions. Configure the NTFS permissions as necessary, and then click OK. Click Next.

4. On the Share Protocols page, you can choose whether to share the folder by using Windows protocol (indicated as SMB, which stands for Server Message Block) or using a UNIX protocol (indicated as NFS, or Network File System). Typically, SMB will suffice, even for UNIX clients. NFS is available only when the Services For Network File System role service is installed. Click Next.

5. On the SMB Settings page, click Advanced if you want to change the default settings for the number of simultaneous users permitted, offline files, or access-based enumeration. Access-based enumeration hides shared folders that a user does not have permission to access. Click Next.

6. On the SMB Permissions page, as shown in Figure 11-12, select the permissions you want to assign. To define custom permissions, select Users And Groups Have Custom Share Permissions, and then click the Permissions button. Click Next.

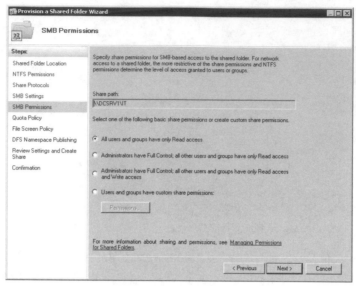

FIGURE 11-12 The SMB Permissions page

7. On the Quota Policy page, select the Apply Quota check box if you want to define a quota. Then, select a quota template. Click Next.

8. On the File Screen Policy page, select the Apply File Screen check box if you want to allow only specific types of files in the folder. Then, select the file screen you want to use. Click Next.

> **NOTE CONFIGURING FILE SCREENING**
>
> You can configure file screening using the Roles\File Services\Share And Storage Management\File Server Resource Manager\File Screening Management node of Server Manager. You can use the FileScrn.exe command-line tool in scripts or when running Windows Server 2008 Server Core.

9. On the DFS Namespace Publishing page, select the Publish The SMB Share To A DFS Namespace check box if desired. Then, provide the DFS namespace information. Click Next.

10. On the Review Settings And Create Share page, click Create. Then click Close.

Sharing Folders from a Command Prompt or Script

You can share folders from a script or a command prompt (for example, when running Server Core) using the Net Share command.

To view existing shares, type the following command:

```
net share
```

To create a share, use the following syntax:

```
net share ShareName=Path [/GRANT:user,[READ|CHANGE|FULL]]
[/CACHE:Manual|Documents|Programs|None]
```

For example, to share the C:\Shared folder by using the share name Files, type the following command:

```
net share Files=C:\Shared
```

To share the same folder with read access for everyone but disallow Offline Files, type the following command:

```
net share Files=C:\Shared /GRANT:Everyone,Read /CACHE:None
```

To remove a share, specify the share name and the /DELETE parameter. The following example would remove the share named Files:

```
net share Files /DELETE
```

For complete usage information, type the following command:

```
net share /?
```

Connecting to Shared Folders

Client computers connect to shared folders across the network by using the Universal Naming Convention (UNC) format: \\<server_name>\<share name>. For example, if you share the folder MyDocs from the server MyServer, you would connect to it by typing **\\MyServer \MyDocs**.

You can use UNC format just as you would specify any folder name. For example, you could open a file in Notepad by providing the path \\MyServer\MyDocs\MyFile.txt. At a command prompt, you could view the contents of the shared folder by running the following command:

```
dir \\MyServer\MyDocs
```

Most users prefer to access shared folders by using a network drive. Network drives map a drive letter to a shared folder. For example, although the C drive is typically a local hard disk, you could assign the Z drive to a shared folder. Client computers can connect to shared folders from Windows Explorer by clicking the Map Network Drive button on the toolbar or by clicking the Tools menu and then choosing Map Network Drive. Alternatively, you can map a network drive by using the Net command at a command prompt with the following syntax:

```
net use <drive_letter>: \\<server_name>\<share_name>
```

For example, the following command would map the Z drive to the \\MyServer\MyDocs shared folder:

```
net use Z: \\MyServer\MyDocs
```

Classification Management

Regulations require many businesses and government agencies to classify files in different ways. Windows Server 2008 R2 includes the File Classification Infrastructure to help automate this process. With the File Classification Infrastructure, you define a custom set of classification properties and then create classification rules to apply different values for each of those properties to specific files.

Creating Classification Properties

Because you define the properties used to classify files, you can create any categories that you might need. For example, to classify files as being either confidential or not confidential, you could create a Yes/No property named Is Confidential. However, to categorize files as Classified, Sensitive, or Public, you would create an Ordered List property named Confidentiality Level that provides for the choosing one of the three options.

You can create the following property types:

- **Yes/No** More commonly known as a Boolean or binary value, allows you to define a property that can be either yes or no.
- **Date-time** Allows you to specify a date using a property. You might do this to define the date a file needs to be deleted, reviewed, or audited.
- **Number** Allows you to specify a number.
- **Multiple Choice List** Allows you to specify a list of values and select zero, one, or more than one for any given file.
- **Ordered List** Allows you to specify a list of values and select only one.
- **String** Allows you to specify a single string.
- **Multi-string** Allows you to specify multiple strings.

To create a property, follow these steps:

1. In Server Manager, right-click Roles\File Services\Share And Storage Management\File Server Resource Manager\Classification Management\Classification Properties, and then choose Create Property. The Create Classification Property Definition dialog box appears.
2. Type a name and description. Then, choose a property type. Depending on the property type, you might need to add more information. For example, if you choose Multiple Choice List or Ordered List, you will need to type each of the possible values.
3. Click OK.

Creating Classification Rules

Rules apply property values to files that match criteria you specify. When you create a rule, you specify the scope to choose which folders the rule will apply to. You can choose two different classification mechanisms:

- **Folder Classifier**   Applies property values to files based on their folder.
- **Content Classifier**   Applies property values to files based on their content. Windows will search file contents for strings and regular expressions and apply property values when it finds a match.

To create a classification rule, follow these steps:

1. In Server Manager, right-click Roles\File Services\Share And Storage Management\File Server Resource Manager\Classification Management\Classification Rules, and then choose Create A New Rule. The Classification Rule Definitions dialog box appears.

2. On the Rule Settings tab, type a name and description. Click the Add button to specify the folder to apply the rule to. You can select multiple folders.

3. On the Classification tab, choose a classification mechanism. Then, choose a property and the value to be assigned when the rule matches a file.

4. Click the Advanced button. On the Evaluation Type tab, select the Re-evaluate Existing Property Values check box if you want to evaluate files that have already been assigned properties. You can then choose to overwrite the existing rules or aggregate the values. If you chose Content Classifier as the classification mechanism in the previous step, follow the next three steps as well:

   a. In the Additional Rule Parameters dialog box, select the Additional Classification Parameters tab.

   b. In the Name box, type one of the following: **String**, **StringCaseSensitive**, or **RegularExpression**. In the Value box, type your string or regular expression. Repeat to add multiple strings. Figure 11 13 shows each of the three criteria types configured; however, only one is required.

   c. Click OK.

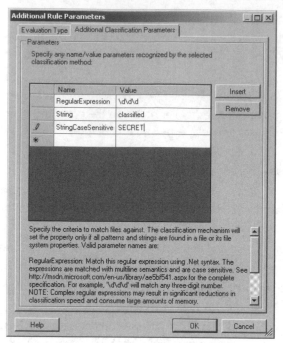

FIGURE 11-13 Specifying content matching criteria

5. Click OK.

After you create your classification rules, you can apply the rules using the File Server Resource Manager snap-in by right-clicking Classification Management\Classification Rules and then clicking Run Classification With All Rules Now. You can then choose either to wait while Windows runs the rule classification or to run the rule classification in the background. After you run the rule classification, Windows displays an HTML report showing the number of files that matched your rules and the sizes of each group.

To automatically classify files on a schedule you specify, right-click Classification Management \Classification Rules, and then click Configure Classification Schedule. In the File Server Resource Manager Options dialog box, on the Automatic Classification tab, click the Create button to specify a schedule. Figure 11-14 shows the dialog box with a sample schedule.

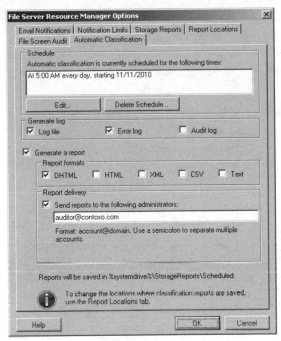

FIGURE 11-14 Creating a file classification schedule

Distributed File System

Large organizations often have dozens, or even hundreds, of file servers. This can make it very difficult for users to remember which file server specific files are stored on.

DFS provides a single namespace that allows users to connect to any shared folder in your organization. With DFS, all shared folders can be accessible using a single network drive letter in Windows Explorer. For example, if your Active Directory domain is contoso.com, you could create the DFS namespace \\contoso.com\dfs. Then, you could create the folder \\contoso.com \dfs\marketing and map it to shared folders (known as *targets*) at both \\server1\marketing and \\server2\marketing.

Besides providing a single namespace to make it easier for users to find files, DFS can provide redundancy for shared files by using replication. Replication also allows you to host a shared folder on multiple servers and have client computers automatically connect to the closest available server.

Installing DFS

You can install DFS when adding the File Services server role by using the Add Roles Wizard, or you can add the role service later using Server Manager by right-clicking Roles\File Services and then choosing Add Role Services. Whichever method you use, follow these steps to complete the wizard pages:

1. On the DFS Namespaces page, choose whether to create a namespace. Click Next.

2. If the Namespace Type page appears, choose whether to use a domain-based namespace (for Active Directory environments) or a stand-alone namespace (for workgroup environments). If all DFS servers for the namespace are running Windows Server 2008 or Windows Server 2008 R2, enable Windows Server 2008 mode to support access-based enumeration. Click Next.

3. If the Credentials page appears, select a Domain Admin user account, and then click Next.

4. If the Namespace Configuration page appears, you can click the Add button to add folders. You can also do this later by using the DFS Management snap-in. Click Next.

If you don't create a DFS namespace or add folders, you can add them later by using the DFS Management console in Server Manager.

Creating a DFS Namespace

The DFS namespace forms the root of shared folders in your organization. Although you might need only a single DFS namespace, you can create multiple DFS namespaces. To create a DFS namespace, follow these steps:

1. In Server Manager, right-click Roles\File Services\DFS Management\Namespaces, and then choose New Namespace. The New Namespace Wizard appears.

2. On the Namespace Server page, type the name of the server that will host the namespace. You can add servers later to host the namespace for redundancy. Users do not reference the server name when accessing the DFS namespace. Click Next.

3. On the Namespace Name And Settings page, type a name. This name acts as the share name when users access the DFS namespace—for example, *domain_name**namespace_name*. Click the Edit Settings button to configure the permissions for the namespace. Click Next.

4. On the Namespace Type page, choose whether to create a domain-based namespace or a stand-alone namespace. Domain-based namespaces use the Active Directory domain name as their root, and stand-alone namespaces use the server as their root. Click Next.

5. On the Review Settings And Create Namespace page, click Create.

6. On the Confirmation page, click Close.

After creating a namespace, you can adjust settings by right-clicking the namespace and then choosing Properties. The Properties dialog box for the namespace has three tabs:

- **General** Type a description for the namespace.
- **Referrals** Control how multiple targets in a referral list are ordered.

When a client accesses the root of a namespace or a folder with targets, the client receives a referral from the domain controller. Clients always attempt to access the first target computer in the referral list and, if the first target computer does not respond, they access computers farther down the list. This tab gives you control over how multiple targets in a referral list are ordered. The Cache Duration setting defines how long clients wait before requesting a new referral. Select one of the following options from the Ordering Method drop-down list:

- **Random Order**   Distributes referrals evenly among all targets (with targets in the same site listed first).

- **Lowest Cost**   Directs clients to the closest target computer based on site link costs, which you can define by using the Active Directory Sites And Services console.

- **Exclude Targets Outside Of The Client's Site**   Causes client requests to fail instead of accessing a target in a different Active Directory site.

Folders inherit the ordering method from the namespace root by default, but you can also edit the properties of individual folders.

EXAM TIP

Know the different referral order types for the exam!

- **Advanced**   Choose from two polling configurations: Optimize For Consistency or Optimize For Scalability. Optimize For Consistency configures namespace servers to query the primary domain controller (PDC) each time the namespace changes, which reduces the time it takes for changes to the namespace to be visible to users. Optimize For Scalability reduces the number of queries (thus improving performance and reducing utilization of your PDC) by querying the closest domain controller at regular intervals.

Adding Folders to a DFS Namespace

Before your namespace is useful, you must add folders to it. Folders can be *organizational*, which means they exist only within the DFS namespace, or they can be associated with a shared folder on a server. When users connect to a DFS namespace, these folders appear exactly like folders in a traditional file system.

To add folders to a DFS namespace, follow these steps:

1. In Server Manager, select Roles\File Services\DFS Management\Namespaces.

2. In the details pane, right-click the namespace, and then choose New Folder. The New Folder dialog box appears.

3. Type the name for the folder. If the folder is to be used only for organizational purposes (for example, it will contain only other folders), you can click OK. If you want the folder to contain files, click the Add button to associate it with a shared folder. If you add multiple folder targets, you can configure automatic replication between the folders.

4. Click OK.

Configuring DFS Root Permissions

By default, only local, domain, and enterprise administrators can create new DFS roots. To allow other users or groups to create DFS roots, follow these steps:

1. In Server Manager, right-click Roles\File Services\DFS Management\Namespaces, and then click Delegate Management Permissions. The Delegate Management Permissions dialog box appears.
2. Click the Add button. The Select Users Or Groups dialog box appears.
3. Type the name of the group to which you want to grant permissions, and then click OK.
4. Click OK again.

   The group you specified will be allowed to create new DFS roots. You can return to the Delegate Management Permissions dialog box to remove the group.

To view who can edit a DFS root's properties or add DFS folders to the DFS root, select the DFS root in Server Manager, and then select the Delegation tab in the details pane. Remove any group by right-clicking it and then clicking Remove. Add groups by right-clicking the namespace and selecting Delegate Management Permissions.

Use share permissions and NTFS file permissions to configure who can add physical files and folders to a DFS root.

Configuring DFS from a Command Prompt or Script

You can use the DFSUtil tool to configure DFS from a command prompt or script. DFSUtil has replaced DFSCmd included with Windows Server 2003.

To use DFSUtil to view the DFS roots in a domain, run the following command:

`dfsutil domain <domain_name>`

To view the roots on a specific server, run the following command:

`dfsutil server <server_name>`

To view the targets in a namespace, run the following command:

`dfsutil target \\<domain_name>\<namespace_root>`

To view the targets for a folder, run the following command:

`dfsutil link \\<domain_name>\<namespace_root>\<folder>`

To view which Active Directory site a client participates in, run the following command:

`dfsutil client siteinfo <client_name>`

For complete usage information, type **dfsutil /?** at a command prompt. To troubleshoot DFS, use the DFSDiag command-line tool. For more information, type **dfsdiag /?** at a command prompt.

Generating Health Reports for DFS Replication

You can generate a diagnostic report for DFS replication that shows how successful or unsuccessful DFS replication has been at copying files to the different DFS servers. Health reports allow you to detect problems such as files that aren't being copied and DFS servers that are not receiving updates. To create a diagnostic report, follow these steps:

1. In Server Manager, select Roles\File Services\DFS Management\Replication.

2. Right-click a replication group, and then click Create Diagnostic Report.

3. On the Type Of Diagnostic Report Or Test Page, select Health Report. Click Next.

> **NOTE TESTING PROPAGATION**
>
> On the Type Of Diagnostic Report Or Test page, you can select Propagation Test to actively test replication by generating a test file. After the test has completed, you can return to this wizard page and generate a Propagation Report to examine the results of the test.

4. On the Path And Name page, select a folder to save the report in and provide a name. Click Next.

5. On the Members To Include page, remove any servers that you do not want included in the report. Click Next.

6. On the Options page, you can choose to count backlogged files and replicated files. Note that when there are large numbers of either, the report could take a long time to generate. Click Next.

7. On the Review Settings And Create Report page, click Create.

    The wizard displays the DFS Replication Health Report using the default browser. Depending on the number of files and errors, the details of the report might take 10 minutes or longer to appear.

There are several ways you can automate health monitoring for DFS replication:

- Use Scheduled Tasks to run the DfsrAdmin.exe with the Health parameter on a regular basis. For detailed information, read "Automating DFS Replication Health Reports" at *http://blogs.technet.com/b/filecab/archive/2006/06/19/437213.aspx*

- Use the Performance Monitor snap-in and data collector sets to monitor the DFS Replicated Folders, DFS Replication Connections, and DFS Replication Service Volumes counters. For more information, read Lesson 2, "Monitoring Performance and Reliability," in Chapter 10.

- If you use the Microsoft System Center Operations Manager 2007 enterprise monitoring tool, you can automatically monitor DFS health by using the DFS Replication Management Pack. To download the DFS Replication Monitoring Management Pack, visit *http://www.microsoft.com/downloads/details.aspx?FamilyID=c97b22a1-1fd6-426f-94ab-2a6e6db4aed0*.

- If you have WMI scripting skills, use the DFS Replication (DFSR) WMI provider. For detailed information, visit *http://msdn.microsoft.com/library/bb540028.aspx*.

Configuring Failover Clustering for DFS

Windows Server 2008 R2 supports failover clustering for DFS servers. As shown in Figure 11-15, failover clusters connect two computers to a single storage system; however, only one server at a time accesses the shared storage. If the primary server fails, the secondary server starts, connects to the shared storage, and assumes the cluster's host name and IP address. In this way, failover clusters can bring a service back online a few minutes after total hardware failure of the primary server. Administrators can fix the problem with the primary server at their leisure while users access shared folders transparently using the secondary server.

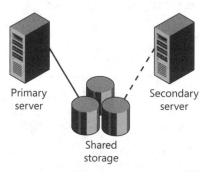

Primary
server

Secondary
server

Shared
storage

FIGURE 11-15 Failover clustering for DFS

Failover clusters require two servers to be physically connected to a single shared storage system. Typically, you will use a fibre channel or iSCSI disk drive subsystem. Individual hard drives in these subsystems are identified by using logical unit numbers (LUNs). To manage the LUNs, use the Storage Manager For SANs console, available in Server Manager in the Roles \File Services\Share And Storage Management node.

EXAM TIP

The 70-642 exam does not cover how to configure clusters. However, you should be familiar with the fact that Windows Server 2008 R2 supports failover clustering for DFS. For detailed instructions, read "Deploying DFS Replication on a Windows Failover Cluster" at *http://blogs.technet.com/b/filecab/archive/2009/06/29/deploying-dfs-replication-on-a-windows-failover-cluster-part-i.aspx.*

Offline Files

Mobile users might need access to shared folders even when they're disconnected from your internal network. Offline Files makes this possible by allowing client computers to automatically cache a copy of files on shared folders and by providing transparent access to the files when the user is disconnected from the network. The next time the user connects to the network, Offline Files synchronizes any updates and prompts the user to manually resolve any conflicts.

Server administrators can configure Offline Files at the shared folder, and users of client computers can configure Offline Files when connected to a shared folder. To configure Offline Files caching behavior for a shared folder, follow these steps:

1. In Server Manager, select Roles\File Services\Share And Storage Management.

2. In the details pane, right-click the share you want to configure, and then choose Properties.

3. On the Sharing tab, click Advanced.

4. In the Advanced dialog box, click the Caching tab, shown in Figure 11-16. Select one of the following three options, and then click OK twice:

   - **Only The Files And Programs That Users Specify Are Available Offline**   Users must manually select the files they want to access while offline. This option works well when users understand how to use Offline Files. If you select this option, you can also enable BranchCache, which can cache the files at remote BranchCache servers throughout your network.

   - **No Files Or Programs From The Share Are Available Offline**   Prevents users from accessing Offline Files. This option is the best choice for confidential documents that should not be stored on mobile computers.

   - **All Files And Programs That Users Open From The Share Are Automatically Available Offline**   Files that users access while connected to the network are automatically cached for a limited amount of time. This option works well when users do not understand how to use Offline Files. If you select this option, you can also select the Optimize For Performance check box, which causes clients to use the local cache to run executable files located on a shared folder.

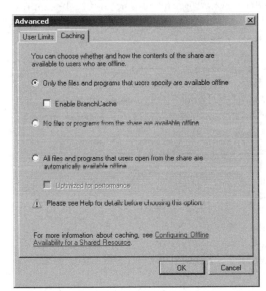

FIGURE 11-16 Configuring Offline Files behavior for a shared folder

You can also access the same settings from Windows Explorer by clicking Advanced Sharing on the Sharing tab of the shared folder's properties dialog box and then clicking the Caching button.

If you choose Only The Files And Programs That Users Specify Are Available Offline, users must configure mapped drives for use with Offline Files if they want to access files while offline. In Windows 7, configure a network drive, folder, or file for Offline Files by right-clicking it and choosing Always Available Offline. Windows will immediately synchronize the file or folder. Users can return to the Offline Files tab later and click Synch Now to copy the latest version of the file. To monitor synchronized files, use the Sync Center tool in Control Panel.

BranchCache

BranchCache stores copies of files shared by remote file or web servers (including servers running Windows Server Update Services [WSUS]) that are running Windows Server 2008 R2 and shares them with clients in the same office. When clients access a file stored on a file or web server in a remote office, BranchCache attempts to retrieve a cached copy from the local BranchCache server or from another client on the local network. BranchCache always verifies that cached files are up to date, so you never need to worry that clients are accessing outdated files.

BranchCache can reduce WAN utilization by reducing the number of files that must be transferred from a remote file server across the WAN.

 REAL WORLD

Tony Northrup

In most enterprise file-sharing scenarios, BranchCache does not noticeably improve network responsiveness for users accessing remote files. However, if many users at a remote office are downloading a large file across a low-bandwidth WAN connection simultaneously, BranchCache can improve responsiveness by eliminating the bandwidth bottleneck.

Therefore, you should enable BranchCache at only those remote offices connected by low bandwidth links, where many different clients access the same files from remote servers running Windows Server 2008 R2.

Using BranchCache Modes

BranchCache can operate in two modes: Distributed Cache and Hosted Cache. In Distributed Cache mode, BranchCache clients cache a copy of remote files and share them with other clients in the same office. In Hosted Cache mode, a server running Windows Server 2008 R2 with the BranchCache feature installed maintains a central cache of files accessed by clients in the same office.

The sections that follow describe Distributed Cache and Hosted Cache mode in more detail.

DISTRIBUTED CACHE MODE

Distributed Cache mode uses peer-to-peer file sharing to exchange copies of files from file servers located on remote networks. When clients running Windows 7 need to read a file from a server in a remote office, those clients retrieve only a file identifier from the remote server. The clients then broadcast a request to other computers running Windows 7 on the same network. If any of those computers have cached a copy of the file, they send it directly to the client across the local network.

At a detailed level, successfully retrieving a cached document using Distributed Cache mode follows these four steps, illustrated in Figure 11-17:

1. A client running Windows 7 connects to the content server and requests a file (or part of a file), exactly as it would if it were to retrieve the file without using BranchCache. After authorizing the user, the server returns an identifier that the client uses to search for the file on the local network. Because this is the first time any client has attempted to retrieve the file, it is not already cached on the local network. Therefore, the client retrieves the file directly from the content server and caches it using BranchCache.

2. A second client running Windows 7 requests the same file from the content server. Again, the content server authorizes the user and returns an identifier.

3. The requesting client sends a request to its peers on the local network for the required file by using the Web Services Dynamic Discovery (WS-Discovery) multicast protocol.

4. The client that previously cached the file becomes the serving client and sends the file to the requesting client. The data is encrypted by using an encryption key derived from the hashes. The client decrypts the data, validates it, and passes it up to the application.

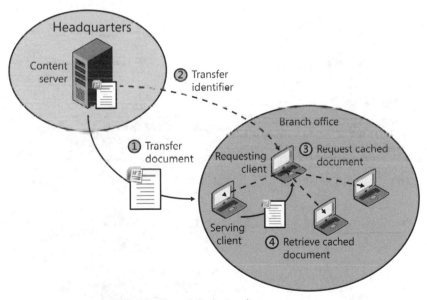

FIGURE 11-17 BranchCache Distributed Cache mode

HOSTED CACHE MODE

Hosted Cache mode uses a client-server architecture to exchange copies of files from file servers located on remote networks. When clients running Windows 7 need to read a file from a server in a remote office, the clients retrieve only a file identifier from the remote server. The clients then send the identifier to the local BranchCache Hosted Cache server. If the Hosted Cache server has a cached copy of the file, it sends the copy to the client. If the Hosted Cache server does not have a copy of the file, the client copies the file from the remote server and then provides a copy to the BranchCache server so that the server can satisfy future requests.

At a detailed level, successfully retrieving a cached document by using Hosted Cache mode follows these four steps, illustrated in Figure 11-18:

1. The client running Windows 7 connects to the content server and requests a file (or part of a file), exactly as it would if it were to retrieve the file without using BranchCache. After authorizing the user, the server returns an identifier that the client uses to search for the file on the Hosted Cache. Because this is the first time any client has retrieved the file, the file is not already cached. Therefore, the client retrieves the file directly from the content server.

2. The client caches the file to the Hosted Cache.

3. A second client running Windows 7 requests the same file from the content server. Again, the content server authorizes the user and returns an identifier.

4. The client uses the identifier to request the data from its Hosted Cache server. The Hosted Cache encrypts the data and returns it to the client. The client then validates the data by using the hash provided as part of the identifier to verify that it has not been modified.

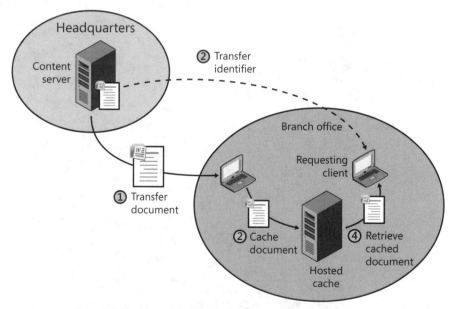

FIGURE 11-18 BranchCache Hosted Cache mode

Distributed Cache mode does not require you to configure a BranchCache Hosted Cache server in remote offices. Therefore, you should use it in remote offices that do not have a computer running Windows Server 2008 R2.

In remote offices that do have a computer running Windows Server 2008 R2, you should use Hosted Cache mode because it provides these benefits:

- **Increased cache reliability**   Hosted Cache mode increases the cache efficiency because content is available even when the client that originally requested the data is offline.

- **Caching for the entire branch office**   Distributed Cache mode operates on a single subnet only. If a branch office using Distributed Cache has multiple subnets, a client on each subnet would need to download a separate copy of each file. With Hosted Cache, all clients in a branch office can access a single cache, even if they are on different subnets.

Configuring BranchCache

A computer running Windows Server 2008 R2 can serve one of four different BranchCache roles, each requiring a slightly different configuration:

- A file server that allows shared files to be cached
- A web server that allows web content to be cached
- A Hosted Cache server that stores cached files in a remote office
- A BranchCache client that retrieves and caches remote files

Because all BranchCache capabilities are disabled by default, you will need to follow the steps in the next four sections to enable them.

INSTALLING REQUIRED COMPONENTS FOR A FILE SERVER

To allow shared files to be cached by BranchCache clients, install the File Services server role on the file server, and then add the BranchCache For Network Files role service. If you are installing the File Services role for the first time, select BranchCache For Network Files on the Select Role Services page of the Add Roles Wizard. If you have already installed the File Services role without the role service, right-click Roles\File Services in Server Manager, and then click Add Role Services. On the Select Role Services page, select BranchCache For Network Files.

INSTALLING REQUIRED COMPONENTS FOR A WEB SERVER OR HOSTED CACHE SERVER

To configure a computer to act as a Hosted Cache server, and to allow BranchCache clients to cache files on Internet Information Services (IIS) websites hosted on a server, install the BranchCache feature. In Server Manager, right-click Features, and then click Add Features. In the Add Features Wizard, select the BranchCache feature.

CONFIGURING BRANCHCACHE SERVERS

After installing the role service or feature that you need for your file servers, web servers, and Hosted Cache servers, use Group Policy settings to configure BranchCache. You will need to enable BranchCache for all file and web servers that should allow cached content.

In the Group Policy Object Editor, enable the Computer Configuration\Policies\Administrative Templates\Network\Lanman Server\Hash Publication For BranchCache policy. Once enabled, you can select three different levels of BranchCache support:

- **Allow Hash Publication For All Shared Folder** Enables BranchCache support for all shared files.

- **Allow Hash Publication Only For Shared Folders On Which BranchCache Is Enabled** Enables BranchCache support only for those files you have chosen to support, as described in the section "Offline Files," earlier in this lesson.

- **Disallow Hash Publication On All Shared Folders** Prevents BranchCache support.

CONFIGURING BRANCHCACHE CLIENTS

You can also use Group Policy settings to enable BranchCache on client computers by enabling the Computer Configuration\Policies\Administrative Templates\Network\BranchCache\Turn On BranchCache policy.

If you plan to use Distributed Cache mode, enable the Set BranchCache Distributed Cache Mode policy. You can then configure the size of the local cache using the Set Percentage Of Disk Space Used For Client Computer Cache policy.

If you plan to use Hosted Cache mode, enable the Set BranchCache Hosted Cache Mode policy. Then, specify the host name of the client's local Hosted Cache server. The host name you specify must match the name of the server specified in the certificate for the BranchCache server, and the client must trust that certificate.

Because BranchCache has the potential to slow down network requests while it looks for a local copy of a file, BranchCache attempts to find cached files only when the remote server is located across a slow network link. That threshold is defined by the Configure BranchCache For Network Files policy. The default of 80 ms is typically sufficient.

PRACTICE Working with Shared Folders

In this practice, you create a redundant DFS namespace.

EXERCISE 1 Adding the Distributed File System Role Service

In this exercise, you must add the File Services server role and Distributed File System role service on both Dcsrv1 and Boston. Then, you create a DFS namespace that is hosted on both computers and create shared folders that will be part of that namespace. The shared folders will automatically replicate files between each other, providing redundancy for clients who need to access the files.

To complete this exercise, Dcsrv1 should be configured as a domain controller and Boston should be configured as a domain member.

1. On Dcsrv1, in Server Manager, right-click Roles, and then choose Add Roles. The Add Roles Wizard appears.

2. On the Before You Begin page, click Next.

3. On the Server Roles page, select the File Services check box. Click Next.

4. On the File Services page, click Next.

5. On the Select Role Services page, select the role services File Server, Distributed File System, and File Server Resource Manager check boxes. Click Next.

6. On the Create A DFS Namespace page, type the namespace name **Public**. Click Next.

7. On the Namespace Type page, leave the default settings selected. Click Next.

8. If the Credentials page appears, click Select and provide Domain Admin credentials. Click Next.

9. On the Namespace Configuration page, click Next.

10. On the Configure Storage Usage Monitoring page, select the check boxes for all local disks, and then click Next.

11. On the Report Options page, click Next.

12. On the Confirmation page, click Install.

13. On the Results page, click Close.

Repeat the previous steps on Boston, except do not create a namespace on the Create A DFS Namespace page.

EXERCISE 2 Adding a Server to the DFS Namespace

Add a server to the DFS namespace by following these steps:

1. On Dcsrv1, in Server Manager, right-click Roles\File Services\DFS Management\ NameSpaces\\\<*domain*>\Public, and then choose Add Namespace Server. The Add Namespace Server dialog box appears.

2. Click the Browse button. In the Select Computer dialog box, type **Boston**, and then click OK. If you're prompted to start the DFS Namespace service on Boston, click Yes. Click OK again to close the Add Namespace Server dialog box.

3. In the details pane, click the Namespace Servers tab. Note that both servers are listed. If one of the servers is offline, clients will be able to connect to the second server. This provides redundancy for critical DFS namespaces.

EXERCISE 3 Adding a Replicated Folder to the DFS Namespace

After you create the DFS namespace and host it on two servers, you create a shared folder named Files on both Dcsrv1 and Boston, add the shared folder to the DFS namespace, and configure it for replication.

1. On Dcsrv1, in Server Manager, right-click Roles\File Services\Share And Storage Management, and then click Provision Share. The Provision A Shared Folder Wizard appears.

2. On the Shared Folder Location page, type **C:\Files**. Click Next. When prompted, click Yes to create the folder.

3. On the NTFS Permissions page, select Yes, Change NTFS Permissions. Click Edit Permissions, and grant the Users group Allow Modify permissions. Click OK. Then, click Next.

4. On the Share Protocols page, type a share name of **Files**. Click Next.

5. On the SMB Settings page, click Advanced. On the Caching tab, select No Files Or Programs From The Share Are Available Offline. This prevents mobile computers from keeping a locally cached copy of files. Click OK, and then click Next.

6. On the SMB Permissions page, select Administrators Have Full Control; All Other Users And Groups Have Only Read Access. Click Next.

7. On the Quota Policy page, select the Apply Quota check box. Select Auto Apply Template To Create Quotas On Existing And New Subfolders. Then, in the Derive Properties From This Quota Template drop-down list, select 200 MB Limit With 50 MB Extension. Click Next.

8. On the File Screen Policy page, select the Apply File Screen check box. In the Derive Properties From This File Screen Template drop-down list, select Block Executable Files. Click Next.

9. On the DFS Namespace Publishing page, select the Publish The SMB Share To A DFS Namespace check box. In the Parent Folder In Namespace box, type **\\nwtraders.msft \Public** (or substitute your domain name). In the New Folder Name box, type **Files**. Click Next.

10. On the Review Settings And Create Share page, click Create.

11. Click Close.

12. On Boston, open a command prompt with administrative privileges and run the following commands to create a folder, assign Users the Modify NTFS permission, and then share the folder. This duplicates the shared folder you created on Dcsrv1 using the Provision A Shared Folder Wizard.

```
mkdir C:\Files
icacls C:\Files\ /grant users:M
net share Files=C:\Files /GRANT:Users,READ /GRANT:Administrators,FULL /CACHE:None
```

Now, on Dcsrv1, add the \\Boston\Files shared folder as a folder target for the \\nwtraders.msft \Public\Files folder.

1. On Dcsrv1, in Server Manager, right-click \\nwtraders.msft\Public, and then choose Refresh.

2. In Server Manager, right-click \\nwtraders.msft\Public\Files, and then choose Add Folder Target.

3. In the New Folder Target dialog box, type **\\Boston\Files**. Click OK.

4. In the Replication dialog box, click Yes to create a replication group between the Dcsrv1 and Boston servers. The Replicate Folder Wizard appears.

5. On the Replication Group And Replicated Folder Name page, click Next.

6. On the Replication Eligibility page, click Next.

7. On the Primary Member page, select Dcsrv1. Click Next.

8. On the Topology Selection page, select Full Mesh. Click Next. Note that if you have more than two or three replication partners and you will always be updating one server, a hub and spoke topology can be more efficient.

9. On the Replication Group Schedule And Bandwidth page, click Next. Note that you have the option to limit bandwidth (to reduce impact on other network applications) or to replicate only during nonpeak hours.

10. On the Review Settings And Create Replication Group page, click Create.

11. On the Confirmation page, click Close.

12. In the Replication Delay dialog box, click OK.

13. In Server Manager, select the DFS Management\Namespaces\\\nwtraders.msft\Public \Files folder, and then select the Replication tab in the details pane. Note that both Dcsrv1 and Boston are listed as replication members.

14. In Server Manager, select the DFS Management\Replication\nwtraders.msft\public \files node. In the details pane, browse each of the four tabs to view more information about the replication group that the Replicate Folder Wizard automatically created.

EXERCISE 4   Testing DFS Replication

In this exercise, you connect to the DFS namespace and create a file to verify that it auto matically replicates.

1. On Dcsrv1, while logged on as any account other than Administrator, click Start, and then choose Computer.

2. In the Computer window, click Map Network Drive on the toolbar.

3. In the Map Network Drive window, type **\\nwtraders.msft\Public\Files**. Then, click Finish. Windows Explorer maps the Z drive to the shared folder.

4. In the new mapped drive, create a text file by right-clicking the details pane, choosing New, and then choosing Text Document. Because UAC limits your privileges to those of a standard user and the Users group has only the Read share permission (even though Users have Modify NTFS permissions), you will be unable to create the file.

5. In the Windows Explorer window, select the C:\Files folder. Then, right-click the details pane, choose New, and choose Text Document. Assign the document the name Text File. Then, open the file and type "Hello, world." Save and close the file.

6. On Boston, open Windows Explorer and view the C:\Files folder. Notice that the Text File has been replicated. (This might take a few minutes.) Open the file to verify that it contains the text you typed.

Lesson Summary

- The File Services server role installs tools for managing shared folders, disk quotas, file screening, and storage reports.

- You can define quota thresholds to notify users and administrators when a user con-sumes more than a specified amount of disk space. Although hard quotas will cause applications to fail, you can create them to block users from saving files once the users exceed a limit that you define. You can manage quotas by using Windows Explorer, the Quota Management console, or the DirQuota command-line tool.

- Classification Management adds custom properties to files based on rules you specify. Typically, organizations use the technology only when regulations require it.

- DFS defines a namespace that can consist of different shared folders located throughout your organization. By adding multiple targets for a single folder, you can replicate files between multiple file servers, providing redundancy and allowing users to connect to the shared folder even when one of the servers fails.

- Offline Files is a Windows feature that copies network files and folders to the local computer so that users can access them when disconnected from the network. Offline Files can automatically synchronize files when the user is online.

- BranchCache can reduce WAN utilization by sharing remote files between computers on a local area network (LAN). BranchCache clients must be running Windows 7 or Windows Server 2008 R2. File and web servers must be running Windows Server 2008 R2. If a remote office has a local computer running Windows Server 2008 R2, you can configure it as a Hosted Cache server to cache files accessed by any client in the office.

Lesson Review

You can use the following questions to test your knowledge of the information in Lesson 2, "Sharing Folders." The questions are also available on the companion CD if you prefer to review them in electronic form.

> **NOTE ANSWERS**
>
> Answers to these questions and explanations of why each answer choice is correct or incorrect are located in the "Answers" section at the end of the book.

1. You create a folder named Marketing and configure NTFS permissions to grant the Domain Users group Read permission and the Marketing group Modify permission. You share the folder and grant the Everyone group the Reader share permission. Mary, a user account who is a member of both the Marketing group and the Domain Users group, needs to access files in the folder from across the network. What effective permissions will Mary have?

   A. No Access

   B. Read

   C. Write

   D. Full Control

2. You are running Windows Server 2008 Server Core. You need to create a shared folder. Which command should you use?

   A. Net

   B. Netsh

   C. Share

   D. Ipconfig

3. Your organization has a central headquarters with seven regional offices. You deploy a DFS server to the headquarters and each regional office and add a DFS namespace that is hosted on each of the DFS servers. You want clients to connect to their local DFS server when it is available and then connect to any other DFS server when the local DFS server is not available. Which ordering method should you choose?

   A. Random Order

   B. Lowest Cost

   C. Excludes Targets Outside Of The Client's Site

   D. Clients Fall Back To Preferred Targets

4. To better control disk utilization, you need to use disk quotas to send an email to users when they have consumed 80 MB of disk space and to prevent users from consuming more than 100 MB of disk space. What is the most efficient way to do this?

   A. Create a hard quota with an 80-MB limit and a second hard quota with a 100-MB limit.

   B. Create a soft quota with an 80-MB limit and a second soft quota with a 100-MB limit.

   C. Create a single hard quota with a 100-MB limit. Create a warning at 80 percent.

   D. Create a single soft quota with a 100-MB limit. Create a warning at 80 percent.

5. You need to configure quotas on a computer running Windows Server 2008 Server Core. Which tool should you use?

   A. FileScrn

   B. DirQuota

   C. DFSUtil

   D. Net

Lesson 3: Backing Up and Restoring Files

With previous versions of Windows, administrators needed to rely on non-Microsoft software to back up servers. With Windows Server 2008 and Windows Server 2008 R2, the operating system has useful backup capabilities built in. You can back up specific files and folders to local hard disks or shared folders on remote computers. You can also back up the entire system volume to a second local hard disk and quickly restore it by starting the computer from the Windows Server 2008 R2 setup media.

> **After this lesson, you will be able to:**
> - Manage shadow copy storage.
> - Use Windows Server Backup to restore files and volumes.
>
> **Estimated lesson time: 30 minutes**

Shadow Copies

Shadow copies allow backup software to access files that are in use. If backup software (including Windows Server Backup and non-Microsoft applications) needs to access a file that's in use by a different application, Volume Shadow Copy creates a shadow copy of the file in its current state and then gives the backup process access to the shadow copy. This allows the application that's using the file to make updates without affecting the backup.

If an application updates a file after a shadow copy is made, Windows must store both the original and changed portion of the file. Because shadow copies store only changes to files, the storage requirements are significantly less than the full size of files being accessed.

Managing Shadow Copies from Windows Explorer

You can manage shadow copies by using the Windows Explorer interface. Follow these steps:

1. In Windows Explorer, right-click a volume (such as your C drive), and then choose Configure Shadow Copies. Alternatively, you can view the volume's properties and then select the Shadow Copies tab. The Shadow Copies dialog box appears.

2. In the Select A Volume list, select the volume you want to configure. Then, do either of the following:

   - Click Enable, and then click Yes to enable shadow copies on the volume. Similarly, you can click Disable and then click Yes to turn shadow copies back off.

   - Click Settings to define where shadow copies are stored, how much space they will consume, and how often they will be created.

3. Click Create Now to immediately create a shadow copy.

4. Click OK.

Managing Shadow Copies from a Command Prompt

You can manage shadow copies from the command prompt by using the VSSAdmin tool. For example, to create a shadow copy of the C volume, run the following command with administrative privileges:

`vssadmin create shadow /For=C:`

To view the storage currently allocated to shadow copies, run the following command:

`vssadmin list shadowstorage`

To view available shadow copies and the time they were created, run the following command:

`vssadmin list shadows`

That command lists shadow copy IDs, which you need to specify when reverting to a shadow copy. For example, if a shadow copy ID is {56036723-cdcc-49ef-98a4-445b1645770e}, you could revert to the shadow copy by using the following command:

`vssadmin revert shadow /Shadow={56036723-cdcc-49ef-98a4-445b1645770e}`

For complete usage information, type **VSSAdmin /?** at a command prompt.

Windows Server Backup

Windows Server Backup copies an entire disk volume (for example, the volume Windows is installed on) to a .vhd file on a second local disk. After performing a backup, you can restore individual files or an entire volume. If Windows cannot start (for example, the system volume has failed), you can start the computer from the Windows installation media, restore the system volume from the backup, and have the operating system up and running in less than an hour.

The sections that follow describe how to install the Windows Server Backup features, manually initiate a backup, schedule automatic backups, and recover files and volumes.

Installing Windows Server Backup Features

To install the Windows Server Backup Features, follow these steps:

1. In Server Manager, right-click Features, and then choose Add Features. The Add Features Wizard appears.

2. On the Features page, expand Windows Server Backup Features. Then, select either the Windows Server Backup check box (for graphical tools) or the Command-Line Tools check box (to script backups), or both check boxes. If you're prompted to install additional features to support the command-line tools, click Add Required Features. Click Next.

3. On the Confirmation page, click Install.

4. On the Results page, click Close.

Now you can access the Windows Server Backup tool from the Administrative Tools folder on the Start menu or in Server Manager at Storage\Windows Server Backup. You can run the Wbadmin backup tool from a command prompt or script.

Manually Performing a Backup

To manually perform a backup, follow these steps:

1. In Server Manager, select the Storage\Windows Server Backup node.

2. In the Actions pane, click Backup Once. The Backup Once Wizard appears.

3. On the Backup Options page, choose whether to use the same or new options, and then click Next. If you choose to use the same options, skip to step 9.

4. On the Server Backup Configuration page, either back up the full server or select Custom to select specific volumes. If you are backing up to a local disk, you should select Custom so that you can exclude the backup volume from the backup. Click Next.

5. If the Select Backup Items page appears, select the check boxes for the volumes you want to back up, and then click Next.

6. On the Specify Destination Type page, choose whether to back up locally (for example, to a different volume) or to a shared folder on the network. Click Next.

7. Depending on the choice you made in the previous step, you will see either the Select Backup Destination page or the Specify Remote Folder page. Specify your backup location, and then click Next.

8. On the Confirmation page, click Backup.

9. On the Backup Progress page, you can watch the backup progress (as shown in Figure 11-19) or click Close to allow the backup to continue in the background.

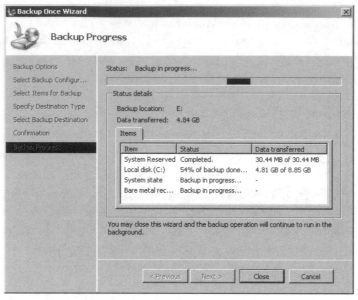

FIGURE 11-19 Manually running a backup

Windows creates a WindowsImageBackup folder in the root of the backup media. Inside that folder, Windows creates a folder with the current computer's name. It then creates a Catalog folder containing the GlobalCatalog and BackupGlobalCatalog files as well as a folder named Backup *<year>-<month>-<date> <time>* that contains the .vhd disk image file. The format is exactly the same as a system image backup created in Windows 7.

If you want to access the contents of the .vhd disk image without restoring it, attach the file as a new drive. In Server Manager, right-click Roles\File Services\Share And Storage Management\Disk Management, and then click Attach VHD. From a command prompt, run DiskPart, and then use the Attach command.

Scheduling Backups

To schedule a backup to run automatically, follow these steps:

1. In Server Manager, select the Storage\Windows Server Backup node.

2. In the Actions pane, click Backup Schedule. The Backup Schedule Wizard appears.

3. On the Getting Started page, click Next.

4. On the Select Backup Configuration page, either back up the full server or select Custom to select specific volumes. If you are backing up to a local disk, you should select Custom so that you can exclude the backup volume from the backup.

5. If the Select Backup Items page appears, select the check boxes for the volumes you want to back up, and then click Next.

6. On the Specify Backup Time page, select the time and frequency of your backups, as shown in Figure 11-20. Click Next.

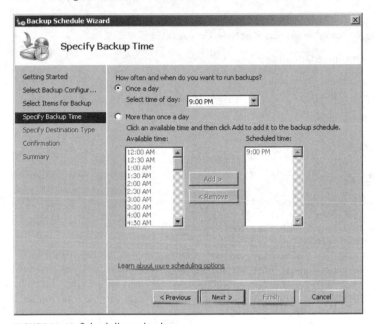

FIGURE 11-20 Scheduling a backup

7. On the Select Destination Type page, choose where to save the backup file. You will get the best performance if you choose to dedicate a disk for backups, however, the disk will be reformatted, all data will be lost, and the disk will no longer appear in Windows Explorer. Click Next.

8. The pages that follow will vary depending on the destination type. Respond to the prompts that appear.

9. On the Confirmation page, click Finish.

10. On the Summary page, the Backup Schedule Wizard formats the backup destination disk. Click Close.

You can view the scheduled task that initiates the backup by using the Task Scheduler console. The backup task is available in the \Configuration\Task Scheduler Library\Microsoft\Windows \Backup node in Server Manager and calls the Wbadmin tool to perform the backup.

Performing Backups from a Command Prompt or Script

You can use the Wbadmin tool to initiate backups from a script or at a command prompt (such as when using Windows Server 2008 Server Core). For example, to initiate a backup of the C drive to the L drive, you would run the following command prompt from an elevated command prompt:

```
wbadmin start backup -backupTarget:L: -include:C: -quiet
```

The output resembles the following:

```
wbadmin 1.0 - Backup command-line tool
(C) Copyright 2004 Microsoft Corp.

Retrieving volume information...

This would backup volume Local Disk(C:) to L:.

Backup to L: is starting.

Running shadow copy of volumes requested for backup.
Running backup of volume Local Disk(C:), copied (0%).
Running backup of volume Local Disk(C:), copied (18%).
Running backup of volume Local Disk(C:), copied (40%).
Running backup of volume Local Disk(C:), copied (77%).
Running backup of volume Local Disk(C:), copied (98%).
Backup of volume Local Disk(C:) completed successfully.
Backup completed successfully.

Summary of backup:
------------------

Backup of volume Local Disk(C:) completed successfully.
```

Run the following command to back up all critical files to the L drive:

```
wbadmin start backup -backupTarget:L: -allCritical -quiet
```

To schedule a backup, run the command **wbadmin enable backup**. To restore a backup, run **wbadmin start recovery** and specify the -version, -items, and -itemtype parameters. To view the available backup versions, run the following command:

```
wbadmin get versions
```

The output resembles the following:

```
wbadmin 1.0 - Backup command-line tool
(C) Copyright 2004 Microsoft Corp.

Backup time: 6/23/2010 12:00 AM
Backup target: Fixed Disk labeled 1.5TB backup(D:)
Version identifier: 06/23/2010-05:00
Can recover: Volume(s), File(s), Application(s), Bare Metal Recovery, System State
Snapshot ID: {e219fd5f-0ed7-4b31-adc4-0fafad5f8827}
```

```
Backup time: 2/14/2011 9:50 AM
Backup target: Fixed Disk labeled 2TB-offsite(I:)
Version identifier: 02/14/2011-14:50
Can recover: Volume(s), File(s), Application(s), Bare Metal Recovery, System State
Snapshot ID: {f9f08d64-1f98-43be-9a67-d39d57c7438f}

Backup time: 3/2/2011 1:00 AM
Backup target: Fixed Disk labeled RAID5(H:)
Version identifier: 03/02/2011-06:00
Can recover: Volume(s), File(s), Application(s), Bare Metal Recovery, System State
Snapshot ID: {7c05730c-d719-497e-a155-8bc0a0fd68a4}
```

The following command demonstrates how to recover a user's documents folder and all its contents from a specific backup version:

```
wbadmin start recovery -version:03/31/2005-09:00 -itemType:File -items:c:\users\user1\
documents\ -recursive
```

The -itemType parameter can be Volume, App, or File.

To perform a backup of the system state, run **wbadmin start systemstatebackup**. To restore a system state backup, run **wbadmin start systemstaterecovery**. To delete a system state backup, run **wbadmin delete systemstatebackup**.

For complete usage information, type **wbadmin /?** at a command prompt.

 Quick Check

1. What command should you run to configure shadow copies?

2. What command should you run to initiate a backup?

Quick Check Answers

1. You should run *vssadmin*.

2. You should run *wbadmin*.

Recovering Individual Files

You can restore individual files from a backup or a recent shadow copy by following these steps:

1. In Windows Explorer, right-click a file you want to restore, and then choose Restore Previous Versions. The properties dialog box appears with the Previous Versions tab selected.

2. As shown in Figure 11-21, select the version you want to restore, and then click Restore.

FIGURE 11-21 Restoring a file with Previous Versions

3. When prompted, click Restore.

4. Click OK twice.

   The previous version of the file is restored.

Recovering Files or Volumes

To recover a server from a backup, follow these steps:

1. In Server Manager, select the Storage\Windows Server Backup node.

2. In the Actions pane, click Recover. The Recovery Wizard appears.

3. On the Getting Started page, select the server to recover, and then click Next.

4. On the Select Backup Date page, choose the backup from which to recover. Click Next.

5. On the Select Recovery Type page, choose one of the following three options, and then click Next:

   - **Files And Folders**   Browse files that have been backed up and select specific files, folders, or both to be recovered.

   - **Applications**   Applications can register with Windows Server Backup to store application-specific data. This option allows you to selectively restore application data.

   - **Volumes**   Allows you to restore an entire volume. However, you cannot use this to restore the operating system volume. To do that, follow the instructions in the next section of this lesson, "Recovering from a Backup When Windows Will Not Start."

6. If the Select Items To Recover page appears, browse the backup to select a folder or files to recover, as shown in Figure 11-22. Then, click Next. If a dialog box appears, click OK.

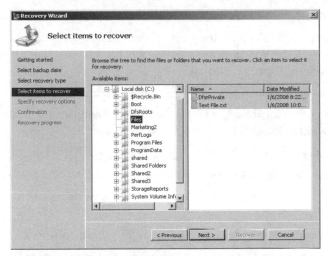

FIGURE 11-22 Selecting files to recover

7. If the Specify Recovery Options page appears, as shown in Figure 11-23, choose the backup destination and whether existing files will be overwritten. Click Next.

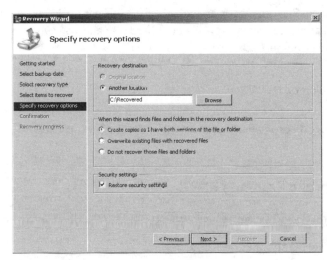

FIGURE 11-23 Selecting recovery options

8. If the Select Volumes page appears, select the volume check box, and then click Next.

9. On the Confirmation page, click Recover.

10. On the Recovery Progress page, click Close.

Recovering from a Backup When Windows Will Not Start

If Windows cannot start or you need to recover the entire system volume from a backup, you can start the computer from the Windows Server 2008 R2 DVD and use the System Image Recovery wizard to recover the operating system. Follow these steps:

1. Insert the Windows Server 2008 R2 media, and restart the computer.

2. When the Press Any Key To Boot From The CD Or DVD prompt appears, press a key. After a brief delay, the Install Windows Wizard appears.

3. On the language selection page, click Next.

4. Click Repair Your Computer in the lower-left corner.

5. In the System Recovery Options dialog box, select the operating system instance, and then click Next.

6. Click System Image Recovery. The Re-Image Your Computer Wizard appears.

7. On the Select A System Image Backup page, use the default setting to restore the most recent backup. Alternatively, click Restore A Different Backup if you need to restore an older backup (for example, if the most recent backup is corrupted or you need to restore to a date prior to a security compromise). Click Next.

8. On the Choose Additional Restore Options page, select the Format And Repartition Disks check box if you are restoring to a replacement hard disk and you previously used a custom partition scheme. Click Next.

9. On the final page, click Finish.

10. In the confirmation dialog box, click Yes.

Windows restores your backup by overwriting the volumes you are recovering. After the restoration is complete, Windows automatically restarts using the state it was in at the time of the backup.

PRACTICE **Backing Up and Restoring Files**

In this practice, you back up and restore files by using shadow copies and Windows Server Backup.

EXERCISE 1   Restoring a File from a Shadow Copy

In this exercise, you create a file, perform a volume shadow copy, and then restore the file.

1. Create a text document on your desktop. Open the text document, add the text **Before**, and save and close the document.

2. Open a command prompt with administrative privileges. Then, run the following command to create a shadow copy of your C drive:

   ```
   vssadmin create shadow /For=C:
   ```

3. Open the text document that you saved to the desktop. Change the text to **After**, and then save and close the document.

4. Right-click the document, and then choose Restore Previous Versions. The properties dialog box appears with the Previous Versions tab selected.

5. Select the most recent version (there will probably be only one because the file is new), and then click Restore.

6. When prompted, click Restore.

7. Click OK twice.

8. Open the text file to verify that the document was restored to the state it was in before you created the shadow copy.

EXERCISE 2 Backing Up and Restoring Files

In this exercise, you must back up Dcsrv1, restore individual files, and then restore the entire system volume. Prior to performing this exercise, configure Dcsrv1 with a second hard disk to provide a backup target.

1. In Server Manager, select the Storage\Windows Server Backup node.

2. In the Actions pane, click Backup Schedule. The Backup Schedule Wizard appears.

3. On the Getting Started page, click Next.

4. On the Select Backup Configuration page, select Custom.

5. On the Select Backup Items page, click Add Items. Select the Bare Metal Recovery check box, and then click OK. Click Next.

6. On the Specify Backup Time page, specify a time five minutes in the future. Click Next.

7. On the Select Destination Type page, select Back Up To A Hard Disk That Is Dedicated For Backups. Click Next.

8. On the Select Destination Disk page, click Show All Available Disks. Select the backup target disk, and click OK. Select the disk again, and then click Next.

9. Click Yes when prompted.

10. On the Label Destination Disk page, click Next.

11. On the Confirmation page, click Finish.

12. On the Summary page, the Backup Schedule Wizard formats the backup destination disk. Click Close.

Wait until the backup begins and completes. You can monitor the backup progress by using the Windows Server Backup console.

After the backup has completed, follow these steps to remove and then restore a file. These steps assume you have completed the Lesson 1 practice. If you have not, you can delete any file on the disk instead of the suggested files.

1. Delete the C:\Users\EfsUser\Documents folder.

2. In Server Manager, select the Storage\Windows Server Backup node.

3. In the Actions pane, click Recover. The Recovery Wizard appears.

4. On the Getting Started page, click Next.

5. On the Select Backup Date page, notice that the most recent backup is already selected. Click Next.

6. On the Select Recovery Type page, select Files And Folders, and then click Next.

7. If the Select Items To Recover page appears, browse the backup to select the C:\Users \EfsUser\Documents folder. Then, click Next. If a dialog box appears, click OK.

8. If the Specify Recovery Options page appears, specify the backup destination C:\Users \EfsUser. Click Next.

9. On the Confirmation page, click Recover.

10. On the Recovery Progress page, click Close.

Now open Windows Explorer to verify that the C:\Users\EfsUser\Documents folder has been recovered. Then delete the C:\Users\EfsUser\Documents folder again and perform the following steps to restore the entire Windows system volume. This simulates a complete recovery—for example, a recovery from a failed hard disk.

1. Insert the Windows Server 2008 R2 media, and restart the computer.

2. When the Press Any Key To Boot From The CD Or DVD prompt appears, press a key. After a brief delay, the Install Windows wizard appears.

3. On the language selection page, click Next.

4. Click Repair Your Computer.

5. In the System Recovery Options dialog box, select the operating system instance, and then click Next.

6. Click System Image Recovery. The Re-Image Your Computer Wizard appears.

7. On the Select A System Image Backup page, click Next to use the most recent backup.

8. On the Choose Additional Restore Options page, click Next.

9. On the final page, click Finish.

10. In the dialog box, click Yes.

Wait several minutes for the volume to be rewritten from the backup. After Windows restarts, verify that the C:\Users\EfsUser\Documents folder was recovered. The restore would have been successful even if a new hard disk had been used.

Lesson Summary

- Windows automatically creates shadow copies when backup software needs to access files that are in use. Although you might never need to manage shadow copies, you can use the VSSAdmin tool to manually create shadow copies or manage the shadow copy storage space.

- Windows Server Backup creates a .vhd image file containing a copy of the disk volume being backed up. You can then restore individual files or the entire volume. Use the Wbadmin tool to manage backups from a command prompt.

Lesson Review

You can use the following questions to test your knowledge of the information in Lesson 3, "Backing Up and Restoring Files." The questions are also available on the companion CD if you prefer to review them in electronic form.

> **NOTE ANSWERS**
>
> Answers to these questions and explanations of why each answer choice is correct or incorrect are located in the "Answers" section at the end of the book.

1. You are planning to modify several critical configuration files on a computer running Windows Server 2008 R2. Which tool can you use to allow you to restore files to their previous state if necessary?
   - **A.** StorRept
   - **B.** FileScrn
   - **C.** DirQuota
   - **D.** VSSAdmin

2. You use the Windows Server Backup tool to manually perform a backup to the D drive on a computer named FileServer. In which folder is the backup stored?
   - **A.** D:\WindowsFileBackup\FileServer\
   - **B.** D:\WindowsImageBackup\FileServer\
   - **C.** D:\WindowsImage\Backup\FileServer\
   - **D.** D:\FileServer\WindowsImage\Backup\

3. You are using the Windows Server Backup tool to restore data. Which of the following tasks can you perform? (Choose all that apply.)
   - **A.** Restore individual files.
   - **B.** Restore the system volume.
   - **C.** Restore a nonsystem volume.
   - **D.** Overwrite files that are currently in use.

Chapter Review

To further practice and reinforce the skills you learned in this chapter, you can perform the following tasks:

- Review the chapter summary.
- Review the list of key terms introduced in this chapter.
- Complete the case scenarios. These scenarios set up real-world situations involving the topics of this chapter and ask you to create a solution.
- Complete the suggested practices.
- Take a practice test.

Chapter Summary

- NTFS file permissions provide access control while the operating system is online, and EFS protects files from unauthorized access when an attacker bypasses the operating system. Use NTFS file permissions as the primary method for file security, and use EFS to protect mobile computers that might be stolen or computers that otherwise might be physically accessible to an attacker.

- Windows Server 2008 provides much more powerful shared folder capabilities. After installing the File Services server role, you can manage disk quotas for individual folders, automatically notifying users and administrators when a user exceeds a specified threshold. You can now provision shared folders, complete with quotas and file security, using a simplified wizard interface. With DFS you can create a single namespace that provides users access to all the shared folders in your organization. Mobile users can enable Offline Files to configure Windows to automatically create a local copy of shared files so that they can be accessed while the user is disconnected from the network.

- Shadow copies allow backup software to access files that are currently in use, and they can be used to create quick backups on the local disk. The Windows Server Backup tool provides powerful backup capabilities that allow you to restore individual files or entire volumes.

Key Terms

Do you know what these key terms mean? You can check your answers by looking up the terms in the glossary at the end of the book.

- hard quota
- referral
- soft quota
- targets

Case Scenarios

In the following case scenarios, you will apply what you've learned about how to plan and deploy file services. You can find answers to these questions in the "Answers" section at the end of this book.

Case Scenario 1: Planning File Services

You are a systems engineer for City Power & Light. Currently, your organization uses departmental servers for file sharing. Because each department has its own file server, your organization has hundreds of shared folders. Users are easily confused about which mapped drives contain the files they need, and systems administrators have a difficult time providing security for folders. Additionally, if a departmental server fails, the shared folder is offline until the server can be restored from a backup.

Answer the following questions for your manager.

1. How can you reduce the number of shared folders users must connect to?

2. If you use a DFS namespace, how can you ensure users do not connect to other department's shared folders?

3. How can you provide redundancy?

Case Scenario 2: Planning Disaster Recovery

You are a systems administrator for Northwind Traders. Your organization is beginning to deploy servers running Windows Server 2008 R2. Your manager is very concerned about recovering a server that fails because of a failed hard disk.

Answer the following questions for your manager:

1. When purchasing servers, what are the hardware requirements for scheduling backups using Windows Server Backup?

2. After performing a backup, how will you recover a server with a failed system disk?

3. Can the same backup be used to restore files that become corrupted or are accidentally deleted?

Suggested Practices

To help you successfully master the exam objectives presented in this chapter, complete the following tasks.

Configure a File Server

For this task, you should complete both practices.

- **Practice 1**   Use EFS to encrypt a file. Then, either start the computer from a CD that allows you to view files or reinstall Windows. Attempt to access the encrypted file.

- **Practice 2**   Log on using standard user privileges and attempt to edit files in your own user folders, other users' folders, program files folders, and Windows system folders. Examine the NTFS file permissions for each folder.

Configure Distributed File System

For this task, you should complete Practices 1 and 2 to gain practical experience with DFS. For practice working with the DFSUtil command-line tool, complete Practice 3. Complete Practice 4 to gain experience troubleshooting DFS problems.

- **Practice 1**   Create a DFS namespace in your production environment and add shared folders to the namespace.

- **Practice 2**   Create a shared folder with three or more target folders and configure replication between the folders. Add files of different sizes and determine how long it takes for files to replicate.

- **Practice 3**   Use DFSUtil to configure a complete DFS namespace, complete with multiple targets and folders.

- **Practice 4**   Use DFSDiag to diagnose problems with your DFS namespace.

Configure Shadow Copy Services

For this task, you should complete Practices 1 and 2 on a computer in a practice environment. For additional practice working with VSSAdmin, complete Practice 3.

- **Practice 1**   Use VSSAdmin to decrease the storage space allowed for shadow copies.
- **Practice 2**   Use VSSAdmin to remove all shadow copies.
- **Practice 3**   Use Restore Previous Versions to restore a file of more than 200 MB from a shadow copy. While the restoration is taking place, type the command **Vssadmin Query Reverts /For=C:** to view the status.

Configure Backup and Restore

For this task, you should complete all three practices to gain experience using the Wbadmin command-line tool for managing backup and restore actions.

- **Practice 1**   Schedule a daily backup by using the Wbadmin command.
- **Practice 2**   Use the Wbadmin command to back up system state, and then restore it.
- **Practice 3**   Using an installation of Windows Server 2008 Server Core, use Wbadmin to back up the system volume. Then, restore a specific file from the backup.

Manage File Server Resources

For this task you should complete all three practices to gain experience working with disk quotas.

- **Practice 1**   Create a custom quota template to send an email notification to the user when the user consumes 80 MB, send an email notification to both the user and administrators when they consume 90 MB, and prevent the user from saving more data when the user consumes 100 MB. Apply the quota template, and then test it to verify that it works as expected and you receive the notifications. Notice the behavior of different applications as you try to save a file to the folder protected by the quota.
- **Practice 2**   Apply the template you created in Practice 1 using the DirQuota command-line tool.
- **Practice 3**   Review the Storage Manager for SANs Step-by-Step Guide at *http://technet.microsoft.com/library/cc771928.aspx.*

Take a Practice Test

The practice tests on this book's companion CD offer many options. For example, you can test yourself on just the content covered in this chapter, or you can test yourself on all the 70-642 certification exam content. You can set up the test so that it closely simulates the experience of taking a certification exam, or you can set it up in study mode so that you can look at the correct answers and explanations after you answer each question.

> **MORE INFO**   **PRACTICE TESTS**
>
> For details about all the practice test options available, see "How to Use the Practice Tests" in this book's Introduction.

CHAPTER 12

Managing Printers

Printers are one of an organization's most complex management challenges. Because printers must be located physically near users, they're impossible to centralize. Printers require almost constant maintenance because ink must be replaced, paper must be refilled, and hardware must be fixed.

Although printers will always be a challenge, Windows Server 2008 R2 provides sophisticated tools to improve manageability and to allow you to quickly detect problems. This chapter describes how to install, share, and manage printers.

Exam objectives in this chapter:

- Configure and monitor print services.

Lessons in this chapter:

- Lesson 1: Managing Printers **632**

Before You Begin

To complete the lesson in this chapter, you should be familiar with Windows networking and be comfortable with the following tasks:

- Adding roles to a Windows Server 2008 R2 computer
- Configuring Active Directory directory service domain controllers and joining computers to a domain
- Basic network configuration, including configuring IP settings

You will also need the following nonproduction hardware, connected to test networks:

- A computer named Dcsrv1 that is a domain controller in the Nwtraders.msft domain. This computer must have at least one network interface.

> **NOTE COMPUTER AND DOMAIN NAMES**
>
> The computer and domain names you use will not affect these exercises. The practices in this chapter refer to these computer names for simplicity, however.

- A computer named Boston that is a member of the Nwtraders.msft domain.
- Optionally, one or more printers.

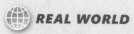

REAL WORLD
Tony Northrup

Because they are full of moving parts and must be physically distributed, printers are always going to be a management challenge. Use these best practices to minimize print management costs:

- Deploy two or more identical printers to each location and configure them as printer pools. *Printer pools* allow users to continue printing even when one printer fails—and hardware problems are extremely common with printers.

- Try to use only one or two printer models throughout your organization. This will simplify the ink and replacement parts you need to stock, as well as minimize your employees' training requirements.

- Connect printers directly to wired networks instead of connecting them to servers. This will provide more flexibility for choosing the location of your printers and allow you to physically secure your servers.

- Train users to perform basic printer management tasks, including refilling paper, replacing ink, and fixing jammed paper. This will reduce the number of printer-related support calls.

Lesson 1: Managing Printers

Windows Server 2008 R2 includes the Print And Document Services server role, which adds the Print Management snap-in to provide sophisticated printer management capabilities. There are also a variety of command-line tools for scripting print management tasks and managing computers running Windows Server 2008 R2 Server Core. Although you can still use Control Panel to install, share, and manage printers, the Print Management snap-in provides a more full-featured user interface. This lesson describes how to use Control Panel, the Print Management snap-in, and command-line tools to manage printers.

Installing the Print And Document Services Server Role

Windows Server 2008 R2 can share printers without adding any server roles. However, adding the Print And Document Services server role adds the Print Management snap-in, which simplifies printer configuration. To install the Print And Document Services server role, follow these steps:

1. In Server Manager, right-click Roles, and then choose Add Roles. The Add Roles Wizard appears.

2. If the Before You Begin page appears, click Next.

3. On the Server Roles page, select the Print And Document Services check box. Click Next.

4. On the Print And Document Services page, click Next.

5. On the Select Role Services page, select the appropriate check boxes for the following roles, and then click Next:

   - **Print Server** Installs the Print Management snap-in, described later in this lesson. This is sufficient for allowing Windows and many non-Windows clients to print.

   - **LPD Service** Allows clients to print using the Line Printer Daemon (LPD) protocol, which is commonly used by UNIX clients. To act as an LPD client, you must install the Line Printer Remote (LPR) Port Monitor feature, as described in "Installing Printers" later in this chapter.

   - **Internet Printing** Allows clients to print using Internet Printing Protocol (IPP) and creates a website where users can manage print jobs using their web browsers. This role service requires Internet Information Services (IIS).

   - **Distributed Scan Server** Allows you to manage network scanners, configure scan processes, and route documents from network scanners to the correct destination. If you to install this role service, you need to create an Active Directory account for it, generate an SSL certificate, and specify an email server.

6. If you are prompted to install the Web Server (IIS) role service, click Add Required Role Services, and then click Next.

7. If the Specify Service Account page appears because you chose to install the Distributed Scan Server role service, specify a domain user account that has permissions to scan processes in Active Directory Domain Services and to specify the scan destinations. Typically, you should create a new account specifically for this purpose. Click Next.

8. If the Specify Temporary Folder Settings page appears because you chose to install the Distributed Scan Server role service, select a folder to temporarily store scan files and specify a size limit for the folder. Click Next.

9. If the Specify E-Mail Server For Scan Server page appears because you chose to install the Distributed Scan Server role service, specify your Simple Mail Transport Protocol (SMTP) server. Click Next.

10. If the Choose A Server Authentication Certificate For SSL Encryption page appears because you chose to install the Distributed Scan Server role service.

11. If the Web Server (IIS) page appears because you selected the Internet Printing role service, click Next. Then, on the Select Role Services page, configure the required IIS role services by using the default settings, and click Next again.

12. On the Confirm Installation Selections page, click Install.

13. On the Installation Results page, click Close.

14. If prompted, restart the computer.

Before attempting to use the Print And Document Services management tools, close and reopen Server Manager. You can access the Print And Document Services tools by using the Roles\Print And Document Services node in Server Manager.

Installing Printers

To allow printers to be physically accessible to users while keeping print servers secured, most modern printers are connected to the network. Although users can print directly to network printers, using a print server gives you stronger management capabilities. The following sections describe how to install printers using either Control Panel or the Print Management snap-in.

To install a network printer shared by the LPD service on a computer running LINUX, UNIX, or Windows, you must add the LPR Port Monitor feature. To install the LPR Port Monitor feature, open Server Manager. Then, right-click Features, and choose Add Features. In the Add Features wizard, select the LPR Port Monitor feature, click Next, and then click Install.

Installing a Printer by Using Control Panel

After connecting a printer either to the network or to a server, follow these steps to install the printer by using Control Panel:

1. Click Start, and then choose Devices And Printers.

2. Click Add A Printer. The Add Printer wizard appears.

3. On the What Type Of Printer Do You Want To Install page, if the printer is attached directly to the server, click Add A Local Printer. If the printer is wireless or attached to the network, click Add A Network, Wireless, Or Bluetooth Printer.

4. If the Choose A Printer Port page appears, select the physical port to which the printer is attached, as shown in Figure 12-1. Click Next.

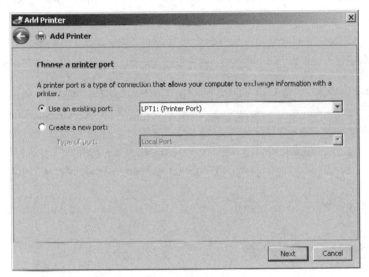

FIGURE 12-1 The Choose A Printer Port page

5. If you are installing a network printer, select the printer or click The Printer That I Want Isn't Listed and specify the network location of the printer. Click Next.

6. If you are installing a network printer and you select Add A Printer Using A TCP/IP Address Or Hostname, you next see the Find A Printer By Name Or TCP/IP Address page. You can choose to find the printer in Active Directory directory services, specify the printer's network location (such as *server**printer*), or specify the server's host name or IP address. Click Next.

> **NOTE** **SEARCHING FOR NETWORK PRINTERS**
>
> The Network Printer Installation Wizard, described in the following section, "Installing a Printer by Using the Print Management Snap-in," does a much better job of finding network printers than the Find A Printer By Name Or TCP/IP Address page.

7. If the Install The Printer Driver page appears, select a manufacturer and printer if you plan to use a driver included with Windows Server 2008 R2. To retrieve updated drivers from the Microsoft website, click Windows Update. To use a driver included with the printer or downloaded from the manufacturer's website, click Have Disk, select the driver, and then click OK. Click Next.

8. The Which Version Of The Driver Do You Want To Use page appears if you have previously installed the same driver. Choose whether to use the existing driver or to replace it, and then click Next.

9. On the Type A Printer Name page, type a name for the printer, and then click Next.

10. On the Printer Sharing page, choose whether to share the printer. If you do share the printer, type a location that allows users to physically find the printer. Click Next.

11. Click Finish.

The printer is immediately available for use from the server. If you chose to share the printer, it is also accessible to authorized users.

Installing a Printer by Using the Print Management Snap-in

After connecting a printer either to the network or to a server, follow these steps to install it using the Print Management snap-in:

1. In Server Manager, right-click Roles\Print And Document Services\Print Management \Print Servers\<*Server*>, and then choose Add Printer. The Network Printer Installation Wizard appears.

2. On the Printer Installation page, shown in Figure 12-2, choose an installation method, and then click Next.

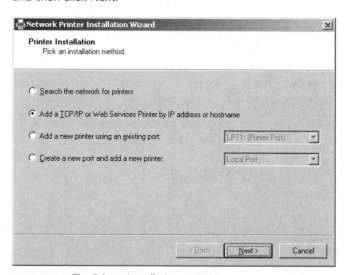

FIGURE 12-2 The Printer Installation page

3. The pages that follow will vary depending on the printer installation method you chose. For example, if you chose to search for a network printer, the Network Printer Search page (as shown in Figure 12-3) appears. Respond to the prompts and click Next.

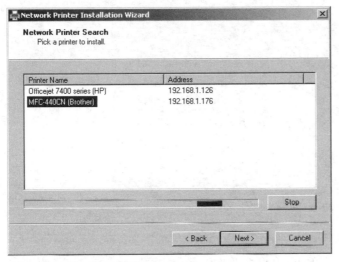

FIGURE 12-3 The Network Printer Search page

4. On the Printer Driver page, choose whether to use an existing driver, install a new driver, or use the printer driver that the wizard selected. Then, click Next.

5. If you choose to install a new driver, the Printer Installation page appears. Select a driver by first selecting the appropriate manufacturer and then selecting the printer model. Click Next.

6. On the Printer Name And Sharing Settings page, type a name for the printer. To immediately share the printer, select the Share This Printer check box and type a name and location. Click Next.

7. On the Printer Found page, click Next.

8. Depending on the type of printer, you might also be prompted to perform printer-specific configuration, as illustrated by Figure 12-4.

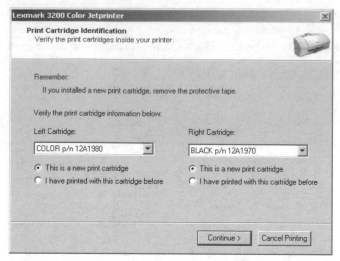

FIGURE 12-4 Performing printer-specific configuration

9. On the Completing The Network Printer Installation Wizard page, click Finish.

After completing the wizard, the printer is ready to be used.

Sharing Printers

You can share printers by using both Control Panel and the Print Management snap-in. From Control Panel, right-click the printer, choose Printer Properties, and then select the Sharing tab. To share a printer by using the Print Management snap-in, right-click the printer, and then choose Manage Sharing.

Whichever method you choose, you will see a dialog box resembling Figure 12-5. To share the printer, select the Share This Printer check box. Select the Render Print Jobs On Client Computers check box to allow clients to handle the processor-intensive rendering process, or clear the check box to push the processing to the print server. Select the List In The Directory check box to allow the printer to be found in Active Directory. To add a driver for a processor type other than the operating system's default, click the Additional Driver's button. Then, click OK.

If the client's operating system uses the same driver as the server, the client can automatically download the driver the first time the client connects to the printer. If a client requires a different driver—for example, if a client computer uses a 32-bit version of Windows and the server uses a 64-bit version of Windows—you should install the additional driver on the server to allow the client to automatically install the driver. From the Sharing tab, click the Additional Drivers button, select the check boxes for the platforms you want to support (as shown in Figure 12-6), click OK, and then select the printer driver.

FIGURE 12-5 The Sharing tab

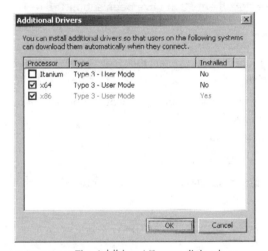

FIGURE 12-6 The Additional Drivers dialog box

 EXAM TIP

Windows 7 and Windows Server 2008 R2 include location-aware printing. The concept is really simple: instead of having a single default printer, users have a different default printer for each network that they connect to. This allows a mobile user to print to work and home printers automatically without having to choose a different default printer. Location-aware printing is on the exam objectives, but there's not much more to know about it, and it's available only for mobile computers—which servers are not likely to be. For more information, read *http://technet.microsoft.com/library/ee424313.aspx*.

Configuring Print Server and Printer Permissions

In a manner that is similar to configuring NTFS file permissions, you can configure printer and print server permissions. For example, you could use printer permissions to grant only your Human Resources group access to print to a departmental printer and grant IT the right to manage the printer. To configure the permissions for either the print server or the printer, right-click the object in the Print Management console, and then click Properties. Then, select the Security tab.

By default, everyone can print to a printer and view the print server. Users can manage their own documents in the print queue but not documents of other users. Administrators can manage any user's documents in the print queue and configure the printer itself.

You can configure the following printer permissions:

- **Print**   Users can print.
- **Manage Printers**   Users can change printer configuration settings.
- **Manage Documents**   Users can remove documents that have been submitted to the printer.

Print servers also have the Print, Management Printers, and Manage Documents permissions. However, these options define only the default settings for new printers that you create. Changing these permissions does not impact any existing printers.

In addition to the default printer permissions, you can configure the following print server permissions to delegate management to nonadministrators:

- **View Server**   Users can view the server and shared printers.
- **Manage Server**   Users can manage the print server features.

Print server and printer permissions are in effect regardless of whether users are logged on locally or are accessing folders across the network.

Adding Printer Drivers

You should install drivers for all client platforms you intend to support so that clients can automatically download the driver and install the printer the first time they connect. To add printer drivers by using the Print Management snap-in, follow these steps:

1. In Server Manager, right-click Roles\Print And Document Services\Print Management \Print Servers\<*ServerName*>\Drivers, and then choose Add Driver. The Add Printer Driver Wizard appears.

2. On the Welcome To The Add Printer Driver Wizard page, click Next.

3. On the Processor And Operating System Selection page, select the check boxes for the processors and operating systems that will be using the driver. Click Next.

4. On the Printer Driver Selection page, click the Have Disk button, select the folder containing the printer driver, and then click OK. Select the printer, and then click Next.

> **NOTE** **FINDING PRINTER DRIVERS**
>
> Typically, you can find the latest driver at the printer manufacturer's website. You can also find drivers for a different Windows platform (for example, a 64-bit version of Windows) from that platform's installation media.

5. On the Completing The Add Printer Driver Wizard page, click Finish.

If the driver is not digitally signed, the Add Printer Driver Wizard will warn you that the driver might be dangerous. Drivers can be unreliable or malicious, and using digitally signed drivers significantly reduces those risks. If you choose to use drivers that are not signed, be certain you trust the source.

The Add Printer Driver Wizard might prompt you to install drivers for different versions of Windows, as shown in Figure 12-7. If prompted, provide the path to the driver files, and then click OK.

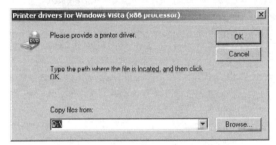

FIGURE 12-7 Providing drivers for different versions of Windows

In the original release of Windows Server 2008, a single failed printer driver could cause an entire server to stop printing. Windows Server 2008 R2 adds print driver isolation, which prevents a failed printer driver from impacting other printer drivers. Therefore, if one printer driver fails, users can continue to print to different printers. To enable print driver isolation, right-click the driver, highlight Set Driver Isolation, and then choose Isolated.

If a user connects to a shared printer and you have not added the required driver, the user will be prompted to install the driver, as shown in Figure 12-8. You can disable the Computer Configuration\Policies\Windows Settings\Security Settings\Local Policies\Security Options \Devices: Prevent Users From Installing Printer Drivers policy to allow users to install printer drivers without administrative privileges.

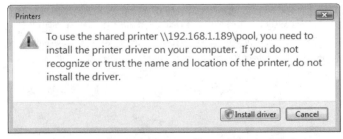

FIGURE 12-8 Prompting the user to confirm a driver installation

Configuring Printer Pooling

A printer pool consists of two or more identical printers that users can print to as if they were a single printer. Typically, you should physically locate the printers next to each other. Although any single print job will always print through a single printer, having multiple printers reduces the likelihood that users will need to wait for a large print job to complete before retrieving their own print jobs.

Printers in a printer pool should use the same print driver. Although the printers do not have to be identical, client computers will install only a single driver for all printers in the print pool. Sometimes a single printer driver will work with multiple printer models from a single manufacturer, allowing you to use different printers as part of a single printer pool.

To create a printer pool, follow these steps:

1. Install each of the printers that will be in the pool.

2. In Server Manager, select Print And Document Services\Print Management\Print Servers\<*ServerName*>\Printers. In the details pane, right-click one of the printers in the pool, and then choose Properties. The printer properties dialog box appears.

3. Click the Ports tab, and select the Enable Printer Pooling check box.

4. Select the port check box for each printer in the printer pool, as shown in Figure 12-9. Click OK.

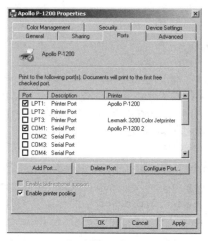

FIGURE 12-9 Enabling printer pooling

You need to share only the printer for which you enabled printer pooling. The reason is that any print jobs submitted to that shared printer will be sent to the first available printer in the printer pool. If you share individual printers in the printer pool, users can print to a specific printer, bypassing the pool.

Configuring Printer Priorities

When several documents are in a printer queue, you can use printer priorities to print higher-priority documents before lower-priority ones. For example, you could use this capability to allow documents printed by members of the Managers group to print before documents printed by members of the Employees group.

To configure printer priorities, follow these steps:

1. Install the printer that will have multiple priorities. Then, install the same printer again using the same port. You should have one logical printer for each priority level you need, even though you have only a single physical printer. You will assign each of the logical printers a different priority level.

2. In Server Manager, right-click one of the logical printers, and then choose Properties. The printer properties dialog box appears.

3. Click the Advanced tab, and specify a priority for the logical printer. All print jobs sent to a higher-priority logical printer will print before any lower-priority logical printer begins to print its jobs. The highest priority is 99; the lowest is 1.

4. Repeat steps 2 and 3 for each of the logical printers.

5. Connect higher-priority users to the higher-priority logical printer and lower-priority users to the lower-priority logical printer. Configure printer permissions to restrict access to specific groups.

Although higher-priority print jobs are always placed above lower-priority print jobs in the print queue, after a print job begins printing, it cannot be interrupted. For example, if a user prints a 100-page document to a low-priority logical printer and no higher-priority documents are in the print queue, the printer immediately begins printing the 100-page document. If another user then submits a higher-priority print job, the 100-page low-priority document will finish printing before the higher-priority document is printed.

Managing Internet Printing

If you install the Internet Printing role service, you can manage printers by using a web browser to visit the URL http://<ServerName>/Printers. As shown in Figure 12-10, the webpage lists the printers shared by a server and their current status.

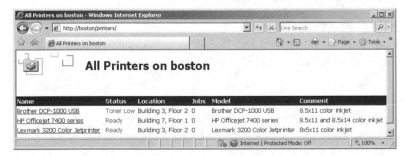

FIGURE 12-10 Managing printers from a web browser

Click a printer to view more detailed information about that printer, including the current print queue, as well as to pause, resume, or cancel printing. As shown in Figure 12-11, clicking Connect prompts the user to install the printer if it is not already installed. To connect to the printer, Internet Explorer must be configured to allow add-ons to run. Connecting to a printer using a web browser is convenient for guests, but you should use Group Policy settings to configure printers for client computers that you manage. For more information, read "Deploying Printers with Group Policy" later in this lesson.

To connect directly to a printer shared with Internet printing, provide the URL in the format http://<*ServerName*>/Printers/<*PrinterName*>/.printer.

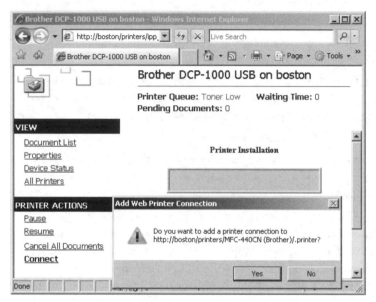

FIGURE 12-11 Installing a printer from a web browser

Generating Notifications

You can use custom filters to generate email notifications or to automatically run scripts when specific conditions are met on a printer. For example, you could send an email to a printer administrator when a printer is out of paper or jammed.

First, create a custom filter by following these steps:

1. In Server Manager, right-click Roles\Print And Document Services\Print Management \Custom Filters, and then choose Add New Printer Filter. The New Printer Filter Wizard appears.

2. On the Filter Name And Description page, type a name for the filter, and then click Next.

3. On the Define A Filter page, configure the Filter Criteria, one row at a time, as described here:

- **Field** Defines the criteria being compared. The most useful Field is Queue Status, which indicates the printer's current state.

- **Condition** Conditions vary depending on the value you select for Field, but they can be Is Exactly, Is Not Exactly, Begins With, Contains, and many others.

- **Value** The value the Field and Condition must match for a printer to meet the filter criteria.

4. When you have configured the filter criteria, click Next. Figure 12-12 shows a filter criteria that would match only shared printers that have paper jams and a location beginning with Boston.

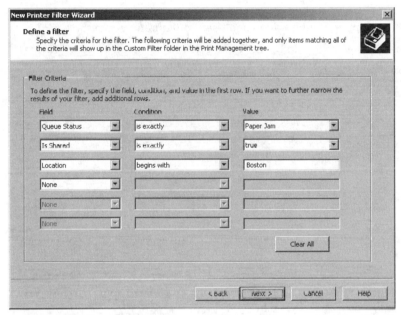

FIGURE 12-12 Defining a printer filter

5. On the Set Notifications (Optional) page, choose whether to send an email notification, whether to run a script when a printer matches the criteria you defined on the previous page, or both. For example, if you configured the filter as shown in Figure 12-12, you could use this page to send an email notification to an administrator in Boston who could fix the paper jam. Click Finish.

Deploying Printers with Group Policy

Enterprise environments should use Group Policy settings to deploy shared printers to clients. To deploy a printer with Group Policy settings, follow these steps:

1. In Server Manager, select Roles\Print And Document Services\Print Management\Print Servers\<*ServerName*>\Printers. In the details pane, right-click the printer, and then choose Deploy With Group Policy.

2. In the Deploy With Group Policy dialog box, click the Browse button to select the Group Policy object (GPO) that you want to use. Then, click OK.

3. To deploy the printer to all users who log on to a particular computer, select the The Computers That This GPO Applies To check box. To deploy the printer to specific users regardless of which computers they log on to, select the The Users That This GPO Applies To check box. You can select both check boxes to deploy the printer using both the Computer Configuration and User Configuration nodes in a GPO.

4. Click the Add button to add the GPO to the list, as illustrated in Figure 12-13.

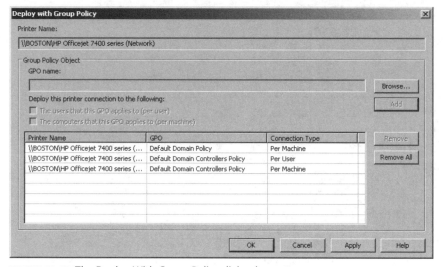

FIGURE 12-13 The Deploy With Group Policy dialog box

5. Repeat steps 2 and 3 to deploy the printer to additional GPOs.

6. Click OK.

7. Click OK to confirm that the printers were successfully added to the GPO, and then click OK again to close the Deploy With Group Policy dialog box.

The next time computers refresh Group Policy settings, the printer will be added to the list of available printers. You can view the deployed printers by editing a GPO in the Group Policy Management Editor and selecting the Policies\Windows Settings\Deployed Printers node in either the Computer Configuration (for printers deployed to computers) or User Configuration (for printers deployed to users) node.

Migrating Printers

To allow you to quickly migrate a print server from one computer to another, you can export a list of printers and drivers from the current print server and then import them into the new print server. You can automatically migrate all configuration settings, including whether a printer is published in the Active Directory. The sections that follow describe how to export and then import printers.

Exporting Printers

To export print queues and printer settings to a file, follow these steps:

1. In Server Manager, right-click Print Management, and then choose Migrate Printers. The Printer Migration wizard appears.
2. On the Getting Started With Printer Migration page, select Export Printer Queues And Printer Drivers To A File. Click Next.
3. On the Select A Print Server page, select a server, and then click Next.
4. On the Review The List Of Items To Be Exported page, click Next.
5. On the Select The File Location page, type a file name, and then click Next.
6. On the final page, click Finish.

You can also export printers at a command prompt or from a script using the PrintBRM tool, which is located in the %SystemRoot%\System32\spool\tools\ folder. To export printers to a file, run PrintBRM with the -B parameter, as the following example demonstrates:

```
cd %SystemRoot%\System32\spool\tools\
printbrm -b -f printers.printerexport
```

For complete usage information, type **PrintBRM -?**.

Importing Printers

To import print queues and printer settings from a file, follow these steps:

1. In Server Manager, right-click Print Management, and then choose Migrate Printers. The Printer Migration wizard appears.
2. On the Getting Started With Printer Migration page, select Import Printer Queues And Printer Drivers From A File. Click Next.
3. On the Select The File Location page, type the name of the exported file, and then click Next.
4. On the Review The List Of Items To Be Imported page, click Next.
5. On the Select A Print Server page, select a server, and then click Next.
6. On the Select Import Options page, as shown in Figure 12-14, click the Import Mode drop-down list to choose whether to keep or overwrite existing printers. Then, choose whether to list the imported printers in the Active Directory. Click Next.

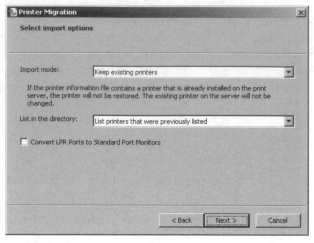

FIGURE 12-14 The Select Import Options page

7. On the final page, click Open Event Viewer to review any errors that might have occurred during the import process (all errors will have the source PrintBRM). Then, click Finish.

You can also simply double-click the .PrinterExport file created when you exported the printers and follow the prompts that appear.

To import printers at a command prompt or from a script, run **PrintBRM** with the -R parameter, as the following example demonstrates:

```
cd %SystemRoot%\System32\spool\tools\
printbrm -r -f printers.printerexport
```

For complete usage information, type **PrintBRM -?**.

Managing Printers from a Command Prompt or Script

Windows Server 2008 R2 includes seven tools for managing printers from a command prompt. The following scripts are stored in the %SystemRoot%\System32\Printing_Admin_Scripts \en-US\ folder:

- **PrnMngr.vbs** Adds and removes printers.

- **PrnCnfg.vbs** Configures printers. For example, you can change printer names or locations, configure a separator page, or grant print permissions to users.

- **PrnDrvr.vbs** Adds, removes, or lists printer drivers. For example, you can add a driver to make it available for automatic installation by a client.

- **PrnJobs.vbs** Manages print jobs. For example, you can list and cancel documents in the print queue.

- **PrnPort.vbs** Manages printer ports. For example, you can create a port for a network printer.

- **PrnQctl.vbs** Prints a test page, pauses or resumes a printer, and clears a printer queue.
- **PubPrn.vbs** Publishes a printer to the Active Directory.

Each of these tools is a Microsoft Visual Basic script. To use them, run the **CScript** command and pass the full path to the script file as the first parameter. Then, provide any script parameters. For example, to view usage information for the PrnCnfg.vbs script, run the following command:

```
cscript %SystemRoot%\System32\Printing_Admin_Scripts\en-US\prncnfg.vbs -?
```

> **NOTE SET CSCRIPT AS THE DEFAULT APPLICATION**
>
> If you don't want to have to type *cscript* before the script names, run the command cscript //H:cscript //S to configure Script as the default application to run .vbs files. After that, you can just call the script name.

To add a printer named Printer1 that is connected to LPT1 on the local computer and requires a printer driver called Printer Driver1, type:

```
cscript %SystemRoot%\System32\Printing_Admin_Scripts\en-US\prnmngr.vbs -a -p Printer1 _
    -m "Printer Driver1" -r lpt1:
```

To configure a printer named MyPrinter so that the spooler in the remote computer named MyServer keeps print jobs after they have been printed, type:

```
cscript %SystemRoot%\System32\Printing_Admin_Scripts\en-US\prncnfg.vbs -t -s MyServer _
    -p MyPrinter +keepprintedjobs
```

To list all drivers on the \\PrintServer1 server, type:

```
cscript %SystemRoot%\System32\Printing_Admin_Scripts\en-US\prndrvr.vbs -l -s \\ _
    PrintServer1
```

To add a version 3 Windows x64 printer driver for the "Laser Printer Model 1" model of printer using the C:\temp\LaserPrinter1.inf driver information file for a driver stored in the C:\temp folder, type:

```
cscript %SystemRoot%\System32\Printing_Admin_Scripts\en-US\prndrvr.vbs -a -m "Laser _
    Printer Model 1" -v 3 -e "Windows x64" -i c:\temp\LaserPrinter1.inf -h c:\temp
```

 Quick Check

1. Which role service should you install to allow clients to manage printers using their web browser?
2. What script would you run to publish a printer to Active Directory?

Quick Check Answers

1. The Internet Printing role service.
2. The PubPrn.vbs script.

Monitoring Printers

You can monitor printer usage in real time using the Performance Monitor snap-in. The most useful counters offered by the Print Queue object are:

- **Job Errors and Out Of Paper Errors** The total number of job errors or out of paper errors since the last restart.

- **Jobs and Jobs Spooling** The number of jobs currently in a print queue. You can monitor these counters to determine whether a particular printer is being overused and might need to be replaced with a faster printer or added to a printer pool.

- **Total Pages Printed and Total Jobs Printed** The total number of pages and jobs printed by a printer.

You can view the counters for a specific printer by selecting the printer in the Instances Of Selected Object list in the Add Counters dialog box. For detailed information about using Performance Monitor, read Lesson 2, "Monitoring Performance and Reliability," in Chapter 10, "Monitoring Computers."

PRACTICE **Installing and Sharing a Printer**

In this practice, you share a printer pool from Dcsrv1 and then connect and print to it from Boston.

EXERCISE 1   Installing the Print And Document Services Server Role

In this exercise, you install the Print And Document Services server role with the Print Server and Internet Printing role services.

1. On Dcsrv1, in Server Manager, right-click Roles, and then choose Add Roles. The Add Roles Wizard appears.

2. If the Before You Begin page appears, click Next.

3. On the Server Roles page, select the Print And Document Services check box. Click Next.

4. On the Print And Document Services page, click Next.

5. On the Select Role Services page, select the Print Server and Internet Printing check boxes. Click Next.

6. If IIS isn't currently installed, in the Add Roles Wizard dialog box, click Add Required Role Services.

7. On the Select Role Services page, click Next.

8. On the Web Server (IIS) page, click Next.

9. On the Select Role Services page, you're prompted to select the role services you want to install to support IIS. Click Next to accept the default settings.

10. On the Confirmation page, click Install.

11. On the Results page, click Close.

EXERCISE 2 Installing Two Printers

In this exercise, you install two printers. If you have a printer (either a network printer or a printer connected directly to your server), you can substitute that printer for the non-existent printer described in this exercise.

1. On Dcsrv1, close and then reopen Server Manager. In Server Manager, right-click Roles \Print And Document Services\Print Management\Print Servers\Dcsrv1\Printers, and then choose Add Printer. The Network Printer Installation Wizard appears.

2. On the Printer Installation page, select Add A New Printer Using An Existing Port. Select the LPT:1 port, which corresponds to the parallel port present on most computers. Click Next.

3. On the Printer Driver page, select Install A New Driver. Click Next.

4. On the Printer Installation page, select the Apollo P-1200 driver. Click Next.

5. On the Printer Name And Sharing Settings page, select the Share This Printer check box. Click Next.

6. On the Printer Found page, click Next.

7. On the Completing The Network Printer Installation Wizard page, select the Add Another Printer check box. Click Finish.

8. On the Printer Installation page, select Add A New Printer Using An Existing Port. Select the LPT2 port, and then click Next.

9. On the Printer Driver page, select Use An Existing Printer Driver On The Computer. Select Apollo P-1200, and then click Next.

10. On the Printer Name And Sharing Settings page, clear the Share This Printer check box. Click Next.

11. On the Printer Found page, click Next.

12. On the Completing The Network Printer Installation Wizard page, click Finish.

Now you have configured Dcsrv1 to simulate having two identical printers connected to LPT1 and LPT2.

EXERCISE 3 Configuring a Printer Pool

In this exercise, you configure a printer pool on Dcsrv1.

1. On Dcsrv1, in Server Manager, select Roles\Print And Document Services\Print Management\Print Servers\Dcsrv1\Printers. In the details pane, right-click Apollo P-1200, and then choose Properties.

2. Select the Ports tab. Select the Enable Printer Pooling check box. Then, select both LPT1 and LPT2. Click OK.

Now, any print jobs submitted to the first Apollo P-1200 printer will be sent to either of the two printers you created, depending on which printer is available.

EXERCISE 4   Printing to the Printer Pool

In this exercise, you will install a network printer and then print to the printer pool from Boston.

1. On Boston, click Start, and then choose Devices And Printers.

2. Click Add A Printer. The Add Printer wizard appears.

3. On the What Type Of Printer Do You Want To Install page, click Add A Network, Wireless, Or Bluetooth Printer.

4. Click The Printer That I Want Isn't Listed.

5. On the Find A Printer By Name Or TCP/IP Address page, select Select A Shared Printer By Name. Type **\\Dcsrv1\Apollo P-1200**. Click Next. Notice that the printer driver is automatically installed.

6. On the Type A Printer Name page, click Next.

7. On Dcsrv1, select the Apollo P-1200 printer in the Print Management snap-in and watch the job queue. On Boston, click Print A Test Page several times to watch the client submit the jobs to the printer. Click Finish.

EXERCISE 5   Using Group Policy Settings to Configure a Client Printer

In this exercise, you will use Group Policy settings to configure Boston with a connection to a shared printer.

1. On Dcsrv1, in Server Manager, select Roles\Print And Document Services\Print Management\Print Servers\Dcsrv1\Printers. In the details pane, right-click Apollo P-1200 (Copy 1), and then choose Deploy With Group Policy.

2. In the Deploy With Group Policy dialog box, click the Browse button. Select Default Domain Policy, and then click OK.

3. Select both the The Computers That This GPO Applies To (Per Machine) and The Users That This GPO Applies To (Per User) check boxes.

4. Click the Add button to add the GPO to the list.

5. Click OK.

6. Click OK to confirm that the printers were successfully added to the GPO. Then, click OK one more time to close the Deploy With Group Policy dialog box.

Restart Boston. When it restarts, log on and open Control Panel\Printers to verify that the second copy of the Apollo P-1200 printer was added using Group Policy.

EXERCISE 6 Managing Internet Printing

In this exercise, you will use a web browser to manage a shared printer from a remote computer.

1. On Boston, click Start, and then choose Internet Explorer.

2. In the Address bar, type **http://Dcsrv1/Printers**, and then press Enter.

3. On the All Printers On Dcsrv1 page, click Apollo P-1200.

4. Click the different links in the left pane to view more information about the printer and to pause and resume the printer.

Lesson Summary

- You can use Server Manager to install the Print And Document Services server role, which adds the Print Management snap-in.

- Installing a printer requires you to select a port (which can be a physical or network port) and a print driver.

- Sharing printers allows users to print from across the network.

- You can use printer permissions to control which users can print to and manage a printer.

- Different Windows platforms require different drivers. For example, 32-bit and 64-bit versions of Windows require separate drivers. To allow clients to automatically download and install the correct driver, you should install drivers for all Windows platforms that you support.

- A printer pool uses a single logical printer to print to multiple physical printers. Windows will print to the first available printer.

- You can prioritize documents by creating multiple logical printers for a single physical printer and then assigning different priorities to each of the logical printers. Documents sent to the high-priority logical printer will always complete before any documents sent to the low-priority logical printer are processed. Use printer permissions to control who can print to the high-priority logical printer.

- If you install the Internet Printing Protocol (IPP) role service, clients can use HTTP to submit print jobs and manage print queues.

- You can use custom filters to generate notifications when specific printers have problems.

- Use Group Policy settings to configure clients to connect to shared printers.

- Windows Server 2008 R2 includes both graphical and command-line tools to migrate printers from one server to another.

- To manage printers from a command prompt, use the scripts provided in the %SystemRoot%\System32\Printing_Admin_Scripts\en-US\ folder.

- You can monitor printers by using the Performance Monitor snap-in.

Lesson Review

You can use the following questions to test your knowledge of the information in Lesson 1, "Managing Printers." The questions are also available on the companion CD if you prefer to review them in electronic form.

> **NOTE ANSWERS**
>
> Answers to these questions and explanations of why each answer choice is correct or incorrect are located in the "Answers" section at the end of the book.

1. Currently, you manage eight Windows Server 2008 R2 print servers. You plan to centralize management by moving all printers to a single print server running Windows Server 2008 R2 Server Core. After exporting the printers on each of the eight original print servers, how can you import them on the new print server?

   A. **printui -b -f** *<file name>*

   B. **printbrm -r -f** *<file name>*

   C. **printbrmengine -r -f** *<file name>*

   D. **netsh print import** *<file name>*

2. You need to write a script to publish several printers to the Active Directory. Which tool should you use?

   A. PrnMngr.vbs

   B. PrnCnfg.vbs

   C. PrnQctl.vbs

   D. PubPrn.vbs

3. You share a printer, MyPrinter, from a computer named MyServer. MyServer runs Windows Server 2008 R2 and has the Internet Printing role service installed. You need to configure a client computer to print to the shared printer from behind a firewall that allows only web connections. When configuring the client, what path to the printer should you provide?

   A. http://MyServer/Printers/MyPrinter/.printer

   B. http://MyServer/MyPrinter

   C. \\MyServer\Printers\MyPrinter\.printer

   D. \\MyServer\MyPrinter

4. You would like to be notified by email when a specific printer runs out of paper or has a paper jam. How can you do this?

   A. Configure a notification from the driver properties.

   B. Use the PrintBRM tool to configure an email notification.

   C. Configure a notification from the printer properties.

   D. Create a custom filter.

Chapter Review

To further practice and reinforce the skills you learned in this chapter, you can perform the following tasks:

- Review the chapter summary.
- Review the list of key terms introduced in this chapter.
- Complete the case scenarios. These scenarios set up real-world situations involving the topics of this chapter and ask you to create a solution.
- Complete the suggested practices.
- Take a practice test.

Chapter Summary

To install, share, and manage printers connected to a Windows Server 2008 computer, install the Print Services server role. This adds the Print Management snap-in to the Server Manager console. You can also manage printers from Control Panel or by using command-line tools.

Key Terms

Do you know what these key terms mean? You can check your answers by looking up the terms in the glossary at the end of the book.

- Internet Printing Protocol (IPP)
- Line Printer Daemon (LPD)

Case Scenario

In the following case scenario, you will apply what you've learned about how to plan and deploy printer sharing. You can find answers to these questions in the "Answers" section at the end of this book.

Case Scenario: Managing Network Printers

You are a systems administrator for Northwind Traders, a medium-sized organization with approximately 200 employees in a single facility. The employees share about 20 printers. Most of the printers are for general use by any employee, but each of the five executives has an office printer that should be accessible only to the executive and the executive's assistant.

Currently, client computers print directly to the network printers, but managing the printers has been a challenge. If a printer jams or runs out of paper, nobody is notified—and users often simply choose to print to a different printer rather than solve the problem. Another challenge is that the Marketing department often creates large print jobs of more than 100 pages, requiring other users to wait until the print job completes to retrieve their documents. Several executives have complained that other employees print to their private printers because the printers show up when users search the network for a printer.

Your manager calls you into her office to discuss possible solutions to these problems. Answer the following questions for your manager:

1. How can we centralize management of the network printers?

2. How can we notify an administrator when a printer runs out of paper or is jammed?

3. How can you control access to private printers?

4. How can you reduce the impact of large print jobs?

Suggested Practices

To help you successfully master the exam objectives presented in this chapter, complete the following tasks.

Configure and Monitor Print Services

For this task, you should complete Practices 1, 2, and 3. Although clusters will probably not be covered on your exam, you can complete Practice 4 to gain experience creating highly available print servers.

- **Practice 1**   Install Windows Server 2008 R2 Server Core and use command-line tools to configure the server as a print server and share a printer.

- **Practice 2**   If you have multiple printers that use the same driver (or two printers that are the same model), configure them as a printer pool. Then, print several documents of different lengths in rapid succession and examine how Windows Server 2008 R2 distributes the print jobs.

- **Practice 3**   Install and share a printer. Then, use Performance Monitor to monitor usage of the printer. Submit several print jobs to the printer.

- **Practice 4**   If you have the hardware available, configure a print server failover cluster to provide redundancy when a print server fails. For detailed instructions, read "Failover Cluster Step-by-Step Guide: Configuring a Two-Node Print Server Failover Cluster" at *http://technet.microsoft.com/library/cc771509.aspx*.

Take a Practice Test

The practice tests on this book's companion CD offer many options. For example, you can test yourself on just the content covered in this chapter, or you can test yourself on all the 70-642 certification exam content. You can set up the test so that it closely simulates the experience of taking a certification exam, or you can set it up in study mode so that you can look at the correct answers and explanations after you answer each question.

> **MORE INFO   PRACTICE TESTS**
>
> For details about all the practice test options available, see "How to Use the Practice Tests" in this book's Introduction.

Answer

Chapter 1: Lesson Review Answers

Lesson 1

1. **Correct Answer: A**

    A. **Correct:** The address shown is an APIPA address, which is assigned automatically to a DHCP client if a DHCP server cannot be found. An APIPA address usually results in a loss of connectivity to network resources. To fix the problem, you should first attempt to obtain a new address from a DHCP server. To do that, use the **Ipconfig /renew** command.

    B. **Incorrect:** This command will merely verify that you can connect to your own address. It will not help establish network connectivity.

    C. **Incorrect:** This command will merely verify that you can trace a path to your own address. It will not help establish network connectivity.

    D. **Incorrect:** This command displays the list of IP address-to-MAC address mappings stored on the computer. It will not fix any problems in network connectivity.

2. **Correct Answer: D**

    A. **Incorrect:** You should not configure a DNS server as a DHCP client. A DNS server needs the most stable address available, which is a manually configured static address.

    B. **Incorrect:** An APIPA address is an address that signifies a network problem. It is not a stable address and should not be assigned to a server.

    C. **Incorrect:** An alternate configuration is not a stable address because it can be replaced by a DHCP-assigned address. You should assign the most stable address type—a static address—to a DNS server.

    D. **Correct:** The addresses of infrastructure servers such as DHCP and DNS servers should never change. Therefore, these server types should be assigned manual or static addresses because these address types do not change.

Lesson 2

1. **Correct Answer: D**

    A. **Incorrect:** A /23 network can support 512 addresses but only 510 devices.

    B. **Incorrect:** A /22 network can support 1024 addresses but only 1022 devices.

    C. **Incorrect:** A /23 network can support 510 devices, but a /22 network can support more.

    D. **Correct:** A /22 network can support 1024 addresses but only 1022 devices because two addresses in every block are reserved for network communications.

2. **Correct Answer: B**

   A. Incorrect: A /28 network supports 16 addresses and 14 computers. You need to support 18 addresses and 16 computers.

   B. Correct: You need to support 18 addresses and 16 computers. A /27 network supports 32 addresses and 30 computers. This is the smallest option that provides you with the address space you need.

   C. Incorrect: A /26 network supports 64 addresses and 62 computers. This is larger than you need, so it would violate company policy.

   D. Incorrect: The current /29 network supports eight addresses and six computers. It cannot support the 16 computers you need.

3. **Correct Answer: D**

   A. Incorrect: Remote users cannot connect to the server because the server is not configured on the same subnet as its default gateway. With a subnet mask of 255.255.255.224, the server sees itself on a subnet with the 32 addresses from 192.168.1.64 to 192.168.1.95. By changing the server address to 192.168.1.62, the server would see itself on a subnet with the 32 addresses from 192.168.1.32 to 192.168.1.63. Because the default gateway is assigned 192.168.1.1, however, this action doesn't solve the problem.

   B. Incorrect: Remote users cannot connect to the server because the server is not configured on the same subnet as its default gateway. With a subnet mask of 255.255.255.224, the server sees itself on a subnet with the 32 addresses from 192.168.1.64 to 192.168.1.95. By changing the server address to 192.168.1.34, the server would see itself on a subnet with the 32 addresses from 192.168.1.32 to 192.168.1.63. Because the default gateway is assigned 192.168.1.1, however, this action doesn't solve the problem.

   C. Incorrect: Remote users cannot connect to the server because the server is not configured on the same subnet as its default gateway. With a subnet mask of 255.255.255.224, the server sees itself on a subnet with the 32 addresses from 192.168.1.64 to 192.168.1.95. By switching to a 26-bit subnet mask or 255.255.255.192, the server would see itself on a subnet with the 64 addresses from 192.168.1.64 to 192.168.1.127. Because the default gateway is assigned 192.168.1.1, however, this action doesn't solve the problem.

   D. Correct: As originally configured, the server and the default gateway are on different subnets. A subnet mask of 255.255.255.224 creates a block of 32 addresses. Computers configured with this subnet mask see other addresses in the same subnet when the first three octets are identical and the last octet value is equally divisible by 32, dropping any remainder. If you switch the server configuration to a 25-bit subnet mask or 255.255.255.128, the block size becomes 128 addresses. In this case, the server would see itself on a subnet with the 128 addresses from 192.168.1.0 to 192.168.1.127. This range includes the addresses of both the server and the default gateway, so the problem would be solved.

4. **Correct Answer: A**

   A. Correct: Segment A needs to support 600 computers and therefore requires a block size of 1024, which describes a /22 network. Adding 1024 or 4 x 256 to the starting address of 131.107.168.0 brings you to the starting address of Segment B, 131.107.172.0. Segment B needs to support 300 hosts and therefore requires a block size of 512, or a /23 network. Adding 512 or 2 x 256 to the starting address of Segment B brings you to the starting address of Segment C, 131.107.174.0. Segment C needs to support 150 hosts, for which a block size of 256 (a /24 network) is needed. Adding 256 to the starting address of Segment C brings you to the starting address of Segment D, 131.107.175.0. Segment D needs to support 75 hosts, for which a block size of 128 is needed. A /25 network is used for this block size.

   B. Incorrect: See the explanation for A.

   C. Incorrect: See the explanation for A.

   D. Incorrect: See the explanation for A.

Lesson 3

1. **Correct Answer: A**

   A. Correct: Global addresses are routable addresses that can communicate directly with IPv6-only hosts on public networks. This is the kind of address you need if you want a static IPv6 address to which other computers can connect from across the IPv6 Internet.

   B. Incorrect: A link-local address is not routable and cannot be used on a public network.

   C. Incorrect: A unique-local address is routable but cannot be used on a public network.

   D. Incorrect: A site-local address is a version of a unique local address, but these address types are being phased out.

2. **Correct Answer: C**

   A. Incorrect: You would need global addresses only if you wanted your network to connect to the public IPv6 network.

   B. Incorrect: Link-local addresses are not routable, so they would not allow your subnets to intercommunicate.

   C. Correct: Unique local addresses resemble private address ranges in IPv4. They are used for private routing within organizations.

   D. Incorrect: Site-local addresses were once defined as a way to provide routing within a private network, but this address type has been deprecated.

3. **Correct Answer: B**

   A. **Incorrect:** Configuring the firewalls with an IPv6 address would be insufficient. Every computer in the company would also need to have a global address, and the three firewalls would need to be connected to the IPv6 Internet.

   B. **Correct:** The purpose of Teredo is to provide clients behind an IPv4 NAT device to communicate directly on the IPv6 Internet. If all three firewalls could enable communication between internal clients and external Teredo servers, internal clients would all be provided with a global IPv6 address and would be able to communicate with each other directly.

   C. **Incorrect:** Unique local addresses would not enable computers in each office to communicate across the Internet. Unique local addresses resemble private IPv4 addresses in that they are used only within private networks.

   D. **Incorrect:** An ISATAP router connects an IPv6 network to an IPv4 network. An ISATAP router would not allow clients behind separate NAT devices to communicate directly with each other.

4. **Correct Answer: C**

   A. **Incorrect:** IPv6 addresses that begin with "fa00" are currently undefined.

   B. **Incorrect:** IPv6 addresses that begin with "fb80" are currently undefined.

   C. **Correct:** IPv6 addresses that begin with "fd00" are unique local addresses. These addresses are used within private sites and can be routed among many segments. However, they cannot be used to communicate on the public IPv6 Internet.

   D. **Incorrect:** IPv6 addresses that begin with "fe80" are link-local addresses. These addresses can be used to communicate only on the local LAN. They cannot be used to communicate with hosts on other network segments.

5. **Correct Answer: A**

   A. **Correct:** If you have four subnets, you need to claim 2 bits for subnetting. In this case, the network prefix used in the subnetted space must be /52 + 2, or /54. For a /54 subnetting scheme, the increment between subnets is 2^{64-54} or 2^{10}, which in hexadecimal is written as 400. The subnet 1 address must be 3f04:4d12:95a5:a000::/54, and then using the hexadecimal increment, you can determine that the subnet 2 address is 3f04:4d12:95a5:a400::/54, the subnet 3 address is 3f04:4d12:95a5:a800::/54, and the subnet 4 address is 3f04:4d12:95a5:ac00::/54.

   B. **Incorrect:** The network prefix should be /54 because you should claim only 2 bits for subnetting. If you claimed a third bit for subnetting, eight subnets would be created, and the increment between subnets would be 200 in hexadecimal. The address of subnet 3 in that case would be 3f04:4d12:95a5:a400::/55.

   C. **Incorrect:** This is the address of subnet 4.

   D. **Incorrect:** See the explanations for answers A and B.

Chapter 1: Case Scenario Answers

Case Scenario: Working with IPv4 Address Blocks

1. /29 (255.255.255.248)
2. You need a /28 network (subnet mask 255.255.255.240).
3. This address block would support 16 addresses and 14 hosts.

Chapter 2: Lesson Review Answers

Lesson 1

1. **Correct Answer: A**

    A. **Correct:** This command flushes the DNS server cache. If you know that a DNS server is responding to queries with outdated cache data, it's best to clear the server cache. This way, the next time the DNS server receives a query for the name, it will attempt to resolve that name by querying other computers.

    B. **Incorrect:** Restarting the DNS Client service will flush the DNS client cache on the computer in question. It won't affect the way the DNS server responds to the query for that computer's name.

    C. **Incorrect:** Typing **ipconfig /flushdns** simply clears the DNS client cache. It won't affect the way the DNS server responds to the query for that computer's name.

    D. **Incorrect:** Restarting all client computers will not fix the problem. It merely has the effect of clearing the DNS client cache on all computers. This could fix problems related to outdated client cache data, but it will not fix the problem on the DNS server itself.

2. **Correct Answer: D**

    A. **Incorrect:** When you enable IPv6 on a computer running Windows Server 2008, no extra functionality is enabled in connections to a computer running Windows XP.

    B. **Incorrect:** IPv6 never blocks network functionality, so disabling it would never enable a feature like connectivity through a UNC.

    C. **Incorrect:** Enabling LLMNR on WS08A could enable UNC connectivity to another computer running Windows Server 2008, Windows Vista, or Windows 7, but it would not enable UNC connectivity to a computer running Windows XP.

    D. **Correct:** If NetBIOS were disabled, it would block UNC connectivity to a computer running Windows XP.

3. **Correct Answer: A**

   A. Correct: By not specifying a DNS server, you prevent Research01 from registering with a DNS server and thereby keep other computers from resolving the name of Research01 through DNS. By configuring the HOSTS file on the five authorized computers, you enable just those five computers to resolve the name Research01 to an IP address.

   B. Incorrect: Adjusting the properties of the A record for Research01 in DNS will not prevent other computers from being able to read the record. The properties of a resource record are used to allow or deny other computers from updating the record.

   C. Incorrect: Research01 is not a DNS server, so blocking DNS requests will have no effect on the ability of other computers to resolve the name Research01.

   D. Incorrect: You can use IPsec to block network access to all but a select group of computers, but you cannot use IPsec to prevent other computers from resolving the name of a particular computer.

Lesson 2

1. **Correct Answer: A**

   A. Correct: The file Cache.dns, located in the %systemroot%\system32\dns\ folder, contains the list of the root DNS servers that the local DNS server will query if it cannot itself answer a query. By default, this file contains the list of Internet root servers, but you can replace it with the list of your company root servers.

   B. Incorrect: A HOSTS file specifies a list of resolved names that are preloaded into the DNS client cache. It does not specify root servers.

   C. Incorrect: The Lmhosts file is used to resolve NetBIOS names. It does not specify DNS root servers.

   D. Incorrect: Specifying a forwarder is not the same as specifying root servers. If the connection to a forwarder fails, a DNS server will query its root servers.

2. **Correct Answer: C**

   A. Incorrect: This option does not provide a way to resolve Internet names. It also does not provide a way for the New York DNS servers to resolve the names in the Sacramento office.

   B. Incorrect: This option does not provide a way for computers in each office to resolve names of the computers in the other office.

   C. Correct: This is the only solution that enables the DNS servers to effectively resolve names in the local domain, in the remote domain, and on the Internet.

   D. Incorrect: This option does not provide an effective way for computers to resolve Internet names.

3. **Correct Answer: C**

   A. Incorrect: This command will set the pool of random ports used for DNS queries at 2500. DNS socket pooling increases DNS security by making it harder to spoof a DNS server performing a query. However, it doesn't change the security of data stored on your DNS server. In addition, the SocketPoolSize value of 2500 is the default, so this command does not improve security over the default setting.

   B. Incorrect: This command will exclude a port range or set of ranges from being selected as a random port used in a DNS server query. It does not affect the security of data stored on a DNS server.

   C. Correct: Cache locking prevents resource records stored in a DNS server cache from being overwritten for a percentage of the records' TTL value. By making a cache entry incapable of being modified for a high percentage of its lifetime, you can improve the integrity of data in your DNS database. A setting of 90 (percent) or higher is recommended.

   D. Incorrect: This command will enable netmask ordering, a feature in which a DNS server will order DNS responses by prioritizing IP addresses that match the client's subnet. This setting does not affect security, and the feature is already enabled by default.

Lesson 3

1. **Correct Answer: B**

   A. Incorrect: Configuring conditional forwarding would allow computers in one domain to resolve names in the other domain. However, the question states that this functionality is already being achieved. Conditional forwarding by itself would not enable clients to connect to resources by using a single-tag name.

   B. Correct: If you specify west.cpandl.com on the DNS suffix search list, that suffix will be appended to a DNS query. This option would enable a user to submit a single-tag name query in a UNC path and have the client automatically append the name of the west.cpandl.com domain.

   C. Incorrect: This option merely ensures that the client's own name is registered in DNS. It does not enable a user to connect to resources in the remote domain.

   D. Incorrect: By default, the client will append a single-tag name query with the client's own domain name. If that query fails, the client will append the single-tag name query with the parent domain name. Neither of these options would enable the query for a computer in the remote domain to be resolved properly.

2. **Correct Answer: D**

   A. **Incorrect:** Merely configuring a connection-specific suffix does not enable a computer to register with DNS if all the other settings are left at the default values.

   B. **Incorrect:** Enabling this option registers a connection-specific suffix only if one is configured. If the other settings are left at the default values for a non-DHCP client, this setting would have no effect.

   C. **Incorrect:** This option is already enabled if the DNS client settings are left at the default values.

   D. **Correct:** This answer choice provides the only solution that is not a default value and that, when configured, enables a DNS client to register its static address with a DNS server.

3. **Correct Answer: B**

   A. **Incorrect:** This search list will not reduce latency of negative responses because it is the same search list that is used by default.

   B. **Correct:** The devolution level determines the minimum number of tags or labels within the local DNS domain suffix that a DNS client will append to an unqualified single name that it wants to resolve. When you set the devolution level to 3, clients in the local domain will append only "Dublin.ie.fabrikam.com" and "ie.fabrikam.com" to single-name queries. By appending only four- and three-tag suffixes instead of the default of four- three- and two-tag suffixes, the latency of negative responses is reduced.

   C. **Incorrect:** Configuring this option will not reduce the latency of negative responses because this option is already selected by default.

   D. **Incorrect:** This option will only increase the latency of negative responses. When a client is configured with a connection-specific suffix, that suffix is appended to the unqualified single-name before the parent suffixes of the primary DNS suffix. As a result, more queries are performed, which requires more time before a negative response can be achieved.

Chapter 2: Case Scenario Answers

Case Scenario 1: Troubleshooting DNS Clients

1. Enable the Use This Connection's DNS Suffix In DNS Registration setting.
2. Configure the Windows 7 clients with the address of the WINS server.

Case Scenario 2: Deploying a DNS Server

1. You should deploy a caching-only server.
2. Configure conditional forwarding so that all queries for the fabrikam.com network are directed to DNS servers on the internal network at the main office.

Chapter 3: Lesson Review Answers

Lesson 1

1. **Correct Answer: D**

   A. Incorrect: Disabling scavenging on the zone will affect all records. You want to prevent a single record from being scavenged.

   B. Incorrect: Disabling scavenging on the server will prevent all records on the server from being scavenged. You want to prevent only a single record from being scavenged.

   C. Incorrect: On a zone where aging is enabled, statically-addressed clients create the same time stamps that DHCP clients do. Assigning a computer a static address does not affect scavenging behavior.

   D. Correct: Manually created records are never scavenged. If you need to prevent a certain record from being scavenged in a zone, the best way to achieve that is to delete the original record and re-create it manually.

2. **Correct Answers: A, B, F**

   A. Correct: To prevent computers outside of the Active Directory domain from registering with a DNS server, you need to configure the zone to accept secure dynamic updates only. You can configure a zone to accept secure dynamic updates only if you store it in Active Directory. You can store a zone in Active Directory only if the DNS server is also an Active Directory domain controller.

   B. Correct: To prevent computers outside of the Active Directory domain from registering with a DNS server, you need to configure the zone to accept secure dynamic updates only. This option is available only if you store the DNS zone in Active Directory, and this last option is available only if you create the zone on a domain controller.

   C. Incorrect: If you don't store the zone in Active Directory, you won't be able to require secure updates for the zone.

   D. Incorrect: If you disable dynamic updates for the zone, no computers will be able to register and you will have to create and update every record manually. This is not the best way to solve this problem because it creates too much administrative overhead.

   E. Incorrect: You don't want to choose this option because you want to prevent nonsecure updates. When you allow nonsecure updates, you allow computers outside of the local Active Directory domain to register in the zone.

   F. Correct: To prevent computers outside of the Active Directory domain from registering with a DNS server, you need to configure the zone to accept secure dynamic updates only. This option is available only if you store the DNS zone in Active Directory, and this last option is available only if you create the zone on a domain controller.

3. **Correct Answer: D**

   A. Incorrect: If you created a second, identical record for mailserver1 and mailserver2 with round robin enabled, you would distribute the workload 40 percent to mailserver1, 40 percent to mailserver2, and 20 percent to mailserver3. No server would be used as a backup.

   B. Incorrect: If you created a second, identical record for mailserver1 and mailserver2 with round robin disabled, mailserver1 would receive 100 percent of the workload, because that would always be the first server listed in the response list in DNS.

   C. Incorrect: If you assigned a preference value of *1* to mailserver3, you would make that server the preferred mail server. The other two servers would both act as backup mail servers.

   D. Correct: If you assign a preference value of *20* to mailserver3, that server is used as a backup server when an SMTP application is unable to contact either of the preferred servers. The workload is divided between the other two servers through round robin DNS.

Lesson 2

1. **Correct Answer: A**

   A. Correct: This is the only solution that will improve name resolution response times, keep an updated list of remote name servers, and minimize zone transfer traffic.

   B. Incorrect: Conditional forwarding would improve name resolution response times and minimize zone transfer traffic, but it would not allow you to keep an updated list of remote name servers.

   C. Incorrect: A secondary zone would improve name resolution response times and allow you to keep an updated list of remote name servers, but it would not minimize zone transfer traffic because the entire zone would need to be copied periodically from the remote office.

   D. Incorrect: You cannot perform a delegation in this case. You can perform a delegation only for a child domain in the DNS namespace. For example, a child domain of the ny.us.nwtraders.msft domain might be uptown.ny.us.nwtraders.msft.

2. **Correct Answer: C**

   A. Incorrect: When you choose this option, computers running Windows 2000 Server cannot see the ForestDnsZones partition in which zone data is stored.

   B. Incorrect: When you choose this option, computers running Windows 2000 Server cannot see the DomainDnsZones partition in which zone data is stored.

   C. Correct: When you choose this option, zone data is stored in the domain partition, which is visible to computers running Windows 2000 Server.

   D. Incorrect: Computers running Windows 2000 Server would not be able to see any new application directory partitions that you create, so creating one and choosing the associated option would not resolve the problem.

3. **Correct Answer: C**

   A. **Incorrect:** The Reload command reloads data from the local zone data. It does not populate a zone with initial data when the Transfer From Master command does not work.

   B. **Incorrect:** The Transfer New Copy Of Zone From Master command performs a zone transfer from the secondary zone even when there have been no updates to the zone. It does not populate a zone with initial data if the Transfer From Master command does not work.

   C. **Correct:** By default, DNS zones are configured not to allow zone transfers. Unless this default setting is changed, the new secondary zone will not be able to load the zone data.

   D. **Incorrect:** Notifications are used to inform secondary servers whenever a zone update has occurred. Notifications cannot help when the zone data cannot be loaded on a new secondary zone.

Lesson 3

1. **Correct Answer: A, C**

   A. **Correct:** Windows Server 2008 does not support the latest version of DNSSEC, which Is based on RFC 4033, RFC 4034, and RFC 4035. To implement the latest version of DNSSEC, you need to upgrade to Windows Server 2008 R2.

   B. **Incorrect:** You need to configure at least one trust anchor from another domain for your DNS server to perform validation of that remote domain and its delegated subdomains. However, the trust anchor can originate from any domain. It does not have to be from the public root server.

   C. **Correct:** Windows Vista is not compatible with the latest version of DNSSEC. To configure clients to request DNSSEC validation, you need to upgrade all clients to Windows 7.

   D. **Incorrect:** You need to configure at least one trust anchor from another domain for your DNS server to perform validation of that remote domain and its delegated subdomains. However, the trust anchor can originate from any domain. It does not have to be from the top-level domain servers.

2. **Correct Answer: D**

   A. **Incorrect:** To validate responses from Northwindtraders.com, you need to configure a public key from that organization as a trust anchor on your DNS server.

   B. **Incorrect:** To validate responses from Northwindtraders.com, you need to configure a public key from that organization as a trust anchor on your DNS server.

   C. **Incorrect:** You need to import a public key from Northwindtraders.com, but should use the KSK as a trust anchor. A KSK is updated less frequently and will decrease administrative effort in the future.

   D. **Correct:** You need to import a public key from Northwindtraders.com and configure it as a trust anchor if you want to validate the DNS responses received from that zone. You should use a KSK because this type of key is updated less frequently and therefore will decrease the administrative effort required to maintain DNSSEC.

3. **Correct Answer: B**

   A. **Incorrect:** If you create a rule that matches the FQDN "fabrikam.com," clients will not request DNSSEC when they query for any particular host name such as "www.fabrikam.com" in this domain. They will request DNSSEC only when they query specifically for "fabrikam.com."

   B. **Correct:** This Name Resolution Policy rule configures DNS clients to request DNSSEC validation whenever they query for a name that ends in "fabrikam.com." This rule therefore applies to every name queried for in the fabrikam.com domain.

   C. **Incorrect:** Importing the trust anchor from fabrikam.com enables the local DNS server to establish an island of trust with the DNS servers in the fabrikam.com domain. It does not configure clients to request DNSSEC validation.

   D. **Incorrect:** Exporting the trust anchor from your domain to the DNS servers at fabrikam.com enables the remote servers to establish trust with you so that they can validate your DNS responses. This action will not configure any clients to request DNSSEC validation.

Chapter 3: Case Scenario Answers

Case Scenario 1: Managing Outdated Zone Data

1. The best way to remove stale records that you know to be outdated is to delete them manually.

2. You can enable aging and scavenging on each server and in the zone to prevent the accumulation of such records in the future.

3. The No-Refresh interval should be left at the default of 7 days. The Refresh interval should be configured as 14 days.

Case Scenario 2: Configuring Zone Transfers

1. You should host a secondary zone at the Rochester site.

2. Configure notifications on the primary zone at the headquarters so that the server hosting the secondary zone is notified whenever changes occur.

Chapter 4: Lesson Review Answers

Lesson 1

1. **Correct Answer: A**

   A. **Correct:** If computers cannot communicate beyond the local subnet even when you specify an IP address, the problem is most likely that the computers do not have a default gateway specified. To assign a default gateway address to DHCP clients, configure the 003 Router option.

B. Incorrect: If the DHCP clients needed to have a DNS server assigned to them, they would be able to connect to computers when specified by address but not by name.

C. Incorrect: The 015 Domain Name option provides DHCP clients with a connection-specific DNS suffix assigned to them. If clients needed such a suffix, the problem reported would be that clients could not connect to servers when users specified a single-label computer name such as "Server1" (instead of a fully qualified domain name [FQDN] such as "Server1.contoso.com").

D. Incorrect: The 044 WINS/NBNS Server option configures DHCP clients with the address of a WINS server. A WINS server would not enable you to connect to computers on remote subnets when you specify those computers by address.

2. **Correct Answer: C**

   A. Incorrect: You know that clients are already configured as DHCP clients because they have received addresses in the APIPA range of 169.254.0.0/16.

   B. Incorrect: Dhcp1 does not need to be running the DHCP client service because it is not acting as a DHCP client.

   C. Correct: If you want the DHCP server to assign addresses to computers on the local subnet, the server needs to be assigned an address that is also located on the same subnet. With its current configuration, the server is configured with an address in the 10.10.0.0/24 subnet but is attempting to lease addresses in the 10.10.1.0/24 range. To fix this problem, you can either change the address of the DHCP server or change the address range of the scope.

   D. Incorrect: This command would enable other computers to connect to Dhcp1 if a user specified Dhcp1 by name. However, the ability to connect to a DHCP server by specifying its name is not a requirement for DHCP to function correctly. DHCP exchanges do not rely on computer names.

3. **Correct Answer: A**

   A. Correct: In stateless addressing, DHCPv6 clients self-configure their IPv6 addresses with the help of neighboring IPv6 routers. However, they can still obtain DHCPv6 options from a DHCPv6 server.

   B. Incorrect: In stateful addressing, DHCPv6 clients obtain IPv6 addresses and potentially also DHCPv6 options from a DHCPv6 server.

   C. Incorrect: This command instructs a DHCPv6 client to obtain an IPv6 address from a DHCPv6 server. It does not affect how DHCPv6 options are obtained.

   D. Incorrect: This command instructs a DHCPv6 client not to obtain DHCPv6 options from a DHCPv6 server. It does not affect how IPv6 addresses are obtained.

Lesson 2

1. **Correct Answer: D**

   A. **Incorrect:** Configuring a scope option that assigns clients the DNS server address does nothing to prevent the potential conflict of the scope leasing out the same address owned by the DNS server.

   B. **Incorrect:** It is not recommended to assign reservations to infrastructure servers such as DNS servers. DNS servers should be assigned static addresses.

   C. **Incorrect:** You can configure only one contiguous address range per scope.

   D. **Correct:** Creating an exclusion for the DNS server address is the simplest way to solve the problem. When you configure the exclusion, the DHCP server will not lease the address and the DNS server preserves its static configuration.

2. **Correct Answer: B**

   A. **Incorrect:** This command configures the DHCP Server service to start automatically when Windows starts.

   B. **Correct:** This is a command you can use on a Server Core installation of Windows Server 2008 to install the DHCP Server role.

   C. **Incorrect:** This command starts the DHCP Server service after it is already installed.

   D. **Incorrect:** You can use this command on a full installation of Windows Server 2008 to install the DHCP Server role. You cannot use this command on a Server Core installation.

3. **Correct Answer: A**

   A. **Correct:** Name protection prevents clients that are not running Windows and are assigned a duplicate name on the network from being registered in DNS.

   B. **Incorrect:** This option will prevent clients that are not running Windows from being registered in DNS at all, which is not the best solution to the problem.

   C. **Incorrect:** This option would make the problem worse by allowing any computer with a duplicate name to overwrite the resource record of the original owner of that name.

   D. **Incorrect:** This option removes security information from the records created by the DHCP server. It will not prevent duplicate names from being registered by clients that are not running Windows.

Chapter 4: Case Scenario Answers

Case Scenario 1: Deploying a New DHCP Server

1. Configure the scope with a default gateway option (the 003 Router option).

2. Delete the leases. This will force the DHCP clients to renew their leases and obtain a default gateway address.

Case Scenario 2: Configuring DHCP Options

1. You should configure these options at the server level (the Server Options folder) because they apply to all scopes.

2. Create a new user class for these 30 computers. In the user class, configure the 015 DNS Domain Name option that specifies the special connection-specific suffix. On the 30 clients, use the **Ipconfig /setclassid** command to configure those clients as members of the class.

Chapter 5: Lesson Review Answers

Lesson

1. **Correct Answer: B**
   A. **Incorrect:** This answer has the incorrect router. The router with the IP address 192.168.1.1 is currently the default gateway, so all traffic will be sent to that router anyway.
   B. **Correct:** When using the Route Add command, specify the destination network first and then the subnet mask. Finally, provide the router that will be used to access the remote network.
   C. **Incorrect:** The parameters are reversed—the destination network should be listed as the first parameter after Route Add.
   D. **Incorrect:** The parameters are reversed, and the wrong router is listed.

2. **Correct Answers: A and D**
   A. **Correct:** PathPing uses ICMP to detect routers between your computer and a specified destination. Then PathPing computes the latency to each router in the path.
   B. **Incorrect:** Ping tests connectivity to a single destination. You cannot easily use Ping to determine the routers in a path.
   C. **Incorrect:** Although you can use Ipconfig to determine the default gateway, you cannot use it to determine all routers in a path.
   D. **Correct:** Tracert provides very similar functionality to PathPing, using ICMP to contact every router between your computer and a specified destination. The key difference between Tracert and PathPing is that PathPing computes accurate performance statistics over a period of time, whereas Tracert sends only three packets to each router in the path and displays the latency for each of those three packets.

3. **Correct Answer: C**
   A. **Incorrect:** NAT allows clients with private IP addresses to connect to computers on the public Internet. NAT does not automatically configure routing.
   B. **Incorrect:** Although OSPF is a routing protocol and would meet the requirements of this scenario, Windows Server 2008 does not support OSPF. Earlier versions of Windows do support OSPF.

C. Correct: RIP is a routing protocol. Routing protocols allow routers to communicate a list of subnets that each router provides access to. If you enable RIP on a computer running Windows Server 2008, RIP can automatically identify neighboring routers and forward traffic to remote subnets.

D. Incorrect: Although you could use static routes to reach remote subnets, the question requires you to configure Windows Server 2008 to automatically identify the remote networks.

Case Scenario 1: Adding a Second Default Gateway

- If the computers are configured with static IP addresses, you can use the Advanced TCP/IP Settings dialog box to configure multiple default gateways. If the computers are configured with dynamically assigned DHCP IP addresses, you can define multiple default gateways using DHCP scope options. Clients will automatically detect a failed default gateway and send traffic through the second default gateway.

Case Scenario 2: Adding a New Subnet

1. Yes, you can create a static route on the client computers specifying that the router with IP address 192.168.1.2 is the correct path to the 192.168.2.0/24 network. As long as 192.168.1.1 remains the default gateway, all other communications will be sent to 192.168.1.1.

2. You should run the following command:

```
route -p add 192.168.2.0 MASK 255.255.255.0 192.168.1.2
```

Chapter 6: Lesson Review Answers

Lesson

1. **Correct Answer: B**

   A. Incorrect: AH provides data authentication but not data encryption.

   B. Correct: ESP is the protocol that provides encryption for IPsec.

   C. Incorrect: A server-to-server type connection security rule is used to authenticate data between two endpoints on a network. It cannot be used to encrypt all traffic in a domain.

   D. Incorrect: A tunnel type connection security rule is used to authenticate data between a tunnel endpoint and a client or set of clients. It cannot be used to encrypt all traffic in a domain.

2. **Correct Answer: A**

   A. Correct: If both domains are in the same Active Directory forest, you can use the Kerberos protocol built into Active Directory to provide authentication for IPsec communication.

   B. Incorrect: You do not need to configure certificates for authentication. Active Directory already provides the Kerberos protocol that you can use with IPsec.

C. Incorrect: You do not need to configure a preshared key as the authentication method. The Kerberos protocol is already available, and it is more secure than a preshared key.

   D. Incorrect: NTLM is a backup authentication method for Active Directory, but it is not a valid authentication method for IPsec.

3. **Correct Answer: D**

   A. Incorrect: By default, Connection Security Rules do not encrypt traffic.

   B. Incorrect: By default, Connection Security Rules do not encrypt traffic.

   C. Incorrect: A rule that specifies an IP filter action of Permit allows the traffic specified in the rule to pass without IPsec encryption or authentication.

   D. Correct: A rule that specifies an IP filter action of Request Security will attempt to encrypt traffic with other computers. If the associated GPO is applied to the domain, all domain computers are configured with the same policy, and encryption is successfully negotiated for domain traffic.

Chapter 6: Case Scenario Answers

Case Scenario: Implementing IPsec

1. Kerberos (because the IPsec communications are limited to an Active Directory environment).
2. Assign the Client (Respond Only) IPsec policy.

Chapter 7: Lesson Review Answers

Lesson 1

1. **Correct Answer: C**

   A. Incorrect: The wireless client cannot log detailed information about authentication failures because RADIUS does not provide detailed information about why credentials were rejected. Instead, you should examine the Security event log on the RADIUS server.

   B. Incorrect: Same as answer A.

   C. Correct: The Windows Server 2008 RADIUS service adds events to the local Security event log. These events have information useful for identifying the cause of the problem, such as the user name submitted.

   D. Incorrect: The Windows Server 2008 RADIUS service adds events to the local Security event log, not to the System event log.

2. **Correct Answer: D**

   A. Incorrect: 128-bit WEP provides much better security than 64-bit WEP. However, 128-bit WEP is still considered extremely unsecure because it uses static keys and can be cracked in a relatively short time.

   B. Incorrect: WPA-PSK uses static keys, making it vulnerable to brute force attacks. WPA-PSK should be used only for testing.

   C. Incorrect: 64-bit WEP is the original wireless security standard, and it is now considered outdated. 64-bit WEP uses small, static keys and contains several cryptographic weaknesses that allow it to be cracked in a short time.

   D. Correct: WPA-EAP (and WPA2-EAP) provide the highest level of security by authenticating users to a central RADIUS server, such as a server running Windows Server 2008. As of the time of this writing, breaking WPA-EAP security using brute force techniques would be much more difficult than any other wireless security standard.

3. **Correct Answer: B**

   A. Incorrect: WEP provides authentication and encryption, however, users need to provide a static security key when they first connect to the network.

   B. Correct: WPA-EAP and WPA2-EAP authenticate using a RADIUS server. You can configure Windows Server 2008 R2 to act as a RADIUS server to the authentication computer and user domain accounts.

   C. Incorrect: Like WEP, WPA-PSK authenticates users with a static key that they must type.

   D. Incorrect: Like WEP and WPA-PSK, WPA2-PSK authenticates users with a static key that they must type.

Lesson 2

1. **Correct Answers: A and C**

   A. Correct: Enabling ICS changes the IP address of the internal network adapter to 192.168.0.1.

   B. Incorrect: Enabling ICS does not change the IP address of the external network adapter, which is typically a public IP address defined by your ISP.

   C. Correct: Enabling ICS automatically enables a DHCP server on your internal interface so that clients on the internal network can receive the proper IP configuration.

   D. Incorrect: Enabling ICS enables a DHCP server on your internal interface but not on your external interface.

2. **Correct Answer: A**

   A. Correct: By default, NAT does not allow connections from the Internet to the intranet. You can support them, however, by configuring port forwarding on the NAT server. With port forwarding, the NAT device accepts the TCP connection and forwards it to a specific server on the intranet.

   B. Incorrect: NAT allows clients to establish TCP connections to servers on the Internet.

C. Incorrect: Streaming video often uses User Datagram Protocol (UDP), which often fails when a NAT device is in use. However, streaming video connections that use TCP should always work. For that reason, most streaming media protocols support both UDP (for performance) and TCP (for compatibility with NAT).

D. Incorrect: HTTPS functions exactly like any other TCP connection. Therefore, NAT clients do not have any problem establishing an HTTPS connection to a server on the Internet.

3. **Correct Answer: C**

A. Incorrect: The Internet network adapter should have the IP address that was assigned by your ISP, not on the internal network adapter.

B. Incorrect: You should configure the ICS server to send queries to the DNS server, and client computers to send DNS queries to the ICS server. However, you should not configure the internal network adapter with the DNS server's IP address.

C. Correct: ICS always assigns the IP address 192.168.0.1 to the internal network adapter.

D. Incorrect: 192.168.0.0/24 is the internal network that ICS assigns to clients. However, 192.168.0.0 is not a valid IP address.

Lesson 3

1. **Correct Answers: A and D**

A. Correct: A VPN server allows clients on the public Internet to connect to your intranet while providing authentication and encryption.

B. Incorrect: Clients never submit requests directly to a RADIUS server. Instead, a wireless access point, VPN server, or other access provider submits authentication requests to the RADIUS server on the client's behalf. Additionally, without a VPN connection, client computers would not have access to the internal network.

C. Incorrect: Configuring your own modem bank and telephone circuits would provide the required connectivity. However, the capital expense would be significant. A more cost-effective alternative is to outsource the dial-up access to an ISP.

D. Correct: ISPs can provide dial-up access with integrated VPN connections to clients and authenticate to your internal RADIUS server. With Windows Server 2008, the RADIUS server can, in turn, authenticate to an Active Directory domain controller.

2. **Correct Answers: B and D**

A. Incorrect: VPN connections almost always provide better performance than dial-up connections. However, dial-up connections are not adequate for streaming video.

B. Correct: Dial-up connections can connect directly to a server on your intranet, bypassing the Internet entirely.

C. Incorrect: VPNs include encryption, preventing an attacker with access to the transmission from interpreting the data.

D. Correct: Both VPN and dial-up servers can authenticate to a central RADIUS server.

3. **Correct Answers: C and D**

   A. **Incorrect:** Windows XP Professional does not support SSTP.

   B. **Incorrect:** Windows 2000 Professional does not support SSTP.

   C. **Correct:** Windows Vista with Service Pack 1 supports being an SSTP VPN client. It does not support being a VPN server. Windows Vista without Service Pack 1 does not support SSTP.

   D. **Correct:** Windows Server 2008 R2 supports being either an SSTP VPN client or server.

Lesson 4

1. **Correct Answer: C**

   A. **Incorrect:** Teredo is used for clients behind a NAT device. Most public hotspots do use NAT. However, the scenario states that only HTTP and HTTPS communications are allowed through the firewall. Therefore, while Teredo would provide better performance, DirectAccess will use IP-HTTPS because Teredo requires communications that those firewalls would block.

   B. **Incorrect:** ISATAP provides IPv6 tunneling across IPv4 networks. However, it would be blocked by a firewall that only allowed HTTP and HTTPS communications.

   C. **Correct:** IP-HTTPS tunnels IPv6 communications across HTTPS, which Web browsers and servers use for authenticated and encrypted communications. Because it is so widely used on the Internet, it is almost universally available on Internet-connected networks.

   D. **Incorrect:** 6-to-4 is only useful for clients that are connected directly to the public IPv4 Internet and have a public IP address. Public hotspots typically use NAT, and the scenario limits communications to HTTP and HTTPS, which means 6-to-4 would be blocked.

2. **Correct Answers: B and C**

   A. **Incorrect:** Although DirectAccess does require an Active Directory domain, it does not need to be at the Windows Server 2008 functional level. You do, however, need to have at least one domain controller running Windows Server 2008 with Service Pack 2 or Windows Server 2008 R2.

   B. **Correct:** The DirectAccess server must have two alphabetically consecutive public IP addresses.

   C. **Correct:** DirectAccess uses IPsec to authenticate and encrypt communications. IPsec, in turn, requires clients and servers to have computer certificates.

   D. **Incorrect:** DirectAccess does require an Active Directory domain. However, no domain controller may be accessible from the DirectAccess server's public network adapter. Therefore, the DirectAccess server itself cannot be a domain controller.

3. **Correct Answer: D**

   A. **Incorrect:** The Network Connections service manages local and remote network connections. Although it is important for mobile client computers that might connect to different networks, you do not need to restart the service after installing DirectAccess.

   B. **Incorrect:** IPsec and the IPsec Policy Agent are required for DirectAccess to work. However, you do not need to restart the service to allow clients to connect to DirectAccess.

C. **Incorrect:** Windows uses the Workstation service to allow clients to connect to shared folders and printers. It is not directly involved with DirectAccess.

D. **Correct:** The IP Helper services configures IPv6 settings when it starts, and it never refreshes them unless you restart it. The DirectAccess setup wizard updates Group Policy settings to modify IPv6 settings on clients. Therefore, to apply the updated IPv6 settings, you must restart the IP Helper service on client computers.

Chapter 7: Case Scenario Answers

Case Scenario 1: Connecting a Branch Office to the Internet

1. The ISP might be able to provide you with a block of more than 50 IP addresses. However, the additional cost probably wouldn't be worth it because you do not need to accept incoming connections. Although you always need at least one public IP address, additional IP addresses are required only if you plan to host a server that will be accessible from the Internet.

2. You should configure a NAT server on the boundary between the public Internet and your intranet. The NAT server can translate the private IP addresses to its public IP address, allowing complete connectivity for outgoing connections.

3. Typically, for an office with only 50 computers, you would choose a router that has NAT capabilities built in. Alternatively, you could choose to deploy NAT by using a Windows Server 2008 computer. That would be advisable only if you planned to connect the server to the Internet anyway.

Case Scenario 2: Planning Remote Access

1. The sales staff will need dial-up access because they might be in hotel rooms that have only an analog modem connection. For better performance for computers running versions of Windows released prior to Windows 7, you should also recommend supporting a VPN server. To provide transparent intranet connectivity for Windows 7 clients, add DirectAccess.

2. The VPN server will need to be connected to both the Internet and your private intranet. You already have several servers that are configured this way, so you could configure an existing server to accept VPN connections and route the communications to the intranet. To address the concerns about maintaining a separate user name and password, you could authenticate users to the Active Directory domain controller (for PPTP connections) or using client certificates (for L2TP connections).

3. You could choose to connect a bank of 50 modems to a dial-up server that is connected to your private intranet, you could purchase a separate modem bank and have it authenticate to a RADIUS server, or you could establish a service agreement with a dial-up ISP and have the ISP authenticate against your RADIUS server.

4. Probably, because most wireless networks connect to the Internet. The firewall might block VPN connections, however. In that case, SSTP connections (available for only Windows Vista and Windows Server 2008 clients) might be compatible with the firewall. DirectAccess will allow Windows 7 clients to connect as long as HTTPS is supported.

Chapter 8: Lesson Review Answers

Lesson 1

1. **Correct Answer: B**

   A. Incorrect: The computer running Windows Server 2008 R2 will need to make outbound connections on TCP port 290; however, Windows Firewall allows outbound connections by default. Therefore, you do not need to create a firewall rule.

   B. Correct: By default, Windows Server 2008 R2 will block inbound connections that do not have a firewall rule. There is no firewall rule for TCP port 39 by default. Therefore, you will need to add one.

   C. Incorrect: The computer running Windows Server 2008 R2 needs to make outbound connections on TCP port 290, but it does not need to allow inbound connections on that port.

   D. Incorrect: Windows 7 allows any outbound connection by default. Therefore, you do not need to create a firewall rule to allow outbound connections.

2. **Correct Answers: A and C**

   A. Correct: Selecting Allow Only Secure Connections requires IPsec, which you must use to require domain authentication at the firewall level.

   B. Incorrect: Specifying a profile for the firewall rule simply means the rule won't apply when the server isn't connected to the domain network. You can't use profiles to require client connection authentication.

   C. Correct: After requiring IPsec on the General tab, you can use this tab to limit connections only to users who are members of specific groups.

   D. Incorrect: Configuring scope can be a very powerful tool for limiting connections from users. Although it might be advisable to also limit scope to connections from client computers on your internal network, doing so doesn't necessarily require users to be a member of your domain. Additionally, you would need to configure the Remote IP Address settings, not the Local IP Address settings.

3. **Correct Answer: D**

   A. Incorrect: Both Windows XP (configured using the Windows Firewall node) and Windows 7 (configured using either the Windows Firewall node or the Windows Firewall With Advanced Security node) support filtering UDP traffic.

   B. Incorrect: Both the Windows Firewall and the Windows Firewall With Advanced Security nodes support creating a rule for an executable.

   C. Incorrect: Both the Windows Firewall and the Windows Firewall With Advanced Security nodes support configuring scope for a rule.

   D. Correct: The Windows Firewall With Advanced Security node supports firewall features available only for Windows Vista, Windows 7, Windows Server 2008, and Windows Server 2008 R2, but not Windows XP. One of the most important features is the ability to require IPsec connection security and to authenticate and authorize users or computers using IPsec.

Lesson 2

1. **Correct Answer: A**

   A. **Correct:** Setting NAP Enforcement to Allow Limited Access limits the client to the remediation servers you list. If you do not list any remediation servers, clients will be completely denied network access.

   B. **Incorrect:** Setting the Access Permission to Deny Access prevents clients from performing a health check. Therefore, both compliant and noncompliant clients will be blocked.

   C. **Incorrect:** The Session Timeout disconnects remote access connections after a specific amount of time. You cannot set a Session Timeout of 0.

   D. **Incorrect:** IP filters should be used for remote access connections. They do not apply to NAP network policies.

2. **Correct Answers: B and C**

   A. **Incorrect:** Health policies apply only to NAP-capable computers.

   B. **Correct:** Computers that do not support NAP require a separate network policy with a NAP-Capable Computers condition that matches Only Computers That Are Not NAP-Capable.

   C. **Correct:** Remediation server groups define the servers that are accessible to computers with limited access. To meet the requirements of this scenario, you would need to create a network policy with a NAP-Capable Computers condition matching Only Computers That Are Not NAP-Capable, set the NAP Enforcement for that network policy to Allow Limited Access, and then configure the network policy with the new remediation server group.

   D. **Incorrect:** You can use a single connection request policy for computers that both are and are not NAP-capable. Therefore, you do not need to create a new connection request policy. Additionally, the NAP-Capable Computers condition is not available for connection request policies.

3. **Correct Answers: A and B**

   A. **Correct:** Because NPS and DHCP are running on separate computers, you must install NPS on the DHCP server and then configure a RADIUS proxy on the DHCP server to forward RADIUS requests to the primary NPS server.

   B. **Correct:** Same as answer A.

   C. **Incorrect:** HRA is required only for IPsec enforcement.

   D. **Incorrect:** DHCP enforcement does not require certificate services.

Chapter 8: Case Scenario Answers

Case Scenario 1: Evaluating Firewall Settings

1. You will need to create a Program firewall rule that allows inbound connections for the web service. Although you could create a Port firewall rule that allows inbound connections for TCP port 81, it's typically more efficient to create a Program firewall rule.

2. You do not need to create a firewall rule on the client computers because they allow outbound connections by default.

Case Scenario 2: Planning NAP

1. The computer running Windows XP didn't have an important update installed, and the attacker exploited a vulnerability. It could have been prevented in a couple of ways. First, if the computer running Windows XP had been recently updated, the vulnerability would have been removed. Second, if that same computer had been updated to Windows Vista or Windows 7, which supports a public Windows Firewall profile that automatically drops all unrequested incoming connections when connected to untrusted networks, the attack would have been dropped regardless of whether the update were applied.

2. Yes, you could enable outbound firewall rules and block outbound traffic by default. This would require you to create firewall rules for all applications that are allowed to communicate on your network.

3. NAP can be used to perform health checks on client computers before granting them network access. The default SHV can verify that Windows Firewall is enabled, recent updates have been installed, and antivirus software is running. NAP could have prevented the infected computer from connecting to the internal network and accessing confidential documents.

4. Probably, because most organizations have computers that would not meet even the most basic health checks. To prevent that, implement NAP in monitoring-only mode. After you have identified computers that fail health checks, you can update them and verify that they now pass the health check. There will probably be computers that cannot pass the health check or are not NAP-capable. You will need to create exceptions to allow those computers to connect to your network.

5. You will probably need to use a combination of several NAP enforcement methods. IPsec and 802.1X enforcement provide excellent security. To protect remote access connections, you will need to use VPN enforcement. If you have networks that cannot support IPsec or 802.1X enforcement, you can make use of DHCP enforcement.

Chapter 9: Lesson Review Answers

Lesson 1

1. **Correct Answer: D**

   A. **Incorrect:** Because you have a centralized IT department, having local IT departments manage the WSUS servers would be inefficient. Instead, you should configure the remote offices as replicas of the WSUS server at the headquarters, allowing you to manage all updates using a single WSUS server.

   B. **Incorrect:** Although this architecture would work, it would be extremely wasteful of Internet bandwidth. The bandwidth required for 1200 client computers to each download a service pack from the Internet would be so extreme that for many computers the updates might never succeed.

   C. **Incorrect:** Like answer B, this architecture would work. However, the WAN links would likely be saturated with update traffic as every computer at each remote office transfers large updates. To resolve this, place WSUS servers at each office.

   D. **Correct:** To make best use of WAN and Internet bandwidth, configure a WSUS server at each office and have each computer download updates from your central WSUS server.

2. **Correct Answer: B**

   A. **Incorrect:** Enabling this setting configures the Windows Update client to immediately install updates that do not require the computer to be restarted.

   B. **Correct:** This Group Policy setting allows you to configure whether updates are installed automatically and when they are installed. By default, however, Windows Update clients will notify users of the updates and prompt them to perform the installation.

   C. **Incorrect:** Enabling this setting prevents the Windows Update client from automatically restarting the computer. By default, this setting is disabled, which is required for auto matically restarting computers, as outlined in the scenario.

   D. **Incorrect:** You can use this setting to configure client computers as members of a com-puter group. It has no impact on how updates are installed.

3. **Correct Answers: C and D**

   A. **Incorrect:** Windows 95 does not support acting as a WSUS client.

   B. **Incorrect:** Windows 98 does not support acting as a WSUS client.

   C. **Correct:** Windows 2000, with Service Pack 3 or later, can act as a WSUS client.

   D. **Correct:** Windows XP can act as a WSUS client without any service pack.

Lesson 2

1. **Correct Answers: A, B, and D**

   A. Correct: The System log contains high-level information generated by the Windows Update client.

   B. Correct: The Windows Update Operational log contains detailed information generated by the Windows Update client.

   C. Incorrect: In this scenario, only the client computer would be able to report on the cause of the error. Therefore, the information cannot be available on the WSUS server.

   D. Correct: The WindowsUpdate.log file has extremely detailed information generated by the Windows Update client.

2. **Correct Answers: A and D**

   A. Correct: The Update Status Summary report shows a description of every update and which computer groups the update is approved for.

   B. Incorrect: The Update Status Summary report does not show specifically which computers installed an update, though it does provide the total number of computers. However, the Update Detailed Status report does provide this information.

   C. Incorrect: The Update Status Summary report does not show whether an update can be removed using WSUS.

   D. Correct: The Update Status Summary report shows a pie chart with the number of computers the update failed and succeeded for.

3. **Correct Answers: B and C**

   A. Incorrect: You can use the Configure Automatic Updates policy to control whether client computers download updates and notify users or automatically install updates. You cannot use the policy to define computer group memberships, however.

   B. Correct: Configuring the Enable Client-Side Targeting Group Policy setting and then specifying a target group name for the computer will place all computers the GPO is applied to in the specified computer group.

   C. Correct: Selecting Change Membership allows you to specify the computer groups a computer will be placed in.

   D. Incorrect: You cannot use the drag-and-drop feature to move computers in the Update Services console.

Chapter 9: Case Scenario Answers

Case Scenario 1: Planning a Basic WSUS Infrastructure

1. WSUS can act as a distribution point for updates on your LAN. Clients can then retrieve the updates without connecting to Microsoft on the Internet. Although the WSUS server will still need to download updates across the Internet, it will use much less bandwidth than 250 computers individually would.

2. A single WSUS server can serve all 250 computers on your LAN. Although you could configure two WSUS servers redundantly (by configuring a round-robin DNS entry that contained the IP addresses of both WSUS servers), it's typically unnecessary because a WSUS server can go offline for short periods without affecting client computers.

3. Click the Options node in the Update Services console. Then, in the details pane, click Automatic Approvals. You can simply enable the Default Automatic Approval Rule (which approves all critical and security updates), or you can create your own customized rules.

Case Scenario 2: Planning a Complex WSUS Infrastructure

1. Each of the five offices should have a WSUS server.

2. The New York City office can be a replica of the London office. However, the other three offices will need to have an independently managed WSUS server.

Chapter 10: Lesson Review Answers

Lesson 1

1. Correct Answer: A
   A. **Correct:** You can use the Wecutil utility to automatically configure a computer to collect events.
   B. **Incorrect:** This command should be run on the forwarding computer.
   C. **Incorrect:** This command should be run on the forwarding computer.
   D. **Incorrect:** You don't need to add the forwarding computer to the Event Log Readers group. Only the collecting computer should be a member of that group.

2. Correct Answers: B and C
   A. **Incorrect:** You should run this command on the collecting computer.
   B. **Correct:** You should run this command on the forwarding computer.
   C. **Correct:** You should run this command on the forwarding computer.
   D. **Incorrect:** You don't need to add the forwarding computer to the Event Log Readers group. Only the collecting computer should be a member of that group.

3. **Correct Answer: A**

A. **Correct:** As described in the section "Creating an Event Subscription" in Chapter 10, "Monitoring Computers," you should use the Wecutil tool to customize a subscription interval.

B. **Incorrect:** WinRM is used to configure the forwarding computer.

C. **Incorrect:** The Net tool is useful for stopping and starting services and for changing group memberships at the command line. It cannot configure subscriptions.

D. **Incorrect:** The Event Viewer console allows you to configure many aspects of a subscription, but it does not allow you to customize the subscription interval.

Lesson 2

1. **Correct Answer: B**

A. **Incorrect:** You can use Performance Monitor to view performance counters in real time or to analyze performance data saved as part of a Data Collector Set. However, Performance Monitor cannot tell you when an application was installed.

B. **Correct:** Reliability Monitor tracks application installations (assuming they use Windows Installer). With a few clicks, you can determine whether any applications were installed recently and exactly when the installation occurred.

C. **Incorrect:** Data Collector Sets capture current performance and configuration data. They cannot tell you when an application was installed.

D. **Incorrect:** Network Monitor, discussed in Chapter 10, Lesson 3, "Using Network Monitor and Simple Network Management Protocol," captures network traffic. It does not have information about application installations.

2. **Correct Answers: A and C**

A. **Correct:** Performance Monitor views real-time data by default, but you can also use it to view data recorded using a Data Collector Set.

B. **Incorrect:** Reliability Monitor records and displays application installations and various type of failures. It does not record performance data.

C. **Correct:** Data Collector Sets record performance data. After the data is recorded, you can view it using the Performance Monitor tool. To be able to analyze two sets of data against each other, create a custom Data Collector Set that records the necessary performance information. Then run the Data Collector Set during peak usage times and at night. You can open two instances of Performance Monitor to view each of the reports and compare them to each other.

D. **Incorrect:** Network Monitor, discussed in Chapter 10, Lesson 3, "Using Network Monitor and Simple Network Management Protocol," captures network traffic. It does not record performance data.

3. **Correct Answers: B and D**

   A. Incorrect: Although application failures are recorded, errors within an application (that do not cause an application to fail) are not recorded in Reliability Monitor.

   B. Correct: Application installs and uninstalls are recorded in Reliability Monitor.

   C. Incorrect: Services starting and stopping are typically recorded in the event log but are not tracked by Reliability Monitor.

   D. Correct: Reliability Monitor records device driver failures.

Lesson 3

1. **Correct Answers: A and C**

   A. Correct: Regardless of the network infrastructure, you can always capture communications to and from your local computer.

   B. Incorrect: By default, Layer 2 switches will not send HostC any communications between HostA and HostB. You would need to enable as a monitoring port the port that HostC is connected to.

   C. Correct: All computers connected to a hub can see all other computers' communications. Therefore, with P-Mode enabled, HostC would be able to capture communications sent to and from HostA.

   D. Incorrect: HostC must be connected to the same hub as either HostA or HostB. The switch would not forward communications destined for either HostA or HostB to HostC.

2. **Correct Answer: B**

   A. Incorrect: Netmon is the Network Monitor executable file, and it starts the graphical tool. You cannot run it from a command prompt.

   B. Correct: NMCap allows you to capture communications from a command prompt and save them to a .CAP file.

   C. Incorrect: Nmconfig is used to install and uninstall Network Monitor. You cannot use it to capture data.

   D. Incorrect: Nmwifi.com configures wireless scanning options, and you typically access it by viewing a wireless network adapter's properties from within Network Monitor.

3. **Correct Answer: D**

   A. Incorrect: This filter would show all HTTP communications and any communications that came from the IP address 192.168.10.12.

   B. Incorrect: This filter would show only HTTP communications from the IP address 192.168.10.12. The scenario requires you to view communications sent both to and from the client computer, and this filter would not show communications sent to the client computer (which would have a destination IP address of 192.168.10.12).

C. Incorrect: This filter would show all HTTP communications and any communications that came from or were sent to the IP address 192.168.10.12.

D. Correct: The && operator requires that both parameters be met for a frame to be shown. In this case, the filter meets your requirements because the frames must be HTTP and must have either a source or destination IP address of 192.168.10.12. The IPv4.Address parameter can match either the source or destination IP address.

Chapter 10: Case Scenario Answers

Case Scenario 1: Troubleshooting a Network Performance Problem

1. You can use Data Collector Sets to record a baseline when the server is performing normally. Then run the same Data Collector Set when the performance problem occurs. You can then use Performance Monitor to analyze the two sets of results and identify the factors that differentiate the two.

2. A protocol analyzer, such as Network Monitor, would allow you to analyze the individual frames.

Case Scenario 2: Monitoring Computers for Low Disk Space

1. You can use event forwarding to send low disk space events to a central computer. Then the IT department can monitor that single event log to identify computers with low disk space conditions.

2. Windows XP, Windows Server 2003, Windows Vista, Windows 7, Windows Server 2008, and Windows Server 2008 R2 can support event forwarding. Windows XP must have Service Pack 2 and WS-Management 1.1 installed. Windows Server 2003 either must be Windows Server 2003 R2 or have Service Pack 1 or later installed. Windows Server 2003 also requires WS-Management 1.1.

Chapter 11: Lesson Review Answers

Lesson 1

1. **Correct Answer: C**

   A. Incorrect: Users have No Access permission if no access control entry applies to them or if they explicitly have a Deny permission assigned. In this case, Mary has Write access because she has the Modify NTFS permission assigned.

   B. Incorrect: Share permissions apply only when users access a folder across the network. Because Mary is accessing the folder from the local computer, only NTFS permissions apply. The Marketing group is granted Modify NTFS permissions, which allows Mary to write to the folder (in addition to being able to read the contents of the folder).

C. **Correct:** Through Mary's membership in the Marketing group, Mary has the Modify NTFS permission. Because Mary is not accessing the files using the share, share permissions do not affect Mary's effective permissions. Therefore, Mary can write to the folder.

D. **Incorrect:** Full Control permissions allow users to change permissions. Having this level of access would require Mary to have Full Control NTFS permissions.

2. **Correct Answer: B**

A. **Incorrect:** This procedure would add NTFS permissions for the user. However, the user already has the necessary NTFS permissions.

B. **Correct:** Whether EFS-protected files are accessed from the local computer or across the network, you must add the user's certificate to the file to allow them to decrypt it.

C. **Incorrect:** Although removing encryption would allow the user to access the file, it would also reduce security.

D. **Incorrect:** Refer to the explanation for answer B.

3. **Correct Answers: B and D**

A. **Incorrect:** The Full Control share permission would allow users to change permissions on files contained within the shared folder when the users also had sufficient NTFS privileges.

B. **Correct:** The Change share permission grants users the ability to read, update, and create files in the shared folder. Users must also have sufficient NTFS privileges.

C. **Incorrect:** The Full Control NTFS permission would allow users to change permissions on files contained within the shared folder. Users would be able to use the privileges only when they were accessing the file locally or when they also had sufficient share privileges.

D. **Correct:** The Change NTFS permission grants users the ability to read, update, and create files in the shared folder. When users are accessing the folder across the network, they must also have sufficient share privileges.

Lesson 2

1. **Correct Answer: B**

A. **Incorrect:** Users have No Access permission when no access control entry applies to them or when they explicitly have a Deny permission assigned. In this case, Mary has Read access because she has both NTFS and share permissions assigned.

B. **Correct:** When connecting to a shared folder, users always have the fewest privileges allowed by both share permissions and NTFS permissions. In this case, only the share permission grants the Everyone group Reader access—which limits Mary's permission to read-only.

C. **Incorrect:** If Mary were to log on locally to the computer and access the files on the local hard disk, share permissions would not be a factor, and Mary would be able to update the files. However, because Mary is accessing the folder using a share and the share has only Reader permissions assigned, Mary will be able to only read the files.

D. **Incorrect:** Full Control permissions allow users to change permissions. Having this level of access would require Mary to have both Full Control NTFS permissions and Full Control share permissions.

2. **Correct Answer: A**

A. **Correct:** You can use the Net Share command to create shared folders.

B. **Incorrect:** You can use Netsh for a wide variety of network configuration tasks, but you cannot use it to share folders.

C. **Incorrect:** Share is an executable program used for file locking by older MS-DOS applications.

D. **Incorrect:** The Ipconfig tool displays IP configuration information, but it cannot be used to add shares.

3. **Correct Answer: A**

A. **Correct:** Random Order configures clients to connect to DFS servers at their local site first. If no local DFS server is available, clients randomly choose another DFS server.

B. **Incorrect:** The Lowest Cost algorithm uses Active Directory site costs to determine which DFS server to connect to when no DFS server is available at the local site. Although this algorithm is often more efficient than Random Order, the scenario requires clients to randomly connect to DFS servers at different sites.

C. **Incorrect:** This algorithm prevents clients from connecting to DFS servers at different sites.

D. **Incorrect:** Selecting this check box configures how clients connect to DFS servers when a DFS server is offline and then later online. It does not configure how clients initially select a DFS server.

4. **Correct Answer: C**

A. **Incorrect:** Creating a hard quota at 80 MB would prevent the user from saving more than 80 MB of files, which does not meet your requirements.

B. **Incorrect:** Creating a soft quota with a 100-MB limit would not prevent users from exceeding the quota.

C. **Correct:** The most efficient way to meet your requirements is to create a single hard quota with a 100-MB limit. The hard quota prevents users from saving files when they exceed their quota limit. Creating a warning at 80 percent would allow you to configure the quota to send an email to the user when the user has consumed 80 MB of disk space.

D. **Incorrect:** Soft quotas allow the user to continue to save files after the user has exceeded the quota. For this reason, it would not meet your requirements.

5. **Correct Answer: B**

   A. Incorrect: Use the FileScrn tool to configure file screening for folders, which configures Windows to block specific file types.

   B. Correct: You can use the DirQuota tool configure disk quotas from the command prompt.

   C. Incorrect: The DFSUtil tool configures DFS, not quotas.

   D. Incorrect: You can use the Net tool to configure folder sharing from the command prompt. It cannot configure disk quotas.

Lesson 3

1. **Correct Answer: D**

   A. Incorrect: The StorRept tool configures storage reports from the command prompt.

   B. Incorrect: FileScrn is a command-line tool for configuring file screening. It cannot be used to create backups.

   C. Incorrect: You can use DirQuota to configure disk quotas. It does not create backups, however.

   D. Correct: VSSAdmin allows you to initiate a shadow copy, which you can use to restore files after they have been modified.

2. **Correct Answer: B**

   A. Incorrect: Refer to the explanation for answer B.

   B. Correct: Windows creates a WindowsImageBackup folder in the root of the backup media. Inside that folder, it creates a folder with the current computer's name.

   C. Incorrect: Refer to the explanation for answer B.

   D. Incorrect: Refer to the explanation for answer B.

3. **Correct Answers: A and C**

   A. Correct: You can use the Windows Server Backup tool to restore individual files. You can also simply right-click a file and then choose Restore Previous Versions.

   B. Incorrect: Windows cannot overwrite system files while the operating system is running. Therefore, to restore the system volume, you must perform a recovery by starting the computer from the Windows Server 2008 installation media.

   C. Correct: You can restore nonsystem volumes while the operating system is running.

   D. Incorrect: Windows Server Backup cannot overwrite files that are currently in use. Instead, you will be prompted to save the recovered files to a different folder.

Chapter 11: Case Scenario Answers

Case Scenario 1: Planning File Services

1. You can create a DFS namespace that contains multiple shared folders even if they're hosted by different servers. Then, users can map a network drive to the namespace and use the single network drive to connect to any shared folder.

2. You can use share permissions and NTFS file permissions.

3. You can add multiple targets to a shared folder and enable replication between them. Users who connect to the shared folder can automatically be connected to the server at their local site. If that server is unavailable, the client computer can connect to another target server and access the same files.

Case Scenario 2: Planning Disaster Recovery

1. You will need an additional hard disk with sufficient capacity to store a backup of the system volume and any other volumes that you plan to back up.

2. After replacing the failed disk, you will need to start the computer from the Windows Server 2008 installation media and then use the system recovery tools to restore the system volume.

3. Yes, if you restore the file before another backup is performed. If a backup is performed after the file becomes corrupted, the corrupted file might overwrite the valid version of the file.

Chapter 12: Lesson Review Answers

Lesson

1. **Correct Answer: B**

   A. **Incorrect:** The PrintUI command is a graphical interface and cannot be called from a command line. Also, the -b parameter is used to export printer configurations, not to import them.

   B. **Correct:** You use the PrintBRM command to export and import printer settings from a command prompt. Use the -R parameter to specify an import.

   C. **Incorrect:** The PrintBRMEngine executable file is used by PrintBRM and PrintBMRUI, but it cannot be directly called.

   D. **Incorrect:** Netsh is used to configure network settings and cannot be used to import or export printer settings.

2. **Correct Answer: D**

   A. Incorrect: The PrnMngr.vbs tool adds and removes printers.

   B. Incorrect: The PrnCnfg.vbs tool configures printer names, locations, permissions, and other basic configuration settings.

   C. Incorrect: The PrnQctrl.vbs tool prints a test page, pauses or resumes a printer, and clears the print queue.

   D. Correct: The PubPrn.vbs tool publishes a printer to the Active Directory.

3. **Correct Answer: A**

   A. Correct: To allow a client to connect from behind a firewall that allows only web connections, you will need to use Internet printing. To connect to printers shared with Internet printing, specify the path in the format http://<*ServerName*>/Printers/<*PrinterName*>/.printer.

   B. Incorrect: Although connecting through the firewall will require you to use HTTP, you must specify the URL using the format http://<*ServerName*>/Printers/<*Printer* Name>/.printer.

   C. Incorrect. You do not need to specify the Printers folder or the printer name as part of a Universal Naming Convention (UNC) path. Also, a UNC path would not allow you to bypass the firewall.

   D. Incorrect: This would be the correct format if you were connecting to a printer across a local area network using a standard Universal Naming Convention (UNC) path. However, you must specify a URL to use Internet printing, which will allow you to bypass the firewall.

4. **Correct Answer: D**

   A. Incorrect: You cannot configure notifications directly from the driver's properties. Instead, you should create a custom filter and then create a notification for the filter.

   B. Incorrect: PrintBRM is used to export and import printer settings and cannot configure email notifications.

   C. Incorrect: You cannot configure notifications directly from the printer's properties. Instead, you should create a custom filter and then create a notification for the filter.

   D. Correct: You can create a custom filter with criteria that match the printer name and a problem status. Then, you can create a notification for the custom filter to send an email.

Chapter 12: Case Scenario Answers

Case Scenario: Managing Network Printers

1. You can use Windows Server 2008 R2 as a print server. If you install each of the network printers and then share them, users can connect to the Windows Server 2008 R2 computer and submit print jobs to the server. The server can then manage the print queues for each of the printers.

2. You can create custom filters that match printers with problems and then configure an email notification to be sent to an administrator. Alternatively, you can use the notification to run a script or an executable file that is integrated into a custom management infrastructure.

3. Windows Server 2008 R2 supports using permissions to control which users can print to and manage printers. You can deny access to all users except the executive, the assistant, and the IT personnel who need to manage the printer. This wouldn't, however, prevent users from connecting directly to printers. To control direct access, you would need to modify the printer's configuration to allow connections only from the print server. Alternatively, if your network supports virtual local area networks (VLANs) or another access control technology, you could restrict access to the printers using your network infrastructure.

4. You could configure multiple similar printers as part of a printer pool. Any print jobs submitted to the printer pool would be sent to the first available printer. This would allow small print jobs to print to one printer while another printer handled the large print job.

Glossary

A

address block A group of contiguous addresses that can be expressed with a single network address and a subnet mask. An example of an address block is 10.10.10.192 /26.

aging The process of tracking the age of resource records in a zone.

application directory partition A partition in Active Directory that is reserved for use with a specific application, such as DNS. In Windows Server 2003, Windows Server 2008, and Windows Server 2008 R2, domain controllers that are DNS servers include two application directory partitions by default: DomainDnsZones and ForestDnsZones.

Authentication Header (AH) The security protocol in IPsec that ensures data authentication and integrity.

Authoritative server A DNS server that contains complete information about a particular zone in its local database (as opposed to its cache).

Automatic Private IP Addressing (APIPA) An auto-configured IPv4 address in the range 169.254.0.0 /16. An APIPA address offers limited connectivity and is normally a sign that a DHCP server cannot be reached.

B

broadcast A type of network transmission in which a signal is sent to all computers on a local subnet.

D

Default User class An options class to which all DHCP clients belong. When you assign a DHCP option to the Default User class, all DHCP clients receive the option.

defense-in-depth A security technique that reduces risk by providing multiple layers of protection. With defense-in-depth, if one security layer fails, another layer continues to provide protection.

Domain Name System (DNS) The hierarchical (multi-tag) naming and name resolution system used on the Internet and in Windows networks.

downstream server The server that synchronizes updates from an upstream server when you are designing WSUS architectures.

dynamic updates The feature in which DNS clients can automatically register and update their own resource records in DNS.

E

Encapsulating Security Payload (ESP) The security protocol in IPsec that provides data encryption.

exclusion An IP address that falls within the range of a DHCP server scope but that is configured not to be leased to DHCP clients.

F

firewall A security tool used to filter unwanted traffic while allowing legitimate traffic.

forwarder A DNS server (not a root server) to which unresolved queries are sent by a forwarding DNS server.

forwarding For a DNS server, the process of sending to another specified DNS server (not the root server) any query that the original DNS server cannot answer.

fully qualified domain name (FQDN) A computer's host name concatenated with its DNS suffix. An FQDN is a name that can be queried for in a DNS infrastructure. An example of an FQDN is server1.contoso.com.

G

gateway A synonym for router; a device that forwards communications between networks.

H

hard quota A storage limit that prevents users from creating more files after they reach a threshold.

hop A router or gateway.

host name In DNS, the first or single-tag name assigned to a computer. For example, "clientA" is a host name.

host route A route that directs traffic to a single IP address. DHCP NAP enforcement uses host routes to allow a noncompliant computer to access remediation resources.

HOSTS A manually configured file sometimes used by the local system to map DNS names to IP addresses.

I

Internet Control Message Protocol (ICMP) The messaging protocol built into IP on which the Ping and Tracert utilities are based.

Internet Printing Protocol (IPP) A printing protocol that uses Hypertext Transfer Protocol (HTTP). HTTP can work through most proxy servers and firewalls.

Internet Protocol Security (IPsec) An Internet Engineering Task Force (IETF) standards-based suite of protocols whose purpose is to provide data authentication and encryption for IP networks.

IPv4 The Layer 3 protocol that currently forms the backbone of the Internet and almost every computer network in the world. IPv4 provides addressing and routing services, but its addresses are becoming exhausted.

IPv6 A Layer 3 protocol that offers a virtually unlimited supply of addresses and that, in the long term, will replace IPv4 on public networks.

K

Kerberos The data authentication protocol native to Active Directory.

key pair In asymmetric cryptography, a combination of keys generated by an organization and used together for encryption and decryption.

key rollover The process of renewing keys in advance of their expiration.

key signing key (KSK) A key pair used to digitally sign keys in a DNSSEC-enabled zone. The KSK can protect the security of the zone without needing to be updated frequently. The public key portion of a KSK can be stored on other DNSSEC-enabled servers as a means to validate the signature of another key (the ZSK) that is used to sign a remote zone.

L

latency The delay when a packet travels from a client to a server.

lease The use of an IP address that is assigned to a DHCP client by a DHCP server. An address lease has a finite length and must be renewed periodically.

Line Printer Daemon (LPD) A printing protocol commonly used by older UNIX operating systems. Most newer operating systems, including UNIX, can connect to shared printers by using standard Windows sharing.

Link Local Multicast Name Resolution (LLMNR) A name resolution service for computers running Windows Vista, Windows 7, Windows Server 2008, and Windows Server 2008 R2. LLMNR resolves names only on the local subnet.

Lmhosts A manually configured file sometimes used by the local system to map NetBIOS names to IP addresses.

M

master zone A zone, usually a primary zone, from which a transfer is performed to a secondary or stub zone.

monitoring port A port on a Layer 2 switch that receives all communications even when they are not directed to that port. You can use a monitoring port with Network Monitor to capture communications between other computers.

N

name resolution The process of translating a computer name into a computer address.

Name Resolution Policy Table (NRPT) A table enforced in Group Policy that configures DNS clients to handle certain DNS queries in a special way. The NRPT is used to configure clients to request DNSSEC validation with specific queries. It is also used to configure clients to use DirectAccess.

NetBIOS An older set of network services still present in Windows networks today. NetBIOS includes, among other features, a naming system and a name resolution system.

Network Address Translation (NAT) A technology deployed on a router that hides the addresses on one network and allows computers on private ranges to communicate with computers on the Internet.

O

option A configuration setting other than an address assigned to a DHCP client through a DHCP lease.

options class A category of DHCP clients that enables a DHCP server to assign options only to particular clients within a scope.

P

P-Mode When using Network Monitor, a promiscuous mode that records communications sent between hosts other than the computer running Network Monitor. P-Mode is disabled by default.

Preshared Key A shared password that is also used to encrypt and decrypt data.

primary DNS suffix The main domain name assigned to a computer. The primary DNS suffix is tied to domain membership and enables automatic DNS registration in a zone.

primary zone A read-write copy of a zone that provides the original source data for a portion of a DNS namespace.

private address ranges Specific IPv4 ranges that can be employed by any organization for private use.

private key In public key cryptography, a key that is generated locally as part of a key pair and kept secret. The private key is used to encrypt files that can be decrypted only with the corresponding public key. It is also the only key that decrypts files encrypted with the corresponding public key. A private key is used to create digital signatures.

public key In public key cryptography, a key that is generated locally as part of a key pair and then made available to the world at large. The public key is used to encrypt files that can be decrypted only with the corresponding private key. It is also the only key that decrypts files encrypted with the corresponding private key. A public key is used to validate digital signatures.

R

recursion For a DNS server, the process of accepting a name query from a client and then querying other servers on behalf of the client.

referral A list of servers, provided by an Active Directory domain controller, that can serve a DFS request.

replication The automatic synchronization of data that occurs among domain controllers in an Active Directory domain.

reservation An IP address that is configured always to be assigned to a DHCP client by a DHCP server.

resolver In general, a service that resolves names for a computer. In Windows, the resolver is the DNS Client service.

Resource record An entry in a DNS server database that gives information about a computer name. Most records equate a computer name to an IP address or a computer alias to a main computer name.

root hints A file that contains the list of root servers in a DNS namespace. The root servers are queried by default when a DNS server cannot itself answer a query.

router A device that forwards communications between networks.

routing table A list of IP destinations and the network interface a computer can use to reach each destination.

S

scavenging The process of deleting outdated records in a zone.

secondary zone A standard zone stored in a text file that provides a read-only copy of zone data.

Security Association (SA) A set of security standards agreed upon by two computers communicating through IPsec.

soft quota A storage limit that allows users to create more files after they reach a threshold. Soft quotas are used to send notifications or add events.

stub zone A zone that includes only a list of servers authoritative for names in a specific DNS domain.

subnet mask A 32-bit number used by a host on an IPv4 network to differentiate the network ID portion of an IPv4 address from the host ID portion.

T

targets Destination shared folders referenced by nodes in a DFS namespace.

Time to Live (TTL) The number of seconds for which a resource record is configured to remain in a DNS cache.

Transport mode The traditional mode of IPsec that provides end-to-end security between computers on a network.

trust anchor In DNSSEC, a public key from another zone that is used to validate digital signatures from that zone. Every server configured with DNSSEC must have at least one trust anchor configured.

Tunnel mode A mode of IPsec that provides compatibility for some VPN gateways.

U

upstream server The server that provides update files to all downstream servers when you are designing WSUS architectures. Microsoft's own Microsoft Update servers are the final upstream servers.

user class A user-defined options class that is populated by DHCP clients sharing a particular class ID set by an administrator.

V

vendor class An options class that is made up of members belonging to a vendor group. "Microsoft Windows 2000 Options" is an example of a vendor class.

W

Wi-Fi Protected Access (WPA) A wireless security standard that uses either static keys (in the case of WPA-PSK) or dynamic keys (WPA-EAP).

WINS server A name server used to resolve NetBIOS names on Windows networks.

Windows Server Update Services (WSUS) Software that provides automated support for installing the latest critical updates and security updates to Windows 7, Windows Server 2008 R2, and earlier versions of Windows through Windows 2000.

Wired Equivalent Protection (WEP) A wireless security standard that uses static keys.

worm A type of malware that replicates by attacking vulnerable computers across a network.

Z

zone A database on a DNS server that includes the authoritative data for computer name-to-address mappings of a particular portion of a DNS namespace. A zone is assigned the same names as the domain for which it contains the data.

zone signing key (ZSK) A key pair used in DNSSEC to digitally sign the resource records in a zone. A ZSK should be updated relatively frequently to reduce the risk of being compromised.

zone transfers The periodic zone copies that must occur between a master and a secondary zone in order to keep zone data current.

Index

A

ABE (Access-based Enumeration), 573
aborting TCP sessions, 12
access control lists (ACLs) and NAP enforcement, 447
Access-based Enumeration (ABE), 573
ACK flag, 11–12
AcknowledgmentNumber fields in TCP headers, 12
ACLs (access control lists) and NAP enforcement, 447
Active Directory
    DNS zone integration with, 179
    partitions. *See* partitions
Active Directory Diagnostics Data Collector Set, 543
Active Directory Domain Services (AD DS)
    as SRV-aware application, 195
    backing up BitLocker with, 581
    deploying DNS servers in, 137–138
    user accounts, 105
Active Directory Domain Services server role, 137
Active Directory forests, and DNS forwarders, 148
Active Directory replication
    forcing, 176
    scope, setting, 180–181
    tools for, 176
AD DS. *See* Active Directory Domain Services (AD DS)
AD DS Installation Wizard, 137
ad hoc wireless networks, 352, 362. *See also* wireless
    networks
Add Roles Wizard, 139
address blocks, 53
    determining size of, 56–59
    host capacity of, 59
    host capacity of, determining (practice exercise), 80–81
    reference chart for, 54–56
    size requirements, determining, 59–61
    subnets and, 53
address classes, 43

address exclusions, 270–271
address leases, 256
    deleting, 273
    durations, changing, 273
    for remote access clients, 257
    reservations for, 271–272
Address Resolution Protocol. *See* ARP (Address Resolution
        Protocol) protocol
address space, 53
    dividing, calculations for, 68–76
    subnetting. *See* subnets
aging
    defined, 196
    enabling, 196
    properties, setting, 198
AH (Authentication Header) protocol, 321
alias (CNAME) resource records, 192–193
aliases for Network Monitor IP addresses, 560
alternate configurations, assigning (practice exercise), 37
answer files, creating for Dcpromo, 140
APIPA addresses
    automatic updating and, 166
    defaulting to, 27
    defined, 24
    as problem indicator, 28
    repairing connection when present, 29
application directory partitions. *See* partitions
Application event log
    troubleshooting WSUS with, 510
    WSUS server health, adding to, 508
application layer (Layer 7), 13
application layer protocols, 13
approving security updates
    overview of, 504–506
    practice exercise for, 515–516

ARP (Address Resolution Protocol) protocol
    defined 33
    monitoring traffic via, 35
Arp utility, 33–34
asymmetric encryption. *See* key pairs
auditing events, 523
authentication
    with AH (Authentication Header) protocol, 321
    block period, setting, 364
    caching, preventing, 364
    for DirectAccess, 407
    event forwarding and, 534
    exempting, 332
    with IPsec. *See* IPsec (Internet Protocol Security);
        IPsec Policies
    logging attempts, 359–361
    preference order, setting, 333
    requiring, 333
    restricting connections by type of, 397
    vs. securing connections, 320
    specifying method, 333
    for VPNs (virtual private networks), 392
    for wired networks, 363–364
    for wireless networks, 351, 353–356
Authentication Exemption rule, 332
Authentication Header (AH) protocol, 321
authoritative DNS servers, 122
authorizing connections, 436–438
Automatic Private IP Addressing addresses. *See* APIPA
    (Automatic Private IP Addressing) addresses
Automatic Updates client. *See* Windows Update client

B

backing up. *See also* shadow copies; Windows Server
    Backup
    automatically, 618–619
    certificates, 237
    from command prompt, 620–621
    DNS zones, 234
    file encryption keys, 574
    practice exercise for, 625–626
    restoring after, 621–623
    restoring after, when Windows will not start, 624
    scheduling, 618–619
    system state, 621
BaseNetworkTShoot filter for Network Monitor, 560

bidirectional model of networking, 3
binary notation
    compared to other notations, 48
    converting to decimal notation, 44–46
    for subnet masks, 43
BitLocker
    backing up computer before enabling, 581
    configuring on computer without TPM chip, 579
    enabling, 581–582
    Group Policy settings, 579
    modes for, 579
    overview of, 578
    performance impact of, 578
    recovery password, setting, 582
    turning off, 582
    volume integrity, checking, 581
    when to use, 578
    Windows editions containing, 579
BitLocker-To-Go, 582
blocking outbound connections
    overview of, 435
    practice exercise for, 441–442
blocking reauthentication, 364
b-node (NetBIOS), 118
booting from recovery DVD, 624
BranchCache
    client configuration, 610
    configuring, 609–610
    Distributed Cache mode, 607
    Group Policy settings, 610
    Hosted Cache mode, 608–609
    overview of, 587, 606
    when to use, 606
bridging network connections, 18–20
broadcasts
    address for, 59
    limiting, with subnets, 64
    overview of, 25

C

CA (Certification Authority), 456–457
cache locking, 151
cache poisoning
    Arp, 34
    preventing, 151

Cache.dns file
  overview of, 128
  viewing contents of, 144
caching, DNS, 131–132
caching-only servers
  configuring, 142–143
  when to use, 143
calculating subnet addresses, 68–76
caller ID, restricting connections by, 397
canonical names, 192–193
capturing network traffic
  from command prompt, 557–558
  from command prompt, practice exercise for, 564
  filtering when, 560–561
  with friendly aliases, 560
  without full Network Monitor installation, 558
  with Network Monitor, 555–558
certificate revocation list. See CRL (certificate
      revocation list)
certificates
  backing up, 237
  DirectAccess setup, 413
  DirectAccess setup, practice exercise for, 417–418
  IPsec authentication with, 323
Certification Authority (CA), 456–457
Change.txt file for WSUS, 510
Checksum fields
  in IP headers, 9
  in TCP headers, 13
classification management, 596–598
Classless Inter Domain Routing (CIDR) notation, 43
Client For Microsoft Networks, 18
clients. See network clients
CNAME resource records, 192–193
collusion, 577
computer groups
  client-side targeting, 502–503
  creating, 502
  server-side targeting, 502–503
  for WSUS, configuring, 502–503
computer names, creating, 160
conditional forwarding, 149–150
Configure A DNS Server wizard, 183
connection request policies, 358–359
Connection Security Rules, 316, 320
  configuring for NAP, 458–459
  creating, 330–334
  encryption, requiring, 336
    exporting, 320
    IPsec settings for, 334–336
    naming, 334
    practice exercise for, 341–342
    profiles, 334
    setting by protocols/ports, 334
    types of, 331
connectionless communication, 13
connection-oriented communication, 11
connection-specific suffixes, 161–162
connectivity. See also network connections
  configuring, 17
  Network Connections area, 17
  testing, 397–402
  troubleshooting, 2
country domains, 121
Create IP Security Rule Wizard, 326–330
CRL (certificate revocation list)
  overview of, 410
  practice exercise for, 418
  publishing, 419
CScript, as default application, 649

D

Data Collector Sets
  built-in, 543–544
  creating, 544–546
  customizing, 546
  data sources, adding to, 546
  importing/exporting, 549
  Logman command-line tool for, 549
  overview of, 543
  reports, viewing, 547
  running, practice exercise for, 551–552
  specifying location for, 545
  starting, 544, 546
  stopping, 544
  templates for, 545
  types of, 546
  viewing reports for, 544
data link layer (Layer 2)
  overview of, 6
  standards defined at, 6
  switches, and Network Monitor, 556–557
Data Recovery Agents. See DRAs (Data Recovery Agents)
datagrams. See packets; TCP packets

DataOffset fields in TCP headers, 12
day and time restrictions on network connections, 396
Dcdiag tool, 176
Dcpromo.exe
    answer files, creating, 140
    overview of, 137
    on Server Core installations of Windows Server 2008,
        140–141
deadlines for security updates, defining, 505
declining security updates, 506
default gateway. *See also* routers
    configuring, 24
    defined, 53, 291
    for DHCP scopes, defining, 262
    network ID, 51
    overview of, 50
    in routing table, 303
    unconfigured, 51
Default Response Rule in IPsec, 326
Default User class, 276
defense-in-depth, 437
delaying DHCP responses, 280
delegating DNS zones
    implementing, 214–215
    structure of, 213–214
    when to do, 213
delegating subdomains, 123
Delegation Signer (DS) records, 227–232
demand-dial routing, 299–300
    enabling, 386–387, 392
    filters, configuring, 300
    overview, 299–300
deploying DNS servers
    on domain controllers, 137–138
    on Server Core installations of Windows Server 2008,
        140–141
    on stand-alone servers, 139
deploying NAP (Network Access Protection), 450
deprecated IPv6 address state, 91
DestinationAddress fields
    in Ethernet headers, 7
    in IP headers, 9
device map, 16
devolution of DNS suffixes, 163
DFS (Distributed File System)
    command-line configuration, 602
    failover clustering, configuring, 604
    health monitoring, configuring, 603

installing, 600
namespace configuration, 600–601
overview of, 599
polling configurations, 601
practice exercise for, 610–611
referral order, 601
replication, generating health reports for, 603
root permissions, configuring, 602
testing propagation, 603
testing propagation, practice exercise for, 613
DFSCmd command-line tool, 602
DFSUtil command-line tool, 602
DHCID records, 284
DHCP (Dynamic Host Configuration Protocol)
    address assignment process, 254–255
    Delay Configuration setting, 280
    enabling, practice exercise for, 268
    ICS (Internet Connection Sharing) and, 374
    MAC filtering, 279–280
    name protection, 284
    negotiation, example of, 255
    options classes, 276
    options for, 257
    options inheritance, 274
    scope options, 274–275
    user classes, 276–279
    vendor classes, 276
    for VPNs (virtual private networks), 393
DHCP clients
    Default User class, 276
    DNS address configuration, 158
    network broadcasts and
    overview of, 25
    troubleshooting, 29
DHCP messages, 254–256
DHCP Server role
    adding, practice exercise for, 266–268, 476–477
    overview of, 258–265
DHCP servers
    acknowledgment message, 255
    address leases. *See* address leases
    authorizing, 265
    backup, 281
    discovery of, 255
    DNS suffix, setting, 259
    DnsUpdateProxy security group, adding, 284–285
    dynamic DNS updates, 282–283
    exclusion ranges, 270–271

installing/configuring, 258–265
IPv6 protocol and, 254
NAP configuration, practice exercise for, 477–478
NAP enforcement and, 448, 460–461
for NAT (Network Address Translation), configuring, 377–378
network connection bindings, configuring, 259
options inheritance, 274
releasing IP addresses, 256
scopes, 257, 261–262
on Server Core installation, 285
split-scope configuration, 281
WINS server configuration, 260
DHCPv6
stateless mode, configuring, 262–264
stateless mode vs. stateful mode, 267
dialog box notifications for events, 525
dial-up connections
advantages and disadvantages, 383
architecture of, 382
caller ID, 397
configuring, 385–391
creating manually, 390–391
enabling ICS (Internet Connection Sharing) for, 375–376
encryption, configuring, 390
filtering traffic for, 389
IP configuration, 386
modem configuration, 387–388
multilink settings, 397
RADIUS server configuration, 388–390
routing, 299–300
Routing And Remote Access Services configuration, 385–386
DifferentiatedService fields in IP headers, 9
digital signatures, 225
DirectAccess
advantages of, 406, 411
authentication, 407
certificate setup, 413
certificate setup, practice exercise for, 417–418
client configuration, practice exercise for, 420–421
configuration videos, 415
configuring, practice exercise for, 415–418
connection types, 407–408
end-to-edge protection, 407
end-to-end protection, 407
firewall configuration, 412–413

firewall configuration, practice exercise for, 416
hardware and software requirements, 410–411
ICMP configuration, practice exercise for, 416
IPsec protection, enabling, 409
on IPv4 networks, 408–409
IPv6 protocol and, 406, 408–409
limitations of, 412
name resolution, 409
NLS (Network Location Server), 410
operating system compatibility, 406
overview of, 405–406
propagating settings, 414
server configuration, practice exercise for, 418–420
setting up, 413–414
setting up, practice exercise for, 419–420
directory partitions. *See* partitions
DirQuota command-line tool, 590
disabling IPv6 protocol, 134
disk quotas
command-line configuration, 590
configuring with Windows Explorer, 590–592
creating, 589–590
event triggers for, 591
Group Policy settings, 592
overview of, 587
performance impact of, 570
Quota Management console, 587–590
templates for, 588–589
thresholds, adding, 589
Distributed File System. *See* DFS (Distributed File System)
Distributed Scan Server role service, 633
dividing address spaces, 68–76
DNS cache locking, 151
DNS client cache
clearing, 168
flushing, 168
overview of, 131–132
practice exercise for, 168–169
viewing, 168
DNS clients
DNSSEC configuration, 240–241
DNSSEC configuration, practice exercise for, 245
dynamic update settings, 184–185
single-label name tags, 199
updating, 165–167
updating manually, 185
DNS console, clearing DNS server cache with, 132

DNS forwarders
    conditions, configuring, 149–150
    configuring, 145–148
    NAT (Network Address Translation), 378
    security and, 146
    when to use, 146–148
DNS Manager
    aging/scavenging settings, 196
    Conditional Forwarders container, 149–150
    connecting to DNS server from, 141
    opening, 138
    partitions, browsing, 205
DNS namespace. *See also* DNS zones
    canonical names, 192–193
    overview of, 121
    private, 122
    root hints, 127–128, 144
    subdomains, 121
    top-level domain names, 121
    trailing dot, 121
    zones, 123
DNS queries
    components of, 124
    with delegated subdomains, 213–214
    example of, 128–130
    forwarding. *See* forwarders
    IPsec protection, enabling, 409
    process for, 124–127
DNS recursion, 127–128, 144
DNS resolution. *See also* DNS suffixes; name resolution
    via DNSSEC, 227–232
    example of, 128–130
    methods of, 124
    NSEC (Next Secure) records, 233
    overview of, 120
    security and, 146, 151
    WINS resolution as backup for, 195
DNS resolvers, 123, 125
DNS server cache, 132
DNS Server Core role, 141, 378
DNS servers. *See also* deploying DNS servers
    adding to list of, 158
    address configuration, 158
    authoritative, 122
    caching-only, configuring, 142–143
    caching-only, when to use, 143
    configuring manually, 23, 139
    connecting to from DNS Manager, 141

defined, 122
deploying, 137–141
domain controller deployment, 183
dynamic update settings, 165, 184–185
forwarders, configuring, 145–148
function of, 122
IP configuration, 143
manually configuring, 23, 139
multihomed, 143
primary, naming, 186
promoting to domain controllers, 137
properties, configuring, 143–150
refresh interval, setting, 187
reviewing configuration, practice exercise for,
        153–154
root hints, 127–128, 144
single-label names for, 199
source port randomization, 151
trust anchors, configuring, 238–240
trust relationships, 226
DNS socket pooling, 151
DNS suffixes, 160–161. *See also* DNS resolution
    configuring for DHCP servers, 259
    connection-specific, 161–162
    custom search lists, 164
    devolution, 163
    Group Policy configuration, 164
    search lists, configuring, 162–163
DNS zone replication
    default partitions, 205
    partitions, pattern of, 206
    scope, setting, 180–181, 207–209
    to Windows 2000 Server, 207
DNS zones. *See also* DNS namespace
    @ symbol in, 193
    Active Directory-integrated, 179
    Active Directory-integrated, advantages of, 205
    aging, enabling, 196
    backing up, 234
    creating, 177
    creating, practice exercise for, 243
    defined, 177
    delegating, 213–215
    forward lookup, 123, 139, 181–182
    GlobalNames, 199–202
    host records, 165
    masters, 179
    name server (NS) records, 188, 221

naming, 183
overview of, 123
pointer records. *See* pointer records
primary, 178
public keys in, 224, 228. *See also* public keys
read-only domain controllers and, 179
refresh interval, setting, 187
replication. *See* DNS zone replication
resource records. *See* resource records
retry interval, setting, 187
reverse lookup, 123, 181–182
round robin distribution, 193
scavenging, enabling, 196
secondary, 178–179
secondary, setting expiration time for, 187
serial number for, 186
signing files, 237–238
signing files, practice exercise for, 244
standard, 180
structuring, 213
stubs, 179
time stamping records, 198
type, choosing, 178–180
verifying, practice exercise for, 156
WINS records in, 195
zone transfers, 100, 188, 210–212
Dnscmd tool
key generation with, 235–237
overview of, 132
signing zone files with, 237–238
subcommands for, 176
DNSKEY resource records, 224
DNSSEC
certificates, backing up, 237
client configuration for, 240–241
configuring, 234–240
configuring, practice exercise for, 245
defined, 223
Delegation Signer (DS) records, 227–232
IPSec authentication, enforcing, 241
key generation switches/options, 235–237
key rollover, configuring, 234–235
name resolution with, 227–232
NSEC (Next Secure) records, 233
Resource Record Signature (RRSIG) records, 227–232
trust relationships, 226
validating remote domains with, 226

DnsUpdateProxy security group, 284–285
Documents folder, encrypting, 576
domain administrator account, creating (practice exercise), 154–155
domain controllers
creating, practice exercise for, 152–153
deploying DNS servers on, 137–138, 183
firewall configuration, 432
partitions in, 205
read-only, 179
setting replication scope for, 180–181
Domain firewall profile, 431
domain isolation, 332
domain names
fully qualified (FQDNs), 121
fully qualified (FQDNs), generation of, 124
registrars, 122
top-level, 121
trailing dot, 121
Domain network profile, 15
domain suffixes. *See* DNS suffixes
DomainDnsZones partition, 205
domains, adding computers to (practice exercise), 155–156
dotted-decimal notation
block size, determining, 58–59
compared to other notations, 48
converting subnet masks into, 43
converting subnet masks into (practice exercise), 78
converting to binary notation, 44–46
converting to slash notation, 49–50
overview of, 40
DRAs (Data Recovery Agents)
adding manually, 578
assigning two people to, 577
configuring, 577–578
configuring, practice exercise for, 582–583
overview of, 577
practice exercise for, 584
DS (Delegation Signer) records, 227–232
dynamic DNS updates, 165, 184–185
configuring for DHCP servers, 282–283
forcing with Ipconfig, 185
Dynamic Host Configuration Protocol. *See* DHCP (Dynamic Host Configuration Protocol); DHCP clients; DHCP servers

E

EAP-MSCHAP v2 authentication, 356
EFS (Encrypting File System)
    applying, 574
    applying, practice exercise for, 583
    encryption key, backing up, 574, 576
    Group Policy configuration, 575–577
    indexing encrypted files, 577
    locking desktop to prevent bypass of, 576
    operating system compatibility, 573
    overview of, 573
    performance impact of, 570
    recovering encrypted files, 577–578
    sharing files protected by, 574–575
    smart cards, requiring, 576
email notifications for events, 525
Encapsulating Security Payload (ESP) protocol, 321
Encrypting File System. *See* EFS (Encrypting File System)
encryption. *See also* BitLocker; EFS (Encrypting File System); key pairs
    for dial-up connections, 390
    with ESP (Encapsulating Security Payload) protocol, 321
    for event forwarding, 531
    for HRA server, 454–455
    IPsec and, 321–322
    for Network Monitor, 557
    Network Monitor and, 522
    for wireless networks, 350
    for WSUS, 509–510
endpoints, specifying, 333
enumerating subnets, 68–76, 96, 99–101
ESP (Encapsulating Security Payload) protocol, 321
Ethernet frames
    analyzing, 559
    example of, 6–7
    filtering, 560–561
    IP protocol in, 8–10
    vs. packets, 559
Ethernet protocol, 6–7
EthernetType fields in Ethernet headers, 7
event forwarding
    configuring collecting computer, 528
    configuring forwarding computer, 527
    firewall exceptions for, 534

HTTPS protocol for, 531
    normal delay in, 532
    overview of, 526
    practice exercise for, 536
    privileges, verifying, 533
    protocols and ports for, 526
    query validity, verifying, 534–535
    troubleshooting, 532–535
    on Windows XP/Windows Server 2003 computers, 526
event logs, filtering, 524–525
event monitoring. *See also* event forwarding
    event subscriptions, creating, 528–531
    overview of, 523
    practice exercises for, 535–537
Event Viewer
    Applications And Services Logs, 523
    automatically responding to events in, 525–526
    custom views, 525
    event subscriptions, creating, 528–531
    event subscriptions, practice exercise for, 536–537
    event triggers, practice exercise for, 535–536
    filtering event logs, 524–525
    opening, 523
    saving filters, 525
    viewing events in, 523–524
exclusion ranges
    creating, 270–271
    creating, practice exercise for, 286
exporting
    certificates, 237
    DNS zones, 234
    printers, 647
    security update metadata, 508

F

failover clustering for DFS servers, 604
fault tolerance
    DHCP server backups and, 281
    NAP (Network Access Protection) and, 450
fields. *See* IP headers; TCP headers; *specific fields*
File And Printer Sharing
    as default service, 18
    enabling/disabling locally, 15

file classification
    properties for, 596
    rules, creating, 597–598
    scheduling, 598
file permissions
    Access-based Enumeration (ABE), 573
    applying, 572–573
    command-line configuration, 573
    default, 571
    precedence when in conflict, 572
file screening
    configuring, 594
    performance impact of, 570
file security, 570. *See also* BitLocker; EFS (Encrypting File
        System); NTFS file permissions
File Services server role, 586–587
file sharing, 38. *See also* folder sharing
Filter Action Wizard, 339–340
filtering
    event logs, 524–525
    inbound traffic, 432–434
    inbound traffic, practice exercise for, 440–441
    IP traffic. *See* IPsec (Internet Protocol Security);
        IPsec Policies; IPsec rules
    network captures, 560–561
    outbound traffic, 434–435
    outbound traffic, practice exercise for, 441–442
filters, 393–394
FIN flag, 12
firewall exceptions
    for DirectAccess, 412–413
    enabling, 32, 393–394
    for event forwarding, 527, 534
    ICMP and, 38
    overview of, 32
    practice exercise for, 38
    for WSUS, 499–500
firewall rules
    actions available for, 433
    automatically enabled, 441
    connection authorization, configuring, 436–438
    creating, 433–434
    default, 432
    for inbound traffic, 433–434
    for inbound traffic, practice exercise for, 440–441

for outbound traffic, 434–435
    for outbound traffic, practice exercise for, 441–442
    port-based, 439–440
    scope, configuring, 435–436
    types of, 433
firewalls. *See also* Windows Firewall with Advanced
        Security (WFAS)
    defined, 431
    domain controller configuration, 432
    Group Policy configuration, 438
    importance of, 431
    profiles for, 431–432
    scope, configuring, 435–436
    server configuration, 432
    verifying, 467
flags. *See specific flags*
flash drives, encrypting, 582
flushing DNS client cache, 168
folder sharing. *See also* DFS (Distributed File System)
    from command prompt, 594–595
    connecting to folders, 595
    File Servers server role for, 586–587
    mapping network drive for, 595
    with Provision A Shared Folder Wizard, 593
    from Windows Explorer, 592–593
ForestDnsZones partition, 205
forward lookup zones, 123
    adding, 139
    creating, 181–182
    GlobalNames. *See* GlobalNames zone
    naming, 183
    overview of, 123
    WINS servers in, 195
forwarders
    conditions, configuring, 149–150
    configuring, 145–148
    NAT (Network Address Translation), 378
    security and, 146
    when to use, 146–148
forwarding events. *See* event forwarding
FQDNs (fully qualified domain names), 121, 124
fragmentation of packets, 9
FragmentedFlag fields in IP headers, 9
frames. *See* Ethernet frames
fully qualified domain names. *See* FQDNs (fully qualified
        domain names)

G

gateway. *See* default gateway; routers
gateway-to-gateway tunneling, 322
geographical domains, 121
global IPv6 addresses, 87–88
GlobalNames zone
    adding records, practice exercise for, 202
    creating, practice exercise for, 201
    deploying, 200
    deploying, practice exercise for, 201
    overview of, 199
    populating, 200
    testing, practice exercise for, 202
glue records, 213
GPOs (Group Policy Objects)
    client-side targeting with, 503
    creating Connection Security Rules with, 330–334
    creating, practice exercise for, 338
    defining Connection Security Rules with, 320
    IPsec Policy in, 317, 324–326
    NAP client configuration with, 463–465
    WMI filters and, 438
Group Policy
    BitLocker policies, 579
    BranchCache policies, 610
    disk quota policies, 592
    DNS suffix search lists in, 164
    DNSSEC configuration policies, 240–241
    EFS policies, 575–577
    firewall policies, 438
    LLMNR disabling policies, 116
    printer policies, 646
    refreshing, 414
    SNMP policies, 563
    Windows Update policies, 490–491
    wired network policies, 363–364
    wireless connection policies, 361–362
    wireless connection policies, practice exercise for, 368–369
    WSUS configuration, verifying, 511
Group Policy Objects. *See* GPOs (Group Policy Objects)
groups, computer, 502–503

H

handshake process for TCP protocol, 11–12
headers. *See EthernetType* fields in Ethernet headers; IP headers; *specific headers*; TCP headers
health certificates, requiring for servers, 458–459
Health Policies template (NPS), 365
Health Registration Authority role service. *See* HRA (Health Registration Authority) role service
    configuring, 456–457
    installing, 453–455
health requirement policies
    updating, 466–472
    updating, practice exercise for, 480
hexadecimal numbering
    overview of, 87
    translating powers of 2 into, 97–98
h-node (NetBIOS), 119
HopLimit field in IP headers, 10
host ID, 41–42. *See also* interface ID (IPv6)
host names, retrieving, 160
host records
    defined, 165
    function of, 190
host routes, 448
hostname command, 160
hosts, 445
Hosts file
    vs. Lmhosts file, 132
    location of, 131
    updating, 131
HRA (Health Registration Authority) role service
    configuring, 456-457
    installing, 453-455
HTTPS protocol
    for event forwarding, 531
    tunneling protocol for (IP-HTTPS), 95

I

IANA (Internet Assigned Numbers Authority), 121
IASNAP.log file, 361
Icacls command-line tool, 573

ICANN (Internet Corporation for Assigned Names and Numbers), 121–122
ICMP (Internet Control Message Protocol)
    defined, 31
    DirectAccess configuration, practice exercise for, 416
    enabling request response, 295
    exempting from authentication, 336
    firewall exceptions, practice exercise for, 38
    traffic, defined, 327
ICS (Internet Connection Sharing)
    architecture of, 374
    configuring NAT with, 374–375
    DHCP service for, 374
    enabling for remote access connections, 375–376
    internal network interface address, 374
    for intranet servers, 375
    IP addresses for, 375
    overview of, 373
    port number settings, 375
    vs. Routing And Remote Access Services, 376
Identification fields in IP headers, 9
idle time-outs, setting, 397
IEEE 802.1X standards, 363–364
    configuring, practice exercise for, 366–367
    NAP enforcement, 446–447, 459–460
    overview of, 363–364
IGMP (Internet Group Management Protocol), 296, 298–299
IIS (Internet Information Services), 496
IKE (Internet Key Exchange) protocol, 321–322, 394
importing printers, 647–648
inbound traffic
    filtering, 432–434
    filtering, practice exercise for, 440–441
indexing encrypted files, 577
installing DNS servers. *See also* deploying DNS servers
    on domain controllers, 137–138
    on Server Core installations of Windows Server 2008, 140–141
    on stand-alone servers, 139
installing Network Monitor, 554
installing printers
    with Control Panel, 635–636
    overview of, 634
    practice exercise for, 651
    with Print Management snap-in, 636–638

installing WSUS (Windows Server Update Services)
    planning for, 495–496
    practice exercise for, 513–514
    process for, 499–500
interface ID (IPv6), 88
international domains, 121
Internet
    preventing access to, Open Systems Interconnect (OSI) model, 4
    overview of, 2–4
Internet Assigned Numbers Authority (IANA), 121
Internet Connection Sharing. *See* ICS (Internet Connection Sharing)
Internet Control Message Protocol. *See* ICMP (Internet Control Message Protocol).
Internet Group Management Protocol (IGMP), 296, 298–299
Internet Information Services (IIS), 496
Internet Key Exchange (IKE) protocol, 321–322, 394
Internet layer (Layer 3), 7–8
Internet printing
    managing, 643–644
    practice exercise for, 653
Internet Printing Protocol (IPP), 633
Internet Printing role service, 643
Internet Protocol Security. *See* IPsec (Internet Protocol Security)
intranet
    example of, 292
    servers, accessing Internet with, 375
Intra-Site Automatic Tunnel Addressing Protocol (ISATAP), 92–93
IP addresses. *See also* IP protocol; IPv6 addresses; subnet masks
    address block reference chart, 54–56
    address blocks, 53
    calculating for subnets, 68–76, 99–101
    compared to ZIP codes, 41–42
    DHCP assignment of, 254–255
    DHCP configuration, 24–25
    for dial-up connections, 386
    for DNS requests, specifying, 143
    exclusion ranges, 270–271
    filtering Network Monitor by, 560
    firewall scope, configurin, 436
    for ICS (Internet Connection Sharing), 375

IP addresses *(continued)*
    leases, ending, 273
    leasing, 256
    leasing duration, 273
    leasing, for remote access clients, 257
    MAC address associations, 271–272
    network and host IDs, 41–42
    for network broadcasts, 59
    private, 52, 372
    public, 52
    ranges, defining, 262
    releasing, 256, 400
    renewing, 400
    reservations for, 271–272
    resolving names. *See* DNS resolution; name
        resolution
    for routers, 293, 301
    scopes, 257
    scopes, splitting, 281
    static, 22–24
    static, practice exercise for, 36
    structure of, 40–41
    subnet verification, 76
    for subnets, 59
    unicast, 51
IP configuration
    manually assigning, 22–24
    manually assigning, practice exercise for, 36
    practice exercise for, 36
    renewing, 29
    viewing, 20–21
IP filter lists
    adding IP addresses to, 327
    filter actions, 328, 330
    managing, 330
    mirrored filters, 328
    overview of, 318–319
    predefined filters, 328
IP Filters template (NPS), 365
IP headers
    Checksum fields, 9
    DestinationAddress fields, 9
    DifferentiatedService fields, 9
    FragmentedFlag fields, 9
    HopLimit fields, 10
    Identification fields, 9
    NextProtocol fields, 9

    overview of, 8–10
    PayloadLength fields, 10
    SourceAddress fields, 9
    TimeToLive fields, 9
    TotalLength fields, 9
IP mapping, repairing, 34IP packets. *See* packets;
    TCP packets
IP protocol. *See also* IPv6 protocol
    alternate configurations, assigning
    alternate configurations, practice exercise for, 37
    communication with IPv6, 92–93
    in Ethernet headers, 8–10
    loopback addresses, 92
    manually configuring, 22–24
    overview of, 8
IP registries, 52
IP routing. *See* routing
IP-address-to-name resolution, 121
Ipconfig, 20
    /release argument, 400
    /renew argument, 29, 400
    clearing/viewing DNS client cache with, 168
    forcing DNS update with, 185
    reading output (practice exercise), 101–102
    renewing connection with, 29
    running, 398–400
IP-HTTPS protocol, 95
IPP (Internet Printing Protocol), 633
IPsec (Internet Protocol Security)
    Authentication Header (AH) protocol, 321
    authentication, 323, 329
    client configuration for NAP, 457
    connection establishment, 321–322
    Connection Security Rules, 316, 320, 334–336
    Default Response Rule, 326
    default settings, 335
    DNSSEC enforcement, 227, 241
    enabling for NAP, 457
    Encapsulating Security Payload (ESP) protocol, 321
    encryption, 321–322
    Internet Key Exchange (IKE) protocol, 321–322
    Kerberos authentication, 323
    NAP enforcement, 446
    NAP enforcement, configuring, 453–459
    negotiating security, 318
    on non-Windows computers, 317
    overview of, 317

preshared keys, 323
requirements for, 446
Security Associations (SAs), 321
services provided by, 317
transport mode, 322
tunnel authorization, 336
tunnel mode, 322
for WSUS, 496
IPsec Policies. *See also* IPsec rules
assigning, 317
assigning multiple, 324
configuring, 326
creating, 325–326
creating, practice exercise for, 338
example of, 319
IP filter lists, 318–319, 330
Negotiate Security option, 318
predefined, 324
predefined filters, 328
testing, practice exercise for, 340–341
IPsec rules. *See also* Connection Security Rules; IPsec
    Policies
creating, 326–330
creating, practice exercise for, 338–340
filter actions, 339–340
filter actions, practice exercise for, 339–340
overview of, 318–319
IPv4 protocol. *See* IP protocol
IPv6 addresses. *See also* IP addresses
global, 87–88
link local, 88–89
link-local, pinging (practice exercise), 102
overview of, 86–87
shortening, 87
site-local, as deprecated, 91
states of, 91
structure of, 87
syntax of, 86–87
unique local, 90–91
unique local, assigning (practice exercise), 102–103
IPv6 hosts
autoconfiguration flags, 264
stateful addressing, 264
IPv6 protocol. *See also* IP protocol
Arp cache poisoning and, 35
communication with IPv4, 92–93
configuring, 87

DHCP servers and, 254
DirectAccess and, 406
disabling, 134
DNS server settings, 264
header example, 9–10
ICMP and, 31
LLMNR (Link Local Multicast Name Resolution)
    compatibility with, 116
loopback addresses, 92
manually configuring, 23
NAT and, 372
NetBIOS incompatibility with, 110, 120
overview of, 8
purpose of, 86
renewing configuration, 29
router compatibility, 92
subnets and, 96–101
transition technologies, 92–95, 408–409
ISATAP (Intra-Site Automatic Tunnel Addressing
    Protocol) protocol, 92–93
Isolation rules, 332
iteration, 127

K

Kerberos authentication, 333
key pairs
digital signatures and, 225
generating, 235–237
Key Signing Keys and Zone Signing Keys, 228
overview of, 224
rollover configuration, 234–235
Key Signing Keys (KSKs), 228
generating, 235
rollover configuration, 234–235
keys. *See* private keys; public keys

L

L2TP (Layer Two Tunneling Protocol), 391
languages for security updates, configuring, 496
LANs, viewing device map, 16
latency
event subscriptions and, 530
VPNs and, 385

Layer 1 (physical layer), 6
Layer 2 (data link layer)
  overview of, 6
  standards defined at, 6
  switches, and Network Monitor, 556–557
Layer 3 (Internet layer), 7–8
Layer 4 (transport layer), 10
Layer 7 (application layer), 13
Layer Two Tunneling Protocol (L2TP), 391
layered networking, pinging (practice exercise), 102
leases
  deleting, 273
  durations, changing, 273
  for remote access clients, 257
  reservations for, 271–272
limited connectivity with APIPA address, 29
Line Printer Daemon (LPD) protocol, 633
Link Layer Topology Discovery (LLTD) Mapper, 16
Link Local Multicast Name Resolution. See LLMNR (Link
    Local Multicast Name Resolution)
link-local addresses, 88–90
LLMNR (Link Local Multicast Name Resolution)
  advantages and disadvantages, 116
  disabling, 116
  Network Discovery and, 112
  overview of, 110, 112
  practice exercise for, 133–134
  responses over IP protocols, 114–115
  when to use, 112
Lmhosts files
  vs. Hosts file, 132
  overview of, 117
load balancing for SMTP mail servers, 193–194
local IP addresses, configuring firewall scope for, 436.
    See also IP addresses
location-aware printing, 639
logging. See also monitoring
  NAP (Network Access Protection), 474–476
  Windows Firewall traffic, 439
Logman command-line tool, 549
loopback addresses
  overview of, 92
  in routing table, 303
LPD (Line Printer Daemon) protocol, 633
LPR Port Monitor feature, 634

M

MAC addresses
  associating with IP addresses, 271–272
  in Ethernet headers, 7
  filtering DHCP traffic by, 279–280
  routing with, 294
MAC filtering, 279–280
mail exchange (MX) resource records, 193–194
man in the middle attacks, preventing, 409
manual backups, 617–618
manually configuring IP addresses, 22–24
mapping
  network devices, 16
  network drives, 595
masks. See subnet masks
master zones, 179
Maximum Transmission Unit (MTU) packet size, 9
MBSA (Microsoft Baseline Security Analyzer), verifying
    updates with, 497
Media Streaming, enabling/disabling locally, 15
Microsoft Baseline Security Analyzer (MBSA), verifying
    updates with, 497
Microsoft Report Viewer Redistributable 2008, 499
Microsoft Update, 489. See also WSUS (Windows Server
    Update Services)
Microsoft Update Improvement Program, 501
migrating printers, 647–648
mirrored filters, 328
m-node (NetBIOS), 119
modem banks, 388
modem configuration, 387–388
monitoring. See also event monitoring; Network Monitor;
    Performance Monitor
  with Data Collector Sets, 543–549
  NAP (Network Access Protection), 450, 472–473
  ports, 556
  printers, 650
  with Reliability Monitor, 542–543
  with Resource Monitor, 541
MTU (Maximum Transmission Unit) packet size, 9
multicast addresses in routing table, 303
multihomed servers, configuring, 143
Multilink And Bandwidth Allocation Protocol (BAP), 397
MX (mail exchange) resource records, 193–194
My Network Places, 116

N

name protection, 284
name resolution. *See also* DNS resolution
    defined, 111
    DirectAccess and, 409
    with DNSSEC, 227–232
    filtering Network Monitor by, 560
    LLMNR (Link Local Multicast Name Resolution),
        112–116
    NetBIOS, 110, 116–120
    NSEC (Next Secure) records, 233
    overview of, 109
    Windows methods for, 111–112
Name Resolution Policy Table (NRPT)
    adding rules to, 240–241
    DirectAccess configuration, 408–409
    DNSSEC requests through, 227–232
    rules, viewing, 409
name root servers, public, 2
name server (NS) records
    creating, 188
    creating, practice exercise for, 221
name servers. *See* DNS servers
namespace, DNS. *See also* DNS zones
    canonical names, 192–193
    overview of, 121
    private, 122
    root hints, 127–128, 144
    subdomains, 121
    top-level domain names, 121
    trailing dot, 121
    zones, 123
naming DNS zones, 183
NAP (Network Access Protection)
    802.1X access point enforcement, 446–447
    802.1X configuration, 459–460
    ACLs, quarantining with, 447
    analyzing costs of, 473
    architecture of, 445
    autoremediation, enabling, 452
    client configuration, 463–465
    Configure NAP Wizard, 455–456
    configuring, 451–453
    connection process, 449
    deploying, 450

DHCP configuration, practice exercise for, 477–478
DHCP enforcement, 448
DHCP enforcement, configuring, 460–461
enforcement, disabling, 472–473
enforcement types, 446
error code resolution settings, 467
fault tolerance, 450
health requirement policies, 466–472
health requirement policies, practice exercise for, 480
health state changes, 448
health validation, 448–449
implementation of, 445
installing, 450–451
IPsec enforcement, 446
IPsec enforcement, configuring, 453–459
logging, 361, 474–476
monitoring, 450
monitoring-only status, 472–473
network policy configuration, 470
noncompliant computers, identifying, 474–476
RADIUS servers as, 450
remediation, configuring, 468–470
Remote Desktop Gateway enforcement, 448
security updates, enforcing, 468
testing, practice exercise for, 479–480
verifying updates with, 497
VLANs, quarantining with, 447
VPN server enforcement, 447, 462
NAS (Network Access Server), restricting connections
        by port type, 397
NAT (Network Address Translation). *See also* private IP
        addresses
    client computers, configuring, 378
    client configuration, practice exercise for, 380
    configuring as server, practice exercise for, 379–380
    configuring, with Internet Connection Sharing (ICS),
        374–375
    configuring, with Routing And Remote Access
        Services, 376–377
    DHCP server, configuring, 377–378
    DNS forwarding with, 378
    as hardware vs. as server, 373
    IPv6 and, 372
    logging, configuring, 379
    overview of, 372
Neighbor Solicitation message, 91

Net Share command, 594–595
NetBIOS
    advantages and disadvantages, 120
    broadcasts over IPv4, 117
    configuring, 118
    defined, 116
    enabling/disabling, 110, 118
    history of, 110
    IPv6 incompatibility, 120
    Lmhosts files, 117
    methods of name resolution, 117
    node types, 118–119
    practice exercise for, 133–134
    responses over IP protocols, 116–117
    when to use, 116
    WINS servers, 117
NetBT. See NetBIOS
Netsh utility
    enabling wireless Single Sign On, 353
    IP configuration with, 24–25
    NAP client configuration, viewing, 464
    practice exercise for, 38
    syntax, 24
Netstat, identifying ports with, 439–440
Network Access Protection. See NAP (Network Access
    Protection)
Network Access Protection Agent service
    overview of, 463
    trace logging, 475–476
Network Access Server (NAS), restricting connections
    by port type, 397
network adapters, configuring for DHCP servers, 259
Network Address Translation. See NAT (Network
    Address Translation)
Network and Sharing Center
    Change Advanced Sharing Settings option, 15
    opening, 15
    See Full Map option, 16
network authentication. See authentication
network broadcasts
    address for, 59
    limiting, with subnets, 64
    overview of, 25
network clients
    overview of, 18
    viewing, for connections, 17

Network Connection Details dialog box, 20
network connections
    alternate configurations
    authenticating. See authentication
    bindings, configuring, 259
    bridging, 18–20
    day and time restrictions, 396
    default components of, 17–18
    default configuration of, 23
    idle time-outs, setting, 397
    IP configuration, 20–21, 24–25
    IP configuration, practice exercise for, 36
    on-demand, 301
    properties of, 17, 20–21
    repairing, 29
    restrictions, configuring, 395–397
    security, 363–364
    sharing. See ICS (Internet Connection Sharing)
    testing connectivity, 397–402
    troubleshooting, 29–35
    verifying, practice exercise for, 38
Network Connections area, 17
network connectivity
    configuring, 17
    Network Connections area, 17
    testing, 397–402
    troubleshooting, 2
Network Discovery
    enabling/disabling locally, 15
    LLMNR (Link Local Multicast Name Resolution)
        and, 112
network ID, 41–42. See also subnet ID
    for default gateways, 51
    identifying, 42
    IP routing and, 50
    subnet verification, 76
network interface layer
    overview of, 6
    standards defined at, 6
    switches, and Network Monitor, 556–557
network layer (Layer 3), 7–8
network layers. See also specific layers
    numbering scheme, 5
    overview of, 2
Network Location Server (NLS), 410
Network Map, 16

Network Monitor
  analyzing data from, 558–559
  capture file size, configuring, 556
  capturing network traffic with, 555–557
  command-line administration, 557–558
  command-line administration, practice exercise
      for, 564
  DHCP exchange display, 255
  encryption, 522, 557
  filtering data from, 560–561
  installing, 554
  IP addresses, translating, 560
  Layer 2 switches and, 556–557
  OneClick tool, 558
  P-Mode capturing, 558
  practice exercise for, 563–564
  starting, 555
  stopping data capture, 556
  unscrambling packets, 522
Network Monitor 3 Driver, 554
network policies
  configuring, 396–397
  for NAP, 470
Network Policy And Access Services role (practice
      exercise), 476–477
Network Policy Server (NPS)
  installing, practice exercise for, 366–368
  Security event log, 359
  templates for, 365
network prefix notation, 43, 97
network printers. *See* printers
network profiles, 15
network protocols, 18. *See* protocols; *specific protocols*
network segments, 6. *See also* packets; TCP packets
network services
  overview of, 18
  viewing, for connections, 17
networks. *See also* subnets; wireless networks
  /n, determining size of, 56–57
  host capacity, determining, 59
  host capacity, determining (practice exercise),
      80–81
  size requirements, determining, 59–61
  size requirements, determining (practice exercise),
      82–83
New Connection Security Rule Wizard, 331–334

New Resource Record dialog box, 189
New Zone Wizard, 177–185
Next Generation TCP/IP stack, 5, 8, 92
Next Secure (NSEC) records, 233
NextProtocol fields in IP headers, 9
NFS (Network File System) services, enabling, 587
NLS (Network Location Server), 410
NMCap command-line tool, 557–558
No-Broadcasts filter for Network Monitor, 560
node types for NetBIOS, 118–119
notifications
  for disk quota thresholds, 589
  for events, 525
  for printer events, 644–645
  for Windows Update, configuring, 490–491
  for zone transfers, 212
NPS (Network Policy Server)
  installing, practice exercise for, 366–368
  Security event log, 359
  templates for, 365
NRPT. *See* Name Resolution Policy Table (NRPT)
NS (name server) records, 188, 221
NSEC (Next Secure) records, 233
NTFS file permissions
  Access-based Enumeration (ABE), 573
  applying, 572–573
  command-line configuration, 573
  default, 571
  precedence when in conflict, 572
numbering of network layers, 5

O

octet values for subnet masks, 49, 54–55
octets, in IP addresses, 10
Offline Files
  configuring, 604–606
  encrypting, 577
Open Shortest Path First (OSPF) protocol, 296
Open Systems Interconnect (OSI) model, 4
Operational event log, troubleshooting with, 532
organizational domains, 121
OSI (Open Systems Interconnect) model, 4
OSPF (Open Shortest Path First) protocol, 296
outbound traffic, filtering, 434–435

P

packet filtering
configuring, 397
for VPNs (virtual private networks), 393–394
packet forwarding. *See also* routing
Layer 2 and Layer 3 addresses, 294
process for, 293
tracing, 294–295
packet loss, tracking, 33
packets. *See also* Ethernet frames; TCP packets
vs. Ethernet frames, 559
fragmentation, 9
Maximum Transmission Unit (MTU) size, 9
overview of, 3
page file
configuring, 550–551
monitoring, 550
overview of, 549
partitions
creating, 206, 209
creating, practice exercise for, 218
default, 205
defined, 205
domain, storing DNS data in, 207
FQDNs for, 205
permissions for creating, 209
referencing local server name for, 209
replication pattern, 206
setting replication scope for, 207–209
storing zones in, 209
storing zones in, practice exercise for, 218
for virtual memory, avoiding, 551
passwords for wireless networks, 350–351
PathPing utility
output example, 33, 294–295
practice exercise for, 306
testing network connectivity with, 33
as Tracert alternative, 402
Windows Firewall and, 32
PayloadLength field in IPv6 header, 10
PEAP (Protected EAP) authentication, 355
Performance Monitor
configuring, 540–541
counters, bolding, 539
overview of, 539

page file, monitoring, 550
virtual memory configuration, 549–551
permissions
NTFS, 571–573
printer, 640
persistent connection, configuring VPN as, 300
Pfirewall.log file, 439
physical layer (Layer 1), 6
physical memory, analyzing usage, 549
Ping utility
output example, 400–401
practice exercise for, 38
running, 400–401
testing network connectivity with, 30–31
troubleshooting, 192
Windows Firewall and, 32
pinging link-local addresses (practice exercise), 102
p-node (NetBIOS), 118
pointer records
99 in, 194
defined, 165
referencing in zone files, 194
update behavior for, 166–167
Point-to-Point Tunneling Protocol (PPTP), 391
poisoned ARP cache example, 34
ports. *See* TCP ports
postal codes, compared to IP addresses, 41–42
power management, and Windows Update client, 491
powers of 2, translating hexadecimal into, 56, 97–98
PPTP (Point-to-Point Tunneling Protocol), 391
preferred IPv6 address state, 91
preshared keys, 323
primary DNS server, naming, 186
primary DNS zones, 178
Print And Document Services server role
installing, 633–634
installing, practice exercise for, 650
Print Management snap-in
installing, 633
printer driver installation with, 640–641
printer installation with, 636–638
printer sharing with, 638
print server permissions, 640
PrintBRM command-line tool, 647–648
printer drivers
digitally signed, 641
finding, 641

installing, 636–638, 640–641
isolation of, 641
for printer pools, 642
printer pools, 632
configuring, 642
configuring, practice exercise for, 651
drivers for, 642
printing to, practice exercise for, 652
printers
best practices for, 632
command-prompt management, 648–649
counters, viewing, 650
exporting, 647
filters for, 644–645
Group Policy settings, 646
Group Policy settings, practice exercise for, 652
importing, 647–648
installing, 634–636
installing, practice exercise for, 651
Internet management of, 643–644
Internet management of, practice exercise for, 653
location-aware printing with, 639
LPR Port Monitor feature, 634
monitoring, 650
network, finding, 635
notifications, configuring, 644–645
permissions, configuring, 640
print queues, 643
priorities, configuring, 643
scripts for, 648–649
sharing, 636, 638
private domain namespace, 122
Private firewall profile, 432
private IP addresses, 52. See also NAT (Network Address
    Translation)
address ranges for, 372
unique local addresses, 90–91, 102–103
private keys. See also public keys
digital signatures and, 225
location of, 224
overview of, 224
rollover configuration, 234–235
Process Monitor, 522
profiles, network, 15
Protected EAP (PEAP) authentication, 355
protected wireless networks, 362–363. See also wireless
    networks

protocols. See also specific protocols
application layer, 13
defined, 2
network, 18
viewing, for connections, 17
Provision A Shared Folder Wizard, 593
PSH flag, 12
Public firewall profile, 432
Public Folder Sharing, 15
public IP addresses, 52. See also global IPv6 addresses
public key cryptography, 224–226. See also private keys;
    public keys
public keys. See also private keys
configuring for wireless networks, 352–353
digital signatures and, 225
Key Signing Keys and Zone Signing Keys, 228
overview of, 224
rollover configuration, 234–235
trust anchors, 226
trust anchors, configuring, 238–240
publishing CRL (certificate revocation list), 419

Q

QoS Packet Scheduler, setting as default, 18
querying DNS servers. See DNS queries
Quota Management console, 587–590
quotas. See disk quotas

R

RAC (Reliability Analysis Component), 543
RADIUS Clients template (NPS), 365
RADIUS servers
backups for, 360
configuring Windows Server as, 354–355
configuring, practice exercise for, 366–368
dial-up configuration, 388–390
log files, 360–361
logons, monitoring, 359–361
modem banks, connecting to, 388–390
as NAP (Network Access Protection) servers, 450
proxy configuration, 356–359
Security event log, 359

RADIUS servers *(continued)*
  Security event log, practice exercise for, 370
  server groups, adding, 358
  trace logging, enabling, 361
  UDP port for, 356
  wireless network authentication, 351, 354–356
RD (Remote Desktop) Gateways and NAP enforcement,
    448, 462
read-only domain controllers (RODCs), 179
recovering encrypted files. *See* DRAs (Data Recovery
    Agents)
recovery DVD, booting from, 624
recursion, DNS, 127–128, 144
refreshing
  Group Policy, 414
  resource record timestamps, 198
releasing IP addresses, 400
Reliability Analysis Component (RAC), 543
Reliability Monitor, 542–543
reloading DNS zones, 212
remediation networks. *See also* NAP (Network Access
    Protection)
  automatic connection to, 452
  infrastructure for, 445
Remediation Server Groups template (NPS), 365
remediation servers, 469
remote access. *See also* dial-up connections; VPNs
    (virtual private networks)
  clients, address leasing, 257. *See also* address leases
  clients, filtering traffic to, 389
  granting for VPN users, 394
  overview of, 382
Remote Desktop (RD) Gateways, and NAP enforcement,
    448, 462
remote hosts, pinging, 400–401
Remote RADIUS Servers template (NPS), 365
renewing
  IP addresses, 400
  IPv6 configuration, 29
Repadmin tool, 176
repairing network connection, 29
replication, Active Directory
  forcing, 176
  scope, setting, 180–181
  tools for, 176
replication, DNS zone
  default partitions, 205
  partitions, pattern of, 206

scope, setting, 180–181, 207–209
  to Windows 2000 Server, 207
reports
  for Data Collector Sets, viewing, 547
  for WSUS, viewing, 506–508
reservations, 271–272
resolvers, DNS, 123, 125
resolving names. *See* DNS resolution; name resolution
Resource Monitor, 541
Resource Record Signature (RRSIG) records, 227–232
resource records, 123, 185–195. *See also* name server
    (NS) records; *specific resource records*
  caching, 132
  CNAME, 192–193
  created automatically, 189
  creating, 189
  deleting outdated. *See* scavenging
  dynamic update settings, 165
  host (A or AAAA), 190–191
  MX (mail exchange), 193
  name protection, 284
  owner of, 185
  pointer (PTR). *See* pointer records
  responsible person (RP), 187
  scavenging, 196, 198–199
  security permissions, 184
  service (SRV), 195
  Start of Authority (SOA) records, 185–186
  time stamping, 196, 198
responsible person (RP) resource record, 187
restarting computer after updates, 490
restoring backups
  from shadow copies, 624–625
  of files, 621–622
  of volumes, 622–623
  when Windows will not start, 624
restrictions on network connections, day and time, 396
reverse domains, 121
reverse lookup zones, 123
  creating, 181–182
  overview of, 123
reverse lookups, 121
RIP (Routing Internet Protocol), 296–298
RODCs (read-only domain controllers), 179
role services, adding, 366
roles, server. *See* server roles
root hints, 127–128, 144
root servers

locating, 127–128
public, for troubleshooting, 2
updating list of, 144
rootkits, 578
round robin DNS, 193
Route Add command, 304
Route command, 301–304
Route Print command, 301, 303–304
routers. *See also* default gateway
advertisements, filtering, 298
configuring Windows Server as, 296–299
defined, 7, 291
hardware-based, benefits of, 291
IP addresses for, 293, 301
neighbors, listing, 298
routing protocols, 295–296
subnet configuration, 304
routing
demand-dial, 299–300, 386–387, 392
example of, 292
Layer 2 and Layer 3 addresses, 294
overview of, 50–51, 293
persistent vs. nonpersistent routes, 304
static, 301–305
Routing And Remote Access Services
advantages of, 376
configuring static routing with, 305
dial-up connection configuration, 385–386
enabling NAT (Network Address Translation) with,
376–377
installing, 296–297
overview of, 373
Routing Internet Protocol (RIP), 296–298
routing table, 293, 301, 305
RP (responsible person) resource record, 187
RST flag, 12
rules. *See specific rules*
rules, classification, 597–598
rules, security. *See* Connection Security Rules; IPsec
Policies

S

SAs (Security Associations)
details, viewing, 342
establishing, 321–322
overview of, 321

Scan Management snap-in, 634
scavenging
automatic, enabling, 198
defined, 196
enabling, 196
manually, 199
properties, setting, 198
scheduling backups, 618–619
Schtasks command-line tool, 526
scope, firewall, 435–436
scopes, DHCP, 257, 261–262
secondary DNS zones. *See also* zone transfers
creating, practice exercise for, 219
deploying, practice exercise for, 219
enabling transfers to, 188
enabling transfers to, practice exercise for, 220
expiration time, setting, 187
manually updating, 212
overview of, 178–179
Secure Socket Tunneling Protocol (SSTP), 391
Secured Password authentication, 356
Security Associations (SAs)
details, viewing, 342
establishing, 321–322
overview of, 321
Security event log
for Network Policy Server, 359
viewing, practice exercise for, 370
Security Rule Wizard, 326–330
security rules. *See* Connection Security Rules; IPsec
Policies
security updates. *See also* NAP (Network Access
Protection); WSUS (Windows Server Update
Services)
approving, 504–506
approving, practice exercise for, 515–516
auditing, 496–497
automatic, configuring, 490, 501
auto-restart after, configuring, 490
deadlines, defining, 505
declining, 505–506
deployment process, 502
enforcing, 468
importance of, 488
installed, viewing, 512
Knowledge Base (KB) number, finding, 513
metadata, exporting, 508
for off-network computers, 495

security updates *(continued)*
 removing, 506, 513
 reports, viewing, 506–508
 sorting list of, 505
 storing locally, 495, 501
 troubleshooting, 510–512
segments, 6. *See also* packets; TCP packets
SequenceNumber fields in TCP headers, 12
serial number for DNS zones, 186
Server Cleanup Wizard (WSUS), 501
Server Core installation of Windows Server 2008, 285
server roles
 Active Directory Domain Services, 137
 DHCP Server, 258–268, 476–477
 DNS Server Core, 141
 File Services, 586–587
 Print And Document Services, 633–634
 Print And Document Services, practice exercise
  for, 650
server firewall configuration, 432
servers, DNS. *See* DNS servers
Server-To-Server rule, 333
service (SRV) resource records, 195
services, network
 overview of, 18
 viewing, for connections, 17
shadow copies
 command-prompt management, 616
 IDs, viewing list of, 616
 overview of, 616
 restoring from, practice exercise for, 624–625
 Windows Explorer management, 616
Shared Secrets template (NPS), 365
sharing
 EFS-protected files, 574–575
 folders. *See* folder sharing
 Internet connections. *See* ICS (Internet Connection
  Sharing)
 printers, 636, 638
SHAs (System Health Agents), 448
SHVs. *See* System Health Validators (SHVs)
signatures, digital, 225
signing zone files
 overview of, 237–238
 practice exercise for, 244
Simple Network Management Protocol (SNMP),
 configuring, 561–563

single-label computer names, resolving.
  See GlobalNames zone
site-local addresses (deprecated), 91
6to4 protocol, 93
slash notation for subnet masks, 43
 compared to other notations, 48
 converting to (practice exercise), 79
 converting to dotted-decimal, 49–50
sliding windows in TCP protocol, 13
smart cards
 requiring for EFS (Encrypting File System), 576
 for wireless security, 351, 356
SMTP servers, 193
SNMP (Simple Network Management Protocol),
  configuring, 561–563
SOA (Start of Authority) records. *See* Start of Authority
  (SOA) records
socket pooling, 151
sockets, 151
software notifications for updates, 491
SoftwareDistribution.txt file for WSUS, 510
SourceAddress fields
 in Ethernet headers, 7
 in IP headers, 9
split-scope DHCP configuration, 281
SRV (service) resource record, 195
SSL certificates
 installing, 455
 for WSUS, 509–510
SSTP (Secure Socket Tunneling Protocol), 391
stability, monitoring with Reliability Monitor, 542–543
stack, TCP/IP, 5, 8, 92
stale resource records. *See* aging; scavenging
standard DNS zones, 180
Start of Authority (SOA) records, 185
 opening, 186
 serial number, changing, 186
stateless mode
 defined, 262
 for DHCPv6, 262–264
 vs. stateful mode, 267
static DNS servers, 23
static IP addresses
 assigning, 22–24
 practice exercise for, 36
static keys for wireless encryption, 350–351

static routing
  configuring, 301–304
  configuring, practice exercise for, 306–309
  in routing table, 303
stub DNS zones
  example of, 215–217
  name resolution improvement with, 217
  overview of, 179
  uses for, 216
subdomains, 121. *See also* delegating DNS zones
subnet ID. *See also* network ID
  in IPv6 addresses, 88, 96
  number of bits, determining, 96–97
  overview of, 65
subnet masks
  address classes, as deprecated, 43
  assigning (practice exercise), 77
  commonly used, 16
  for DHCP scopes, defining, 262
  dotted-decimal, converting to (practice exercise), 78
  dotted-decimal, determining size of, 58–59
  enumerating address ranges, 68–76
  identifying network ID with, 42
  midrange values for, 46–47
  notation comparison, 48
  notations for, 43
  octet values, 48–49
  octet values, calculating, 54–55
  overview of, 42
  restricting broadcast traffic with, 64
  size required, determining, 59–61
  size required, determining (practice exercise), 82–83
  slash notation, converting to (practice exercise), 79
  slash notation, converting to binary, 43
  slash notation, converting to dotted-decimal, 49–50
  variable-length, creating, 67–68
subnets
  address space calculations, 68–76
  creating, 61–62
  defined, 53
  determining number of, 66
  effect on address space, 66
  enumerating address ranges, 68–76, 96, 99–101
  equally-sized, creating, 66–67
  hexadecimal increment, determining, 97–99
  in IPv6 protocol, 96–101
  IP address for, 59

network prefix, determining, 97
  vs. networks, 54
  ownership verification, 76
  physical topology considerations, 64
  reference table, creating, 68
  routers on, 304
  for variable numbers of hosts, 67–68
  vs. virtual LAN (VLAN) switches, 64
subscribing to events
  overview of, 528–531
  practice exercise for, 536–537
suffixes, DNS. *See* DNS suffixes
switches as layer 2 devices, 6
SYN flag, 11
sysdm.cpl command, 160
System Diagnostics Data Collector Set, 544
System event log, 378–379, 395
system file encryption. *See* BitLocker
System Health Agents (SHAs), 448
System Health Validators (SHVs)
  configuring, 466–467
  overview of, 448
  Windows SHV, 467–468
System Image Recovery wizard, 624
System Performance Data Collector Set, 543
System Properties dialog box, changing computer
    name in, 160
system reliability, monitoring, 542
System Stability Report, 542
system state, backing up, 621

T

Task Manager, viewing physical memory usage in, 549
Task Scheduler, 520–526
TCP flags, 12
TCP headers
  AcknowledgmentNumber fields, 12
  Checksum fields, 13
  DataOffset fields, 12
  DstPort fields, 12
  SequenceNumber fields, 12
  SrcPort fields, 12
  vs. UDP headers, 13
  Window fields, 13
  for WSUS, 509

TCP packets. *See also* packets
  encapsulation of, 14
  header example, 12
  number of protocols in, 14
TCP ports
  configuring, for DNS, 151
  for event forwarding, 526
  for HTTP traffic, 12
  for ICS (Internet Connection Sharing), 375
  identifying, 439–440
  monitoring, 556
  overview of, 10
  for VPNs (virtual private networks), 392–393
TCP protocol
  connection-oriented nature of, 11
  handshake process, 11–12
  overview of, 10
TCP sessions, aborting, 12
TCP/IP layers. *See* network layers
TCP/IP protocol encapsulation, 14
TCP/IP stack, 5, 8, 92
Telnet Server, installing (practice exercise), 440–441
Telnet services, installing (practice exercise), 337
templates, NPS, 365. *See also* NPS (Network Policy
    Server)
tentative IPv6 address state, 91
Teredo protocol, 94–95
Terminal Services Gateway. *See* RD (Remote Desktop)
    Gateways, and NAP enforcement
testing network connectivity, 397–402
thumb drives, encrypting, 582
Time to Live (TTL) values, 132, 187
time stamping resource records, 198
TimeToLive fields in IP headers, 9
top-level domain names, 121
TotalLength fields in IP headers, 9
TPM (Trusted Platform Module) chips, 579
trace logging
  enabling, 361
  for Network Access Protection Agent service,
    475–476
Tracert utility
  -d switch, 32
  DNS lookups, turning off, 401
  output example, 32

  practice exercise for, 306
  running, 401–402
  testing network connectivity with, 32
  Windows Firewall and, 32
tracing packets, 294–295. *See also* PathPing utility;
    Tracert utility
trailing dot in domain names, 121
transition technologies, 92–95
transport layer (Layer 4), 10
troubleshooting
  DHCP connections, 29
  network connections, 29–35
  TCP/IP connectivity, 2
trust anchors
  configuring, 238–240
  location of, 238
  overview of, 226
Trusted Platform Module (TPM) chips, 579
TTL (Time to Live) values, 132, 151
tunneling protocols, 92–95
  authorizing, 336
  overview of, 92–95

U

UDP headers, vs. TCP headers, 13
UDP protocol
  header example, 13
  overview of, 10
unicast addresses, 51
unique local addresses
  assigning, 90–91
  assigning (practice exercise), 102–103
updates. *See* security updates; WSUS (Windows Server
    Update Services)
updating DNS zones, 212
URG flag, 12
UrgentPointer field in TCP headers, 13
user classes
  implementing, 276–279
  populating, 279
  predefined, 277
user credentials, preventing caching of, 364
user permissions. *See* NTFS file permissions

V

validating digital signatures, 225
validating DNS data, 226
virtual LAN (VLAN)
  configuring, 356
  NAP enforcement and, 447
  switches, vs. subnets, 64
virtual machines, configuring, 307
virtual memory
  configuring, 550–551
  overview of, 549
  partitioning and, 551
virtual private networks (VPNs)
  advantages and disadvantages, 384–385
  architecture of, 384
  authentication, 392
  client configuration, 394
  client configuration, practice exercise for, 403
  configuring router, 299–300
  connecting to, 394
  DHCP relay agent configuration, 393
  enabling ICS (Internet Connection Sharing) for,
    375–376
  latency and, 385
  NAP enforcement, 462
  packet filter configuration, 393–394
  port configuration, 392–393
  protocols for, 391
  reconnecting automatically, 394–395
  routing configuration and, 301
  server configuration, 392–393
  server configuration, practice exercise for, 402–403
  server enforcement of NAP, 447
  troubleshooting, 395
Visual Basic scripts for printing, 648–649
VLAN (virtual LAN)
  configuring, 356
  NAP enforcement and, 447
  switches, vs. subnets, 64
volume backups, restoring, 622–623
volume encryption. *See* BitLocker
volume integrity, checking, 581
Volume Shadow Copy. *See* shadow copies
VPN Reconnect, 394–395
VPNs. *See* virtual private networks (VPNs)
VSSAdmin command-line tool, 616

W

WANs (wireless area networks)
  BranchCache and, 606
  WSUS architecture for, 492
WAPs (wireless access points). *See also* wireless
    networks
  bridging into single network, 18–20
  configuring, practice exercise for, 368
  connecting to, practice exercise for, 369
  as RADIUS clients, 355–356
  security standards, 350–352
Wbadmin command-line tool, 620–621
Web pages, filtering Network Monitor by, 560
WEP (Wired Equivalent Protection), 350
Windows Firewall with Advanced Security. *See* WFAS
    (Windows Firewall with Advanced Security)
wi-fi. *See* wireless networks
Wi-Fi Protected Access (WPA), 351
Window fields in TCP headers, 13
Windows 2000 Server, replicating DNS zones to, 207
Windows Defender, 467
Windows Event Collector
  for event forwarding, 526, 528
  practice exercise for, 536
Windows Firewall with Advanced Security (WFAS), 527.
    See also firewalls
  connection authorization, configuring, 436–438
  Connection Security Rule configuration, 320
  Connection Security Rule export, 320
  creating inbound rules in, 433–434
  creating outbound rules in, 435
  default behavior of, 432, 434
  DirectAccess configuration, 412–413
  DirectAccess configuration, practice exercise for, 416
  Group Policy configuration, 438
  ICMP and, 32
  IPsec settings for Connection Security Rules, 334–336
  logging, enabling, 439
  rule scope, configuring, 435–436
Windows Internal Database, security update storage
    in, 495
Windows logs, viewing, 523
Windows PowerShell, configuring WSUS APIs with, 509
Windows Remote Management
  configuration, verifying, 532–533
  for event forwarding, 526–527

Windows Search Service, 587
Windows Server
    dashboard for, 15–16
    Server Core installation, deploying DNS servers on,
        140–141
Windows Server 2003 File Services, 587
Windows Server 2008
    Name Protection feature, 284
    as RADIUS proxy, 356–359
    as RADIUS server, 354–355
    as router. *See* routers
    Server Core installation, installing DHCP on, 285
Windows Server Backup
    features, installing, 617
    manually backing up with, 617–618
    overview of, 617
    scheduling backups with, 618–619
Windows Server Update Services (WSUS). *See* WSUS
    (Windows Server Update Services)
Windows System Health Validator (SHV), 467–468
Windows Update client. *See also* security updates;
    WSUS (Windows Server Update Services)
    automatic updates, configuring, 490
    blocking user access to, 491
    client-side targeting, 491, 502–503
    Group Policy settings, 490–491
    history, viewing, 512
    Install Updates And Shut Down option,
        disabling, 491
    notification settings, configuring, 490–491
    power management and, 491
    server-side targeting, 502–503
    troubleshooting, 511–512
    verifying updates with, 496
    WSUS server location, specifying, 490
Windows XP computers, on Network Map, 16
WindowsImageBackup folder, 618
WinRM command-line tool, 527
WINS servers
    configuring, 260
    DHCP specification for, 257
    in DNS zones, 195
    overview of, 117
Wired Equivalent Protection (WEP), 350
wired networks, requiring authentication for, 363–364
wireless access points. *See* WAPs (wireless access points)

wireless area networks. *See* WANs (wireless area
    networks)
Wireless Diagnostics Data Collector Set, 544
wireless networks. *See also* WAPs (wireless access points)
    ad hoc mode, 352
    authentication, 353–356
    configuring, 361–362
    connecting automatically, 361–362
    deploying, 362–363
    Group Policy settings, 361–362
    Group Policy settings, practice exercise for, 368–369
    infrastructure mode, 352
    logons, monitoring, 359–361
    password protecting, 350–351
    public key infrastructure (PKI) configuration,
        352–353
    RADIUS authentication, 351
    security standards, 350–352
    Single Sign On, 353
    troubleshooting, 544
    unprotected, 350
    WPA-EAP deployment, 362–363
wizards. *See specific wizards*
worms
    defined, 431
    propagation of, 434
WPA (Wi-Fi Protected Access), 351
WPA2 (IEEE 802.11i), 351
WPA-EAP (Extensible Authentication Protocol), 351
    autoenrollment, configuring, 352–353
    configuring, practice exercise for, 366–370
    deploying wireless networks with, 362–363
    Security event log, 359
WPA-Personal (WPA-PSK), 351
WSUS (Windows Server Update Services). *See also*
    security updates
    APIs, accessing, 509
    approving updates, 504–506
    approving updates, practice exercise for, 515–516
    architecture of, 492–494
    auditing updates, 496–497
    client computers, configuring, 504, 515
    command-line administration, 508–509
    computer groups, configuring, 502–503
    configuration overview, 500
    database location, 496

declining updates, 505–506
exporting data from, 508
firewall exceptions, 499–500
health monitoring, configuring, 508
IIS website for, 496
inactive approvals, managing, 509
installation planning, 495–496
installing, 499–500
installing, practice exercise for, 513–514
languages, configuring, 496
moving files, 508
for multiple IT departments, 494
for multiple offices, 492–494
new features in, 489
notification settings, configuring, 501
overview of, 489
personalizing, 501
ports, configuring, 509
products updated, configuring, 496, 501
redundancy and, 492
removing updates, 506, 513
replication, configuring, 495
reports, viewing, 506–508
requirements for, 494–495
secure communications for, 496
Server Cleanup Wizard, 501
Server Configuration Wizard, 501
server registry key, updating, 508
servers, viewing list of, 508
for single offices, 492
sorting updates, 505
source and proxy server, configuring, 501
SSL certificate configuration, 509–510
synchronization, scheduling, 501

synchronization, viewing report on, 508
troubleshooting, 510
update source, configuring, 495
update storage, configuring, 495, 501
verifying connection to, 511
WAN architecture, 492
Windows Internal Database storage, 495
Windows Update client, 490–491
WSUSUtil tool, 508–509
WSUSUtil command-line tool, 508–509

Z

ZIP codes, compared to IP addresses, 41–42
zone ID (IPv6), 89–90
zone replication
    default partitions, 205
    partitions, pattern of, 206
    scope, setting, 180–181, 207–209
    to Windows 2000 Server, 207
Zone Signing Keys (ZSKs), 228, 234–235
zone transfers, 179
    enabling, 188, 211
    forcing, 186
    initiation of, 211
    notifications for, 212
    options for, 211
    practice exercise for, 220
    retry interval, setting, 187
    when to use, 210
zones, 176. *See also* DNS zones
ZSKs (Zone Signing Keys), 228, 234–235

About the Authors

TONY NORTHRUP, MCITP, MCTS, MCPD, MCSE, and CISSP, is a Windows consultant and author living in Waterford, Connecticut, in the United States. Tony started programming before Windows 1.0 was released, but has focused on Windows administration and development for the last 15 years. He has written more than two dozen books covering Windows development, networking, and security. Among other titles, Tony is coauthor of the *Windows 7 Resource Kit* (Microsoft Press, 2009) and *Windows Server 2008 Networking and Network Access Protection (NAP)* (Microsoft Press, 2008). Tony has a technology blog at *www.vistaclues.com*.

J.C. MACKIN, MCITP, MCTS, MCSE, and MCDST, is a writer and Microsoft Certified Trainer. He is coauthor of many titles from Microsoft Press, including the *Self-Paced Training Kits* for Exams 70-291, 70-622, 70-643, and 70-685.

What do you think of this book?

We want to hear from you!

To participate in a brief online survey, please visit:

microsoft.com/learning/booksurvey

Tell us how well this book meets your needs—what works effectively, and what we can do better. Your feedback will help us continually improve our books and learning resources for you.

Thank you in advance for your input!

Stay in touch!

To subscribe to the *Microsoft Press® Book Connection Newsletter*—for news on upcoming books, events, and special offers—please visit:

microsoft.com/learning/books/newsletter